THE JOHN HARVARD LIBRARY

Bernard Bailyn
Editor-in-Chief

PAMPHLETS OF THE
AMERICAN REVOLUTION

Volume I

1750–1765

The John Harvard Library

PAMPHLETS OF THE
AMERICAN REVOLUTION
1750-1776

Edited by
BERNARD BAILYN

with the assistance of
Jane N. Garrett

Volume I
1750-1765

THE BELKNAP PRESS OF
HARVARD UNIVERSITY PRESS
Cambridge, Massachusetts
1965

TO
Oscar Handlin

FOREWORD

It was longer ago than I like to recall that Howard Mumford Jones, then Editor-in-Chief of the John Harvard Library, invited me to prepare a collection of pamphlets of the American Revolution for publication in that series. Like all students of American history I knew well perhaps a half dozen of the most famous pamphlets of the Revolution, obviously worth republication, and I knew also of others, another half dozen or so, that would probably be worth considering. The project was attractive to me, it did not appear to be particularly burdensome, and since in addition it was related to a book I was then preparing on eighteenth-century politics, I agreed to undertake it.

The starting point of the work was the compilation of a complete bibliography of the pamphlets. This alone proved to be a considerable task, and it was in assembling this list that I discovered the magnitude of the project I had embarked on. The full bibliography of pamphlets relating to the Anglo-American struggle published in the colonies through the year 1776 contains not a dozen or so items but over four hundred; in the end I concluded that no fewer than seventy-two of them ought to be republished. But sheer numbers were not the most important measure of the magnitude of the project. The pamphlets include all sorts of writings — treatises on political theory, essays on history, political arguments, sermons, correspondence, poems — and they display all sorts of literary devices. But for all their variety they have in common one distinctive characteristic: they are, to an unusual degree, *explanatory*. They reveal not merely positions taken but the reasons why positions were taken; they reveal motive and understanding: the assumptions, beliefs, and ideas that lay behind the manifest events of the time. As a result I found myself, as I read through these many documents, viewing the Revolutionary movement with something like surprise, for the "interior" view, from the vantage point of the pamphlets, was different from what I had expected. The task, consequently, took on an increasing excitement, for much of the history of the American Revolution has fallen into the condition that overtakes so many of the great events of the past; it is, as Professor Trevor-Roper has written in another connection, taken for granted: "By our explanations, interpretations, assumptions we gradually make it seem automatic, natural, inevitable; we remove from it the sense of wonder, the unpredictability, and therefore the freshness it ought to have." Study of the pamphlets appeared to lead back into the unpredictable reality of the Revolution, and posed a variety of new problems of interpretation. More, it seemed to me, was called for in preparing this edition than simply reproducing accurately and annotating a selected group of texts.

Study of the pamphlets confirmed my rather old-fashioned view that the American Revolution was above all else an ideological-constitutional struggle and not primarily a controversy between social groups undertaken to force changes in the organization of society. It confirmed too my belief that intellectual developments in the decade before Independence led to a radical idealization and rationalization of the previous century and a half of American experience, and that it was this intimate relationship between Revolutionary thought and the circumstances of life in eighteenth-century America that endowed the Revolution with its peculiar force and made of it a transforming event. But if the pamphlets confirmed this belief, they filled it with unexpected details and gave it new meaning. They shed light on the question of the sources and character of Revolutionary thought. Most commonly the thought of the Revolution has been seen as an expression of the natural rights philosophy: the ideas of the social contract, inalienable rights, natural law, and the contractual basis of government. But some have denounced this interpretation as "obtuse secularism," and, reading the sermons of the time with acute sensitivity, argue that it was a respect for world opinion that led the Founders to put their case "in the restricted language of the rational century," and that the success of the Revolutionary movement is comprehensible only in terms of the continuing belief in original sin and the need for grace. Yet others have described the sermons as a form of deliberate propaganda by which revolutionary ideas were fobbed off on an unsuspecting populace by a "black regiment" of clergy committed, for reasons unexplained, to the idea of rebellion. And still others deny the influence of both Enlightenment theory and theology, and view the Revolution as no revolution at all, but rather as a conservative movement wrought by practitioners of the common law and devoted to preserving it, and the ancient liberties embedded in it, intact.

The pamphlets do reveal the influence of Enlightenment thought, and they do show the effective force of certain religious ideas, of the common law, and also of classical literature; but they reveal most significantly the close integration of these elements in a pattern of, to me at least, surprising design — surprising because of the prominence in it of still another tradition, interwoven with yet still distinct from these more familiar strands of thought. This distinctive influence had been transmitted most directly to the colonists by a group of early eighteenth-century radical publicists and opposition politicians in England who carried forward into the eighteenth century and applied to the politics of the age of Walpole the peculiar strain of anti-authoritarianism bred in the upheaval of the English Civil War. This tradition, as it developed in the British Isles, has been the subject of extensive research by Caroline Robbins, forming the substance of her *Eighteenth-Century Commonwealthman;* but it had not hitherto been applied to the origins of the American Revolution. Convinced of the importance of this influence, I thought it would be useful to identify and classify all the references found in the pamphlets and associated documents, and on the basis of such a study present in both the annotation to the texts and in essay form an inter-pretation of the sources and character of the pamphleteers' thought. This essay became the nucleus of the General Introduction, where it appears now as Chapters III and IV; the same themes reappear and are further detailed in several of the individual Introductions, particularly those to Pamphlets 1 and 14.

It was in the context of the sources and pattern of ideas presented in Chapter III and IV that I began to see a new meaning in phrases that I, like most historians, had readily dismissed as mere rhetoric and propa-ganda: "slavery," "corruption," "conspiracy." These inflammatory words were used so forcefully by pamphleteers of so great a variety of social statuses, political positions, and religious persuasions; they fitted so logi-cally into the pattern of radical and opposition thought; and they re-flected so clearly the realities of life in an age in which monarchical autocracy flourished, in which the stability and freedom of England's "mixed" constitution was a recent and remarkable achievement, and in which the fear of conspiracy against constituted authority was built into the very structure of politics, that I began to suspect that they meant something very real to both the writers and their readers: that there were real fears, real anxieties, a sense of real danger behind these phrases, and not merely the desire to influence by rhetoric and propaganda the inert minds of an otherwise passive populace. The more I read, the less useful, it seemed to me, was the whole idea of propaganda in its modern mean-ing when applied to the writings of the American Revolution — a view which I have touched on in several places in this volume (particularly

in the Introduction to Pamphlet 12) and which I hope to develop at
length on another occasion. In the end I was convinced that the fear of a
comprehensive conspiracy against liberty throughout the English-speaking
world — a conspiracy believed to have been nourished in corruption, and
of which, it was felt, oppression in America was only the most immediately visible part — lay at the heart of the Revolutionary movement. This
too seemed to me to be worth developing. It appears as Chapter V of
the General Introduction, extended in the Note on Conspiracy, and it
forms parts of several of the Introductions to the individual pamphlets.

Beyond all of this, however, I found in the pamphlets evidence of a
transformation that overtook the inheritance of political and social thought
as it had been received in the colonies by the early 1760's. Indeliberately,
half-knowingly, as responses not to desire but to the logic of the situation, the leaders of colonial thought in the years before Independence
forced forward alterations in, or challenged, major concepts and assumptions of eighteenth-century political theory. They reached — then, before
1776, in the debate on the problem of imperial relations — new territories
of thought upon which would be built the commanding structures of the
first state constitutions and of the Federal Constitution. This too deserved
to be explored, it seemed to me; the results appear in Chapter VI. Finally
there was evidence that this transformation of thought, which led to
conclusions so remarkably congruent with the realities of American life,
was powerfully contagious. It affected areas not directly involved in the
Anglo-American controversy; areas as gross as the institution of chattel
slavery and as subtle as the assumptions of human relations. This "spill-
over" effect I have tried to analyze in the final chapter of the General
Introduction.

At no point in the General Introduction have I attempted to describe
all shades of opinion on any of the problems discussed. I decided at the
start to present what I took to be the dominant or leading ideas of those
who made the Revolution. There were of course articulate and outspoken
opponents of the Revolution, and at times I have referred to their ideas;
but the future lay not with them but with the leaders of the Revolu-
ionary movement, and it is their thought at each stage of the developing
rebellion that I have attempted to present, using often the shorthand
phrase "the colonists" to refer to them and their ideas.

At the start of the work on the pamphlets, when I first began to encounter difficulties in tracking down the references that appear in them,

I turned to Jane N. Garrett, Assistant to the Director of the Boston Athenaeum, for help. She willingly assisted, and soon I found her aid indispensable in locating editions of works cited in the pamphlets, checking the pamphleteers' quotations, preparing documentation for the notes, and reading the manuscript and proof sheets for accuracy. She became in effect co-proprietor of the enterprise, and her name therefore appears where it belongs, on the title page.

Clifford K. Shipton in at least two ways made the whole project possible. Though I have the good fortune to live in a community replete with archives of the colonial past, I could not have made a comprehensive study of the pamphlets without using Mr. Shipton's microcard edition of American imprints before 1800. Like every student of early American history I am beholden to Mr. Shipton for providing this invaluable aid to scholarship. In addition, Mr. Shipton facilitated my work by making available to me the originals of pamphlets owned by the American Antiquarian Society, over whose splendid collection he presides, and by allowing me to read in manuscript his biography of Benjamin Church, which is to appear in volume XIII of *Sibley's Harvard Graduates*.

The General Introduction was read in its entirety at an early stage by Oscar Handlin and Gordon S. Wood, both of whom were in the midst of studies of their own using some of the same materials I was using and treating similar topics. I profited by their informed and penetrating criticism. John Clive read the manuscript at a later stage, and, perhaps realizing that it was too late to save me from major errors, contented himself with pointing out several dozen infelicities, non sequiturs, and assorted solecisms; I am grateful to him for his discriminating comments.

At times Mrs. Garrett and I reached dead ends in running down references in the pamphlets, and turned to experts on particular subjects for help. We wish to thank in this connection Charles Blitzer, Reuben A. Brower, Paul F. Cooper, Jr., Mason Hammond, Leonard Krieger, Jacob M. Price, Samuel E. Thorne, L. Kinvin Wroth, and Hiller B. Zobel. On some of the stickier problems members of the reference department of the Boston Athenaeum gave us valuable assistance. Thomas R. Adams, Director of the John Carter Brown Library, not only responded swiftly and generously to requests I made of that institution, but allowed me to use the galley proofs of his own bibliography of Revolutionary pamphlets which is to be published in a forthcoming volume of the *Publications of the Colonial Society of Massachusetts* and subsequently as a separate book. Though I unfortunately heard of Mr. Adams' authoritative work on the bibliography of the pamphlets only when I had finished compiling my own list, I benefited greatly by being able to check my entries against his. J. G. A. Pocock kindly shared with me in correspondence his own thoughts on certain of the topics treated in the General Introduction, and allowed me to read his unpublished paper "Machiavelli, Harrington and English Political Ideologies in the Eighteenth Century." Francelia Mason went far beyond her duties as Assistant Editor of the John Harvard Library in suggesting improvements in the manuscript and in handling the complications of getting such a book properly into print. Carol S. Thorne, Julie S. Cohen, Janet Marshall, and Kristine Marsden took care of the transcription of the documents and the typing of the editorial material. Mrs. Thorne helped also in other ways, particularly in checking the final proofs; and Mrs. Marsden helped prepare the index.

Lotte Bailyn, who has kept a sharp eye on the whole enterprise, forced me to make two decisions on questions of format that not only improved the book but greatly sped up publication; and she made it possible for me to continue working on the book through a difficult time.

B. B.

A NOTE ON THE TEXTS

SELECTION

Several principles aside from the primary one of relevance to the Anglo-American controversy guided the selection of the pamphlets that are to appear in these volumes. (Those to be included in volumes II–IV are listed on pp. 749–752.) Contemporary fame was one: no collection of pamphlets would be complete without James Otis' *Rights of the British Colonies* or John Dickinson's *Farmer's Letters* even if they had not been important in the history of political theory. Representativeness was another: effort has been made to include specimens of each of the main categories of constitutional arguments and literary genres that appear in the pamphlet literature. Literary distinction was a third. Originality of thought, whether recognized at the time or not, was a fourth. Two restrictions only were set down at the start: the pamphlets selected must be American imprints, and they must be reproduced in their entirety. These were useful, indeed indispensable, rules, but both were deliberately broken at least once: the former to permit the use of a Dublin imprint (Pamphlet 32) identical with its Boston original except for the reduction of repetitious appendixes, the latter to allow for the separate republication of an especially important piece (Pamphlet 52) that happened to have been published originally as an appendix to a sermon of no distinction whatever.

No two people making such a selection would agree on all the items to be included; the present choice, like any such choice, may be open to criticism. But it is hoped that if errors have been made in the selection they are errors of commission rather than omission.

With a few exceptions, explained in the end notes, the first editions of the pamphlets were used as the bases for the present reprinting.

PRESENTATION

One of the most difficult and important questions that had to be answered in planning these volumes was how the texts should be edited. The pamphlets were to be reprinted in their entirety, and the language of the originals was to be scrupulously respected; but a slavish reproduction of all the typographical idiosyncrasies found in the pamphlets would have been ridiculous. In certain respects the appearance of the words obviously resulted from the vagaries of eighteenth-century typesetting; in others it

merely reflected archaic printing conventions. The pamphleteers themselves were often quite casual about the details of their writing; Jonathan
Mayhew, in preparing the second printing of his *Discourse Concerning
Unlimited Submission,* ignored the punctuation altogether, announcing
that he was leaving errors of that sort "to be corrected by the reader." Yet
certain aspects of typography were just as clearly essential to the authors'
meaning. In the end the following rules for editing were decided on; they
have been used throughout.

Spelling has been altered to conform to current American usage, but
not so as to affect the choice of words. Thus *steared* becomes *steered,
colour* becomes *color;* but *amongst* does not become *among,* nor *catched
caught,* and the phrase "an hundred" remains as it is. Punctuation has
been modernized, but only where it was felt that modern usage would
assist in conveying the writer's thought; for the most part this has meant
eliminating excessive commas and standardizing terminal punctuation.
When the meaning of a passage was in doubt, the punctuation has been
left unaltered or the changes enclosed in brackets. The capitalization of
initial letters has also been modernized, but, except for one group of
cases,[1] the italicization and capitalization of whole words have been retained. For italics were used not only, as they are now, for emphasis, but
also to indicate both direct quotations and paraphrases, and it proved
impossible to distinguish among these intentions in order to modernize
the printing forms; and the capitalization of whole words — both in full
and small capitals — was used deliberately by the pamphleteers to convey degrees of stress. Other minor printing conventions (affecting, for
example, regnal numbers, statute titles, £, s., d.) have been put into
standard modern form, unusual contractions (except in poetry) have been
spelled out, and typographical errors silently corrected. But to avoid
bibliographical confusion all book and pamphlet titles cited have been
rendered in their original orthography.

For ease in locating cited passages of the pamphlets, the original page
numbers have been retained; they appear in shaded brackets easily distinguishable from the normal brackets which enclose editorial insertions.
Arabic superscript numbers refer to editorial notes printed at the back of
the volume. The archaic indicators — stars, daggers, etc. — regrouped in
regular sequences, refer to the original notes reproduced at the bottom
of the pages.

---

[1] In a number of the pamphlets the names of all persons and places, and all adjectives
formed from place names, were printed routinely in italics. In pamphlets in which this
purely mechanical italicization seemed likely to encumber the reader, it has been uniformly
removed.

CONTENTS

PAMPHLETS OF
THE AMERICAN REVOLUTION

1750

1760

1763

1764

1765

Original title pages

of pamphlets reprinted in this volume

A

DISCOURSE

CONCERNING

Unlimited Submiſſion

AND

Non-Reſiſtance

TO THE

HIGHER POWERS:

With ſome REFLECTIONS on the RESISTANCE made to

King CHARLES I.

AND ON THE

Anniverſary of his Death :

In which the MYSTERIOUS Doctrine of that Prince's Saintſhip and Martyrdom is UNRIDDLED :

The Subſtance of which was delivered in a SERMON preached in the Weſt Meeting-Houſe in *Boſton* the LORD'S-DAY after the 30th of *January*, 1749 | 50.

Publiſhed at the Requeſt of the Hearers.

By JONATHAN MAYHEW, A. M.

Paſtor of the Weſt Church in *Boſton*.

Fear GOD, honor the King.   Saint PAUL.
He that ruleth over Men, muſt be juſt, ruling in the Fear of GOD.
                                        Prophet SAMUEL.
I have ſaid, ye are Gods— but ye ſhall die like Men, and fall like one of the PRINCES.   King DAVID.

Quid memorem inſandas cædes? quid facta TYRANNI
Effera ? Dii CAPITI ipſius GENERIQUE reſervent—
Necnon Threïcius *longa cum veſte* SACERDOS
Obloquitur——   *Rom. Vat. Prin.*

BOSTON, Printed and Sold by D. FOWLE in Queen ſtreet ; and by D. GOOKIN over-againſt the South-Meeting-Houſe. 1750.

Pamphlet 1.   Courtesy Harvard College Library

A

LETTER,

To the People of ∨

PENNSYLVANIA;

Occafioned by the ASSEMBLY's paffing
that Important ACT, .

FOR

CONSTITUTING the JUDGES

OF THE

SUPREAM COURTS and COMMON-PLEAS,

During GOOD BEHAVIOUR.

I charged your Judges at that Time, faying, Hear the Caufes between your
Brethren, and judge Righteoufly between every Man and his Brother, and the
Stranger that is with him : Ye fhall not Refpect Perfons in Judgment, but you
fhall hear the Small as well as the Great ; you fhall not be afraid of the Face of
Man, for the Judgment is GOD's. Deut. i. 16, 17.

PHILADELPHIA : Printed in MDCCLX.

VERSES

ON

Doctor MAYHEW's

BOOK of OBSERVATIONS

On the CHARTER and CONDUCT

OF THE

SOCIETY

FOR THE

PROPAGATION of the GOSPEL in FOREIGN PARTS :

With NOTES, critical and explanatory.

By a Gentleman of *Rhode-Island* Colony.

PROVIDENCE, in NEW-ENGLAND :

Printed and fold by WILLIAM GODDARD, at the Sign of SHAKESPEAR's Head.   1763.

Pamphlet 3.   Courtesy Harvard College Library

THE
Colonel Dismounted:
OR THE
Rector Vindicated.
In a Letter addressed to His REVERENCE:

CONTAINING

A Dissertation upon the CONSTITUTION
of the COLONY.

By COMMON SENSE.

Quodcunque ostendis mihi sic, incredulus odi.

HOR.

WILLIAMSBURG:
Printed by JOSEPH ROYLE, MDCCLXIV.

Pamphlet 4. Courtesy American Antiquarian Society

Lot 31 Condy

CONSIDERATIONS

UPON

The Act of Parliament,

WHEREBY

A Duty is laid of *six Pence*
Sterling per Gallon on Molasses, and *five
Shillings* per Hundred on Sugar of foreign
Growth, imported into any of the British
Colonies.

SHEWING,

Some of the many Inconveniencies necessarily resulting from the Operation of the
said Act, not only to those Colonies, but
also to the British Sugar-Islands, and
finally to *Great-Britain*.

❑   ❑

BOSTON:

Printed and Sold by EDES and GILL, in Queen
Street, M,DCC,LXIV.

1764

Pamphlet 5.   Courtesy American Antiquarian Society

REASONS

WHY

The *BRITISH* COLONIES,

IN

AMERICA,

SHOULD NOT BE CHARGED WITH

INTERNAL TAXES,

BY AUTHORITY OF

PARLIAMENT;

HUMBLY OFFERED,

For CONSIDERATION,

In Behalf of the COLONY of

CONNECTICUT.

NEW-HAVEN:
Printed by B. MECOM. M,DCC,LXIV.

Pamphlet 6.   Courtesy Harvard College Library

THE

RIGHTS

OF THE

British Colonies

Afferted and proved.

By James Otis, *Efq*;

---

*Hæc omnis regio et celfi plaga pinea montis
Cedat amicitiæ Teucrorum : et fœderis æquas
Dicamus leges, fociófque in regna vocemus.
Confidant, fi tantus amor, et mœnia condant.*

VIRG.

B O S T O N:
Printed and Sold by EDES and GILL, in Queen-Street.
M,DCC,LXIV.

Pamphlet 7. Courtesy Harvard College Library

THE

SENTIMENTS

OF A

British American.

O. Thacher Esquire

Aſellum in prato timidus paſcebat ſenex.
Is, hoſtium clamore ſubito territus,
Suadebat aſino fugere, ne poſſent capi.
At ille lentus : quæſo num binas mihi
Clitellas impoſiturum victorem putas ?
Senex negavit. Ergo quid refert mea
Cui ſerviam ? clitellas dum portem meas.

PHÆDRUS.

B O S T O N:

Printed and Sold by EDES & GILL, next to the
Priſon in Queen-Street. 1764.

[Price Six Pence.]

Pamphlet 8. Courtesy Harvard College Library

THE

RIGHTS

OF

COLONIES

EXAMINED.

PUBLISHED BY AUTHORITY.

PROVIDENCE:
PRINTED BY *WILLIAM GODDARD.*
M.DCC.LXV.

A

LETTER

FROM A

GENTLEMAN at *Halifax*,

TO HIS

FRIEND in *Rhode-Island*,

CONTAINING

REMARKS UPON A PAMPHLET,

ENTITLED,

THE RIGHTS OF COLONIES

EXAMINED.

NEWPORT:

PRINTED AND SOLD BY S. HALL.   M.DCC.LXV.

A
VINDICATION

OF THE

Britiſh Colonies,

AGAINST

The Aſperſions of

THE

Halifax GENTLEMAN,

IN

His Letter to a *Rhode-Iſland* FRIEND.

By James Otis.

Sed fugite, ô miſeri, fugite, atque ab litore funem
Rumpite !
Clamorem immenſum tollit, quo pontus et omnes
Intremuere undæ, penitúſque exterrita tellus
Italiæ curvíſque immugiit Ætna Cavernis.
—— *fluit æs rivis, aurique metallum*
Vulnificúſque chalybs vaſtâ fornace liqueſcit
—— *Alii ventoſis follibus auras*
Accipiunt reddúntque. alii ſtridentia tingunt
Æra lacu : gemit impoſitis incudibus antrum.
Illi inter ſeſe multâ vi brachia tollunt
In numerum. verſántque tenaci forcipe maſſam.   VIRGIL.

BOSTON:
Printed and Sold by EDES and GILL, in Queen-Street, 1765.

Pamphlet 11. Courtesy Harvard College Library

Liberty and Property vindicated, and the St--pm-n burnt.

A

DISCOURSE

OCCASIONALLY MADE

On burning the *Effige* of the

ST--PM-N.

IN

NEW-LONDON,

IN THE COLONY OF

CONNECTICUT.

XXXXXXXXXXXXXXXXXXXXXXXXXXX

By a Friend to the LIBERTY of his Country.

[Benjamin Church]

XXXXXXXXXXXXXXXXXXXXXXXXXXX

BOSTON: Re-printed and Sold at the Newest Printing-Office in Milk-Street. 1765.

Pamphlet 12. Courtesy American Antiquarian Society

CONSIDERATIONS

ON THE

PROPRIETY

OF IMPOSING

TAXES

IN THE

Britiſh COLONIES,

For the Purpoſe of raiſing a REVENUE, by
ACT OF PARLIAMENT.

———*Haud Totum Verba reſignent
Quod latet arcanâ, non enarrabile, fibrâ.*

North-America: Printed by a North-American.
MDCCLXV.

Pamphlet 13. Courtesy John Carter Brown Library

THE
LATE REGULATIONS

RESPECTING THE

BRITISH COLONIES

ON THE CONTINENT OF

AMERICA

CONSIDERED;

In a Letter from a Gentleman in PHILADELPHIA
to his Friend in LONDON.

Prosunt minus recte excogitata; cum alios incitent saltem
ad veritatis investigationem. FULB. A BARTOL.

PHILADELPHIA:

Printed and Sold by WILLIAM BRADFORD, at the Corner of
Market and Front-Streets. M.DCC.LXV.

Pamphlet 14. Courtesy Boston Athenaeum

GENERAL INTRODUCTION

THE TRANSFORMING RADICALISM
OF THE AMERICAN REVOLUTION

ABBREVIATIONS

Adams, "Bibliographical Study": Thomas R. Adams, "American Independence, The Growth of an Idea: A Bibliographical Study of the American Political Pamphlets Published between 1764 and 1776 Dealing with the Dispute between Great Britain and Her Colonies." To be published in a forthcoming volume of the *Publications of the Colonial Society of Massachusetts* and subsequently as a separate volume.

Adams, *Diary and Autobiography:* Lyman H. Butterfield, *et al.,* eds., *Diary and Autobiography of John Adams.* 4 vols. Cambridge, 1961.

Adams, *Works:* Charles Francis Adams, ed., *The Works of John Adams.* 10 vols. Boston, 1850–1856.

Coke, *Inst.:* Edward Coke, *The Institutes of the Laws of England.* 4 parts. First published London, 1628–1644.

Coke's Reports: *The Reports of Sir Edward Coke . . . of Divers Resolutions and Judgements . . . of Cases in Law . . .* First published in its entirety in English in London, 1658.

D.A.B.: Allen Johnson and Dumas Malone, eds., *Dictionary of American Biography.* 22 vols. N.Y., 1928–1944.

D.N.B.: Leslie Stephen and Sidney Lee, eds., *The Dictionary of National Biography.* 63 vols. London, 1885–1900.

Evans: Charles Evans, comp., *American Bibliography: A Chronological Dictionary of All Books, Pamphlets and Periodical Publications Printed in the United States of America [1639–1800].* 14 vols. Chicago and Worcester, Mass., 1903–1959. (Volumes XIII and XIV were compiled by Clifford K. Shipton.)

Gipson, *British Empire:* Lawrence H. Gipson, *The British Empire before the American Revolution.* 10 vols., in progress. Caldwell, Idaho, and New York, 1936–. Volume X (New York, 1961), most frequently cited, is subtitled *The Triumphant Empire: Thunder-Clouds Gather in the West, 1763–1766.*

Inst.: (See Coke, *Inst.*)

Mod.: *Modern Reports; or, Select Cases Adjudged in the Courts of King's Bench, Chancery, Common Pleas, and Exchequer [1669–1732].* [Standardized title of the London, 1793–1796 (T. Leach) edition.] 12 parts. First published London, 1682–1738.

Morgan, *Stamp Act:* Edmund S. Morgan and Helen M. Morgan, *The Stamp Act Crisis.* Chapel Hill, 1953.

N.E.Q.: New England Quarterly

Pa. Mag.: Pennsylvania Magazine of History and Biography

Sabin: Joseph Sabin, *et al.,* comps., *A Dictionary of Books Relating to America, from Its Discovery to the Present Time.* 29 vols. New York, 1868–1936.

Salkeld: William Salkeld, *Reports of Cases Adjudg'd in the Courts of King's Bench, with Some Special Cases in the Courts of Chancery, Common Pleas and Exchequer . . . [1689–1712].* 2 vols. First published [London], 1717.

Vaughan: Edward Vaughan, ed., *Reports and Arguments of . . . Sir John Vaughan Kt. Late Chief Justice of His Majesties Court of Common Pleas . . . [1665–1674].* First published London, 1677.

W.M.Q.: William and Mary Quarterly

CHAPTER I

THE PAMPHLETS OF THE REVOLUTION

WHATEVER deficiencies the leaders of the American Revolution may have had, reticence, fortunately, was not one of them. They wrote easily and amply, and turned out in the space of scarcely a decade and a half and from a small number of presses a rich literature of theory, argument, opinion, and polemic. Every medium of written expression was put to use. The newspapers, of which by 1775 there were thirty-eight in the mainland colonies, were crowded with columns of arguments and counter-arguments appearing as letters, official documents, extracts of speeches and sermons. Broadsides — single sheets on which were often printed not only large-letter notices but, in three or four columns of minuscule type, essays of several thousand words — appeared everywhere; they could be found posted or passing from hand to hand in the towns of every colony.[1] Above all, there were pamphlets: booklets consisting of a few printer's sheets, folded in various ways so as to make various sizes and numbers of pages, and sold — the pages stitched together loosely, unbound and uncovered — for a few pence, at most for a shilling or two.[2]

It was in this form — as pamphlets — that much of the most important and characteristic writing of the American Revolution appeared. For the Revolutionary generation as for its predecessors back to the early sixteenth century, the pamphlet had peculiar virtues as a medium of communication. Then, as now, it was seen that the pamphlet allowed one to do things that were not possible in any other form.

The pamphlet [George Orwell, a modern pamphleteer, has written] is a one-man show. One has complete freedom of expression, including, if one chooses, the freedom

---

[1] Arthur M. Schlesinger, *Prelude to Independence* (New York, 1958), pp. 215–216, part ii; Philip Davidson, *Propaganda and the American Revolution* (Chapel Hill, 1941), pp. 216–224. Cf. Chester N. Greenough, "New England Almanacs, 1766–1775, and the American Revolution," *Proceedings of the American Antiquarian Society,* new ser., 45 (1935), 288–316.

[2] The precise bibliographical definition of a pamphlet is the following: a booklet formed by the folding and stitching loosely together of between two and five printers sheets, which "gives to a pamphlet, in extreme, twenty pages when printed in folio; forty pages when printed in quarto; and eighty pages when printed in octavo." Charles Evans and Clifford K. Shipton, Comps., *American Bibliography* . . . (Chicago and Worcester, Mass., 1903–1959), V, xv. Cf. Lester Condit, *A Pamphlet about Pamphlets* (Chicago, 1939), chap. i.

to be scurrilous, abusive, and seditious; or, on the other hand, to be more detailed, serious and "highbrow" than is ever possible in a newspaper or in most kinds of periodicals. At the same time, since the pamphlet is always short and unbound, it can be produced much more quickly than a book, and in principle, at any rate, can reach a bigger public. Above all, the pamphlet does not have to follow any prescribed pattern. It can be in prose or in verse, it can consist largely of maps or statistics or quotations, it can take the form of a story, a fable, a letter, an essay, a dialogue, or a piece of "reportage." All that is required of it is that it shall be topical, polemical, and short.[3]

The pamphlet's greatest asset was perhaps its flexibility in size, for while it could contain only a very few pages and hence be used for publishing short squibs and sharp, quick rebuttals, it could also accommodate much longer, more serious and permanent writing as well. Some pamphlets of the Revolutionary period contain sixty or even eighty pages, on which are printed technical, magisterial treatises. Between the extremes of the squib and the book-length treatise, however, there lay the most commonly used, the ideally convenient, length: from 5,000 to 25,000 words, printed on anywhere from ten to fifty pages, quarto or octavo in size.

The pamphlet of this middle length was perfectly suited to the needs of the Revolutionary writers. It was spacious enough to allow for the full development of an argument — to investigate premises, explore logic, and consider conclusions; it could accommodate the elaborate involutions of eighteenth-century literary forms; it gave range for the publication of fully wrought, leisurely-paced sermons; it could conveniently carry state papers, collections of pseudonymous newspaper columns, and strings of damaging or exonerating personal correspondence. It was in this form, consequently, that "the best thought of the day expressed itself"; it was in this form that "the solid framework of constitutional thought" was developed; it was in this form that "the basic elements of American political thought of the Revolutionary period appeared first."[4] And yet pamphlets of this length were seldom ponderous; whatever the gravity

[3] George Orwell, "Introduction," in George Orwell and Reginald Reynolds, eds., *British Pamphleteers* (London, 1948–1951), I, 15. Orwell's spirited introductory essay was sparked by his belief that in twentieth-century society the press does not adequately represent all shades of opinion. "At any given moment there is a sort of all-prevailing orthodoxy, a general tacit agreement not to discuss some large and uncomfortable fact." He looked back to the days of vigorous, highly individualistic pamphleteering with nostalgia, and hoped that people "would once again become aware of the possibilities of the pamphlet as a method of influencing opinion, and as a literary form." A. J. P. Taylor's introduction to volume II of the same collection is an acerb comment on Orwell's nostalgia.

[4] Davidson, *Propaganda*, pp. 209–210; Moses C. Tyler, *The Literary History of the American Revolution, 1763–1783* (New York, 1897), I, 17 ff.; Homer L. Calkin, "Pamphlets and Public Opinion during the American Revolution," *Pa. Mag.*, 64 (1940), 22–42.

of their themes or the spaciousness of their contents, they were always polemical, always essentially intimate, and aimed at immediate and rapidly shifting targets: at suddenly developing problems, unanticipated arguments, and swiftly rising, controversial figures. The best of the writing that appeared in this form, consequently, had a rare combination of spontaneity and solidity, of dash and detail, of casualness and care.

Highly flexible, easy to manufacture, and cheap, pamphlets were printed in the American colonies wherever there were printing presses, intellectual ambitions, and political concerns. But in their origins most of them may be grouped within three categories. The largest number were direct responses to the great events of the time. The Stamp Act touched off a heavy flurry of pamphleteering in which basic American positions in constitutional theory were staked out; its repeal was celebrated by the publication of at least eleven thanksgiving sermons, all of them crowded with political theory; the Townshend Duties led to another intense burst of pamphleteering, as did the Boston Massacre and the precipitating events of the insurrection itself — the Tea Party, the Boston Port Act, and the meeting of the first Continental Congress.[5]

But if the writing of the pamphlets had been only a response to these overt public events, their numbers would have been far smaller than in fact they were. They resulted also, and to a considerable extent, from what might be called chain-reacting personal polemics: strings of individual exchanges — arguments, replies, rebuttals, and counter-rebuttals — in which may be found heated personifications of the larger conflict. A bold statement on a sensitive issue was often sufficient to start such a series, which characteristically proceeded with increasing shrillness until it ended in bitter personal vituperation. Thus East Apthorp's tract of 1763 on the Church of England's Society for the Propagation of the Gospel, inflaming as it did New Englanders' fears of an American bishopric, was answered at once by Jonathan Mayhew in a 176-page blast, and then, in the course of the next two years, by no less than nine other pamphleteers writing in a melée of thrusts and counterthrusts. Similarly, a succession of seven or eight searing pamphlets followed Richard Bland's attack on the Reverend

<hr />

[5] See, in general, Evans, *American Bibliography,* vols. III–V; and Thomas R. Adams, ed., "American Independence, the Growth of an Idea: A Bibliographical Study of the American Political Pamphlets Published between 1764 and 1776 . . . ," to appear in a forthcoming volume of the *Publications of the Colonial Society of Massachusetts.* (This work is cited hereafter as Adams, "Bibliographical Study.") The published sermons delivered at the repeal of the Stamp Act are listed in William D. Love, Jr., *The Fast and Thanksgiving Days of New England* (Boston and New York, 1895), pp. 541–542.

John Camm in the Two-Penny Act controversy in Virginia. Any number of people could join in such proliferating polemics, and rebuttals could come from all sides. Thomas Paine's *Common Sense* was answered not merely by two exhaustive refutations by Tories but also by at least four pamphlets written by patriots who shared his desire for independence but not his constitutional and religious views or his assumptions about human nature.[6]

A third type of pamphlet — besides those that surrounded the great public events and those that appeared in polemical series — was distinguished by the ritualistic character of its themes and language. In the course of the Revolutionary controversy, the regular, usually annual, publication in pamphlet form of commemorative orations came to constitute a significant addition to the body of Revolutionary literature. In an earlier period such publications had consisted mainly of sermons delivered on election day in New England together with a few of those preached on official thanksgiving and fast days. But from the mid-1760's on, celebrations of more secular anniversaries were added: the anniversary of the repeal of the Stamp Act, of the Boston Massacre, of the landing of the Pilgrims, and of an increasing number of fast and thanksgiving days marking political rather than religious events.[7]

Such commemorative orations were stylized; but in the heat of controversy the old forms took on new vigor, new relevance and meaning: some of the resulting pamphlets of this type have remarkable force and originality. Massachusetts and Connecticut had been publishing sermons preached on election days for one hundred years before Independence; by 1760 these pamphlets had arrived not only at an apparent fulfillment in style but, in content, at a classically monitorial attitude to political authority as well. Yet Andrew Eliot's use of the familiar formulas in his

---

[6] Adams, "Bibliographical Study," contains a separate listing of "Pamphlet Exchanges." On the Apthorp-Mayhew and Bland-Camm controversies, see below, Introductions to Pamphlets 3 and 4, and pp. 61–62, 154–158; other exchanges are discussed in the Introductions to Pamphlets 10, 11, and 13.

[7] Love, *Fast and Thanksgiving Days, passim;* Robert W. G. Vail, "A Check List of New England Election Sermons," *Proceedings of the American Antiquarian Society,* new ser., 45 (1935), 233–266. The Massacre Orations were delivered annually from 1771 to 1784, when they were superseded by Fourth of July Orations. In 1785 Peter Edes published a collection of Massacre Orations under the title *Orations Delivered at the Request of Inhabitants . . .* (Boston, [1785]). Accounts of the orators and of the circumstances of their speaking appear in James S. Loring, *The Hundred Boston Orations Appointed by the Municipal Authorities . . .* (Boston, 1852). On the Pilgrim celebrations and the general significance of the pre-Revolutionary commemorations, see Wesley Frank Craven, *The Legend of the Founding Fathers* (New York, 1956), chap. ii.

election sermon of 1765 infused them with more direct power and gave them new point; for to proclaim from the pulpit in the year of the Stamp Act and before the assembled magistrates of Massachusetts that when tyranny is abroad "submission . . . is a crime" was an act of political defiance strengthened rather than weakened by the sanction of time and tradition the words had acquired. Similarly the title of John Carmichael's Artillery Company sermon, *A Self-Defensive War Lawful,* though it merely repeated a traditional phrase, was, in 1775, in itself provocative; and the concluding passage of the pamphlet constitutes a significant transition in which clichés about the duties of Christian soldiers acquire the fervor of battlefield prayers. And if one of the later commemorative celebrations, that of the Boston Massacre, quickly became the occasion for the outpouring of some of the most lurid and naïve rhetoric heard in eighteenth-century America, another of them, a thanksgiving day appointed by the Continental Congress, inspired an obscure Salem parson to write, in the most dignified and moving prose, a paean to the promise of American life, and to devise an original blend of theological and constitutional principles. Everywhere in New England, clerical orators celebrating these anniversary events invoked the power of the ancient "jeremiad" to argue that "any vindication of provincial privileges was inextricably dependent upon a moral renovation." [8]

Not all the pamphlets, of course, fall into these three categories. Some, like the *Votes and Proceedings of the Freeholders . . . of . . . Boston* (1772), written for circulation in pamphlet form, were in themselves political events to which other pamphleteers responded. Others, like Jefferson's *Summary View . . .* (1774), written as an instruction to the Virginia delegates to the first Continental Congress, were political "position" papers whose quality justified their wide circulation. And in addition there were literary pieces — poems like John Trumbull's *M'Fingall* and plays like Mercy Otis Warren's *The Blockheads* and *The Group* — which, though manifestly political, sprang from more deeply personal inspiration.

Expressing vigorous, polemical, and more often than not considered views of the great events of the time; proliferating in chains of personal

---

[8] Andrew Eliot, *A Sermon Preached before His Excellency Francis Bernard . . .* (Boston, 1765), pp. 47–48; John Carmichael, *A Self-Defensive War Lawful . . .* (Lancaster, Mass., [1775]), especially p. 25; Samuel Williams, *A Discourse on the Love of Our Country . . .* (Salem, 1775); Perry Miller, "From the Covenant to the Revival," in *The Shaping of American Religion* (James W. Smith and A. Leland Jamison, eds., *Religion in American Life,* I, Princeton, 1961), 327.

vituperation; and embodying to the world the highly charged sentiments uttered on commemorative occasions, pamphlets appeared year after year and month after month in the crisis of the 1760's and 1770's. Several hundred of them bearing on the Anglo-American controversy were published between 1750 and 1776; over 1500 by 1783.[9] Explanatory as well as declarative, and expressive of the beliefs, attitudes, and motivations as well as of the professed goals of those who led and supported the Revolution, they reveal, more clearly perhaps than any other single group of documents, the contemporary meaning of that transforming event.

[9] The present collection is based on study of somewhat over 400 pamphlets; on the figures for the later years, see Calkin, "Pamphlets and Public Opinion," p. 23.

CHAPTER II

LITERARY QUALITIES

IMPORTANT above all else for their revelation of the ideas, attitudes, and motivations that lay at the heart of the American Revolution, the pamphlets published in the two decades before Independence are primarily political, not literary, documents. But form and substance are never wholly separate. The literary qualities of the pamphlets are also important, not only in themselves but for what they reveal of the people who wrote them, their goals and style of mind.

These pamphlets form part of that vast body of English polemical and journalistic literature of the seventeenth and eighteenth centuries to which the greatest men of letters contributed. Milton, Halifax, Locke, Swift, Defoe, Bolingbroke, Addison were all pamphleteers at least to the extent that Bland, Otis, Dickinson, the Adamses, Wilson, and Jefferson were. But there are striking differences in the quality of the British and American polemical writings considered simply as literature.

The differences do not lie simply in the presence or absence of literary techniques. One of the surprising aspects of the American writings is the extent to which they include the stylistic modes associated with the great age of English pamphleteering. Of satire, the protean artifice that dominated the most creative pamphleteering of the time, one scholar has identified no fewer than 530 examples published in America during the period 1763–1783; a large percentage of these appeared originally, or were reprinted, in pamphlets.[1] In addition to satire there is an abundance of other devices: elusive irony and flat parody; extended allegory and direct vituperation; sarcasm, calculated and naïve. All the standard tropes and a variety of unusual figurations may be found in the pamphlet literature.

The results are at times remarkable. Who has ever heard of Ebenezer Chaplin? He was parson of the second parish of the town of Sutton, Massachusetts, in the years before the Revolution; in conventional form he preached regularly and published occasionally on the problems of the church. But in a sermon published as a pamphlet in 1773 he suddenly

[1] Bruce I. Granger, *Political Satire in the American Revolution, 1763–1783* (Ithaca, 1960), p. viii.

revealed a remarkably self-conscious literary bent. The sermon is entitled *The Civil State Compared to Rivers,* and in it Chaplin managed for the better part of twenty-four pages to sustain the single simile announced in the title; the figure winds steadily through the argument, dramatizing it, coloring it, raising the aesthetic level of the piece far above what could have been attained by direct exposition. It is a noteworthy literary invention, and it gleams amid the hundreds of artistically drab sermons of the period.[2]

Similarly unexpected in its literary effects, though of a quite different genre, is Philip Livingston's *Other Side of the Question,* which appeared in the heavy bombardment of polemics of 1774. Where most of the writers in those exchanges used invective, Livingston used ironic ridicule, and he did so with such agility and lightness of touch that a device reminiscent of *Tristram Shandy* fits in naturally; two scatological passages seem normal exaggerations of a smart and worldly style.[3]

Effective in another way is the extended sham of a Christian catechism that was published anonymously in 1771 as an attack on sycophantic officemongering. No work of genius, it nevertheless gave a twist of originality to a familiar theme, exaggerating the abjectness of bought loyalty by its burlesque of sacred obligations. In a somewhat similar vein is what has been described as "the most ambitious and nearly successful of half a dozen Biblical imitations which appeared in the Revolutionary period," *The First Book of the American Chronicles of the Times,* a parody in six parts of an entire book of the Bible. It is so complete in its plot and characterization as to make identification of people and places an engaging puzzle. By its extensiveness and detail, by the sheer number of its imaginative touches, it attains a considerable effect.[4]

[2] Ebenezer Chaplin, *The Civil State Compared to Rivers, All under God's Control and What People Have To Do When Administration Is Grievous* . . . (Boston, 1773).

[3] [Philip Livingston], *The Other Side of the Question* . . . (New York, 1774), p. 11: "Pray read the eighth and ninth pages ——— ——— ——— ——— ——— ——— ——— ——— Have you read them? ——— Why now, your honor, I will undertake to confute everything contained there." See also pp. 20, 25.

[4] *A Ministerial Catechise, Suitable To Be Learned by All Modern Provincial Governors, Pensioners, Placemen, etc. Dedicated to T[homas] H[utchinson], Esq.* (Boston, 1771); *The First Book of the American Chronicles of the Times* (1774–1775); Granger, *Political Satire,* p. 70. *The First Book,* which was enormously popular, was published in six chapter segments in Philadelphia, Boston, Newbern, North Carolina, and Norwich, Connecticut. On the complicated printing history of this pamphlet, or series of pamphlets, see J. R. Bowman, "A Bibliography of *The First Book* . . . ," *American Literature,* I (1929–30), 69–74. Political satire in the form of Biblical parodies was popular throughout the Revolutionary period, as it had been in earlier years. Cf. Davidson, *Propaganda,* p. 212; Granger, *Political Satire,* pp. 34–35, 68–70, 236–237. For an example characteristic of the earlier years, see

In other ways, by other devices, literary effects were sought and achieved. The most commonly attempted was the satire associated with pseudonymous authorship. Governor Stephen Hopkins of Rhode Island, for example, fell upon the opportunity offered to him when his antagonist, Judge Martin Howard, Jr., characterized him as a "ragged country fellow"; he replied with an earthy, vicious attack which he justified by the argument that rags go together with a crude directness of speech. And Richard Bland, in what was probably the most intricate literary conceit written in the entire period, succeeded to such an extent in ridiculing his antagonist by reversing roles with him and condemning him from his own mouth that his victim was forced to reply weakly by explaining to his readers who was really who. Even the more common and transparent forms of pseudonymity provided an opportunity for literary invention. The pastoral pose was more useful to the Reverend Samuel Seabury, arguing the case for the agrarian interests in New York against non-importation, than it had been to the most famous "farmer" of them all, John Dickinson; it provided not only a consistent point of view but figures of speech and the opportunity for fanciful self-characterization.[5]

All sorts of literary twists and turns were used. Thomas Bradbury Chandler's *The American Querist,* one of the most popular of the Tory pamphlets, consisted of an even one hundred rhetorical questions aimed at the pretensions of the first Continental Congress; the queries were printed for emphasis as one hundred separate paragraphs spread across twenty-one octavo pages. Elephantine footnoting attached to nine stanzas of lampooning verse was the form one response took to Mayhew's extended attacks on the Society for the Propagation of the Gospel. Dramatic dialogues — *"Between the Ghost of General Montgomery, Just Arrived from the Elysian Fields, and An American Delegate"; "Between a Southern Delegate and His Spouse"* — were convenient frames for lurid caricatures, and since they made fewer demands on the skills of the

---

Stephen Hopkins', or his party's, *The Fall of Samuel the Squomicutite, and the Overthrow of the Sons of Gideon,* referring to Samuel Ward and Gideon Wanton, described in Edward Field, ed., *State of Rhode Island and Providence Plantations . . .* (Boston, 1902), I, 209–210.

[5] [Stephen Hopkins], *A Letter to the Author of the Halifax Letter . . .* ([Newport], 1765); [Richard Bland], *The Colonel Dismounted: or, the Rector Vindicated* (Williamsburg, 1764: JHL Pamphlet 4); [John Camm], *Critical Remarks on a Letter Ascribed to Common Sense . . . with a Dissertation on Drowsiness . . .* (Williamsburg, 1765), pp. vi–ix; [Samuel Seabury], *Free Thoughts on the Proceedings of the Continental Congress Held at Philadelphia September 5, 1774 . . .* ([New York], 1774), reprinted in Clarence H. Vance, ed., *Letters of a Westchester Farmer (1774–1775) (Publications of the Westchester County Historical Society,* VIII, White Plains, 1930), pp. 43–68.

dramatist, they were on the whole more successful than the half-dozen more fully evolved plays that were written for pamphlet publication.[6]

And all the detailed linguistic tactics of the classic era of English pamphleteering were present. The pamphlets abound in aphorisms: a section of one sermon is in effect nothing but a mosaic of aphorisms.[7] There are apostrophes, hyperboles, and vivid personifications. There are subtle transitions that seek to ease the flow of thought, and others contrived to interrupt it, to surprise and fix attention. Even the most crudely bombastic harangues contain artful literary constructions.

And yet, for all of this — for all of the high self-consciousness of literary expression, the obvious familiarity with cosmopolitan models and the armory of sophisticated belles-lettres — the pamphlets of the American Revolution that seek artistic effects are not great documents. Next to the more artful pamphlets of eighteenth-century England they are pallid, imitative, and crude. And the higher, the more technically demanding the mode of expression, the more glaring the contrast. There is nothing in the American literature that approaches in sheer literary skill such an imaginatively conceived and expertly written pamphlet as Swift's *Modest Proposal,* or even such a lesser piece as Defoe's *Shortest Way with the Dissenters;* there is no allegory as masterful as Arbuthnot's *History of John Bull,* and no satire as deft as his *Art of Political Lying.* Indeed, there are not many of the American pamphlets that are as successful in technique as any number of the less imaginative, straight expository essays published in seventeenth- and eighteenth-century England, essays of which Shebbeare's *Letter to the People of England,* lamenting corruption and excoriating the mismanagement of Braddock's expedition, may be taken as average in quality and Swift's *Conduct of the Allies* as a notable refinement. Why this should be so — why the more imaginative and self-consciously literary of the pamphlets of the Revolution should be manifestly inferior in quality to the English models — is an important even if not a wholly answerable question. For it helps

[6] [Thomas Bradbury Chandler], *The American Querist: or, Some Questions Proposed* . . . ([New York], 1774); [John Aplin], *Verses on Doctor Mayhew's Book of Observations* (Providence, 1763: JHL Pamphlet 3). The dialogues, in the order cited, were published in Philadelphia, 1776 (cf. Richard Gimbel, *Thomas Paine: A Bibliographical Check List of Common Sense* . . . , New Haven, 1956, CS 9, p. 74) and [New York], 1774. They are reprinted in *Magazine of History,* 13 [Extra Number 51] (1916); and 18 [Extra Number 72] (1920–21).

[7] Samuel Cooke, *A Sermon Preached at Cambridge, in the Audience of His Honor Thomas Hutchinson Esq.* . . . . (Boston, 1770), pp. 11 ff.

locate and explain the qualities of these documents that are of the greatest distinction.

First and foremost, the American pamphleteers, though participants in a great tradition, were amateurs next to such polemicists as Swift and Defoe. Nowhere in the relatively undifferentiated society of colonial America had there developed before 1776 a group of penmen professional in the sense that Defoe or Franklin's friend James Ralph were professional: capable, that is, of earning their living by their pens, capable of producing copy on order as well as on inspiration, and taught by the experience of dozens of polemical encounters the limits and possibilities of their craft. The closest to having attained such professionalism in the colonies were a few of the more prominent printers; but with the exception of Franklin they did not transcend the ordinary limitations of their trade: they were rarely principals in the controversies of the time. The American pamphleteers were almost to a man lawyers, ministers, merchants, or planters heavily engaged in their regular occupations. For them political writing was an uncommon diversion, peripheral to their main concerns. They wrote easily and readily, but until the crisis of Anglo-American affairs was reached, they had had no occasion to turn out public letters, tracts, and pamphlets in numbers at all comparable to those of the English pamphleteers. The most experienced polemical writer in the colonies was probably William Livingston of New York, who, together with two or three of his friends, had sustained *The Independent Reflector* through enough issues in 1752 and 1753 to fill one good-sized volume.[8] But Swift's formal prose work alone fills fourteen volumes, and Defoe is known to have written at least 400 tracts, pamphlets, and books: his contributions to a single periodical during a ten year period totals 5,000 printed pages, and that represents less than half of what he wrote in those years. It appears to have been no great matter for a professional like James Ralph, who attained success as a paid political writer after years of effort in poetry, drama, and criticism and who late in life published an eloquent *Case of Authors by Profession or Trade,* to turn out, amid a stream of pamphlets and periodical pieces, a massive *History of England* whose bibliographical and critical introduction alone covers 1078 folio pages.[9]

[8] William Livingston, *et al., The Independent Reflector* . . . (Milton M. Klein, ed., Cambridge, 1963).
[9] On the professionalism of the English political writers in general, see Laurence Hanson,

No American writer in the half century between the death of Cotton Mather and the Declaration of Independence had anything like such experience in writing; and it is this amateurism, this lack of practiced technique, that explains much of the crudeness of the Revolutionary pamphlets considered simply as literature. For while the colonial writers were obviously acquainted with and capable of imitating the forms of sophisticated polemics, they had not truly mastered them; they were rarely capable of keeping their literary contrivances in control. All of the examples cited above for their literary qualities (and as self-conscious artistic efforts they are among the most noteworthy documents of the group) suffer from technical weaknesses. By virtue of its extended simile Chaplin's *Civil State* shines among the sermons of the time, but in the end the effect is almost overcome by insistence; the figure is maintained too long; it becomes obtrusive, and the reader ends more aware of it than of the thought it is supposed to be illuminating. The *Ministerial Catechism* lacks the verbal cleverness necessary to keep it from falling into a jog-trotting substitution-play of words. And while the *First Book of . . . American Chronicles* is a more intricate and extended burlesque, its diction, one critic has noted, "has a synthetic ring and at one point a brief passage of French dialect is jarring." [10] Most of the pseudonymous poses, including Hopkins' cited above, were transparent to begin with, and they were unevenly, even sloppily, maintained; often, they were simply cast aside after the opening passages, to be snatched up again hurriedly at the end in a gesture of literary decorousness. Even Bland, as artful a litterateur as America produced in the period, was incapable of fully controlling his own invention. If his elaborate conceit threw his intended victim into confusion, it must have had a similar effect on many of its other readers, for at times the point is almost lost in a maze of true and facetious meanings. Chandler's *Querist* is notably original, but strings of syntactically identical questions can become monotonous unless their contents are unusually clever; fifty of them are almost certain to become wearying; Chandler's one hundred will exhaust the patience of any reader.

Government and the Press 1695–1763 (Oxford, 1936) (on Defoe's productivity, p. 94); William T. Laprade, *Public Opinion and Politics in Eighteenth Century England* (New York, 1936); Robert R. Rea, *The English Press in Politics 1760–1774* (Lincoln, Nebraska, 1963). On James, whose *History* was used by the colonists (see below, *Letter to the People of Pennsylvania*, JHL Pamphlet 2, text note 1) and whose career stands in such striking contrast to those of the American pamphleteers, see Robert W. Kenny, "James Ralph . . . ," *Pa. Mag.*, 64 (1940), 218–242.   [10] Granger, *Political Satire*, p. 70.

And these are among the strongest of the efforts made to attain literary effects. The weakest are, on technical grounds, quite remarkably bad. The poetry — or, more accurately, the versification — is almost uniformly painful to read. There is scarcely a single group of stanzas that can be read with any satisfaction as poetry. Most of the verses are a kind of limping jingle-jangle in which sense and sound are alternatively sacrificed to each other, and both, occasionally, to the demands of termination. The dramatic dialogues, whatever their political importance might be, as literary expressions are wooden and lifeless. And the plays, especially the verse plays, are almost totally devoid of characterization or any other form of verisimilitude.

But there is more than amateurism behind the relative crudeness of the artistic efforts in the American pamphlets. For if writers like Adams and Jefferson were amateur pamphleteers, their writings in other ways display formidable literary talents. Jefferson had an extraordinary gift for supple and elegant if abstract expression; it was well known and appreciated at the time. And Adams, seemingly so stolid and unimaginative an embodiment of prosaic virtues, had a basically sensuous apprehension of experience which he expressed in brilliantly idiomatic and figurative prose — but in diary notations and in letters. Neither, as pamphleteers, sought literary effects: Jefferson's sole effort is a straightforward if gracefully written political policy statement, and Adams' major piece is a treatise on government.[11]

It is not simply a question of the presence or absence of literary imagination or technical skill but of their employment. The more deliberately artful writings were in a significant way — for reasons that reach into the heart of the Revolutionary movement — peripheral to the main lines of intellectual force developing through the period. They were peculiarly incongruous to the deeper impulses of the time, and they never attracted the major talents nor fully excited those that were drawn to them. Beneath the technical deficiencies of the belleletristic pieces lies an absence of motivating power, of that "peculiar emotional intensity" that so dis-

[11] Jefferson's style has been frequently discussed, most fully by Carl Becker, *The Declaration of Independence* (New York, 1922), chapter v. Cf. Bernard Bailyn, "Boyd's Jefferson: Notes for a Sketch," *N.E.Q.,* 33 (1960), 392–393. On Adams' prose, see Bernard Bailyn, "Butterfield's Adams: Notes for a Sketch," *W.M.Q.,* 3d ser., 19 (1962), 246–247. The writings referred to are Jefferson's *A Summary View of the Rights of British America . . .* (Williamsburg, [1774]), reprinted in Paul L. Ford, ed., *Writings of Thomas Jefferson* (New York, 1892–1899), I, 429–447, and Adams' *Thoughts on Government . . .* (Philadelphia, 1776), in *Works,* IV, 193–200.

tinguishes the political writing of Jonathan Swift.[12] The American pamphlets are essentially decorous and reasonable. Not that they are all mild in tone, prissy, anemic, or lacking in emphasis. Vigor of one sort or another was common enough; at times, as in the frantic Tory outpouring of 1774–1775, there was something akin to verbal violence. And mudslinging invective was everywhere; for in an age when gross public accusations were commonplace, it took a degree of restraint no one sought to employ to keep from depicting George Washington as the corrupter of a washerwoman's daughter, John Hancock as both impotent and the stud of an illegitimate brood, William Drayton as a disappointed office seeker whose fortune had been ruined by "the nicks of *seven* and *eleven*," and Judge Martin Howard, Jr., as a well-known card-sharper.[13]

But mere vigor and lurid splash are not in themselves expressions of imaginative intensity. Among all those who wrote pamphlets, in fact, there appear to have been only three — James Otis, Thomas Paine, and that strange itinerant Baptist John Allen — who had anything like the concentrated fury that propelled Swift's thought and imagination through the intensifying indirections of literary forms. And in all three cases there were singular circumstances. Otis' passion, the wildness that so astonished his contemporaries, already by 1765 was beginning to lack control: it would soon slip into incoherence. The "daring impudence," the "uncommon frenzy" which gave *Common Sense* its unique power, Paine brought with him from England in 1774; it had been nourished in another culture, and was recognized at the time to be an alien quality in American writing. And Allen too — in any case no equal, as a pamphleteer, of Paine — had acquired his habits of literary expression abroad.[14]

[12] F. R. Leavis, "The Irony of Swift," *Determinations: Critical Essays* (London, 1934), p. 81.

[13] *The Battle of Brooklyn, A Farce in Two Acts* . . . (New York, 1776), p. 11 (cf. Allen French, "The First George Washington Scandal," *Proceedings of the Massachusetts Historical Society*, 65 [1932–1936], 469 ff.); [John Mein], *Sagittarius's Letters and Political Speculations* . . . (Boston, 1775), pp. 103–104; Thomas Bolton, *An Oration Delivered March Fifteenth, 1775* . . . ([Boston], 1775), p. 5; *Some Fugitive Thoughts on a Letter Signed Freeman* . . . ([Charleston], 1774), p. 10; Hopkins, *Letter to the Author of the Halifax Letter*, p. 7.

[14] On Otis, see below, Introductions to Pamphlets 7 and 11. The quoted phrases on Paine are from John Adams, *Diary and Autobiography*, III, 330–335, and Charles Inglis, *The True Interest of America* . . . *Strictures on a Pamphlet Intitled Common Sense* . . . (Philadelphia, 1776), vi. Inglis notes later in the pamphlet that Paine's "main attack is upon the passions of his readers, especially their pity and resentment . . . he seems to be everywhere transported with rage—a rage that knows no limits, and hurries him along like an impetuous torrent . . . such fire and fury . . . indicate that some mortifying disap-

The American writers were profoundly reasonable people. Their pamphlets convey scorn, anger, and indignation; but rarely blind hate, rarely panic fear. They sought to convince their opponents, not, like the English pamphleteers of the eighteenth century, to annihilate them. In this rationality, this everyday, businesslike sanity so distant from the imaginative mists where artistic creations struggle into birth, they were products of their situation and of the demands it made in politics. For the American Revolution, which transformed American life and introduced a new era in human history, was to a remarkable extent an affair of the mind. Its dominant goals were not the overthrow of the existing order but the establishment in principle of existing matters of fact, and its means were the communication of understanding. Its great expressions embodied in the best of the pamphlets are therefore expository and explanatory: didactic, systematic, and direct, rather than imaginative and metaphoric. They take the form most naturally of treatises and sermons, not poems; of descriptions, not allegories; of explanations, not burlesques. The reader is led through arguments, not images. The pamphlets aim to persuade.

What was essentially involved in the American Revolution was not the disruption of society, with all the fear, despair, and hatred that that entails, but the realization, the comprehension and fulfillment, of what was taken to be America's destiny in the context of world history. The great social shocks that in the French and Russian Revolutions sent the foundations of thousands of individual lives crashing into ruins had taken place in America in the course of the previous century, slowly, silently, almost imperceptibly, not as a sudden avalanche but as myriads of individual changes and adjustments which had gradually transformed the order of society. By 1763 the great landmarks of European life — the church and the idea of orthodoxy, the state and the idea of authority: much of the array of institutions and ideas that buttressed the society of

---

pointment is rankling at heart, or that some tempting object of ambition is in view, or probably both" (p. 34). Allen, author of *The American Alarm . . . by the British Bostonian* and the immensely popular *Oration upon the Beauties of Liberty,* both published in 1773, left London in 1769, where he had been a Baptist preacher, after various vicissitudes, including a trial for forgery and some time in debtor's prison. Before arriving in the colonies he had published *The Spiritual Magazine . . .* (3 vols.) and a half-dozen pamphlets, and during his tumultuous stay in New York, 1770–1772, added *The Spirit of Liberty, or Junius's Loyal Address* (1770). His wanderings after he left Boston in 1773 are obscure, but apparently he continued to publish religious tracts; a poem, *Christ the Christian's Hope . . .* (Exeter, N.H., 1789), may also be his. See Walter Wilson, *The History and Antiquities of Dissenting Churches and Meeting Houses, London . . .* (London, 1814), IV, 426–428; and *Biographical Memoirs of the Late Rev. John Gano . . .* (New York, 1806), pp. 89–90.

the *ancien régime* — had faded in their exposure to the open, wilderness environment of America. But until the disturbances of the 1760's these changes had not been seized upon as grounds for a reconsideration of society and politics. Often they had been condemned as deviations, as retrogressions back toward a more primitive condition of life. Then, after 1760 — and especially in the decade after 1765 — they were brought into open discussion as the colonists sought to apply advanced principles of society and politics to their own immediate problems.[15]

The original issue of the Anglo-American conflict was, of course, the question of the extent of Parliament's jurisdiction in the colonies. But that could not be discussed in isolation. The debate involved eventually a wide range of social and political problems, and it ended by 1776 in what may be called the conceptualization of American life. By then Americans had come to think of themselves as in a special category, uniquely placed by history to capitalize on, to complete and fulfill, the promise of man's existence. The changes that had overtaken their provincial societies, they saw, had been good: elements not of deviance and retrogression but of betterment and progress; not a lapse into primitivism, but an elevation to a higher plane of political and social life than had ever been reached before. Their rustic blemishes had become the marks of a chosen people. "The liberties of mankind and the glory of human nature is in their keeping," John Adams wrote in the year of the Stamp Act. "America was designed by Providence for the theatre on which man was to make his true figure, on which science, virtue, liberty, happiness, and glory were to exist in peace." [16]

The effort to comprehend, to communicate, and to fulfill this destiny was continuous through the entire Revolutionary generation — it did not cease, in fact, until in the nineteenth century its creative achievements became dogma. But there were three phases of particular concentration: the period up to and including 1776, centering on the discussion of Anglo-American differences; the devising of the first state governments, mainly in the years from 1776 to 1780; and the reconsideration of the state constitutions and the reconstruction of the national government in the last half of the decade of the eighties. In each of these phases important contributions were made not only to the skeletal structure of consti-

[15] Bernard Bailyn, "Political Experience and Enlightenment Ideas in Eighteenth-Century America," *American Historical Review*, 67 (1961–62), pp. 339–351.

[16] *Diary and Autobiography*, I, 282.

tutional theory but to the surrounding areas of social thought as well. But in none was the creativity as great, the results as radical and as fundamental, as in the period before Independence. It was then that the premises were defined and the assumptions set. It was then that explorations were made in new territories of thought, the first comprehensive maps sketched, and routes marked out. Thereafter the psychological as well as intellectual barriers were down. It was the most creative period in the history of American political thought. Everything that followed assumed and built upon its results.

In the pamphlets published before Independence may be found the fullest expressions of this creative effort. There were other media of communication; but everything essential to the discussion of those years appeared, if not originally then as reprints, in pamphlet form. The treatises, the sermons, the speeches, the exchanges of letters published as pamphlets — even some of the most personal polemics — all contain elements of this great, transforming debate.

It is the purpose of the sections that follow to examine the common elements of these writings, to present the basic issues and problems as they were seen by the writers, and to trace certain fundamental shifts in understanding that they reveal.

CHAPTER III

SOURCES AND TRADITIONS

THE intellectual history of the years of crisis from 1763 to 1776 is the story of the clarification and consolidation under the pressure of events of a view of the world and of America's place in it only vaguely and partially seen before. Elements of this picture had long been present in the colonies — some of them dated from as far back as the settlements themselves — but they had existed in balance, as it were, with other, conflicting views, and they had not been fully formulated. Expressed in fragmentary form on occasions of controversy, they had appeared as partisan arguments, without unique appeal or status or claim to legitimacy. Then, in the intense political heat of the decade after 1763 these long popular, though hitherto inconclusive, controversial, and imperfectly harmonized, ideas about the world and America's place in it were fused into a comprehensive view, unique in its moral and intellectual appeal. It is the development of this view to the point of overwhelming persuasiveness to the majority of American leaders and the meaning this view gave to the events of the time, and not simply an accumulation of grievances, that explains the origins of the American Revolution. For this peculiar configuration of ideas constituted in effect an intellectual switchboard wired so that certain combinations of events would activate a distinct set of signals — danger signals, indicating hidden impulses and the likely trajectory of events impelled by them. Well before 1776 the signals registered on this switchboard led to a single, unmistakable conclusion — a conclusion that had long been feared and to which there could be only one rational response.

What were the sources of this world view? From whom, from what, were the ideas and attitudes derived?

Study of the sources of the colonists' thought as expressed in the informal as well as the formal documents, in the private as well as the public utterances, and above all in the discursive, explanatory pamphlets, reveals, at first glance, a massive, seemingly random eclecticism. To judge simply from an enumeration of the colonists' citations, they had at their finger tips, and made use of, a large portion of the inheritance of western

culture, from Aristotle to Molière, from Cicero to "Philoleutherus Lipsiensis" [Richard Bentley], from Virgil to Shakespeare, Ramus, Pufendorf, Swift, and Rousseau. They liked to display authorities for their arguments, citing and quoting from them freely; at times their writings become almost submerged in annotation: in certain of the writings of John
Dickinson the text disappears altogether in a sea of footnotes and footnotes
to footnotes.[1] But ultimately this profusion of authorities is reducible to
a few, distinct groups of sources and intellectual traditions dominated and
harmonized into a single whole by the influence of one peculiar strain of
thought, one distinctive tradition.

Most conspicuous in the writings of the Revolutionary period was the
heritage of classical antiquity. Knowledge of classical authors was universal among colonists with any degree of education, and references to
them and their works abound in the literature. From the grammar schools,
from the colleges, from private tutors and independent reading came a
general familiarity with and the habit of reference to the ancient authors
and the heroic personalities and events of the ancient world. "Homer,
Sophocles, Plato, Euripides, Herodotus, Thucydides, Xenophon, Aristotle,
Strabo, Lucian, Dio, Polybius, Plutarch, and Epictetus, among the Greeks;
and Cicero, Horace, Vergil, Tacitus, Lucan, Seneca, Livy, Nepos, Sallust,
Ovid, Lucretius, Cato, Pliny, Juvenal, Curtius, Marcus Aurelius, Petronius,
Suetonius, Caesar, the lawyers Ulpian and Gaius, and Justinian, among the
Romans" — all are cited in the Revolutionary literature; many are di-
rectly quoted. "It was an obscure pamphleteer indeed who could not mus-
ter at least one classical analogy or one ancient precept."[2]

But this elaborate display of classical authors is deceptive. Often the
learning behind it was superficial; often the citations appear to have been
dragged in as "window dressing with which to ornament a page or a
speech and to increase the weight of an argument," for classical quotation,
as Dr. Johnson said, was "the *parole* of literary men all over the world."
So Jonathan Mayhew casually lumped Plato with Demosthenes and Cicero

[1] Most notably in his *Essay on the Constitutional Power of Great-Britain over the
Colonies in America* . . . (Philadelphia, 1774), reprinted in *Pennsylvania Archives*, 2d ser.,
III, 565 ff. See also Josiah Quincy, Jr.'s *Observations on the Act of Parliament Commonly
Called the . . . Boston Port-Bill* . . . (Boston, 1774), reprinted in Josiah Quincy, *Memoir
of the Life of Josiah Quincy Jun.* . . . (Boston, 1825), pp. 355 ff.
[2] Charles F. Mullett, "Classical Influences on the American Revolution," *Classical Jour-
nal*, 35 (1939–1940), 93, 94. On the classics in general in colonial and Revolutionary America,
see Richard M. Gummere, *The American Colonial Mind and the Classical Tradition*
(Cambridge, 1963); on the teaching of the classics in the secondary schools, see Robert
Middlekauff, *Ancients and Axioms* (New Haven, 1963).

as the ancients who in his youth had initiated him "in the doctrines of civil liberty"; Oxenbridge Thacher too thought Plato had been a liberty-loving revolutionary, while Jefferson, who actually read the *Dialogues,* discovered in them only the "sophisms, futilities, and incomprehensibilities" of a "foggy mind" — an idea concurred in with relief by John Adams, who in 1774 had cited Plato as an advocate of equality and self-government but who was so shocked when he finally studied the philosopher that he concluded that the *Republic* must have been meant as a satire.[3]

Yet Jefferson was a careful reader of the classics, and others too — James Otis, for example, who wrote treatises on Latin and Greek prosody — were thorough scholars of the ancient texts. What is basically important in the Americans' reading of the ancients is the high selectivity of their real interests and the limitation of the range of their effective knowledge. For though the colonists drew their citations from all portions of the literature of the ancient world, their detailed knowledge and engaged interest covered only one era and one small group of writers. What gripped their minds, what they knew in detail, and what formed their view of the whole of the ancient world was the political history of Rome from the conquests in the east and the civil wars in the early first century B.C. to the establishment of the empire on the ruins of the republic at the end of the second century A.D. For their knowledge of this period they had at hand, and needed only, Plutarch, Livy, and above all Cicero, Sallust, and Tacitus — writers who had lived either when the Republic was being fundamentally challenged or when its greatest days were already past and its moral and political virtues decayed. They had hated and feared the trends of their own time, and in their writing had contrasted the present with a better past, which they endowed with qualities absent from their own, corrupt era. The earlier age had been full of virtue: simplicity, patriotism, integrity, a love of justice and of liberty; the present was venal, cynical, and oppressive.[4]

For the colonists, arguing the American cause in the controversies of the 1760's and 1770's, the analogies to their own times were compelling. They saw their own provincial virtues — rustic and old-fashioned, sturdy and effective — challenged by the corruption at the center of power, by the threat of tyranny, and by a constitution gone wrong. They found their

---

[3] Mullett, "Classical Influences," pp. 93, 99; Peter Gay, *The Party of Humanity* (New York, 1963), p. 10; Lester J. Cappon, ed., *The Adams-Jefferson Letters* (Chapel Hill, 1959), II, 433, 437. Cf. Gummere, *Classical Tradition,* pp. 178–179.

[4] Mullett, "Classical Influences," pp. 96 ff. Cf. Harold T. Parker, *The Cult of Antiquity and the French Revolutionaries* (Chicago, 1937), pp. 22, 23.

ideal selves, and to some extent their voices, in Brutus, in Cassius, and in
Cicero, whose Catilinarian orations the enraptured John Adams, aged 23,
declaimed aloud, alone at night in his room. They were simple, stoical
Catos, desperate, self-sacrificing Brutuses, silver-tongued Ciceros, and terse,
sardonic Tacituses eulogizing Teutonic freedom and denouncing the de-
cadence of Rome. England, the young John Dickinson wrote from London in 1754, is like Sallust's Rome: " 'Easy to be bought, if there was but
a purchaser.' " Britain, it would soon become clear, was to America "what
Caesar was to Rome." [5]

The classics of the ancient world are everywhere in the literature of the
Revolution, but they are everywhere illustrative, not determinative, of
thought. They contributed a vivid vocabulary but not the logic or grammar of thought, a universally respected personification but not the source
of political and social beliefs. They heightened the colonists' sensitivity to
ideas and attitudes otherwise derived.

More directly influential in shaping the thought of the Revolutionary
generation were the ideas and attitudes associated with the writings of
Enlightenment rationalism — writings that expressed not simply the rationalism of liberal reform but that of enlightened conservatism as well.

Despite the efforts that have been made to discount the influence of the
"glittering generalities" of the European Enlightenment on eighteenth-
century Americans, their influence remains, and is profusely illustrated in
the pamphlet literature. It is not simply that the great *virtuosi* of the
American Enlightenment — Franklin, Adams, Jefferson — cited the classic
Enlightenment texts and fought for the legal recognition of natural rights
and for the elimination of institutions and practices associated with the
ancien régime. They did so; but they were not alone. The ideas and
writings of the leading secular thinkers of the European Enlightenment —
reformers and social critics like Voltaire, Rousseau, and Beccaria as well
as conservative analysts like Montesquieu — were quoted everywhere in
the colonies, by everyone who claimed a broad awareness. In pamphlet
after pamphlet the American writers cited Locke on natural rights and
on the social and governmental contract, Montesquieu and later Delolme
on the character of British liberty and on the institutional requirements
for its attainment, Voltaire on the evils of clerical oppression, Beccaria on

[5] Adams, *Diary and Autobiography*, I, 63; Mullett, "Classical Influences," p. 102; H.
Trevor Colbourn, ed., "A Pennsylvania Farmer at the Court of King George: John
Dickinson's London Letters, 1754–1756," *Pa. Mag.*, 86 (1962), 268. Quincy, *Observations*,
in Quincy, *Memoir*, p. 435. American views of corruption in English life are described
below, pp. 56–58, 79–82.

the reform of criminal law, Grotius, Pufendorf and Vattel on the laws of nature and of nations, and Burlamaqui on the limitations on public authority necessary for a free society.

The pervasiveness of such citations is at times astonishing. In one of the two pamphlets by James Otis reprinted in the present volume, for example, Locke, Rousseau, Grotius, and Pufendorf are cited as authorities, and in the other their earlier opponents — spokesmen, such as Filmer, for more traditional ideas of political authority — are denounced. Similarly, Josiah Quincy, Jr., cites with approval a whole library of enlightened authors, among them Beccaria, Rousseau, Montesquieu, and the historian Robertson; and the young Alexander Hamilton, seeking to score points against his venerable antagonist, Samuel Seabury, recommends with arch condescension that his adversary get himself at the first opportunity to some of the writings of Pufendorf, Locke, Montesquieu, and Burlamaqui to discover the true principles of politics. Examples could be multiplied almost without end. Citations, respectful borrowings from, or at least references to, the eighteenth-century European illuminati are everywhere in the pamphlets of Revolutionary America.[6]

The citations are plentiful, but the knowledge they reflect, like that of the ancient classics, is at times superficial. Locke is cited often with precision on points of political theory, but at other times he is referred to in the most offhand way, as if he could be relied on to support anything the writers happened to be arguing.[7] Bolingbroke and Hume are at times lumped together with radical reformers, and popularizers like Burlamaqui are treated on a level with Locke.[8] Nor were the critical, reforming writings of the Enlightenment, even some of the most radical, used exclusively by the left wing of the Revolutionary movement. Everyone, whatever his position on Independence or his judgment of Parliament's actions, cited them as authoritative; almost no one, Whig or Tory, disputed them or in-

---

[6] Otis, *Rights of the British Colonies* (JHL Pamphlet 7), pp. 9, 15, 22–23, 25, 26, 27, 30, 37; *A Vindication of the British Colonies* (JHL Pamphlet 11), pp. 10–12; Quincy, *Observations,* in Quincy, *Memoir,* pp. 394, 402, 404, 406, 415, 452; [Hamilton], *The Farmer Refuted . . .* (New York, 1775), reprinted in *Works* (H. C. Lodge, ed., New York and London, 1904), I, 59.

[7] Thus Simeon Howard validates his offhand description of the state of nature with the footnote "See Locke on government." *Sermon Preached to the Ancient and Honorable Artillery-Company . . .* (Boston, 1773), p. 8.

[8] Hume was greatly respected in America, but his *History of Great Britain,* though often referred to, was commonly believed to be, in Daniel Dulany's words, "a studied apology for the Stuarts, and particularly Charles I." Elihu S. Riley, ed., *Correspondence of "First Citizen" — Charles Carroll of Carrollton, and "Antilon" — Daniel Dulany, Jr. . . .* (Baltimore, 1902), p. 191. On Bolingbroke, see below, note 21.

troduced them with apology. Writers the colonists took to be opponents of Enlightenment rationalism — primarily Hobbes, Filmer, Sibthorpe, Mandeville, and Mainwaring — were denounced as frequently by loyalists as by patriots; but almost never, before 1776, were Locke, Montesquieu, Vattel, Beccaria, Burlamaqui, Voltaire, or even Rousseau.[9] Mercy Otis Warren listed the contents of a hypothetical Tory library in her play *The Group;* but with the exception of Filmer none of the authors she mentions there were in fact referred to favorably by the Tories. James Chalmers, the Maryland loyalist, attacked Paine not with Hobbes, Sibthorpe, Wedderburn's speeches, and the statutes of Henry VIII, which, according to Mrs. Warren he should have done, but with Montesquieu, Hutcheson, even Voltaire and Rousseau. The Pennsylvania Loyalist Joseph Galloway cited Locke and Pufendorf as readily as his antagonists did; and when Charles Inglis looked for the source of Paine's anti-monarchism in order to attack it, he found it not in Enlightenment theory, whose exponents he praised, but in an obscure treatise by one John Hall, "pensioner under Oliver Cromwell."[10]

Referred to on all sides, by writers of all political viewpoints in the colonies, the major figures of the European Enlightenment and many of the lesser, contributed substantially to the thought of the Americans; but except for Locke's, their influence, though more decisive than that of the authors of classical antiquity, was neither clearly dominant nor wholly determinative.

Also prominent and in certain ways powerfully influential was yet another group of writers and ideas. Just as the colonists cited with enthusi-

---

[9] On those universally despised apologists of Stuart authoritarianism, Robert Sibthorpe and Roger Mainwaring, minor figures of the time of Charles I made famous by the condemnations of both Locke and Sidney, see JHL Pamphlet 1, Introduction note 6. The only sustained attack on Locke and systematic effort to justify Filmer in the Revolutionary literature is Jonathan Boucher's remarkable sermon of 1775, "On Civil Liberty, Passive Obedience, and Nonresistance," published in his *View of the Causes and Consequences of the American Revolution* . . . (London, 1797), which is discussed at length below, Chap. VII, sec. 4.

[10] [Mercy Otis Warren], *The Group, A Farce* . . . (Boston, 1775), reprinted in Montrose J. Moses, ed., *Representative Plays by American Dramatists* . . . *1765–1819* (New York, 1918), p. 227; [James Chalmers], *Plain Truth* . . . *Containing Remarks on* . . . *Common Sense* (Philadelphia, 1776), pp. 1–3, 67, 72; [Joseph Galloway], *A Candid Examination of the Mutual Claims* . . . (New York, 1775), pp. 21–22 (see also 4–5, 8, 15, 17–18); [Charles Inglis], *The True Interest of America* . . . (Philadelphia, 1776), p. 22. For a particularly striking example of a favorable reference to Locke by a Tory who believed that "in the *body politic* all inferior jurisdictions should flow from *one superior fountain,*" see Isaac Hunt, *The Political Family; or* . . . *the Reciprocal Advantages Which Flow from an Uninterrupted Union Between Great-Britain and Her American Colonies* (Philadelphia, 1775), pp. 6, 7.

asm the theorists of universal reason, so too did they associate themselves, with offhand familiarity, with the tradition of the English common law. The great figures of England's legal history, especially the seventeenth-century common lawyers, were referred to repeatedly — by the colonial lawyers above all, but by others as well. Sir Edward Coke is everywhere in the pamphlets: "Coke upon Littleton," "my Lord Coke's Reports," "Lord Coke's 2nd Institute" — the citations are almost as frequent as, and occasionally even less precise than, those to Locke, Montesquieu, and Voltaire. The earlier commentators Bracton and Fortescue are also referred to, casually, as authorities, as are Coke's contemporary Francis Bacon, and his successors as Lord Chief Justice, Sir Matthew Hale, Sir John Vaughan, and Sir John Holt.[11] In the later years of the Revolutionary period, Blackstone's *Commentaries* and the opinions of Chief Justice Camden became standard authorities. Throughout the literature, trial reports — Raymond's, Salkeld's, Williams', Goldsboro's — are referred to, and use is made of standard treatises on English law: Sullivan's *Lectures on the Laws of England;* Gilbert's *Law of Evidence;* Foster's *Crown Law;* Barrington's *Observations on the More Ancient Statutes.*

The common law was manifestly influential in shaping the awareness of the Revolutionary generation. But, again, it did not in itself determine the kinds of conclusions men would draw in the crisis of the time. Otis and Hutchinson both worshiped Coke, but for reasons that have nothing to do with the great chief justice, they read significantly different meanings into his opinion in *Bonham's Case*.[12] The law was no science of what to do next. To the colonists it was a repository of experience in human dealings embodying the principles of justice, equity, and rights; above all, it was a form of history — ancient, indeed immemorial, history; constitutional and national history; and, as history, it helped explain the movement of events and the meaning of the present. Particularly revealing, therefore, though vague in their intent, are the references in the pamphlets to the seventeenth-century scholars of the law, especially of the history of the law, whose importance in the development of English historical thought we have only recently become aware: Henry Spelman, Thomas Madox, Robert Brady, and William Petyt. English law — as authority, as legitimizing precedent, as embodied principle, and as the framework of historical

---

[11] On Coke, see Charles F. Mullett, "Coke and the American Revolution," *Economica,* 12 (1932), 457–471. Of the other jurists mentioned (on whom see Index listings in the present volume) Hale was a particularly well known and attractive figure; the *Newport Mercury* ran a biography of him, January 23 and 30, 1764.

[12] See Introduction to Otis' *Rights of the British Colonies* (JHL Pamphlet 7).

understanding — stood side by side with Enlightenment rationalism in the minds of the Revolutionary generation.[13]

Still another tradition, another group of writers and texts, that emerges from the pamphlet literature as a major source of ideas and attitudes of the Revolutionary generation stemmed ultimately from the political and social theories of New England Puritanism, and particularly from the ideas associated with covenant theology. For the elaborate system of thought erected by the first leaders of settlement in New England had been consolidated and amplified by a succession of writers in the course of the seventeenth century, channeled into the main stream of eighteenth-century political and social thinking by a generation of enlightened preachers, and softened in its denominational rigor by many hands until it could be received, with minor variations, by almost the entire spectrum of American Protestantism.[14]

In one sense this was the most limited and parochial tradition that contributed in an important way to the writings of the Revolution, for it drew mainly from local sources and, whatever the extent of its newly acquired latitudinarianism, was yet restricted in its appeal to those who continued to understand the world, as the original Puritans had, in theological terms. But in another sense it contained the broadest ideas of all, since it offered a context for everyday events nothing less than cosmic in its dimensions. It carried on into the eighteenth century and into the minds of the Revolutionaries the idea, originally worked out in the sermons and tracts of the settlement period, that the colonization of British America had been an event designed by the hand of God to satisfy his ultimate aims. Reinvigorated in its historical meaning by newer works like Daniel Neal's *History of the Puritans* (1732-1738), his *History of New England* (1720), and Thomas Prince's uncompleted *Chronological History of New England in the Form of Annals* (1736), this powerful strain of thought, found everywhere in the eighteenth-century colonies, stimulated confidence in the idea that America had a special place, as yet not fully revealed, in

[13] J. G. A. Pocock, *The Ancient Constitution and the Feudal Law* (Cambridge, 1957), p. 31, chap. viii; David C. Douglas, *English Scholars 1660-1730* (rev. ed., London, 1951), chaps. vi, xi. For instances of the use of the seventeenth-century scholars by the American pamphleteers, see, besides references indexed in the present volume, Maurice Moore, *The Justice and Policy of Taxing the American Colonies* . . . (Wilmington, N.C., 1765), p. 3; Richard Bland, *An Inquiry into the Rights of the British Colonies* . . . (Williamsburg, 1766), pp. 7, 22; and Riley, *Correspondence of "First Citizen"* . . . *and "Antilon,"* pp. 84-85, 193, 231-232.

[14] Perry Miller, "From the Covenant to the Revival," in *The Shaping of American Religion* (James W. Smith and A. Leland Jamison, eds., *Religion in American Life,* I, Princeton, 1961), pp. 322-334.

the architecture of God's intent. "Imparting a sense of crisis by revivifying Old Testament condemnations of a degenerate people," it prepared the colonists for a convulsive realization by locating their parochial concerns at a critical juncture on the map of mankind's destiny. Their own history, it was clear, would provide the climax for those remarkable *"Connections"* from which they liked to quote, Samuel Shuckford's *Sacred and Profane History of the World Connected* (which contains a map fixing the exact geographical location of the garden of Eden) and Humphrey Prideaux's *The Old and New Testament Connected.*[15]

But important as all of these clusters of ideas were, they did not in themselves form a coherent intellectual pattern, and they do not exhaust the elements that went into the making of the Revolutionary frame of mind. There were among them, in fact, striking incongruities and contradictions. The common lawyers the colonists cited, for example, sought to establish right by appeal to precedent and to an unbroken tradition evolving from time immemorial, and they assumed, if they did not argue, that the accumulation of the ages, the burden of inherited custom, contained within it a greater wisdom than any man or group of men could devise by the power of reason. Nothing could have been more alien to the Enlightenment rationalists whom the colonists also quoted — and with equal enthusiasm. These theorists felt that it was precisely the heavy crust of custom that was weighing down the spirit of man; they sought to throw it off and to create by the unfettered power of reason a framework of institutions superior to the accidental inheritance of the past. And the covenant theologians differed from both in continuing to assume the ultimate inability of man to improve his condition by his own powers and in deriving the principles of politics from divine intent and from the network of obligations that bound redeemed man to his maker.

What brought these disparate strands of thought together, what dominated the colonists' miscellaneous learning and shaped it into a coherent whole, was the influence of still another group of writers, a group whose thought overlapped with that of those already mentioned but which was yet distinct in its essential characteristics and unique in its determinative power. The origins of this tradition lay in the radical social and political thought of the English Civil War and of the Commonwealth period, and

---

[15] E.g., Benjamin Trumbull, *A Discourse Delivered at . . . the Town of New-Haven . . .* (New Haven, 1773), pp. 7–8; Dan Foster, *A Short Essay on Civil Government, the Substance of Six Sermons . . .* (Hartford, 1775), pp. 23, 61. Miller, "From the Covenant to the Revival," p. 340.

it had developed in the early eighteenth century through a succession of
writers associated with religious dissent and opposition politics, eventuat-
ing in the extreme "left" under George III. Among the seventeenth-
century progenitors of this line of eighteenth-century radical theorists and
opposition politicians united in criticism of the status quo, Milton was an
important figure — not Milton the poet so much as Milton the radical
tractarian, author of *Eikonoklastes* and *The Tenure of Kings and Magistrates* (both published in 1649). The American Revolutionary writers
referred with similar respect if with less understanding to the more systematic writing of Harrington and to that of the like-minded Henry
Neville; above all, they referred to the doctrines of Algernon Sidney, that
"martyr to civil liberty" whose *Discourses Concerning Government* (1698)
became, in Caroline Robbins' phrase, a "textbook of revolution" in
America.[16]

The colonists identified themselves with these seventeenth-century heroes
of liberty: but they felt closer to the early eighteenth-century transmitters
of this tradition of seventeenth-century radicalism — writers who modified
and enlarged this earlier body of ideas, fused it into a whole with other,
contemporary strains of thought, and applied it to the problems of
eighteenth-century English politics. These early eighteenth-century writers
— coffee-house radicals and opposition politicians revered by the disaffected and despised by the establishment throughout the eighteenth
century — faded into obscurity in the nineteenth century and are almost
entirely unknown today. But as much as any single group of writers they
shaped the mind of the American Revolutionary generation.

To the colonists the most important of these publicists and intellectual
middlemen were those spokesmen for extreme libertarianism, John Trenchard (1662–1723) and Thomas Gordon (d. 1750). The former, a west-
country squire of ample means and radical ideas, was a 57-year-old
veteran of the pamphlet wars that surrounded the Glorious Revolution

---

[16] George Sensabaugh, *Milton in Early America* (Princeton, 1964), chaps. ii, iii; cf., e.g.,
Howard, *Sermon*, p. 28; Quincy, *Observations*, in Quincy, *Memoir*, p. 411; *Proceedings
of the Massachusetts Historical Society*, 69 (1956), 116, 117, 125; *Collections of the
Massachusetts Historical Society*, 4th ser., IV, 403, 412–413. On Harrington, see H. F.
Russell Smith, *Harrington and his Oceana: . . . and Its Influence in America* (Cambridge,
England, 1914), chaps. vii, viii; cf., e.g., Otis, *Rights of the British Colonies* (JHL Pam-
phlet 7), p. 15 and text note 6; *Novanglus and Massachusettensis . . .* (Boston, 1819),
pp. 81–82. On Sidney, see Caroline Robbins, "Algernon Sidney's *Discourses. . . ,*" *W.M.Q.*,
3d ser., 4 (1947), 267–296; and cf., e.g., [Stephen Hopkins], *The Rights of Colonies
Examined* (Providence, 1765: JHL Pamphlet 9), p. 4; William Stearns, *A View of the
Controversy . . .* (Watertown, 1775), p. 18; *Novanglus and Massachusettensis*, pp. 62–65.

when in 1719 he met Gordon, "a clever young Scot . . . fresh from Aberdeen University, [who had come] to London to make his fortune, equipped with little but a sharp tongue and a ready wit." They joined forces to produce, first, the weekly *Independent Whig* to attack High Church pretensions and, more generally, the establishment of religion, fifty-three papers of which were published in book form in 1721; and *Cato's Letters*, a searing indictment of eighteenth-century English politics and society written in response to the South Sea Bubble crisis, which appeared first serially in *The London Journal* and then, beginning in 1720, in book form.[17] Republished entire or in part again and again in the colonies, "quoted in every colonial newspaper from Boston to Savannah," and referred to repeatedly in the pamphlet literature, the writings of Trenchard and Gordon ranked in the minds of the Americans with the treatises of Locke as the most authoritative statement of the nature of political liberty and above Locke as an exposition of the social sources of the threats it faced.[18]

Standing with Trenchard and Gordon as early eighteenth-century "preceptors of civil liberty" was the liberal Anglican bishop, Benjamin Hoadly. This "best hated clergyman of the century amongst his own order," as Leslie Stephen described him, achieved fame, or notoriety, in England for his role in the elaborate clerical polemics of the "Bangorian Controversy" (1717–1720), in which he had been assisted by Gordon. In the course of this bitter and voluminous debate he had become an object of scorn and vituperation as well as of admiration in England; but in the colonies he

[17] Charles B. Realey, *The London Journal and Its Authors, 1720–1723* (Bulletin of the University of Kansas, XXXVI, no. 23, Dec. 1, 1935), pp. 1–34; J. M. Bulloch, *Thomas Gordon, the "Independent Whig"* (Aberdeen, 1918); William T. Laprade, *Public Opinion and Politics in Eighteenth Century England* (New York, 1936), pp. 237–269; Caroline Robbins, *The Eighteenth-Century Commonwealthman* (Cambridge, 1959), pp. 115–125, 392–393.

[18] Elizabeth C. Cook, *Literary Influences in Colonial Newspapers 1704–1750* (New York, 1912), pp. 81–83, 89, 125–126, 129, 137, 139, 159, 257, 265. On the Quaker merchants' interest in these writers, see Frederick B. Tolles, *Meeting House and Counting House* (Chapel Hill, 1948), pp. 178–179. On their influence on William Livingston and others in New York, see William Livingston, *et al.*, *The Independent Reflector* . . . (Milton M. Klein, ed., Cambridge, 1963), pp. 21–28, 365, 450–452. For examples of the use of *Cato's Letters* by the American pamphleteers, see, besides those indexed in the present volume, [Joseph Galloway], *A True and Impartial State of the Province of Pennsylvania* . . . (Philadelphia, 1759), title page; H. Trevor Colbourn, "The Historical Perspective of John Dickinson," *Early Dickinsoniana* (The Boyd Lee Spahr Lectures in Americana, Dickinson College, 1951–1961, Carlisle, Pa., 1961), pp. 13, 14, 18; Jonathan Mayhew to Thomas Hollis, August 19, 1765, *Proceedings of the Massachusetts Historical Society*, 69 (1956), 176; [John Dickinson], *Letters from a Farmer in Pennsylvania* . . . (Philadelphia, 1768), in Paul L. Ford, ed., *The Writings of John Dickinson* (Memoirs of the Historical Society of Pennsylvania, XIV, Philadelphia, 1895), p. 343n; Chalmers, *Plain Truth*, p. 72.

was widely held to be one of the notable figures in the history of political thought. Anglicans in America, it was true, like their co-denominationalists at home, could scarcely endorse his extraordinary denial of sacerdotal powers for the Church hierarchy or his almost unbelievable repudiation of the whole idea of the church visible, nor could they, in theory at least, accept his extreme toleration of dissent. But their attention focused not on his views of the Church but on the crucial battles he had fought early in the century against the nonjurors and their doctrines of divine right and passive obedience, and on the extreme statements of Whig political theory in his treatise *The Original and Institution of Civil Government Discussed* (1710) and in certain of his many tracts, especially *The Measures of Submission to the Civil Magistrates Considered* (1705). Ultimately, Hoadly came to embody physically the continuity of the tradition of English radical and opposition thought, for though he had been active at the end of the seventeenth century, he lived on until 1761, associating in his very old age with the English radicals of Jefferson's generation and establishing contact with such spokesmen of advanced American thought as Jonathan Mayhew.[19]

With Hoadly, among his contemporaries, though below him in importance to the Americans, was the outstanding opponent in Parliament of Walpole's administration, the leader of a coterie of early eighteenth-century free-thinking Whigs, Robert Viscount Molesworth. Friend of Trenchard and Gordon, encomiast of *Cato's Letters* (they were frequently attributed to him), he was known particularly in the colonies for his *Account of Denmark* (1694), which detailed the process by which free states succumb

[19] Leslie Stephen, *History of English Thought in the Eighteenth Century* (London, 1876), II, 152. Hoadly has yet to be excavated from the scorn and abuse Stephen heaped on him, but some indication of his importance emerges from Norman Sykes's essay in F. J. C. Hearnshaw, ed., *Social and Political Ideas of Some English Thinkers . . . 1650–1750* (London, 1928), chap. vi. For illustrations of the way Hoadly's ideas entered into the mainstream of American Revolutionary thought, see Jonathan Mayhew's *Discourse Concerning Unlimited Submission* (Boston, 1750: JHL Pamphlet 1), Introduction and notes 11 and 12; [John Allen], *The American Alarm . . .* (Boston, 1773), 4th sec., p. 10; Gad Hitchcock, *A Sermon Preached before . . . Gage . . .* (Boston, 1774), pp. 23, 27; Howard, *Sermon,* p. 23; [John Dickinson], "Letters to the Inhabitants of the British Colonies," in Ford, *Writings,* pp. 494–496nn; and R. C. Nicholas' reply to "Hoadleianus" in *Virginia Gazette* (R), June 10, 1773. There is perhaps no better testimony to Hoadly's role in the growth of a Revolutionary frame of mind than the recollection of the arch-Tory Jonathan Boucher, who, hearing that a rival preacher proposed to deliver a sermon against absolute monarchy, concluded that he must have "found such a sermon in Hoadly, and having transcribed it, showed it to the Committee, by whom it was approved, as any and every thing was and would have been, however loose and weak, that but seemed to be against power and for liberty." Jonathan Bouchier, ed., *Reminiscences of an American Loyalist . . .* (Boston and New York, 1925), p. 120.

to absolutism.[20] An opposition leader of another sort who contributed in a more complicated way to the colonists' inheritance of early eighteenth-century thought was Bolingbroke, who, though a leader of the extreme right in English politics, joined with the radicals in decrying the corruption of the age and the oppressiveness of Walpole's government.[21] The Scottish philosopher, Francis Hutcheson, and the nonconformist schoolmaster, Philip Doddridge, were also figures of this generation the colonists knew and cited in the same general context, as was Isaac Watts, the hymnologist and writer on questions of church and education.[22]

The tradition continued into the Revolutionaries' own generation, powerfully promoted by Richard Baron, republican and dissenter, associate and literary heir of Thomas Gordon, who republished in the 1750's political works of Milton and Sidney and issued also an anthology of the writings of the later radicals, including Jonathan Mayhew; and by that extraordinary one-man propaganda machine in the cause of liberty, the indefatigable Thomas Hollis. A group of forceful writers active in the 1760's and 1770's renewed the earlier ideas, extended them still further, and, together with the leading spokesmen for the colonies, applied them to the Anglo-American controversy. Foremost among these later advocates of reform in politics and religion were Richard Price, Joseph Priestley, and John Cartwright; but the key book of this generation was the three-volume *Political Disquisitions* published in 1774 by the schoolmaster, political theorist, and moralist, James Burgh.[23] The republican historian

[20] On Molesworth, see Robbins, *Commonwealthman,* chap. iv, pp. 393–394; and Realey, *London Journal,* pp. 4–5. Cf. *Newport Mercury,* July 30, 1764; John Dickinson, *A Speech Delivered in the House of Assembly . . . 1764* (Philadelphia, 1764), in Ford, *Writings,* p. 24; Arthur Lee, *An Appeal to the Justice and Interests of the People of Great Britain . . .* (New York, 1775), p. 32.

[21] On Bolingbroke, whose *Freeholder's Political Catechism* (1733) was reprinted in New London in 1769, see, e.g., Colbourn, "Historical Perspective," p. 11; "Dickinson's London Letters," pp. 246–247; *Newport Mercury,* July 30, 1764; Quincy, *Observations,* in Quincy, *Memoir,* p. 386. On the use made of Bolingbroke and Pulteney's *The Craftsman,* see Paul S. Boyer, "Borrowed Rhetoric: The Massachusetts Excise Controversy of 1754," *W.M.Q.,* 3d ser., 21 (1964), 328–351.

[22] All of these figures are discussed in Robbins' *Commonwealthman,* but on the link to America the same author's essay on Hutcheson in *W.M.Q.,* 3d ser., 11 (1954), 214–251 is especially important.

[23] On Baron and Hollis, see Mayhew, *Discourse* (JHL Pamphlet 1), Introduction and references in notes 16 and 17; and the Eliot-Hollis correspondence in *Collections of the Massachusetts Historical Society,* 4th ser., IV, 399–461. The later radicals are discussed in Robbins' *Commonwealthman;* but see particularly Oscar and Mary F. Handlin, "James Burgh and American Revolutionary Theory," *Proceedings of the Massachusetts Historical Society,* 73 (1961), 38–57; and Nicholas Hans, "Franklin, Jefferson, and the English Radicals at the End of the Eighteenth Century," *Proceedings of the American Philosophical Society,* 98 (1954), 406–426.

Catharine Macaulay was also an important figure of this generation to the colonists, but among the many Whig historians the Americans knew and referred to — including Bulstrode Whitelock, William Guthrie, and James Ralph — their preference was for the exiled Huguenot, Paul de Rapin-Thoyras. His "inestimable treasure," the vast, radically Whiggish *Histoire d'Angleterre,* published in English between 1725 and 1731, together with his earlier sketch of the whole, *A Dissertation on the . . . Whigs and Tories* (reprinted in Boston in 1773), provided indisputable proof of the theories of all of the radical and anti-establishment writers by demonstrating their validity through a thousand years of English history.[24] But all history, not only English history, was vital to the thought of the Revolutionary generation, and it is a matter of particular consequence that among the best, or at least the most up-to-date, translations of Sallust and Tacitus available to the colonists were those by the ubiquitous Thomas Gordon, "under whose hands [Tacitus] virtually became an apologist for English Whiggery"; he prefaced his translations with introductory "Discourses" of prodigious length in which he explained beyond all chance of misunderstanding the political and moral meaning of those ancient historians.[25]

It would be difficult to exaggerate the importance of this tradition of

[24] "Rapin . . . in my opinion . . . carries the palm among the writers of our story, and wants nothing but a reduction of his enormous bulk to about half the present size, and to have his language a little enlivened . . . to render him an inestimable treasure of knowledge." William Livingston to Noah Welles, August 18, 1759, quoted by Klein in Livingston, *Independent Reflector,* p. 284. H. Trevor Colbourn, "John Dickinson, Historical Revolutionary," *Pa. Mag.,* 83 (1959), 277, 281, 282, 289; "Dickinson's London Letters," pp. 448–449; Dickinson, *Farmer's Letters,* in Ford, *Writings,* pp. 391, 393. [James Wilson], *Considerations on the Nature and the Extent of . . . Parliament* (Philadelphia, 1774), p. 5; John Lathrop, *A Sermon Preached to the Ancient and Honorable Artillery-Company . . .* (Boston, 1774), p. 20; [John Joachim Zubly], *Calm and Respectful Thoughts on the Negative of the Crown . . .* [Savannah, 1772], p. 14. For Jefferson's admiration of Rapin and his widely shared dislike of Hume's *History,* see E. M. Sowerby, ed., *Catalogue of the Library of Thomas Jefferson* (Washington, D.C., 1952–1959), I, 156–157; cf. Dulany's opinion of Hume, above, note 8. For a revealing and characteristic use of Rapin by John Adams, see *Works,* III, 543. Rapin's *Dissertation* is an effort to explain the party structure under George I as the logical outcome of England's entire ideological and constitutional history; its stress on the "formed design" of the Tories to restore Stuart absolutism to the throne made it, for reasons explained in Chapter V below, of particular relevance to American Revolutionary thought.

[25] Tolles, *Meeting House and Counting House,* p. 189. For examples of the use of these translations, see [Stephen Hopkins'] compliment to the "fine English" of Gordon's *Tacitus,* in his letter to Goddard, *Providence Gazette,* April 8, 1765; Charles Carroll, in Riley, *Correspondence of "First Citizen" . . . and "Antilon,"* p. 48; Colbourn, "Dickinson, Historical Revolutionary," p. 280; Colbourn, "Thomas Jefferson's Use of the Past," *W.M.Q.,* 3d ser., 15 (1958), 61–62 (and see pp. 60, 64–65 for Jefferson's more general involvement with this radical tradition); Quincy, *Observations,* in Quincy, *Memoir,* pp. 443, 444.

radical dissent to the thought of the American Revolutionaries. Testimonies to their unique influence are everywhere in the literature. Sometimes they are explicit, as when Jonathan Mayhew wrote that he had been
"initiated, in youth, in the doctrines of civil liberty, as they were taught
by such men . . . as Sidney and Milton, Locke, and Hoadly, among the
moderns; I liked them, they seemed rational"; or when John Adams insisted, against what he took to be the massed opinion of informed Englishmen, that the root principles of good government could be found only in
"Sidney, Harrington, Locke, Milton, Nedham, Neville, Burnet, and
Hoadly"; or again, when he listed the great political thinkers of 1688 as
"Sidney, Locke, Hoadly, Trenchard, Gordon, Plato Redivivus [Neville]";
or when Josiah Quincy, Jr., bequeathed to his son in 1774 "Algernon
Sidney's works, — John Locke's works, — Lord Bacon's works, — Gordon's
Tacitus, — and *Cato's Letters.* May the spirit of liberty rest upon him!" [26]
More often, the evidence is implicit, in the degree to which the pamphlet-
eers quoted from, plagiarized, and modeled their writings on *Cato's
Letters* and *The Independent Whig.* Above all, their influence may be
seen in the way the peculiar bent of mind of the writers in this tradition
was reflected in the ideas and attitudes of the Americans.

The fact is easily mistaken because on major points of theory the
eighteenth-century contributors to this tradition — those the colonists knew
best: Trenchard and Gordon, Molesworth, Hoadly, and Rapin — were
not original. Borrowing heavily from more original thinkers, they were
often, in their own time and after, dismissed as mere popularizers. Their
key concepts — natural rights, the contractual basis of society and government — were commonplaces of the liberal thought of the time. But if the
elements of their thought were ordinary, the emphasis placed upon them
and the use made of them were not. So far in fact were their conclusions
from being commonly accepted that they served to alienate their advocates
not merely from political influence in mid-century England but even from
political respectability. Not one of these writers would have agreed with
the sentiment expressed by the Lord Chancellor of England in 1766 and
concurred in by the overwhelming majority of eighteenth-century Englishmen: "I seek for the liberty and constitution of this kingdom no
farther back than the [Glorious] Revolution; there I make my stand."
These writers so employed the ideas they had inherited from the seven-

[26] Jonathan Mayhew, *The Snare Broken* . . . (Boston, 1766), p. 35; John Adams,
Thoughts on Government . . . (Philadelphia, 1776), in *Works,* IV, 194; *Works,* VI, 4;
Quincy, *Memoir,* p. 350.

teenth century as to refuse to accept the Glorious Revolution and the lax political pragmatism that followed as the final solution to the political problems of the time. They refused to believe that the transfer of sovereignty from the crown to Parliament provided a perfect guarantee that the individual would be protected from the power of the state. Ignoring the complacency and general high level of satisfaction of the time, they called for vigilance against the government of Walpole equal to what their predecessors had shown against the Stuarts. They insisted, at a time when government was felt to be less oppressive than it had been for two hundred years, that it was necessarily — by its very nature — hostile to human liberty and happiness; that, properly, it existed only on the tolerance of the people whose needs it served; and that it could be, and reasonably should be dismissed — overthrown — if it attempted to exceed its proper jurisdiction.

It was the better to maintain this vigil against government that they advocated reforms beyond anything admissible in Walpole's age — or indeed in any age that followed in England until well into the nineteenth century. At one time or another, one or another of them argued for adult manhood suffrage; elimination of the rotten borough system and the substitution of regular units of representation systematically related to the distribution of population; the binding of representatives to their constituencies by residential requirements and by instructions; alterations in the definition of seditious libel so as to permit full freedom of the press to criticize government; the total withdrawal of government control over religion; and the broadening of popular education.

Such ideas, based on extreme solicitude for the individual and an equal hostility to government, were expressed in a spirit of foreboding and fear for the future. For while they acknowledged the existing stability and prosperity of England, they nevertheless grounded their thought in pessimism concerning human nature and in the discouraging record of human weakness. Their resulting concern was only deepened by the scenes they saw around them. Politics may have been stable, but the stability rested on corruption, which, they warned, if left unchecked, would eat away the foundations of liberty. Everywhere there was self-indulgence, effeminizing luxury, and gluttonous pursuit of gain. If nothing were done to stop the growth of these evils, England would follow so many other nations into a tyranny from which there would be no recovery.

But if these dark thoughts, in the England of Walpole and Gibbon, attained popularity in certain opposition, radical, and nonconformist circles, they had relatively little political influence in the country at large. In the mainland colonies of North America, however, they were immensely popular and influential. There, an altered condition of life made what in England were considered to be extreme, dislocating ideas sound like simple statements of fact. There, the spread of independent landholding had insensibly created a broad electorate. There, the necessity of devising systems of representation at a stroke and the presence of persistent conflict between the legislatures and the executives had tended to make representation regular and responsible and had limited the manipulative influence of any group in power. There, the multiplicity of religious groupings, the need for continuous encouragement of immigration, and the distance from European centers of ecclesiastical authority had weakened the force of religious establishments below anything known in Europe. There politics, far from being stable, was a constant churn of petty factions in which the dignity and authority of a state stripped of much of its powers of political manipulation was continuously compromised, dragged down willy-nilly into the mire of provincial discord. There, finally, the moral basis of a healthy, liberty-preserving polity seemed already to exist in the unsophisticated lives of the independent, uncorrupted, landowning yeoman farmers who comprised so large a part of the colonial population.

In such a situation the writings of the English radical and opposition leaders seemed reasonable, even if still controversial, and they quickly became influential. Wherever groups appeared seeking justification for and enlargement of the changes that had taken place in the colonies, they turned to these writers. When in 1735 John Peter Zenger's lawyer sought theoretical grounds for attacking the traditional concept of seditious libel, he turned for authority to Trenchard and Gordon's *Cato's Letters*. When in 1750 Jonathan Mayhew sought to work out, in his celebrated *Discourse Concerning Unlimited Submission,* a full rationale for resistance to constituted government, he drew on — indeed, cribbed wholesale — not Locke, whose ideas would scarcely have supported what he was saying, but a sermon of Benjamin Hoadly, from whom he borrowed not only ideas and phrases but, in abusing the nonjuror Charles Leslie, the Bishop's enemies as well. And when in 1752–1753 William Livingston and his friends undertook to publish in a series of periodical essays a sweeping critique of public life in New York, and in particular to assault the concept of a privileged state, they modeled their publication, *The Independent Re-*

flector, on Trenchard and Gordon's *Independent Whig* (which already had had two American editions), and borrowed from it specific formulations for their central ideas.[27] Everywhere in America the tradition that had originated in seventeenth-century radicalism and that had been passed on, with elaborations, by a small group of publicists and politicians of the early eighteenth century, brought forth congenial responses and provided grounds for opposition politics.

But it did more. It provided also a harmonizing force for the other, discordant elements in the political and social thought of the Revolutionary generation. Within the framework of these ideas, Enlightenment abstractions and common law precedents, covenant theology and classical analogy — Locke and Abraham, Coke and Brutus — could all be brought together into a comprehensive theory of politics. It was in terms of this pattern of ideas and attitudes — originating in the English Civil War and carried forward with additions and modifications not on the surface of English political life but in its undercurrents stirred by doctrinaire libertarians, disaffected politicians, and religious dissenters — that the colonists responded to the new regulations imposed by England on her American colonies after 1763.

[27] Leonard W. Levy, *Legacy of Suppression* (Cambridge, 1960), pp. 115–121, 129–137; Stanley N. Katz, ed., *A Brief Narrative of the Case and Trial of John Peter Zenger* (Cambridge, 1963), pp. 15, 9, 10. Mayhew's use of Hoadly's *Measures of Submission to the Civil Magistrates* is detailed in the Introduction to his *Discourse Concerning Unlimited Submisson* (JHL Pamphlet 1). On Livingston's reliance on Trenchard and Gordon, see Klein's comments in Livingston, *Independent Reflector,* pp. 21–28, 450–452; and Livingston's quotation, p. 365.

CHAPTER IV

POWER AND LIBERTY:
A THEORY OF POLITICS

THE theory of politics that emerges from the pamphlets of the pre-Revolutionary years rests on the belief that what lay behind every political scene, the ultimate explanation of every political controversy, was the disposition of power. The acuteness of the colonists' sense of this problem is, perhaps, for the twentieth-century reader, the most striking thing to be found in these eighteenth-century pamphlets: it serves to link the Revolutionary generation to our own in the most intimate way.

The colonists had no doubt about what power was and about its central, dynamic role in any political system. Power was not to be confused, James Otis pointed out, with unspecified physical capacity — with the "mere physical quality" described in physics. The essence of what they meant by power was perhaps best revealed inadvertently by John Adams as he groped for words in drafting his *Dissertation on the Canon and Feudal Law*. Twice choosing and then rejecting the word "power," he finally selected as the specification of the thought he had in mind "dominion," and in this association of words the whole generation concurred. "Power" to them meant the dominion of some men over others, the human control of human life: ultimately force, compulsion.[1] And it was, consequently, for them as it is for us "a richly connotative word": some of its fascination may well have lain for them, as it has been said to lie for us, in its "sado-masochistic flavor," [2] for they dwelt on it endlessly, almost compulsively; it is referred to, discussed, dilated on at length and in similar terms by writers of all backgrounds and of all positions in the Anglo-American controversy.

Most commonly the discussion of power centered on its essential characteristic of aggressiveness: its endlessly propulsive tendency to expand itself beyond legitimate boundaries. In expressing this central thought,

---

[1] [James Otis], *Brief Remarks on the Defence of the Halifax Libel* . . . (Boston, 1765), p. 24; Adams, *Diary and Autobiography*, I, 255. Cf. Charles Carroll: "power (understood as force)," *Maryland Historical Magazine*, 12 (1917), 187.

[2] K. R. Minogue, "Power in Politics," *Political Studies*, 7 (1959), 271.

which explained more of politics, past and present, to them than any
other single consideration, the writers of the pamphlets outdid themselves in verbal ingenuity. All sorts of metaphors, similes, and analogies
were used to express this view of power. The image most commonly
used was that of the act of trespassing. Power, it was said over and over
again, has "an encroaching nature"; ". . . if at first it meets with no
control [it] creeps by degrees and quick subdues the whole." Sometimes
the image is of the human hand, "the hand of power," reaching out to
clutch and to seize: power is "grasping" and "tenacious" in its nature;
"what it seizes it will retain." Sometimes power "is like the ocean, not
easily admitting limits to be fixed in it." Sometimes it is "like a cancer,
it eats faster and faster every hour." Sometimes it is motion, desire, and
appetite all at once, being "restless, aspiring, and insatiable." Sometimes
it is like "jaws . . . always opened to devour." It is everywhere in public life, and everywhere it is threatening, pushing, and grasping; and
too often in the end it destroys its benign — necessarily benign — victim.[3]

What gave transcendent importance to the aggressiveness of power
was the fact that its natural prey, its necessary victim, was liberty, or
law, or right. The public world these writers saw was divided into distinct, contrasting, and innately antagonistic spheres: the sphere of power
and the sphere of liberty or right. The one was brutal, ceaselessly active,
and heedless; the other was delicate, passive, and sensitive. The one
must be resisted, the other defended, and the two must never be confused.
"Right and power," Richard Bland stated, "have very different meanings, and convey very different ideas"; "power abstracted from right cannot give a just title to dominion," nor is it possible legitimately, or even
logically, to "build right upon power." When the two are intermingled,
when "brutal power" becomes "an irresistible argument of boundless

[3] The examples quoted here, selected from innumerable discussions of power in the
literature before 1776, are from: *America. A Poem. By Alexander Martin . . . to Which
Is Added Liberty. A Poem. By Rusticus* [Philadelphia, 1769?], p. [17]; [William Hicks],
Considerations upon the Rights of the Colonists . . . (New York, 1766), p. 15; Richard
J. Hooker, ed., "John Dickinson on Church and State," *American Literature,* 16 (1944–
45), 90; John Adams, *Dissertation on the Canon and Feudal Law,* in *Works,* III, 457;
[Moses Mather], *America's Appeal to an Impartial World . . .* (Hartford, 1775), p. 22;
and John Adams ("Novanglus"), in *Novanglus and Massachusettensis . . .* (Boston,
1819), p. 34. So also Jonathan Mayhew: "Power is of a grasping, encroaching nature . . .
[it] aims at extending itself and operating according to mere *will* wherever it meets with
no balance, check, control, or opposition of any kind." *The Snare Broken . . .* (Boston,
1766), p. 34; and "Power is like avarice, its desire increases by gratification," *Newport
Mercury,* July 30, 1764. Cf. *Cato's Letters* (London, 1723–1724), numbers 25, 31, 33, 44;
Benjamin Hoadly, *Works* (John Hoadly, ed., London, 1773), II, 25.

right" as it did, John Dickinson explained, under the Cromwellian dictatorship, innocence and justice can only sigh and quietly submit.[4]

Not that power was in itself — in some metaphysical sense — evil. It was natural in its origins, and necessary. It had legitimate foundations "in compact and mutual consent" — in those covenants among men by which, as a result of restrictions voluntarily accepted by all for the good of all, society emerges from a state of nature and creates government to serve as trustee and custodian of the mass of surrendered individual powers. Power created legitimately by those voluntary compacts which the colonists knew from Lockean theory to be logical and from their own experience to be practical, power in its legitimate form inhered naturally in government and was the possession and interest of those who controlled government, just as liberty, always weak, always defensive, always, as John Adams put it, "skulking about in corners . . . hunted and persecuted in all countries by cruel power," inhered naturally in the people and was their peculiar possession and interest. Liberty was not, therefore, for the colonists, as it is for us, professedly the interest and concern of all, governors and governed alike, but only of the governed. The wielders of power did not speak for it, nor did they naturally serve it. Their interest was to use and develop power, no less natural and necessary than liberty but more dangerous. For "as great a blessing as government is," the Rev. Peter Whitney explained, "like other blessings, it may become a scourge, a curse, and severe punishment to a people." What made it so, what turned power into a malignant force, was not its own nature so much as the nature of man — his susceptibility to corruption and his lust for self-aggrandizement.[5]

On this there was absolute agreement. Everyone, of course, knew that if "weak or ignorant men are entrusted with power" there will be "universal confusion," for "such exaltation will . . . make them giddy and vain and deprive them of the little understanding they had before." But it was not simply a question of what the weak and ignorant will do. The problem was more systematic than that; it concerned "mankind in gen-

[4] [Richard Bland], *An Inquiry into the Rights of the British Colonies* . . . (Williamsburg, 1766), pp. 5, 25; [John Joachim Zubly], *An Humble Enquiry* . . . ([Charleston?], 1769), p. 26; [John Dickinson], *An Essay on the Constitutional Power of Great-Britain* . . . (Philadelphia, 1774), p. 108 (reprinted in *Pennsylvania Archives,* 2d ser., III, 610). See also, [William Hicks], *The Nature and Extent of Parliamentary Power Considered* . . . (Philadelphia, 1768), pp. 21, 27.

[5] Andrew Eliot, *A Sermon Preached before His Excellency Francis Bernard* . . . (Boston, 1765), p. 17; Adams, *Diary and Autobiography,* I, 282; II, 58; Peter Whitney, *The Transgressions of a Land* . . . *Two Discourses* . . . (Boston, 1774), pp. 21–22.

eral." And the point they hammered home time and again, and agreed on — free-thinking Anglican literati no less than neo-Calvinist theologians — was the incapacity of the species, of mankind in general, to withstand the temptations of power. Such is "the depravity of mankind," Samuel Adams, speaking for the Boston Town Meeting, declared, "that ambition and lust of power above the law are . . . predominant passions in the breasts of most men." These are instincts that have "in all nations combined the worst passions of the human heart and the worst projects of the human mind in league against the liberties of mankind." Power always and everywhere had had a pernicious, corrupting effect upon men. It "converts a good man in private life to a tyrant in office." It acts upon men like drink: it "is known to be intoxicating in its nature" — "too intoxicating and liable to abuse." And nothing within man is sufficiently strong to guard against these effects of power — certainly not "the united considerations of reason and religion," for they have never "been sufficiently powerful to restrain these lusts of men." [6]

From these central premises on the nature of power and man's weakness in face of its temptations, there followed a series of important conclusions. Since power "in proportion to its extent is ever prone to wantonness," Josiah Quincy wrote, and since in the last analysis "the supreme power is ever possessed by those who have arms in their hands and are disciplined to the use of them," the absolute danger to liberty lay in the absolute supremacy of "a veteran army" — in making "the civil subordinate to the military," as Jefferson put it in 1774, "instead of subjecting the military to the civil power." Their fear was not simply of armies but of *standing armies,* a phrase that had distinctive connotations, derived, like so much of their political thought, from the seventeenth century and articulated for them by earlier English radicals — in this case most memorably by Trenchard in his famous *An Argument Shewing That a*

[6] Eliot, *Sermon,* pp. 10–11; [Daniel Dulany], *Considerations on the Propriety of Imposing Taxes* (Annapolis, 1765: JHL Pamphlet 13), p. 41: "for mankind are generally so fond of power that they are oftener tempted to exercise it beyond the limits of justice than induced to set bounds to it from the pure consideration of the rectitude of forbearance"; *The Votes and Proceedings of the Freeholders . . . of . . . Boston . . .* (Boston, [1772]), p. 20; [Jonathan Boucher], *A Letter from a Virginian . . .* ([New York], 1774), p. 7; Oliver Noble, *Some Strictures upon the . . . Book of Esther . . .* (Newburyport, 1775), p. 5; *The Genuine Principles of the Ancient Saxon, or English Constitution . . .* (Philadelphia, 1776), p. 5 (quoting [Obadiah Hulme's] *An Historical Essay on the English Constitution* [1771]); Josiah Quincy, Jr., *Observations on the . . . Boston Port-Bill . . .* (Boston, 1774), in Josiah Quincy, *Memoir of the Life of Josiah Quincy Jun. . . .* (Boston, 1825), pp. 372–373; Whitney, *Transgressions,* pp. 21–22; Zabdiel Adams, *The Grounds of Confidence and Success in War . . .* (Boston, 1775), p. 5; Adams, *Diary and Autobiography,* II, 59.

Standing Army Is Inconsistent with a Free Government . . . (1697). With him the colonists universally agreed that "unhappy nations have lost that precious jewel *liberty* . . . [because] their necessities or indiscretion have permitted a standing army to be kept amongst them." There was, they knew, no "worse state of thraldom than a military power in any government, unchecked and uncontrolled by the civil power"; and they had a vivid sense of what such armies were: gangs of restless mercenaries, responsible only to the whims of the rulers who paid them, capable of destroying all right, law, and liberty that stood in their way.[7]

This fear of standing armies followed directly from the colonists' understanding of power and of human nature: on purely logical grounds it was a reasonable fear. But it went beyond mere logic. Only too evidently was it justified, as the colonists saw it, by history and by the facts of the contemporary world. Conclusive examples of what happened when stand-

[7] Quincy, *Observations,* in Quincy, *Memoir,* pp. 373, 428; [Thomas Jefferson], *A Summary View of the Rights of British America* . . . (Philadelphia, 1774), in Paul L. Ford, ed., *Writings of Thomas Jefferson* (New York, 1892–1899), I, 445. [John Trenchard and Walter Moyle], *An Argument,* p. 4 (reprinted in *The Pamphleteer* . . . , X [1817], 114); [Samuel Seabury], *An Alarm to the Legislature of the Province of New-York* . . . (New York, 1775), in Clarence H. Vance, ed., *Letters of a Westchester Farmer (Publications of the Westchester County Historical Society,* VIII, White Plains, 1930), p. 159. For other examples of the almost obsessive concern in the colonies with standing armies, see *No Standing Army in the British Colonies* . . . (New York, 1775); Noble, *Some Strictures,* pp. 28–29; *Genuine Principles,* p. 23; Simeon Howard, *A Sermon Preached to the Ancient and Honorable Artillery-Company* . . . (Boston, 1773), pp. 26–28; (quoting Trenchard); James Lovell, *An Oration* . . . (Boston, 1771), pp. 8–9 (also quoting Trenchard); and above all, Quincy, *Observations,* in Quincy, *Memoir,* pp. 400–445. Caroline Robbins, *The Eighteenth-Century Commonwealthman* (Cambridge, 1959) discusses the English background of the problem at many points (see index under Militia). But the fullest discussion of the ideological meaning of standing armies is that of J. G. A. Pocock, in "Machiavelli, Harrington and English Political Ideologies in the Eighteenth Century," a paper read to the Australian and New Zealand Association for the Advancement of Science, January 21, 1964. Pocock, who dates the origins of "that concept or bogey" in 1675, argues that by the end of the seventeenth century it had come to mean not praetorians or janissaries but "a permanent professional force maintained by the administration and supplied out of the public exchequer"; as such, standing armies were feared as instruments in the systematic corruption of Parliament by the administration and hence of the overthrow of the balanced constitution. The colonists echoed this concern: see specifically John Dickinson's association of standing armies and excise collection in his *Letters from a Farmer* . . . *(Philadelphia,* 1768), in Paul L. Ford, ed., *Writings of John Dickinson (Memoirs of the Historical Society of Pennsylvania,* XIV, Philadelphia, 1895), p. 391; and Simeon Howard's definition of a standing army as "a number of men paid by the public to devote themselves wholly to the military profession," who, though "really servants of the people and paid by them," come to think of themselves as the King's men exclusively and become "the means, in the hands of a wicked and oppressive sovereign, of overturning the constitution of a country and establishing the most intolerable despotism." *Sermon,* pp. 26, 27. But the phrase was also commonly used loosely to mean simply the personal troops of the prince in states already lacking balanced constitutions; e.g., John Hancock, *An Oration* . . . (Boston, 1774), pp. 13–14.

ing armies were permitted to dominate communities were constantly
before their minds' eyes. There was, first and foremost, the example of
the Turks, whose rulers — cruel, sensuous "bashaws in their little divans"
— were legendary, ideal types of despots who reigned unchecked by right
or law or in any sense the consent of the people; their power rested on
the swords of their vicious janissaries, the worst of standing armies. So
too had the French kings snuffed out the liberties of their subjects "by
force" and reduced to nothing the "puny privilege of the French parliaments." The ranks of "despotic kingdoms" included also Poland, Spain,
and Russia; India and Egypt were occasionally mentioned too.

More interesting than these venerable despotisms, bywords for the rule
of force unrestrained by countervailing influences, were a number of
despotic states that had within living memory been free and whose
enslavement, being recent, had been directly observed. Venice was one:
it had once, not so long ago, been a republic, but now it was governed
"by one of the worst of despotisms." Sweden was another; the colonists
themselves could remember when the Swedish people had enjoyed liberty
to the full; but now, when the pamphlets were being written, they were
known to "rejoice at being subject to the caprice and arbitrary power of
a tyrant, and kiss their chains." But the most vivid of these sad cases,
because the most closely studied, was that of Denmark. The destruction
of parliamentary liberties in Denmark had in fact taken place a century
before, but that event, carefully examined in a treatise famous in radical
circles and in America, was experienced as contemporary by the colonists.

Molesworth's *An Account of Denmark* (1694) established the general
point, implicit in all similar histories but explicit in this one, that the
preservation of liberty rested on the ability of the people to maintain
effective checks on the wielders of power, and hence in the last analysis
rested on the vigilance and moral stamina of the people. Certain forms
of government made particularly heavy demands on the virtue of the
people. Everyone knew, from Montesquieu if from no other source, that
democracy — direct rule by all the people — required such spartan, self-
denying virtue on the part of all the people that it was likely to survive
only where poverty made upright behavior necessary for the perpetuation
of the race. Other forms, aristocracies, for example, made less extreme
demands; but even in them virtue and sleepless vigilance on the part of
at least the ruling class was necessary if privilege was to be kept responsible and the inroads of tyranny perpetually blocked off. It had been
the lack of this vigilance that had brought liberty in Denmark to its

knees, for there a corrupt nobility, more interested in using its privileges for self-indulgence than for service to the state, had dropped its guard and allowed in a standing army which quickly destroyed the constitution and the liberties protected by it.

The converse of all of this was equally true and more directly relevant. The few peoples that had managed to retain their liberties in the face of all efforts of would-be tyrants propelled by the lust for power had been doughty folk whose vigilance had never relaxed and whose virtue had remained uncontaminated. The Swiss, a rustic people locked in mountain sanctuaries, were ancient members of this heroic group; they had won their liberty long ago and had maintained it stubbornly ever after. The Dutch were more recent members, having overthrown the despotic rule of Spain only a century earlier; they too were industrious people of stubborn, Calvinist virtue, and they were led by an alert aristocracy. More recent in their emergence from darkness were the Corsicans, whose revolt against Genoese overlords backed by French power had begun only in 1729; they were still, at the time of the Stamp Act, struggling under the leadership of Pasquale Paoli to maintain their independence and liberty.[8]

Above all, however, there were the English themselves. The colonists' attitude to the whole world of politics and government was fundamentally shaped by the root assumption that they, as Britishers, shared in a unique inheritance of liberty. The English people, they believed, though often threatened by despots who had risen in their midst, had managed

[8] On Turkey, see, for example, [William H. Drayton], *A Letter from Freeman* . . . (Charleston, 1774), p. 8; and [Richard Bland], *The Colonel Dismounted* (Williamsburg, 1764: JHL Pamphlet 4), p. 26. On the long history of such attitudes to the Turks, see J. G. A. Pocock, *The Ancient Constitution and the Feudal Law* (Cambridge, 1951), p. 132; John Gough, *Fundamental Law in English Constitutional History* (Oxford, 1955), pp. 48–49; and *Cato's Letters,* number 50. For an elaborate discussion of the "awful lesson" of Poland entirely in the spirit of the Revolutionary pamphleteers, see Mercy Warren, *History of the . . . American Revolution* (Boston, 1805), II, 182–184. On France and the other familiar tyrannies, see, for example, Quincy, *Observations,* in Quincy, *Memoir,* pp. 443, 450–451; Dickinson, *Farmer's Letters,* in Ford, *Writings,* pp. 321, 369; [Stephen Johnson], *Some Important Observations* . . . (Newport, 1766), p. 11; Alexander Hamilton, *Farmer Refuted* (1774), in *Works* (H. C. Lodge, ed., New York and London, 1904), I, 113. On the more recent despotisms, especially Denmark and Sweden, see *Votes and Proceedings of Boston,* p. 35; Dulany, *Considerations* (JHL Pamphlet 13), p. 46n; Samuel Williams, *Discourse* . . . (Salem, 1775), p. 21. On the surviving free states, see, for example, John Joachim Zubly, *The Law of Liberty* . . . (Philadelphia, 1775), appendix, pp. 33–41; [Carter Braxton], *An Address* . . . (Philadelphia, 1776), p. 18; [James Chalmers], *Plain Truth* . . . (Philadelphia, 1776), pp. 9 ff.; [Charles Inglis], *The True Interest of America* . . . (Philadelphia, 1776), pp. 46, 61. For a detailed discussion of Molesworth's *Account of Denmark,* see Robbins, *Commonwealthman,* pp. 98–109, 393–394.

to maintain, to a greater degree and for a longer period of time than any other people, a tradition of the successful control of power and of those evil tendencies of human nature that would prevent its proper uses.

In view of the natural obstacles that stood in the way of such a success and in view of the dismal history of other nations, this, as the colonists saw it, had been an extraordinary achievement. But it was not a miraculous one. It could be explained historically. The ordinary people of England, they believed, were descended from simple, sturdy Saxons who had known liberty in the very childhood of the race and who, through the centuries, had retained the desire to preserve it. But it had taken more than desire. Reinforcing, structuring, expressing the liberty-loving temper of the people, there was England's peculiar "constitution," described by John Adams, in words almost every American agreed with before 1763, as "the most perfect combination of human powers in society which finite wisdom has yet contrived and reduced to practice for the preservation of liberty and the production of happiness." [9]

The word "constitution" and the concept behind it was of central importance to the colonists' political thought; their entire understanding of the crisis in Anglo-American relations rested upon it. So strategically located was this idea in the minds of both English and Americans, and so great was the pressure placed upon it in the course of a decade of pounding debate that in the end it was forced apart, along the seam of a basic ambiguity, to form the two contrasting concepts of constitutionalism that have remained characteristic of England and America ever since.

At the start of the controversy, however, the most distinguishing feature of the colonists' view of the constitution was its apparent traditionalism. Like their contemporaries in England and like their predecessors for centuries before, the colonists at the beginning of the Revolutionary controversy understood by the word "constitution" not, as we would have it, a written document or even an unwritten but deliberately contrived design of government and a specification of rights beyond the power of ordinary legislation to alter; they thought of it, rather, as the constituted — that is, existing — arrangement of governmental institutions, laws, and customs together with the principles and goals that animated them. So John Adams wrote that a political constitution is

---

[9] Adams, *Works*, III, 477. For characteristic encomiums on the constitution and descriptions of its operating balance, see James Otis, *Rights of the British Colonies* (Boston, 1764: JHL Pamphlet 7), p. 47; Dulany, *Considerations* (JHL Pamphlet 13), p. 15; Johnson, *Observations*, pp. 27 ff.; Whitney, *Transgressions*, p. 10; Mather, *America's Appeal*, pp. 7–8, 34 ff.

like "the constitution of the human body"; "certain contextures of the nerves, fibres, and muscles, or certain qualities of the blood and juices" some of which "may properly be called *stamina vitae,* or essentials and fundamentals of the constitution; parts without which life itself cannot be preserved a moment." A constitution of government, analogously, Adams wrote, is "a frame, a scheme, a system, a combination of powers for a certain end, namely, — the good of the whole community." [10]

The elements of this definition were traditional, but it was nevertheless distinctive in its emphasis on the animating principles, the *stamina vitae,* those "fundamental laws and rules of the constitution, which ought never to be infringed." Belief that a proper system of laws and institutions should be suffused with, should express, essences and fundamentals — moral rights, reason, justice — had never been absent from English notions of the constitution. But not since the Levellers had protested against Parliament's supremacy in the mid-seventeenth century had these considerations seemed so important as they did to the Americans of the 1760's. Nor could they ever have appeared more distinct in their content. For if the ostensible purpose of all government was the good of the people, the particular goal of the English constitution — "its end, its use, its designation, drift, and scope" — was known to all, and declared by all, to be the attainment of liberty. This was its peculiar "grandeur" and excellence; it was for this that it should be prized "next to our Bibles, above the privileges of this world." It was for this that it should be blessed, supported and maintained, and transmitted "in full, to posterity." [11]

But how had this been achieved? What was the secret of this success of the British constitution? It lay in its peculiar capacity to balance and check the basic forces within society. It was common knowledge, expressed in such familiar clichés, a Virginian complained, "that the merest sciolist, the veriest smatterer in politics must long since have had them all by rote," [12] that English society consisted of three social orders, or estates, each with its own rights and privileges, and each embodying

---

[10] Adams, *Works,* III, 478–479. On the emergence of American ideas of constitutionalism, see below, Chap. VI, sec. 2.

[11] *A Letter to the People of Pennsylvania* (Philadelphia, 1760: JHL Pamphlet 2), p. 3; Adams, *Works,* III, 479; Otis, *Rights* (JHL Pamphlet 7), p. 47; Johnson, *Observations,* p. 28.

[12] [Robert Carter Nicholas], *Considerations on the Present State of Virginia Examined* ([Williamsburg], 1774), in the Earl G. Swem edition (New York, 1919), p. 40.

within it the principles of a certain form of government: royalty, whose natural form of government was monarchy; the nobility, whose natural form was aristocracy; and the commons, whose form was democracy. In the best of worlds, it had been known since Aristotle, each of these forms independently was capable of creating the conditions for human happiness; in actuality all of them, if unchecked, tended to degenerate into oppressive types of government — tyranny, oligarchy, or mob rule — by enlarging their own rights at the expense of the others' and hence generating not liberty and happiness for all but misery for most. In England, however, these elements of society, each independently dangerous, entered into government in such a way as to eliminate the dangers inherent in each. They entered simultaneously, so to speak, in a balanced sharing of power. The functions, the powers, of government were so distributed among these components of society that no one of them could dominate the others and strip them of their rights. Each pressed competitively against the other two, and the result was a stable equilibrium of poised forces each of which, in protecting its own rights against the encroachments of the others, contributed to the preservation of the rights of all.

Such was the theoretical explanation, universally accepted in the eighteenth century, of the famous "mixed" constitution of England.[13] It was an arrangement of power that appeared to the colonists as it did to most of Europe as "a system of consummate wisdom and policy." But if the theory was evident and unanimously agreed on, the mechanics of its operation were not. It was not clear how the three social orders were related to the functioning branches of government. The modern assumption of a tripartite division of the functions of government into legislative, executive, and judicial powers did not exist for the colonists; even the terminology was vague: the term "legislative" was used to mean the whole of government as well as the lawmaking branch. And in any case the balance of the constitution was not expected to be the result of the symmetrical matching of social orders with powers of government: it was not assumed that each estate would singly dominate

[13] On the origins of this theory of the English constitution, see Corinne C. Weston, "Beginnings of the Classical Theory of the English Constitution," *Proceedings of the American Philosophical Society,* 100 (1956), 133–144, and the same author's article in the *English Historical Review,* 75 (1960), 410–425. On its popularity in the eighteenth century, see Stanley Pargellis, "The Theory of Balanced Government," in Conyers Read, ed., *The Constitution Reconsidered* (New York, 1938), pp. 37–49. Cf. below, Chap. VII, sec. 3.

one of the branches or functions of government.[14] What was agreed on primarily and most significantly was that all three social orders did and should enter into and share, by representation or otherwise, the legislative branch. In the legislative functioning of government, Moses Mather explained in terms that commanded universal assent, power was

so judiciously placed as to connect the force and to preserve the rights of all; each estate, armed with a power of self-defense against the encroachments of the other two, by being enabled to put a negative upon any or all of their resolves, neither the King, Lords, or Commons could be deprived of their rights or properties but by their own consent in Parliament and no laws could be made or taxes imposed but such as were necessary and in the judgment of the three estates in Parliament, for the common good and the interest of the realm.[15]

It was also agreed that the executive function was largely if not completely the proper responsibility of the first order of society, the crown. The rights exercised there were understood to be the rights of power: prerogative rights, privileges properly enjoyed by the monarch and his servants. But there the agreement stopped. There were several explanations of how the balance of social forces worked to check the undue exercise of prerogative power. Some writers found a sufficient balance and check in the fact that executive action was confined to bounds laid down by laws in the making of which all three powers had shared. But others were able to perceive a subtler kind of check upon prerogative power. For John Adams an essential point was that the commons, or the democracy, of society shared too in the execution of laws through the institution of trial by jury. This ancient device was critical, as Adams saw it, in establishing the equipoise of the English constitution in that it introduced into the "executive branch of the constitution . . . a mixture of popular power" and as a consequence "the subject is guarded in the execution of the laws." [16] Most writers, however, turned for explanation not so much to the popular recruitment of juries and hence to a social balance within the executive branch as to the pressure exerted against the executive from outside, by an independent judiciary. It was

[14] The matching of social powers with powers of government was inadequately worked out even by Montesquieu, though he clearly defined the functions of government as legislative, executive, and judicial. See *Spirit of the Laws* (Franz Neumann, ed., New York, 1949), bk. xi, sec. 6 (especially p. 156; cf. p. lviii). For a detailed account of the intense discussion of Montesquieu and the doctrine of the separation of powers in Massachusetts in 1763, see Ellen E. Brennan, *Plural Office-Holding in Massachusetts 1760–1780* (Chapel Hill, 1945), chap. ii.

[15] Mather, *America's Appeal*, p. 8.

[16] Adams, *Works*, III, 481; cf. *Four Letters on Interesting Subjects* (Philadelphia, 1776), p. 21.

taken as a maxim by all, whether or not they used the point to explain how the executive branch entered into the separation of powers, that it was the function of the judges "to settle the contests between prerogative and liberty, . . . to ascertain the bounds of sovereign power, and to determine the rights of the subject," and that in order for them to perform this duty properly they must be "perfectly free from the influence of either." The threat to this independence — liberty being passive and power active — came most commonly from prerogative because of the effect of "its natural weight and authority" working upon the almost universal "love of promotion and private advantage." Unless the judiciary could stand upon its own firm and independent foundations — unless, that is, judges held their positions by a permanent tenure in no way dependent upon the will and pleasure of the executive — it would be ridiculous "to look for strict impartiality and a pure administration of justice, to expect that power should be confined within its legal limits, and right and justice done to the subject . . ."[17]

The difficulty of explaining how, precisely, the natural divisions of society expressed themselves in the English government so as to pit power against power for the mutual benefit of all was compounded when the unit involved was seen to be not the single community of Britain but an empire of communities each with its own separate social groupings and governmental institutions yet each part of a greater society and government as well. But until the Revolutionary crisis was well under way no one sought to settle this complicated constitutional problem.[18] The colonists were content to celebrate the wonderful balance of forces they understood to exist in England, and to assume that in some effective way the same principles operated both in epitome within each colony and in the over-all world of the empire as well.

[17] *Letter to the People of Pennsylvania* (JHL Pamphlet 2), pp. 4, 5, 7.

[18] Thus Dickinson: ". . . the government here is not only *mixed* but *dependent,* which circumstances occasions a *peculiarity in its form* of a very delicate nature" (*Farmer's Letters,* in Ford, *Writings,* p. 386). For an example of the critical importance that, at the height of the crisis, would be attached to the question of how the colonies shared in "the democracy" of the English constitution, see Adams ("Novanglus"), *Novanglus and Massachusettensis,* pp. 79 ff. A common assumption, which would evolve into a central point of Revolutionary theory, was that the colonists upon leaving England had "totally disclaim[ed] all *subordination* to and dependence upon the two inferior estates of their mother country" (Hicks, *Nature and Extent of Parliamentary Power,* p. 6). Behind the lack of definition of the imperial constitution before 1763 and of the colonies' involvement in it lay the more basic question of the meaning of the British "empire" itself. The concept when applied to the American colonies had only a special and restricted meaning. See Richard Koebner, *Empire* (Cambridge, England, 1961), chap. iii, esp. pp. 77 ff.

The result of this balanced counterpoise of social and governmental forces in the British constitution was the confinement of social and political powers to specified, limited spheres. So long as the crown, the nobility, and the democracy remained in their designated places in government and performed their designated political tasks liberty would continue to be safe in England and its dominions. But if any of them reached beyond the set boundaries of their rightful jurisdictions; if, particularly, the agencies of power — the prerogative, administration — managed, by corrupt practices, to insinuate their will into the assembly of the commons and to manipulate it at pleasure, liberty would be endangered.

The very idea of liberty was bound up with the preservation of this balance of forces. For political liberty, as opposed to the theoretical liberty that existed in a state of nature, "doth not consist in a freedom from all laws and government, but in a freedom from unjust law and tyrannical government." Liberty was "a power of acting agreeable to the laws which are made and enacted by the consent of the PEOPLE, and in no ways inconsistent with the natural rights of a single person, or the good of the society." Liberty, that is, was the capacity to exercise "natural rights" within limits set not by the mere will or desire of men in power but by non-arbitrary law — law enacted by legislatures containing within them the proper balance of forces.[19]

But what were these all-important "natural rights"? They were defined in a significantly ambiguous way. They were understood to be at one and the same time the inalienable, indefeasible rights inherent in people as such, and the concrete specifications of English law. Rights, John Dickinson wrote,

are created in us by the decrees of Providence, which establish the laws of our nature. They are born with us; exist with us; and cannot be taken from us by any human power without taking our lives. In short, they are founded on the immutable maxims of reason and justice.

Such God-given, natural, inalienable rights, distilled from reason and justice through the social and governmental compacts, were expressed in the common law of England, in the statutory enactments of Parliament, and in the charters of privileges promulgated by the crown. The

[19] Levi Hart, *Liberty Described and Recommended* . . . (Hartford, 1775), p. 13 (cf. p. 9); [John Allen], *The Watchman's Alarm* . . . (Salem, 1774), p. [5]. As Allen points out, his definition of liberty — "the true etymology of the word" — was taken from Daniel Fenning's *Royal English Dictionary* (London, 1761). On the antecedents to such definitions of Montesquieu, Rapin, and Bolingbroke, see Neumann's introduction to *The Spirit of the Laws*, p. xlix–liii.

great corpus of common law decisions and the pronouncements of King and Commons were but expressions of "God and nature . . . The natural absolute personal rights of individuals are . . . the very basis of all municipal laws of any great value." Indeed, "Magna Carta itself is in substance but a constrained declaration, or proclamation and promulgation in the name of King, Lords, and Commons of the sense the latter had of their original, inherent, indefeasible, natural rights." [20]

But this relationship between human rights and English law — so simple sounding when expressed in casual phrases like Daniel Dulany's "unalienable rights of the subject" — was in fact complicated even before the events of the 1760's and seventies placed the whole issue under severe pressure. Even then the identification between the two was known to be necessarily incomplete, for the provision of English law did not and properly could not wholly exhaust the great treasury of human rights. No documentary specification ever could. Laws, grants, and charters merely stated the essentials (which everyone summarized, with minor variations in phrasing, as "personal security, personal liberty, and private property") insofar, and only insofar, as they had come under attack in the course of English history. They marked out the minimum not the maximum boundaries of right. To claim more, to assert that all rights might be written into a comprehensive bill or code was surely, James Otis declared, "the insolence of a haughty and imperious minister . . . the flutter of a coxcomb, the pedantry of a quack, and the nonsense of a pettifogger." The "strange gallimaufry" of "codes, pandects, novels, decretals of popes, and the inventions of the d——l" may be suitable for "the cold bleak regions [of] Brandenburg and Prussia or the scorching heats of Jamaica or Gambia," but not for Britain's more temperate climate." [21]

Conceiving of liberty, then, as the exercise, within the boundaries of the law, of natural rights whose essences were minimally stated in English law and custom, the colonists saw in the balance of powers of the British constitution "a system of consummate wisdom" that provided an effective "check upon the power to oppress." [22] Yet they were far from

[20] [John Dickinson], *An Address to the Committee of Correspondence in Barbados . . .* (Philadelphia, 1766), in Ford, *Writings,* p. 262; [James Otis], *A Vindication of the British Colonies* (Boston, 1765: JHL Pamphlet 11), p. 8; *Votes and Proceedings of Boston,* pp. 7–8.

[21] Dulany, *Considerations* (JHL Pamphlet 13), p. 30; *Votes and Proceedings of Boston,* p. 8; Otis, *Vindication* (JHL Pamphlet 11), p. 32.

[22] Mather, *America's Appeal,* p. 8; Lovell, *Oration,* p. 11.

optimistic about the future of liberty under the constitution. They looked ahead with anxiety rather than with confidence, for they knew from Rapin and from other historians in the same tradition how embattled liberty had been throughout English history and by how small a margin it had been retrieved in its last, recent period of trial; and they knew too from the radical writings and from direct observation the dangers it faced in their own time.

The historical phasing of the defense of liberty in England was a matter of great importance to the colonists not merely because it illustrated the characteristic dangers liberty faced but also because it made clear their own special role in history. "Liberty," James Otis wrote in a sentence that reveals much of the structure of the colonists' historical thought, "was better understood and more fully enjoyed by our ancestors before the coming in of the first Norman tyrants than ever after, till it was found necessary for the salvation of the kingdom to combat the arbitrary and wicked proceedings of the Stuarts." The period before the Norman conquest was the greatest age of English history.

. . . it is a fact as certain as history can make it that the present civil constitution of England derives its original from those Saxons who . . . established a form of government in [England] similar to that they had been accustomed to live under in their native country . . . This government, like that from whence they came, was founded upon principles of the most perfect liberty. The conquered lands were divided among the individuals in proportion to the rank they held in the nation, and every freeman, that is, every freeholder, was a member of their Witanmoot or Parliament.

Political liberty, based upon a landholding system "the wisest and most perfect ever yet devised by the wit of man, as it stood before the eighth century," had flourished in this ancient elysium. But then had come the conquest, and with it the imposition of feudal tyranny upon gothic liberty. "The spirit of the English nation, depressed and broken by the Norman conquest, for many years quietly gave way to the rage of despotism, and peaceably submitted to the most abject vassallage." Not only had the King himself been rapacious and cruel, eagerly snatching at the liberties of the ancient, Saxon constitution, but the barons, "domineering and turbulent . . . capricious and inconstant . . . sometimes abetted the King in his projects of tyranny, and at other times excited the people to insurrections and tumults. For these reasons the constitution was ever fluctuating from one extreme to another. Now despotism, now anarchy prevailed." Gradually, safeguards against such evils were built up — that great array of documents starting with Magna Carta that outlined the inner boundaries of English liberties — which remained effective until, in the seventeenth century, that "execrable race of the Stuarts" precipiated a "formidable, violent, and bloody" struggle between the people and the confederacy "of temporal and spiritual tyranny." In the end liberty, as all the world knew, had been re-established in England, for the Glorious Revolution had created " that happy establishment which Great Britain has since enjoyed." But it had been a close victory which would require the utmost vigilance to maintain.[23]

[23] Otis, *Rights* (JHL Pamphlet 7), p. 31; Bland, *Inquiry*, p. 7; Jefferson to Edmund Pendleton, August 13, 1776, *Papers of Thomas Jefferson* (Julian P. Boyd, ed., Princeton, 1950–), I, 492; Hicks, *Considerations*, p. 2; [James Wilson], *Considerations on the . . . Authority of the British Parliament* (Philadelphia, 1774), p. 12; Adams, *Dissertation*, in *Works*, III, 451; Otis, *Rights* (JHL Pamphlet 7), p. 70.
The pamphlets contain a good deal of discussion of English history, for much of the intellectual coherence of the colonists' political arguments rested on their views of the past. The ancient, presumably Saxon, origins of the English constitution was of particular importance to them, though, as John Adams pointed out, the Saxon constitution was "involved in much obscurity . . . the monarchical and democratic factions in England, by their opposite endeavors to make the Saxon constitutions swear for their respective systems, have much increased the difficulty of determining . . . what that constitution, in many important particulars, was" (*Works*, III, 543). Most agreed with Charles Carroll that "the liberties which the English enjoyed under their Saxon kings were wrested from them by the Norman conqueror," but differed with him on the idea that only at the close of the reign of Henry III was there "the first faint traces of the House of Commons" (Elihu S. Riley, ed., *Correspondence of "First Citizen" . . . and "Antilon" . . .*, Baltimore, 1902, p. 212). Maurice Moore cited Spelman and Madox to the effect that the commons in the ancient constitution, while not apparently meeting regularly, was summoned when taxation was to be discussed, a practice abolished at the conquest and only slowly thereafter recovered (*The Justice and Policy of Taxing* [Wilmington, N.C., 1765], pp. 3–4). Richard Bland cited Petyt, Brady, Rapin, and particularly Tacitus to establish the ancient, Saxon antecedents of the actual representation of all freeholders in Parliament, but, concentrating on the lack of such a franchise in eighteenth-century England ("the putrid part of the constitution"), ignored the conquest altogether (*Inquiry*, pp. 7–10). William Hicks too passed silently over the "Saxon" era and wrote vaguely of the establishment of constitutional liberty in post-conquest struggles (*Considerations*, pp. 2–4; *Nature and Extent of Parliamentary Power*, p. 3). But the view most characteristic of the Revolutionary pamphleteers is that summarized in the passage above, which postulated an ideal constitution complete with an elected House of Commons in Saxon England, destroyed by the conquest, regained with modifications in the course of centuries of struggle that culminated in the Glorious Revolution, and that was once again challenged by the corruption of eighteenth-century politics. In accepting this view the colonists sought not to undermine Parliamentary authority as such but to establish its true character in its ancient origins in such a way as to emphasize the corruptions of the Parliament of George III. For detailed examinations of John Dickinson's and Thomas Jefferson's rendering of this history and of the sources of their ideas, see H. Trevor Colbourn's articles, "John Dickinson, Historical Revolutionary," *Pa. Mag.*, 83 (1959), 280–292; and "Thomas Jefferson's Use of the Past," *W.M.Q.*, 3d ser., 15 (1958), 56–70. For Rapin's influential account of the ancient origins of the English constitution, linking pre-conquest institutions to eighteenth-century politics, see his *Dissertation on the . . . Whigs and Tories* [1717] (Boston, 1773), pp. 6–16; for his elaborate and inconclusive discussion of the pre-conquest

It had been at this critical juncture in the history of England and of liberty, when Englishmen had been forced to struggle with tyranny as they had not since the conquest, that America had been settled. The conjunction had not been accidental. "It was this great struggle that peopled America . . . a love of universal liberty, and a hatred, a dread, a horror, of the infernal confederacy [of temporal and spiritual tyranny] projected, conducted, and accomplished the settlement of America." Just as their Saxon ancestors had left "their native wilds and woods in the north of Europe," the settlers of America had emigrated to create in a new land civil and ecclesiastical governments purer, more free than those they had left behind. The transplantation had been made from an undefiled branch of the nation, strong, healthy, brimming with the juices of liberty, and it had been placed in a soil perfect for its growth. In the colonies, "sought and settled as an asylum for liberty, civil and religious," virtue continued to be fortified by the simplicity of life and the lack of enervating luxury.[24]

This was not merely a parochial view. Though the idea that America was a purer and freer England came largely from local, nonconformist readings of history, it was reinforced by powerful elements within Enlightenment thought. European illuminati continued to identify America, as John Locke had done, with something approximating a benign state of nature and to think of the colonies as special preserves of virtue and liberty. They could not help but note the refreshing simplicity of life and the wholesome consequences of the spread of freehold tenure. Nor could they deny the argument of Trenchard that the colonies demonstrated the military effectiveness of militia armies whose members were themselves the beneficiaries of the constitution and hence not likely to wish to destroy it.[25] No less a figure than Voltaire stated that America

origins of Parliament, see his *Dissertation on the Government, Laws . . . of the Anglo-Saxons. Particularly, the Origin, Nature, and Privileges of their Wittena-Gemot, or Parliament . . .* , published in volume II (London, 1728) of his *History of England,* pp. [135]–210. On the historiographical background of these views, see Pocock, *Ancient Constitution,* especially chap. ii; Christopher Hill, "The Norman Yoke," *Puritanism and Revolution* (London, 1958), chap. iii; David C. Douglas, *English Scholars 1660–1730* (London, 1951), especially chap. vi; and Samuel Kliger, *The Goths in England* (Cambridge, 1952), chap. ii, especially pp. 146 ff.

[24] Adams, *Dissertation,* in *Works,* III, 451; Jefferson, *Summary View,* in Ford, *Writings,* I, 430; Amos Adams, *A Concise Historical View of the . . . Planting . . .* (Boston, 1769), p. 51. See also Judah Champion, *A Brief View of the Distresses . . . Our Ancestors Encountered in Settling New-England . . .* (Hartford, 1770), pp. 10 ff.; and, for an even more local application of the same point of view, James Dana, *A Century Discourse . . .* (New Haven, [1770]), pp. 18 ff.

[25] *An Argument,* pp. 21–22 (in *The Pamphleteer,* X, 132–133).

was the refinement of all that was good in England, writing in his *Lettres philosophiques* that Penn and the Quakers had actually brought into existence "that golden age of which men talk so much and which probably has never existed anywhere except in Pennsylvania." At lower levels of sophistication too — in the propaganda turned out by promoters of emigration — the idea was broadcast that inhabitants of the colonies enjoyed a unique simplicity and rectitude in their social life and a special freedom in their politics.

Not all, of course, agreed. A contrary picture of the colonists as provincial rustics steadily degenerating in a barbarous environment distant from civilizing influences persisted.[26] But on the eve of the Revolutionary controversy Americans, if not all Europeans and if not the crown officials who legally ruled them, could see themselves as peculiarly descended, and chosen for a special destiny. English successes in the Seven Years' War made this seem particularly realistic, for it seemed reasonable, after the conquest of Canada, to envision, as Jonathan Mayhew did in 1759, "a mighty empire" in America "(I do not mean an independent one) in numbers little inferior perhaps to the greatest in Europe, and in felicity to none." There would be "a great and flourishing kingdom in these parts of America," with cities "rising on every hill . . . happy fields and villages . . . [and] religion professed and practiced throughout this spacious kingdom in far greater purity and perfection than since the times of the apostles." [27]

It was at least possible. What would in fact happen in England and America would of course be the result, the colonists knew, of the degree of vigilance and the strength of purpose the people could exert. Believing with Trenchard that "what happened yesterday will come to pass again, and the same causes will produce like effects in all ages," [28] they assumed that the preservation of liberty would continue to be a struggle with adversity; and if at the moment the prospects for success

---

[26] Durand Echeverria, *Mirage in the West* (Princeton, 1957), chap. i; Koebner, *Empire*, pp. 93–96.

[27] *Two Discourses Delivered October 25, 1759* . . . (Boston, 1759), pp. 60, 61.

[28] *An Argument,* p. 5 (in *The Pamphleteer,* X, 115); cf., e.g., James Otis: "the laws of nature are uniform and invariable. The same causes will produce the same effects from generation to generation." *Vindication* (JHL Pamphlet 11), p. [3]. See also the Carrolls' remarks to the same effect quoted directly below, and [James Chalmers], *Additions to Plain Truth* . . . (Philadelphia, 1776), p. 128. For an explanation of this belief, see Daniel J. Boorstin, *The Mysterious Science of the Law* (Cambridge, 1941), chap. ii, especially pp. 32–33; on the relation of this notion to the emerging idea of progress, see Stow Persons, "The Cyclical Theory of History in Eighteenth Century America," *American Quarterly,* 6 (1954), 147–163.

in that struggle seemed excellent in the colonies, they were poor indeed in the home country. By 1763, before any of the major problems of Anglo-American relations had appeared, the belief was widespread in America that circumstances in England were far from conducive to the maintenance of political freedom, that it was likely, indeed, that a new crisis of liberty was approaching. Radical writings, from *Cato's Letters* to Hollis' influential correspondence with leading colonists four decades later, insisted that the environment of eighteenth-century England was, to a dangerous degree, hostile to liberty: that Jacobite remnants flourished, that effeminizing luxury and slothful negligence continued to soften the moral fiber of the nation, and that politics festered in corruption. Specifically, the colonists were told again and again that the prime requisite of constitutional liberty, an independent Parliament free from the influence of the crown's prerogative, was being undermined by the successful efforts of the administration to manipulate Parliamentary elections to its advantage and to impose its will on members in Parliament. Nor was this sense of threat to the liberty-preserving balance of the constitution conveyed merely by reports by disaffected Englishmen. It was experienced directly by Americans themselves visiting England in the 1750's and 1760's.

John Dickinson, in England in the election year 1754 as a student of law, was enthralled by the sophistication and variety of life in London, and "filled with awe and reverence" by his contact with scenes of ancient greatness and by the opportunity to hear "some of the greatest men in England, perhaps in the world." But he was shocked, too, beyond all expectation, by Hogarthian election scenes and by the callous disregard of freedom exhibited in Parliament. Over £1,000,000, he wrote his father, had been expended in efforts to manipulate the general election. The starting price for the purchase of votes in one northern borough, he reported, was 200 guineas.

It is astonishing to think what impudence and villainy are practiced on this occasion. If a man cannot be brought to vote as he is desired, he is made dead drunk and kept in that state, never heard of by his family or friends till all is over and he can do no harm. The oath of their not being bribed is as strict and solemn as language can form it, but is so little regarded that few people can refrain from laughing while they take it. I think the character of Rome will equally suit this nation: "Easy to be bought, if there was but a purchaser."

The fact that over seventy elections were disputed, he continued a few months later, is "one of the greatest proofs perhaps of the corruption of the age that can be mentioned."

Bribery is so common that it is thought there is not a borough in England where it is not practiced, and it is certain that many very flourishing ones are ruined, their manufactories decayed, and their trade gone by their dependence on what they get by their votes. We hear every day in Westminster Hall leave moved to file informations for bribery, but it is ridiculous and absurd to pretend to curb the effects of luxury and corruption in one instance or in one spot without a general reformation of manners, which everyone sees is absolutely necessary for the welfare of this kingdom. Yet Heaven knows how it can be effected. It is grown a vice here to be virtuous . . . People are grown too polite to have an old-fashioned religion, and are too weak to find out a new, from whence follows the most unbounded licentiousness and utter disregard of virtue, which is the unfailing cause of the destruction of all empires.

And in the House of Lords he heard speeches that could only be interpreted as acquiescence in the creation of a standing army. "But such is the complacency these great men have for the smiles of their prince that they will gratify every desire of ambition and power at the expense of truth, reason, and their country." [29]

So too Charles Carroll of Carrollton wrote from London in 1760 after twelve years of study and travel abroad that "a change in our constitution is I think near at hand. Our dear-bought liberty stands upon the brink of destruction." His father, who had also been educated abroad, agreed: "Things seem to be tending hastily to anarchy in England;" he wrote his son in 1763, "corruption and freedom cannot long subsist together . . . for my part I think an absolute government preferable to one that is only apparently free; and this must be the case of your present constitution, if it be true that whoever presides in the treasury can command in Parliament." At home in Maryland two years later it seemed more evident than ever to the younger Carroll that the English constitution was "hastening to its final period of dissolution, and the symptoms of a general decay are but too visible." Sell your estate in England, he advised an English friend, and

purchase lands in this province where liberty will maintain her empire till a dissoluteness of morals, luxury, and venality shall have prepared the degenerate sons of some future age to prefer their own mean lucre, the bribes, and the smiles of corruption and arbitrary ministers to patriotism, to glory, and to the public weal. No doubt the same causes will produce the same effects, and a period is already set to the reign of American freedom; but that fatal time seems to be at a great distance. The present generation at least, and I hope many succeeding ones, in spite of a corrupt Parliament, will enjoy the blessings and the sweets of liberty.

Later, Carroll's father, further informed of the realities of European life not only by his well-traveled son but by "daily papers, periodical and

[29] H. Trevor Colbourn, "A Pennsylvania Farmer at the Court of King George: John Dickinson's London Letters, 1754–1756," *Pa. Mag.*, 86 (1962), 257, 268, 421, 445.

occasional pamphlets" as well, enlarged upon the theme in letters to his English friends:

What must be the end of this shameless, long-continued want of honor, public spirit, and patriotism? Will not your profligacy, corruption, and versatility sink you into anarchy and destruction? All states laboring under the same vices have met with the fate which will be your lot. That fate is impending; it cannot be far off. The same causes will ever produce similar effects . . . are you not a people devoted to and on the brink of destruction? I began to be acquainted with the world in the year 1720, memorable by the ruin of not only the unthinking adventurers in the South Sea stock but of numberless widows, helpless minors, and innocent infants . . . Soon after Sir Robert Walpole was made premier he reduced corruption into a regular system which since his time to the present period has been improved and founded on so broad and solid a basis as to threaten the constitution with immediate ruin and already to have left to the people little more than the appearance of liberty.[30]

In the context of such beliefs the question inevitably arose "whether we are obliged to yield," as Jonathan Mayhew put it in his famous *Discourse* of 1750, "an absolute submission to our prince, or whether disobedience and resistance may not be justifiable in some cases." The answer was clear. Submission is not required "to all who bear the *title* of rulers in common, but only to those who *actually* perform the duty of rulers, by exercising a reasonable and just authority for the good of human society." When government fails to serve its proper ends then "a regard to the public welfare ought to make us withhold from our rulers that obedience and subjection which it would, otherwise, be our duty to render to them." In such situations one is "bound to throw off [his] allegiance"; not to do so would be tacitly to conspire "in promoting slavery and misery."

For a nation thus abused to arise unanimously and to resist their prince, even to the dethroning him, is not criminal, but a reasonable way of vindicating their liberties and just rights; it is making use of the means, and the only means, which God has put into their power, for mutual and self-defense. And it would be highly criminal in them not to make use of this means. It would be stupid tameness and unaccountable folly for whole nations to suffer *one* unreasonable, ambitious, and cruel man to wanton and riot in their misery. And in such a case it would, of the

[30] Charles Carroll of Carrollton to Charles Carroll, Sr., London, January 29, 1760. *Maryland Historical Magazine,* 10 (1915), 251; Charles Carroll, Sr., to Charles Carroll of Carrollton, September 3, 1763, Thomas M. Field, ed., *Unpublished Letters of Charles Carroll of Carrollton* . . . (New York, 1902), p. 78; Charles Carroll of Carrollton to Mr. Bradshaw, November 21, 1765, *ibid.,* p. 97; Charles Carroll, Sr., to William Graves, December 23, 1768, *Maryland Historical Magazine,* 12 (1917), 185. On the generality of such views, see William L. Sachse, *The Colonial American in Britain* (Madison, 1956), pp. 204–207.

two, be more rational to suppose that they that did NOT *resist* [rather] than that they who did, would *receive to themselves damnation.*

When tyranny is abroad, "submission," Andrew Eliot wrote quite simply in 1765, "is a crime." [31]

[31] *A Discourse Concerning Unlimited Submission* (Boston, 1750: JHL Pamphlet 1), pp. 13, 20, 29, 30, 40; Eliot, *Sermon*, pp. 47–48.

CHAPTER V

THE LOGIC OF REBELLION

I T is the meaning imparted to the events after 1763 by this integrated
group of attitudes and ideas that lies behind the colonists' rebellion.
In the context of these ideas, the controversial issues centering on the
question of Parliament's jurisdiction in America acquired as a group new
and overwhelming significance. The colonists believed they saw emerging
from the welter of events during the decade after the Stamp Act a pattern
whose meaning was unmistakable. They saw in the measures taken by
the British government and in the actions of officials in the colonies something for which their peculiar inheritance of thought had prepared them
only too well, something they had long conceived to be a possibility in
view of the known tendencies of history and of the present state of affairs
in England. They saw about them, with increasing clarity, not merely
mistaken, or even evil, policies violating the principles upon which freedom rested, but what appeared to be evidence of nothing less than a
deliberate conspiracy launched surreptitiously by plotters against liberty
both in England and in America. The danger to America, it was believed,
was in fact only the small, immediately visible part of the greater whole
whose ultimate manifestation would be nothing less than the destruction
of the English constitution with all the rights and privileges embedded
in it.

This belief transformed the meaning of the colonists' struggle, and it
added an inner accelerator to the movement of opposition. For, once
grasped, it could not be easily dispelled: denial only confirmed it, since
what conspirators profess is not what they believe; the ostensible, for them,
is not the real; and the real is deliberately malign.

It was this — the overwhelming evidence, as they saw it, that they were
faced with conspirators against liberty determined at all costs to gain ends
which their words dissembled — that was signaled to the colonists after
1763, and it was this above all else that in the end propelled them into
Revolution.

Suspicion that an active conspiracy of power against liberty existed and
involved the colonies directly was deeply rooted in the consciousness of a

large segment of the American population; it had assumed specific form before any of the famous political events of the struggle with England took place. No adherent of a nonconformist church or sect in the eighteenth century was free from suspicion that the Church of England, an arm of the English state, was working to bring all subjects of the crown into the community of the Church; and since toleration was official and nonconformist influence in English politics formidable, it was doing so by stealth, disguising its efforts, turning to improper uses devices that had been created for benign purposes. In particular, the Society for the Propagation of the Gospel in Foreign Parts, an arm of the Church created in 1701 to aid in bringing the Gospel to the pagan Indians, was said by 1763 to have "long had a formal design to root out Presbyterianism, etc., and to establishing both episcopacy and bishops." [1]

This suspicion, which had smoldered in the breasts of New Englanders and nonconformists throughout the colonies for half a century or more, had burst into flame repeatedly, but never so violently as in 1763, in the Mayhew-Apthorp controversy which climaxed years of growing anxiety that plans were being made secretly to establish an American episcopate. To Mayhew, as to Presbyterian and Congregational leaders throughout the colonies, there could be little doubt that the threat was real. Many of the facts were known, facts concerning maneuvers in London and in America. Anglican leaders in New York and New Jersey had met almost publicly to petition England for an American episcopate, and there could be little doubt also of the role of the Society for the Propagation of the Gospel in this undercover operation. For if the ostensible goal of the Society was the gospelizing of the pagan Indians and Negroes, its true goal was manifestly revealed when it established missions in places like Cambridge, Massachusetts, which had not had a resident Indian since the seventeenth century and was well equipped with "orthodox" preachers. Such missions, Mayhew wrote, have "all the appearance of entering wedges . . . carrying on the crusade, or spiritual siege of our churches, with the hope that they will one day submit to an episcopal sovereign." Bishops, he wrote unblinkingly in reply to the Archbishop of Canterbury, have commonly been instruments in arbitrary reigns of "establishing a tyranny over the bodies and souls of men," and their establishment in America would mark the end of liberty in Massachusetts and elsewhere. By 1765, when the final exchanges in this pamphlet war were published,

[1] Jonathan Mayhew, *Observations on the Charter and Conduct of the Society for the Propagation of the Gospel in Foreign Parts* . . . (Boston, 1763), pp. 103–108.

it was commonly understood in New England and elsewhere that "the stamping and episcopizing [of] our colonies were . . . *only different branches of the same plan of power."* [2]

Fear of an ecclesiastical conspiracy against American liberties, latent among nonconformists through all of colonial history, thus erupted into public controversy at the very same time that the first impact of new British policies in civil affairs was being felt. And though it was, in an obvious sense, a limited fear (for large parts of the population identified themselves with the Anglican church and were not easily convinced that liberty was being threatened by a plot of Churchmen) it nevertheless had a profound indirect effect everywhere, for it stimulated among highly articulate leaders of public opinion, who would soon be called upon to interpret the tendency of civil affairs, a general sense that they lived in a conspiratorial world in which what the highest officials professed was not what they in fact intended, and that their words masked a malevolent design.[3]

Reinforcement for this belief came quickly. Even for those who had in no way been concerned with the threat of an episcopal establishment, the passage of the Stamp Act was not merely an impolitic and unjust law that threatened the priceless right of the individual to retain possession of his property until he or his chosen representative voluntarily gave it up to another; it was to many, also, a danger signal indicating that a more general threat existed. For though it could be argued, and in a sense proved by the swift repeal of the act, that nothing more was involved than ignorance or confusion on the part of people in power who really knew better and who, once warned by the reaction of the colonists, would not repeat the mistake — though this could be, and by many was, concluded, there nevertheless appeared to be good reason to suspect that more was involved. For from whom had the false information and evil

[2] Mayhew, *Observations,* p. 57; Jonathan Mayhew, *Remarks on an Anonymous Tract . . . Being a Second Defence . . .* (Boston, 1764), p. 12; Alden Bradford, *Memoir of the Life and Writings of Rev. Jonathan Mayhew . . .* (Boston, 1838), p. 372. For a full account of "the Anglican Plot," see Carl Bridenbaugh, *Mitre and Sceptre* (New York, 1962), chaps. vii–ix. See also Introduction to [John Aplin], *Verses on Doctor Mayhew's Book of Observations* (Providence, 1763: JHL Pamphlet 3), and pp. 156–158 below.

[3] Thus John Adams drew the theme of his *Dissertation on the Canon and Feudal Law* (1765) from the association of the episcopal "plot" and the Stamp Act; see especially the concluding section ("there seems to be a direct and formal design on foot to enslave all America") in *Works,* III, 464. On this association in general, see Bridenbaugh, *Mitre and Sceptre,* chap. ix: "Bishops and Stamps, 1764–1766." For Adams' final summary of the Mayhew-Apthorp affair, see below, p. 158.

advice come that had so misled the English government? From officials in the colonies, said John Adams, said Oxenbridge Thacher, James Otis, and Stephen Hopkins — from officials bent on overthrowing the constituted forms of government in order to satisfy their own lust for power, and not likely to relent in their passion. Some of these local plotters were easily identified. To John Adams, Josiah Quincy, and others the key figure in Massachusetts from the beginning to the end was Thomas Hutchinson who by "serpentine wiles" was befuddling and victimizing the weak, the avaricious, and the incautious in order to increase his notorious engrossment of public office. In Rhode Island it was, to James Otis, that "little, dirty, drinking, drabbing, contaminated knot of thieves, beggars, and transports . . . made up of Turks, Jews, and other infidels, with a few renegado Christians and Catholics" — the Newport junto, led by Martin Howard, Jr., which had already been accused by Stephen Hopkins and others in Providence of "conspiring against the liberties of the colony." [4]

But even if local leaders associated with power elements in England had not been so suspect, there were grounds for seeing more behind the Stamp Act than its ostensible purpose. The official aim of the act was, of course, to bring in revenue to the English treasury. But the sums involved were in fact quite small, and "some persons . . . may be inclined to acquiesce under it." But that would be to fall directly into the trap, for the smaller the taxes, John Dickinson wrote in the most influential pamphlet published in America before 1776, the more dangerous they were, since they

---

[4] For a succinct explanation of the manifest threat of the Stamp Act, see Stephen Hopkins, *Rights of Colonies Examined* (Providence, 1765: JHL Pamphlet 9), pp. 16–17. Adams' almost paranoiac suspicions of Hutchinson's hidden motives run through his *Diary and Autobiography*; e.g., I, 306; II, 39; III, 430. See also *Novanglus and Massachusettensis* . . . (Boston, 1819), pp. 49–50, 68; *Works*, X, 285–286, 298. It is the generality of such suspicions that accounts for the furor caused by the publication in 1773 of Hutchinson's innocuous letters of 1768 — letters in which, the publishers wrote in the pamphlet's title, "*the Judicious Reader Will Discover the Fatal Source of the Confusion and Bloodshed.*" Josiah Quincy thought he saw the final proof of Hutchinson's conspiratorial efforts in his maneuverings with the North administration in London in 1774 and 1775: "Journal of Josiah Quincy Jun. . . . in England . . . ," *Proceedings of the Massachusetts Historical Society*, 50 (1916–1917), 444, 446, 447, 450, 452. Thacher's suspicions of Hutchinson (whom he called "Summa Potestatis," or "Summa" for short), are traced in the Introduction to his *Sentiments of a British American* (Boston, 1764: JHL Pamphlet 8). Otis' phrase is quoted from his abusive pamphlet, *Brief Remarks on the Defence of the Halifax Libel* . . . (Boston, 1765), p. 5. The charge against Howard appeared in the *Providence Gazette*, Sept. 15, 1764, and is part of the intense antipathy that built up in Providence against the royalist group in Newport. See, in general, Morgan, *Stamp Act*, chap. iv; and Introduction to Howard's *Letter from a Gentleman at Halifax* (Newport, 1765: JHL Pamphlet 10).

would the more easily be found acceptable by the incautious, with the result that a precedent would be established for making still greater inroads on liberty and property.

Nothing is wanted at home but a PRECEDENT, the force of which shall be established by the tacit submission of the colonies . . . If the Parliament succeeds in this attempt, other statutes will impose other duties . . . and thus the Parliament will levy upon us such sums of money as they choose to take, *without any other* LIMITATION *than their* PLEASURE.[5]

But by then, in 1768, when Dickinson's *Farmer's Letters* were published as a pamphlet, more explicit evidence of a wide-ranging plot was accumulating rapidly. Not only had another revenue act, the Townshend Duties, been passed by Parliament despite all the violence of the colonists' reaction to the Stamp Act, but it was a measure that enhanced the influence of the customs administration, which for other reasons had already come under suspicion. There had been, it was realized by the late 1760's, a sudden expansion in the number of "posts in the [colonial] 'government' . . . worth the attention of persons of influence in *Great Britain*" — posts, Franklin explained, like the governorships, filled by persons who were

generally strangers to the provinces they are sent to govern, have no estate, natural connection, or relation there to give them an affection for the country . . . they come only to make money as fast as they can; are sometimes men of vicious characters and broken fortunes, sent by a minister merely to get them out of the way.[6]

By the late 1760's, in the perspective of recent events, one could see that the invasion of customs officers "born with long claws like eagles," had begun as far back as the last years of the Seven Years' War and was now being reinforced by the new tax measures. The wartime Orders in Council demanding stricter enforcement of the Navigation Laws; the Sugar Act of 1764, which had multiplied the customs personnel; and the American Board of Customs Commissioners created in 1767 with "power," Americans said, "to constitute as many under officers as they please" — all of these developments could be seen to have provided for an "almost incredible number of inferior officers," most of whom the colonists believed to be "wretches . . . of such infamous characters that the merchants can-

[5] *Letters from a Farmer in Pennsylvania* . . . (Philadelphia, 1768), in Paul L. Ford, ed., *Writings of John Dickinson* (*Memoirs of the Historical Society of Pennsylvania*, XIV, Philadelphia, 1895), 382.

[6] Dickinson, *Farmer's Letters*, in Ford, *Writings*, p. 380; Albert H. Smyth, ed., *Writings of Benjamin Franklin* (New York, 1905–1907), V, 83. Cf. Verner W. Crane, *Benjamin Franklin's Letters to the Press, 1758–1775* (Chapel Hill, 1950), pp. 106–107, 277.

not possibly think their interest safe under their care." More important by far, however, was their influence on government.

For there was an obvious political and constitutional danger in having such "a set of *idle drones,*" such "lazy, proud, worthless *pensioners* and *placemen,*" in one's midst. It was nothing less than "a general maxim," James Wilson wrote,

that the crown will take advantage of every opportunity of extending its prerogative in opposition to the privileges of the people, [and] that it is the interest of those who have *pensions* or *offices at will* from the crown to concur in all its measures.

These "baneful harpies" were instruments of power, of prerogative. They would upset the balance of the constitution by extending *"ministerial influence* as much beyond its former bounds as the late war did the *British* dominions." Parasitic officeholders, thoroughly corrupted by their obligations to those who had appointed them, would strive to *"distinguish themselves* by their sordid zeal in defending and promoting measures which *they know beyond all questionsi* to be *destructive* to the *just rights* and *true interest* of their country." Seeking to *"serve the ambitious purposes of great men* at home," these *"base-spirited wretches"* would urge — were already urging — as they logically had to, the specious attractions of "SUBMISSIVE behavior." They were arguing

with a plausible affection of *wisdom* and *concern* how *prudent* it is to please the *powerful* — how *dangerous* to provoke them — and then comes in the perpetual incantation that freezes up every generous purpose of the soul in cold, inactive expectation — "that if there is any request to be made, compliance will obtain a favorable attention."

In the end, this extension of executive patronage, based on a limitless support of government through colonial taxation, would make the whole of government "merely a ministerial engine"; by throwing off the balance of its parts, it would destroy the protective machinery of the constitution.[7]

[7] [Silas Downer], *Discourse Delivered in Providence . . . at the Dedication of the Tree of Liberty* . . . (Providence, 1768), p. 10; Ebenezer Baldwin, *An Appendix Stating the Heavy Grievances* . . . , published in Samuel Sherwood, *A Sermon Containing Scriptural Instructions to Civil Rulers* . . . (New Haven, [1774]), pp. 52–53; *Observations on Several Acts of Parliament . . . and Also on the Conduct of the Officers of the Customs . . .* ([Boston], 1769), p. 15; William Gordon, *Discourse Preached December 15th 1774 . . .* (Boston, 1775), p. 11; [James Wilson], *Considerations on the . . . Legislative Authority of the British Parliament* (Philadelphia, 1774), pp. 6–7; Dickinson, *Farmer's Letters,* in Ford, *Writings,* pp. 382, 398n, 399–400; *Votes and Proceedings of . . . Boston . . .* (Boston, [1772]), p. 21. See also, among the voluminous expressions of resentment and fear of petty officeholders in the colonies, [Henry Laurens], *Extracts from the Proceedings of the High Court of Vice-Admiralty in Charlestown . . . with . . . Observations on American Custom-House Officers . . .* (Charleston, 1769); and *A Ministerial Catechise, Suitable To Be Learned by All . . . Pensioners, Placemen . . .* (Boston, 1771).

But even this did not exhaust the evidence that a design against liberty was unfolding. During the same years the independence of the judiciary, so crucial a part of the constitution, was suddenly seen to be under heavy attack, and by the mid-1760's to have succumbed in many places.[8]

This too was not a new problem. The status of the colonial judiciary had been a controversial question throughout the century. The Parliamentary statute of 1701 which guaranteed judges in England life tenure in their posts had been denied to the colonies, in part because properly trained lawyers were scarce in the colonies, especially in the early years, and appointments for life would prevent the replacement of ill-qualified judges by their betters, when they appeared; and in part because, judicial salaries being provided for by temporary legislative appropriations, the removal of all executive control from the judiciary, it was feared, would result in the hopeless subordination of the courts to popular influences. The status of the judiciary in the eighteenth century was therefore left open to political maneuvering in which, more often than not, the home government managed to carry its point and to make the tenure of judges as temporary as their salaries. Then suddenly, in the early 1760's, the whole issue exploded. In 1759 the Pennsylvania Assembly declared that the judges of that province would thereafter hold their offices by the same permanence of tenure that had been guaranteed English judges after the Glorious Revolution. But the law was disallowed forthwith by the crown. Opposition newspapers boiled with resentment; angry speeches were made in the Assembly; and a pamphlet appeared explaining in the fullest detail the bearing of judicial independence on constitutional freedom.

In New York the issue was even more inflamed and had wider repercussions. There, the judges of the Supreme Court, by a political maneuver of 1750, had managed to secure their appointments for life. But this tenure was interrupted by the death of George II in 1760 which required the reissuance of all crown commissions. An unpopular and politically weak lieutenant governor, determined to prevent his enemies from controlling the courts, refused to recommission the judges on life tenure. The result was a ferocious battle in which the opposition asserted New York's *"undoubted right* of having the judges of our courts on a constitutional basis," and demanded the "liberties and privileges" of Englishmen in this connection as in all others. But they were defeated, though not by

---

[8] For further details on the problem of the judiciary, and for documentation of the paragraphs that follow, see the Introduction and notes to *A Letter to the People of Pennsylvania* (Philadelphia, 1760: JHL Pamphlet 2).

the governor. In December 1761 orders were sent out from the King in Council to all the colonies, permanently forbidding the issuance of judges' commissions anywhere on any tenure but that of "the pleasure of the crown." [9]

All the colonies were affected. In some, like New Jersey, where the governor's incautious violation of the new royal order led to his removal from office, or like North Carolina, where opposition forces refused to concede and managed to keep up the fight for permanent judicial tenure throughout the entire period from 1760 to 1776, the issue was directly joined. In others, as in Massachusetts, where specific supreme court appointments were vehemently opposed by anti-administration interests, the force of the policy was indirect. But everywhere there was bitterness at the decree and fear of its implications, for everywhere it was known that judicial tenure "at the will of the crown" was "dangerous to the liberty and property of the subject," and that if the bench were occupied by "men who depended upon the smiles of the crown for their daily bread," the possibility of having an independent judiciary as an effective check upon executive power would be wholly lost.[10]

This fear was magnified by the rumor, which was circulating vigorously as early as 1768, that it was part of the administration's policy to have the salaries of the colonial judges "appointed for them by the crown, independent of the people." If this ever happened, the Boston Town Meeting asserted when the rumor was becoming actuality, it would "complete our slavery." The reasoning was simple and straightforward:

if taxes are to be raised from us by the Parliament of Great Britain without our consent, and the men on whose opinions and decisions our properties, liberties, and lives in a great measure depend receive their support from the revenues arising from these taxes, we cannot, when we think of the depravity of mankind, avoid looking with horror on the danger to which we are exposed!

"More and more," as the people contemplated the significance of crown salaries for a judiciary that served "at pleasure," was it clear that "the designs of administration [were] totally to subvert the constitution." Any

---

[9] Milton M. Klein, "Prelude to Revolution in New York: Jury Trials and Judicial Tenure," *W.M.Q.*, 3d ser., 17 (1960), 452.

[10] [William H. Drayton], *A Letter from Freeman of South-Carolina* . . . (Charleston, 1774), pp. 10, 20. For other characteristic expressions of the fear of a corrupt judiciary, see [John Allen], *An Oration upon the Beauties of Liberty* . . . (Boston, 1773), pp. 21 ff.: *The Conduct of Cadwallader Colden* . . . ([New York], 1767), reprinted in *Collections of the New-York Historical Society*, X (New York, 1877), 433–467; [John Allen], *The American Alarm* . . . (Boston, 1773), 1st sec., pp. 17, 20, 27, 28; *Votes and Proceedings of Boston*, pp. 37–38; Adams, *Diary and Autobiography*, II, 36, 65–67; III, 297 ff.

judge, the House in Massachusetts ultimately stated, who accepted such salaries would thereby declare "that he has not a due sense of the importance of an impartial administration of justice, that he is an enemy to the constitution, and has it in his heart to promote the establishment of an arbitrary government in the province." [11]

Long before this, however, another aspect of the judicial system was believed also to have come under deliberate attack. The jury system, it was said, in New York particularly but elsewhere as well, was being systematically undermined. In New York the same executive who had fought the permanent tenure of judges insisted on the legality of allowing jury decisions, on matters of fact as well as of law, to be appealed to the governor and Council. This effort, though defeated within a year by action of the Board of Trade in England, had a lasting impact on the political consciousness of New Yorkers. It was publicly assailed, in the year of the Stamp Act, as "arbitrary" and "scandalous" in its deliberate subversion of the British constitution.[12]

Associated with this but more important because more widespread in its effect was the extension and enforcement of the jurisdiction of the vice-admiralty courts — "prerogative" courts composed not of juries but of single judges whose posts were "political offices in the hands of the royal governors, to be bestowed upon deserving friends and supporters." Since these courts had jurisdiction over the enforcement of all laws of trade and navigation as well as over ordinary marine matters, they had always been potentially threatening to the interests of the colonists. But in the past, by one means or another, they had been curtailed in their effect, and much of their business had been shunted off to common law courts dominated by juries. Suddenly in the 1760's they acquired a great new importance, for it was into their hands that the burden of judicial enforcement of the new Parliamentary legislation fell. It was upon them, consequently, and upon the whole principle of "prerogative" courts that abuse was hurled as the effect of their enhanced power was felt. "What has America done," victims of the decisions of these courts asked, "to be thus particularized, to be disfranchised and stripped of so invaluable a privilege as the trial by jury?" The operations of the vice-admiralty courts, it was felt, especially after their administrative reorganization in 1767, denied Americans a cru-

---

[11] *Votes and Proceedings of Boston*, p. 20; Thomas Hutchinson, *History of . . . Massachusetts-Bay* (Lawrence S. Mayo, ed., Cambridge, 1936), III, 278, 279.

[12] Klein, "Prelude to Revolution in New York," pp. 453–459.

cial measure of the protection of the British constitution. "However respectable the judge may be, it is however an hardship and severity which distinguishes [defendants before this court] from the rest of Englishmen." The evils of such prerogative invasion of the judiciary could hardly be exaggerated: their "enormous created powers . . . threatens future generations in America with a curse tenfold worse than the Stamp Act." [13]

The more one looked the more one found evidences of deliberate malevolence. In Massachusetts, Thomas Hutchinson's elaborate patronage machine, long in existence but fully organized only after the arrival of Governor Francis Bernard in 1760, appeared to suspicious tribunes like Oxenbridge Thacher and John Adams to constitute a serious threat to liberty. The Hutchinsons and the Olivers and their ambitious allies, it was said (and the view was widely circulated through the colonies), had managed, by accumulating a massive plurality of offices, to engross the power of all branches of the Massachusetts government thereby building a "foundation sufficient on which to erect a tyranny."

Bernard had all the executive, and a negative of the legislative; Hutchinson and Oliver, by their popular arts and secret intrigues, had elevated to the [Council] such a collection of crown officers, and their own relations, as to have too much influence there; and they had three of a family on the superior bench . . . This junto therefore had the legislative and executive in their control, and more natural influence over the judicial than is ever to be trusted to any set of men in the world.

With encouragement, no doubt, from England, they were stretching their power beyond all proper bounds, becoming "conspirators against the public liberty." [14]

The same evil of plural officeholding, tending to destroy the protective mechanism of the separation of powers, was observed to be at work in South Carolina. In both cases the filiation between the engrossing of offices in England and in America could be said to be direct. The self-seeking monopolists of office in the colonies, advancing themselves and their faithful adherents "to the exclusion of much better men," Adams wrote somewhat plaintively, were as cravenly obedient to their masters in power

[13] Carl Ubbelohde, *The Vice-Admiralty Courts and the American Revolution* (Chapel Hill, 1960), pp. 112, 125–126. For further expressions of antipathy to the admiralty courts, see especially the Laurens pamphlet cited in note 7 above, and also, besides the references indexed in the present volume, Adams, *Works,* III, 466–467; *Votes and Proceedings of Boston,* p. 24.

[14] John Adams ("Novanglus"), *Novanglus and Massachusettensis,* pp. 49–50; Ellen E. Brennan, *Plural Office-Holding in Massachusetts 1760–1780* (Chapel Hill, 1945), chaps. i, ii. See also references to Hutchinson, above, note 4.

in England as their own despicable "creatures" were to them.[15] How deep this issue ran, how powerful its threat, could be seen best when one noted the degree to which it paralleled cognate developments in England.

John Wilkes's career was crucial to the colonists' understanding of what was happening to them; his fate, the colonists came to believe, was intimately involved with their own.[16] Not only was he associated in their minds with general opposition to the government that passed the Stamp Act and the Townshend Duties, that was flooding the colonies with parasitic placemen, and that appeared to be making inroads into the constitution by weakening the judiciary and bestowing monopolies of public offices on pliant puppets — not only was he believed to be a national leader of opposition to such a government, but he had entered the public arena first as a victim and then as the successful antagonist of general warrants, which, in the form of writs of assistance, the colonists too had fought in heroic episodes known throughout the land. He had, moreover, defended the sanctity of private property against confiscation by the government. His cause was their cause. His *Number 45 North Briton* was as celebrated in the colonies at it was in England, and more generally approved of; its symbolism became part of the iconography of liberty in the colonies. His return from exile in 1768 and subsequent election to Parliament were major events to Americans. Toasts were offered to him throughout the colonies, and substantial contributions to his cause as well as adulatory letters were sent by Sons of Liberty in Virginia, Maryland, and South Carolina. A stalwart, independent opponent of encroaching government power and a believer in the true principles of the constitution, he was expected to do much in Parliament for the good of all: so the Bostonians wrote him in June 1768 "your perseverance in the *good old cause* may still prevent the great system from dashing to pieces. 'Tis from your endeavors we hope for a royal 'Pascite, ut ante, boves,' and from our attachment to 'peace and good order' we wait for a constitutional redress: being determined that the King of Great Britain shall have subjects but not slaves in these remote parts of his dominions." [17]

[15] Drayton, *Letter from Freeman,* pp. 9, 18–19, 32–33; Edward McCrady, *The History of South Carolina Under the Royal Government 1719–1776* (New York, 1899), pp. 533–535, 710–713; Adams, *Diary and Autobiography,* I, 306; II, 39.

[16] For a detailed discussion of the Wilkes affair in the context of the present discussion, see Pauline Maier, "John Wilkes and American Disillusionment with Britain," *W.M.Q.,* 3d ser., 20 (1963), 373–395.

[17] Boston Sons of Liberty to Wilkes, June 6, 1768, *Proceedings of the Massachusetts Historical Society,* 47 (1913–1914), 191. The quotation is from Virgil, *Eclogues* i, 45: "pasture your cattle as of old."

By February 1769 it was well known that *the fate of Wilkes and America must stand or fall together."* [18] The news, therefore, that by the maneuvers of the court party Wilkes had been denied the seat in Parliament to which he had been duly elected came as a profound shock to Americans. It shattered the hopes of many that the evils they saw around them had been the result not of design but of inadvertence, and it portended darker days ahead. When again, and then for a second, a third, and a fourth time Wilkes was re-elected to Parliament and still denied his seat, Americans could only watch with horror and agree with him that the rights of the Commons, like those of the colonial Houses, were being denied by a power-hungry government that assumed to itself the privilege of deciding who should speak for the people in their own branch of the legislature. Power had reached directly and brutally into the main agency of liberty. Surely Wilkes was right: the constitution was being deliberately, not inadvertently, torn up by its roots.

Meanwhile an event even more sinister in its implications had taken place in the colonies themselves. On October 1, 1768, two regiments of regular infantry, with artillery, disembarked in Boston. For many months the harassed Governor Bernard had sought some legal means or excuse for summoning military help in his vain efforts to maintain if not an effective administration then at least order in the face of Stamp Act riots, circular letters, tumultuous town meetings, and assaults on customs officials. But the arrival of troops in Boston increased rather than decreased his troubles. For to a populace steeped in the literature of English radicalism the presence of troops in a peaceful town had such portentous meaning that resistence instantly stiffened. It was not the physical threat of the troops that affected the attitudes of the Bostonians; it was the bearing their arrival had on the likely tendency of events. Viewed in the perspective of Trenchard's writings, these were not simply soldiers assembled for police duties; they were precisely what history had proved over and over again to be prime movers of the process by which unwary nations lose "that precious jewel *liberty*." Here, in bold, stark actuality, was a standing army — just such a standing army as had snuffed out freedom in Denmark. True, British regulars had been introduced into the colonies on a permanent basis at the end of the Seven Years' War; that in itself had been disquieting. But it could then be argued that troops were needed to police the newly acquired territories, and that they were not in any case to

[18] William Palfrey to Wilkes, February 21, 1769, *Proceedings of the Massachusetts Historical Society*, 47 (1913–1914), 197.

be regularly garrisoned in peaceful, populous towns.[19] No such defense could be made of the troops sent to Boston in 1768. No simple, ingenuous explanation would suffice. The true motive was only too apparent for those with eyes to see. One of the classic stages in the process of destroying free constitutions of government had been reached.

And again significant corroboration could be found in developments in England, and support furnished for the belief that events in America were only part of a larger whole. On May 10, 1768, a mob assembled in St. George's Fields, London, in support of the imprisoned Wilkes was fired upon by the regiment of Foot Guards that had been summoned by the nervous magistrates. Several deaths resulted, the most dramatic being that of a boy, wrongly identified as a leader of the mob, who was tracked down and shot to death on orders of the commander. The political capital made of this misfortune by the Wilkesites and other anti-government groups in London was echoed loudly in the colonies, the more so when it appeared that convictions of the guilty soldiers by normal processes of the law courts were being quashed by the government. Could it be believed to be a coincidence that in February 1770 a young Bostonian was also shot to death by officers of the state? This was more than a parallel to what had happened in London: the two events were two effects of the same cause.[20]

And then, a few weeks later, came the Boston Massacre. Doubts that the troops in Boston constituted a standing army and that it was the purpose of standing armies to terrify a populace into compliance with tyrannical wills were silenced by that event. The narrative of the Massacre written by James Bowdoin and others, which was distributed everywhere in the English-speaking world, stressed the deliberateness of the shooting and the clarity of the design that lay behind the lurid event; nor was the parallel to the St. George's Fields murders neglected. The acquittal of the indicted soldiers did not alter the conviction that the Massacre was the logical work of a standing army, for it accentuated the parallel with the English case which also had concluded with acquittal; and in Boston too there was suspicion of judicial irregularities. How the murderers managed to escape was known to some, it was said, but was "too dark to explain." [21]

---

[19] Gipson, *British Empire*, X, 200–201, 328–329, 408; cf. Bernhard Knollenberg, *Origin of the American Revolution, 1759–1766* (New York, 1960), pp. 87–96.

[20] George Rudé, *Wilkes and Liberty* (Oxford, 1962), pp. 49 ff.; Maier, "Wilkes and American Disillusionment," pp. 386–387.

[21] Allen, *Oration upon the Beauties of Liberty*, p. xiii. [Bowdoin, *et al.*], *Short Narrative of the Horrid Massacre in Boston* . . . (Boston, 1770), reprinted within the year three times in Boston, three times in London and once (retitled) in Dublin, appears also in Frederic Kidder, *History of the Boston Massacre* . . . (Albany, 1870); for the direct as-

Unconstitutional taxing, the invasion of placemen, the weakening of the judiciary, plural officeholding, Wilkes, standing armies — these were major evidences of a deliberate assault of power upon liberty. Lesser testimonies were also accumulating at the same time: small episodes in themselves, they took on a large significance in the context in which they were received. Writs of assistance in support of customs officials were working their expected evil: "our houses, and even our bedchambers, are exposed to be ransacked, our boxes, trunks, and chests broke open, ravaged and plundered by wretches whom no prudent man would venture to employ even as menial servants." Legally convened legislatures had been "adjourned . . . to a place highly inconvenient to the members and greatly disadvantageous to the interest of the province"; they had been prorogued and dissolved at executive whim. Even the boundaries of colonies had been tampered with, whereby *"rights of soil"* had been eliminated at a stroke. When in 1772 the Boston Town Meeting met to draw up a full catalogue of the "infringements and violations" of the "rights of the colonists, and of this province in particular, as men, as Christians, and as subjects," it approved a list of twelve items, which took seventeen pamphlet pages to describe.[22]

But then, for a two-year period, there was a *détente* of sorts created by the repeal of the Townshend Duties, the withdrawal of troops from Boston, and the failure of other provocative measures to be taken. It ended abruptly, however, in the fall and winter of 1773, when, with a terrifying rush, the tendencies earlier noted were brought to fulfillment. In the space of a few weeks, all the dark, twisted roots of malevolence were finally revealed, plainly, for all to see.

The turning point was the Boston Tea Party in December 1773. Faced by this defiant resistance to intimidation, the powers at work in England, it was believed, gave up all pretense of legality — "threw off the mask," John Adams said — and moved swiftly to complete their design. In a period of two months in the spring of 1774 Parliament took its revenge

sociation of the Massacre with the problem of standing armies, see Kidder, *History*, p. 27. The annual Massacre Day orators played up this association in lurid detail: see, for example, Joseph Warren, *An Oration* . . . (Boston, 1772), pp. 11–12; John Hancock, *An Oration* . . . (Boston, 1774), pp. 13–15. The view of the Massacre held by John Adams and Josiah Quincy, Jr., the lawyers who successfully defended the soldiers in court, is especially important. Both thought the Massacre was "the strongest of proofs of the danger of standing armies" despite their efforts on the soldiers' behalf; Adams saw nothing incompatible between the verdict of the jury and his being invited to deliver one of the orations commemorating the Massacre. Josiah Quincy, *Memoir of the Life of Josiah Quincy Jun.* . . . (Boston, 1825), p. 67; Adams, *Diary and Autobiography*, II, 74, 79.

[22] *Votes and Proceedings of Boston*, pp. 13–30.

in a series of coercive actions no liberty-loving people could tolerate: the
Boston Port Act, intended, it was believed, to snuff out the economic life
of the Massachusetts metropolis; the Administration of Justice Act, aimed
at crippling judicial processes once and for all by permitting trials to be
held in England for offenses committed in Massachusetts; the Massachusetts Government Act, which stripped from the people of Massachusetts
the protection of the British constitution by giving over all the "democratic" elements of the province's government — even popularly elected
juries and town meetings — into the hands of the executive power; the
Quebec Act, which, while not devised as a part of the coercive program,
fitted it nicely, in the eyes of the colonists, by extending the boundaries of
a "papist" province, and one governed wholly by prerogative, south into
territory claimed by Virginia, Connecticut, and Massachusetts; finally, the
Quartering Act, to take effect in all colonies, which permitted the seizure
for the use of troops of all buildings, public and private, deserted and
occupied.

Once these coercive acts were passed there could be little doubt that "the
system of slavery fabricated against America . . . is the offspring of
mature deliberation." To the leaders of the Revolutionary movement
there was, beyond question, "a settled, fixed plan for *enslaving* the
colonies, or bringing them under arbitrary government, and indeed the
nation too." By 1774 the idea "that the British government — the *King,
Lords,* and *Commons* — have laid a regular plan to enslave America, and
that they are now deliberately putting it in execution" had been asserted,
Samuel Seabury wrote wearily but accurately, "over, and over, and over
again." The less inhibited of the colonial orators were quick to point out
that "the MONSTER of a standing ARMY" had sprung directly from "a
PLAN . . . systematically laid and pursued by the British ministry near
twelve years for enslaving America"; the Boston Massacre, it was claimed,
had been "planned by Hillsborough and a knot of treacherous knaves in
Boston." Careful analysts like Jefferson agreed on the major point; in one
of the most closely reasoned of the pamphlets of 1774 the Virginian stated
unambiguously that though "single acts of tyranny may be ascribed to the
accidental opinion of a day . . . a series of oppressions begun at a distinguished period and pursued unalterably through every change of ministers
too plainly prove a deliberate and systematical plan of reducing us to
slavery." And the fastidious and scholarly John Dickinson, though in
1774 he still clung to the hope that inadvertence, at least on the part of the
King, was involved, believed that "a plan had been deliberately framed

and pertinaciously adhered to, unchanged even by frequent changes of ministers, unchecked by any intervening gleam of humanity, to sacrifice to a passion for arbitrary dominion the universal property, liberty, safety, honor, happiness, and prosperity of us unoffending yet devoted Americans." Some sought to date the origins of the plot. Josiah Quincy found it in the Restoration of Charles II; and though John Adams, with one eye on Thomas Hutchinson, wrote in 1774 that "the conspiracy was first regularly formed and begun to be executed in 1763 or 4," later he traced it back to the 1750's and forties and the administration of Governor Shirley of Massachusetts. Nor were the stages of its development neglected. They could be traced, if in no other place then in the notorious Hutchinson letters of 1768–69, those "profoundly secret, dark, and deep" letters which, published in 1773, totally exposed Hutchinson's "machiavellian dissimulation," John Adams wrote, and convicted him of "junto conspiracy"; they gave proof, the Boston Committee of Correspondence wrote, that God had "wonderfully interposed to bring to light the plot that has been laid for us by our malicious and invidious enemies." [23]

But who, specifically, were these enemies, and what were their goals? Local plotters like Hutchinson were clearly only "creatures" of greater figures in England coordinating and impelling forward the whole effort. There were a number of specific identifications of these master influences. One, which appeared in 1773, claimed that at the root of the evil stood the venerable John Stuart, Lord Bute, whose apparent absence from politics during the previous decade could be seen as one of his more successful dissimulations: "he has been aiming for years . . . to destroy the

[23] [Alexander Hamilton], *A Full Vindication of the Measures of the Congress* . . . (New York, 1774), in H. C. Lodge, ed., *Works* (New York and London, 1904), I, 10; Baldwin, *Appendix*, p. 67; [Samuel Seabury], *A View of the Controversy* . . . (New York, 1774), in Clarence H. Vance, ed., *Letters of a Westchester Farmer* . . . *(1774–1775)* (*Publications of the Westchester County Historical Society*, VIII, White Plains, 1930), p. 123; Oliver Noble, *Some Strictures upon the* . . . *Book of Esther* . . . (Newburyport, 1775), pp. 28, 26; Hancock, *Oration*, p. 9; [Jefferson], *A Summary View* . . . (Williamsburg, 1774), in Paul L. Ford, ed., *Writings of Thomas Jefferson* (New York, 1892–1899), I, 435; on the development of Dickinson's understanding of the cause of the crisis, see Introduction to his *Late Regulations* (Philadelphia, 1765: JHL Pamphlet 14); Quincy, *Observations on the* . . . *Boston Port-Bill with Thoughts on* . . . *Standing Armies* (Boston, 1774), in Quincy, *Memoir*, p. 446 (cf. pp. 464–465); Adams, *Works*, X, 242–243 (for Adams' full elaboration of the ministry's "dark intrigues and wicked machinations" so clearly dovetailed with the Hutchinson clique's maneuverings, see *Novanglus and Massachusettensis*, pp. 15 ff., 49–50, 55, 71–72; *Diary and Autobiography*, II, 80, 90, 119); John C. Miller, *Origins of the American Revolution* (Boston, 1943), p. 332. For other expressions of the fear of "a constant, unremitted, uniform aim to enslave us," see *Votes and Proceedings of Boston*, pp. 30, 37; Allen, *American Alarm*, 1st sec., pp. 8–9, 17, 18, 33; Edmund S. Morgan, *The Gentle Puritan* (New Haven, 1962), pp. 263–265. See also the Note on Conspiracy that follows this chapter.

ancient right of the subjects," and now was finally taking steps to "over-throw both . . . King and state; to bring on a revolution, and to place another whom he [is] more nearly allied to upon the throne." Believing the people to "have too much liberty," he intended to reduce them to the "spiritless SLAVES" they had been "in the reign of the *Stuarts*." [24] A more general version of this view was that a Stuart-Tory party, the "corrupt, Frenchified party in the nation," as it was described in 1766, was at work seeking to reverse the consequences of the Glorious Revolution. It was this notion that led to the republication of Rapin's *Dissertation on . . . the Whigs and Tories* in Boston in 1773; and it was this notion that furnished Jefferson with his ultimate understanding of the "system" that sought to destroy liberty in America.[25] Still another explanation emphasized the greed of a "monied interest" created by the crown's financial necessities during the Seven Years' War. The creation of this group was accompanied "by levying of taxes, by a host of tax gatherers, and a long train of dependents of the crown. The practice grew into system, till at length the crown found means to break down those barriers which the constitution had assigned to each branch of the legislature, and effectually destroyed the independence of both Lords and Commons." [26]

The most common explanation, however — an explanation almost universally accepted even after the Declaration of Independence placed responsibility officially on the King himself — located "the spring and cause

[24] Allen, *American Alarm*, 1st sec., pp. 18–19; cf. the same author's reference to *"Scotch barbarian troops"* at the St. George's Fields riot, in *Oration upon the Beauties of Liberty*, p. xiii.

[25] [Stephen Johnson], *Some Important Observations* . . . (Newport, 1766), p. 15. Jefferson's explanation appeared first as notes he jotted down on reading François Soulé's *Histoire des troubles de l'Amérique anglaise* (London, 1785) at the point where George III's education is mentioned: "The education of the present King was Tory. He gave decisive victories to the Tories. To these were added sundry rich persons sprung up in the E. I. America would have been too formidable a weight in the scale of the Whigs. It was necessary therefore to reduce them by force to concur with the Tories." Later he wrote more formally to Soulé: "The seeds of the war are here traced to their true source. The Tory education of the King was the first preparation for that change in the British government which that party never ceases to wish. This naturally ensured Tory administrations during his life. At the moment he came to the throne and cleared his hands of his enemies by the peace of Paris, the assumptions of unwarrantable right over America commenced; they were so signal, and followed one another so close as to prove they were part of a system either to reduce it under absolute subjection and thereby make it an instrument for attempts on Britain itself, or to sever it from Britain so that it might not be a weight in the Whig scale. This latter alternative however was not considered as the one which would take place. They knew so little of America that they thought it unable to encounter the little finger of Great Britain." *The Papers of Thomas Jefferson* (Julian P. Boyd, ed., Princeton, 1950–), X, 373n2, 369.

[26] [Carter Braxton], *An Address to . . . Virginia; on the Subject of Government* . . . (Philadelphia, 1776), p. 10.

of all the distresses and complaints of the people in England or in America" in "a kind of fourth power that the constitution knows nothing of, or has not provided against." This "overruling arbitrary power, which absolutely controls the King, Lords, and Commons," was composed, it was said, of the "ministers and favorites" of the King, who, in defiance of God and man alike, "extend their usurped authority infinitely too far," and, throwing off the balance of the constitution, make their "despotic will" the authority of the nation.

For their power and interest is so great that they can and do procure whatever laws they please, having (by power, interest, and the application of the people's money to *placemen* and *pensioners*) the whole legislative authority at their command. So that it is plain (not to say a word of a particular reigning arbitrary *Stuarchal* power among them) that the rights of the people are ruined and destroyed by ministerial *tyrannical* authority, and thereby . . . become a kind of slaves to the ministers of state.

This "junto of courtiers and state-jobbers," these "court-locusts," whispering in the royal ear, "instill in the King's mind a divine right of authority to command his subjects" at the same time as they advance their "detestable scheme" by misinforming and misleading the people.[27]

It was a familiar notion that had served in England for generations to justify opposition to a crown that could do no wrong, and it had recently been revived by both Pitt and Burke echoing the earlier eloquence of Bolingbroke. It had, moreover, a particular familiarity in New England, and elsewhere in the colonies, where people generally were acquainted with the Book of Esther and hence had a model for a ministerial conspiracy in the story of that "tyrannic *bloodthirsty* MINISTER OF STATE," Haman, at the court of Ahasuerus. There he was, wrote the Newbury, Massachusetts, minister Oliver Noble in 1775, "*Haman the Premier,* and his junto of court *favorites, flatterers,* and *dependents* in the royal city, together with *governors* of the provinces, *councilors, boards of trade, commissioners* and their *creatures, officers* and *collectors* of REVENUE, *solicitors,* assistants, *searchers,* and *inspectors,* down to tide-waiters and their *scribes,* and the good Lord knows whom and how many of them, together with the coachmen and servants of the whole . . ." — [*footnote:*] "Not that I am certain the *Persian* state had all these *officers* . . . or that the underofficers of state rode in *coaches* or chariots . . . But as the Persian monarchy was despotic . . . it is highly probable . . ." The story was so well known: ". . . now behold the DECREE obtained!

[27] Allen, *American Alarm,* 1st sec., pp. 8–9; Noble, *Some Strictures,* p. 6; Allen, *Oration upon the Beauties of Liberty,* p. 29.

The *bloody* PLAN ripened!" The *"cruel perpetrators of the horrid* PLOT and a *banditti* of ministerial tools through the provinces" had everything in readiness. "But behold! . . . A merciful GOD heard the cries of this oppressed people . . ." The parallels were closely drawn; Haman: Lord North; Esther and the Jews: the colonists; and Mordicai: Franklin.[28]

But why were not these manipulators of prerogative satisfied with amassing power at home? Why the attention to faraway provinces in America? Several answers were offered, besides the general one that power naturally seeks to drive itself everywhere, into every pocket of freedom. One explanation was that the court, having reached a limit in the possibilities of patronage and spoils in the British Isles, sought a quarrel with the colonies as an excuse for confiscating their wealth. "The long and scandalous list of placemen and pensioners and the general profligacy and prodigality of the present reign exceed the annual supplies. England is drained by taxes, and Ireland impoverished to almost the last farthing . . . America was the only remaining spot to which their oppression and extortion had not fully reached, and they considered her as a fallow field from which a large income might be drawn. . ." When the colonists' reaction to the Stamp Act proved that "raising a revenue in America quietly" was out of the question, it was decided to destroy their power to resist: the colonies were to be "politically broken up." And so the Tea Act was passed, not to gain a revenue but to provoke a quarrel. The ministry wished "to see America in arms . . . because it furnished them with a pretense for declaring us rebels; and persons conquered under that character forfeit their all, be it where it will or what it will, to the crown." England did not desire an accommodation of any sort, Lord North's conciliatory plan notwithstanding. "From motives of political avarice," she sought an excuse for conquest: "it is on this ground only that the continued obstinacy of her conduct can be accounted for." [29]

But perhaps the most explicit and detailed explanation of the assault upon America by a conspiratorial ministry came from the pen of a country parson in Connecticut writing "to enlighten the people of a country town not under the best advantages for information from the newspapers and other pieces wrote upon the controversy." Seeking to rouse the villagers "to a sense of the danger to which their liberties are now involved," the

---

[28] Archibald S. Foord, *His Majesty's Opposition, 1714–1830* (Oxford, 1964), pp. 37–38, 51, 53–54, 147–148, 170, 291, 318–319; Noble, *Some Strictures*, pp. 10, 17–18, 12. See also Richard Salter, *A Sermon* . . . (New London, 1768); Johnson, *Some Important Observations*, pp. 39, 55–56; Elisha Fish, *Joy and Gladness* . . . (Providence, 1767).

[29] *Four Letters on Interesting Subjects* (Philadelphia, 1776), p. 5.

Rev. Ebenezer Baldwin of Danbury explained that during the last war "the state of the colonies was much more attended to than it had been in times past," and "a very exalted idea of the riches of this country" had been conveyed back to England by the returning officers and soldiers. This exciting information fitted the plans of the ministry neatly, for

notwithstanding the excellency of the British constitution, if the ministry can secure a majority in Parliament who will come into all their measures [and] will vote as they bid them, they may rule as absolutely as they do in *France* or *Spain,* yea as in *Turkey* or *India.* And this seems to be the present plan: to secure a majority of Parliament, and thus enslave the nation with their own consent. The more places or pensions the ministry have in their gift the more easily they can *bribe* a majority of Parliament by bestowing those places on them or their friends. This makes them erect so many new and unnecessary offices in America, even so as to swallow up the whole of the revenue . . . by bestowing these places — places of considerable profit and no labor — upon the children or friends or dependents of the members of Parliament, the ministry can secure them in their interest. This doubtless is the great thing the ministry are driving at, to establish arbitrary government with the consent of Parliament. And to keep the people of England still, the first exertions of this power are upon the colonies.[30]

Thus the balance of the constitution had been thrown off by a gluttonous ministry usurping the prerogatives of the crown and systematically corrupting the independence of the Commons. Corruption was at the heart of it — the political corruption built on the general dissoluteness of the populace, so familiar in the history of tyranny and so shocking to observers of mid-eighteenth-century England. The evil, public and private, that had appalled Dickinson in 1754 had ripened, it seemed clear, in the subsequent decade. As early as 1766 there had been nervous speculation in the colonies about what would happen

if the British empire should have filled up the measure of its iniquity and become ripe for ruin: . . . if a proud, arbitrary, selfish, and venal spirit of corruption should ever reign in the British court and diffuse itself through all ranks in the nation; if lucrative posts be multiplied without necessity, and pensioners multiplied without bounds; if the policy of governing be by bribery and corruption, and the trade and manufactures of the nation be disregarded and trampled under foot; if all offices be bought and sold at a high and extravagant price . . . and if, to support these shocking enormities and corruptions, the subjects in all quarters must be hard squeezed with the iron arms of oppression.

Two years later it was stated that

The present involved state of the British nation, the rapacity and profuseness of many of her great men, the prodigious number of their dependents who want to be gratified with some office which may enable them to live lazily upon the labor of others, must convince us that we shall be taxed so long as we have a penny to pay,

[30] Baldwin, *Appendix,* p. 51, 67–68.

and that new offices will be constituted and new officers palmed upon us until the number is so great that we cannot by our constant labor and toil maintain any more.

By 1769 a Boston correspondent of Wilkes commented on "that torrent of corruption which 'like a general flood, has deluged all' to the eternal disgrace of the British nation," and suggested that the reason the "arbitrary and despotic" English government had "extended their ravages to America" was because they had found the British Isles too restricted an area for the full gratification of their "incessant cravings of luxury, extravagance and dissipation." [31]

That by 1774 the final crisis of the constitution, brought on by political and social corruption, had been reached was, to most informed colonists, evident; but if they had not realized it themselves they would soon have discovered it from the flood of newspapers, pamphlets, and letters that poured in on them from radical sources in England. Again and again reports from the home country proclaimed that the English nation had departed, once and for all and completely, from the true principles of liberty: the principles not of "certain modern Whigs," as one English pamphlet of 1774, reprinted in the colonies seven times within the year of its first appearance, explained, but of "Whigs before the [Glorious] Revolution and at the time of it; I mean the principles which such men as Mr. Locke, Lord Molesworth, and Mr. Trenchard maintained with their pens, Mr. Hampden and Lord [William] Russell with their blood, and Mr. Algernon Sidney with both." To those Englishmen who in the 1770's most directly inherited and most forcefully propagated these radical principles — Richard Price, Joseph Priestley, James Burgh — the situation at home if not abroad justified, even exaggerated, the worst fears for the future of liberty that their predecessors had expressed. For these latter-day radicals had witnessed personally the threatening rise of prerogative influence in the English government and its dramatic manifestation in the Wilkes affair; and they had seen revealed the rapacity and bankruptcy of the swollen East India Company, a revelation which illuminated to them the corruption of their era as dramatically as the collapse of the South Sea Company had revealed the rottenness of the era of George I to Trenchard and Gordon. Everywhere there was cynicism and gluttonous self-seeking. What more was needed to convince

[31] Johnson, *Some Important Observations*, p. 20; Thomas Bradbury, *The Ass, or, the Serpent* . . . (1712: reprinted in Boston, 1768), p. 12n; William Palfrey to Wilkes, February 21 and April 12, 1769, *Proceedings of the Massachusetts Historical Society*, 47 (1913-1914), 197, 199.

one that affairs in Britain were plummeting toward complete and irrecoverable collapse? The long-awaited signs of the total degeneration of the moral qualities necessary to preserve liberty were unmistakable, and these English radicals said so, vigorously, convincingly, in a series of increasingly shrill pamphlets and letters that were read avidly, circulated, published and republished, in America.[32]

There, these ideas carried conviction to a far larger part of the population, and bore more dramatic implications than they did in England. "Liberty," John Adams wrote, "can no more exist without virtue and independence than the body can live and move without a soul," and what liberty can be expected to flow from England where "luxury, effeminacy, and venality are arrived at such a shocking pitch" and where "both electors and elected are become one mass of corruption"? It was not hard to see where England stood: it was, Adams declared, precisely at the point "where the Roman republic was when Jugurtha left it and pronounced it a venal city ripe for destruction, if it can only find a purchaser." The analogy to the decline and fall of Rome and its empire was intriguing and informative; others carried it further and became more specific. Like Rome in its decline, England, "from being the nursery of heroes, became the residence of musicians, pimps, panders, and catamites." The swift decline of her empire, which, it was observed, had reached its peak only between 1758 and the Stamp Act, resulted from the same poison that had proved so fatal to free states in classical antiquity: the corruption, effeminacy, and languor that came from "the riches and luxuries of the East" and led to a calamitous "decay of virtue" and the collapse of the constitution. So often, so stridently, and so convincingly was it said in the colonies that in England "luxury has arrived to a great pitch; and it is a universal maxim that luxury indicates the declension of a state" — so often was it argued that vigor was gone, ex-

---

[32] [Matthew Robinson-Morris, Lord Rokeby], *Considerations on the Measures Carrying on with Respect to the British Colonies in North America* (2d ed., London, 1774), p. 10. This pamphlet was reprinted three times in Boston, twice in Philadelphia, and once in New York and Hartford in 1774 and 1775. For Abigail Adams' awareness of the identity between Rokeby's views and those of her husband writing as "Novanglus," see her letter of May 22, 1775, in L. H. Butterfield, *et al.*, eds., *Adams Family Correspondence* (Cambridge, 1963), I, 202, 203n11. See also [Joseph Priestley], *An Address to Protestant Dissenters* (Boston, 1774), p. 6; this pamphlet, first published in London in 1773, appeared in three American editions in 1774. And see, in general, Oscar and Mary F. Handlin, "James Burgh and American Revolutionary Theory," *Proceedings of the Massachusetts Historical Society*, 73 (1961), 38–57; H. Trevor Colbourn, "John Dickinson, Historical Revolutionary," *Pa. Mag.*, 83 (1959), 284; Caroline Robbins, *The Eighteenth-Century Commonwealthman* (Cambridge, 1959), chap. ix.

haustion and poverty approaching, that those who would defend British policy were obliged to debate the point: to assert the health and strength of English society, arguing, as Samuel Seabury did, that England was a "vigorous matron, just approaching a green old age; and with spirit and strength sufficient to chastise her undutiful and rebellious children" and not at all, as his adversary Alexander Hamilton had pictured her, "an old, wrinkled, withered, worn-out hag." [33]

The fact that the ministerial conspiracy against liberty had risen from corruption was of the utmost importance to the colonists. It gave a radical new meaning to their claims: it transformed them from constitutional arguments to expressions of a world regenerative creed. For they knew that England was one of the last refuges of the ancient gothic constitution that had once flourished everywhere in the civilized world. By far "the greatest part of the human race," it was known, already lies in "total subjection to their rulers." Throughout the whole continent of Asia people are reduced "to such a degree of abusement and degradation"

that the very idea of liberty is unknown among them. In *Africa,* scarce any human beings are to be found but barbarians, tyrants, and slaves: all equally remote from the true dignity of human nature and from a well-regulated state of society. Nor is *Europe* free from the curse. Most of her nations are forced to drink deep of the bitter cup. And in those in which freedom seem to have been established, the vital flame is going out. Two kingdoms, those of *Sweden* and *Poland,* have been betrayed and enslaved in the course of one year. The free towns of *Germany* can remain free no longer than their potent neighbors shall please to let them. *Holland* has got the forms if she has lost the spirit of a free country. *Switzerland* alone is in the full and safe possession of her freedom.

And if now, in this deepening gloom, the light of liberty went out in Britain too — in Britain, where next to "self-preservation, political liberty is the main aim and end of her constitution" — if, as events clearly portended and as "senators and historians are repeatedly predicting . . . continued corruption and standing armies will prove mortal distempers in her constitution" — what then? What refuge will liberty find?

"To our own country," it was answered, "must we look for the biggest part of that liberty and freedom that yet remains, or is to be expected, among mankind . . . For while the greatest part of the nations of the earth are held together under the yoke of universal slavery, the North

---

[33] Adams ("Novanglus"), *Novanglus and Massachusettensis,* pp. 25, 22, 43; William Hooper of North Carolina, quoted in Charles F. Mullett, "Classical Influences on the American Revolution," *Classical Journal,* 35 (1939–1940), 103; William H. Drayton, *A Charge on the Rise of the American Empire* . . . (Charleston, 1776), pp. 2–3; Seabury, *A View of the Controversy,* in Vance, *Letters of a Westchester Farmer,* p. 140.

American provinces yet remain *the country of free men:* the *asylum,* and the last, to which such may yet flee from the common deluge." More than that: "our native country . . . bids the fairest of any to promote *the perfection and happiness of mankind.*" No one, of course, can predict "the state of mankind in future ages." But insofar as one can judge the ultimate "designs of providence by the number and power of the causes that are already at work, we shall be led to think that the perfection and happiness of mankind is to be carried further in America than it has ever yet been in any place." Consider the growth the colonies had enjoyed in so short a time — growth in all ways, but especially in population: a great natural increase it had been, supplemented by multitudes from Europe, "tired out with the miseries they are doomed to at home," migrating to America "as the only country in which they can find food, raiment, and rest." Consider also the physical vigor of the people. But above all consider the moral health of the people and of the body politic.

The fatal arts of luxury and corruption are but comparatively beginning among us . . . Nor is corruption yet established as the common principle in public affairs. Our representatives are not chosen by bribing, corrupting, or buying the votes of the electors. Nor does it take one half of the revenue of a province to manage her house of commons . . . We have been free also from the burden and danger of standing armies . . . Our defenses has been our *militia* . . . the general operation of things among ourselves indicate strong tendencies towards a state of greater perfection and happiness than mankind has yet seen.

No one, therefore, can conceive of the cause of America as "the cause of a mob, of a party, or a faction." The cause of America "is the cause of *self-defense,* of *public faith,* and of the *liberties of mankind* . . . 'In our destruction, liberty itself expires, and human nature will despair of ever-more regaining its first and original dignity.'" [34]

This theme, elaborately orchestrated by the colonial writers, marked the fulfillment of the ancient idea, deeply embedded in the colonists' awareness, that America had from the start been destined to play a special role in history. The controversy with England, from its beginning in the early 1760's, had lent support to that belief, so long nourished by so many different sources: the covenant theories of the Puritans, certain strands of Enlightenment thought, the arguments of the English radicals, the condition of life in the colonies, even the conquest of Canada. It had

[34] Samuel Williams, *A Discourse on the Love of Our Country* . . . (Salem, 1775), pp. 21, 22, 23, 25, 26. Cf., e.g., Thomas Coombe, *A Sermon Preached* . . . (Philadephia, 1775), pp. 19–20; [Richard Wells], *A Few Political Reflections* . . . (Philadelphia, 1774), pp. 38–40, 50.

been the Stamp Act that had led John Adams to see in the original settlement of the colonies "the opening of a grand scene and design in providence for the illumination of the ignorant and the emancipation of the slavish part of mankind all over the earth." And Jonathan Mayhew, celebrating the conclusion of the same episode, had envisioned future streams of refugees escaping from a Europe sunk in "luxury, debauchery, venality, intestine quarrels, or other vices." It was even possible, Mayhew had added, "who knows?" that "our liberties being thus established, . . . on some future occasion . . . we or our posterity may even have the great felicity and honor to . . . keep Britain herself from ruin." [35]

Now, in 1774, that "future occasion" was believed to be at hand. After the passage of the Coercive Acts it could be said that "all the spirit of patriotism or of liberty now left in England" was no more than "the last snuff of an expiring lamp," while "the same sacred flame . . . which once showed forth such wonders in Greece and in Rome . . . burns brightly and strongly in America." Who ought then to suppress as "whimsical and enthusiastical" the belief that the colonies were to become "the foundation of a great and mighty empire, the largest the world ever saw to be founded on such principles of liberty and freedom, both civil and religious . . . [and] which shall be the principal seat of that glorious kingdom which Christ shall erect upon earth in the latter days"? It was the hand of God that was "in America now giving a new epocha to the history of the world." [36]

In the invigorating atmosphere of such thoughts, the final conclusion of the colonists' logic could be drawn not with regret but with joy. For while everyone knew that when tyranny is abroad "submission is a crime"; while they readily acknowledged that "no obedience is due to arbitrary, unconstitutional edicts calculated to enslave a free people"; and while they knew that the invasion of the liberties of the people "constitutes a state of war with the people" who may properly use "all the power which God has given them" to protect themselves — nevertheless they hesitated to come to a final separation even after Lexington and Bunker Hill. They hesitated, moving slowly and reluctantly, protesting "before God and the world that the utmost of [our] wish is that things may return to their old channel." They hesitated because their *"senti-*

[35] Adams, *Dissertation,* in *Works,* III, 452n; Jonathan Mayhew, *The Snare Broken* . . . (Boston, 1766), pp. 36, 38.

[36] Rokeby, *Considerations,* p. 148; Ebenezer Baldwin, *The Duty of Rejoicing under Calamities and Afflictions* . . . (New York, 1776), p. 38.

ments of duty and affection" were sincere; they hesitated because their respect for constituted authority was great; and they hesitated too because their future as an independent people was a matter of doubt, full of the fear of the unknown.[37]

What would an independent American nation be? A republic, necessarily — and properly, considering the character and circumstances of the people. But history clearly taught that republics were delicate polities, quickly degenerating into anarchy and tyranny; it was impossible, some said, to "recollect a single instance of a nation who supported this form of government for any length of time or with any degree of greatness." Others felt that independence might "split and divide the empire into a number of petty, insignificant states" that would easily fall subject to the will of "some foreign tyrant, or the more intolerable despotism of a few American demogogues"; the colonies might end by being "parceled out, Poland-like."

But if what the faint-hearted called "the ill-shapen, diminutive brat *independency"* contained within it all that remained of freedom; if it gave promise of growing great and strong and becoming the protector and propagator of liberty everywhere; if it were indeed true that "the cause of America is in a great measure the cause of all mankind"; if " 'Tis not the concern of a day, a year, or an age; posterity are virtually involved in the contest, and will be more or less affected even to the end of time by our proceedings now" — if all of this were true, ways would be found by men inspired by such prospects to solve the problems of a new society and government. And so let every lover of mankind, every hater of tyranny,

stand forth! Every spot of the old world is overrun with oppression. Freedom hath been hunted round the globe. Asia and Africa have long expelled her. Europe regards her like a stranger, and England hath given her warning to depart. O! receive the fugitive, and prepare in time an asylum for mankind.[38]

---

[37] Johnson, *Some Important Observations*, pp. 21, 23; [Robert Carter Nicholas], *Considerations on the Present State of Virginia Examined* ([Williamsburg], 1774), in Earl G. Swem reprint (New York, 1919), pp. 68, 42.

[38] Braxton, *Address*, p. 19; Seabury, *View*, in Vance, *Letters of a Westchester Farmer*, p. 112; Daniel Leonard ("Massachusettensis"), in *Novanglus and Massachusettensis*, p. 185; [Joseph Galloway], *A Candid Examination of the Mutual Claims of Great-Britain and the Colonies* . . . (New York, 1775), p. 31; [Thomas Paine], *Common Sense* . . . (Philadelphia, 1776), in Moncure D. Conway, ed., *The Writings of Thomas Paine* (New York, 1894–1896), I, 68, 84–85, 100–101.

A NOTE ON CONSPIRACY

The conviction on the part of the leaders of the Revolutionary movement that they were faced with a deliberate conspiracy aimed at eliminating their freedom had deep and widespread roots. As the pamphlets in the present volume make clear, it existed at the very beginning of the Anglo-American controversy. As early as 1765 pro-administration partisans like Martin Howard, Jr., were obliged to confront it directly (*Halifax Letter,* JHL Pamphlet 10, p. 6), and in 1764 pro-Americans like Oxenbridge Thacher felt it necessary "to suppose," for the sake of discussion, "that no design is formed to enslave them" (*Sentiments of a British American,* JHL Pamphlet 8, p. 4). The conviction grew steadily everywhere in the colonies, though most quickly where the polarization of politics was extreme and where radical leaders were least inhibited in expressing and reinforcing general apprehensions. Thus in 1770 the Boston Town Meeting in its instructions to its representatives to the General Court wrote that recent events "afford great reason to believe that a deep-laid and desperate plan of imperial despotism has been laid, and partly executed, for the extinction of all civil liberty . . . the august and once revered fortress of English freedom — the admirable work of ages — the BRITISH CONSTITUTION seems fast tottering into fatal and inevitable ruin." *A Report of the Record Commissioners of the City of Boston . . .* [vol. XVIII] (Boston, 1887), p. 26 (cf. the 1772 instructions, pp. 83–86).

But if such beliefs developed most fully and quickly in centers of agitation like Boston, they were by no means confined to these centers. As the annotation to the present chapter indicates, the idea was generally accepted by sympathizers of the American cause, even by such cautious and reluctant Revolutionaries as John Dickinson, who understood perfectly the psychological and political effects of a conspiratorial frame of mind (see *Farmer's Letters,* in Ford, *Writings,* pp. 387–388). Opponents of the Revolutionary movement were obliged to argue the point. "I should hardly expect," Daniel Dulany wrote in 1773 (he was then neutral in his sympathies) "to find [substantial merchants] in a plot against liberty, since commerce is ever engrafted on the stock of liberty and must

86

feel every wound that is given to it." Elihu S. Riley, ed., *Correspond-ence of "First Citizen" — Charles Carroll of Carrollton, and "Antilon" — Daniel Dulany, Jr. . . .* (Baltimore, 1902), p. 35.

Nor was the fear of conspiracy local to the American situation. It was deeply rooted in the political awareness of eighteenth-century Britons, involved in the very structure of their political life. Its origins went back at least to the apprehensions of the secret maneuvers of the Tories under James II and of that "extensive network of conspiracy that spread out over western Europe" in the first quarter of the eighteenth century, of which "the Jacobite party in Britain was but one element" (Foord, *His Majesty's Opposition,* pp. 82, 70, and pages cited in note 28 above; note also in this connection the significance, touched on above, Chap. III, 24n, of Rapin's *Dissertation on the . . . Whigs and Tories,* first published in 1717 and reprinted in Boston in 1773). Under George III, George Rudé has pointed out, it was

widely believed . . . that the influence of the Crown was being used to staff the administration with new Favourites and "King's Friends," who formed a secret Closet party, beyond the control of Parliament and guided behind the scenes by the sinister combination of the Earl of Bute (who had resigned office in 1763) and the Princess Dowager of Wales. Opponents of the new system talked darkly of a repeti-tion of "the end of Charles II's reign" — and such talk was not confined to the circle of the Duke of Newcastle and others, who might be inclined to identify the eclipse of their own public authority with that of the national interest.

Such expressions, Rudé concludes, "were common currency and abound throughout this period both in the press, in Burke's *Thoughts on the Present Discontents* (1770), in personal correspondence, pamphlet litera-ture and speeches in Parliament" (*Wilkes and Liberty,* p. 186). Burke's *Thoughts* is particularly relevant to the American situation, for the language throughout that piece is largely interchangeable with that of innumerable Revolutionary pamphleteers: "A new project . . . devised by a certain set of intriguing men . . . *to secure to the court the un-limited and uncontrolled use of its own vast influence under the sole direction of its own private favor* . . . a faction ruling by the private inclinations of a court, against the general sense of the people . . . pur-sues a scheme for undermining all the foundations of our freedom . . ." So widespread were such ideas among the opposition in England, espe-cially when the American problem was broached, that even so cool, well-informed, and hard-headed an observer as Dr. John Fothergill had to explain that he did "not quite" credit the ministry with "endeavoring to enslave [the colonists] by system," and to point out that the government "are very happy if they can find expedients for the present moment" (to Lt. Col. Ironside, Dec. 22, 1774, *Bulletin of the Friends Historical Society*, 5, 1913, p. 5).

Paradoxically, however, and significantly, the opponents of the Revolution — the administration itself — were equally convinced that they were victims of conspiratorial designs. Officials in the colonies, and their superiors in England, were persuaded as the crisis deepened that they were confronted by an active conspiracy of intriguing men whose professions masked their true intentions. As early as 1760 Governor Bernard of Massachusetts had concluded that a "faction" had organized a conspiracy against the customs administration, and by the end of the decade he and others in similar positions (including that "arch-conspirator" Thomas Hutchinson) had little doubt that at the root of all the trouble in the colonies was the maneuvering of a secret, power-hungry cabal that professed loyalty to England while assiduously working to destroy the bonds of authority and force a rupture between England and her colonies. The writings of officials abound with references to the work of a seditious faction; they reach the extreme of vilification in Chief Justice Peter Oliver's scurrilous *Origin & Progress of the American Rebellion* and attain the ultimate in respectability in George III's statement to Parliament of October 26, 1775 — a statement that may be taken as the precise obverse of Jefferson's claim, in the Declaration of Independence, that there was a "design to reduce [the colonies] under absolute despotism."

The authors and promoters of this desperate conspiracy [George III informed Parliament] have in the conduct of it derived great advantage from the difference of our intentions and theirs. They meant only to amuse, by vague expressions of attachment to the parent state and the strongest protestations of loyalty to me, whilst they were preparing for a general revolt . . . The rebellious war now levied is . . . manifestly carried on for the purpose of establishing an independent empire. (Merrill Jensen, ed., *American Colonial Documents to 1776, English Historical Documents*, IX, London, 1955, 851.)

The precise effect this mutuality of fears may have had on the course of events is difficult to assess, but something like an "escalation" of distrust toward a disastrous deadlock was anticipated by Burke as early as 1769. "The Americans have made a discovery, or think they have made one, that we mean to oppress them: we have made a discovery, or think we have made one, that they intend to rise in rebellion against us . . . we know not how to advance; they know not how to retreat." *Sir Henry*

Cavendish's Debates of the House of Commons . . . (John Wright, ed., London, 1841–1843), I, 398. For a particularly full "exposure" of the Americans' conspiracy, see Joseph Galloway, *Historical and Political Reflections on the Rise and Progress of the American Rebellion* . . . (London, 1780). In *A Reply to* . . . *Sir William Howe* . . . (London, 1780) Galloway dilates on the association of the colonial conspirators with the opposition faction in England, and relates all of this to the suspicious conduct of General Howe on the field of battle.

CHAPTER VI

TRANSFORMATION

I T was an elevating, transforming vision: a new, fresh, vigorous, and above all morally regenerate people rising from obscurity to defend the battlements of liberty and then in triumph standing forth, heartening and sustaining the cause of freedom everywhere. In the light of such a conception everything about the colonies and their controversy with the mother country took on a new appearance. Provincialism was gone: Americans stood side by side with the heroes of historic battles for freedom and with the few remaining champions of liberty in the present. What were once felt to be defects — isolation, institutional simplicity, primitiveness of manners, multiplicity of religions, weakness in the authority of the state — could now be seen as virtues, not only by Americans themselves but by enlightened spokesmen of reform, renewal, and hope wherever they might be — in London coffeehouses, in Parisian *salons,* in the courts of German princes. The mere existence of the colonists suddenly became philosophy teaching by example. Their manners, their morals, their way of life, their physical, social, and political condition were seen to vindicate eternal truths and to demonstrate, as ideas and words never could, the virtues of the heavenly city of the eighteenth-century philosophers.

But the colonists' ideas and words counted too, and not merely because they repeated as ideology the familiar utopian phrases of the Enlightenment and of English libertarianism. What they were saying by 1776 was familiar in a general way to reformers and illuminati everywhere in the western world. But it was different, too. Words and concepts had been reshaped in the colonists' minds in the course of a decade of pounding controversy — strangely reshaped, turned in unfamiliar directions, toward conclusions they could not themselves clearly perceive. They found a new world of political thought as they struggled to work out the implications of their beliefs in the years before Independence. It was a world not easily possessed; often they withdrew in some confusion to more familiar ground. But they touched its boundaries, and, at certain points, probed its interior. Others, later — writing and revising the first state constitutions, drafting and ratifying the federal constitution, and debating in detail, exhaustively, the merits of these efforts — would resume the search for resolutions of the problems the colonists had broached before 1776.

This critical probing of traditional concepts — part of the colonists' effort to express reality as they knew it and to shape it to ideal ends — became the basis for all further discussions of enlightened reform, in Europe as well as in America. The radicalism the Americans conveyed to the world in 1776 was a transformed as well as a transforming force.

I. REPRESENTATION AND CONSENT

The question of representation was the first serious intellectual problem to come between England and the colonies, and while it was not the most important issue involved in the Anglo-American controversy (the whole matter of taxation and representation was "a mere incident," Professor McIlwain has observed, in a much more basic constitutional struggle[1]), it received the earliest and most exhaustive examination and underwent a most revealing transformation. This shift in conception took place rapidly; it began and for all practical purposes concluded in the two years of the Stamp Act controversy. But the intellectual position worked out by the Americans in that brief span of time had deep historical roots; it crystallized, in effect, three generations of political experience. The ideas the colonists put forward, rather than creating a new condition of fact, expressed one that had long existed; they articulated and in so doing generalized, systematized, gave moral sanction to what had emerged haphazardly, incompletely and insensibly, from the chaotic factionalism of colonial politics.

What had taken place in the earlier years of colonial history was the partial re-creation, as a matter of fact and not of theory, of a kind of representation that had flourished in medieval England but that had faded and been superseded by another during the fifteenth and sixteenth centuries. In its original, medieval, form elective representation to Parliament had been a device by which "local men, locally minded, whose business began and ended with the interests of the constituency," were enabled, as attorneys for their electors, to seek redress from the royal court of Parliament, in return for which they were expected to commit their constituents to grants of financial aid. Attendance at Parliament of representatives of the commons was for the most part an obligation unwillingly performed, and local communities bound their representatives to

[1] Charles H. McIlwain, "The Historical Background of Federal Government," *Federalism as a Democratic Process* (New Brunswick, N.J., 1942), p. 35.

local interests in every way possible: by requiring local residency or the ownership of local property as a qualification for election, by closely controlling the payment of wages for official services performed, by instructing representatives minutely as to their powers and the limits of permissible concessions, and by making them strictly accountable for all actions taken in the name of the constituents. As a result, representatives of the commons in the medieval Parliaments did not speak for that estate in general or for any other body or group larger than the specific one that had elected them.[2] Changing circumstances, however, drastically altered this form and practice of representation. By the time the institutions of government were taking firm shape in the American colonies, Parliament in England had been transformed. The restrictions that had been placed upon representatives of the commons to make them attorneys of their constituencies fell away; members came to sit "not merely as parochial representatives, but as delegates of all the commons of the land." Symbolically incorporating the state, Parliament in effect had become the nation for purposes of government, and its members virtually if not actually, symbolically if not by sealed orders, spoke for all as well as for the group that had chosen them. They stood for the interest of the realm; for Parliament, in the words by which Edmund Burke immortalized this whole concept of representation, was not "a *congress* of ambassadors from different and hostile interests, which interests each must maintain, as an agent and advocate, against other agents and advocates; but Parliament is a *deliberative* assembly of *one* nation, with *one* interest, that of the whole, where, not local purposes, not local prejudices ought to guide, but the general good, resulting from the general reason of the whole." Gradually the restrictions once placed upon representatives to make them attorneys of their constituencies fell away.[3]

But the colonists, reproducing English institutions in miniature, had been led by force of circumstance to move in the opposite direction. Starting with seventeenth-century assumptions, out of necessity they drifted

[2] *Interim Report . . . on House of Commons Personnel . . .* (London, 1932), quoted in George L. Haskins, *The Growth of English Representative Government* (Philadelphia, 1948), p. 130; also pp. 111, 76–77.

[3] S. B. Chrimes, *English Constitutional Ideas in the Fifteenth Century* (Cambridge, England, 1936), p. 131. On the political functioning of this form of representation, see Samuel H. Beer, "The Representation of Interests in British Government: Historical Background," *American Political Science Review*, 51 (1957), 614–628. Burke's statement is from his speech to the electors of Bristol, 1774. For the continuity in the eighteenth century of this conception, cf. Speaker Onslow's almost identical understanding of "the constant notion and language of Parliament," in W. C. Costin and J. Steven Watson, eds., *The Law and Working of the Constitution: Documents, 1660–1914* (London, 1952), I, 392.

backwards, as it were, toward the medieval forms of attorneyship in representation. Their surroundings had recreated to a significant extent the conditions that had shaped the earlier experiences of the English people. The colonial towns and counties, like their medieval counterparts, were largely autonomous, and they stood to lose more than they were likely to gain from a loose acquiescence in the action of central government. More often than not they felt themselves to be the benefactors rather than the beneficiaries of central government, provincial or imperial; and when they sought favors from higher authorities they sought local and particular — in effect private — favors. Having little reason to identify their interests with those of the central government, they sought to keep the voices of local interests clear and distinct; and where it seemed necessary, they moved — though with little sense of innovating or taking actions of broad significance, and nowhere comprehensively or systematically — to bind representatives to local interests. The Massachusetts town meetings began the practice of voting instructions to their deputies to the General Court in the first years of settlement, and they continued to do so whenever it seemed useful throughout the subsequent century and a half. Elsewhere, with variations, it was the same; and elsewhere, as in Massachusetts, it became customary to require representatives to be residents of, as well as property owners in, the localities that elected them, and to check upon their actions as delegates. With the result that disgruntled contemporaries felt justified in condemning Assemblies composed "of plain, illiterate husbandmen, whose views seldom extended farther than to the regulation of highways, the destruction of wolves, wildcats, and foxes, and the advancement of the other little interests of the particular counties which they were chosen to represent." [4]

All of this, together with the associated experience common to all of the colonies of selecting and controlling agents to speak for them in

[4] Kenneth Colegrove, "New England Town Mandates," *Publications of the Colonial Society of Massachusetts,* XXI (*Transactions,* 1919), 411–436; William Smith, *History of New-York* . . . (Albany, 1814), p. 371. See in general the material assembled in Hubert Phillips, *The Development of a Residential Qualification for Representatives in Colonial Legislatures* (Cincinnati, 1921); for an excellent account in detail, see Richard P. McCormick, *The History of Voting in New Jersey* (New Brunswick, 1953), chap. ii. The pamphlets published in Massachusetts in 1754 over the controversial excise bill of that year are particularly revealing of the tendency of thought on representation before the Revolution. See Evans listings 7176, 7186, 7227, 7296, 7303, 7304, 7312, 7319, 7332, 7418; the last of these, *An Appendix to the Late Total Eclipse of Liberty . . . Thoughts on . . . the Inherent Power of the People . . . Not Given Up to Their Representatives . . .* (Boston, 1756), written by the harassed printer Daniel Fowle, was reprinted in 1775.

England, formed the background for the discussion of the first great issue of the Anglo-American controversy. For the principal English argument put forward in defense of Parliament's right to pass laws taxing the colonies was that the colonists, like the "nine tenths of the people of Britain" who do not choose representatives to Parliament, were in fact represented there. The power of actually voting for representatives, it was claimed, was an accidental and not a necessary attribute of representation, "for the right of election is annexed to certain species of property, to peculiar franchises, and to inhabitancy in certain places." In what really counted there was no difference between those who happened to live in England and those in America: "none are actually, all are virtually represented in Parliament," for, the argument concluded,

every Member of Parliament sits in the House not as representative of his own constituents but as one of that august assembly by which all the commons of *Great Britain* are represented. Their rights and their interests, however his own borough may be affected by general dispositions, ought to be the great objects of his attention and the only rules for his conduct, and to sacrifice these to a partial advantage in favor of the place where he was chosen would be a departure from his duty.[5]

In England this conception of "virtual" representation articulated the existing fact, and it raised no widespread objection. It was its opposite, the idea of representation as attorneyship, that was seen as "a new sort of political doctrine strenuously enforced by modern malcontents." But in the colonies the situation was reversed. There, where political experience had led to a different expectation of the process of representation and where the workings of virtual representation in the case at hand were seen to be damaging, the English argument was met at once with flat and universal rejection, ultimately with derision. It consists, Daniel Dulany wrote in a comprehensive refutation of the idea, "of facts not true and of conclusions inadmissible." What counts, he said in terms with which almost every pamphleteer in America agreed, was the extent to which representation worked to protect the interests of the people against the encroachments of government. From this point of view the analogy between the nonelectors in England and those in America was utterly specious, for the interests of Englishmen who did not vote for members of Parliament were intimately bound up with those who

[5] [Thomas Whately], *The Regulations Lately Made Concerning the Colonies and the Taxes Imposed upon Them, Considered* (London, 1765), p. 109. For a discussion of Whately's pamphlet and others arguing the same point, together with Dulany's reply to them, see Introduction to [Daniel Dulany], *Considerations on the Propriety of Imposing Taxes* (Annapolis, 1765: JHL Pamphlet 13).

did and with those chosen to sit as representatives. The interests of all three, "the nonelectors, the electors, and the representatives, are individually the same, to say nothing of the connection among the neighbors, friends, and relations. The security of the nonelectors against oppression is that their oppression will fall also upon the electors and the representatives. The one can't be injured and the other indemnified." But no such "intimate and inseparable relation" existed between the electors of Great Britain and the inhabitants of the colonies. The two groups were by no means involved in the same consequences of taxation: "not a single actual elector in England might be immediately affected by a taxation in America imposed by a statute which would have a general operation and effect upon the properties of the inhabitants of the colonies." [6]

Once a lack of natural identity of interests between representatives and the populace was conceded, the idea of virtual representation lost any force it might have had; for by such a notion, James Otis wrote, you could "as well prove that the British House of Commons in fact represent all the people of the globe as those in America." The idea, in such situations, was "futile" and "absurd" — the work of a "political visionary." And perhaps not only in such situations; logically one could lead the argument further and say that the whole conception of virtual representation, wherever or however it might be applied, was defective. If it was wrong in America it was wrong in England too, and should be rooted out no less thoroughly in the one place than in the other. "To what purpose," James Otis asked in a celebrated passage, "is it to ring everlasting changes to the colonists on the cases of Manchester, Birmingham, and Sheffield, who return no members? If those now so considerable places are not represented, they ought to be." For, as John Joachim Zubly, the Swiss-born pastor of Savannah, Georgia, wrote in an almost verbatim denial of what Burke five years later would describe as the proper function of representatives,

[6] William Seal Carpenter, *The Development of American Political Thought* (Princeton, 1930), 47n; Dulany, *Consideration* (JHL Pamphlet 13), pp. 7, 10. Thus also, e.g., [Ebenezer Devotion], *The Examiner Examined* . . . (New London, 1766): "There is nothing, say the colonists, that can give a proper representation but the actual choice of a representative, or in failure of this, an obvious sameness of interest in him that represents and the party represented, or at least an interwoven, inseparable interest between the nonelector and him that elects" (p. 16). And see, among the many other refutations of virtual representation, Maurice Moore, *The Justice and Policy of Taxing the American Colonies* (Wilmington, N.C., 1765); Richard Bland, *An Inquiry into the Rights of the British Colonies* . . . (Williamsburg, 1766); *Some Observations of Consequence in Three Parts* . . . ([Philadelphia], 1768), pp. 23 ff.

every representative in Parliament is not a representative for the whole nation, but only for the particular place for which he hath been chosen. If any are chosen for a plurality of places, they can make their election only for one of them . . . no member can represent any but those by whom he hath been elected; if not elected, he cannot represent them, and of course not consent to anything in their behalf . . . representation arises entirely from the free election of the people.[7]

So widely believed, indeed, — such a simple matter of fact — was it that " 'virtual representation' " anywhere, under any conditions, was "too ridiculous to be regarded," that the American Tories gladly used it as a basis of protest against the assumed representativeness of the makeshift Provincial and Continental Congresses. For it was not much of an exaggeration of Otis' earlier arguments to claim in New York in 1775 that by the patriots' reasoning "every man, woman, boy, girl, child, infant, cow, horse, hog, dog, and cat who *now* live, or ever *did* live, or ever *shall* live in this province are fully, freely, and sufficiently represented in this present glorious and august Provincial Congress." [8]

But the colonists' discussion of representation did not stop with the refutation of the claims made for virtual representation. The debate broadened into a general consideration of the nature and function of representation — in situations where interests of electors and elected, franchised and disfranchised, coincided as well as where they did not. The virtues of binding representatives by instructions were now explicitly explored. Some approached the question cautiously, arguing that, though the idea "that the constituent can bind his representative by instructions" may in recent years have become "an unfashionable doctrine," nevertheless, "in most cases" the "persuasive influence" if not the "obligatory force" of instructions should be insisted upon: "a representative who should act against the explicit recommendation of his constituents would most deservedly forfeit their regard and all pretension to their future confidence." Others expressed hesitancy in other ways, resolving the issue ambiguously by admitting the validity of virtual representation in cases where the nonvoters knew who their virtual representatives were and could "indiscriminately with the freeholders, at any time, instruct them what part to act in cases of importance." But the dominant voices were

---

[7] [James Otis], *Considerations on Behalf of the Colonists* . . . (London, 1765), pp. 9, 6; Benjamin Church, *An Oration Delivered March Fifth 1773* . . . (Boston, 1773), p. 15; [John Joachim Zubly], *An Humble Enquiry into the Nature of the Dependency of the American Colonies* . . . ([Charleston?], 1769), p. 17 (see also pp. 11, 16, 22).

[8] [John Dickinson], *An Essay on the Constitutional Power of Great-Britain* . . . (Philadelphia, 1774), in *Pennsylvania Archives*, 2d ser., III, 594; *The Triumph of the Whigs; or, T'Other Congress Convened* (New York, 1775), p. 8.

direct and decisive. Constituents, it was argued, had nothing less than "an inherent right to give instructions to their representatives." For representatives, James Wilson concluded, were properly to be considered the "creatures" of their constituents, and they were to be held strictly "accountable for the use of that power which is delegated to them." [9]

But what did that mean? There were far-reaching implications, some of which, first drawn out during this decade of debate, would remain persistent problems until finally resolved in the full realization of American democracy in the nineteenth and twentieth centuries. It was seen, even in the 1760's and 1770's, that if a representative were kept to strict accountability, he would in effect be acting "in every respect as the persons who appointed him . . . would do were they present themselves." With the result, it was concluded, that a representative assembly "should be in miniature an exact portrait of the people at large. It should think, feel, reason and act like them." If the population shifted in composition, so too should the character of the assembly, for "equal interests among the people should have equal interests in it." There might well be, in fact, "some permanent ratio by which the representatives should . . . increase or decrease with the number of inhabitants." [10]

And what if such were the case? The result would be, if not a wholly original contribution to advanced thought, at least a reversion to a radical concept that had long since disappeared from the mainstream of English political theory. For such arguments led to a recovery and elaboration of conceptions of government by the consent of the governed that had flourished briefly a century earlier, during the Commonwealth period, and had then faded during the Restoration and been lost sight of in the struggle in which the supremacy of Parliament had been permanently established. The view of representation developing in America implied if it did not state that direct consent of the people in government was not

[9] Dulany, *Considerations* (JHL Pamphlet 13), p. [3]; Moore, *Justice and Policy,* p. 11; [Stephen Johnson], *Some Important Observations* . . . (Newport, 1766), p. 32; [James Wilson], *Considerations on the Nature and Extent of the Legislative Authority of the British Parliament* (Philadelphia, 1774), p. 9.

[10] Moore, *Justice and Policy,* p. 7; [John Adams], *Thoughts on Government* . . . (Philadelphia, 1776), in *Works,* IV, 195; *Four Letters on Interesting Subjects* (Philadelphia, 1776), pp. 21–22. See also the importance attached by Jefferson to the crown's denial of an increase of representation in the colonial assemblies to reflect the growth and spread of the population. [Jefferson], *A Summary View of the Rights of British America* . . . (Williamsburg, [1774]), in Paul L. Ford, ed., *Writings of Thomas Jefferson* (New York, 1892–1899), I, 441. So too Adams felt that a truly representative imperial Parliament would reflect in its size and complexity the variety of peoples represented in it: Adams ("Novanglus"), *Novanglus and Massachusettensis* . . . (Boston, 1819), p. 80.

restricted, as Locke would have had it, to those climactic moments when government was overthrown by the people in a last final effort to defend their rights, nor even to those repeated, benign moments when a government was peaceably dissolved and another chosen in its place. Where government was such an accurate mirror of the people, sensitively reflecting their desires and feelings, consent was a continuous, everyday process. In effect the people were present through their representatives, and were themselves, step by step and point by point, acting in the conduct of public affairs. No longer merely an ultimate check on government, they *were* in some sense the government. Government had no separate existence apart from them; it was *by* the people as well as *for* the people; it gained its authority from their continuous consent. The very nature and meaning of law was involved. The traditional sense, proclaimed by Blackstone no less than by Hobbes, that law was a command "prescribed by source superior and which the inferior is bound to obey" — such a sense of law as the declaration of a person or body existing somehow independently above the subjects of law and imposing its will upon them, was brought into question by the developing notion of representation. Already in these years there were adumbrations of the sweeping repudiation James Wilson and others would make of Blackstone's definition of law, and of the view they would put in its place: the view that the binding power of law flowed from the continuous assent of the subjects of law; the view "that the only reason why a free and independent man was bound by human laws was this — that he bound himself." [11]

These were deep-lying implications of making representation — systematically, in principle as well as in fact — "a substitute for legislation by direct action of the people." They were radical possibilities, glimpsed but not wholly grasped, thrown up in the creative clash of ideas that preceded the Revolution, and drawn into the discussion of the first state constitutions even before Independence was declared. They were perhaps, in these early years, understood most clearly by the more perceptive of the Tories, who stood outside and viewed with apprehension the tendency

---

[11] E.g., Locke, *Second Treatise of Government*, xiii, 149. Cf. Otis' discussion of the Glorious Revolution in his *Rights of the British Colonies* (Boston, 1764: JHL Pamphlet 7), 15 ff., quoting Locke on the dissolution of government, p. 23. Wilson on Blackstone, in Andrew C. McLaughlin, *The Foundations of American Constitutionalism* (New York, 1932), pp. 83–84; cf. [Moses Mather], *America's Appeal* . . . (Hartford, 1775), p. 39. See in general on the points involved, Carpenter, *Development of American Political Thought,* pp. 91 ff.; J. W. Gough, *Fundamental Law in English Constitutional History* (Oxford, 1955), pp. 175–176, 120; Charles H. McIlwain, *Constitutionalism and the Changing World* (New York, 1939), pp. 64–65.

of events and the drift of theory. "The position," the Anglican minister Samuel Seabury wrote in 1774, "that we are bound by no laws to which we have not consented either by ourselves or our representatives is a novel position unsupported by any authoritative record of the British constitution, ancient or modern. It is republican in its very nature, and tends to the utter subversion of the English monarchy."[12]

2. CONSTITUTIONS AND RIGHTS

Certain of the Tories understood also with special clarity the meaning of changes that were taking place in other areas of thought. They grasped, and exclaimed against in protest, the transformation of the notion of what a constitution was and of the nature of the rights that constitutions existed to protect. "What is the constitution," Charles Inglis demanded in his anguished reply to *Common Sense* — what is "that word so often used — so little understood — so much perverted? It is, as I conceive — *that assemblage of laws, customs, and institutions which form the general system according to which the several powers of the state are distributed and their respective rights are secured to the different members of the community."* [13] It was still for him, as it had been for John Adams a decade earlier, "a frame, a scheme, a system, a combination of powers": the existing arrangement of governmental institutions, laws, and customs together with the animating principles, the *stamina vitae,* that gave them purpose and direction. But so far toward a different conception of constitutionalism had American thought shifted after 1765 that by 1776 Inglis' quite traditional definition could only be uttered as the *cri de coeur* of one bypassed by history.

The first suggestions of change came early in the period, the full conclusion only at the very end. At the start what would emerge as the central feature of American constitutionalism was only an emphasis and a peculiarity of tone within an otherwise familiar discourse. While some writers, like Richard Bland, continued to refer to "a legal constitution, that is, a legislature," and others spoke of "the English constitution . . . a nice piece of machinery which has undergone many changes and alterations," most of the pamphleteers saw the necessity of emphasizing principles above institutions, and began to grasp the consequences of doing

[12] Carpenter, *Development of American Political Thought,* pp. 43, 91; [Samuel Seabury], *A View of the Controversy* . . . (New York, 1774), in Clarence H. Vance, ed., *Letters of a Westchester Farmer (Publications of the Westchester County Historical Society,* VIII, White Plains, 1930), p. 111.
[13] [Charles Inglis], *The True Interest of America* . . . (Philadelphia, 1776), p. 18.

so.[14] The confusions and difficulties inherent in this process are dramatically illustrated in the troubled career of James Otis.[15]

The heart of the problem Otis faced in the early 1760's was the extent to which, indeed the sense in which, the "constitution" could be conceived of as a limitation on the power of lawmaking bodies. In the writs of assistance case in 1761 he had struck a bold and confident note — so bold, indeed, that John Adams later wrote, rather romantically, that "then and there the child Independence was born." On that famous occasion Otis had said not only than an act of Parliament "against the constitution is void" but that it was the duty of the courts to "pass such acts into disuse," for the "reason of the common law [could] control an act of Parliament." But what was the "constitution" which an act of Parliament could not infringe? Was it a set of fixed principles and rules distinguishable from, antecedent to, more fundamental than, and controlling the operating institutions of government? And was there consequently a "constitutional" limitation on Parliament's actions? Otis' answers were ambiguous, and proved to be politically disastrous. The main authority for his statement in the writs case that an act of Parliament against the constitution was void was Coke, reinforced by later judges expounding the great chief justice's dictum in *Bonham's Case*. But in that pronouncement Coke had not meant, as Professor Thorne has made clear, "that there were superior principles of right and justice which Acts of Parliament might not contravene." Thinking in terms of private law, not constitutional construction, Coke had meant only that the courts would interpret statutes "in such a way as not to conflict with those same accepted principles of reason and justice which . . . were presumed to underlie all law"; and by saying that the courts might "void" a legislative provision that violated the constitution he had meant only that the courts were to construe statutes so as to bring them into conformity with recognized legal principles.[16]

Otis, drawing the language of seventeenth-century law into the constitu-

[14] [Richard Bland], *The Colonel Dismounted* . . . (Williamsburg, 1764: JHL Pamphlet 4), p. 22; [William Hicks], *Considerations upon the Rights of the Colonists* . . . (New York, 1766), p. 1.

[15] Otis' constitutional thought is discussed in detail in the Introductions to his *Rights of the British Colonies* (JHL Pamphlet 7) and his *Vindication of the British Colonies Against the Aspersions of the Halifax Gentleman* (Boston, 1765: JHL Pamphlet 11). The reader is referred to these essays for full elaboration and documentation of the interpretation that follows.

[16] Adams, *Works*, X, 248; Josiah Quincy, Jr., *Reports of Cases* . . . *in the Superior Court of Judicature* . . . *Between 1761 and 1772* (Samuel M. Quincy, ed., Boston, 1865), p. 474; Samuel E. Thorne, "Dr. Bonham's Case," *Law Quarterly Review*, 54 (1938), 545,

tional struggle of the eighteenth century, found himself veering toward positions he was neither intellectually nor politically prepared to accept. "If the reasons that can be given against an act are such," he wrote in his *Rights of the British Colonies* in 1764, "as plainly demonstrate that it is against *natural* equity, the executive courts will adjudge such act void." And again, in an Appendix to the same pamphlet, originally written as a memorial to the Massachusetts agent in London, commenting on the statement that "judges will strain hard rather than interpret an act void, *ab initio*," he wrote: *"This is granted, but still [Parliament's] authority is not boundless if subject to the control of judges in any case."* Was this not to limit the power of Parliament by the provisions of a fixed constitution distinct from and superior to the legislature, a constitution interpreted and applied by the courts? Others, in time, would say it was. Indeed, a contemporary authority whom Otis quoted at length in the Appendix to his pamphlet could hardly have said this more clearly. Does the power of legislators extend to fundamental law, and if so may they "change the constitution of the state?" Otis asked in the words of the Swiss theorist Emmerich de Vattel. No, was the answer: "they ought to consider the fundamental laws as sacred if the nation has not in very express terms given them the power to change them. For the constitution of the state ought to be fixed; and since that was first established by the nation, which afterwards trusted certain persons with the legislative power, the fundamental laws are excepted from their commission."

But though Otis quoted this passage from Vattel he did not draw its implications. He ignored them, in fact, in working out his own view of the constitution and of the limits of Parliament's powers. If an act of Parliament violated natural laws, "which are *immutably* true," he wrote, it would thereby violate "eternal truth, equity, and justice," and would be "consequently void."

. . . and so it would be adjudged by the Parliament itself when convinced of their mistake. Upon this great principle Parliaments repeal such acts as soon as they find they have been mistaken . . . When such mistake is evident and palpable . . . the judges of the executive courts have declared the act "of a whole Parliament void." See here the grandeur of the British constitution! See the wisdom of our ancestors! . . . If the supreme legislative errs, it is informed by the supreme executive in the King's courts of law . . . This is government! This is a constitution! to preserve which . . . has cost oceans of blood and treasure in every age; and the blood and the treasure have upon the whole been well spent.

549, 551. See also Thorne's *A Discourse upon the . . . Statutes . . .* (San Marino, 1942), pp. 85–92.

Parliament was thus itself part of the constitution, not a creature of it, and its power was "uncontrollable but by themselves, and we must obey. They only can repeal their own acts . . . let the Parliament lay what burdens they please on us, we must, it is our duty to submit and patiently bear them, till they will be pleased to relieve us." Yet Parliament's enactments against the constitution — against, that is, the whole system of laws, principles, and institutions based on reason and justice of which it was a part — were void, Otis argued; the courts will adjudge them so, and Parliament itself, by the necessity of the system, will repeal them.[17]

It was a strange argument, comprehensible only as an effort to apply seventeenth-century assumptions to eighteenth-century problems. For Otis continued to assume, with Coke, that Parliament was effectively a supreme judicial as well as a supreme legislative body and hence by definition involved in judicial processes. He continued to believe, too, that moral rights and obligations were not "differentiated as they would be today from legal rights and obligations," and that they naturally radiated from, rather than restricted, enacted law.[18] And he expected fundamental, or higher, law to "control" positive acts of government not in the sense of furnishing judges with grounds for declaring them nonexistent because they conflicted with the "constitution" but only in the sense of providing judges with principles of interpretation by which to modify gross inequities and to interpret "unreasonableness" and self-contradiction in ways that would allow traditional qualities of justice to prevail.

But these assumptions were no longer applicable, in the same way, in the eighteenth century. Parliament was in reality no longer a court but an all powerful sovereign body, and the problem at hand concerned the structure and authority of government, not private law. Otis' theory of the constitution that included a self-correcting Parliament sensitive to the principles of justice and responsive to the admonitions of the courts was, insofar as it was realistic at all, an anachronism, and it came under attack by both the administration, which charged him with attempting to restrict the power of Parliament, and by the colonial radicals, who accused him of preaching passive obedience and nonresistance.

Otis had been faithful, in this way, to the seventeenth-century sources of constitutional thought which he, like so many Americans, revered. Others — poorer scholars, perhaps, but better judges of the circumstances

[17] Otis, *Rights* (JHL Pamphlet 7), pp. 41, 73n, 72n, 47, 39–40.
[18] Gough, *Fundamental Law,* pp. 45, 35–36.

that surrounded them — were less faithful, and in the end more creative. The dominant view of the constitution in 1764 was still the traditional one, unencumbered by Otis' complexities. While Otis was quoting Coke together with Vattel without grasping the implications of their conjunction, others were referring to constitutions as "a sort of fundamental laws"; as the common law; as Parliament; and as the whole complex of existing laws and public institutions.[19] The transition to more advanced ground was forced forward by the continuing need, after 1764, to distinguish fundamentals from institutions and from the actions of government so that they might serve as limits and controls. Once its utility was perceived and demonstrated, this process of disengaging principles from institutions and from the positive actions of government and then of conceiving of them as fixed sets of rules and boundaries, went on swiftly.

In 1768, Samuel Adams, accustomed to drawing more extreme conclusions than most of his contemporaries, wrote in a series of letters in behalf of the Massachusetts House of Representatives that "the constitution is fixed; it is from thence that the supreme legislative as well as the supreme executive derives its authority," and he incorporated the same language into the famous Massachusetts Circular Letter of that year. At the same time a Philadelphian, William Hicks, wrote that if one were to concede that statutes were "a part of [the] constitution" simply because they were once promulgated by government, one would have no basis for restraining the actions of any government. There is nothing sacrosanct, he wrote, in the "variant, inconsistent form of government which we have received at different periods of time"; they were accidental in origins, and their defects should be corrected by comparison with ideal models. In 1769 the emerging logic was carried further by Zubly, who flatly distinguished legislatures from the constitution, and declared that the existing Parliament "derives its authority and power from the constitution, and not the constitution from Parliament." The constitution, he wrote, "is permanent and ever the same," and Parliament "can no more make laws which are against the constitution or the unalterable privileges of British subjects than it can alter the constitution itself . . . The power of Parliament, and of every branch of it, has its bounds assigned by the constitution."[20]

[19] Andrew Eliot, *A Sermon Preached Before His Excellency* (Boston, 1765), p. 19; [Martin Howard, Jr.,], *A Letter From a Gentleman at Halifax* (Newport, 1765: JHL Pamphlet 10), p. 10; Bland, *Colonel Dismounted* (JHL Pamphlet 4), pp. 27, 29.

[20] Samuel Adams, quoted in Randolph G. Adams, *Political Ideas of the American Revolution* (3d ed., New York, 1958), p. 138; the texts of the letters are in Adams' *Writings* (H. A. Cushing, ed., New York, 1904–1908), I, 152 ff. (see especially p. 156); the Circular

In 1770 the constitution was said to be "a line which marks out the enclosure"; in 1773, it was "the standing measure of the proceedings of government" of which rulers are "by no means to attempt an alteration . . . without public consent"; in 1774 it was a "model of government"; in 1775 it was "certain great first principles" on whose "certainty and permanency . . . the rights of both the ruler and the subjects depend; nor may they be altered or changed by ruler or people, but [only] by the whole collective body . . . nor may they be touched by the legislator." Finally, in 1776 there came conclusive pronouncements. Two pamphlets of that year, brilliant sparks thrown off by the clash of Revolutionary politics in Pennsylvania, lit up the final steps of the path that led directly to the first constitutions of the American states. "A constitution and a form of government," the author of *Four Letters on Important Subjects* wrote, "are frequently confounded together and spoken of as synonymous things, whereas they are not only different but are established for different purposes." All nations have governments, "but few, or perhaps none, have truly a constitution." The primary function of a constitution was to mark out the boundaries of governmental powers — hence in England, where there was no constitution, there were no limits (save for the effect of trial by jury) to what the legislature might do. In order to confine the ordinary actions of government, the constitution must be grounded in some fundamental source of authority, some "higher authority than the giving out temporary laws." This special authority could be gained if the constitution were created by "an act of *all*," and it would acquire permanence if it were embodied "in some written charter." Defects, of course, might be discovered and would have to be repaired: there would have to be some procedure by which to alter the constitution without disturbing its controlling power as fundamental law. For this, the means "are easy":

some article in the constitution may provide that at the expiration of every seven or any other number of years a *provincial jury* shall be elected to inquire if any inroads have been made in the constitution, and to have power to remove them; but not to make alterations, unless a clear majority of all the inhabitants shall so direct.

Thus created and thus secured, the constitution could effectively designate what "part of their liberty" the people are to sacrifice to the necessity of having government, by furnishing answers to "the two following ques-

Letter is at pp. 184–188. [William Hicks], *The Nature and Extent of Parliamentary Power* . . . (Philadelphia, 1768), p. 31; Zubly, *Humble Enquiry,* p. 5.

tions: first, what shall the form of government be? And secondly, what shall be its power?" In addition, "it is the part of a constitution to fix the manner in which the officers of government shall be chosen, and determine the principal outlines of their power, their time of duration, manner of commissioning them, etc." Finally, "all the great rights which man never mean, nor ever ought, to lose should be *guaranteed,* not *granted,* by the constitution, for at the forming a constitution, we ought to have in mind that whatever is left to be secured by law only may be altered by another law." [21]

The same ideas, in some ways even more clearly worked out, appear in the second Pennsylvania pamphlet of 1776, *The Genuine Principles of the Ancient Saxon or English Constitution,* which was largely composed of excerpts from Obadiah Hulme's *An Historical Essay on the English Constitution,* published in London in 1771, a book both determinative and representative of the historical understanding that lay behind the emerging American constitutionalism. Here too was stated the idea of a constitution as a *"set of fundamental rules* by which even the supreme power of the state shall be governed" and which the legislature is absolutely forbidden to alter. But in this pamphlet there are more explicit explanations of how such documents come into being and of their permanence and importance. They are to be formed "by a convention of the delegates of the people appointed for that express purpose," the pamphlet states, and they are never to be "added to, diminished from, nor altered in any respect by any power besides the power which first framed [them]." They are to remain permanent, and so to have the most profound effect on the lives of people. "Men entrusted with the formation of civil constitutions should remember they are PAINTING FOR ETERNITY: that the smallest defect or redundancy in the system they frame may prove the destruction of millions." [22]

[21] Samuel Cooke, *A Sermon Preached at Cambridge* . . . (Boston, 1770), p. 11; Charles Turner, *A Sermon Preached Before* . . . *Hutchinson* . . . (Boston, 1773), pp. 16, 17, 18–19; Peter Whitney, *The Transgressions of a Land* . . . (Boston, 1774), p. 8; Mather, *America's Appeal,* pp. 22–23; *Four Letters on Important Subjects,* pp. 18, 15–16, 19, 22.

[22] *Genuine Principles,* pp. 4, 35, 34; on Hulme and the influence of his *Essay,* see Caroline Robbins, *The Eighteenth-Century Commonwealthman* (Cambridge, 1959), pp. 363–365. Among the many other statements of the idea of a fixed constitution published by 1776, see especially those of the Tories; e.g., Seabury, *A View,* in Vance, *Letters of a Westchester Farmer,* p. 123; and [Thomas Bradbury Chandler], *What Think Ye of the Congress Now?* . . . (New York, 1775), p. 44. But for a dramatic illustration of the speed with which Revolutionary ideas were maturing, compare Chandler's and Seabury's understanding with that expressed by the Concord Town Meeting in 1776, in S. E. Morison, ed., *Sources and Documents of the American Revolution* . . . (Oxford, 1923), p. 177.

Accompanying this shift in the understanding of constitutionalism, and part of it, was another change, which also began as a relocation of emphasis and ended as a contribution to the transforming radicalism of the Revolution. The rights that constitutions existed to protect were understood in the early years of the period, as we have seen, to be at once the inalienable, indefeasible rights inherent in all people by virtue of their humanity, and the concrete provisions of English law as expressed in statutes, charters, and court decisions; it was assumed that the "constitution" in its normal workings would specify and protect the inalienable rights of man. But what if it did not? What if this sense proved false, and it came to be believed that the force of government threatened rather than protected these rights? And what if, in addition, the protective machinery of rights — the constitution — came to be abstracted from the organs of government and to be seen not as an arrangement of institutions and enactments but as a blueprint for institutions, the ideal against which the actual was to be measured?

These questions were first posed early in the controversy, in the course of one of the most vituperative exchanges of constitutional views of the entire period. It is true, Judge Martin Howard, Jr., of Rhode Island wrote in response to Stephen Hopkins' *Rights of Colonies Examined* (1765), that the common law carries within it and guarantees with special force the "indefeasible" personal rights of men; for Britons it is the common law that makes these natural rights operative. But Parliament's power is no less a part of that same common law. "Can we claim the common law as an inheritance, and at the same time be at liberty to adopt one part of it and reject the other?" If Parliament is rejected, so too must political and even personal rights. If rights are accepted as inextricable parts of laws and institutions, the laws and institutions must be accepted in all their normal workings.[23]

James Otis accepted the challenge. But in his stinging reply — a bitter, sarcastic, half-wild polemic — he again displayed a commitment to tradition that kept him from following through the logic of his own argument; again, he succeeded in dramatizing but not in resolving the issue. The judge's "truly *Filmerian*" performance, he wrote, has "inaccuracies in abundance, declamation and false logic without end . . . and the most indelicate fustian . . ." His central error is that he "everywhere confounds the terms rights, liberties, and privileges, which, in legal as well as vulgar acceptation, denote very different ideas." The source of this confusion,

[23] Howard, *Halifax Letter* (JHL Pamphlet 10), p. 11.

Otis said, was a misreading of Blackstone; from his *Commentaries* Howard had mistakenly derived the idea that the rights of natural persons are the same as those of artificial persons: that is, "bodies politic and corporate." Corporate rights are indeed "matters of the mere favor and grace of the donor or founder"; but that is not to say that the rights of natural people are too. Britons are entitled to their "natural absolute personal rights" by virtue of "the laws of God and nature, as well as by the common law and the constitution of their country so admirably built on the principles of the former." Only such a one as Judge Howard, with his "Filmerian sneer," who "cannot see any difference between power and right, between a blind, slavish submission and a loyal, generous, and rational obedience" — only such a person could fail to understand that the origin of "the inherent, indefeasible rights of the subject" lay in "the law of nature and its author. This law is the grand basis of the common law and of all other municipal laws that are worth a rush. True it is that every act of Parliament which names the colonies . . . binds them. But this is not so, strictly and properly speaking, by the common law as by the law of nature and by the constitution of a parliament or sovereign and supreme legislative in a state." [24]

Otis had shifted the emphasis of discussion to the priority of abstract rights, but he had not attempted to follow through the implications of his own thought: he continued to assume that the actual law would express, and naturally protect, the universal rights of man. But if he did not draw the conclusions implicit in his own logic, others did: there is in the proliferating discussion of constitutionalism a steadily increasing emphasis on the universal, inherent, indefeasible qualities of rights. John Dickinson, also a lawyer — indeed, a more professionally trained lawyer than Otis — attacked in a more knowing and thorough way the idea that rights are matters of "favor and grace." True, in 1764 he had vehemently defended the charter of Pennsylvania against the attacks of Joseph Galloway and others, but not because he believed that "the liberties of the subject were mere favors granted by charters from the crown." The liberties of Pennsylvanians, he had proclaimed in a ringing oration in the Pennsylvania Assembly, are "founded on the acknowledged rights of human nature." The value of a charter like that of Pennsylvania was that it stated the true character of such liberties beyond any misunderstanding, and freed them from the entanglements of those ancient, archaic customs "that our ancestors either had not moderation or leisure enough to un-

---

[24] Otis, *Vindication* (JHL Pamphlet 11), pp. 4, 3–4, 8, 9, 13, 14.

twist." Two years later (1766) he elaborated the point significantly. Charters, he wrote in his *Address to the Committee of Correspondence in Barbados,* like all aspects of the law, are *"declarations* but not *gifts* of liberties." Kings and Parliaments cannot give "the *rights essential to happiness."*

We claim them from a higher source — from the King of kings, and Lord of all the earth. They are not annexed to us by parchments and seals. They are created in us by the decrees of Providence, which establish the laws of our nature. They are born with us; exist with us; and cannot be taken from us by any human power without taking our lives. In short, they are founded on the immutable maxims of reason and justice.

Written laws — even the great declarations like Magna Carta — do not create liberties; they "must be considered as only declaratory of our rights, and in affirmance of them." [25]

Ultimately, the conclusion to be drawn became obvious: the entire legitimacy of positive law and legal rights must be understood to rest on the degree to which they conformed to the abstract universals of natural rights. Not all were willing, even in 1774, to go as far as Alexander Hamilton, who wrote in bold, arresting capitals that "THE SACRED RIGHTS OF MANKIND ARE NOT TO BE RUMMAGED FOR AMONG OLD PARCHMENTS OR MUSTY RECORDS. THEY ARE WRITTEN, AS WITH A SUNBEAM, IN THE WHOLE VOLUME OF HUMAN NATURE, BY THE HAND OF DIVIN- ITY ITSELF, AND CAN NEVER BE ERASED OR OBSCURED BY MORTAL POWER." But if some found this statement too enthusi- astic, few by 1774 — few even of the Tories — disagreed with the calmer formulation of the same idea, by Philip Livingston. Had he understood his antagonist, the Rev. Thomas Bradbury Chandler, correctly? Had Chandler really meant to say "that any right . . . if it be not confirmed by some statute law is not a legal right"? If so, Livingston declared, "in the name of America, I deny it." Legal rights are "those rights which we are entitled to by the eternal laws of right reason"; they exist independent of positive law, and stand as the measure of its legitimacy.[26]

[25] [John Dickinson], *An Address to the Committee of Correspondence in Barbados . . .* (Philadelphia, 1766), in Paul L. Ford, ed., *Writings of John Dickinson (Memoirs of the Historical Society of Pennsylvania,* XIV, Philadelphia, 1895), pp. 261, 262; John Dickinson, *A Speech Delivered . . . 1764,* in *ibid.,* p. 34; [Silas Downer], *Discourse Delivered in Providence . . .* (Providence, 1768), p. 6.

[26] [Alexander Hamilton], *The Farmer Refuted . . .* (New York, 1775), in *Works* (H. C. Lodge, ed., New York and London, 1904), I, 113; [Philip Livingston], *The Other Side of the Question . . .* (New York, 1774), p. 9.

Neither Hamilton nor Livingston, nor any of the other writers who touched on the subject, meant to repudiate the heritage of English common and statutory law. Their claim was only that the source of rights be recognized, in Jefferson's words, as "the laws of nature, and not as the gift of their chief magistrate," and that as a consequence the ideal must be understood to exist before the real and to remain superior to it, controlling it and limiting it. But what was the ideal? What precisely were the ideal rights of man? They were, everyone knew, in some sense Life, Liberty, and Property. But in what sense? Must they not be specified? Must not the ideal now be reduced from a radiant presence and a conglomerate legal tradition to specific enumerated provisions? Must not the essential rights of man be specified and codified if they were to serve effectively as limits on the actions of courts and legislatures? In 1765 James Otis had fulminated at the mere suggestion that a document might profitably be drawn up stating the "rights of the colonies with precision and certainty." Insolence, he had called it, pedantry and nonsense; Britons had no need for "codes, pandects, novels, decretals of popes." "The common law is our birthright, and the rights and privileges confirmed and secured to us by the British constitution and by act of Parliament are our best inheritance." But thought had shifted in the decade that followed, and no voice was raised to object when in 1776 the idea was proclaimed, and acted upon, that "all the great rights . . . should be *guaranteed*" by the terms of a written constitution.[27]

These closely related changes — in the view of what a constitution was and of the proper emphasis in the understanding of rights — were momentous; they would shape the entire future development of American constitutional thought and practice. Yet they did not seem to be momentous at the time. They were not generally experienced as intrusive or threatening alterations. They were hardly seen as changes at all: they drifted into consciousness gradually and easily and were accepted without controversy. For here too, as in so many other developments in political and social thought, the way had been paved by the peculiar circumstances of colonial life. Whatever Otis may have thought of the issue when he

[27] Jefferson, *Summary View*, in Ford, *Writings*, I, 446; Otis, *Vindication* (JHL Pamphlet 11), p. 32; *Four Letters on Interesting Subjects*, p. 22. Later there would be doubts about the value of enumerating rights just as there would be about other of the ideas developing before 1776. See particularly Madison's penetrating analysis in his letter to Jefferson of October 17, 1788, *Papers of Thomas Jefferson* (Julian P. Boyd, ed., Princeton, 1950–), XIV, 18–19, especially arguments 2 and 4.

came to consider it in theoretical terms, the fact was that written constitutions — documents not different essentially from the "codes, pandects,
novels" he denounced — had existed, had been acted upon, had been
assumed to be proper and necessary, for a century or more. Some, like
the charter of the Massachusetts Bay Colony, had originated as commercial charters, concessions of powers by the crown to enterprisers
willing to undertake the risks of exploration and settlement. These, in
the colonial setting, had quickly changed their original character, and
"by some metamorphosis or feat of legerdemain had . . . become the
frame of government for a state." The Massachusetts Bay charter in
particular "approximated a popular constitution," Professor McIlwain has
written, "more closely than any other instrument of government in actual
use up to that time in America or elsewhere in modern times." It is
hardly surprising, he concludes, that the Fundamental Orders of Connecticut of 1639, " 'the first American constitution accepted by the people,' " should have been written by men who emigrated from Massachusetts.[28]

Later crown charters, like those of Connecticut and Rhode Island, were
designed in the first place to be basic instruments of government; and if
the seventeenth-century proprietary grants — those of New York, Maryland, and the Carolinas — were anachronistic in their feudal terminology,
they too created "governing powers" and provided for public institutions
that were expected to be "incapable of alteration or amendment except
by concession from the grantor." Most important of all, because most
deliberately "constitutional" in character, were the foundations laid down
by William Penn for the establishment of government in New Jersey and
Pennsylvania. This remarkable man — courtier and sectarian; saint,
schemer, and scholar — whose imaginative grasp of the possibilities of
constitution-making led him eventually to propose not only a "Plan of
Union for the Colonies" but also a scheme for "The Establishment of a
European Diet, Parliament, or Estates," devoted himself enthusiastically
to constructing a proper framework of government for the Quaker colonies. In consultation with the leading political theorists of his time, he

[28] Charles M. Andrews, *The Colonial Period of American History* (New Haven, 1934–
1938), I, 440; McIlwain, *Constitutionalism and the Changing World*, p. 241 (cf. Andrews,
Colonial Period, II, 102 ff.). See, in general, Benjamin F. Wright, Jr., "The Early History
of Written Constitutions in America," *Essays . . . in Honor of Charles Howard McIlwain*
(Cambridge, 1936), pp. 344–371. For the claim that "to Plymouth belongs the credit for
having established what may fairly be described as the first American constitution" (the
code of laws of 1636), see George L. Haskins, "The Legacy of Plymouth," *Social Education*, 26 (1962), 9.

drew up and published a series of concessions, frames of government, and charters, which were, in effect, blueprints for "civil administration, elections, court procedure, the exercise of justice, fines, penalties, and . . . the duties and obligations of office-holders." These schemes, again and again revised in an effort to adjust soaring idealism to the demands of ordinary human realities, could hardly have been more clearly fundamental, more manifestly constituent, in nature.[29]

By the Revolutionary period, the surviving charters, which in origins had been the instruments of the aggressive creation, or legitimation, of power, had become defensive bulwarks against the misuse of power. In Connecticut, Rhode Island, and Massachusetts they were cherished still, as they had been for a century and more, as special confirmations of "the ancient common law of England, and of the common rights of Englishmen." In Pennsylvania, in the years immediately preceding the Stamp Act, the attack launched against the Penn family's tax privileges, which had been written into the original charter, was fended off by impassioned pleas, like that of John Dickinson, to preserve intact, tax privileges and all, the "laws and liberties framed and delivered down to us by our careful ancestors . . . Any body of men acting under a charter must surely tread on slippery ground when they take a step that may be deemed a surrender of that charter." Nor were the benefits of these famous compacts "between the sovereign and the first patentees" valued only in the particular provinces in which they had survived. Everywhere in the colonies the existing charters were prized as "evidential of the rights and immunities belonging to all the King's subjects in America." [30]

For some people, in fact, the charters had acquired, in the course of the years, an additional, transcendent sanction. Those who viewed the world in the light of covenant theology could see the colonial charters as valid not merely in the eyes of the law but in the eyes of God as well: "our charter . . . was a solemn *covenant* between [the King] and our *fathers*" — a "sacred" covenant by which the crown had contracted with

[29] Andrews, *Colonial Period*, II, 137 (cf. 49), 283n; III, 269, 287n–288n, 286. On the Duke's Laws of New York, see A. E. McKinley, "The Transition from Dutch to English Rule in New York," *American Historical Review*, 6 (1900–1901), 704 ff.

[30] [Thomas Fitch, *et al.*], *Reasons Why the British Colonies Should Not Be Charged with Internal Taxes* (New Haven, 1764: JHL Pamphlet 6), p. 9; Dickinson, *Speech Delivered . . . 1764*, in Ford, *Writings*, p. 30; Cooke, *Sermon Preached at Cambridge*, p. 33. Dickinson's assumption in 1764 that Pennsylvania's Charter of Privileges of 1701 was in effect unalterable fundamental law is particularly important. See David L. Jacobson, "John Dickinson's Fight against Royal Government, 1764," *W.M.Q.*, 3d ser., 19 (1962), 72–74.

a morally regenerate people to maintain their "rights, liberties, and privileges . . . inviolably firm and free from the least innovations, in the same manner that King David stood engaged by the covenant of the people." For "the covenant people of God" in particular, these charters, on the eve of the Revolution, were known to contain "the first great principles, or stamina, of their governments . . . prescribing the forms of their several governments, determining and bounding the power of the crown over them within proper limits, and ascertaining and securing their rights, jurisdictions, and liberties." [31]

It took no wrench of mind, no daring leap, to accept, by then, the concept of a fixed, written constitution limiting the ordinary actions of government. Famous examples of the fact had long been present: the explicit idea, following, brought this experience into consciousness, gave it new meaning and propulsive power.

The same, though perhaps less obviously so, was true of the change in emphasis in the meaning of rights. The abstraction of rights from their embodiments in ancient, customary law, and their purposeful compilation and publication were not entirely new things for the colonists. Experience in such matters was buried deep in the colonial past; the process, and its results, had been familiar a century before it became systematically important in constitutional theory.

Denied the guidance of experts in the law, lacking sure ideas of what precisely the law provided and what rights were theirs, yet passionately devoted to the belief that English laws and English rights *were* theirs if they would but claim them, the first settlers in British America had found it necessary to compile the law they knew, enumerate its provisions, and specify some, at least, of the rights it guaranteed. The process could hardly have begun earlier than in fact it did. The Pilgrims, responding not to theory but to the practical needs of everyday life, drew up a code of law as early as 1636: "it contains," a leading authority on the early history of American law has written, "a rudimentary bill of rights," which, when elaborated and enlarged in the later years of the seventeenth

---

[31] Samuel Webster, *The Misery and Duty of an Oppressed and Enslav'd People* . . . (Boston, 1774), pp. 10 ff. (the quotation is at 22); Mather, *America's Appeal*, p. 24. See also Johnson, *Some Important Observations*, pp. 42 ff.; and, for a full presentation of this theme and of the political significance of the renewal of "jeremiad" preaching on the eve of the Revolution, Perry Miller, "From the Covenant to the Revival," *The Shaping of American Religion* (James W. Smith and A. Leland Jamison, eds., *Religion in American Life,* I, Princeton, 1961).

century, became "a recognizably modern bill of rights." The Puritans did the same, also within two decades of settlement. Their *Laws and Liberties* of 1648 was in design an abridgement of the laws they had themselves enacted; but, "the culmination of an extraordinarily creative period" of legal and constitutional thought, it went beyond restating and digesting the laws in force, to define "the just rights and privileges of every freeman." It quickly became famous, and influential, in all the colonies. It proved to be

the fountainhead of Massachusetts law during most of the seventeenth century, and even thereafter, and its provisions were widely copied by other colonies, or used by them as models in framing their own laws. Through such intercolonial borrowing, its influence spread into other parts of New England, beyond to New York and even to Delaware and Pennsylvania.[32]

But the other colonies were not entirely dependent on New England models. Acting independently, in response to needs similar to those that had motivated the Massachusetts codifiers, they too drew up, on various occasions, their own formulations of rights. The ill-fated "Charter of Liberties and Privileges" passed by the first General Assembly of New York in 1683, contained not only "the outlines of a constitution for the province" but a "bill of rights" as well. Even more elaborate, and explicit, were the provisions of the "Rights and Privileges of the Majesty's Subjects" enacted eight years later, in 1691, by the same body. This remarkable statute, objected to in England because of its "large and doubtful expressions" and disallowed there, listed the rights of the individuals in the form of a series of categorical prohibitions on government: the individual was to be free from unlawful arrest and imprisonment, arbitrary taxation, martial law and the support of standing armies in time of peace, feudal dues, and restrictions on freehold tenure; in addition, he was guaranteed due process of law, especially trial by jury, and, if Protestant, full liberty to "enjoy his or their opinion, persuasions, [and] judgments in matters of conscience and religion throughout all this province." [33]

But, again, it was William Penn who saw farthest and accomplished the most. His "Laws, Concessions, and Agreements" for the province of

[32] Haskins, "Legacy of Plymouth," pp. 9–10, 22; Andrews, *Colonial Period,* I, 458; George L. Haskins, *Law and Authority in Early Massachusetts* (New York, 1960), pp. 136 ff., 120.

[33] Andrews, *Colonial Period,* III, 117, 119; *The Colonial Laws of New York* . . . (Charles Z. Lincoln, *et al.,* eds., Albany, 1894–1896), I, 244–248; *Documents Relative to the Colonial History of the State of New-York* . . . (E. B. O'Callaghan and Berthod Fernow, eds., Albany, 1853–1887), IV, 263–264.

West New Jersey, drafted and published in 1677, provided not only for the distribution of land and the organization of government, but also, and in great detail, for "the common laws or fundamental rights and privileges" of the inhabitants. The central purpose of this enlightened document was, in fact, to state, so that they might be known and be preserved intact in the New World, "such liberties as were guaranteed by law for the good government of a people, in accord with, as near as conveniently might be, 'the primitive, ancient, and fundamental laws of the people of England.'" Most explicit of all were Penn's statements of rights and privileges in the provisions he made for his own province of Pennsylvania. In his original Concessions and in his Frames of Government, but even more in the so-called "Laws Agreed upon in England" and in the Charter of Liberties and the Charter of Privileges, he laid out, point by point, the rights, duties, and proper regulations of "every phase of human life, civil and social." [34]

By no means all of these documents were bills of rights as we know them. Most of them were not thought of as defining rights antecedent to government and law, rights to which government and law must accommodate themselves. The most common assumption behind them was, rather, that these were rights that the law — English law if not colonial — already provided for and that were now being compiled simply to make them better known and more readily available for reference in a wilderness environment. Presumed to be neither "basic" in some special way nor logically comprehensive, they were mainly devoted to eliminating arbitrary procedures in the enactment and execution of laws. But some of them are nevertheless astonishingly modern, containing some of the precise prohibitions on governmental powers and some of the exact guarantees of individual action that would later come to be thought of as necessary parts of fully evolved bills of rights. The eighteenth century would add nothing to William Penn's declaration, in his "Concessions . . . or Fundamental Rights" of West New Jersey, that "no men nor number of men upon earth hath power or authority to rule over men's conscience in religious matters"; nor would much improvement be made in his clause providing that no one "shall be deprived or condemned of life, limb, liberty, estate, [or] property . . . without a due trial and judgment passed by twelve good and lawful men of his neighborhood." And

[34] *The Grants, Concessions, and Original Constitutions of the Province of New Jersey* . . . (Aaron Leaming and Jacob Spicer, eds. [Somerville, N.J., 1881]), pp. 382–409; Andrews, *Colonial Period*, III, 273–274 (cf. 167), 286; *The Federal and State Constitutions, Colonial Charters* . . . (F. N. Thorpe, comp., Washington, D.C., 1909), V, 3044 ff.

it is doubtful if James Madison, writing a full century later, would better the statements in New York's *Act Declaring What Are the Rights and Privileges* guaranteeing "due course of law," trial by jury, and freedom from the obligation to quarter troops in peacetime.[35]

All of these codes and declarations — whatever the deliberate assumptions of their authors, and however archaic or modern-sounding their provisions — were, at the very least, efforts to abstract from the deep entanglements of English law and custom certain essentials — obligations, rights, and prohibitions — by which liberty, as it was understood, might be preserved. As English law in America became better known in the eighteenth century through the work of an increasingly professional bar, and as governmental and judicial processes became stabilized in the colonies, the original need that had given rise to these documents faded. Except where they were embedded in, or protected by, crown charters, they tended to drop from prominence — but not from awareness. In some places surviving intact from the settlement period to the Revolution, well remembered in others where they had been eliminated from the statutes, and everywhere understood to be reasonable and beneficent, these documents formed a continuous tradition in colonial American life, and drifted naturally into the thought of the Revolutionary generation. So in 1774 Alexander Hamilton asserted, as a conclusive argument, that New York's "very remarkable" Act of 1691 "confutes all that has been said concerning the novelty of our present claims, and proves that the injurious reflections on the [Continental] Congress for having risen in their demands are malicious and repugnant to truth." [36]

3. SOVEREIGNTY

Representation and consent, constitution and rights — these were basic problems, consideration of which led to shifts in thought that helped shape the character of American radicalism. But of all the intellectual problems the colonists faced, one was absolutely crucial: in the last analysis it was over this issue that the Revolution was fought. On the pivotal question of sovereignty, which is the question of the nature and location of the ultimate power in the state, American thinkers attempted to depart sharply from one of the most firmly fixed points in eighteenth-century political thought; and though they failed to gain acceptance for their strange and awkward views, they succeeded nevertheless in opening

[35] *Grants of New Jersey*, pp. 394, 395; *Colonial Laws of New York*, I, 247.
[36] Hamilton, *Farmer Refuted*, in Lodge, *Works*, I, 174.

this fundamental issue to critical discussion, preparing the way for a new departure in the organization of power.

The idea of sovereignty current in the English-speaking world of the 1760's was scarcely more than a century old. It had first emerged during the English Civil War, in the early 1640's, and had been established as a canon of Whig political thought in the Revolution of 1688. It was composed essentially of two components. The first was the notion that there must reside somewhere in every political unit a single, undivided, final power, higher in legal authority than any other power, subject to no law, a law unto itself. Derived in part from the political theory of classical antiquity, in part from Roman law, and in part from medieval thought, this idea came to England most directly in the sixteenth-century writings, especially those of Jean Bodin, that sought to justify and fortify monarchial supremacy.

But in these early writings the concept of sovereignty still retained important limitations derived from its legal, religious, and pre-national origins. By sovereign Bodin had meant supreme, but not arbitrary: not without restrictions or controls, that is; the action of the sovereign state, he assumed, must still "embody the law of nature and of God." Bodin's theory, Professor McIlwain writes, for all its efforts to establish a power beyond appeal, "is a theory of law not of might, the theory of the *Rechtsstaat;* and it is this theory which . . . for two generations after Bodin dominated even English thought." But then, in the mid-seventeenth-century crisis in England, a change came. In the desperate necessity to isolate a reliable source of order, the permeation of might with right ended; a generation of cold-eyed analysts stripped the idea of sovereignty of its moral and legalistic qualities and laid bare the doctrine of naked force. Hobbes and Filmer are the names most obviously associated with this change in English thought; but it was not their work alone. The familiar restrictions had been attacked and undermined, if not eliminated, by earlier defenders of the royal prerogative — Roger Mainwaring and Robert Sibthorpe (whom the colonists would frequently denounce as pre-eminent absolutists), Francis Bacon, and James I himself. Yet it was, nevertheless, Hobbes who, in a series of writings in the mid-seventeenth century, first went beyond the immediate claims of monarchy to argue systematically that the only essential quality of sovereignty as such — whoever or whatever its possessor might be — was the capacity to compel obedience; and it was with his name, and with Filmer's, that the colonists came to associate the conception of the *Machtstaat* in its most blatant form.[37]

Final, unqualified, indivisible power was, however, only one part of the notion of sovereignty as it was understood by Englishmen on the eve of the American Revolution. The other concerns its location. Who, or what body, was to hold such powers? For the absolutists of James I's time, as later for Filmer, the answer was, of course, the crown. But others who also believed with Hobbes that "the preservation of life itself depended essentially upon power and not upon law" feared that an absolutely un-fettered King would become an absolute despot — precisely the sort of ruler that Charles I had sought to become. In the extraordinary outburst of political theorizing that took place in 1642 when the final break with the crown was made, a new conclusion was drawn from the argument that there must necessarily be "an arbitrary power in every state some-where." If this power fell to "one man or to a few there may be danger in it, but the Parliament is neither one nor few," and as a result "no inconvenience" would follow from placing arbitrary power in Parliament's hands. Parliament is "so equally and geometrically proportionable" in its composition, "and all the [e]states do so orderly contribute their due parts therein" that its absolute, arbitrary power "is not dangerous nor need to be restrained." [38]

The words are those of Henry Parker, taken from the pamphlet of 1642 in which he "worked out for the first time in English history a theory of Parliamentary sovereignty." He, and others with him, devel-oped the idea further under the pressure of attacks that came, on the one hand from extreme Royalists, now defenders of fundamental law as a necessary qualification on sovereignty, and on the other from extreme libertarians, determined to protect the individual against government in any form. Parker's view survived and flourished, and the result, by the Restoration, was a conception of Parliament that would have been in-conceivable a generation earlier: a body absolute and arbitrary in its sovereignty; the creator and interpreter, not the subject, of law; the su-perior and master of all other rights and powers within the state. It was

[37] McIlwain, *Constitutionalism and the Changing World*, pp. 26–29, 52–55, 72 ff.; Gough, *Fundamental Law*, pp. 117 ff.; Margaret A. Judson, *The Crisis of the Constitution . . . 1603–1645* (New Brunswick, N.J., 1949), chaps. iv, v; George L. Mosse, *The Struggle for Sovereignty in England* (East Lansing, Mich., 1950), chap. iv.

[38] Margaret A. Judson, "Henry Parker and the Theory of Parliamentary Sovereignty," *Essays [to] McIlwain*, pp. 152, 144, 150, 151.

this conception of Parliamentary sovereignty that triumphed in the Glorious Revolution; and it was this conception, justified in the end by the theory of an ultimate supremacy of the people — a supremacy, that is, normally dormant and exercised only at moments of rebellion against tyrannical government — that was carried on into the eighteenth century and into the debates that preceded the American Revolution.[39]

It had been a gradual development, and it had ended in a significant inversion. The earliest tradition, Professor McIlwain writes in one of his most striking essays, had been that of Hooker and Coke, Eliot and Hale, who

would have repudiated all arbitrary government whatsoever, whether by king or parliament; Filmer had declared that any government in England must be both arbitrary and royal; for Hobbes it must be arbitrary but not necessarily royal; for many Whigs a century later it must be arbitrary and cannot be royal. Thus after 1689, and the revolution settlement which marked the final triumph of the Whigs, the arbitrary power of Hobbes and Filmer was for the first time "engrafted into the English constitution" . . . and vested in the national assembly . . . For the Whigs the only real sovereign must be the Parliament, that is all.

By the mid-eighteenth century this Whig conception of a sovereign Parliament had hardened into orthodoxy. In the year of the Stamp Act, it was given its classic formulation by Blackstone, who wrote in his *Commentaries* that "there is and must be in all [forms of government] a supreme, irresistible, absolute, uncontrolled authority, in which the *jura summi imperii,* or the rights of sovereignty, reside," and that in England this "sovereignty of the British constitution" was lodged in Parliament, the aggregate body of King, Lords, and Commons, whose actions "no power on earth can undo." [40]

The formula seemed incontrovertible, and it quickly became the foundation of the English claim against America. For there were few who would deny that "a power to tax is a necessary part of every supreme legislative authority." Therefore if Parliament "have not that power over America they have none, and then America is at once a kingdom of itself." The logic of the Declaratory Act, consequently, was impeccable: Parliament "had, hath, and of right ought to have, full power and authority to make

[39] Judson, "Henry Parker," pp. 153, 163, 164; Gough, *Fundamental Law,* pp. 176 ff.

[40] McIlwain, *Constitutionalism and the Changing World,* pp. 63–64; on the complexities of Blackstone's position, see Ernest Barker, *Essays on Government* (Oxford, 1945), pp. 137–138; for Blackstone's application of these ideas to the question of Parliament's control of the colonies, see Lawrence H. Gipson, "The Great Debate . . . on the Stamp Act, 1766, as Reported by Nathaniel Ryder," *Pa. Mag.,* 86 (1962), 17.

laws and statutes of sufficient force and vitality to bind the colonies and people of America . . . in all cases whatsoever." [41]

How to qualify, undermine, or reinterpret this tenet of English political theory was the central intellectual problem that confronted the leaders of the American cause; and there is no more fascinating spectacle in the history of American political thought than the efforts that were made — starting in the struggle with England over the extent of Parliament's power and continuing into the debates on the ratification of the constitution — to come to terms with this problem. It is a classic instance of the creative adjustment of ideas to reality. For if in England the concept of sovereignty was not only logical but realistic, it was far from that in the colonies. From the beginning of settlement, circumstances in America had run directly counter to the exercise of unlimited and undivided sovereignty. Despite the serious efforts that had been made by the English government in the late seventeenth century to reduce the areas of local jurisdiction in the colonies, local provincial autonomy continued to characterize American life. Never had Parliament or the crown, or both together, operated in actuality as theory indicated sovereign powers should. They had exercised authority, of course. The crown had retained the final power of legalizing or annulling actions of the colonial legislatures and of the colonial courts; it had made appointments to high office; it had laid down rules and policies for its colonial officials to follow; it had held in its own hand major decisions, civil and military, affecting relations with other nations; and it had continued to claim control of, if not actually to control, vast areas of wild land in the west as well as certain settled territories in the east. Similarly, Parliament had created the colonial postal system, regulated naturalization, and laid down rules for certain economic activities in the colonies, of which the laws of trade and navigation were the most important. But these were far from total powers; together they did not constitute governance in depth, nor did they exclude the exercise of real power by lesser bodies or organs of government. They touched only the outer fringes of colonial life; they dealt with matters obviously beyond the competence of any lesser authority; they concerned the final review of actions initiated and sustained by colonial authorities. All other powers were enjoyed, in fact if not in constitutional theory, by local, colonial organs of government. This area of residual authority, con-

[41] [Jared Ingersoll], *Mr. Ingersoll's Letters Relating to the Stamp-Act* (New Haven, 1766), p. 13.

stituting the "internal police" of the community, included most of the substance of everyday life.

It had in fact been local American agencies that effectively created and maintained law and order, for there had been no imperial constabulary, and such elements of England's military power as had appeared in America from time to time had acted for purposes that only incidentally involved the daily lives of the colonists. It had in fact been local, common law courts that administered justice in the colonies; the courts associated with the home government had been condemned as "prerogative," their jurisdiction repeatedly challenged and closely restricted. And it had in fact been local bodies — towns and counties in the first instance, ultimately the provincial Assemblies — that laid down the rules for daily life; rules concerning the production and distribution of wealth, personal conduct, the worship of God — most of the ways in which people deal with the world, animate and inanimate, about them. And these same bodies had been the ones accustomed to tax. Moneys had of course been collected by the home authorities; but they had been fees, dues, and rents — charges, for the most part, incidental to the regulation of overseas trade — not taxes. The power of taxing, from the earliest years of settlement, had been exercised by the representative Assemblies of the various colonies, and exercised without competition — indeed with encouragement — from England.

The condition of British America by the end of the Seven Years' War was therefore anomalous: extreme decentralization of authority within an empire presumably ruled by a single, absolute, undivided sovereign. And anomalous it had been known to be at the time. For decades before 1763 the situation had been remarked on, and reforms proposed by officers of the crown in the colonies as well as by administrators and theorists in England. But since, in the age of Walpole and Newcastle, no sustained effort had been made to alter the situation, the colonists found themselves in 1763 faced not merely with new policies but with a challenge to their settled way of life — a way of life that had been familiar in some places for a century or more. The arguments the colonists put forward against Parliament's claims to the right to exercise sovereign power in America were efforts to express in logical form, to state in the language of constitutional theory, the truth of the world they knew. They were at first, necessarily, fumbling and unsure efforts, for there were no arguments — there was no vocabulary — to resort to: the ideas, the terminology, had to be invented.

How was this to be done? What arguments, what words, could be used to elevate to the status of constitutional principle the division of authority that had for so long existed and which the colonists associated with the freedom they had enjoyed? Here again Otis' pronouncements were among the first and most famous (they are inextricably involved with his statements on rights and the constitution), and they are also among his most confused. In this instance as in others, the curiously anachronistic quality of his thought led him into difficulties he could not resolve and toward conclusions he could not accept. He assumed the validity of the current concept of sovereignty — "a supreme legislative and a supreme executive power must be placed *somewhere* in every commonwealth. Where there is no other positive provision or compact to the contrary, those powers remain in the *whole body of the people.*" And he agreed also that in England this power resided in Parliament. "The power of Parliament is uncontrollable but by themselves, and we must obey. They only can repeal their own acts. There would be an end of all government if one or a number of subjects or subordinate provinces should take upon them so far to judge of the justice of an act of Parliament as to refuse obedience to it." But to say that a sovereign Parliament is absolute, he added, is not to say that it is arbitrary. "The Parliament cannot make 2 and 2, 5," he wrote in a phrase that encapsulates the whole pre-Hobbesian view of sovereignty; "omnipotency cannot do it." The pillars of Parliament "are fixed in judgment, righteousness, and truth." [42]

This position, which reverted to a conception of sovereignty that had been realistic at a time when Parliament's legislative authority had not in fact been supreme, and before the mid-seventeenth-century theorists had asserted the necessity of defining the state in terms of an arbitrary as well as an absolute power, could not in the 1760's be maintained as an effective political argument. It could easily be shown to be self-contradictory. Seeking to maintain it — asserting, that is, the absolute power of what was, by definition, a benign authority — Otis found himself weaving back and forth, fending off attacks from both political extremes. Judged by what he had said about constitutional limitations on legislative power in the writs of assistance case in 1761, his assertion in 1765 that — such is the nature of sovereignty — "it is our duty to submit," appeared to leading

[42] Otis, *Rights of the British Colonies* (JHL Pamphlet 7), pp. 12, 39, 47, 48. See in general on Otis' constitutional arguments the Introductions to his *Rights* and to his *Vindication of the British Colonies* (JHL Pamphlet 11).

patriots to constitute an astonishing reversal, and they could only conclude that he had been "corrupted and bought off" by the ministry.

Otis reacted more keenly, however, to the opposite charge, leveled at him both in England and America, that his view of the self-defining restrictions of Parliament's power amounted to claiming for the colonies "an independent, uncontrollable, provincial legislative." Never, he replied, had he intended to make such a claim. Everyone knows, he wrote in his *Vindication,* that *"imperium in imperio* [is] the greatest of all political solecisms," and that there is, consequently, no limit to Parliament's power of legislation or taxation. England "justly asserts the right and authority to bind her colonies where she really thinks the good of the whole requires it; and of this she remains the supreme judge, from whose final determination there is no appeal" — though, of course, he added, from this it does not follow "that 'tis always expedient and in all circumstances equitable for the supreme and sovereign legislative" to use its power.

By 1766 Otis' argument, grossly distended by the pressures placed upon it, was blatantly self-contradictory. By then he was beseeching his readers to believe that he had never intended so much as to hint at limitations on the "unlimited authority of Parliament over the colonies," apologizing to them if he had inadvertently given a different impression, and proclaiming himself in basic agreement with the Grenville ministry. But simultaneously he lashed out at that "contaminated knot of thieves, beggars and transports" in Newport responsible for such "evil work" as Judge Howard's *Halifax Letter,* which stated essentially the same position he was defending.[43]

It was a bewildering performance, and it is little wonder that he was denounced as a "double-faced Jacobite-Whig." [44] His political judgment, on this occasion as on others, was obviously erratic. But his troubles mainly stemmed, here as in his arguments on other constitutional issues, from his peculiar application of early seventeenth-century ideas and assumptions to eighteenth-century problems. Failing to recognize that the idea of sovereignty had long since acquired as an essential characteristic arbitrariness as well as absolutism, he saw no danger in allowing Parliament to exercise sovereign authority, and to exercise it not only over the nation proper but over distant colonies as well. Parliament might make

---

[43] *Rights,* p. 40; Adams, *Works,* X, 296–297; Otis, *Vindication* (JHL Pamphlet 11), pp. 4, 14, 5; [Otis], *Brief Remarks on the Defence of the Halifax Libel . . .* (Boston, 1765), pp. 22, 5.

[44] Ellen E. Brennan, "James Otis: Recreant and Patriot," *N.E.Q.,* 12 (1939), 722.

occasional mistakes, he admitted, but in the end — such was the wonder of the British constitution — it would necessarily act justly and wisely. If the Stamp Act was in fact wrong, Parliament would repeal it.

The repeal, when it came, was too late to vindicate Otis' position. By then, leading colonial writers were attacking the problem of sovereignty in a different way — a more realistic and pragmatic way. Tacitly acknowledging that by accepted definition sovereignty was both absolute and arbitrary, but convinced nevertheless that there were things that Parliament could not rightly do, they set out, silent on the metaphysics of the problem, to locate pragmatically a line of separation between powers of Parliament that were valid when exercised in America and those that were not. It was only later and gradually, when challenged by informed and articulate opponents, that they faced up to the implications of what they had been doing, and acknowledged that they were in effect calling "sovereignty itself into question" and attempting to reconceive the basic principles of state authority.[45]

The path the colonists took away from the accepted eighteenth-century notions of sovereignty appears now, in retrospect, to have been so clear that it is surprising that it was not seen sooner than it was by the colonists themselves. For, as Otis made abundantly evident, any effort to restrict Parliament's power assumed that sovereignty was in some sense divisible; and to search deliberately for the actual seams along which the fabric of power might be divided was to grope toward a political order in which "powers of government are separated and distinguished and in which these powers are distributed among governments, each government having its quota of authority and each its distinct sphere of activity."[46] But the awareness of this fact was slow in developing: the discussion be-

---

[45] ". . . if, intemperately, unwisely, fatally," Edmund Burke predicted in his Speech on American Taxation, "you sophisticate and poison the very source of government by urging subtle deductions . . . from the unlimited and illimitable nature of supreme sovereignty, you will teach them by these means to call that sovereignty itself in question. When you drive him hard, the boar will surely turn upon the hunters. If that sovereignty and their freedom cannot be reconciled, which will they take? They will cast your sovereignty in your face. Nobody will be argued into slavery."

[46] Andrew C. McLaughlin, "The Background of American Federalism," *American Political Science Review,* 12 (1918), 215. The interpretation in the pages that follow owes much to this essay which argues "that the essential qualities of American federal organization were largely the product of the practices of the old British empire as it existed before 1764" and that "the discussions of the generation from the French and Indian war to the adoption of the federal Constitution, and, more particularly, the discussions in the ten or twelve years before independence" were devoted to the problems of this kind of organization. See also McLaughlin, *Foundations of American Constitutionalism,* chap. vi; McIlwain, "Historical Background of Federal Government."

gan at the level of specific distinctions in the powers of Parliament, and it progressed to more general grounds only after it was shown that these distinctions could not be maintained.

The first distinction advanced in the effort to express in constitutional language the limitations on Parliament's power familiar to the colonists, was extemporized casually by the simple expedient of applying to the constitutional problem at hand one of the most common antonyms in the English language. No distinction could be more obvious or more fundamental than that between things "internal" and things "external." Not only did it appear to separate out conveniently the powers that had been exercised for so long by the colonists' own Assemblies and those that had been exercised by Parliament, but it did so echoing the words of some of the most respected authorities on questions of government.[47] An ordinary distinction already drawn into theoretical discussions, used in all sorts of ways in everyday speech, it quickly drifted into the discussion of Anglo-American relations. It was used loosely throughout the pre-Revolutionary years, applied generally to spheres of government, and it was specified by some to the problem of taxation.

Thus in 1764 Richard Bland, searching for a principle by which to assign exclusive powers to colonial governments and yet retain the colonies' dependency on England, found the distinction between things internal and things external to be essential to his purpose. If Virginians are freemen, he argued, they must have a representative assembly capable of enacting "laws for the INTERNAL government of the colony" — "internal" being defined so as to exclude "all power derogatory to their dependence upon the mother kingdom . . . In every instance, therefore, of our EXTERNAL government we are and must be subject to the authority of the British Parliament, but in no others; for if the Parliament should impose laws upon us merely relative to our INTERNAL government, it deprives us, as far as those laws extend, of the most valuable part of our birthright as

---

[47] Thus Vattel, arguing that nations, like men, are naturally "free and independent of each other" except where a bonded obligation has been incurred, pointed out that such an obligation "and the right correspondent to it . . . is distinguished into *external* and *internal*. The obligation is *internal,* as it binds the conscience, and as it comprehends the rules of our duty; it is *external,* as it is considered relatively to other men, and as it produces some right between them." He then discussed the freedom of action permissible to nations in the light of internal and external obligations. *Law of Nations* (London, 1759, translator unnamed — the edition used by both Otis and Bland), I, Introduction, sections 16–17, 20, 27 (pp. 5–7). For the importance of the distinction to Harrington, see Charles Blitzer, *An Immortal Commonwealth* (New Haven, 1960), pp. 111 ff.

Englishmen . . ." And if Parliament is limited in its legislative power over the colonies to external matters, "then any tax respecting our IN-TERNAL polity which may hereafter be imposed on us by act of Parliament is arbitrary, as depriving us of our rights, and may be opposed."

When the Stamp Act controversy exploded, the distinction naturally became part of the discussion of the rights involved. Stephen Hopkins, writing for the colony of Rhode Island, began by defining stamp duties as internal taxes and hence properly within the jurisdiction of the separate colonial legislatures, which had responsibility for the "internal government" of the colonies. The colonial jurisdiction of Parliament, he wrote, was quite different. Its proper power was over

things of a more general nature, quite out of the reach of these particular legislatures . . . One of this kind is the commerce of the whole British empire, taken collectively, and that of each kingdom and colony in it as it makes a part of that whole. Indeed, everything that concerns the proper interest and fit government of the whole commonwealth, of keeping the peace, and subordination of all the parts towards the whole and one among another, must be considered in this light.

For all such "matters of general nature" there must be some "supreme and overruling authority" to make laws and "compel their execution," and such a supreme power, everyone knows, Hopkins wrote, lies in "that grand and august legislative body," Parliament. He did not at this point develop the idea that if "internal" taxes were denied Parliament, "external" taxes might not be; he was not attempting to distinguish among types of taxes but to deal with the broader issue of spheres of authority within which taxation fell.[48]

Others, however, would make this distinction — casually, almost inadvertently, and not with the sense that it was exclusive, comprehensive, or rigorously logical. Thus Connecticut's protest, published under the title *Reasons Why the British Colonies in America Should Not Be Charged with Internal Taxes,* in effect defined all taxation as "internal" taxation, and though it denied Parliament all right to tax the colonies, conceded to it the right to raise revenue through duties on trade, since such commercial fees, as distinct from taxes, fell properly within the sphere of "external" government. Others agreed, especially when it was understood, as Dulany explained, that the essential difference between internal taxes and trade duties was that the former were levied *"for the*

[48] Bland, *Colonel Dismounted* (JHL Pamphlet 4), p. 22; [Stephen Hopkins], *The Rights of Colonies Examined* (Providence, 1765: JHL Pamphlet 9), pp. 10, 11. For Hopkins' later distinction between taxing the colonies in their "interior police" and in their "foreign importations" see below, pp. 504.

single purpose of revenue" and the latter only "for the regulation of trade." [49]

But discriminating among the intentions of lawmakers was both difficult and dangerous; trade duties — whether called "external taxes" or not — could be as onerous as excise taxes. "They may find duties on trade enough," Thomas Hutchinson warned, "to drain us so thoroughly that it will not be possible to pay internal taxes as a revenue to them or even to support government within ourselves." It was obviously to the benefit of the administration to consolidate the advantage this presumed concession appeared to bestow, no matter how "nonsensical" informed people believed distinctions in revenue-raising powers to be. By 1765 English opponents of American claims were imputing to the distinction between "internal" and "external" taxation, said to be commonly drawn in the colonies, an importance and a rigor that had never been intended for it and that made it vulnerable to attacks no one had expected it to have to withstand. That the usage took on this importance and became the subject of powerful attacks was to a considerable extent the result of the stress placed on it by Benjamin Franklin in the course of his famous three-hour testimony before the House of Commons in February 1766. [50]

No one could have been better informed on the state of American thinking and on the armory of weapons the colonists had devised to attack Parliamentary taxation than Franklin. Having left America only a

[49] On Connecticut's pamphlet and the issues involved, see Introduction to Pamphlet 6 below and the documents cited there; Dulany, *Considerations* (JHL Pamphlet 13), p. 33.

[50] Hutchinson to Ebenezer Silliman, November 9, 1764, quoted in Morgan, *Stamp Act,* p. 216; Thomas Whately to John Temple, May 2, 1767, in *Collections of the Massachusetts Historical Society,* 6th ser., IX, 83. Cf. Edmund S. Morgan, "Colonial Ideas of Parliamentary Power, 1764–1766," *W.M.Q.,* 3d ser., 5 (1948), 311–341, where it is argued that the colonists never admitted Parliament's right to levy external taxes, the presumed concession being an attribution to the colonists by writers and debaters in England, and that the colonists' arguments against Parliamentary taxation appeared fully developed in the Stamp Act crisis. The present interpretation, which owes much to Morgan's, differs from it not so much on whether or not this concession was ever made by the colonists (I find that it was, though uncommonly and, in the ways indicated, indeliberately) but on the more basic question of the development of the colonists' constitutional ideas. In the perspective of the fundamental problem of sovereignty, whether the colonists did or did not admit Parliament's right to impose "external" taxes is less important than that they universally thought in terms of "internal" and "external" spheres of government, and that this distinction, of which the taxing issue was a specification, provided them with the means of discriminating among and qualifying the sovereign powers of Parliament. For an example of the colonists' admission of external taxation, besides those elsewhere cited in this volume, see Charles Carroll's explanation of the propriety of Parliament's taxing the colonies by "disallowing drawbacks and imposing duties on our imports and exports," in his letter to Henry Graves, September 15, 1765, *Unpublished Letters of Charles Carroll of Carrollton* . . . (Thomas M. Field, ed., New York, 1902), p. 90.

few months before he was called upon to testify, and having kept in continuous communication with the colonists and with the other agents in London since his arrival there, he knew the official and unofficial literature of opposition thoroughly. In his blandly confident, adroit, and hardheaded testimony covering the whole range of issues in the controversy, the "internal"–"external" distinction became crucial. Since it allowed him to evade the question of whether or not his countrymen were in principle denying Parliament's right to tax them, he referred to it frequently and was forced to defend it. The colonists were not, he said, denying Parliament's right to collect moneys from them. They had long acknowledged Parliament's right "of laying duties to regulate commerce." What they were objecting to as "unconstitutional and unjust" was Parliament's effort "to lay internal taxes," for such a right "was never supposed to be in Parliament, as we are not represented there." His interrogators pressed him: Did he really believe that such a distinction was valid? Yes, Franklin assured them, he did; the difference between "external" and "internal" taxing was "very great."

An external tax is a duty laid on commodities imported; that duty is added to the first cost and other charges on the commodity, and, when it is offered to sale, makes a part of the price. If the people do not like it at that price, they refuse it; they are not obliged to pay it. But an internal tax is forced from the people without their consent, if not laid by their own representatives.

But may not the colonists "by the same interpretation object to Parliament's right of external taxation?" Franklin's reply was shrewdly evasive:

Many arguments have been lately used here to show them that there is no difference, and that if you have no right to tax them internally, you have none to tax them externally, or make any other law to bind them. At present they do not reason so; but in time they may possibly be convinced by these arguments.[51]

Some, in the colonies, were in fact already approaching such conclusions. Dulany's pamphlet, published only a few months before Franklin spoke, had done more than sophisticate the meaning of "internal" taxation. It had broadened the discussion, and led it to a higher plane of generality. For, Dulany had argued, if there were, as he believed, powers that inferior bodies might exercise "without control or compulsion" — if there were areas where "the authority of the superior can't properly interpose" — does it not follow that the superior authority is actually limited

[51] Albert H. Smyth, ed., *The Writings of Benjamin Franklin* (New York, 1905–1907), IV, 421, 424, 445, 446. On Franklin's constitutional ideas, see Verner W. Crane, ed., *Benjamin Franklin's Letters to the Press, 1758–1775* (Chapel Hill, 1950), pp. xxxvii–xlvi, 60–61, and documents cited there.

in what it can do "by the powers vested in the inferior"? [52] In the light of such a possibility, and in the light of the approaching Townshend Duties — aimed as obviously as the Stamp Act at raising a revenue yet "external" by the colonists' own definition — the inadequacy of the much overstrained distinction between "internal" and "external" taxation for marking the limits of Parliament's power over the colonies became obvious. John Dickinson, in his *Farmer's Letters* (1767-68), flatly and formally repudiated it, and, examining the problem of Parliament's power with greater acuity than any writer had shown before, went on to a new stage in the exploration of the idea of sovereignty.

All taxation, Dickinson wrote in his famous pamphlet, being an "imposition to raise money," is essentially the same, and so there is no difference between "external" and "internal" taxation. Parliament has no right to levy taxes on Americans for any purpose whatsoever: that much was clear. What was not so clear, what needed discussion, and what he followed out in his thought boldly and imaginatively, was the proper role of a central government in a truly imperial constitution. The legislature of an empire, he said, was different from the legislature of a nation. Though the two might exist in the same body, they had different functions and powers as organs of government. Over the American colonies Parliament must have all the power, but only the power, necessary to maintain the essential connections of empire, and this meant the power to regulate commerce and other aspects of the economy "in such a manner as [England] thought most conducive to their mutual advantage and her own welfare." The duties imposed in the course of such regulation, he made clear, would be legitimate, for such "external impositions" do not grant property away but only prevent its acquisition. England's other imperial powers were quite specific, and inhered not in Parliament but in the crown: the power to repeal colonial legislation, to exercise "the executive authority of government," and to sit in appeal "from all judgments in the administration of justice." [53]

In admitting that Parliament had such regulatory authority but yet no taxing powers whatever over America, Dickinson was approaching a conception of sovereignty different in essence from what had been accepted hitherto. For in assuming an empire to be basically different from a unitary nation, he was saying now explicitly that its sovereign body need not be supreme everywhere and in all matters in the territory it

[52] Dulany, *Considerations* (JHL Pamphlet 13), p. 15.
[53] Dickinson, *Farmer's Letters*, in Ford, *Writings*, pp. 332, 337, 338.

controlled, but only on some issues and in some ways, and that other, lesser bodies might exercise absolute and arbitrary powers — sovereign powers in effect — within spheres specifically allotted to them.

Once the discussion had reached this level, a maturing of views took place rapidly. For the reiterated assertions that were soon heard to the effect that even "the boldest advocates for the power of Parliament cannot, at this day, without blushing, assert that it is sovereign and supreme *in every respect whatsoever"* — such assertions required a fuller rationalization and a more cogent explanation of principle than even Dickinson had given them if they were to be kept from degenerating into the more extreme claims, already being heard in 1768, that Parliament "cannot pass *any* laws to bind us." Such a notion, the Reverend John Joachim Zubly stated in 1769, must contain "some fallacy couched under an otherwise specious appearance." For it is not a matter of all or nothing. There are, he wrote in his fumbling yet original and penetrating *Enquiry,* significant gradations in the authority of Parliament derived from the variety of separate national entities it rules. The British "EMPIRE" is an "extensive word"; it refers to "England, Scotland, Ireland, the Islands of Man, Jersey, Guernsey, Gibraltar, and Minorca, etc., in the Mediterranean; Senegal, etc., in Africa; Bombay, etc., in the East Indies; and the islands and colonies in North America, etc." The peoples of these extensive domains are not to be equally affected by Parliament's power. With regard to trade, yes: "the power of making it most beneficial to the head and every branch of the empire is vested in the British Parliament"; and with regard to rights, yes: Parliament must guarantee that "all British subjects everywhere have a right to be ruled by the known principles of their common constitution." But otherwise, the various peoples of the empire are ruled unequally by Parliament; the "nature and degree of [their] dependence" upon Parliament "is not exactly alike," and Parliamentary laws affect them only in cases where they are specifically named, and to the extent of the specification.[54]

By then the departure from the traditional understanding of sovereignty had gone far enough to make a sharp recall to orthodoxy advisable on the part of spokesmen for England. The most notable statement of this sort was written in 1769 by William Knox, a Grenvillite, newly appointed

[54] [William Hicks], *The Nature and Extent of Parliamentary Power Considered . . .* (Philadelphia, 1768), p. xiii (see also p. 23: "while the power of the British Parliament is acknowledged *sovereign and supreme in every respect whatsoever,* the liberty of America is no more than a flattering dream, and her privileges delusive shadows"); Downer, *Discourse,* p. 7; Zubly, *Humble Enquiry,* pp. 2, 4, 6, 9.

undersecretary of state for the colonies. Knox, setting a pattern for subsequent opponents of American claims, began by ridiculing what he understood to have been the shifting American positions on what Parliament could and could not do in regard to the colonies. First, he said, the colonists had attempted to distinguish "internal" taxation from "external"; then, when Parliament "seemed to adopt the distinction" and introduced just such "external" taxing, they changed their minds and decided to distinguish taxation for the purpose of regulating trade from taxation for the purpose of creating a revenue — a distinction, Knox wrote, "of all absurdities the most ridiculous that ever was contended for." Finally, they had rejected taxation altogether and admitted only commercial regulation. There was no logic or law behind such gyrations. What Americans were really objecting to had nothing to do with constitutional principles. Their objection was not to Parliament's constitutional right to levy certain kinds of taxes as opposed to certain others, but to its effort to collect any. Their theoretical position was worthless:

For if the authority of the legislative be not in one instance equally supreme over the colonies as it is over the people of England, then are not the colonies of the same community with the people of England. All distinctions destroy this union; and if it can be shown in any particular to be dissolved, it must be so in all instances whatever. There is no alternative: either the colonies are a part of the community of Great Britain or they are in a state of nature with respect to her, and in no case can be subject to the jurisdiction of that legislative power which represents her community, which is the British Parliament.[55]

It was a rebuttal not so much of the pragmatic efforts that had been made in America to limit the power of Parliament but of attempts like that of Zubly to devise a theoretical justification for dividing sovereign power in any way at all. This abstract problem was at the heart of the controversy between England and the colonies, and once directly confronted, it could not be evaded. As a consequence the major constitutional issue in debate shifted permanently after 1769 from the specific questions of taxes and the administration of government to the correct definition of a concept of political science. While defenders of England's policies followed Knox in insisting on the indivisibility of Parliament's sover-

[55] [William Knox], *The Controversy Between Great Britain and Her Colonies Reviewed* . . . (London, 1769), reprinted in *Old South Leaflets,* no. 210 (S. E. Morison, ed.), pp. 8–9, 10–11 (pp. 34–35, 44, 50 in the original edition). Cf. [John Mein], *Sagittarius's Letters and Political Speculations* . . . (Boston, 1775), p. 12; [Jonathan Boucher], *A Letter from a Virginian* . . . ([New York], 1774), pp. 20, 23; Leonard ("Massachusettensis"), in *Novanglus and Massachusettensis,* pp. 173–174.

eignty, American leaders, gingerly choosing among the alternatives open to them, felt their way toward new conclusions.

The structure of this critical problem of theory is perhaps best revealed in the remarkable series of exchanges between Lieutenant Governor Thomas Hutchinson of Massachusetts and the two Houses of Assembly of that colony in 1773. Smarting under the publication late in 1772 of the belligerent *Votes and Proceedings* of the Boston Town Meeting, Hutchinson on January 6, 1773, launched a formal debate with the legislature on the central question involved.[56] His opening speech was characteristically temperate and lucid. Assuming that "from the nature of government there must be one supreme authority" and that for Britons everywhere it was lodged in Parliament, "of which the King is a constituent part," he explained that the Boston *Votes* were subversive in that some of them deny "the supreme authority of Parliament" and others "speak of this supreme authority . . . in such terms as have a direct tendency to alienate the affections of the people from their sovereign." Methodically, he took up the arguments of the Town Meeting, arguments based in turn on reason, on the charter, on the rights of Englishmen, and on natural rights. He concluded that there was "no line that can be drawn between the supreme authority of Parliament and the total independence of the colonies: it is impossible there should be two independent legislatures in one and the same state for . . . two legislative bodies will make two governments as distinct as the kingdoms of England and Scotland before the Union." He ended in the same spirit of reason in which he had begun, requesting the two Houses, since "independence I may not allow myself to think that you can possibly have in contemplation," to communicate their sentiments to him "with the same freedom and unreservedness as I have communicated mine to you" so that he might be convinced of his error "if I am wrong in my principles of government or in the inference which I have drawn from them."

The two Houses lost no time in replying. The Council, confessing cer-

---

[56] The entire debate was published by order of the House in a 126-page pamphlet entitled *The Speeches of His Excellency Governor Hutchinson to the General Assembly . . . 1773. With the Answers of His Majesty's Council and the House of Representatives Respectively* (Boston, 1773). The same documents, with the exception of the governor's concluding speech of March 6, are reprinted in [Alden Bradford, ed.], *Speeches of the Governors of Massachusetts, from 1765 to 1775 . . .* (Boston, 1818), pp. 336–396. The passages quoted in the paragraphs that follow are from pp. 5, 7, 11, 13, 18, 19, 20, 31, 35, 56–57, 60, 61, 81, 115, of the pamphlet, corresponding to pp. 337, 338, 340, 342, 344, 345, 351, 353, 364, 368, 369, 379 in Bradford's *Speeches*.

tain doubts about some of the Boston Resolves but vehemently defending the town's right to issue such declarations, pointed out that if in insisting that Parliament's indivisible authority was "supreme" Hutchinson had meant to imply that it was "unlimited," he should realize that he was in effect offering the colonies only the choice between slavery (except for the liberties that might be granted them by "the mere grace and favor of their governors") and "a declaration of total independence." The councilors denied that the choice was properly so narrow. There is no such thing, they wrote, as total, absolute authority: "supreme or unlimited authority can with fitness belong only to the sovereign of the universe"; the supreme authority in all human governments, including that of Parliament, is by its very nature limited. The real question is how to state those limitations and thus to define other alternatives than those Hutchinson had offered. To fix "with precision" the limits of Parliament's authority, "to determine the exact lines of right and wrong," was, they admitted, a most difficult task which ordinarily they would not attempt; but the governor's speech having "made it absolutely necessary" for them to do so, they proceeded to review the essential parts of the constitution that demonstrated the illegality of Parliament's taxing the people of Massachusetts.

The House leaders too confessed that "it is difficult to draw a line of distinction between the universal authority of Parliament over the colonies and no authority at all," but they declared that if they were forced to make a choice between all or nothing they would certainly choose the latter, for "there is more reason to dread the consequences of absolute uncontrolled supreme power, whether of a nation or a monarch, than those of total independence." But why this choice? What if, as Hutchinson said, two independent legislatures *did* make two separate governments? If they were "united in one head and common sovereign" and did not interfere with each other, could they not "live happily in that connection and mutually support and protect each other"?

Hutchinson retorted sharply to the Council, informing them that their efforts to separate out permissible from forbidden powers in a sovereign body "rather tend to evince the impracticability of drawing such a line." Logically, what they were saying was that two supreme authorities could act simultaneously over the same people; but this, he insisted, was simply impossible. The claims of the House he could not so easily dismiss, for he understood the importance of the legal arguments that could be mobilized to defend the idea that two absolute legislatures might coexist within an empire if they came into contact only in the person of the King. It took this accomplished lawyer, scholar, and politician twenty-two pages of closely wrought and learned prose to state his reasons for believing that the chartered authority of the Massachusetts government derived and depended not from the King but from "the *crown* of England" and was "consequently subject to the supreme authority of England," that is, to Parliament.

The debate went on in exchanges of messages for two months, until it exhausted the knowledge, ingenuity, and patience of all involved. The final statement was Hutchinson's, and it was prophetic. You believe, he said in his recapitulation, that "a *subordinate* power in government . . . , whilst it keeps within its limits, is not subject to the control of the *supreme* power." This is illogical, for how can there be "a *subordinate* power without a power *superior* to it? Must it not, so far as it is without control, be itself supreme?"

It is essential to the being of government that a power should always exist which no other power within such government can have right to withstand and control. Therefore, when the word *power* relates to the supreme authority of government it must be understood *absolute* and *unlimited*.

The future looked dark, he said, for "no sensible writer upon government has before denied" the principles he was restating, and if the members of the Massachusetts General Court

are still of opinion that two jurisdictions, each of them having a share in the supreme power, are compatible in the same state, it can be to no purpose to reason or argue . . . It's enough to observe that this disagreement in our principles will have its influence upon all the deductions which are made from them.

And so it did. The powerful influence of "this disagreement in our principles" was felt generally in the two years that followed. Leading Americans like John Dickinson continued to insist — though now with increasing desperation — that "the sovereignty over the colonies must be limited," that "a line there must be," in principle as well as in fact, setting off Parliament's powers from those of the colonial legislatures, and that this line gave to the English government control of the commerce and foreign affairs of the colonies and to the colonial Assemblies "exclusive right of internal legislation," including taxing. But the response was as adamant, as rigidly secured to the traditional conception of sovereignty as Hutchinson's had been. By the middle of October 1774, when Dickinson's view was adopted as the official American position by the first Continental Congress, its ineffectiveness was widely conceded. Spokesmen for England repeated, with what appears to have been an almost obsessive and ritualistic regularity, that if the colonial legislatures were not in principle "subordinate to the supreme sovereign authority of the nation . . . there is *imperium in imperio:* two sovereign authorities in the same state; which is a contradiction." Arguments to the contrary, Joseph Galloway wrote, were nothing but "unintelligible jargon and horrid nonsense"; an independent unit of government within the territory of the principal state, he explained, "is a *monster,* a thing *out of nature";* what the Revolutionaries had taken into their *"learned* heads, philosophers-like," to do was to "conceive that the supreme legislative authority, which is indivisible in its nature, was, like matter, divisible *ad infinitum;* and under this profound mistake, you began with splitting and dividing it, until by one slice after another, you have hacked and pared it away to less than an atom." [57]

There was little point, in the face of such inflexibility, in continuing to press for a formal classification and division of Parliament's powers. Defenders of American claims were forced to move on to the politically more extreme position that the Massachusetts House had maintained. Acknowledging the impossibility of convincing the authorities in England that Parliament's sovereignty might be divisible, they pursued, with careful logic and a wealth of legal learning, the idea of an imperial federation of sovereign states sharing and establishing unity in a single monarch. If, Moses Mather argued, two supreme powers within a single state are really "the height of political absurdity" then let Parliament's power be totally excluded from the colonies. But the exclusion of Parliament's authority would not necessarily mean the total elimination of all links to England. For, he explained, a "state" was, after all, only "a country or body of people that are connected and united under one and the same constitution of civil government," and there was therefore no contradiction in conceiving of two such entities sharing the same king. George III derived his authority as "King of the American colonies" from a source different from that which empowers his rule as King of Great Britain. And since, "when several rights or capacities meet and are vested in one and the same person they remain entire and as distinct as though they were vested in different persons," the King's role as the first

[57] Dickinson, *Essay on the Constitutional Power of Great-Britain,* in *Pennsylvania Archives,* 2d ser., III, 603, 569–589. Cf. article 4 of the Declaration and Resolves of the first Continental Congress. Seabury, *View of the Controversy,* in Vance, *Letters of a Westchester Farmer,* p. 119; [Joseph Galloway], *A Reply to an Address to . . . a Candid Examination . . .* (New York, 1775), pp. 17, 26, 20.

of the three estates in Parliament in no way means that the authority
of that body extends to America.[58]

Others arrived by other routes at this total rejection of Parliamentary
authority in favor of what would become the modern notion of Commonwealth relations. James Iredell condemned the "beautiful theory" of
sovereignty as "narrow and pedantic," "calculated to sacrifice to a *point
of speculation* the happiness of millions," and developed the argument
from the inapplicability of the idea of sovereignty "to the case of several
distinct and *independent legislatures* each engaged within a *separate* scale
and employed about *different* objects." The most powerful presentations
were based on legal precedents, especially *Calvin's Case* (1608), which,
it was claimed, proved on the authority of Coke and Bacon that subjects
of the King are by no means necessarily subjects of Parliament. One of
the most notable pamphlets that developed the details of this claim, James
Wilson's *Considerations on the Nature and the Extent of the Legislative
Authority of the British Parliament* (1774), opened with a revealing confession. The maturing of his thought, Wilson wrote in his Preface, had
been an unwilling progression. He had begun, only a few years earlier,
with the

expectation of being able to trace some constitutional line between those cases in
which we ought, and those in which we ought not, to acknowledge the power of
Parliament over us. In the prosecution of [my] enquiries, [I] became fully convinced
that such a line does not exist, and that there can be no medium between *acknowledging* and *denying* that power in all cases.

Under the pressure of insistent declarations that sovereignty was indivisible he had followed out the "principles of reason, of liberty, and of
law," to their natural conclusion, which was that "the only dependency
which [the colonies] ought to acknowledge is a dependency on the
crown." [59]

But the position that Wilson and others had given up — that Parliament's sovereignty did extend to America but was constitutionally limited
by the powers reserved to the colonial legislatures — had not been forgotten. The movement of thought had been so rapid, however, that this
argument, radical for the mid-1760's, had by 1775 become a conservative

[58] Mather, *America's Appeal*, pp. 44, 47, 34, 46.
[59] James Iredell, *Address to the Inhabitants of Great Britain* (n.p., 1774), in Griffith
J. McRee, *Life and Correspondence of James Iredell* (New York, 1857–1858), I, 206, 207,
217, 219; Wilson, *Considerations*, pp. [iii], 31. On the legal-historical argument, see
Bland, *Colonel Dismounted* (JHL Pamphlet 4), text note 25 and documents cited there.
See also Hutchinson's arguments, *Speeches*, pp. 62–83; and, in general, Adams, *Political
Ideas*, chaps. iii, v.

bastion defended not only in point of theory by authentic leaders of the American cause like John Dickinson who hesitated to proceed to the more extreme position but also by outspoken Tories who, continuing to ridicule the theory of divided sovereignty, accepted it in practice as they sought to establish some measure of rapport with the new forces of American life. To "disavow the authority of Parliament" and still claim allegiance to the King, the New York Tory leader Samuel Seabury wrote in 1774, "is another piece of Whiggish nonsense"; and he cited Pitt's speeches in Parliament and Dickinson's *Farmer's Letters* to defend the argument, now comfortably old-fashioned, that the line to be drawn — in fact if not in theory — between "the supremacy of Great Britain and the dependency of the colonies" should leave "all internal taxation . . . in our own legislatures, and the right of regulating trade . . . [and] enacting all general laws for the good of the colonies" in Parliament. So also, with minor variations, wrote the English traveler John Lind; so too wrote Daniel Leonard in Massachusetts; so too Joseph Galloway in Pennsylvania; so too Thomas Bradbury Chandler in New York; and so too, in the end — though still ambiguously and much too late — did the government of George III.[60]

Through all these years of crisis, when American thought had moved steadily from Otis' archaisms and confusions to Wilson's advanced speculations on imperial federalism, the British ministry, fortified by fresh, militant assertions such as Dr. Johnson's that "in sovereignty there are no gradations," had remained adamant in its refusal even to consider infringing the Declaratory Act. Its final, pre-Independence proposals for reconciliation did not compromise the point. Only in 1778 — after Independence had invoked the ultimate sovereignty of the people; after most

[60] Seabury, *View of the Controversy,* in Vance, *Letters of a Westchester Farmer,* pp. 112, 125; [John Lind?], *An Englishman's Answer, to the Address, from the Delegates . . .* (New York, 1775), pp. 14–16; Leonard ("Massachusettensis") in *Novanglus and Massachusettensis,* pp. 202–203; Galloway's Plan of Union, 1774, in Morison, *Sources and Documents,* pp. 116–118; [Thomas Bradbury Chandler], *What Think Ye of the Congress Now? . . .* (New York, 1775), p. 44. The distinction between fact and theory in accepting a division of sovereignty was drawn with particular clarity by Thomas Pownall, replying to Dickinson's *Essay,* in the 1774 edition of his *Administration of the British Colonies,* II, 89–111. Pownall, an ex-governor of Massachusetts and in general sympathetic to the colonies (see Introduction to Dulany's *Considerations,* Pamphlet 13) conceded that "in the ordinary exercise" of government, Parliament would respect the line Dickinson described, but "that *in the intendment and remembrance of law,* the power of Parliament, as *a supreme censorial or remedial power,* must be supposed to have a right to go to all cases whatsoever." Similarly, though England has "given up forever" the levying of internal taxes on the colonies, she would never allow herself to suffer the "open test of humiliation" involved in formally renouncing that right (pp. 95–96).

of the states had organized their own governments, and the Articles of Confederation of the new nation had been drawn up and submitted to the states for ratification; and only under the pressure of the catastrophe at Saratoga and of France's entrance into the war — only then, in the instructions to the ill-fated Carlisle Commission, did the North administration relent sufficiently to endorse, though still not in theory, the position that Dickinson had advanced so long ago in the *Farmer's Letters*.

Such a grudging concession was by then grotesquely irrelevant to the realities of the situation. The idea that Americans would at that late date be willing, as the instructions to the Carlisle Commission put it, "to return to their condition of 1763" and to do so in such a way that "the sovereignty of the mother country should not be infringed" was unthinkable.[61] The course of intellectual, as well as of political and military, events had brought into question the entire concept of a unitary, concentrated, and absolute governmental sovereignty. It had been challenged, implicitly or explicitly, by all those who had sought constitutional grounds for limiting Parliament's power in America. In its place had come the sense, premised on the assumption that the ultimate sovereignty — ultimate yet still real and effective — rested with the people, that it was not only conceivable but in certain circumstances salutary to divide and distribute the attributes of governmental sovereignty among different levels of institutions. The notion had proved unacceptable as a solution of the problem of Anglo-American relations, but it was acted upon immediately and instinctively in forming the new union of sovereign states. The problems, intellectual and political, inherent in such an arrangement would persist; some were scarcely glimpsed when the nation was formed. The belief that *"imperium in imperio"* was a solecism and the assumption that the "sovereignty of the people" and the sovereignty of an organ of government were of the same order of things would remain to haunt the efforts of those who would struggle to build a stable system of federal government. But the initial challenges to the traditional eighteenth-century notion of sovereignty had been made. Later analysts, starting where the colonists had left off before Independence and habituated to think in terms of "qualified sovereignty," "lesser sovereignties," "the divisibility of sovereignty," would continue the effort to make federalism a logical as well as a practical system of government.[62]

[61] Royal Instructions to the Peace Commission of 1778, in Morison, *Sources and Documents,* pp. 192, 200.

[62] On the history of the debate on sovereignty in the later eighteenth century and early

They would not entirely succeed; the task would be a continuing one, never fully completed. Generations later there would still be those, states rightists and nationalists, who would repudiate this legacy of the Revolution and reinvoke in different contexts the theories of Hobbes and Blackstone, of Hutchinson and Knox. But the federalist tradition, born in the colonists' efforts to state in constitutional language the qualification of Parliament's authority they had known — to comprehend, systematize, and generalize the unplanned circumstance of colonial life — nevertheless survived, and remains, to justify the distribution of absolute power among governments no one of which can claim to be in its nature total.

---

nineteenth century, see, e.g., Adams, *Political Ideas,* chaps. vii, viii; *Records of the Federal Convention of 1787* (Max Farrand, ed., New Haven, 1911–1937), I, 27, 323, 328, 331–332, 467; II, 347, 584; *The Federalist,* nos. 9, 15, 20, 31, 32, 39, 40, 44, 45, 62, 81; Jackson T. Main, *The Antifederalists* (Chapel Hill, 1961), pp. 120–125; Charles E. Merriam, *A History of American Political Theories* (New York, 1936), pp. 254 ff.; and above all, Madison's private speculations, written to Jefferson in 1787, on "the due partition of power between the general and local governments," in Boyd, *Jefferson Papers,* XII, 273–279.

CHAPTER VII

THE CONTAGION OF LIBERTY

O N such fundamental issues — representation and consent, the nature of constitutions and of rights, the meaning of sovereignty
— and in such basic ways, did the colonists probe and alter
their inheritance of thought concerning liberty and its preservation. To
conceive of legislative assemblies as mirrors of society and their voices as
mechanically exact expressions of the people; to assume, and act upon
the assumption, that human rights exist above the law and stand as the
measure of the law's validity; to understand constitutions to be ideal
designs of government, and fixed, limiting definitions of its permissible
sphere of action; and to consider the possibility that absolute sovereignty
in government need not be the monopoly of a single all-engrossing agency
but (*imperium in imperio*) the shared possession of several agencies each
limited by the boundaries of the others but all-powerful within its own
— to think in these ways, as Americans were doing before Independence,
was to reconceive the fundamentals of government and of society's relation to government.

These were, to be sure, probings, speculations, theories, by which a
generation convinced of the importance of ideas in politics attempted to
deal with the problems they faced. But they were not mere mental
gymnastics. Not only did they provide the rational grounds of resistance
to the authority of Parliament but by 1776 they had become matters of
the most immediate, local urgency, for by then the colonies — independent states in all but name — had begun their extraordinary work of
constitution writing. Up and down the still sparsely settled coast of British North America, groups of men — intellectuals and farmers, scholars
and merchants, the learned and the ignorant — gathered for the purpose
of constructing enlightened governments. During the single year 1776
eight states drafted and adopted constitutions (two did so even before
Independence). Everywhere there were discussions of the ideal nature of
government; everywhere principles of politics were examined, institutions
weighed, and practices considered. And these debates — which were but
forerunners of discussions that would continue well into the nineteenth

century, until the political and social meaning of the American Revolution would be more fully realized — were direct continuations of the discussions that had preceded Independence. The same issues and the same terms were involved. Indeed, some of the most original pamphlets written in the entire Revolutionary period appeared in the transition years 1775 and 1776, and treat simultaneously, as if they were a single undifferentiated set of problems, the constitutional questions of imperial relations and of the organization of the internal governments of the new states.

The originality of these discussions of the nature of government and the uses of power was self-intensifying. Thinkers at each stage, impelled by a spirit at once quizzically pragmatic and loftily idealistic, built upon the conclusions of their predecessors and grasped implications only vaguely sensed before. The movement of thought was rapid, irreversible, and irresistible. It swept past boundaries few had set out to cross, into regions few had wished to enter.

How infectious this spirit of pragmatic idealism was, how powerful — and dangerous — the intellectual dynamism within it, and how difficult it was to plot in advance the direction of its spread, had become clear well before Independence. Institutions were brought into question and condemned that appeared to have little if any direct bearing on the immediate issues of the Anglo-American struggle. New, and difficult, problems, beyond the range of any yet considered, unexpectedly appeared.

I. SLAVERY

No one had set out to question the institution of chattel slavery, but by 1776 it had come under severe attack by pamphleteers following out the logic of Revolutionary thought. The connection, for those who chose to see it, was obvious. "Slavery" was a crucial concept in eighteenth-century political discourse. The ultimate political threat, the absolute political evil, it was embedded in the structure of political thought; it appears in every statement of political principle, in every discussion of constitutionalism or legal rights, in every exhortation to resistance. Can any power in this province, a Massachusetts polemicist asked in 1754, "make slaves of any part of the [British] nation?" Who would not choose "to dine upon a turnip, with old *Fabricus,* and be a freeman, rather than flow in luxury, and be a slave?" It was the loss of attachment to a free constitution that had plunged Rome from the summit of her glory "into the black gulf of infamy and slavery." Tyrannical governments reduce people to "a kind of slaves to the ministers of state." An ambitious ministry must be taught "that any attempt to enslave us would be as fruitless as it would be impolitic." *"Those* who *are taxed* without their own consent expressed by themselves or their representatives," John Dickinson wrote, "are *slaves. We are taxed* without our consent expressed by ourselves or our representatives. *We* are therefore SLAVES." Yes, Josiah Quincy concluded in 1774, "I speak it with grief — I speak it with anguish — Britons are our oppressors: I speak it with shame — I speak it with indignation — *we are slaves"* — "the most abject sort of slaves," said John Adams.[1]

This was not simply lurid rhetoric. Slavery as a political concept had specific meaning which a later generation would lose. To eighteenth-century Americans it meant, as one pamphleteer put it, "being wholly under the power and control of another as to our actions and properties." [2] It meant the inability to maintain one's just property in material things and abstract rights, rights and things which a proper constitution guaranteed a free people. Both symptom and consequence of disease in the body politic, it was the condition that followed the loss of freedom, when corruption, classically, had destroyed the desire and capacity of the people to retain their independence: most commonly, when the elements of power had destroyed — by bribery, intimidation, or more subtle means — the independence of the "democratical" elements of the constitution.

"Slavery" in this sense, far from being mere exclamation and hyperbole, was a term referring to a specific political condition, a condition characteristic of the lives of contemporary Frenchmen, Danes, and Swedes as well as of Turks, Russians, and Poles. And it applied equally to the black plantation laborers on the southern American colonies. For their condition was only a more dramatic, more bizarre variation of the condition of all who had lost the power of self-determination. Their degradation — painfully visible and unambiguously established in law — was only the

---

[1] *The Eclipse* ([Boston], 1754), p. 7; Joseph Warren, *An Oration . . . To Commemorate the Bloody Tragedy of the Fifth of March, 1770* (Boston, 1772), p. 6; [John Allen], *The American Alarm, or the Bostonian Plea, for the Rights and Liberties of the People . . .* (Boston, 1773), 1st sec., p. 9; *A Serious Address to . . . New York . . .* (New York, 1774), p. 5; [John Dickinson], *Letters from a Farmer in Pennsylvania . . .* (Philadelphia, 1768), in Paul L. Ford, ed., *The Writings of John Dickinson (Memoirs of the Historical Society of Pennsylvania,* XIV, Philadelphia, 1895), p. 357; Josiah Quincy, Jr., *Observations on the . . . Boston Port-Bill . . .* (Boston, 1774), in Josiah Quincy, *Memoir of the Life of Josiah Quincy Jun. . . .* (Boston, 1825), p. 451; John Adams ("Novanglus"), in *Novanglus and Massachusettensis . . .* (Boston, 1819), p. 23. Curiously, Dickinson's phrase in the original, newspaper version of the *Farmer's Letters* was almost identical with Quincy's: "We are therefore — I speak it with grief — I speak it with indignation — we are SLAVES."

[2] [Moses Mather], *America's Appeal to the Impartial World . . .* (Hartford, 1775), p. 48.

final realization of what the loss of freedom could mean everywhere; for there was no such thing "as *partial* liberty": he who has authority "to restrain and control my conduct in any instance without my consent hath in all." From this point of view it made little difference whether one's bondage was private or public, civil or political, or even whether one was treated poorly or well. Anyone "who is bound to obey the will of another," Stephen Hopkins wrote, is "as really a slave though he may have a good master as if he had a bad one; and this is stronger in politic bodies than in natural ones, as the former have perpetual succession and remain the same; and although they may have a very good master at one time, they may have a very bad one at another."[3]

The presence of an enslaved Negro population in America inevitably became a political issue where slavery had this general meaning. The contrast between what political leaders in the colonies sought for themselves and what they imposed on, or at least tolerated in, others became too glaring to be ignored and could not be lightened by appeals to the Lockean justification of slavery as the favorable fate of people who "by some act that deserves death" had forfeited their lives and had been spared by the generosity of their captors.[4] The reality of plantation life was too harsh for such fictions. The identification between the cause of the colonies and the cause of the Negroes bound in chattel slavery — an identification built into the very language of politics — became inescapable.

It was not grasped by all at once, nor did it become effective evenly through the colonies. But gradually the contradiction between the proclaimed principles of freedom and the facts of life in America became generally recognized. How embarrassing this obvious discrepancy could be to enthusiastic libertarians was revealed early in the period. What could the Colonel (Richard Bland) mean, the Reverend John Camm demanded to know, by asserting that under an English government "all *men* are *born free*"? Does he mean

that *Virginia* is not an *English government,* or that Negroes are not under it *born slaves,* or that the said slaves are not men? Whichever of these confident assertions he undertakes to maintain, and one of them he must maintain, he will find insuperable difficulties to oppose him as soon as he is able to cast an eye on the

[3] [Richard Wells], *A Few Political Reflections* . . . (Philadelphia, 1774), p. 82; Mather, *America's Appeal,* p. 48; [Stephen Hopkins], *The Rights of Colonies Examined* (Providence, 1765: JHL Pamphlet 9), p. 16.
[4] Locke, *Second Treatise of Government,* iv, 23.

situation of *Virginia,* the map of America, or on the condition and rational conduct of his own domestics.[5]

It was an unanswerable argument — but Camm did not choose to pursue it. Few in the south did; for while everyone believed in liberty and everyone knew that slavery was its denial, everyone knew also, as a South Carolinian wrote in 1774, that the abolition of slavery would "complete the ruin of many American provinces, as well as the West India islands." Few even of the most enlightened Virginians were willing to declare, as Jefferson did in the instructions he wrote for his colony's delegation to the first Continental Congress, that "the rights of human nature [are] deeply wounded by this infamous practice" and that "the abolition of domestic slavery is the great object in those colonies where it was unhappily introduced in their infant state"; fewer still lent active support to the developing antislavery movement, however logically it followed from the principles of the Revolution. But though Patrick Henry, like the majority of his neighbors, felt that "the general inconvenience of living here without them" rendered the freeing of slaves in the south impractical, nevertheless he could not ignore the contradiction involved in maintaining slavery "at a time when the rights of humanity are defined and understood with precision in a country above all others fond of liberty"; and, confessing his own guilt and inconsistency, he wrote that he looked forward to the time "when an opportunity will be offered to abolish this lamentable evil." Even in the south the contagion of liberty spread to the institution of chattel slavery in no way directly involved in the controversy with England; even in the south there would be efforts, as a result, in some degree to control it.[6]

It was in the northern and middle colonies, however, that arguments against slavery explicitly associated with the Anglo-American political controversy were heard throughout the period, increased steadily in number and intensity, and resulted in material alterations. At first the rele-

[5] [John Camm], *Critical Remarks on a Letter Ascribed to Common Sense* . . . (Williamsburg, 1765), p. 19.

[6] *Some Fugitive Thoughts on a Letter Signed Freeman* . . . ([Charleston], 1774), p. 25; [Thomas Jefferson], *A Summary View of the Rights of America* . . . (Williamsburg, [1774]), in Paul L. Ford, ed., *Writings of Thomas Jefferson* (New York, 1892–1899), I, 440; J. Franklin Jameson, *The American Revolution Considered as a Social Movement* (Princeton, 1926), pp. 32–33. On the successful opposition to the clause condemning the slave trade in the first draft of the Declaration of Independence, see Carl Becker, *The Declaration of Independence* (New York, 1922), pp. 212–213; and Benjamin Quarles, *The Negro in the American Revolution* (Chapel Hill, 1961), pp. 42–43.

vance of chattel slavery to libertarian ideals was noted only in individual passages of isolated pamphlets. While Boston merchants in 1764 were still content to speak in a matter-of-fact way of the economics of the slave trade, James Otis, following out the idea that "by the law of nature" all men are "free born" concluded that by "all men" was meant all human beings "white or black," and he launched forthwith a brief but characteristically fierce attack upon the whole institution of slavery.

Does it follow that 'tis right to enslave a man because he is black? Will short curled hair like wool instead of Christian hair . . . help the argument? Can any logical inference in favor of slavery be drawn from a flat nose, a long or short face? Nothing better [than this] can be said in favor of a trade that is the most shocking violation of the law of nature, has a direct tendency to diminish the idea of the inestimable value of liberty, and makes every dealer in it a tyrant . . .

So corrupting is the evil, he concluded, that "those who every day barter away other men's liberty will soon care little for their own" — which explains, he added, the "ferocity, cruelty, and brutal barbarity that has long marked the general character of the sugar islanders." The only idea of government such people can have is that which they see "exercised over ten thousand of their fellow men, born with the same right to freedom and the sweet enjoyments of liberty and life as their unrelenting taskmasters, the overseers and planters." [7]

At this point, however, the argument, though logical, was still a digression in the Anglo-American debate; the explicit association of the political claims of the colonists with attacks on chattel slavery was not as yet automatically made even in the north. So, in 1766, the Reverend Stephen Johnson of Lyme, Connecticut, preaching on "the general nature and consequences of enslaving measures" and dilating on the iniquity of slavery and on its "shocking ill effects and terrible consequences" to both enslavers and enslaved, drew his illustrations from the Bible, from ancient history, "the oppression of Holland," and the histories of France and of England under "former popish reigns" but not from the life around him; he confined his "application" of these principles and illustrations to "the impending calamities which threaten us": he did not mention the enslavement of Negroes in America. Similarly, John Dickinson, having defined taxation without representation as "a state of the most abject slavery," declared that he could not conceive of "an idea of slavery more *complete,* more *miserable,* more *disgraceful,* than that of a people, where

[7] *Considerations upon the Act of Parliament* (Boston, 1764: JHL Pamphlet 5), pp. 15–16; James Otis, *Rights of the British Colonies* (Boston, 1764: JHL Pamphlet 7), p. 29.

justice is administered, government exercised, and a *standing army main-tained* AT THE EXPENSE OF THE PEOPLE, and yet WITHOUT THE LEAST DEPEND-ENCE UPON THEM." [8]

But increasingly the connection was made. Samuel Cooke, in his Mas-sachusetts election sermon of 1770, argued that in tolerating Negro slavery "we, the patrons of liberty, have dishonored the Christian name, and degraded human nature nearly to a level with the beasts that perish," and he devoted most of his text to "the cause of our African slaves." Pointing out that God "is no respecter of persons," he begged the as-sembled leaders of Massachusetts to take the initiative in this cause of the oppressed so relevant to their own more immediate cause. And Benjamin Rush, in a sweeping condemnation of slavery, "On Slave-Keeping" (1773), begged "Ye advocates for American liberty" to rouse themselves and "espouse the cause of humanity and general liberty." Bear a testimony, he wrote in the language of the Quakers, "against a vice which degrades human nature . . . The plant of liberty is of so tender a nature that it cannot thrive long in the neighborhood of slavery. Re-member, the eyes of all Europe are fixed upon you, to preserve an asylum for freedom in this country after the last pillars of it are fallen in every other quarter of the globe." [9]

By 1774 this cry had become a commonplace in the pamphlet literature of the northern and middle colonies. How can we "reconcile the exercise of SLAVERY with our *professions of freedom,*" Richard Wells, "a citizen of Philadelphia," demanded to know. There was no possible justification for the institution, he said. If, as some claimed, the slaves were bought from those who had a right to sell them, where are the titles to prove it? Even a convict who clearly "has *forfeited his life* to the laws of his country and is respited for transportation" has papers that show his just condemnation. And if the claim that we are inflicting just punishment on Africans for crimes committed in their native lands ("which is the last wretched argument . . . advocates for slavery insist on") could be substantiated, what would it prove except that the colonists had become "*executioners* [for] an Ethiopian savage government"? The only claim the Americans had over the Africans is the claim of "*force* and *power*";

---

[8] [Stephen Johnson], *Some Important Observations* . . . (Newport, 1766), pp. 5, 7, 8, 9, 52; Dickinson, *Farmer's Letters,* in Ford, *Writings,* pp. 371, 372. See also [Silas Downer], *Discourse Delivered in Providence* . . . (Providence, 1768), pp. 10, 12.

[9] Samuel Cooke, *A Sermon Preached at Cambridge . . . May 30th, 1770 . . .* (Boston, 1770), pp. 42, 41; Dagobert D. Runes, ed., *The Selected Writings of Benjamin Rush* (New York, 1947), p. 17.

and that being the case, "what arguments can we advance in *their* favor which will not militate against ourselves, whilst England remains superior by land and by sea?" A remonstrance against the slave trade by the forthcoming Continental Congress and a pledge by the colonists not to import or buy slaves, would, he declared, "breathe such an independent spirit of liberty, and so corroborate our own claims that I should dare to hope for an intervening arm of Providence to be extended in our favor." He concluded by reviewing the laws of manumission passed in Pennsylvania, Maryland, and New Jersey.

Even more vigorous and more harshly abusive of the hypocrisy of colonial claims in the face of domestic slavery was the Baptist preacher and pamphleteer, John Allen. The "iniquitous and disgraceful practice of keeping African slaves," he wrote in *The Watchman's Alarm,* was a total abomination; it violated God's laws, the charter of Massachusetts, the natural and inalienable rights of mankind, and the laws of society and humanity.

Blush ye pretended votaries for freedom! ye trifling patriots! who are making a vain parade of being advocates for the liberties of mankind, who are thus making a mockery of your profession by trampling on the sacred natural rights and privileges of Africans; for while you are fasting, praying, nonimporting, nonexporting, remonstrating, resolving, and pleading for a restoration of your charter rights, you at the same time are continuing this lawless, cruel, inhuman, and abominable practice of enslaving your fellow creatures . . .

It would not be surprising, he warned, if the Africans too took heart from the Biblican injunction to "loose the bands of wickedness, undo the heavy burdens, let the oppressed go free." They had far greater reason than their masters to do so, for "what is a trifling three-penny duty on tea compared to the inestimable blessings of liberty to one captive?" Joyfully he celebrated those "sincere friends to the rights and liberties of mankind" who were known to have freed their slaves.

As the crisis deepened and Americans elaborated their love of liberty and their hatred of slavery, the problem posed by the bondage tolerated in their midst became more and more difficult to evade. What were they to say to the Englishmen who told them flatly to "put away the accursed thing (that horrid oppression) from among them, before they presumed to implore the interposition of divine justice: for, whilst they retain their brethren . . . in the most shameful involuntary servitude, it is profane in them to look up to the merciful Lord of all, and call Him father!" And what reply could Bostonians give to the Loyalist printer John Mein who denounced their hypocrisy in "ground[ing] their rebellions on the 'immutable laws of nature'" and yet ("It cannot be! It is nevertheless very true") themselves owned two thousand Negro slaves? Some found at least a partial excuse in pointing out, with Jefferson, that repeated attempts by certain colonies to ban the slave trade or tax it out of existence had met resounding vetoes in England so that the good of the colonies and the rights of human nature had been sacrificed to "the immediate advantages of a few British corsairs." [10]

But the excuse was weak, and in any case something more than excuses was needed. Action was called for to restrict "the cruel and barbarous slave trade" and to alleviate the sufferings of the "oppressed and injured Africans." And something even more than that was called for by preachers in the North devoted to the covenant theology: repentance, expiation, for sins so long committed. It was on this note, and with the explicit refutation of Locke's justification of slavery as a proper alternative to condemning criminals to death, that the pre-Revolutionary discussion of chattel slavery in the context of Revolutionary ideology climaxed and concluded. Two powerful pamphlets entirely devoted to the subject of slavery, written by two close friends in the Congregational ministry, presented a broad range of antislavery arguments explicitly associated with Revolutionary ideology and centered on key doctrines of neo-Puritan theology. The first originated as a sermon delivered in Farmington, Connecticut, in 1774 on the eve of the meeting of the first Continental Congress. The preacher, Levi Hart, of the village of Griswold, prefaced his remarks by explaining that his aim was "to treat the subject only in a moral and religious view"; he would not pretend to pronounce on politics. But his sermon was a jeremiad in form typical of the sulphurous denunciations and exhortations by which the Puritan clergy had sought, since the end of the seventeenth century, to keep its version of orthodoxy relevant to the vital public affairs of the society.

He began by sharply contrasting liberty and slavery and by offering a variety of definitions of liberty, from which he concluded that any society

[10] Wells, *A Few Political Reflections,* pp. 79–80, 81, 82, 83; [John Allen], *The Watchman's Alarm to Lord N——h . . .* (Salem, 1774), pp. 25, 27, 28; Granville Sharp, *A Declaration of the People's Natural Right To Share in the Legislature . . .* (New York, 1774), p. 14n; [John Mein], *Sagittarius's Letters . . .* (Boston, 1775), pp. 38–39; Jefferson, *Summary View,* in Ford, *Writings,* I, 440. Sharp's pamphlet, originally published in London in 1774, was reprinted four times in the colonies before the year was out (Adams, "Bibliographical Study," entries 139d–g). On the original, English context of Sharp's pamphlet, see Frank J. Klingberg, *The Anti-Slavery Movement in England* (New Haven, 1926), chap. ii.

that permits its members to deprive innocent people of their liberty or property was guilty of tyranny and oppression. Consider then the crime, the sin, involved in the toleration of and connivance in *"the horrible slave trade"* by the public in the British colonies. If facts did not compel him to, he said, he "could never believe that British Americans would be guilty of such a crime." It had no justification whatever. The idea that slavery was a just and generous substitute for a deserved death penalty was irrelevant to the American situation, whatever its merits as a theory might be. "What have the unhappy Africans committed against the inhabitants of the British colonies and islands in the West Indies to authorize *us* to seize them, or bribe them to seize one another, and transport them a thousand leagues into a strange land, and enslave them for life?" It was now "high time for this colony to wake up and put an effectual stop to the cruel business of stealing and selling our fellow men." For how, when the colonists themselves "are the tyrants," could they plead for freedom? "What inconsistence and self-contradiction is this! . . . When, O when shall the happy day come, that Americans shall be *consistently* engaged in the cause of liberty?" Only on that day will American liberties be established on a lasting foundation, for only on that day will "the hard bondage of sin and satan" be thrown off and "the most perfect liberty" be enjoyed. Christ alone is "the giver and supporter of original, perfect freedom." So, then, be wise in season,

bid adieu to the kingdom of darkness, the cause of tyranny and oppression, enlist under the captain of the Lord's host, fight under his banner, you may be sure of victory, and liberty shall be your lasting reward, for whom the Son maketh *free* shall be *free indeed*.[11]

But it was left to Hart's friend and mentor, Samuel Hopkins, student of Jonathan Edwards, rigorous theologian and powerful advocate of his own, "Hopkinsian," version of predestinarian Calvinism, to make the final statement, and to link most securely the religious and secular underpinnings of antislavery. Hopkins' interest in the cause of the Negro had been kindled much earlier, when he had first come to see the social meaning of his doctrines of "disinterested benevolence" and "general atonement." For several years after his arrival in Newport, Rhode Island, he had worked to free the slaves of masters near at hand, and in 1770 undertook the training of Negro missionaries to be sent to Africa as part of a scheme of colonization he promoted with his friend Ezra Stiles.

[11] Levi Hart, *Liberty Described and Recommended; In a Sermon Preached to the Corporation of Freemen in Farmington* . . . (Hartford, 1775), pp. v, 9 ff., 15, 16, 20, 22, 23.

The crisis of American affairs demanded a full clarification of his ideas, for he believed the cause of the colonies and the cause of emancipation to be indissolubly united. Hopkins' explanation came in 1776 in a sixty-three page pamphlet entitled *A Dialogue Concerning the Slavery of Africans; Shewing It To Be the Duty and Interest of the American Colonies To Emancipate All the African Slaves . . .*

He painted a vivid and affecting picture of the reality of Negro slavery; the viciousness of the slave trade, corrupting to both slavers and enslaved; the horrors of the transportation and marketing of the Negroes; and their treatment on the American plantations. Methodically he examined the common arguments in defense of the practice, rejecting as nonsense both the idea that slavery was a means of bringing Christianity to the heathens, and the notion that a "forfeiture" was somehow involved in their bondage. The Negroes, he said, have "never forfeited their liberty or given anyone the right to enslave and sell them." Yet they are held in bondage by those whose own struggle for liberty they daily witness and whose heroic pronouncements that slavery is worse than death they must continuously hear. "Oh, the shocking, the intolerable inconsistence! . . . This gross, barefaced, practiced inconsistence." The slavery we complain of "is lighter than a feather compared to their heavy doom, and may be called liberty and happiness when contrasted with the most abject slavery and inutterable wretchedness to which they are subjected." Our so-called Sons of Liberty: what are they but oppressors of thousands "who have as good a claim to liberty as themselves, [and] are shocked with the glaring inconsistence"? For such a sin, he concluded, multiplied in its evil by the indifference that surrounds it, we are under divine judgment. In such a state, only calamities will attend our efforts. Our cause will never triumph until the evil is expunged, until repentance and restitution are truly made. For the struggle for liberty in America can prosper only under God's protection, and that will never fully be granted while the enslavement of the Negroes continues. If we persist, Hopkins warned, the vengeance of God will be upon us: He will withdraw from us such protection as He has so far given, and "punish us seven times more." The guilt was universal; let repentance be so too.[12]

Such ideas were weapons. By July of 1776 much had already been done to extend the reign of liberty to the enslaved Negroes. In Massachusetts, efforts had been made as early as 1767 to abolish the slave trade, and

[12] Quarles, *Negro in the American Revolution*, pp. 33–35; [Samuel Hopkins], *A Dialogue* . . . (Norwich, 1776), pp. 12, 15, 23, 24, 50, 30, 52, 54.

in 1771 and 1774 the legislature voted conclusively to do so but was re-buffed by the governor's veto. In the same year the Continental Congress pledged itself to discontinue the slave trade everywhere, while Rhode Island, acknowledging that "those who are desirous of enjoying all the advantages of liberty themselves should be willing to extend personal liberty to others," ruled that slaves imported into the colony would thereafter automatically become free. Connecticut did the same; Dela-ware prohibited importation; and Pennsylvania taxed the trade out of existence. There, too, in 1775, the Quakers, long the most outspoken advocates of emancipation though not leaders in the Revolutionary movement, formed the first antislavery society in the western world. In the south there was at least a general acquiescence in the Congress' in-clusion of the slave trade in the nonimportation program and satisfaction on the part of many when in April 1776 Congress fulfilled its earlier pledge and voted "that no slaves be imported into any of the thirteen colonies." [13]

The institution of chattel slavery was not dead, even in the north, nor would it be, for many years to come. But it had been subjected to severe pressure as a result of the extension of Revolutionary ideas, and it bore the marks ever after. As long as the institution lasted the burden of proof would lie with its advocates to show why the statement "all men are created equal" did not mean precisely what it said: *all* men, "white or black." [14]

2. ESTABLISHMENT OF RELIGION

Whatever one's views of sin and retribution, in strictly secular terms the "shocking, the intolerable inconsistence" of chattel slavery could not be denied: in many minds the cause of emancipation came naturally and logically to be associated with the defense of American liberty against the encroachments of the English government. Yet nothing shows the protean, uncontrollable character of the Revolutionary movement more clearly than the position in which certain of the spokesmen for anti-slavery found themselves in regard to another issue which also took fire

[13] Quarles, *Negro in the American Revolution,* pp. 40–41; Thomas E. Drake, *Quakers and Slavery in America* (New Haven, 1950), pp. 85–90; W. E. B. DuBois, *The Suppression of the African Slave-Trade* . . . (New York, 1896), pp. 42–47.

[14] Quarles, *Negro in the American Revolution,* p. 43. On the carry-over of the anti-slavery arguments of the Revolutionary period to the debates of the ante-bellum era, see Philip F. Detweiler, "Congressional Debate on Slavery and the Declaration of Independence, 1819–1821," *American Historical Review,* 63 (1957–1958), 598–616.

in the heat of the Revolution. For if Otis and Cooke, Hart and Hopkins were fervent in the struggle against chattel slavery, they were members, if not leaders, of churches in some degree established, and these, to others, were as inconsistent as slavery with the logic of Revolutionary thought, *"Freedom from Civil and Ecclesiastical Slavery"* being both, one pamphlet proclaimed in its title, *"the Purchase of Christ."* [15]

The establishment of religion had been a problem for Americans almost from the first years of settlement. Though most of the early settlers had carried with them traditional assumptions concerning the state's responsibility for supervising and enforcing orthodox religious institutions, and though most of the original communities had sought to recreate ecclesiastical establishments, there had been difficulties from the start. In some places, as in Virginia, trouble was created by the physical circumstances of the situation: the scattering of population and the distance from ecclesiastical centers in Europe. Elsewhere, as in Massachusetts, where the physical circumstances were favorable, the very intensity of religious motivation and the desire to specify and enforce a letter-perfect orthodoxy led to schismatic challenges to the establishment. Still elsewhere, as in New York, the sheer diversity of religious persuasions in the population made the establishment of any one church problematic.

Only rarely in the settlement period, however, were difficulties created by anti-establishment principles, and only in one colony, Pennsylvania, did systematic, principled opposition to establishments survive to shape the character of instituted religion in the eighteenth century. Elsewhere the pattern of establishments in religion, like that of so many other areas of life in the colonies, was the result of unsystematic, incomplete, pragmatic modifications of a traditional model. By the 1750's so irregular, so ill-defined, and so quickly shifting were the religious establishments in the various colonies that they defy a simple summary. In the Virginia of Jefferson's youth, the Church of England was established; but the law requiring nonconformist organizations to register with the government was often ignored, especially in the western counties where the settlement of dissenters was actively promoted by the government; nonconformists were not barred from their own worship nor penalized for failure to attend the Anglican communion, and they were commonly exempted from parish taxes. Dissent excluded no one from voting or from holding public office: even Roman Catholics were known to occupy government posts despite the laws that excluded them. And Virginia's

[15] Jonathan Parsons' Massacre Day sermon, 1774 (Newburyport, [1774]).

was one of the more conservative establishments. The effective privileges of the Church of England were at least as weak in South Carolina and Georgia; they hardly existed in North Carolina. There was scarcely a vestige of them in the middle colonies, and where they had survived in law, as in four counties of New York, they were either ignored or had become embattled by violent opposition well before the Revolution. And in Massachusetts and Connecticut, where the establishment, being nonconformist according to English law, was legally tenuous to begin with, tolerance in worship and relief from church taxation had been extended to the major dissenting groups early in the century, resulting well before the Revolution in what John Adams described as "the most mild and equitable establishment of religion that was known in the world, if indeed [it] could be called an establishment." [16] And this had been further weakened by the splintering effect of the Great Awakening. Almost everywhere the Church of England, the established church of the highest state authority, was defensive, driven to rely more and more on its missionary arm, the Society for the Propagation of the Gospel, to sustain it against the cohorts of dissent.

That establishments of such irregularity and weakness should have come under fire at all is a measure of the contagiousness of Revolutionary thought. There had been deliberate opposition to establishments before the Revolution, but it had been scattered and ineffective. In Virginia, challenges had been made as early as the 1740's by itinerant New Light Presbyterian preachers who shaped a spontaneous, formless outpouring of evangelical fervor into articulate defiance of ecclesiastical law. In Connecticut and Massachusetts the religious awakening of the mid-century had spawned uncontrollable groups of "Separates," strict Congregationalists who believed their evangelicalism to be the only true orthodoxy and who therefore refused to accept the legal benefits available to officially recognized dissenters; they attacked the establishment with all the arguments they could muster: arguments from "the Bible, natural law, the rights of Englishmen, covenants, charters, and statutes." Claiming liberty of conscience to be an "unalienable right of every rational creature," they

---

[16] Adams, *Diary and Autobiography*, III, 312. That the Congregational establishments in New England were severe was a commonplace, however, especially among the Anglican opponents of the Revolutionary movement. See, e.g., [James Chalmers], *Plain Truth . . .* (Philadelphia, 1776), p. 64: ". . . it were folly supreme, madness, to expect angelic toleration from New England", where she has constantly been detested, persecuted, and execrated"; in matters of toleration the people of New England were "not yet arrived in the seventeenth or eighteenth century."

had often preferred to suffer imprisonment and loss of property rather than to pay taxes in support of a church not their own; some had ended by advocating explicitly the complete separation of church and state.[17]

This final, extreme conclusion had been argued most forcefully, however, not in New England and not by such humble people as the Congregational Separates, but in New York, by a group of sophisticated lawyers in the course of a campaign against the privileges of the Church of England which in 1752 and 1753 they had carried on in the pages of the *Independent Reflector*. The immediate issue had been the founding, with the financial support of the provincial government, of an Anglican college in New York; but to William Livingston and the other opposition pamphleteers the controversy spilled over into the general question of the establishment of religion. Before the battle was over, Livingston and his collaborators had brought into question the right of any one religious group to claim for itself exclusive privileges of public support, and had advanced for the first time in American history the conception that public institutions, because they were "public," should be if not secular at least nondenominational.[18]

All of these episodes form an important background to the attack on establishments of religion that developed in the Revolutionary years. Yet episodes they remained: uncoordinated, for the most part short-lived, and differing in underlying assumptions. Their conclusions were felt to be deviations from what was normal and proper, not advances toward it. They lacked the legitimacy that flows from broad popular approbation, from long familiarity, or from complete and irrefutable logic; they did not spread beyond the situation of their origins, and they quickly faded from prominence. The open hostility of the Virginia evangelicals to the established church — an hostility so little grounded in doctrine that its professors had not known what to call themselves when asked to state "their creed and name" ("Lutherans," they decided when one of them happened to remember favorably Luther's Commentary on Galatians)[19]

[17] Wesley M. Gewehr, *The Great Awakening in Virginia, 1740–1790* (Durham, N.C., 1930), pp. 49 ff.; George M. Brydon, *Virginia's Mother Church* . . . (Richmond and Philadelphia, 1947–1952), II, 159 ff.; Alice M. Baldwin, *The New England Clergy and the American Revolution* (Durham, 1928), pp. 65, 76, 77, 79. For a descriptive account of the Separates, see C. C. Goen, *Revivalism and Separatism in New England, 1740–1800* (New Haven, 1962).

[18] William Livingston, *et al., The Independent Reflector* . . . (Milton M. Klein, ed., Cambridge, 1963), papers 17–22.

[19] They were ultimately convinced by "an old Scot" who offered them hospitality one night that they were really Presbyterians. Brydon, *Virginia's Mother Church*, II, 157.

— their deliberate opposition to the Church of England had dissolved quickly with the arrival in Virginia in 1748 of Samuel Davies, an astute politician as well as preacher, who channeled their fervor into a decorous Presbyterianism well within the boundaries of official dissent. In New England the intensity of Separatist agitations and claims had eased by the 1760's, and the groups themselves were beginning to disappear, either by absorption into the major denominations or as a result of the disintegrating effect of successive splinterings. And in New York, once the government had succeeded in silencing the *Reflector,* the group and the ideas that had sustained it fell victim to the unruly politics of the province and lost their identity in the tumbling chaos of factional disputes.

These were scattered, uncoordinated, and deviant episodes, fading in the permissive atmosphere of the colonies. But then in the decades of the sixties and seventies they were recalled with new relevance. Acquiring in the context of Revolutionary thought a higher justification, a breadth, generality, and intensity they had not had before, they merged into the broad movement, mingling sectarianism and secular reform, that would result, ultimately, in the disestablishment of religion in the states and in the United States of America.

Anti-establishment sentiment and constitutional arguments against Parliamentary power were intimately mingled from the very earliest pre-Revolutionary years; but the relationship at the start was in a significant way the obverse of what it would become. Two powerful explosions, one in Virginia and one in Massachusetts, overlapping in time and in doctrine with the first major constitutional disputes, brought the issue of church-state relations vividly to public attention.

In Virginia the Two-Penny Act of 1759 (discussed in the Introduction to Pamphlet 4) ignited the colonists' smoldering anticlericalism. The clergy's protest against what they claimed was an illegal devaluation of their salaries succeeded not only in forcing the disallowance of the act in England but in eliciting from the Bishop of London a letter denouncing the people of Virginia for disrespect to the Church of England, laxness in dealing with dissenters, and a desire "to lessen the influence of the crown and the maintenance of the clergy." In their slashing defense of the Assembly and its act, Richard Bland and Landon Carter turned in fury not only against the leader of the clerical "cabal," the Reverend John Camm, but against the clergy in general and against the Bishop of London as well. Whose fault is it, Bland demanded to know, if, as the Bishop charged, the clergy in Virginia were not accorded the respect due the ministers of an established church? The respect they receive is the respect they earn, for they "stand upon the same level with other men, and are not superior to them, as I know of, in station or learning." Obviously an established church was of great importance in any state, and the clergy should be held in high esteem; but there would be limits to that even if none of the clergy were a disgrace to their calling, as in fact so many in Virginia were; for "the preservation of the community is to be preferred even to them."

The issue could not be contained. If the Anglican clergy were under attack, Camm wrote, echoing the Bishop of London, so too was the prerogative of the crown, and if that were reduced "to a mere shadow, to something that has no *weight* . . . we should only hereby sap one of the strongest batteries erected for the defense of liberty and property." Bland did not deny that "the royal prerogative is, without doubt, of great weight and power in a dependent and subordinate government," but the overriding consideration must be the good of the people: *"salus populi est suprema lex* . . . every consideration must give place to it" — even royal instructions when they conflict with it, a fact that is surely "evident to reason" and a "clear and fundamental . . . rule in the English constitution."

But the last, and most famous, word in this controversy was neither Bland's nor Camm's. It belonged to a rising young lawyer, Patrick Henry, who, in one of the Parsons' Cause cases, defended a parish sued by its rector for wages lost through the Two-Penny Act. That act, Henry said in the hour-long harangue to the jury that made his reputation and became one of the most renowned, as it was one of the most extravagant, statements of the early Revolutionary years — that act had been passed for the good of the people; the King who disallowed it "from being the father of his people degenerated into a tyrant, and forfeits all rights to his subjects' obedience." As for the ministers of the Church of England, they had been described by their lawyer as benevolent and full of holy zeal; but they were in fact the opposite: rapacious harpies who would, "were their powers equal to their will, snatch from the hearth of their honest parishioner his last hoecake, from the widow and her orphan children their last milch cow! the last bed, nay, the last blanket from the lying-in woman!" In opposing the Two-Penny Act they had acted with characteristic disregard for the public good and thus violated the principle upon which established churches must rest: "the only use of an established church and clergy in society is to enforce obedience to civil sanctions, and . . . when a clergy cease to answer these ends, the community have no further need of their ministry, and may justly strip them of their appointments." For their behavior in the present case "instead of useful members of the state, they ought to be considered as enemies of the community, and . . . very justly deserved to be punished with signal severity." [20]

In Massachusetts the attack on the evil of an over-all establishment of religion was a response of the efforts of the Church of England to extend its influence into the heartland of American dissent.[21] In 1759 the Church had established in Cambridge, on the very doorstep of Harvard College, a mission of its Society for the Propagation of the Gospel. Assignment to this Anglican outpost would have been dangerous even for the wisest and most diplomatic of missionaries; but the person appointed to the position, East Apthorp, was inexperienced, contentious, and supercilious. Inevitably he blundered. He blundered in building for himself a house "more in the fashion of a bishop's palace than that of a simple missionary," and he blundered, also, in the way in which he replied — indeed, in replying at all — to a series of newspaper articles ridiculing the efforts the Society for the Propagation of the Gospel had been making to rescue the *"natives, Africans,* and *heathens"* of Massachusetts from the "barbarism" of their nonconformity. The burden of his argument — that the original charter of the Society for the Propagation of the Gospel had not confined its mandate "to the conversion of heathens" but had empowered it to maintain episcopal ministers "among the *English* subjects in . . . the most populous and settled parts of the continent" — was both weak, and, to the majority of New Englanders, obnoxious. And its offensiveness was magnified by a number of incidental touches: Apthorp's insistent identification of Christian orthodoxy with episcopacy; his equating of New England nonconformity not only with superstition, fanaticism, hypocrisy, and persecution but with "popery or Mohammedanism" as well; and the arrogance of his assertion that the Society was "above censure" and

[20] William S. Perry, ed., *Historical Collections of the American Colonial Church: Volume I, Virginia* ([Hartford], 1870), p. 461; Richard Bland, *A Letter to the Clergy of Virginia* . . . (Williamsburg, 1760), pp. 4, 19, 18; John Camm, *A Single and Distinct View* . . . (Annapolis, 1763), p. 24; Richard L. Morton, *Colonial Virginia* (Chapel Hill, 1960), II, 811; William Wirt Henry, *Patrick Henry* (New York, 1891), I, 41.

[21] On the Mayhew-Apthorp controversy, see above, pp. 61–62 and Introduction to Pamphlet 3. On Mayhew's earlier career, see Introduction to Pamphlet 1.

"incapable of wrong motives in the application of its liberality." Above all else, however, Apthorp's pamphlet played into the profound fears felt by non-Anglicans everywhere in the colonies, and especially in New England, that an American episcopate was about to be established. It was to this deep-lying anxiety, acutely inflamed in 1763 by the known, and even more by the suspected, maneuvers of the Archbishop of Canterbury, that Jonathan Mayhew, pastor of Boston's West Church and long famous for his advanced views in both politics and theology, addressed himself in his pamphlet attacks on Apthorp and the Society for the Propagation of the Gospel.[22]

In the course of his overwhelming reply, *Observations on the Charter and Conduct of the Society,* Mayhew argued that by *orthodox* the founders of the Society had meant not only Anglicans but all Protestants,[23] and that it had not been intended that the Society's funds would go to support episcopal clergymen in places "where a competent provision was already made for a clergy of the congregational or presbyterian persuasion." The sending of missionaries to places like Cambridge was a violation of the Society's charter, and it resulted only in "setting altar against altar" in the hope that one day nonconformists in New England would submit to the establishment of the Church of England. Such a prospect was frightening to Mayhew. The essential character of the Church of England was only too well known, he wrote: a mode of worship completely alien "from the simplicity of the Gospel and the apostolic times"; an "enormous hierarchy [that ascended] by various gradations from the dirt to the skies"; and a leadership that, historically, included those "mitred, lordly SUCCESSORS *of the fishermen of Galilee*" who had driven the colonists' ancestors from "the fair cities, villages, and delightful fields of "Britain" into the "arms of savages and barbarians" as punishment for their nonconformity. If the Church of England were ever established in New England, he warned, religious oaths would be demanded as they were in England "and all of us [would] be taxed for the support of *bishops* and their *underlings.*" Such an over-all establishment could only be created by act of Parliament or by fiat of the crown; but neither Parlia-

[22] Wendell D. Garrett, *Apthorp House, 1760–1960* (Cambridge, 1960), pp. 12, 13; [East Apthorp], *Considerations on the Institution and Conduct of the Society* . . . (Boston, 1763), pp. 7, 10–11, 17, 14, 23.
[23] Significantly, "the etymology of the word *orthodox*" played an important role in the arguments of the Baptists ten years later, disputing not a threatened Anglican establishment but the actual Congregational establishment in Massachusetts of which Mayhew, formally at least, had been a member. Allen, *American Alarm,* 4th sec., p. 11.

ment nor crown had the right to extend the ecclesiastical laws of England to America, or, indeed, to reach in any other way into the internal affairs of the colonies.

It was this association of religious with secular life in the colonies that in the end dominated the controversy. The point, implicit throughout, was made explicit by Mayhew himself:

if bishops were speedily to be sent to America, it seems not wholly improbable, from what we hear of the *unusual* tenor of some late Parliamentary acts and bills for raising money on the poor colonies *without their consent,* that provisions might be made for the support of these bishops, if not of all the Church clergy also, in the *same way.*

John Adams, among contemporaries, passed the final verdict on the affair. The Mayhew-Apthorp controversy, he recollected fifty-four years later,

spread an universal alarm against the authority of Parliament. It excited a general and just apprehension that bishops, and dioceses, and churches, and priests, and tithes, were to be imposed on us by Parliament. It was known that neither King, nor ministry, nor archbishops could appoint bishops in America without an Act of Parliament; and if Parliament could tax us, they could establish the Church of England with all its creeds, articles, tests, ceremonies, and tithes, and prohibit all other churches, as conventicles and schism shops.[24]

These two famous episodes — the Two-Penny Act and the Parsons' Cause in Virginia, and the Mayhew-Apthorp controversy in Massachusetts — dramatized popular resentments against real or potential religious establishments and brought together the issues of civil and ecclesiastical oppression just at the time when the first constitutional arguments against the extension of Parliament's power in America were being worked out. But the local leaders in both these cases soon discovered that their arguments were two-edged swords, and that they themselves were at least as vulnerable as their opponents. For much of what they had alleged against the home authorities was soon used against them with even greater force by dissenters in their own midst who stood to them as they had stood to Camm, to Apthorp, and to the establishment behind them, and who, arguing against the privileges of the locally dominant churches, found in the vocabulary Bland and Mayhew were using in their constitutional claims against England a powerful reinforcement.

The burden of this internal opposition was borne by the radical sectarians: New Light Presbyterians, Separate Baptists, and Strict Congrega-

---

[24] Mayhew, *Observations* . . . (Boston, 1763), pp. 20–21, 26, 155–156; Richard J. Hooker, "The Mayhew Controversy," *Church History,* 5 (1936), 254; Adams, *Works,* X, 288.

tionalists; with the result that the most advanced pre-Revolutionary arguments for disestablishment — arguments that would eventually bear fruit in all the governments of the new nation — were unstable compounds of narrow denominationalism and broad libertarianism. In Virginia a new influx of radical dissenters overturned the ecclesiastical stability of the 1750's. Waves of Separate Baptists, violently hostile to coercion in any form, uninhibited New Light Presbyterians, and finally, after 1770, Methodists, all clamoring for full freedom of religion, put almost insupportable pressures on the hitherto benign establishment. To deal with these increasingly belligerent claims, the Burgesses appointed in 1769 a Committee for Religion, and instructed it to draw up a new, comprehensive act of toleration. It was a powerful committee that included among other leading liberal politicians Camm's old enemy Richard Bland, who in these years confided to a friend in words that the Congregationalist Mayhew would have approved, that though he considered himself "a sincere son of the established church" he nevertheless embraced "her doctrines without approving of her hierarchy, which I know to be a relic of the papal encroachments upon the common law," and argued that the creation of an American episcopate would produce "greater convulsions than anything that has ever, as yet, happened in this part of the globe." Yet the bill the committee submitted in 1772 reflected more concern for guaranteeing social stability in a situation of increasing ecclesiastical controversy than for easing the intensity of anti-establishment feeling. It proposed to write into law new limitations on the freedom of local nonconformists to worship as they pleased. Dissenters would be required to meet only during daylight hours, in licensed meetinghouses with unlocked doors; baptizing and even preaching to slaves was to be prohibited, and dissenters suspected of disloyalty could be forced to take the test oath and to swear to the articles of the Church of England.[25]

A storm of protest followed the publication of the bill. Petitions were received from nonconformists throughout the colony demanding for themselves "and other Protestant dissenting ministers liberty to preach in all places and at all seasons without restraint." The language of these protests at first remained pragmatic, premised on the continuation of a religious establishment in Virginia and aimed at warding off specific disabilities. But gradually these demands were extended and their bearing on the political claims of the colonies made clear. The Presbyterians of

[25] Brydon, *Virginia's' Mother Church*, II, 249 ff., 367 ff.; Gewehr, *Great Awakening*, chap. v, pp. 146–147; *Virginia Magazine of History and Biography*, 6 (1898–1899), 132, 131.

Hanover County led the effective opposition, claiming full freedom of "preaching or teaching at any time or place in this colony," and pointing out that such freedom "in civil affairs . . . has long been so friendly to the cause of liberty." "The interest of American liberty," they concluded, is "certainly most deeply concerned in the matter." Similar, more belligerent, claims were made by the Baptists, and it became clear that the passage of the proposed bill, fortifying the establishment in Virginia, would create the same convulsion in that one colony that Bland had feared for all the colonies.[26]

The bill was dropped, and in the confusion of 1774 and 1775 the issue was momentarily lost sight of. But as Independence approached and the need to draft plans for a new state government became urgent, the discussion was revived. Petitions and protests now flooded the Assembly, and in the atmosphere of impending revolution they acquired a powerful new appeal. They appeared not as deviant claims against what was proper and normal but as legitimate and persuasive proposals, appropriately part of a general effort to realize more fully and universalize the natural tendencies of colonial life.[27] The unstable union of sectarian particularism and political idealism was consummated. The famous clause of the Virginia Declaration of Rights, passed in June of 1776, stating that religion "can be directed only by reason and conviction" and that "all men are equally entitled to the free exercise of religion according to the dictates of conscience," was written, in its crucial phrases, by James Madison, confessedly influenced by the claims of the Presbyterians and the "persecuted Baptists" as well as by enlightenment ideals. A delegation of dissenters from three counties pointed out that now that the government was to be "new-modeled," considerations of justice, of good policy, and of the need for unity in the military struggle for "our liberty, our ALL," urged the granting of "equal privilege" — in religion as in civil affairs — to all:

[26] Brydon, *Virginia's Mother Church*, II, 378–380, 381, 555, 556, 557.

[27] Thus, for example, the militia and freeholders of Augusta County instructed their representatives not to forget, in their efforts to establish American rights and privileges, "the illiberal treatment which a difference in religious sentiments . . . has produced," and ordered them to work for a declaration "that no religious sect whatever be established in this commonwealth." A reply to this, published in Purdy's *Gazette* by a member of the established church, agreed that "it seems somewhat hard and repugnant to liberty to oblige men to pay towards the support of a church to which they do not belong"; his defense of the establishment was based only on the ground that if such an institution was for the general good those who opposed it must concede to it "in consideration of the many advantages they may be supposed to derive from the state." "The Sentiments of the Several Companies of Militia and Freeholders of Augusta, in Virginia . . . ," Peter Force, ed., *American Archives* . . . (Washington, D.C., 1837–1853), 5th ser., II, cols. 815, 816.

it would be a "great injustice" if one denomination were to be established among people "worshiping the same God, and all struggling in the same common cause." In Prince Edward County, dissenters rejoiced that the Bill of Rights had delivered them "from a long night of ecclesiastical bondage," and they requested the House "to raise religious as well as civil liberty to the zenith of glory, and . . . that without delay all church establishments might be pulled down, and every tax upon conscience and private judgment abolished . . ." Others declared "that their hopes have been raised and confirmed by the declarations of this House with regard to equal liberty," and prayed that "the burden of an ecclesiastical establishment . . . as well as every other yoke may be broken, and that the oppressed may go free." Still others condemned establishments as "inconsistent with the spirit of taxation which supposes those on whom impositions are laid to be benefited thereby." And finally, Hanover County's Presbyterians, professing themselves to be "governed by the same sentiments which have inspired the United States of America," pointed out that now that the "yoke of tyranny" had been cast off and government was about to be reconstituted on "equitable and liberal foundations," the House should keep in mind "that every argument for civil liberty gains additional strength when applied to liberty in the concerns of religion." Asking for "no ecclesiastical establishments" in their own behalf, they stated their absolute opposition to permitting any other group to enjoy "exclusive or separate emoluments or privileges . . . to the common reproach and injury of every other denomination." The only just, reasonable, and effective solution was to abolish "all partial and invidious distinctions" at once and for all time.[28]

In the end, a decade later, in Jefferson's great Act for Establishing Religious Freedom and the disestablishing legislation that surrounded it, this goal, sought jointly by spokesmen for minority denominationalism and enlightened reform, was attained in the state of Virginia. In Massachusetts and Connecticut the same conclusion was reached with greater difficulty and after a struggle that lasted into the nineteenth century. But there, paradoxically, the pre-Revolutionary opposition to the internal establishment had been even fiercer than in Virginia, and the contagion of Revolutionary thought more virulent.

The leadership in the fight against the internal establishments in New

[28] William T. Hutchinson, et al., eds., Papers of James Madison (Chicago, 1962–), I, 112, 170–175; Brydon, Virginia's Mother Church, II, 562–563, 564, 565, 566; Journal of the House of Delegates of Virginia. Anno Domini, 1776. (Richmond, 1828), pp. 25, 7, 15, 35, 48, 24–25.

England in the 1760's and 1770's was taken by the Separate Baptists, "the most radical of the despised and illegal Separates." These doctrinally self-conscious predestinarian evangelists of the eighteenth century, like Jehovah's Witnesses in the twentieth, were fiercely belligerent, acutely sensitive to slights, and indefatigable in righting every wrong done them; they became, however limited and parochial their intended goals, spearheads in the drive towards a fuller realization of equality. Inheriting in the mid-1760's the social views of the earlier Strict Congregationalists, reinforced by large increases in membership, and strengthened by a newly perfected group organization and by the leadership of the fantastically energetic proselytizer and pamphleteer Isaac Backus, they threw themselves into the fight for equal rights.[29]

Their work was cut out for them. Complacent leaders of the favored church declared that "liberty is the *fundamental* principle of our establishment" since each congregation was free to organize itself, pick its own minister, and, once it certified itself as a unit of a legitimate dissenting denomination, gain exemption from "ministerial taxes." How much better off, they said, was true Christianity here than in England. Abroad there was discrimination against dissenters and limitations of speech and inquiry; but at home in New England there was "liberty of conscience, the rights of private judgment and [an acknowledgment of] the absurdity of advancing the kingdom of Christ by penal laws." Superior human authority was disdained: "We regard neither pope nor prince as head of the church; nor acknowledge that any Parliaments have power to enact articles of doctrine or forms of discipline or modes of worship or terms of church communion." [30]

But popes and parliaments were hardly the point. Everyone conceded that freedom abounded in America, in religious affairs, at this level even in Massachusetts. What was galling to the Baptists and to others who resented having to receive freedoms as favors from those with the right to choose the beneficiaries, was the extent to which the local civil authorities, rejoicing in the advocacy of civil liberty, themselves exercised the very powers they refused to allow others to exercise over them. The toleration they permitted was not freedom or equality; they retained, and used, the power to say what was "regular" enough to be tolerated, and to tie up in humiliating administrative detail what they could not deny in principle. The established church of Massachusetts, Backus wrote,

[29] Goen, *Revivalism and Separatism,* pp. 269, 208 ff., 273 ff.; on Backus see pp. 215–224.
[30] Amos Adams, *Religious Liberty an Invaluable Blessing . . .* (Boston, 1768), pp. 39, 32.

"has declared the Baptists to be irregular, therefore the secular power still *force* them to support the worship which they conscientiously dissent from." This is not liberty, but hypocrisy: "many who are filling the nation with the cry of LIBERTY and against *oppressors* are at the same time themselves violating that dearest of all rights, LIBERTY of CON-SCIENCE." The same persons who protest "year after year against being taxed without their consent and against the scheme of imposing episco-pacy upon them . . . impose cruelly upon their neighbors, and force large sums from them to uphold a worship which they conscientiously dissent from." Let those who claim liberty for themselves in one sphere grant it to others in another.

The note was sounded again and again. Suppose episcopacy were estab-lished here, Backus argued in one of a series of pamphlets supporting the claims of the Baptists, and suppose the Congregational church were per-mitted to exist only on sufferance and within an elaborate machinery of certification and approval. What kind of liberty would those presently in power consider this to be? How astonishing, he wrote, "that any of the same men should at the same time show worse treatment to the fel-low subjects here than what they complain of from the higher powers!" They protest against taxation without representation; but the representa-tion they are denied is at least possible: "what must it be to deprive them of a right that never can be conveyed to any representative!" They call themselves *"Sons of* LIBERTY, but they treat me like *sons of* VIO-LENCE." [31]

As the Anglo-American controversy deepened in the seventies so too did the frequency and intensity of the arguments that applied the logic of secular liberty to the condition of religion and the churches. In town after town in Massachusetts — Ashfield, Berwick, Bolton, Hadley, Haver-hill, Montague — embattled Baptists fortified their please for full freedom of religion with language borrowed from the larger controversy. The most famous episode took place in Ashfield, a hamlet of some five hun-dred souls in the western hills of Massachusetts. The Baptists of that obscure village, claiming they had settled the town in the first place and under the worst of wartime conditions, had refused to pay taxes to sup-port the church of "men of a contrary persuasion" (Congregationalists)

[31] [Isaac Backus], *A Seasonable Plea for Liberty of Conscience, Against Some Late Op-pressive Proceedings* . . . (Boston, 1770), pp. 8, 3, 14; Isaac Backus, *A Letter to a Gentleman in the Massachusetts General Assembly, Concerning Taxes To Support Religious Worship* ([Boston], 1771), pp. 10 ff., 20, 21, 18.

who had subsequently invaded the place and outvoted them in the town meeting. As a result their property was confiscated. Their adversaries justified the action on the grounds that the Baptists were not a denomination worthy of toleration at all, but only a group of wild schismatics too "fluctuating and unstable" to remain peaceably within any respectable organization, and forming in their so-called church only "a sink for some of the filth of Christianity in this part of the country." The *"natural rights"* the Baptists claim, it was said, threaten anarchy; they would create a situation in which everyone could exempt themselves "from the payment of public taxes if they should happen not to be inclined to pay them." Like everyone else, they must be bound within their civil obligations and not released "to a state of nature." The General Court must deal firmly with them, for just as it is the duty of the legislature to protect "all regular religious societies of Protestants," so too must it cast off those who "cannot, in any tolerable sense, answer the valuable ends of religion to the community."

To such charges the Baptists replied in a campaign of indignant protest and petition that did not cease even after the issue had been taken to London and decided in their favor by no less an authority than the King in Council. The Ashfield remonstrants explained to the General Court in detail the "distressed circumstances which we think cries aloud for some pity to be showed upon us." They pointed out that the local authorities "say they will not favor us because we are of a different opinion in religion from them." Yet they took encouragement "in this our address, from the consideration of the rights of mankind having been *so well* defined in the votes of this honorable House, by which we are taught to think 'that no taxation can be equitable where such restraint is laid upon the taxed as takes from him the liberty of GIVING his *own money freely.'* " [32]

But the heart of the problem, in Ashfield as elsewhere, was the assumption of a justifiable tie between church and state. It was against this that the Ashfield Congregationalists particularly directed their case, and it was this that Backus primarily attacked in his comprehensive *Appeal to the Public for Religious Liberty,* published in 1773. Notice, he pointed out, the implications of the axiom that "religious liberty is so blended with civil that if one falls it is not to be expected that the other will

[32] *The Acts and Resolves, Public and Private, of the Province of the Massachusetts Bay . . .* (Boston, 1869–1922), IV, 1036, 1040, 1038.

continue." The legislature can compel acceptance of its own definition of proper religious practice; and so orthodoxy in effect is decided by majority vote, though God himself said that only a *"few* find the narrow way, while *many* go in the broad way." Yes, some minorities are tolerated in Massachusetts; but some are not, and the procedure of deciding which are and which are not worthy of this privilege gives to a group of civil magistrates — a body which, since each man must speak for himself before God, cannot in the nature of things represent anyone in matters of religion — the power of passing judgment on "the *springs* of their neighbors' actions." You are condemned, he told the Massachusetts magistrates, out of your own mouths, for you say that England cannot in right tax beyond her own domain: "have we not as good right to say you do the *same thing,* and so that wherein you judge others you condemn yourselves?" Just as "the present contest between Great Britain and America, is not so much about the greatness of the taxes already laid as about submission to their taxing power, so . . . our greatest difficulty at present concerns the submitting to a taxing power in ecclesiastical affairs." The two campaigns for liberty are logically and morally one. The success of one is dependent on the other: how can anyone reasonably expect that God "will turn the heart of our earthly sovereign to hear the pleas for liberty of those who will not hear the cries of their fellow subjects under their oppressions?" [33]

The point by this time was too obvious to be ignored, and other forceful pamphleteers hammered it home. John Allen, in his florid declamation, *The American Alarm, or the Bostonian Plea, for the Rights and Liberties of the People,* informed the members of the General Court that they had pleaded "like men — like stewards, like gods, for the natural rights and liberties of the people . . . And yet will you dare to make or enforce any law to take away by force and power the properties of your brethren not only contrary to their consent but contrary to their own consciences, because they will not worship the golden image which you have set up?" A true son of liberty, he said, seeks to protect "the sacred liberties of the conscience of mankind as well as to plead for and preserve their civil liberties and properties." You have no more right either by the word of God or by the law of nature to tax the Baptists, or any other

---

[33] Charles Turner, *A Sermon Preached Before His Excellency Thomas Hutchinson* . . . (Boston, 1773), p. 39; Isaac Backus, *An Appeal* . . . (Boston, 1773), pp. 16 ff., 23, 28, 30 ff., 43–44, 54, 55, 52.

minority group, and force them to support a religious worship not their own than you have to tax the angels or allow one man to cut another's throat.

> You tell your governor that the Parliament of England have no right to tax the Americans . . . because they are not the representatives of America; and will you dare to tax the Baptists for a religion they deny? Are you gentlemen their representatives before GOD, to answer for their souls and consciences any more than the representatives of England are the representatives of America? . . . if it be just in the General Court to take away my sacred and spiritual rights and liberties of conscience and my property with it, then it is surely right and just in the British Parliament to take away by power and force my civil rights and property without my consent; this reasoning, gentlemen, I think is plain.[34]

Yet still not plain enough; and it was to dramatize what was to many, by 1774, the manifestly logical extension into ecclesiastical affairs of the claims Americans were making in civil matters, that the Baptists undertook their invasion of the first Continental Congress in Philadelphia.[35]

It was an extraordinary episode, demonstrating vividly the mutual reinforcement that took place in the Revolution between the struggles for civil and religious liberty. On the evening of October 14, 1774, the Massachusetts delegates were invited to Carpenter's Hall by a group of Philadelphians to do "a little business." When they arrived they found themselves faced by "a great number of Quakers seated at the long table with their broad brimmed beavers on their heads" together with a conclave of Baptists and local Philadelphia dignitaries. The assemblage had gathered to confront the Massachusetts delegates with the discrepancy between the way "in which liberty in general is now beheld" and the way the Baptists were treated in Massachusetts. Our state and her delegates, John Adams, one of the delegates, later recalled, had thus been summoned "before a self-created tribunal, which was neither legal nor constitutional." The lengthy condemnation of Massachusetts for retaining, inconsistently with her professed desire for civil liberty, an oppressive establishment of religion, was read out by the Reverend James Manning, president of the College of Rhode Island, and it was supported by the Quaker leaders as well as by Backus and other Baptists. The charge concluded with the hope that the Massachusetts delegates would assure the conference, in the name of the liberty they had come

---

[34] Allen, *American Alarm,* 4th sec., pp. 2, 3, 7, 8, 9.

[35] The three paragraphs that follow are derived from Adams, *Diary and Autobiography,* III, 311, 312; and Alvah Hovey, *A Memoir of the Life and Times of the Rev. Isaac Backus, A.M.* (Boston, 1858), pp. 205, 210, 220–221.

to Philadelphia to preserve, that the offensive laws would be repealed and things in Massachusetts placed "as they were in Pennsylvania."

The Massachusetts delegates were astonished and acutely embarrassed. Years later Adams reconstructed the main points of the groping speech he extemporized for the occasion. In the first place, he said, we delegates cannot bind our constituents, and so there is no point in our giving assurances of any kind: further, the establishment of religion in Massachusetts is so mild that it can hardly be called an establishment at all; and finally, the people of Massachusetts were as conscientious as those of Pennsylvania: they too were acting in accordance with their consciences, and therefore "the very liberty of conscience" sought by the Baptists demanded, by extension, that the laws in question be retained. It was a shabby performance. To the last point the Quaker leader Isaac Pemberton could only exclaim with disgust "Oh! sir, pray don't urge liberty of conscience in favor of such laws!" The conference lasted five hours, and it so upset Adams' equanimity that thirty years later, when he came to write his autobiography, he still felt it necessary to explain the whole thing away by concluding that it had been a plot hatched by that "artful Jesuit" Pemberton in order "to break up the Congress, or at least to withdraw the Quakers and the governing part of Pennsylvania from us."

But if such a rationalization was effective in later years, it was not at the time. The Massachusetts delegates returned home to face still another challenge by the Baptists, this one addressed to the Provincial Congress and hurled with even more painful accuracy. A tax of three pence a pound on tea has made a great noise in the world: "but your law of last June laid a tax of the same sum every year upon the Baptists in each parish . . . All America are alarmed at the tea tax, though, if they please, they can avoid it by not buying the tea; but we have no such liberty." These taxes we are determined not to pay "not only upon your principle of not being taxed where we are not represented, but also because we dare not render that homage to any earthly power which [we] . . . are fully convinced belongs only to God."

The same charge came from other sources. To the Baptists' clamor was added in 1774 a Presbyterian voice at least as sharp and shrill as theirs. In his *Freedom from Civil and Ecclesiastical Slavery, the Purchase of Christ*, Jonathan Parsons, the dour, eloquent, fiercely predestinarian New Light preacher of Newburyport, turned a sermon commemorating the Boston Massacre into a memorable plea for religious freedom. He spoke in defense of those "true" Calvinists, of whom he was a leader, believed to be heterodox by the establishment but known among themselves to be the only truly orthodox. They had refused to take refuge within the official categories of dissent, and consequently had been taxed for the support of an establishment not of their own choosing. "If this is not enslaving men in their most important interests, in the name of wonder, what is?" Was it not a shocking inconsistency "that a *province* which holds an *ecclesiastical tyranny* beyond all her sister colonies should be foremost in her attempts for *civil* liberty"? The evil must be expunged if any hope is to be held for success in the cause of civil liberty, "for while we plead for liberty on one hand and promote slavery on the other, our principles are too contracted and corrupt; and if we regard oppression in our hearts the Lord will not hear us." The church as well as the state "must be founded on principles of justice, benevolence, and moderation, or there can be no peace . . . O that court and country may break through the prejudices and selfishness of the age!" [36]

The pressure was powerful; and though the politics of the later Revolutionary years would permit a partial establishment of religion to persist in Massachusetts, the ultimate conclusion everywhere was clear. The disestablishment of religion was neither an original goal nor completely a product of the Revolution. Its roots lay deep in the colonial past, in circumstances that Jonathan Parsons described as a "random way of settling ministers and churches, together with a vile contempt of creeds and confessions . . . all seem to jumble together, and make mere *hodgepodge.*" These unplanned, unexpected conditions, lacking in completeness and justification, were touched by the magic of Revolutionary thought, and were transformed. Our ancestors learned through their own suffering and the example of England, Samuel Williams wrote in his prophetic *Discourse on the Love of Our Country* (1775),

what must be the effect of endeavoring to enforce *uniformity* in doctrine or discipline. This, with the gradual improvement of the human mind that has since taken place, has been leading these colonies into that truly righteous and catholic principle, *universal toleration and liberty of conscience;* which, if not already perfect, we are in the sure path to.

No doubt "the fierce and bigoted" of every denomination will remain inflamed with a desire to establish themselves at the expense of others. But their efforts will never succeed. "The different parties among us will

[36] Parsons, *Freedom*, pp. 8–9n, 7, 9–10, 14, 15.

subsist, and grow up into more large and respectable bodies. And the mutual interests and wisdom of all cannot fail to perfect that universal toleration and liberty of conscience which is so generally and well begun." [37]

3. THE DEMOCRACY UNLEASHED

If some were elevated and invigorated by the support given to anti-slavery and disestablishment sentiment by the extension of the colonists' constitutional arguments, others were dismayed and felt threatened. Slaveholders were generally alarmed, and sought to check when they could not simply ignore such disturbing ramifications of thought. Anglicans in Virginia and Congregationalists in Massachusetts found fields other than religion in which to follow out the implications of their views on civil liberty. Yet the threat in both cases was limited, for the ultimate consequences were known, and the possibility of standing fast — for the present at least — remained. But there was another area — an area more directly relevant to the central constitutional questions of the Revolution than either of these — in which such limitations did not exist: where the possibility of standing fast did not remain; where the ultimate resolution of thought could not easily be seen; where the familiar meaning of ideas and words faded away into confusion, and leaders felt themselves peering into a haze, seeking to bring shifting conceptions somehow into focus.

"You and I, my dear friend," John Adams wrote in 1776, "have been sent into life at a time when the greatest lawgivers of antiquity would have wished to live. How few of the human race have ever enjoyed an opportunity of making an election of government . . . When, before the present epoch, had three millions of people full power and a fair opportunity to form and establish the wisest and happiest government that human wisdom can contrive?" [38] But how fair in fact was the oppor-

---

[37] Parsons, *Freedom*, pp. 8–9n; Samuel Williams, *A Discourse on the Love of Our Country* . . . (Salem, 1775), p. 15.

[38] [John Adams], *Thoughts on Government* . . . (Philadelphia, 1776), in *Works*, IV, 200. The sentiment was widely shared. Thus the contemporary historian David Ramsay wrote in his *History of the American Revolution* (Philadelphia, 1789), I, 356: "In no age before, and in no other country, did man ever possess an election of the kind of government under which he would choose to live. The constituent parts of the ancient free governments were thrown together by accident. The freedom of modern European governments was, for the most part, obtained by the concessions or liberality of monarchs or military leaders. In America alone, reason and liberty concurred in the formation of constitutions."

tunity? Everyone knew the basic prescription for a wise and just government. It was so to balance the contending powers in society that no one
power could overwhelm the others and, unchecked, destroy the liberties
that belonged to all. The problem was how to arrange the institutions of
government so that this balance could be achieved. For Americans the
ideal solution had been England's "mixed" government, in which major
elements of society formed a self-balancing equilibrium of governmental
institutions. The question that emerged with unanticipated urgency after
1775 was how this solution could apply in the new governments of the
American states. For the primary assumptions that had been made concerning the nature of the basic social forces in the state could no longer
be maintained. Factions, interests, pressure groups of course existed in
eighteenth-century America as they do in the twentieth century. But
these, to eighteenth-century minds, were the burdensome impedimenta,
the unfortunate but more or less less inevitable details of public life which
must be borne but need scarcely be dignified by a place in formal political
thought; only occasionally were they included, except by way of denunci-
ation, in political and constitutional theory. The categories within which
the colonists thought about the social foundations of politics were inheritances from the medieval past. The primary units of politics, they
believed, were the three basic orders of society: royalty, the nobility, and
the commons. These essential strata were distinct in composition and
interests. Royalty was unique in its sanctity and prerogative power; it
stood for order and authority, and it symbolized and unified the state.
The commons had the power of numbers and of productivity; it was
unique in promoting liberty and individual expression. The nobility,
centrally important to the constitution, had a stalwart independence
guaranteed by inherited wealth and status which enabled it to mediate
the powerful conflicts generated above and below; it acted as a balance
wheel, preventing the commons, on the one hand, from turning society
into a licentious mob, and the crown, on the other, from becoming
tyrannical. Each was essential, and equally essential, in achieving the
equilibrium in government that brings tranquility and happiness to all;
but any of them, released from the counter-pressures of the others, would
degenerate — into a tyranny, or into a self-aggrandizing oligarchy, or
into an anarchic democracy destructive, in the end, to liberty as well as
to property. Somehow, through great historic struggles, these social
forces had been brought into the English government in a perfect bal-

ance, and it was this that accounted, it was believed, for the political stability that nation enjoyed.[39]

This constitutional miracle the colonists felt they shared, for they too lived within the jurisdiction of the British government. But they lived also within their own immediate governments, and therein lay a problem that many had recognized from the earliest years but that became acute only after 1763 when the foundations of government in America came under intense scrutiny. It had long been known that the balance of social forces in the colonial polities were peculiarly skewed, for one of the basic components did not exist in proper form. The commons was obviously and vigorously present; and so too was the crown in the person of the King's vicegerent, the governor; but the nobility was not. Who could qualify? It was generally agreed that the members of the House of Lords were "peers of England and not of America," and while a few noblemen had lived in the colonies from time to time, these individuals could scarcely be mistaken for an order of American society: even if their numbers had been sufficient, their status and political role in the colonies would not have been.[40] Nowhere in eighteenth-century America had the legal attributes of nobility been recognized or perpetuated. The law made no provision for hereditary privileges; no office of government had been guaranteed by birth. Indeed, the situation was almost exactly the reverse of the traditional, for the closest to a privileged order that existed in the colonies were the councilors, the governors' advisors and members of the upper chambers of the legislatures, but their identity as a social group was the creation, rather than the creator, of their role in government. In a number of colonies a few families had tended to dominate the Councils; but they had less legal right to do so than certain royal officials who, though hardly members of an American nobility, sat on the Councils by virtue of their offices. Councilors could be and were removed by simple political maneuver. Council seats were filled either by appointment or election: when appointive, they were vulnerable to political pressure in England; when elective, to the vagaries of public opinion at home. As there were no special privileges, no peculiar group possessions, manners, or attitudes to distinguish councilors from other affluent Americans, so there were no separate political interests expressed in the Councils as such.

---

[39] On the derivation and development of this classical theory of the English constitution see references cited above, Chap. IV, note 13.

[40] Allen, *American Alarm,* 1st sec., p. 12; Warren, *Oration,* pp. 9–10.

Yet these were the bodies expected to maintain, by their independence from pressures generated above and below, the balance of the whole. The fact that they could not do so was considered to be a major failing of colonial government, though precisely in what way differed according to the colony examined and the point of view of the examiner. In the colonies in which the Councils were appointed by the crown, the results were deplored with particular vehemence by those who stood on the side of the commons. Richard Henry Lee's description of the situation in Virginia was typical. The constitution of Virginia, he explained to his brother Arthur Lee in 1766, was modeled on the excellent pattern of England's. "But unhappily for us, my brother, it is an exterior semblance only; when you examine separately the parts that compose this government, essential variations appear between it and the happily poised English constitution." In Britain, the King, with his executive powers, and the Commons, "representing the democratic interest," are prevented from overextending their claims

by a powerful body of nobles, independent in the material circumstances of hereditary succession to their titles and seats in the second bench of the legislature . . . With us, the legislative power is lodged in a governor, Council, and House of Burgesses. The two first [are] appointed by the crown, and their places held by the precarious tenure of pleasure [of the crown] only. That security therefore which the constitution derives in Britain from the House of Lords is here entirely wanting, and the just equilibrium totally destroyed by two parts out of three of the legislature being in the same hands.[41]

The analysis was a commonplace of the time, and so too was the conclusion. Councilors of the royal colonies, one pamphleteer wrote in the same year, being "proud of the dignity annexed to their office and fond of maintaining such a flattering superiority . . . naturally become tools of that ministry upon whose favor their very existence depends, since the same power which raised them to their exalted rank can, for a single act of disobedience, sink them into their original obscurity." The result, it was widely agreed, was that in the royal colonies where the councilors "are the meanest creatures and tools in the political creation, dependent every moment for their existence on the tainted breath of a prime minister . . . the crown has really two branches of our legislature in its power," a situation, which, if it ever became universal and fully exploited, would result in the death of liberty in America. But the complaints in the royal colonies came not only from representatives of "the

[41] James C. Ballagh, ed., *Letters of Richard Henry Lee* (New York, 1912–1914), I, 19.

democracy." Royal officials also objected when they discovered that in order to run their governments at all they had to appoint to their Councils local leaders whose interests proved to be indistinguishable from those of the lower House.[42]

Such complaints by crown officials were as nothing, however, next to those that emanated from Massachusetts, where the Council was elected. From Francis Bernard, the harassed governor of the Bay Colony during the Stamp Act troubles, and from others in his administration, came a stream of bitter denunciations of "the constitutional imbecility of the Council." With such a perverted middle chamber, Bernard wrote after an electoral purge of the Council, good government could not possibly exist. If councilors continued "to be turned out of their places whenever they exercise[d] the dictates of their own judgments in contravention to the fury of a seditious demagogue," the result would be anarchy.[43]

As the Anglo-American troubles multiplied and greater control over government was sought by officialdom on the one hand and popular leaders on the other, more and more thought was given to the means by which "an independent and honest middle branch of legislature" might be created capable of resisting both "the exuberances of popular liberty and . . . the stretches of the government party when . . . either advanced beyond the constitutional line of propriety." Remedies were sought for this constitutional weakness, and proposals were made that reached into the roots of American society. A number of writers came to the conclusion that the only solution was the creation of a privileged social order from which the members of the Council could be chosen. Ideally, Governor Bernard wrote, a hereditary nobility should be created in the colonies. And though he acknowledged that America was not yet "(and probably will not be for many years to come) ripe enough for an hereditary *nobility*," he saw no reason why "a *nobility* for life" could not be established at once. A life peerage "would probably give strength and stability to the American governments as effectually as an hereditary *nobility* does to that of *Great Britain*." It was a logical idea, which others

[42] [William Hicks], *Considerations upon the Rights of the Colonists to the Privileges of British Subjects* . . . (New York, 1766), p. 12–13; Adams ("Novanglus"), *Novanglus and Massachusettensis,* p. 91; Bernard Bailyn, "Politics and Social Structure in Virginia," James M. Smith, ed., *Seventeenth-Century America* (Chapel Hill, 1959), p. 113.

[43] *Letters to the Ministry from Governor Bernard, General Gage, and Commodore Hood* . . . (Boston, 1769 [Evans 11176]), p. 12; *Copies of Letters from Governor Bernard, &c. to the Earl of Hillsborough* [Boston, 1769], p. 9. See also Edward Channing and Archibald C. Coolidge, eds., *The Barrington-Bernard Correspondence* . . . (Cambridge, 1912), pp. 198, 256–258.

too came to believe was the solution to a crucial problem of government. In New York the scurrilous attacker of Alexander McDougall, the pseudo-Wilkes, attributed much of the current troubles to the fact that England's "AUGUST PEERAGE . . . does not obtain, with its due weight, in the royal colonies." Its pale imitation, the Council, is "equal in legislative and judicial authority; but in influence, privileges and stability, vastly inferior." No one, surely, unless his principles were *"verging to democracy"* — ("God forbid that we should ever be so miserable as to sink into a republic!") — would wish anything but strength for this "essential though imperfect branch of the mixed monarchy." Let us hope that "with the increase of numbers and opulence" the colonies will achieve "a perfect *copy* of that *bright original* which is the envy and admiration of the world!" And the one thing, above all others, that would advance the progress toward that goal would be the vesting of the councilors "with their offices for life." [44]

Andrew Oliver, the provincial secretary of Massachusetts and a close political ally of Bernard, in less rhetorical language, went further. In one of the letters whose publication as a pamphlet in 1773 so inflamed public opinion in Massachusetts he stated that the necessary independence of the middle branch could never be achieved under the present circumstances. A way must be found "to put a man of fortune above the common level and exempt him from being chosen by the people into the lower offices" where he might be subject to popular intimidation. The best solution, as he saw it, was to create "an order of patricians or esquires . . . to be all men of fortune or good landed estates" appointed to that rank for life by act of the governor and Council; from among this social order members of the Council would be chosen, and on them would be bestowed "a title one degree above that of esquire."

Many, of course, disagreed with such proposals. John Adams believed that arguments in favor of creating an American life peerage were part of the general plot against liberty hatched in the corrupt centers of power in England. But ideas in favor of creating some kind of social basis for constitutional balance were widespread, even among those who opposed the strengthening of English power in America. William Drayton, who knew well enough that the colonies did "not yet desire

---

[44] [William H. Drayton], *A Letter from Freeman of South-Carolina . . .* (Charleston, 1774), p. 4; *Select Letters on the Trade and Government of America . . . by Governor Bernard . . .* (2d ed., London, 1774), p. 83; *No. 3. The Dougliad. On Liberty . . .* [New York, 1770], pp. 2–3.

dignities, lordships, and dukedoms," believed that the main constitutional difficulty in the colonies lay in the appointment to Council seats of "more strangers from England than men of rank in the colony," and urged that councilors be appointed for life from among those qualified not only by local birth and residence but by local property in sufficient quantity to distinguish them in an unmistakable way from the population at large and make them independent of pressures and temptations from any source.[45]

The idea that constitutional liberty was bound up with the mediating political power of a privileged social order persisted into the turmoil of the Revolutionary crisis, but it came under new pressures and was challenged by the more advanced thinkers of the time. If America breaks free of English control, it was asked, what would become of the liberty-preserving balance? What elements would there be to be balanced? Monarchy as a social order would obviously be gone. The commons, on the other hand, would most certainly and substantially be there. And that great guarantor of liberty, the middle order?

The idea that the newly independent American states, conceived in the spirit of equal rights and privileges and formed out of a remarkably equalitarian tradition, would deliberately create a privileged order was unthinkable. It was even ludicrous, as the Tory author of *What Think Ye of the Congress Now?* exuberantly pointed out in analyzing the Continental Congress's activities. "An American *House of Lords* is in agitation," he wrote, to be composed of hereditary "orders of the American nobility."

> I am ravished and transported at the foresight of the American grandeur . . . Oh! how we shall shine with dukes in America! There will be no less than fifty three of them . . . The Committees of Correspondence will furnish us with marquises; and the Committees of Observation, with earls. The viscounts may consist of heroes that are famed for their exploits in *tarring and feathering;* and the barons, or lowest order, of those whose merit has been signalized in burning such pamphlets as they were unable to answer.

[45] *Copy of Letters Sent to Great-Britain by His Excellency Thomas Hutchinson . . . and Several Other Persons* . . . (Boston, 1773), p. 31; Adams ("Novanglus"), *Novanglus and Massachusettensis,* pp. 21–22; Drayton, *Letter from Freeman,* pp. 32, 18 (cf. 12). Adams' opponent "Massachusettensis" (Daniel Leonard), who in the end advocated nothing more drastic than filling all the Council seats in the colonies by crown appointment, favored that solution because it was at least an approximation of the proper arrangement which was ruled out because "the infant state of the colonies does not admit of a peerage." *Novanglus and Massachusettensis,* p. 194. For Adams' "Sixth principle of revolution . . . *the necessity of resisting the introduction of a royal or Parliamentary nobility or aristocracy into the country,"* see *Collections of the Massachusetts Historical Society,* 5th ser., IV, 344.

No one seriously proposed to create a new social basis for the middle level of government. But what would the result be? Republican states, of course. This in itself — in view of the Commonwealth derivation of some of the colonists' most cherished ideas, in view also of the high esteem in which successful republics were held, and in view of the "genius of the Americans, their republican habits and sentiments" — was a matter, for most Americans, of satisfaction. But it was a matter also of concern, for while the condition of life in America and the moral qualities of the people made the creation of republics peculiarly feasible, other circumstances made their survival problematic.[46]

Republics had always been known to be delicate polities, peculiarly susceptible to inner convulsions and outer pressures. And the larger the state the greater the danger. Monarchy, it was generally agreed, was best suited to extensive domains, popular government to small territories. The great and glorious republics of the past — "the ancient republics — Rome, Carthage, Athens, etc.," and more recently Switzerland and Holland — had all been small in size compared with the united colonies, compared even with most of the individual states. Republican government "may do well enough for a single city or small territory, but would be utterly improper for such a continent as this. America is too unwieldy for the feeble, dilatory administration of democracy."[47]

"Democracy" — this was the point. "Republic" and "democracy" were words closely associated in the colonists' minds; often they were used synonymously; and they evoked a mixed response of enthusiasm and foreboding. For if "republic" conjured up for many the positive features of the Commonwealth era and marked the triumph of virtue and reason, "democracy" — a word that denoted the lowest order of society as well as the form of government in which the commons ruled — was generally associated with the threat of civil disorder and the early assumption of power by a dictator.[48] Throughout the colonial period, and increasingly

[46] [Thomas Bradbury Chandler], *What Think Ye of the Congress Now?* . . . (New York, 1775), pp. 34–35; Ramsay, *History,* I, 350. On the "quick transition from monarchy to republic in form and belief," see Cecelia M. Kenyon, "Republicanism and Radicalism in the American Revolution . . . ," *W.M.Q.,* 3d ser., 19 (1962), 165–166; *Papers of Thomas Jefferson* (Julian P. Boyd, ed., Princeton, 1950–), II, 26.

[47] [Charles Inglis], *The True Interest of America* . . . (Philadelphia, 1776), 17, 49 ff.; Jonathan Boucher, *A View of the Causes and Consequences of the American Revolution* . . . (London, 1797), p. lxix.

[48] Rev. Samuel Johnson to the Archbishop of Canterbury, July 13, 1760, quoted in Oscar Zeichner, *Connecticut's Years of Controversy* (Chapel Hill, 1949), p. 28; Madison to Jefferson, October 24, 1787, Boyd, *Jefferson Papers,* XII, 276–277; *The Federalist,* no. 14; Roy N. Lokken, "The Concept of Democracy in Colonial Political Thought," *W.M.Q.,*

in the early Revolutionary years, the dangers of "democratical despotism" preyed on the minds not merely of crown officials and other defenders of prerogative, but of all enlightened thinkers: clerics like Andrew Eliot, who pointed out the "many inconveniencies which would attend frequent popular elections"; and lawyers like John Dickinson, who believed that "a people does not reform with moderation," or like William Drayton, who stated forthrightly that he was as desirous of checking "the exuberances of popular liberty" as he was the excesses of prerogative. One could not simply "collect and assemble together the tailors and the cobblers and the ploughmen and the shepherds" of a vast domain and expect them to "treat and resolve about matters of the highest importance of state." They would not know enough, they would not be skilled enough in government, they would not be sufficiently disinterested or independent of pressures to manage a government properly. Surely tradition and the lessons of history indicated that without an economically independent, educated, leisured order of society standing securely and permanently above the petty selfishness of multitudes of ordinary men scattered through half a continent, nothing would be expressed in government but "infinite diversity or particular interests [and] dissonant opinions"; and the result might well be chaos.[49]

3d ser., 16 (1959), 570–580. Cf. Robert R. Palmer, "Notes on the Use of the Word 'Democracy,' 1789–1799," *Political Science Quarterly,* 68 (1953), 203–226. For a characteristic description of how democracies succumb to demagogues, see [James Chalmers], *Additions to Plain Truth* . . . (Philadelphia, 1776), pp. 128–129. For John Adams' frantic efforts to keep the distinction between a democracy and a republic clear ("I was always for a free republic, not a democracy, which is as arbitrary, tyrannical, bloody, cruel, and intolerable a government as that of Phalaris with his bull is represented to have been. Robespierre is a perfect exemplification of the character of the first bellwether in a democracy"), and for his bewildering attempts to define republicanism so as to accommodate the balance of the English constitution without "either an hereditary king or an hereditary nobility," see his letters to Mercy Warren, 1807, in *Collections of the Massachusetts Historical Society,* 5th ser., IV, 394, 325, 353, 473. His conclusion that he "never understood" what a republican government was ("and I believe no other man ever did or ever will") appears to be well substantiated by his subsequent statement that "to speak technically, or scientifically, if you will, there are monarchical, aristocratical, and democratical republics" (*Works,* X, 378). Throughout, however, he was grappling with the problem of recreating the "equipoised" balance of the English constitution in the circumstances of the American states. Cf. Robert R. Palmer, *The Age of the Democratic Revolution* . . . *The Challenge* (Princeton, 1959), pp. 58–59, 267–276.

[49] *Copies of Letters from Governor Bernard,* p. 16; [John Randolph], *Considerations on the Present State of Virginia* ([Williamsburg], 1774), in Earl G. Swem edition (New York, 1919), pp. 15, 17; Andrew Eliot, *A Sermon Preached Before His Excellency Francis Bernard* . . . (Boston, 1765), p. 49; Dickinson, *Farmer's Letters,* in Ford, *Writings,* p. 387; Drayton, *Letter from Freeman,* p. 4; Inglis, *True Interest of America,* pp. 24, 53; [John Lind?], *An Englishman's Answer to the Address from the Delegates* . . . (New York, 1775), p. 19; Edward Barnard, *A Sermon Preached Before His Excellency Francis Bernard* . . . (Boston, 1766), p. 13.

How then, in a society where "no distinction of ranks existed . . . and none were entitled to any rights but such as were common to all," and where the government could by definition express only the will of "the democracy" could the liberty-saving balance be preserved? What, indeed, were the elements to be balanced, and by what organs of government should their interests be expressed?[50] The discussion of these crucial questions — questions upon which the future character of public life in America would depend — began when the burning public issue was still the colonies' relation to England and ended a decade or more later in the revisions of the first state constitutions. Between the two points was a continuous, unbroken line of intellectual development and political experience. It bridged two intellectual worlds: the mid-eighteenth-century world of Montesque, still vitally concerned with a set of ideas derived from Aristotelian, Polybian, Machiavellian, and seventeenth-century radical sources, and the quite different world of Madison and Tocqueville. Between the two was not so much a transition of ideas as a transformation of problems, the ultimate characteristics of which may be seen emerging indeliberately and unsurely in the passionate debate touched off by Paine's *Common Sense*.

For the intellectual core of that brilliant pamphlet advocating the independence of the colonies was its attack on the traditional conception of balance as a prerequisite for liberty. The assumption of the admirers of "the so much boasted constitution of England" that the balance of socio-constitutional forces was liberty-preserving, Paine proclaimed, was a fallacy. "The more simple anything is," he argued, "the less liable it is to be disordered, and the easier repaired when disordered." The constitution of England is "so exceedingly complex" that its evils can scarcely be diagnosed. What it consists of, really, is "the base remains of two ancient tyrannies" — "monarchical tyranny in the person of the King . . . [and] aristocratical tyranny in the persons of the peers" — thinly overlaid with "new republican materials in the persons of the commons, on whose virtue depends the freedom of England." The famous notion "that the constitution of England is a *union* of three powers reciprocally *checking* each other is farcical," and he proceeded to specify its emptiness and self-contradiction. What liberty there was in England was *"wholly owing to the constitution of the people, and not to the constitution of the*

---

[50] The majority in all the states, Ramsay wrote, "saw and acknowledged the propriety of a compounded legislature, yet the mode of creating two branches out of a homogeneous mass of people was a matter of difficulty." Ramsay, *History*, I, 351.

government." In America, where the character of the people was ideal for the attainment of liberty, institutions should be devised that conformed not to inherited prejudices and the accidents of history but to the true principles of human liberty. Let the American colonies cast off the chains that tie them to England and its corrupt monarchy and as independent states create unicameral assemblies chosen annually by a "more equal" system of representation than heretofore and presided over by "a president only." And let "a continental charter, or charter of the United Colonies (answering to what is called the Magna Carta of England)" be framed to provide for a unicameral assembly for the nation as well, selected by the same electorate and also presided over by a president, chosen from the various states in rotation. "But where, says some, is the King of America? I'll tell you, friend, he reigns above, and doth not make havoc of mankind like the Royal Brute of Great Britain." [51]

It was a superbly rhetorical and iconoclastic pamphlet whose slashing attack upon the English monarchy — the one remaining link, in early 1776, between England and the colonies — and upon the concept of balance in the constitution made it an immediate sensation. But if Paine was with the exception of Marx "the most influential pamphleteer of all time," [52] he was also one of the most controversial. *Common Sense* had scarcely been published when it came under strong attack, not only by loyalists but by some of the most ardent patriots who feared the tendencies of Paine's constitutional ideas as much as they approved his pleas for Independence.

The Tories' attack began with James Chalmers' ponderous *Plain Truth,* which condemned Paine's views of society and human nature, and defended the English constitution "which with all its imperfections is, and ever will be, the pride and envy of mankind." All the well-known elements of "this beautiful system" were necessary for freedom: without the crown "our constitution would immediately degenerate into democracy" — a plausible enough kind of state no doubt, but one much favored by demagogues who well know that it, above all other forms of government, was susceptible to absolute corruption. "If we examine the republics of Greece and Rome, we ever find them in a state of war, domestic or foreign." Holland, which survived only because of England's support, had participated "in wars the most expensive and bloody ever waged by

[51] [Thomas Paine], *Common Sense* . . . (Philadelphia, 1776), in Moncure D. Conway, ed., *The Writings of Thomas Paine* (New York, 1894–1896), I, 71, 72, 74, 87, 97, 98, 99.
[52] Harold Laski, quoted in Harry H. Clark, ed., *Thomas Paine* (New York, 1961), p. cl.

mankind." Even Switzerland had fared badly: its "bleak and barren mountains" had not preserved its constitution from assault by "ambition, sedition, and anarchy." The "quixotic system" of government proposed by Paine was "really an insult to our understanding" and would soon give way "to government imposed on us by some Cromwell of our armies," for when popular legislatures presumed to create armies they soon became their victims, unless like Holland they somehow managed "to drown [their] garrisons." Even if dictatorship were avoided, Paine's Congress would become the center of controversies that would conclude in "all the misery of anarchy and intestine war." [53]

A more sophisticated Tory attack on Paine's constitutional ideas, Charles Inglis' *True Interest of America,* was less influential since the entire first printing of the pamphlet was destroyed by a Whig mob; by the time a new edition was prepared independence had been declared and the pamphlet was largely ignored. Yet it is in some ways more revealing than *Plain Truth,* for while Inglis too could fulminate and fume, he understood Paine thoroughly, and analyzed with notable clarity the logic and evidence of his views. In the end Inglis endorsed the traditional idea that monarchy alone is suited to the government of an extensive domain and that popular governments can survive only in small territories where the inhabitants form a homogeneous community with a unified economic interest.[54]

Paine's most influential opponents, however, were not Tories but those who agreed with him on the question of independence but who disagreed with his constitutional proposals. John Adams, who distrusted him from the instant he laid eyes on him (or so he said in later years) and called him "*a star of disaster*" whose constitutional ideas flowed either from "honest ignorance or foolish superstition on one hand or

---

[53] Chalmers, *Plain Truth,* pp. 3, 4, 8, 11, 10, 62, 63, 65. "Rationalis," in an essay published as an Appendix to *Plain Truth,* continued the defense of the English constitution, claiming that the trouble with England was not its constitution but the use made of it by corrupt politicians. "The infinite distractions and mischiefs which have happened in the ancient and modern republics" were only too well known: lacking balance and control, these governments bred factions one of which in each case triumphed over the others, and turned itself into "a many-headed monster, a tyranny of many." "Scenes of blood and devastation . . . the fury of one party encountering the rage of another . . . [men] as fierce and savage as wolves and tigers . . . terrible disorders, outrage, and confusion . . . arbitrary power" — these were the fruits of governments dominated by the democracy, in Greece, in Carthage, in Rome, in Holland, and even in England when Cromwell seized the power from the Commonwealth and ruled "with absolute sway" (pp. 71, 75–78).

[54] Inglis, *True Interest,* p. 17. On the printing history of the pamphlet, which was originally entitled *The Deceiver Unmasked* . . . , see Adams, "Bibliographical Study," entries 219a–c.

from willful sophistry and knavish hypocrisy on the other," denounced Paine's advocacy of unicameral assemblies in both states and nation, and, fearing the effect "so popular a pamphlet might have among the people," set about to put things right.

What bothered Adams most about *Common Sense* was that its plan of government "was so democratical, without any restraint or even an attempt at any equilibrium or counterpoise, that it must produce confusion and every evil work." The premise of his own plan, sketched in his *Thoughts on Government*, which circulated among the constitution-makers of several states in manuscript in the spring of 1776, was that it was possible to devise republican governments with inner balances as effective as those of a mixed monarchy. It was possible because a republic was, by proper definition, only "an empire of laws, and not of men," and this permitted "an inexhaustible variety" of institutional forms "because the possible combinations of the powers of society are capable of innumerable variations." In an extensive country, direct assembly of the whole population was out of the question, and so the first step was "to depute power from the many to a few of the most wise and good" who should form in their assembly "an exact portrait of the people at large . . . equal interests among the people should have equal interests in it." Yet however representative of the interests of society this single assembly might be, it should not be given control of all the branches of government, for it was the nature of popular assemblies to be fickle, "productive of hasty results and absurd judgments," avaricious, and ambitious. Difficult for the electorate to control, an unchecked representative assembly would quickly make itself permanent, exempt itself from the burdens it laid on its constituents, and pass and execute laws for its own benefit. And in any case popular assemblies were unsuited to exercise certain of the powers of government: they were too open and inefficient to act as an executive, and too slow in procedure and ignorant of the law to act as a judiciary. The organization of government "ought to be more complex" than a single unicameral assembly. Even separating the executive from the legislative power and placing it in the hands of an organ of government other than the assembly would not be sufficient, for "these two powers will oppose and encroach upon each other until the contest shall end in war." There would have to be also "a distinct assembly . . . as a mediator between these two extreme branches." Chosen by the representative assembly, it "should have a free and independent exercise of its judgment and consequently a negative voice in the legislature." Let the two houses together choose annually an executive capable of exercising independent judgment to the extent of vetoing acts of the legislature. Distinct from all of this should be the judiciary, composed of men of learning, legal experience, and wisdom. "Their minds should not be distracted with jarring interests," and they should be guaranteed independence by life tenures. Such a republican system, expressing but yet controlling and refining the will of the people, would create an "arcadia or elysium" compared with all other governments "whether monarchical or aristocratical." [55]

The proposal was necessarily conjectural — alternative possibilities were suggested throughout — and it was crowded with ambiguities and paradoxes. What was there in the character of the middle branch that distinguished its members from the population in general? What did it represent? How could it retain its independence if it were elected annually by a body extremely sensitive to public opinion? Its similarities to the middle bodies of other governments were superficial, for it could not be thought of as embodying a separate order or interest in a society that consisted of only one order. And it could not constitute a distinct function of government, for those — the legislative, executive, and judicial — were otherwise provided for. What was clear throughout, however, was that Adams was seeking to perpetuate that "balance between . . . contending powers" that had been the glory of England's uncorrupted constitution.

The point was widely endorsed, and in other pamphlets of 1776 more fully explored. In Virginia, Adams' pamphlet arrived amid the "welter of proposed drafts of constitutions" then before the legislature, and it elicited a mixed reaction. Patrick Henry gave it his highest accolade by saying that its ideas were "precisely the same [as those] I have long since taken up," and wrote that he hoped it would help influence those "opulent families" known to be working for the establishment of aristocratic rather than republican forms of government. What precisely these counter-revolutionary anti-republicans had in mind, and the extent of their agreement with Adams on the key point of the anomalous middle chamber, was made clear in what Henry called a "silly thing" and Richard Henry Lee described as a "contemptible little tract," Carter Braxton's *Address to the Convention of . . . Virginia*, written for the specific purpose of refuting Adams' *Thoughts on Government*.

[55] Adams, *Diary and Autobiography*, III, 330, 331, 333; Adams, *Thoughts on Government*, in *Works*, IV, 194, 195, 196, 198, 200.

The present tyranny of the British government, Braxton wrote, is not, as Paine had said, intrinsic to its structure but the result of "a monied interest" having usurped the power of the crown and destroyed "those barriers which the constitution had assigned to each branch" of the government. Let not the whole be condemned for the momentary corruption of a part. Let Virginia, in principle at least, "adopt and perfect that system which England has suffered to be so grossly abused and the experience of the ages has taught us to venerate." Restore the independence of the branches lost in England. Let there be a popular assembly from which the blood-sucking adherents of the moneyed interests would be excluded and the system of representation made "equal and adequate" so that the prerogative would not be able to corrupt it. Let the house of representatives choose a governor to serve for life and a council of state to constitute "a distinct or intermediate branch of the legislature, and hold their places for life in order that they might possess all the weight, stability, and dignity due to the importance of their office" as well as the time and means for the reflective study of policies and laws. Only such an independent, superior "second branch of the legislature" would be able to "mediate and adjust" the differences that might arise between the governor and the house, "investigate the propriety of laws, and often propose such as may be of public utility." Such a government might have certain failings, but it would at least avoid the evils of popular governments, "fraught with all the tumult and riot incident to simple democracy," that some were now advocating. "Democratical" governments have rarely succeeded, for the mass of the people have only rarely had the power of self-denial, the disdain of riches, of luxury, and of dominance over others necessary to sustain such governments. They have survived only in small countries "so sterile by nature" that men, of necessity equally poor, had no temptation to seek and use power in defense of their interests. The very promise of life in America argued against the stability of democratic governments.[56]

Others in Virginia, including some of those who were striving deliberately to establish a government "very much of the democratic kind," agreed that a "second branch of legislation" was necessary. Even Jefferson, whose draft constitution for his state was a far more "radical departure" than could possibly be accepted, not only provided for a "senate"

[56] Boyd, *Jefferson Papers,* I, 333, 335; Adams, *Works,* IV, 201; [Carter Braxton], *An Address to the Convention of . . . Virginia . . .* (Philadelphia, 1776), pp. 10, 13, 11, 22, 20, 23, 15–16, 18.

but so devised the election of its members that they would be, once chosen, "perfectly independent of their electors"; and though he felt that his device — election of the senators by the representatives for a non-renewable term of nine years — would provide the necessary independence, he said that he "could submit, though not so willingly, to an appointment [of senators] for life or to anything rather than a mere creation by and dependence on the people." And the plan George Mason prepared for the state's official drafting committee provided for the election of the upper house not by the people but by a separate group of specifically elected "deputies or sub-electors" whose sole function it would be to choose members of the upper house from among those possessing "an estate of inheritance of lands in *Virginia* of at least two thousand pounds value." [57]

There were almost as many variations in these constitutional programs as there were writers, for all proposals had to be extemporized from unevenly applicable models in circumstances imperfectly understood. Braxton was alarmed at the "democratical" tendencies of Adams' thought, and Adams was horrified by the same drift in Paine's. There were depths below depths, and at the very bottom of the descent from a mixed monarchy *manqué* to a total repudiation of complexity and balance in society and government was an ill-written pamphlet of thirteen pages published, probably in New England, without identification of author, printer, or place of publication.

Dedicated "to the honest *farmer* and *citizen*," *The People the Best Governors* developed, incompletely yet repetitiously, the theme stated in its title. "The people know best their own wants and necessities, and therefore are best able to rule themselves." They must themselves control all branches of government, and if the dispersal of population requires that representation be the basic form of government, safeguards must immediately be erected against any effort of the representatives to act independently of the people. It must be firmly established that the power of representatives "ought never to extend any farther than barely the making of laws," and that they were never to create by their own determination additional organs of government. They might appoint a Council, but only for purposes of advice: "for the representatives to appoint a Council with a negative authority is to give away that power which they have no right to do, because they themselves derived it from the people." It would amount to the creation of an independent upper chamber of the legisla-

[57] *Letters of Richard Henry Lee,* I, 203; Boyd, *Jefferson Papers,* I, 334, 504, 366.

ture: but what, or whom, could such a body represent? It too would be "virtually the representatives of the people," and as such could not be empowered by any other body than the electorate.[58]

But it was in Pennsylvania in 1776 that the full range of possibilities in devising governmental institutions proper for a society lacking the traditional orders of men was most fully explored and most lucidly explained, and it was there that the transformation of the conceptual framework within which all this thought proceeded could be most clearly seen.

Some in Pennsylvania, accepting forthrightly the radical implications of the revolutionary situation but still thinking in traditional terms, concluded that in the American situation "a well-regulated democracy," of all forms of government, "is most equitable." How could it be otherwise? The constitution of Pennsylvania could scarcely make provision for "a representative of a king, for we have none; nor can there be need of a council to represent the house of lords, for we have not, and hope never shall have, a hereditary nobility different from the body of the people." To make "places of power" a prerogative of birth was poor policy indeed, for "wisdom is not a birthright"; nor was life tenure in office advisable since "men's abilities and manners may change." The fact that other governments have "something, a senate, a council, or upper house," was no reason for Pennsylvania to have one too. "Free government can better, much better, subsist without it. Different branches of legislature cause much needless expense, two ways: first, as there are more persons to maintain; and second, as they waste time and prolong a session by their contentions." If Rome had been a "true democracy, without a senate," it would have lasted longer, and now if Americans were to "admit different branches of legislature" the result might well be just the sort of civic degeneration that has taken place in England. The direction thought should take in the present transactions in America ("the most important . . . in any nation for some centuries past") was toward a "truly popular government" where rotation in office would be mandatory and continuous, and where officeholders would be held to strict accountability. Above all, let the organization of government be simple. At present we have no estate of hereditary privilege. If, nevertheless, we create an organ of government modeled on those that elsewhere have served the political interests of privileged orders, there will soon be some here who will learn

[58] *The People the Best Governors: Or, a Plan of Government Founded on the Just Principles of Natural Freedom* ([Hartford?], 1776), pp. [3]–6, and as reprinted in Frederick Chase, *History of Dartmouth College* (Cambridge, 1891), pp. 654–663. The pamphlet appears also in *Magazine of History*, 21 (1922), 165 ff.

how to maintain control of such an institution, and in time become used to thinking of it as somehow peculiarly their own. In the end, therefore, Pennsylvanians may discover that they have artificially created what fate had mercifully spared them.[59]

Another writer, sharing the same assumptions, went to the opposite extreme, proposing an elaborate system of "three different bodies," an assembly, a senate, and a council, all of which were to have initiating and vetoing powers in legislation.[60] But the future lay with two other Pennsylvania pamphleteers, one of whom expressed clearly what was becoming a general agreement concerning the character of the second chamber in an American republic, an agreement which constitution writers would struggle to express adequately in institutions in the years that followed, and the other of whom pointed directly to what, evolving logically from the breakdown of traditional notions of the social basis of English constitutionalism, would become the fundamental conception of a new theory of politics.

The first writer, observing that the colony had "but one order of free-men in it," argued historically, with evidence quoted wholesale from a book published five years earlier in England, that "the best model that human wisdom, improved by experience, has left them to copy" was "the old Saxon form of government" which had been transferred from "the German woods . . . into England about the year four hundred and fifty." At that time England had been a society of "small republics" within which the entire population, "being all equally interested in every question," had met often in council for full and equal discussion, and from which deputies had been sent to "a national Council and legislative authority." Let Pennsylvania's government be the same as this "beautiful system." Let there be extreme decentralization of political power, frequent elections by secret ballot, open debates in assemblies, popularly elected and moderately paid judges and local officers, and militia armies with elected field commanders. As for the perplexing question of "the

---

[59] "The Interest of America," in Force, *American Archives*, 4th ser., VI, cols. 841–843.

[60] The assembly was to be popularly elected; the senate was to be chosen by specially elected deputies from among themselves; and the council, together with the governor and lieutenant governor, was to be chosen by the assembly and senate together from among those who had served as senators. The main duty of the council was to serve as a plural executive but it was to participate also in the legislative process as a third house. The triple-headed complexity of the whole, it was explained, would give "maturity and wisdom to acts of legislation, as also stability to the state, by preventing measures from being too much influenced by sudden passions." *An Essay of a Frame of Government for Pennsylvania* (Philadelphia, 1776), pp. [3], 5 ff., 10, 11 ff.

respective powers of the several branches of the legislature," the most judicious arrangement would be to have, in addition to a representative assembly, a council composed of men distinguished by their "superior degree of acquaintance with the history, laws, and manners of mankind, and by that means they will be more likely to foresee the mischievous consequences that might follow a proceeding which at first view did not appear to have anything dangerous in it." And it would also be a good idea to have, in addition, a "small privy council" to advise and assist the governor in the execution of his duties. The possibility that the members of the upper house would *"inveterate* themselves" could be eliminated by having them elected at short intervals, for that would give the ultimate decision to the people at large, who surely have not forgotten, nor will fail to guard against, "the mischiefs which have overspread the world, from the days of Sylla to the present bloody period, from the same tyrannic source." [61]

The substitution of knowledge, wisdom, and judgment per se for hereditary privileges as the necessary qualifications for membership in the second chamber of the legislature was only the beginning of a solution to the problem, however, for there was as yet no sense of how these qualities could be recognized publicly, isolated, and recruited into a particular branch of government. Nor was it clear that such a solution avoided the perpetuation of a quasi-traditional aristocracy and hence was free of inconsistency with basic Revolutionary principles, for it was difficult to throw off the assumption that superiority was unitary, that "gentlemen of education, . . . leisure, . . . wisdom, learning, and a firmness and consistency of character" were also gentlemen of "fortune." [62] But it was a solution of sorts that pressed against the boundaries of traditional ideas even if it did not penetrate much beyond them. The adumbration of a truly new configuration of ideas became visible at the same time, however, in another pamphlet dealing with the same problem, the remarkably original and cogent *Four Letters on Interesting Subjects.*

The entire discussion of the effects of divisions among and within the branches of government, the author declared, had been clouded by myths and misunderstandings. Arguments against the simplest forms of government are based on the idea that a number of houses check each other

---

[61] *The Genuine Principles of the Ancient Saxon, or English Constitution . . .* (Philadelphia, 1776), pp. 17, 4, 16, 13, 18–19, 23, 36, 37.

[62] "Essex Result," in Theophilus Parsons, *Memoir of Theophilus Parsons . . .* (Boston, 1859), p. 370.

to the general advantage of all. But in fact the notion "has but little weight." For, in the first place, such checking "tends to embarrass and prolong business"; in the second place, it may injure collective "honor and tempers, and thereby produce petulances and ill-will which a more simple form of government would have prevented"; and in the third place, "the more houses, the more parties": different houses may serve only to institutionalize and sharpen conflicts of interests that otherwise might be reconciled. Suppose, the writer went on, "the landed interest would get into one house, and the commercial interest into the other." The result would be that

a perpetual and dangerous opposition would be kept up, and no business be got through. Whereas, were there a large, equal and annual representation in one house *only,* the different parties, by being thus blended together, would hear each others' arguments; which advantage they cannot have if they sit in different houses. To say there ought to be two houses because there are two sorts of interest is the very reason why there ought to be but one, and *that one* to consist of every sort.[63]

Here quietly but profoundly the ground of political thought had shifted. The essential units participating in the constitution were no longer formal orders of society derived from the assumptions of late medieval society but interests, which, organized for political action, became factions and parties. Their constitutional role was not to manipulate independently a separate institution of government but to join in conflict within a single institution and "blend" themselves together into a general consensus. "Balance" was still involved, but with the repudiation of monarchy and nobility and the confinement of society to "the democracy," the notion of what the social powers were that must be balanced and controlled was changing. What were now seen, though still only vaguely, were the shifting, transitory competitive groupings into which men of the eighteenth century actually organized themselves in the search for wealth, prestige, and power.

This shift in ways of thinking about the social basis of politics was part of a more general turn toward realism in political and constitutional thought. By the time the debates on the first state constitutions had been concluded, the sense that public affairs were basically struggles among formal orders of society had begun to fade and with it the whole elaborate paradigm that lay at the heart of eighteenth-century political thought. To be sure, the ancient formulations which Montesquieu had so deeply

---

[63] *Four Letters on Interesting Subjects* (Philadelphia, 1776), pp. 19–20.

engraved on the minds of his contemporaries still continued to be used; Americans of 1776 still referred to the crown, the aristocracy, and the democracy as social categories basic to politics and to observe that each had its own fundamental principle or spirit in government: for monarchy, fear; for aristocracy, honor; for democracy, virtue. And it was still found natural to assume that the ultimate goal of politics was a motionless equilibrium among these entities, and that public controversy deliberately undertaken was essentially malign or aberrant. But the actual problems of government the American faced were now so urgent, so new, and so comprehensive that attention was beginning to concentrate on the visible and real rather than on the traditional and theoretical. The ancient classifications remained in the back of people's minds; but the problems posed by those disreputable and dangerous elements — factions, interests, and parties — were more obtrusive; they threatened the very existence of republics. A republican constitution, to be successful, must contain some provision for their control; it must somehow cope with the fact that the larger the unit of government the greater the number of contending factions and the smaller the chance that a republican government could control them. How could they be mastered or confined? What would prevent them from tearing a government to pieces? Contention as such must be understood; the struggles of men, in whatever groupings they might form, rather than in fixed social categories, must be taken into account, and the functioning of the organs of government in controlling them more fully explored. Politics in its "vague and vulgar acceptation, . . . referring to the wrangling debates of modern assemblies, debates which far too often turn entirely on the narrow, selfish, and servile views of party" — politics in this humble sense rather than in the traditional, "more dignified sense" must be comprehended and dealt with, not explained away as a series of momentary instabilities and aberrations in an otherwise poised and symmetrical system.[64]

Constitutional thought, concentrating on the pressing need to create republican governments that would survive, tended to draw away from the effort to refine further the ancient, traditional systems, and to move toward a fresh, direct comprehension of political reality. Denied, by the urgency of new problems, the satisfactions of elaborating familiar abstractions, Americans edged toward that hard, clear realism in political thought

[64] Boucher, "On Civil Liberty, Passive Obedience, and Nonresistance," *A View of the Causes and Consequences*, p. 499n.

that would reach fulfillment a decade later in the formation of the national government and achieve its classic expression in *The Federalist*. In the process the concept of "democracy" would be transformed.

4. "WHETHER SOME DEGREE OF RESPECT BE NOT ALWAYS DUE FROM INFERIORS TO SUPERIORS"

Yet none of this — not the changes in the concepts of representation and consent, of constitutions and rights, or of sovereignty, nor the unexpected challenge to such a deeply embedded institution as slavery, nor the unplanned defiance of orthodoxy and establishment in religion, nor the tendency to forsake the traditional assumptions concerning the social basis of politics and the constitutional arrangements that followed from these assumptions — none of these developments measure fully the transforming effect of the Revolutionary movement in America, even at its inception. Beyond these specific changes were others: subtler, vaguer, and ultimately, perhaps, even more important.

In no obvious sense was the American Revolution undertaken as a social revolution. No one, that is, deliberately worked for the destruction or even the substantial alteration of the order of society as it had been known. Yet it was transformed as a result of the Revolution, and not merely because Loyalist property was confiscated and redistributed, or because the resulting war destroyed the economic bases of some people's lives and created opportunities for others that would not otherwise have existed. Seizure of Loyalist property and displacements in the economy did in fact take place, and the latter if not the former does account for a spurt in social mobility that led earlier arrivés to remark, "When the pot boils, the scum will rise." Yet these were superficial changes; they affected a small part of the population only, and they did not alter the organization of society.

What did affect the essentials of social organization — what in time would help permanently to transform them — were changes in the realm of belief and attitude. The views men held toward the relationships that bound them to each other — the discipline and pattern of society — moved in a new direction in the decade before Independence.

Americans of 1760 continued to assume, as had their predecessors for generations before, that a healthy society was a hierarchical society, in which it was natural for some to be rich and some poor, some honored and some obscure, some powerful and some weak. And it was believed that superiority was unitary, that the attributes of the favored — wealth, wisdom, power — had a natural affinity to each other, and hence that political leadership would naturally rest in the hands of the social leaders. Movement, of course, there would be: some would fall and some would rise; but manifest, external differences among men, reflecting the principle of hierarchical order, were necessary and proper, and would remain; they were intrinsic to the nature of things.

Circumstances had pressed harshly against such assumptions. The wilderness environment from the beginning had threatened the maintenance of elaborate social distinctions; many of them in the passage of time had in fact been worn away. Puritanism, in addition, and the epidemic evangelicalism of the mid-eighteenth century, had created challenges to the traditional notions of social stratification by generating the conviction that the ultimate quality of men was to be found elsewhere than in their external condition, and that a cosmic achievement lay within each man's grasp. And the peculiar configuration of colonial politics — a constant broil of petty factions struggling almost formlessly, with little discipline or control, for the benefits of public authority — had tended to erode the respect traditionally accorded the institutions and officers of the state.

Yet nowhere, at any time in the colonial years, were the implications of these circumstances articulated or justified. The assumption remained that society, in its maturity if not in its confused infancy, would conform to the pattern of the past; that authority would continue to exist without challenge, and that those in superior positions would be responsible and wise, and those beneath them respectful and content. These premises and expectations were deeply lodged; they were not easily or quickly displaced. But the Revolution brought with it arguments and attitudes bred of arguments endlessly repeated, that undermined these premises of the *ancien régime*.

For a decade or more defiance to the highest constituted powers poured from the colonial presses and was hurled from half the pulpits of the land. The right, the need, the absolute obligation to disobey legally constituted authority had become the universal cry. Cautions and qualifications became ritualistic: formal exercises in ancient pieties. One might preface one's charge to disobedience with homilies on the inevitable imperfections of all governments and the necessity to bear "some injuries" patiently and peaceably. But what needed and received demonstration and defense was not the caution, but the injunction: the argument that when injuries touched on "fundamental rights" (and who could say when they did not?) then nothing less than "duty to God and religion, to themselves, to the community, and to unborn posterity require such to assert and defend their rights by all lawful, most prudent, and effectual means in their power." Obedience as a principle was only too well known; disobedience as a doctrine was not. It was therefore asserted again and again that resistance to constituted authority was "a doctrine according to godliness — the doctrine of the English nation . . . by which our rights and constitution have often been defended and repeatedly rescued out of the hands of encroaching tyranny . . . This is the doctrine and grand pillar of the ever memorable and glorious Revolution, and upon which our gracious sovereign GEORGE III holds the crown of the British empire." What better credentials could there be? How lame to add that obedience too "is an eminent part of Christian duty without which government must disband and dreadful anarchy and confusion (with all its horrors) take place and reign without control" — how lame, especially in view of the fact that one could easily mistake this "Christian obedience" for that "blind, enslaving obedience which is no part of the Christian institution but is highly injurious to religion, to every free government, and to the good of mankind, and is the stirrup of tyranny, and grand engine of slavery." [65]

Defiance to constituted authority leaped like a spark from one flammable area to another, growing in heat as it went. Its greatest intensification took place in the explosive atmosphere of local religious dissent. Isaac Backus spoke only for certain of the Baptists and Congregational Separates and against the presumptive authority of ministers, when, in the course of an attack on the religious establishment in Massachusetts, he warned that

we are not to obey and follow [ministers] in an implicit or customary way, but each one must consider and follow others no further than they see that the end of their conversation is Jesus Christ the same yesterday, and today, and forever more . . . People are so far from being under obligation to follow teachers who don't lead in this way they incur guilt by such a following of them.

It took little imagination on the part of Backus' readers and listeners to find in this a general injunction against uncritical obedience to authority in any form. Others were even more explicit. The Baptist preacher who questioned not merely the authority of the local orthodox church but the very "etymology of the word [orthodoxy]" assured the world that the colonists

[65] Johnson, *Some Important Observations*, pp. 27–28.

have as just a right, before GOD and man, to oppose King, ministry, Lords, and Commons of England when they violate their rights as Americans as they have to oppose any foreign enemy; and that this is no more, according to the law of nature, to be deemed rebellion than it would be to oppose the King of France, supposing him now present invading the land.

But what to the Baptists was the establishment, to Anglicans was dissent. From the establishment in New England, ever fearful of ecclesiastical impositions from without, came as strong a current of anti-authoritarianism as from the farthest left-wing sect. It was a pillar of the temple, a scion of the church, and an apologist for New England's standing order who sweepingly disclaimed "all human authority in matters of faith and worship. We regard neither pope nor prince as head of the church, nor acknowledge that any Parliaments have power to enact articles of doctrine or forms of discipline or modes of worship or terms of church communion," and, declaring that "we are accountable to none but *Christ*" — words that had struck at the heart of every establishment, civil and religious, since the fall of Rome — concluded with the apparent paradox that "*liberty* is the *fundamental* principle of our establishment." [66]

In such declarations a political argument became a moral imperative. The principle of justifiable disobedience and the instinct to question public authority before accepting it acquired a new sanction and a new vigor. Originally, of course, the doctrine of resistance was applied to Parliament, a non-representative assembly 3000 miles away. But the composition and location of the institution had not been as crucial in creating opposition as had the character of the actions Parliament had taken. Were provincial assemblies, simply because they were local and representative, exempt from scrutiny and resistance? Were they any less susceptible than Parliament to the rule that when their authority is extended beyond "the bounds of the law of God and the free constitution . . . 'their acts are, *ipso facto,* void, and cannot oblige any to obedience'"? There could be no doubt of the answer. Any legislature, wherever located or however composed, deserved only the obedience it could command by the justice and wisdom of its proceedings. Representative or not, local or not, any agency of the state could be defied. The freeholders of Augusta, Virginia, could not have been more explicit in applying to local government in 1776 the defiance learned in the struggle with Parliament. They wrote their delegates to Virginia's Provincial Congress that

[66] Isaac Backus, *A Fish Caught in His Own Net* . . . (Boston, 1768), p. 61; Allen, *American Alarm*, 4th sec., p. 11; 1st sec., p. 15; Adams, *Religious Liberty*, pp. 38, 39.

should the future conduct of our legislative body prove to you that our opinion of their wisdom and justice is ill-grounded, then tell them that your constituents are neither guided nor will ever be influenced by that slavish maxim in politics, "that whatever is enacted by that body of men in whom the supreme power of the state is vested must in all cases be obeyed," and that they firmly believe attempts to repeal an unjust law can be vindicated beyond a simple remonstrance addressed to the legislators.[67]

But such threats as these were only the most obvious ways in which traditional notions of authority came into question. Others were more subtly subversive, silently sapping the traditional foundations of social order and discipline.

"Rights" obviously lay at the heart of the Anglo-American controversy: the rights of Englishmen, the rights of mankind, chartered rights. But *"rights,"* wrote Richard Bland — that least egalitarian of Revolutionary leaders — "imply *equality* in the instances to which they belong and must be treated without respect to the dignity of the persons concerned in them." This was by no means simply a worn cliché, for while "equality before the law" was a commonplace of the time, "equality without re-spect to the dignity of the persons concerned" was not; its emphasis on social equivalence was significant, and though in its immediate context the remark was directed to the invidious distinctions believed to have been drawn between Englishmen and Americans, its broader applic-ability was apparent. Others seized upon it, and developed it, especially in the fluid years of transition when new forms of government were being sought to replace those believed to have proved fatal to liberty. "An affectation of rank" and "the assumed distinction of 'men of conse-quence'" had been the blight of the Proprietary party, a Pennsylvania pamphleteer wrote in 1776. Riches in a new country like America sig-nified nothing more than the accident of prior settlement. The accumula-tion of wealth had been "unavoidable to the descendants of the early settlers" since the land, originally cheap, had appreciated naturally with the growth of settlement.

... perhaps it is owing to this accidental manner of becoming rich that wealth does not obtain the same degree of influence here which it does in old countries. Rank, at present, in America is derived more from qualification than property; a sound moral character, amiable manners, and firmness in principle constitute the first class, and will continue to do so till the origin of families be forgotten, and the proud follies of the old world overrun the simplicity of the new.

[67] Johnson, *Some Important Observations,* p. 22; "Sentiments of the Several Companies," Force, *American Archives,* 5th ser., II, col. 817.

Therefore, under the new dispensation, "no reflection ought to be made on any man on account of birth, provided that his manners rises decently with his circumstances, and that he affects not to forget the level he came from." [68]

The idea was, in its very nature, corrosive to the traditional authority of magistrates and of established institutions. And it activated other, similar thoughts whose potential threat to stability lay till then inert. There was no more familiar notion in eighteenth-century political thought — it was propounded in every tract on government and every ministerial exhortation to the civil magistracy — than that those who wield power were "servants of society" as well as "ministers of God," and as such had to be specially qualified: they must be acquainted with the affairs of men; they must have wisdom, knowledge, prudence; and they must be men of virtue and true religion. [69] But how far should one go with this idea? The doctrine that the qualifications for magistracy were moral, spiritual, and intellectual could lead to conflict with the expectation that public leaders would be people of external dignity and social superiority; it could be dangerous to the establishment in any settled society. For the ancient notion that leadership must devolve on men whose "personal authority and greatness," whose "eminence or nobility," was such that "every man subordinate is ready to yield a willing submission without contempt or repining" — ordinary people not easily conceding to an authority "conferred upon a mean man . . . no better than selected out of their own rank" — this traditional notion had never been repudiated, was still honored and repeated. But now, in the heated atmosphere of incipient rebellion, the idea of leaders as servants of the people was pushed to its logical extreme, and its subversive potentialities revealed. By 1774 it followed from the belief that "lawful rulers are the servants of the people" that they were "exalted above their brethren not for their own sakes, but for the benefit of the people; and submission is yielded, not on account of their persons considered exclusively on the authority they are clothed with, but of those laws which in the exercise of this authority are made by them conformably to the laws of nature and equity." In the distribution of offices, it was said in 1770, "merit only in the candidate" should count — not birth, or wealth, or loyalty to the great; but merit

[68] Richard Bland, *An Inquiry into the Rights of the British Colonies* . . . (Williamsburg, 1766), p. 25; *Four Letters on Interesting Subjects*, pp. 2–3.

[69] E.g., Eliot, *Sermon*, pp. 12–30; Charles Turner, *A Sermon Preached Before His Excellency* . . . (Boston, 1773), p. 30.

only. Even a deliberately judicious statement of this theme rang with defiance to traditional forms of authority: "It is not wealth — it is not family — it is not either of these alone, nor both of them together, though I readily allow neither is to be disregarded, that will qualify men for important seats in government, unless they are rich and honorable in other and more important respects." Indeed, one could make a complete inversion and claim that, properly, the external affluence of magistrates should be the consequence of, not the prior qualification for, the judicious exercise of public authority over others.[70]

Where would it end? By 1774 it had become clear to some that declarations "before GOD . . . that it is no rebellion to oppose any king, ministry, or governor that destroys by any violence or authority whatever the rights of the people" threatened the most elemental principles of order and discipline in society.[71] A small group of writers, opposed not merely to the politics of resistance but to the effect it would have on the primary linkages of society — on that patterning of human relations that distinguishes a civilized community from a primitive mob — attempted to recall to the colonists the lessons of the past, the wisdom, as they thought of it, of the ages. Citing adages and principles that once had guided men's thoughts on the structure of society; equating all communities, and England's empire in particular, with families; quoting generously from Filmer; and explaining that anarchy results when social inferiors claim political authority, they argued, with increasing anxiety, that the essence of social stability was being threatened by the political agitation of the time. Their warnings, full of nostalgia for ancient certainties, were ignored if they were heard at all. But in the very extremism of their reaction to the events of the time there lies a measure of the distance Revolutionary thought had moved from an old to a very new world.

One of the earliest such warnings was written by a young Barbadian, Isaac Hunt, only recently graduated from the College of Philadelphia but already an expert in scurrilous pamphleteering. Opening his *Political Family,* an essay published in 1775 though written for a prize competition

---

[70] Bailyn, "Politics and Social Structure in Virginia," p. 94n15; Gad Hitchcock, *A Sermon Preached Before . . . Gage . . .* (Boston, 1774), pp. 27–28; Cooke, *Sermon,* p. 16; Jason Haven, *A Sermon Preached Before . . . Bernard . . .* (Boston, 1769), pp. 46–47; Peter Whitney, *The Transgressions of a Land Punished by a Multitude of Rulers . . .* (Boston, 1774), p. 16.

[71] [John Allen], *An Oration upon the Beauties of Liberty . . .* (Boston, 1773), p. 28.

in 1766, with a discourse on the necessary reciprocity of parts in the body politic he developed as his central point the idea that "in the *body politic* all inferior jurisdictions should flow from *one superior fountain . . .* a due subordination of the less parts to the greater is . . . necessary to the *existence* of BOTH." Colonies were the children and inferiors of the mother country; let them show the gratitude and obedience due to parents, and so let the principle of order through subordination prevail in the greater as in the lesser spheres of life.[72]

This, in the context of the widespread belief in equal rights and the compact theory of government was anachronistic. But it expressed the fears of many as political opposition turned into revolutionary fervor. Arguments such as Hunt's were enlarged and progressively dramatized, gaining in vituperation with successive publications until by 1774 they were bitter, shrill, and full of despair. Three Anglican clergymen wrote wrathful epitaphs to this ancient, honorable, and moribund, philosophy.

Samuel Seabury — Hamilton's anonymous opponent in the pamphlet wars and the future first bishop of the Episcopal Church in America — wrote desperately of the larger, permanent dangers of civil disobedience. The legal, established authorities in New York — the courts of justice, above all — have been overthrown, he wrote, and in their places there were now "delegates, congresses, committees, riots, mobs, insurrections, associations." Who comprised the self-constituted Committee of Safety of New York that had the power to brand innocent people outlaws and deliver them over "to the vengeance of a lawless, outrageous mob, to be *tarred, feathered, hanged, drawn, quartered,* and *burnt*"? A parcel of upstarts "chosen by the weak, foolish, turbulent part of the country people" — "half a dozen fools in your neighborhood." Was the slavery imposed by their riotous wills to be preferred to the tyranny of a king? No: "If I must be devoured, let me be devoured by the jaws of a lion, and not *gnawed* to death by rats and vermin." If the upstart, pretentious committeemen triumph, order and peace will be at an end, and anarchy will result.

Government was intended for the security of those who live under it — to protect the weak against the strong — the good against the bad — to preserve order and decency among men, preventing every one from injuring his neighbor. Every person,

[72] Isaac Hunt, *The Political Family, or a Discourse Pointing Out the Reciprocal Advantages Which Flow from an Uninterrupted Union Between Great-Britain and Her American Colonies* . . . (Philadelphia, 1775), pp. 6, 7, 29–30.

then, owes obedience to the laws of the government under which he lives, and is obliged in honor and duty to support them. Because if *one* has a right to disregard the laws of the society to which he belongs, *all* have the *same* right; and *then* government is at an end.[73]

His colleague, the elegant, scholarly Thomas Bradbury Chandler, was at once cleverer, more thoughtful, and, for those who heeded arguments, more likely to have been convincing. Two of his pamphlets published in 1774 stated with peculiar force the traditional case for authority in the state, in society, and in the ultimate source and ancient archetype of all authority, the family. His *American Querist,* that extraordinary list of 100 rhetorical questions, put the point obliquely. It asked:

Whether some degree of respect be not always due from inferiors to superiors, and especially from children to parents; and whether the refusal of this on any occasion be not a violation of the general laws of society, to say nothing here of the obligations of religion and morality?

And is not Great Britain in the same relation to the colonies as a parent to children? If so, how can such "disrespectful and abusive treatment from children" be tolerated? God has given no dispensation to people under any government "to refuse *honor* or *custom* or *tribute* to whom they are *due;* to contract habits of thinking and *speaking evil of dignities,* and to weaken the natural principle of respect for those in authority." God's command is clear: his will is that we *"submit to every ordinance of man for the Lord's sake;* and require[s] us on pain of *damnation* to be duly *subject to the higher powers,* and *not to resist* their lawful authority."

Chandler's *Friendly Address to All Reasonable Americans* was more direct. It touched the central theme of authority at the start, and immediately spelled out the implications of resistance. The effort "to disturb or threaten an established government by popular insurrections and tumults has always been considered and treated, in every age and nation of the world, as an unpardonable crime." Did not an Apostle, "who had a due regard for the rights and liberties of mankind," order submission even to that cruelest of all despots, Nero? And properly so: "The bands of society would be dissolved, the harmony of the world confounded, and

---

[73] [Samuel Seabury], *Free Thoughts on the Proceedings of the Continental Congress . . .* ([New York], 1774); and *The Congress Canvassed . . .* ([New York], 1774), in Clarence H. Vance, ed., *Letters of a Westchester Farmer (1774–1775)* (*Publications of the Westchester County Historical Society,* VIII, White Plains, 1930), pp. 59, 61, 62, 90–91.

the order of nature subverted, if reverence, respect, and obedience might be refused to those whom the constitution has vested with the highest authority." [74]

The insistence, the violence of language, increased in the heightening crisis. "Rebellion," Daniel Leonard wrote flatly in 1775, "is the most atrocious offense that can be perpetrated by man," except those committed directly against God. "It dissolves the social band, annihilates the security resulting from law and government; introduces fraud, violence, rapine, murder, sacrilege, and the long train of evils that riot uncontrolled in a state of nature." But the end was near. By the spring of 1775 such sentiments, fulminous and despairing, were being driven underground.

Jonathan Boucher's sermon "On Civil Liberty, Passive Obedience, and Nonresistance" had been written in 1775 "with a view to publication," and though it had been delivered publicly enough in Queen Anne's Parish, Maryland, it was promptly thereafter suppressed; "the press," Boucher later wrote, "was shut to every publication of the kind." Its publication twenty-two years afterward in a volume of Boucher's sermons entitled *A View of the Causes and Consequences of the American Revolution* was the result of the French Revolution's reawakening in the author, long since safely established in England, the fears of incipient anarchy and social incoherence that had agitated him two decades before. It was a fortunate result, for the sermon is a classic of its kind. It sums up, as no other essay of the period, the threat to the traditional ordering of human relations implicit in Revolutionary thought.

Boucher sought, first and foremost, to establish the divine origins of the doctrine of obedience to constituted authority — a necessity, he felt, not merely in view of the arguments of the Reverend Jacob Duché whom he was ostensibly refuting, but, more important, in view of the gross misinterpretation rebellious Americans had for years been making of that suggestive verse of Galatians v, 1: "Stand fast, therefore, in the liberty wherewith Christ hath made us free." What had been meant by "liberty" in that passage, he said, was simply and unambiguously freedom from sin, for "every sinner is, literally, a slave . . . the only true liberty is the liberty of being the servants of God." Yet the Gospel does speak to the question of public obligations, and its command could hardly be more unmistakable: it orders, always, "obedience to the laws of every

[74] [Thomas B. Chandler], *The American Querist: Or, Some Questions Proposed . . .* ([New York], 1774), pp. 4, 5, 30; [Thomas B. Chandler], *A Friendly Address to All Reasonable Americans . . .* (New York, 1774), p. 5.

country, in every kind or form of government." The rumor promoted in the infancy of Christianity "that the Gospel was designed to undermine kingdoms and commonwealths" had probably been the work of Judas, and patently mixed up the purpose of the First Coming with that of the Second. Submission to the higher powers is what the Gospel intends for man: "obedience to government is every man's duty because it is every man's interest; but it is particularly incumbent on Christians, because . . . it is enjoined by the positive commands of God."

So much was scriptural, and could be buttressed by such authorities as Edmund Burke, Bishop Butler, "the learned Mr. Selden," and Lancelot Andrewes, whose Biblical exegesis of 1650 was quoted to the effect that "princes receive their power only from God, and are by him constituted and entrusted with government of others chiefly for his own glory and honor, as his deputies and vicegerents upon earth." More complicated was the application of this central thesis to the associated questions of the origins and aims of government and of the equality of men. As for the former, the idea that the aim of government is "the common good of mankind" is in itself questionable; but even if it were correct, it would not follow that government should rest on consent, for common consent can only mean common feeling, and this a "vague and loose" thing not susceptible to proof. Mankind has never yet agreed on what the common good is, and so, there being no "common feeling" that can clearly designate the "common good," one can scarcely argue that government is, or should be, instituted by "common consent."

Similarly popular, dangerous, and fallacious to Boucher was the notion "that the whole human race is born equal; and that no man is naturally inferior, or in any respect subjected to another, and that he can be made subject to another only by his own consent." This argument, he wrote, is "ill-founded and false both in its premises and conclusions." It is hard to see how it could conceivably be true in any sense. "Man differs from man in everything that can be supposed to lead to supremacy and subjection, *as one star differs from another star in glory*." God intended man to be a social animal; but society requires government, and "without some relative inferiority and superiority" there can be no government.

A musical instrument composed of chords, keys, or pipes all perfectly equal in size and power might as well be expected to produce harmony as a society composed of members all perfectly equal to be productive of order and peace . . . On the principle of equality, neither his parents nor even the vote of a majority of the society . . . can have . . . authority over any man . . . Even an implicit consent can bind a man no longer than he chooses to be bound. The same principle of equality . . . clearly entitles him to recall and resume that consent whenever he sees fit, and he alone has a right to judge when and for what reasons it may be resumed.

A social and political system based on the principles of consent and equality would be "fantastic"; it would result in "the whole business of social life" being reduced to confusion and futility. People would first express and then withdraw their consent to an endless succession of schemes of government. "Governments, though always forming, would never be completely formed, for the majority today might be the minority tomorrow, and, of course, that which is now fixed might and would be soon unfixed."

Consent, equality — these were "particularly loose and dangerous" ideas, Boucher wrote; illogical, unrealistic, and lacking in scriptural sanction. There need be no mystery about the origins of government. Government was created by God. "As soon as there were some to be governed, there were also some to govern; and the first man, by virtue of that paternal claim on which all subsequent governments have been founded, was first invested with the power of government . . . The first father was the first king: and . . . it was thus that all government originated; and monarchy is its most ancient form." From this origin it follows directly that resistance to constituted authority is a sin, and that mankind is "commanded to *be subject to the higher powers*." True, "kings and princes . . . were doubtless created and appointed not so much for their own sakes as for the sake of the people committed to their charge: yet they are not, therefore, the creatures of the people. So far from deriving their authority from any supposed consent or suffrage of men, they receive their commission from Heaven; they receive it from God, the source and original of all power." The judgment of Jesus Christ is evident: the most essential duty of subjects with respect to government is simply "(in the phraseology of a prophet) *to be quiet, and to sit still.*"

How simple but yet how demanding an injunction, for men are ever "*prone* to be presumptuous and self-willed, always disposed and ready to despise *dominion,* and *to speak evil of dignities.*" And how necessary to be obeyed in the present circumstance. Sedition has already penetrated deeply; it tears at the vitals of social order. It threatens far more than "the persons invested with the supreme power either legislative or executive"; "the resistance which your political counselors urge you to practice [is exerted] clearly and literally against *authority* . . . you are encouraged to resist not only all authority over us as it now exists, but any and all that it is possible to constitute." [75]

This was the ultimate concern. What Boucher, Leonard, Chandler, and

[75] Leonard ("Massachusettensis"), *Novanglus and Massachusettensis,* pp. 187–188: Boucher, "On Civil Liberty, Passive Obedience, and Nonresistance," *A View of the Causes and Consequences,* pp. lxxxiv, 504, 506, 507–508, 513n, 512n, 512–516, 511, 524, 525, 534, 535, 548, 552–553.

other articulate defenders of the *status quo* saw as the final threat was not so much the replacement of one set of rulers by another as the triumph of ideas and attitudes incompatible with the stability of any standing order, any establishment — incompatible with society itself, as it had been traditionally known. Their fears were in a sense justified, for in the context of eighteenth-century social thought it was difficult to see how any harmonious, stable social order could be constructed from such materials. To argue that all men were equal would not make them so; it would only help justify and perpetuate that spirit of defiance, that refusal to concede to authority whose ultimate resolution could only be anarchy, demagoguery, and tyranny. If such ideas prevailed year after year, generation after generation, the "latent spark" in the breasts of even the most humble of men would be kindled again and again by entrepreneurs of discontent who would remind the people "of the elevated rank they hold in the universe, as men; that all men by nature are equal; that kings are but the ministers of the people; that their authority is delegated to them by the people for their good, and they have a right to resume it, and place it in other hands, or keep it themselves, whenever it is made use of to oppress them." [76] Seeds of sedition would thus constantly be sown, and harvests of licentiousness reaped.

How else could it end? What reasonable social and political order could conceivably be built and maintained where authority was questioned before it was obeyed, where social differences were considered to be incidental rather than essential to community order, and where superiority, suspect in principle, was not allowed to concentrate in the hands of a few but was scattered broadly through the populace? No one could clearly say. But some, caught up in a vision of the future in which the peculiarities of American life became the marks of a chosen people, found in the defiance of traditional order the firmest of all grounds for their hope for a freer life. The details of this new world were not as yet clearly depicted; but faith ran high that a better world than any that had ever been known could be built where authority was distrusted and held in constant scrutiny; where the status of men flowed from their achievements and from their personal qualities, not from distinctions ascribed to them at birth; and where the use of power over the lives of men was jealously guarded and severely restricted. It was only where there was this defiance, this refusal to truckle, this distrust of all authority, political or social, that institutions would express human aspirations, not crush them.

[76] Leonard ("Massachusettensis"), *Novanglus and Massachusettensis*, p. 152.

PAMPHLET I

JONATHAN MAYHEW, *A DISCOURSE CONCERNING UNLIMITED SUBMISSION AND NONRESISTANCE TO THE HIGHER POWERS*

BOSTON, 1750

INTRODUCTION

Jonathan Mayhew's *Discourse Concerning Unlimited Submission* — the most famous sermon preached in pre-Revolutionary America — illustrates dramatically the ultimate sources of American Revolutionary thought and the distinctive emphasis imparted to them in the process of their transmission. In it one may see a gathering of threads that reach back into the earliest periods of American history and that extend forward into the constitutional debate of the 1760's and 1770's, and beyond that, into the construction of new governments in the American Republic.

Jonathan Mayhew (1720–1766) was a descendant of the "ancient governor" and proprietor of Martha's Vineyard and scion of the dynasty of Congregational ministers which for almost a century had preached the Gospel to the villagers and Indians of that island. His native culture was bleak and narrow in its isolation and its austere, fourth-generation Puritanism. But the death of an older brother destined for the ministry allowed Jonathan to transcend this parochial environment by making it possible for him to enroll, in 1740 at the age of twenty, in Harvard College. The character of that institution, still close in spirit to its seventeenth-century past, was quickly changing in response to the influx of new ideas and to the expectations of a more affluent society. The college was exciting in its forward look and fashionable style, and full of contradictions. Mayhew quickly became part of this world: he first welcomed the Great Awakening as a fulfillment of the religion of his forbears, then reviled it, in the person of George Whitefield, as "puerile" and "enthusiastic"; he drank, and was punished for drinking, "prohibited liquors"; he made "impertinent recrimination" of the college authorities; and he read widely in the literature of enlightened thought. The extant fragment of his college reading list and commonplace book includes references to the classics of the Puritan tradition; but in greater numbers it cites latitudinarian and rationalist theologians: Archbishop Tillotson, Samuel Clarke, William Wollaston, and Samuel Parker; scientists and prophets of natural religion: Robert Boyle, John Ray, and John Woodward; and Pascal, whose *Pensées,* to judge by the number of entries in Mayhew's commonplace book, fascinated the young student.[1]

204

Psychologically if not intellectually he had long been inclining toward liberal positions in theology. His practical-minded missionary father, Experience Mayhew, had extemporized a rude brand of Arminianism in preaching to the Indians, and the son was inclined to honor this commitment, especially when Experience's amateur views, published in a controversial treatise of 1744, came under attack by some of the more professional, and supercilious, theologians of Massachusetts. Three years of further study in Cambridge after graduation and the influence of the rationalist preacher Ebenezer Gay confirmed the liberal tendencies of Jonathan's religious thought, and by 1747, when he was installed in the ministry of the fashionable West Church in Boston, he had already acquired such a reputation for heresy that only two preachers could be found to attend his ordination. His first publication, *Seven Sermons* (1749), in which he forthrightly declared Christianity to be "principally an institution of life and manners" and its goal the realization of "the first and great commandment," permanently established the breadth of his latitudinarianism. Arminian he already was, and the path his ideas would take through Arianism toward the gentle, creedless faith of Unitarianism was even then clear.[2]

All of this in mid-century Massachusetts was scandalous, as the young Paul Revere discovered when, according to family tradition, he was whipped for listening to Mayhew preach. But in England, where *Seven Sermons* was immediately republished, Mayhew's views fitted smoothly into a well-established tradition of radical thinking, and they won him an immediate welcome in advanced circles. Dr. Benjamin Avery, chairman of the influential nonconformist political lobby, the Protestant Dissenting Deputies, wrote to congratulate him upon the wisdom and rationality of his sermons and to inform him that his book had been warmly received by no less a personage than the renowned latitudinarian Bishop of Winchester, Benjamin Hoadly. Thus launched, Mayhew's reputation soared, and within a year, in 1750, Avery and other nonconformist leaders, delighted to find proof in Mayhew's writing that "just and rational sentiments" were gaining ground in America, secured for the young preacher an honorary doctorate from Aberdeen University.[3]

It was a remarkable honor, and Mayhew understandably exulted in it. But he could not ignore the condescension that had been implied in Avery's and Hoadly's surprise that such a book had come out of so remote a province and in their delight that "our brethren there were greatly improved in their taste." The "mean opinion" of his country implied by such remarks, Mayhew wrote, was only too well justified: "the clergy, generally, are very contracted in their opinions; and the laity, if possible, more so." In this provincial culture, intellectual struggles long since won in England had to be refought, and it was to extend the battleline of enlightened ideas into still another sector of reactionary thought that he turned, within a few months of the publication of his sermons, to attack the political theory of High Church Anglicanism.[4]

The occasion was the anniversary (January 30) of the execution of Charles I, a day on which it had once been traditional for Tory, High Church, and

Jacobite orators to revive the generally discredited theory of the divine right of kings. At times in English history — at the Restoration, under James II, and in the years of Tory ascendancy under Queen Anne — something of the original enthusiasm for this absolutist doctrine had been rekindled. But in general, the Whig belief that government was justified by a limited contract between rulers and ruled had prevailed in England, even within the Episcopal hierarchy, which under Charles I had originally produced the theory of divine right as a defense of both church and state. In America, where Episcopacy, if not the Anglican establishment as such, was everywhere suspect, divine right preaching had never been prominent; indeed, it had scarcely existed at all.[5] But fear of absolutism and of its justification in divine right had nevertheless been transmitted to the colonies, especially in the blistering polemics of the early eighteenth-century libertarians; and at mid-century it was still very much alive. As a student at Harvard Mayhew had copied carefully from the *Memorials* of the Parliamentarian Bulstrode Whitelock the lessons to be learned from "the character and reign etc. of K.C.I." and from the preaching of "Drs. Sibthorpe and Mainwaring . . . that the King might make laws and do whatever pleaseth him." Fifteen years later he was still absorbed in the literature of radical anti-authoritarianism and still transfixed by the century-old threat of divine right theory. In January 1750, as the anniversary of the death of Charles I approached, he saw in the pronouncements of Boston's Anglicans a "strange sort of frenzy . . . preaching passive obedience, worshiping King Charles I, and cursing the dissenters and puritans for murdering him." The prospect of a series of public professions of divine right theory and of the "sainthood and martyrdom" of King Charles I goaded him, he later explained, into delivering three sermons on the subject, the last of which, preached on the anniversary day itself, he published as *A Discourse Concerning Unlimited Submission.*[6]

In the principles it expresses the pamphlet is a cliché of Whig political theory. Like innumerable sermons and tracts on civil obedience that had been published in England and America since John Milton first attempted in *Eikonoklastes* (1649) to smash the image of Charles's sainthood and divine powers and in *Pro Populo Anglicano Defensio* (1651) to refute the claims for royal absolutism generally, it begins with a gloss on Romans xiii, 1–8, "Let every soul be subject unto the higher powers"; and it proceeds to demonstrate the Lockeanism of St. Paul: "the true ground and reason of our obligation to be subject to the *higher powers* is the usefulness of magistracy (when properly exercised) to human society, and its subserviency to the general welfare." Submission is demanded only to rulers who exercise "a reasonable and just authority for the good of human society"; those who "rob and ruin the public, instead of being guardians of its peace and welfare . . . immediately cease to be the *ordinance* and *ministers of God,* and no more deserve that glorious character than common *pirates* and *highwaymen.*" From this principle kings are in no way exempt, for "the hereditary, indefeasible, divine right of kings, and the doctrine of nonresistance which is built upon the supposition of such a right, are altogether as fabulous and chimerical as transubstantiation, or any of the most absurd reveries of ancient or modern visionaries." Thus Charles I, long before he had met his fate, had in effect *"unkinged* himself" by governing "in a perfectly wild and arbitrary manner, paying no regard to the constitution and the laws of the kingdom, by which the power of the crown was limited." Resistance to such a king was not rebellion but "a most righteous and glorious stand, made in defense of the natural and legal rights of the people, against the unnatural and illegal encroachments of arbitrary power." Why, then, do *"Episcopal clergy* who are very high in the principles of *ecclesiastical authority* continue to speak of this unhappy prince as a *great saint* and *martyr?"* The reason is clear: for these "bigoted clergymen and friends to church power" to argue that Charles had had divine sanctions and had been martyred is to accuse all dissenters of complicity in murder and to brand them as "scismatics . . . traitors and rebels and all that is bad."

These principles of government and of the limits of civil power were commonplaces of Whig thought; for years they had formed the substance of annual election sermons delivered before the Assemblies of Massachusetts and Connecticut and published by order of those governments.[7] Yet if the principles were commonplace, the emphasis in their expression and the focus of the attack were not. It was widely agreed that resistance to tyranny was justified; but not all commentators proclaimed, as Mayhew did, that "subjects in general" were the "proper judges [of] when their governors oppress them and play the tyrant" and that to deny this was "treason against mankind . . . treason against common sense . . . treason against God," nor was it generally concluded that everyone was "bound" to rebel against evil governors, and that failure to do so was "to join . . . in promoting the slavery of . . . society." The emphasis, almost universally, was on the ultimacy of resistance and on the caution with which one properly approached the denial of constituted authority.[8] As for Mayhew's concentrated blast at the hierarchy of the English church — at the deep, half-submerged foundations of its thought and loyalties — this was flagrant provocation, heedless defiance, of the spiritual arm of what was, after all, a singularly indulgent state.

The counterblasts were quick in coming and long sustained. Even before the sermon appeared in print an attack on an unnamed "wrangling *preacher in this town* [known to have] *belched out a flood of* obloquy *upon the pious memory of King* Charles *the first"* was published in a Boston newspaper.[9] Thereafter for six months the town's public prints carried columns of vituperation pro and con Mayhew's sermon and on the related issues of nonresistance and the sainthood of Charles I. Venerable authorities, some dating back to the original controversy that a century earlier had torn both church and state apart in England, were flourished: Lord Clarendon, Bishops Sprat and Burnet, the historian Neal, the loyalist testimony of Falkland and Digby, Charles I himself, and the self-condemnations of Archbishop Laud. The famous issues were reopened: "Whether the King was not a good man and a martyr"; whether the Star Chamber had not invaded the laws of the land; whether Laud had not assaulted English liberties; the value of ecclesiastical *"forms and ceremonies";* whether "in the canons, the liturgy, or the articles of the Church" there can be found "one word favoring the doctrine of unlimited submission"; whether, on the other hand, something cannot be said for this much-abused doctrine, something to the effect that "It is surely *safer, easier* and *honester* to submit and be quiet, even under the most oppressive princes, than to disturb the peace of kingdoms, neighborhoods, and families"; and finally, that classic argument for authority, whether there could be any difference in essence between one kind of assault upon establishment and any other, and hence whether such an attack as Mayhew had made in the guise of radical Protestantism did not hide within it a secret attachment to *"Rome* and the *Pretender." *[10]

Ancient issues, ancient names — but they were vital still. The Anglicans, embarrassed, in Boston's permissive atmosphere, by Mayhew's exposure of the authoritarian theory their church had once professed, lashed back at him, seeking not merely to disprove his argument but to discredit him. Plagiarism was their most revealing if not their most effective charge. On April 16 and 23, 1750, an anonymous writer in the *Boston Evening-Post,* after deprecating the whole controversy ("Must the present generation quarrel because their forefathers did? Savage! and barbarous! This is to perpetuate variance and make strife hereditary"), and after pointing out that if it was true that tyranny results from "unlimited passive obedience" it was also true that licentiousness, ending in slavery, flows from *"speaking evil of dignities* and abusing the sacred characters both of the dead and the living," proceeded to apologize ironically for Mayhew's "undue warmth" by attributing it to "too intense an application to the reading of such authors as have mixed a good deal of fire in their writings, especially when they treat of Church and Churchmen." So deep had Mayhew's immersion in these incendiary writers been, the columnist continued, and so susceptible and retentive was his mind, that he had clearly made what he read "immediately his own," with the result that his famous pamphlet was a mere pastiche of other people's writings. The *"first,* or argumentative part of his Discourse," the writer said, had been taken "both with matter and words" from a tract — *The Measures of Submission to the Civil Magistrate Considered* — written by Benjamin Hoadly, the famous free-thinking bishop of the Church of England who had praised Mayhew's *Seven Sermons;* and "the *latter,* or declamatory part" was so close an imitation in both spirit and language of Trenchard and Gordon's *Independent Whig* that it might properly be said that Mayhew had "taken an *overdose"* of those authors. And as if that were not enough, an anonymous pamphlet published in England four years before — *A Letter to a Clergyman Relating to His Sermon on the Thirtieth of January* — itself a direct derivative of *The Independent Whig* and in addition dedicated to Hoadly, had supplied the substance of Mayhew's definition of the constitutional limitations on the royal power.

It was not a random or casual charge. Pages were cited and paragraphs compared. A full page of parallel columns, matching passages of Mayhew's *Discourse* with sections of Hoadly's *Measures of Submission,* was appended to the April 16 issue, and two more such pages were printed on April 23d. The accusation was undeniable; but denial was not attempted, for what was at stake was not scholarly integrity but guilt by association, and for Mayhew the association that had been demonstrated was not a matter of shame but of pride. It was with evident delight that he sent a copy of his pamphlet to Hoadly himself, asking that his presumption in doing so be excused on the grounds that to have done otherwise would have been a "manifest injustice" in view of the charge "which some here have asserted, viz.: 'that the greater part of it was stolen from your lordship's original.' " [11]

The important thing, as both Mayhew and his critic saw it, was not the fact that he had lifted phrases and borrowed ideas from other people's writings but who these people were. They were pre-eminent figures in the transmission of the intellectual tradition that had originated in the English Civil War and been carried forward not on the surface of English political life but in those radical undercurrents which so deepened and extended the principles of eighteenth-century Whiggism and which flowed directly into the mainstream of American political thought.[12] For Mayhew, who declared the great modern teachers of liberty to be "Sidney and Milton, Locke and Hoadly . . . I liked them; they seemed rational," [13] it was no disgrace to be caught borrowing ideas and phrases from *The Measures of Submission* and from *The Independent Whig.* The public demonstration of his adherence to the views of the unchurchly Churchman and of those notorious authors who "mixed . . . fire in their writings" was more a credit than a discredit, and he reveled in the association.

Mayhew's *Discourse,* as John Adams later recalled, was "read by everybody, celebrated by friends, and abused by enemies." [14] It circulated widely in the colonies, and was reprinted within a few months of its initial appearance. It quickly became regarded as a classic formulation of the necessity and virtue of resistance to oppression; and like all such statements it became in itself something of a force in public affairs. It created for the extreme radical position on the subject of civil disobedience a more attentive public audience than it had had before in America. Thereafter neither the issue nor Mayhew's position was long absent from public discussion. Within two years of the publication of the *Discourse,* essays "Of Passive Obedience and Nonresistance" appeared in New York as part of William Livingston's attack on the Anglican monopoly of the projected King's College, and they were answered vigorously by spokesmen for the Church. By the early sixties the issue that Mayhew had crystallized in 1750 had become a central question in all the colonies, and his argument, that resistance was obligatory when rulers violated their trust, was dominant. A decade later, in 1775, when the pamphlet was once again reprinted, it expressed what was then almost universally considered to be the simple common sense of the matter, and it was indistinguishable from dozens of other publications appearing everywhere in British North America. The only attempt to refute its arguments extensively — Jonathan Boucher's "On Civil Liberty, Passive Obedience, and Nonresistance" (1775)

— which was as direct a throwback to the crown apologists of Charles I's time and to the nonjurors as Mayhew's *Discourse* had been to Hoadly and the radical Whigs — was suppressed, the presses being "shut to every publication of the kind." [15]

For Mayhew personally the publication of the *Discourse* was a major event, second only in importance to the appearance of his maiden effort, *Seven Sermons*. Like the earlier publication it was picked up by the nonconformist and opposition publicists in England, and slipped neatly into the canon of Anglo-American radicalism. Richard Baron, republican and dissenter, associate, friend, and literary heir of Thomas Gordon, was just then beginning his career as an editor and propagandist of Commonwealth writings (he had already, when Mayhew's pamphlet reached him, republished Sidney's *Discourse,* was in the midst of preparing a two-volume edition of Milton's prose work, and was soon to reprint, among a number of other such writings, a newly discovered second edition of *Eikonoklastes*). He included Mayhew's *Discourse* in a two-volume anthology of pamphlets, *The Pillars of Priestcraft and Orthodoxy Shaken,* which he published in 1752. A compendium of eighteenth-century radicalism, the book contained in its final, expanded form (1768) twenty-four tracts, among which, besides Mayhew's pamphlet, were two by Hoadly and two by Gordon.[16]

With the publication of the *Discourse* Mayhew's reputation was complete, and he stood out thereafter as a pre-eminent spokesman in the colonies for everything that was new, bold, and radically nonconformist in matters of church and state. Through Baron he became a correspondent of Thomas Hollis, the indefatigable propagandist for liberty, and was able to keep close ties to the whole movement of radical politics and political thought in England.[17] His radicalism deepened and spread. His hatred of tyrannical kings became a suspicion of the whole institution of monarchy. Within a year of the publication of the *Discourse* he turned to show how "half-fools and idiots" on thrones are praised for wisdom and virtue while "eminent goodness among the vulgar and middle sorts passes wholly unobserved." England appeared to him increasingly as "a nation where infidelity, irreligion, corruption and venality, and almost every kind of vice seems to have been increasing all the time," while America, in its provincial fastness, seemed with equal speed to be becoming a citadel, perhaps the last, of civil liberty. By 1759, with Canada newly conquered and England apparently sinking deeper into corruption, the future of the American provinces seemed increasingly attractive and important. The colonies, Mayhew wrote in 1759, could become:

a mighty empire (I do not mean an independent one) in numbers little inferior perhaps to the greatest in Europe, and in felicity to none . . . mighty cities rising on every hill and by the side of every commodious port . . . happy fields and villages . . . through a vastly extended territory; there the pastures clothed with flocks, and here the valleys covered with corn . . . religion professed and practiced throughout this spacious kingdom in far greater purity and perfection than since the times of the apostles.

When, after 1760, it appeared that deliberate inroads upon both civil and religious freedom were being made in the colonies, Mayhew moved boldly to apply the beliefs he had professed first in 1750. His resounding controversy with the Reverend East Apthorp over the right of the Church of England to proselytize in the colonies, his incendiary oration on the Stamp Act, and his Thanksgiving sermon, *The Snare Broken* (1766), preached on the occasion of the repeal of the Stamp Act, were the fulfillment and application of his *Discourse Concerning Unlimited Submission* — as was, indeed, the American Revolution itself.[18]

A/DISCOURSE/concerning/Unlimited Submission/and/Non-Resistance/to the/ Higher Powers:/With some Reflections on the Resistance made to/King Charles I./And on the/*Anniversary* of his Death:/In which the mysterious Doctrine of that Prince's/Saintship and Martyrdom is unriddled:/The Substance of which was delivered in a Sermon preached in/the West Meeting-House in *Boston* the Lord's-Day after the/30th of *January,* 1749/50./*Published at the Request of the Hearers.*/ By Jonathan Mayhew, A. M./Pastor of the West Church in *Boston.*/

Fear GOD, honor the King. Saint Paul./*He that ruleth over Men, must be just, ruling in the Fear of GOD.*/Prophet Samuel./*I have said, ye are Gods — but ye shall die like Men, and fall like/one of the PRINCES.* King David./Quid memorem infandas caedes? quid facta TYRANNI/Effera? Dii CAPITI ipsius GENERIQUE reservent — /Necnon Threïcius *longa cum veste* SACERDOS/Obloquitur — — *Rom. Vat. Prin.*/

BOSTON, Printed and Sold by D. Fowle in Queen-Street;/and by D. Gookin over-against the South Meeting-House. 1750./

PREFACE

The ensuing discourse is the last of three upon the same subject, with some little alterations and additions. It is hoped that but few will think the subject of it an improper one to be discoursed on in the pulpit, under a notion that this is preaching politics instead of CHRIST. However, to remove all prejudices of this sort, I beg it may be remembered that "all Scripture . . . is profitable for doctrine, for reproof, for CORRECTION, for instruction in righteousness." * Why, then, should not those parts of Scripture which relate to civil government be examined and explained from the desk, as well as others? Obedience to the civil magistrate is a Christian duty: and if so, why should not the nature, grounds, and extent of it be considered in a Christian assembly? Besides, if it be said that it is out of character for a Christian minister to meddle with such a subject, this censure will at last fall upon the holy apostles. They write upon it in their epistles to Christian churches: and surely it cannot be deemed either criminal or impertinent to attempt an explanation of their doctrine.

It was the near approach of the THIRTIETH *of* January *that turned my thoughts to this subject: on which solemnity the slavish doctrine of passive obedience and nonresistance is often warmly asserted; and the dissenters from the established church represented not only as schismatics (with more of triumph than of truth, and of choler than Christianity) but also as persons of seditious, traitorous, and rebellious principles —* GOD *be thanked one may, in any part of the* British *dominions, speak freely (if a decent regard be paid to those in authority) both of government and religion; and even give some broad hints that he is engaged on the side of Liberty, the* BIBLE, *and Common Sense, in opposition to Tyranny, PRIESTCRAFT, and Nonsense, without being in danger either of the* bastille *or the* inquisition — *though there will always be some interested politicians, contracted bigots, and hypocritical zealots for a party, to take offense at such freedoms. Their censure is praise; their praise is infamy. A spirit of domination is always to be guarded against, both in church and state, even in times of the greatest security, such as the present is amongst US, at least as to the latter. Those nations who are now groaning under the iron scepter of tyranny were once free. So they might, probably, have remained, by a seasonable caution against despotic measures. Civil tyranny is usually small in its beginning, like "the drop of a bucket," † till at length, like a mighty torrent or the raging waves of the sea, it bears down all before it and deluges whole countries and empires. Thus it is as to ecclesiastical tyranny also — the most cruel, intolerable, and impious of any. From small beginnings "it exalts itself above all that is called GOD and that is worshiped." ‡ People have no security against being unmercifully* priest-ridden *but by keeping all imperious* BISHOPS *and other* CLERGYMEN *who love to "lord it over God's heritage" from getting their* foot *into the* stirrup *at all. Let them be once fairly* mounted, *and their "beasts, the laiety" § ¹ may prance and* flounce *about to no purpose: and they will, at length, be so* jaded *and* hacked *by these reverend* jockies *that they will not even have* spirits *enough to complain that their* backs *are galled; or, like* Balaam's *ass, to "rebuke the madness of the prophet."* ||

"The mystery of iniquity began to work" ¶ even in the days of some of the apostles. But the kingdom of antichrist was then, in one respect, like the kingdom of heaven, however different in all others: it was "as a grain of mustard seed." * This grain was sown in Italy, *that fruitful field; and though it were "the least of all seeds," it soon became a mighty tree. It has, long since, overspread and* darkened *the greatest part of* Christendom, *so that we may apply to it what is said of the tree which* Nebuchadnezzar *saw in his vision: "The height thereof reacheth unto heaven, and the sight thereof to the end of all the earth — and* THE BEASTS OF THE FIELD *have shadow under it." Tyranny brings* ignorance *and* brutality *along with it. It degrades men from their just rank into the class of brutes. It damps their spirits. It suppresses arts. It extinguishes every spark of noble ardor and generosity in the breasts of those who are enslaved by it. It makes naturally strong and great minds feeble and little, and triumphs over the ruins of virtue and humanity. This is true of tyranny in every shape. There can be nothing great and good where its influence reaches. For which reason it becomes every friend to truth and humankind, every lover of God and the Christian religion, to bear a part in opposing this hateful monster. It was a desire to contribute a mite towards carrying on a war against this common enemy that produced the following discourse. And if it serve in any measure to keep up a spirit of civil and religious liberty amongst us, my end is answered. — There are virtuous and candid men in all sects; all such are to be esteemed: there are also vicious men and bigots in all sects; and all such* ought to be despised.

> To virtue only and her friends, a friend;
> The world beside may murmur or commend.
> Know, all the distant din that world can keep
> Rolls o'er my grotto, and but soothes my sleep. Pope.[2]

JONATHAN MAYHEW

‡ 2 Thess. ii, 4.　§ Mr. *Leslie.*　|| 2 Pet. ii, 16.　¶ 2 Thess. ii, 7.　* Matt. xiii, 31.

Concerning Unlimited Submission and Nonresistance to the *Higher Powers*

R O M . X I I I , I – 8

1. Let every soul be subject unto the higher powers. For there is no power but of God: the powers that be are ordained of God.

2. Whosoever therefore resisteth the power, resisteth the ordinance of God: and they that resist shall receive to themselves damnation.

3. For rulers are not a terror to good works, but to the evil. Wilt thou then not be afraid of the power? Do that which is good, and thou shalt have praise of the same.

4. For he is the minister of God to thee for good. But if thou do that which is evil, be afraid; for he beareth not the sword in vain: for he is the minister of God, a revenger to execute wrath upon him that doth evil.

5. Wherefore ye must needs be subject, not only for wrath, but also for conscience sake.

6. For, for this cause pay you tribute also: for they are God's ministers, attending continually upon this very thing.

7. Render therefore to all their dues: tribute to whom tribute is due; custom to whom custom; fear to whom fear; honor to whom honor.

IT IS evident that the affair of civil government may properly fall under a *moral* and *religious* consideration, at least so far forth as it relates to the general nature and end of magistracy and to the grounds and extent of that submission which persons of a private character ought to yield to those who are vested with [2] authority. This must be allowed by all who acknowledge the divine original of Christianity. For although there be a sense, and a very plain and important sense, in which Christ's *kingdom is not of this world,** his inspired apostles have, nevertheless, laid down some general principles concerning the office of civil rulers and the duty of subjects, together with the reason and obligation of that duty. And from hence it follows that it

---

* John xviii, 36.

is proper for all who acknowledge the authority of Jesus Christ and the inspiration of his apostles to endeavor to understand what is in fact the doctrine which they have delivered concerning this matter. It is the duty of *Christian* magistrates to inform themselves what it is which their religion teaches concerning the nature and design of their office. And it is equally the duty of all *Christian* people to inform themselves what it is which their religion teaches concerning that subjection which they owe to *the higher powers*. It is for these reasons that I have attempted to examine into the Scripture account of this matter, in order to lay it before you with the same *freedom* which I constantly use with relation to other doctrines and precepts of Christianity; not doubting but you will *judge* upon everything offered to your consideration with the same spirit of *freedom* and *liberty* with which it is *spoken*.

The passage read is the most full and express of any in the New Testament relating to rulers and subjects: and therefore I thought it proper to ground upon it what I had to propose to you with reference to the [3] authority of the civil magistrate and the subjection which is due to him. But before I enter upon an explanation of the several parts of this passage, it will be proper to observe one thing which may serve as a key to the whole of it.

It is to be observed, then, that there were some persons amongst the *Christians* of the apostolic age, and particularly those at *Rome* to whom St. *Paul* is here writing, who seditiously disclaimed *all* subjection to civil authority, refusing to pay taxes and the duties laid upon their traffic and merchandise, and who scrupled not to speak of their rulers without any due regard to their office and character. Some of these turbulent *Christians* were converts from *Judaism,* and others from *paganism*. The *Jews* in general had, long before this time, taken up a strange conceit, that being the *peculiar* and *elect* people of God they were, therefore, exempted from the jurisdiction of any *heathen* princes or governors. Upon this ground it was that some of them, during the public ministry of our blessed Saviour, came to Him with that question: *Is it lawful to give tribute unto* Caesar *or not?* † And this notion many of them retained after they were proselyted to the *Christian* faith. As to the *gentile* converts, some of them grossly mistook the nature of that *liberty* which the Gospel promised, and thought that by virtue of their subjection to Christ, the *only* King and head of his church, they were

† Matt. xxii, 17.

wholly freed from subjection to any other prince; as though Christ's *kingdom had been of this* [4] *world* in such a sense as to interfere with the civil powers of the earth, and to deliver their subjects from that allegiance and duty which they before owed to them. Of these visionary *Christians* in general who disowned subjection to the civil powers in being where they respectively lived, there is mention made in several places in the New Testament. The Apostle *Peter* in particular characterizes them in this manner: *them that . . . despise government, presumptuous are they, self-willed, they are not afraid to speak evil of dignities.*‡ Now it is with reference to these doting *Christians* that the Apostle speaks in the passage before us. And I shall now give you the sense of it in a paraphrase upon each verse in its order, desiring you to keep in mind the character of the persons for whom it is designed, that so as I go along you may see how just and natural this address is, and how well suited to the circumstances of those against whom it is leveled.

The Apostle begins thus: *Let every soul* § *be subject unto the higher powers;* || *for there is no power*¶ *but of* [5] *God: the powers that be* * *are ordained of God* † (ver. 1), q.d.: "Whereas some professed *Christians* vainly imagine that they are wholly excused from all manner of duty and subjection to civil authority, refusing to honor their rulers and to pay taxes; which opinion is not only unreasonable in itself but also tends to fix a lasting reproach upon the *Christian* name and profession, I now, as an apostle and ambassador of Christ, exhort every one of you,

‡ 2 Pet. ii, 10.

§ *Every soul.* This is an *Hebraism* which signifies *every man;* so that the Apostle does not exempt the *clergy,* such as were endowed with the gift of prophecy or any other miraculous powers which subsisted in the church at that day. And by using the *Hebrew* idiom, it seems that he had the *Jewish* converts principally in his eye.

|| *The higher powers:* more literally, the *overruling powers;* which term extends to all civil rulers in common.

¶ By *power,* the Apostle intends not lawless *strength* and brutal *force* without regulation or proper direction, but just *authority;* for so the word here used properly signifies. There may be *power* where there is no *authority.* No man has any *authority* to do what is wrong and injurious, though he may have *power* to do it.

* *The powers that be:* those persons who are in fact vested with authority; those who are in possession. And who those are, the Apostle leaves Christians to determine for themselves; but whoever they are, they are to be obeyed.

† *Ordained of God:* as it is not without God's providence and permission that any are clothed with authority, and as it is agreeable to the positive will and purpose of God that there should be *some persons* vested with authority for the good of society: not that any rulers have their commission immediately from God, the supreme Lord of the universe. If any assert that kings or any other rulers are ordained of God in the latter sense, it is incumbent upon them to show the commission which they speak of, under the broad seal of Heaven. And when they do this, they will, no doubt, be believed.

be he who he will, to pay all dutiful submission to those who are vested with any civil office. For there is, properly speaking, no authority but what is derived from God, as it is only by his permission and providence that any possess it. Yea, I may add that all civil magistrates, as such, although they may be *heathens,* are appointed and ordained of God. For it is certainly God's will that so useful an institution as that of magistracy should take place in the world for the good of civil society." The Apostle proceeds: *Whoever, therefore, resisteth the power, resisteth the ordinance* [6] *of God; and they that resist shall receive to themselves damnation* (ver. 2), q.d.: "Think not, therefore, that ye are guiltless of any crime or sin against God when ye factiously disobey and resist the civil authority. For magistracy and government being, as I have said, the ordinance and appointment of God, it follows that to resist magistrates in the execution of their offices is really to resist the will and ordinance of God himself; and they who thus resist will accordingly be punished by God for this sin in common with others." The Apostle goes on: *For rulers are not a terror to good works, but to the evil.‡ Wilt thou then not be afraid of the power? Do that which is good, and thou shalt have praise of the same. For he is the minister of God to thee for good* (ver. 3d, and part of the 4th), q.d.: "That you may see the truth and justness of what I assert (viz., that magistracy is the ordinance of God, and that you sin against him in opposing it), consider that even *pagan* rulers are not, by the nature and design of their office, enemies and a terror to the good and virtuous actions of men, but only to the injurious and mischievous to society. Will ye not, then, reverence and honor magistracy when ye see the good [7] end and intention of it? How can ye be so unreasonable? Only mind to do your duty as members of society, and this will gain you the applause and favor of all good rulers. For while you do thus, they are, by their office as ministers of God, obliged to encourage and protect you; it is for this very purpose that they are clothed with power." The Apostle subjoins: *But if thou do that which is evil, be afraid, for he beareth not the sword in vain. For he is the minister of*

‡ *For rulers are not a terror to good works, but to the evil.* It cannot be supposed that the Apostle designs here, or in any of the succeeding verses, to give the true character of *Nero* or any other civil powers then in being as if they were in fact such persons as he describes, a terror to evil works only and not to the good. For such a character did not belong to them; and the Apostle was no sycophant or parasite of power, whatever some of his pretended successors have been. He only tells what rulers would be, provided they acted up to their character and office.

God, a revenger, to execute wrath upon him that doth evil § (ver. 4, latter part), q.d.: "But upon the other hand, if ye refuse to do your duty as members of society; if ye refuse to bear your part in the support of government; if ye are disorderly, and do things which merit civil chastisement, then, indeed, ye have reason to be afraid. For it is ⟦8⟧ not in vain that rulers are vested with the power of inflicting punishment. They are, by their office, not only the ministers of God for good to those that do well, but also his ministers to revenge, to discountenance and punish those that are unruly and injurious to their neighbors." The Apostle proceeds: *Wherefore ye must needs be subject not only for wrath but also for conscience sake* (ver. 5), q.d.: "Since, therefore, magistracy is the ordinance of God and since rulers are, by their office, benefactors to society by discouraging what is bad and encouraging what is good and so preserving peace and order amongst men, it is evident that ye ought to pay a willing subjection to them, not to obey merely for fear of exposing yourselves to their wrath and displeasure, but also in point of reason, duty, and conscience: ye are under an indispensable obligation, as *Christians,* to honor their office and to submit to them in the execution of it." The Apostle goes on: *For, for this cause you pay tribute also; for they are God's ministers, attending continually upon this very thing* (ver. 6), q.d.: "And here is a plain reason also why ye should pay tribute to them; for they are God's ministers, exalted above the common level of mankind not that they may indulge themselves in softness and luxury and be entitled to the servile homage of their fellow men, but that they may execute an office no less laborious than honorable, and attend continually upon the public welfare. This being their business ⟦9⟧ and duty, it is

§ It is manifest that when the Apostle speaks of it as the office of civil rulers to encourage what is *good* and to punish what is evil, he speaks only of *civil good* and *evil.* They are to consult the good of society *as such;* not to dictate in religious concerns; not to make laws for the government of men's consciences, and to inflict civil penalties for religious crimes. It is sufficient to overthrow the doctrine of the authority of the civil magistrate in affairs of a spiritual nature (so far as it is built upon anything which is here said by St. *Paul* or upon anything else in the New Testament) only to observe that all the magistrates then in the world were *heathen,* implacable enemies to Christianity; so that to give them authority in religious matters would have been, in effect, to give them authority to extirpate the Christian religion and to establish the idolatries and superstitions of paganism. And can anyone reasonably suppose that the Apostle had any intention to extend the authority of rulers beyond concerns merely civil and political, to the overthrowing of that religion which he himself was so zealous in propagating! But it is natural for those whose religion cannot be supported upon the footing of reason and argument to have recourse to power and force, which will serve a bad cause as well as a good one; and indeed much better.

but reasonable that they should be requited for their care and diligence in performing it, and enabled, by taxes levied upon the subject, effectually to prosecute the great end of their institution, the good of society." The Apostle sums all up in the following words: *Render therefore to all their dues; tribute*|| [3] *to whom tribute is due; custom*|| *to whom custom; fear to whom fear; honor to whom honor* (ver. 7), q.d.: "Let it not, therefore, be said of any of you hereafter, that you contemn government, to the reproach of yourselves and of the *Christian* religion. Neither your being *Jews* by nation nor your becoming the subjects of Christ's kingdom gives you any dispensation for making disturbances in the government under which you live. Approve yourselves, therefore, as peaceable and dutiful subjects. Be ready to pay to your rulers all that they may, in respect of their office, justly demand of you. Render tribute and custom to those of your governors to whom tribute and custom belong, and cheerfully honor and reverence all who are vested with civil authority, according to their deserts."

The Apostle's doctrine, in the passage thus explained concerning the office of civil rulers and the duty of [10] subjects, may be summed up in the following observations,¶ viz.:

That the end of magistracy is the good of civil society, *as such.*

That civil rulers, *as such,* are the ordinance and ministers of God, it being by his permission and providence that any bear rule, and agreeable to his will that there should be *some persons* vested with authority in society, for the well-being of it.

That which is here said concerning civil rulers extends to all of them in common: it relates indifferently to monarchical, republican, and aristocratical government, and to all other forms which truly answer the sole end of government, the happiness of society; and to all the different degrees of authority in any particular state, to inferior officers no less than to the supreme.

That disobedience to civil rulers in the due exercise of their authority is not merely a *political sin* but an heinous *offense against God and religion.*

|| *Grotius* observes that the Greek words here used answer to the *tributum* and *vectigal* of the *Romans;* the former was the money paid for the soil and poll; the latter, the duties laid upon some sorts of merchandise. And what the Apostle here says deserves to be seriously considered by all Christians concerned in that common practice of carrying on an *illicit trade* and *running of goods.*

¶ The several observations, here only mentioned, were handled at large in two preceding discourses upon this subject.

That the true ground and reason* of our obligation to be subject to the *higher powers* is the usefulness [11] of magistracy (when properly exercised) to human society and its subserviency to the general welfare.

That obedience to civil rulers is here equally required under all forms of government which answer the sole end of all government, the good of society; and to every degree of authority in any state, whether supreme or subordinate.

(From whence it follows,

That if unlimited obedience and nonresistance be here required as a duty under any one form of government, it is also required as a duty under all other forms, and as a duty to subordinate rulers as well as to the supreme.)

And lastly, that those civil rulers to whom the Apostle enjoins subjection are the persons *in possession;* [12] *the powers that be,* those who are *actually* vested with authority.†

There is one very important and interesting point which remains to be inquired into; namely, the *extent* of that subjection *to the higher*

* Some suppose the Apostle in this passage enforces the duty of submission with *two* arguments quite distinct from each other; one taken from this consideration, that rulers are the ordinance and the ministers of God (ver. 1, 2, and 4), and the other from the benefits that accrue to society from civil government (ver. 3, 4, and 6). And indeed, these may be distinct motives and arguments for submission, as they may be separately viewed and contemplated. But when we consider that rulers are not the ordinance and the ministers of God but only so far forth as they perform God's will by acting up to their office and character and so by being benefactors to society, this makes these arguments coincide and run up into *one* at last, at least so far that the former of them cannot hold good for submission where the latter fails. Put the supposition that any man bearing the title of a magistrate should exercise his power in such a manner as to have no claim to obedience by virtue of that argument which is founded upon the usefulness of magistracy, and you equally take off the force of the other argument also, which is founded upon his being the ordinance and the minister of God. For he is no longer God's ordinance and minister than he acts up to his office and character by exercising his power for the good of society. This is, in brief, the reason why it is said above, in the *singular* number, *that the true ground and reason,* etc. The use and propriety of this remark may possibly be more apparent in the progress of the argument concerning resistance.

† This must be understood with this *proviso,* that they do not grossly *abuse* their power and trust, but exercise it for the good of those that are governed. Who these persons were, whether *Nero,* etc., or not, the Apostle does not say, but leaves it to be determined by those to whom he writes. God does not interpose, in a miraculous way, to point out the persons who shall bear rule and to whom subjection is due. And as to the unalienable, indefeasible right of *primogeniture,* the Scriptures are entirely silent, or rather plainly contradict it, *Saul* being the first king among the *Israelites,* and appointed to the royal dignity during his own father's lifetime; and he was succeeded, or rather superseded, by *David, the* last *born among many brethren.* Now if *God* has not invariably determined this matter, it must, of course, be determined by *men.* And if it be determined by *men,* it must be determined either in the way of *force* or of *compact.* And which of these is the most *equitable* can be no question.

powers which is here enjoined as a duty upon all Christians. Some have thought it warrantable and glorious to disobey the civil powers in certain circumstances, and, in cases of very great and general oppression when humble remonstrances fail of having any effect, and when the public welfare cannot be otherwise provided for and secured, to rise unanimously even against the sovereign himself in order to redress their grievances, to vindicate their natural and legal rights, to break the yoke of tyranny, and free themselves and posterity from inglorious servitude and ruin. It is upon this principle that many royal oppressors have been driven from their thrones into banishment, and many slain by the hands of their subjects. [13] It was upon this principle that *Tarquin* was expelled from *Rome,* and *Julius Caesar,* the conqueror of the world and the tyrant of his country, cut off in the senate house. It was upon this principle that King *Charles* I was beheaded before his own banqueting house. It was upon this principle that King *James* II was made to fly that country which he aimed at enslaving; and upon this principle was that *revolution* brought about which has been so fruitful of happy consequences to *Great Britain*. But, in opposition to this principle, it has often been asserted that the Scripture in general (and the passage under consideration in particular) makes all resistance to princes a crime, in any case whatever. — If they turn tyrants and become the common oppressors of those whose welfare they ought to regard with a paternal affection, we must not pretend to right ourselves unless it be by prayers and tears and humble entreaties; and if these methods fail of procuring redress we must not have recourse to any other, but all suffer ourselves to be robbed and butchered at the pleasure of the *Lord's anointed,* lest we should incur the sin of rebellion and the punishment of damnation. For he has God's authority and commission to bear him out in the worst of crimes, so far that he may not be withstood or controlled. Now whether we are obliged to yield such an absolute submission to our prince, or whether disobedience and resistance may not be justifiable in some cases notwithstanding anything in the passage before us, is an inquiry in which we are all concerned; and this is the inquiry which is the main design of the present discourse.

[14] Now there does not seem to be any necessity of supposing that an absolute, unlimited obedience, whether active or passive, is here enjoined merely for this reason, that the precept is delivered in *absolute terms,* without any *exception* or *limitation* expressly mentioned. We are enjoined (ver. 1) to be *subject to the higher powers,* and (ver. 5) to be *subject for conscience sake.* And because these expressions are absolute

and unlimited (or, more properly, general), some have inferred that the subjection required in them must be absolute and unlimited also, at least so far forth as to make passive obedience and nonresistance a duty in all cases whatever, if not active obedience likewise. Though, by the way, there is here no distinction made betwixt active and passive obedience; and if either of them be required in an unlimited sense, the other must be required in the same sense also by virtue of the present argument, because the expressions are equally absolute with respect to both. But that unlimited obedience of any sort cannot be argued merely from the indefinite expressions in which obedience is enjoined appears from hence, that expressions of the same nature frequently occur in Scripture, upon which it is confessed on all hands that no such absolute and unlimited sense ought to be put. For example, *Love not the world; neither the things that are in the world;*‡ *Lay not up for yourselves treasures upon earth;*§ *Take therefore no thought for the morrow;*‖ are precepts expressed in at least equally absolute and unlimited terms: but it is generally allowed that they are to be understood with certain restrictions and limitations, [15] some degree of love to the world and the things of it being allowable. Nor, indeed, do the *Right Reverend Fathers in God* and other *dignified clergymen* of the established church seem to be altogether averse to admitting of restrictions in the latter case, how warm soever any of them may be against restrictions and limitations in the case of submission to authority, whether civil or ecclesiastical. It is worth remarking, also, that patience and submission under private injuries are enjoined in much more peremptory and absolute terms than any that are used with regard to submission to the injustice and oppression of civil rulers. Thus, *I say unto you, that ye resist not evil; but whosoever shall smite thee on the right cheek, turn to him the other also. And if any man will sue thee at the law, and take away thy coat, let him have thy cloak also. And whosoever shall compel thee to go a mile with him, go with him twain.*¶ Any man may be defied to produce such strong expressions in favor of a passive and tame submission to unjust, tyrannical rulers as are here used to enforce submission to private injuries. But how few are there that understand those expressions literally? And the reason why they do not is because (with submission to the *Quakers*) common sense shows that they were not intended to be so understood.

But to instance in some Scripture precepts which are more directly to the point in hand: Children are commanded to obey their parents, and

‡ 1 John ii, 15.   § Matt. vi, 19.   ‖ Matt. vi, 34.   ¶ Matt. v, 39, 40, 41.

servants their masters, in as absolute and unlimited terms as subjects [16] are here commanded to obey their civil rulers. Thus this same Apostle: *Children, obey your parents in the Lord, for this is right. Honor thy father and mother, which is the first commandment with promise . . . Servants, be obedient to them that are your masters according to the flesh, with fear and trembling, with singleness of your heart, as unto Christ.** Thus also wives are commanded to be obedient to their husbands: *Wives, submit yourselves unto your own husbands as unto the Lord. For the husband is head of the wife, even as* CHRIST IS THE HEAD OF THE CHURCH . . . *Therefore, as the church is subject unto Christ, so let the wives be to their own husbands* IN EVERY THING.† In all these cases, submission is required in terms at least as absolute and universal as are ever used with respect to rulers and subjects. But who supposes that the Apostle ever intended to teach that children, servants, and wives should, in all cases whatever, obey their parents, masters, and husbands respectively, never making any opposition to their will even although they should require them to break the commandments of God or should causelessly make an attempt upon their lives? No one puts such a sense upon these expressions, however absolute and unlimited. Why then should it be supposed that the Apostle designed to teach universal obedience, whether active or passive, to *the higher powers* merely because his precepts are delivered in absolute and unlimited terms? And if this be a good argument in one case, why is it not in others also? If it be said [17] that resistance and disobedience to *the higher powers* is here said positively to be a sin, so also is the disobedience of children to parents, servants to masters, and wives to husbands, in other places of Scripture. But the question still remains whether in all these cases there be not some exceptions. In the three latter, it is allowed there are. And from hence it follows that barely the use of absolute expressions is no proof that obedience to civil rulers is, in all cases, a duty, or resistance, in all cases, a sin. I should not have thought it worth while to take any notice at all of this argument had it not been much insisted upon by some of the advocates for passive obedience and nonresistance: for it is, in itself, perfectly trifling, and rendered considerable only by the stress that has been laid upon it for want of better.

There is, indeed, one passage in the New Testament where it may seem, at first view, that an unlimited submission to civil rulers is enjoined: *Submit yourselves to every ordinance of man for the Lord's sake.*‡

* Eph. vi, 1, etc.   † Eph. v, 22, 23, 24.   ‡ 1 Pet. ii, 13.

— To *every ordinance of man.* However, this expression is no stronger than that before taken notice of with relation to the duty of wives: *So let the wives be subject to their own husbands* — IN EVERY THING. But the true solution of this difficulty (if it be one) is *this:* by *every ordinance of man§* is not meant every command of the civil magistrate without exception, but *every* [18] *order of magistrates appointed by man,* whether *superior* or *inferior;* for so the Apostle explains himself in the very next words: *Whether it be to the king as supreme, or to governors, as unto them that are sent,* etc. But although the Apostle had not subjoined any such explanation, the reason of the thing itself would have obliged us to limit the expression *every ordinance of man* to such human ordinances and commands as are not inconsistent with the ordinances and commands of God, the supreme lawgiver, or with any other higher and antecedent obligations.

It is to be observed, in the next place, that as the duty of universal obedience and nonresistance to the *higher powers* cannot be argued from the absolute unlimited expressions which the Apostle here uses, so neither can it be argued from the scope and drift of his reasoning, considered with relation to the persons he was here opposing. As was observed above, there were some professed *Christians* in the apostolic age who disclaimed all magistracy and civil authority in general, *despising government* and *speaking evil of dignities,* some under a notion that *Jews* ought not to be under the jurisdiction of *gentile* rulers, and others that they were set *free* from the temporal powers by Christ. Now it is with persons of this licentious opinion and character that the Apostle is concerned. And all that was directly to his point was to show that they were bound to submit to magistracy *in general.* This is a circumstance very material to be taken notice of in order to ascertain [19] the sense of the Apostle. For this being considered, it is sufficient to account for all that he says concerning the duty of subjection and the sin of resistance to the *higher powers* without having recourse to the doctrine of unlimited submission and passive obedience in all cases whatever. Were it known that those in opposition to whom the Apostle wrote allowed of civil authority in general and only asserted that there were *some cases* in which obedience and nonresistance were not a duty, there would, then, indeed be reason for interpreting this passage as containing the doctrine of unlimited

§ Literally, *every human institution or appointment.* By which manner of expression the Apostle plainly intimates that rulers derive their authority *immediately* not from *God* but from *men.*

obedience and nonresistance, as it must, in this case, be supposed to have been leveled against such as denied that doctrine. But since it is certain that there were persons who vainly imagined that civil government in general was not to be regarded by them, it is most reasonable to suppose that the Apostle designed his discourse only against *them*. And agreeably to this supposition we find that he argues the usefulness of civil magistracy in general, its agreeableness to the will and purpose of God who is *over all,* and so deduces from hence the obligation of submission to it. But it will not follow that because civil government is, in general, a good institution and necessary to the peace and happiness of human society, therefore there be no supposable cases in which resistance to it can be innocent. So that the duty of unlimited obedience, whether active or passive, can be argued neither from the manner of expression here used nor from the general scope and design of the passage.

[20] And if we attend to the nature of the argument with which the Apostle here enforces the duty of submission to *the higher powers,* we shall find it to be such an one as concludes not in favor of submission to all who bear the *title* of rulers in common, but only to those who *actually* perform the duty of rulers by exercising a reasonable and just authority for the good of human society. This is a point which it will be proper to enlarge upon because the question before us turns very much upon the truth or falsehood of this position. It is obvious, then, in general that the civil rulers whom the Apostle here speaks of, and obedience to whom he presses upon Christians as a duty, are *good rulers,*|| such as are, in the exercise of their office and power, benefactors to society. Such they are described to be throughout this passage. Thus it is said that they are not *a terror to good works but to the evil;* that they are *God's ministers for good, revengers to execute wrath upon him that doth evil; and that they attend continually upon this very thing.* St. *Peter* gives the same account of rulers: they are *for a praise to them that do well, and the punishment of evildoers.*¶ It is manifest that this character and description of rulers agrees only to such as are rulers in fact as well as in name: to such as govern well and act agreeably to their office. And the Apostle's argument for submission to rulers is wholly built [21] and grounded upon a presumption that they do in fact answer this character,

---

|| By *good rulers* are not intended such as are good in a *moral* or *religious* but only in a *political* sense; those who perform their duty so far as their office extends, and so far as civil society, as such, is concerned in their actions.

¶ See the marginal note [footnote], p. 6. See also the marginal note, p. 7.

and is of no force at all upon supposition to the contrary. If *rulers are a terror to good works and not to the evil;* if they are not *ministers for good to society* but for evil and distress by violence and oppression; if they *execute wrath upon* sober, peaceable persons who do their duty as members of society, and suffer rich and honorable knaves to escape with impunity; if, instead of *attending continually upon* the good work of advancing the public welfare, they *attend* only upon the gratification of their own lust and pride and ambition to the destruction of the public welfare — if this be the case, it is plain that the Apostle's argument for submission does not reach them; they are not the same but different persons from those whom he characterizes and who must be obeyed according to his reasoning. Let me illustrate the Apostle's argument by the following *similitude* (it is no matter how far it is from anything which has, in fact, happened in the world). Suppose, then, it was allowed in general that the *clergy* were an useful order of men, that they ought to be *esteemed very highly in love for their work's sake;** and to be decently supported by those whom they serve, *the laborer being worthy of his reward.†* Suppose, farther, that a number of *Reverend* and *Right Reverend Drones,* who *worked not,* who preached, perhaps, but *once a year,* and *then* not the *Gospel* of Jesus Christ, but the *divine right of tithes,* the *dignity of their office as ambassadors of Christ,* the equity of *sinecures* and [22] a *plurality of benefices,* the excellency of the *devotions* in *that prayer book* which some of them hired *chaplains to use for them,* or some favorite point of *church tyranny* and *antichristian* usurpation; suppose such men as these, spending their lives in effeminacy, luxury, and idleness (or when they were not idle, doing that which is worse than idleness), suppose such men should, merely by the merit of *ordination* and *consecration* and a *peculiar, odd habit,* claim great respect and reverence from those whom they civilly called *the beasts of the laiety,‡* and demand thousands *per annum* for that good service which they *never performed* and for which, if they had performed it, this would be much more than a *quantum meruit.* Suppose this should be the case (it is only by way of *simile* and surely it will give no offense); would not everybody be astonished at such insolence, injustice, and impiety? And ought not such men to be told plainly that they could not reasonably expect the esteem and reward due to the ministers of the Gospel unless they did the duties of their office? Should they not be told that their *title* and *habit*

---

* 1 Thess. v, 13.   † 1 Tim. v, 18.   ‡ Mr. *Leslie.*

claimed no regard, reverence, or pay separate from the *care* and *work* and various *duties* of their *function?* And that while they neglected the *latter,* the *former* served only to render them the more ridiculous and contemptible? — The application of this *similitude* to the case in hand is very easy. If those who bear the title of civil rulers do not perform the duty of civil rulers but act directly counter to the sole end and design of their office; if they [23] injure and oppress their subjects instead of defending their rights and doing them good, they have not the least pretense to be honored, obeyed, and rewarded according to the Apostle's argument. For his reasoning, in order to show the duty of subjection to the *higher powers,* is, as was before observed, built wholly upon the supposition that they do *in fact* perform the duty of rulers.

If it be said that the Apostle here uses another argument for submission to the *higher powers* besides that which is taken from the usefulness of their office to civil society when properly discharged and executed, namely, that their *power is from God,* that they *are ordained of God,* and that they *are God's ministers;* and if it be said that this argument for submission to them will hold good although they do not exercise their power for the benefit but for the ruin and destruction of human society — this objection was obviated, in part, before.§ Rulers have no authority from God to do mischief. They are not *God's ordinance* or *God's ministers* in any other sense than as it is by his permission and providence that they are exalted to bear rule, and as magistracy duly exercised and authority rightly applied in the enacting and executing good laws. Laws attempered and accommodated to the common welfare of the subjects must be supposed to be agreeable to the will of the beneficent Author and supreme Lord of the universe whose *kingdom ruleth over all* ‖ and whose [24] *tender mercies are over all his works.*¶ It is blasphemy to call tyrants and oppressors *God's ministers.* They are more properly *the messengers of Satan to buffet us.** No rulers are properly *God's ministers* but such as are *just, ruling in the fear of God.*† When once magistrates act contrary to their office and the end of their institution, when they rob and ruin the public instead of being guardians of its peace and welfare, they immediately cease to be the *ordinance* and *ministers of God* and no more deserve that glorious character than common *pirates* and *highwaymen.* So that whenever that argument for submission fails which is grounded upon the usefulness of magistracy to civil society (as it always

§ See the margin, page 10 [foot]note *.   ‖ Psal. ciii, 19.   ¶ Psal. cxlv, 19.
* 2 Cor. xii, 7.   † 2 Sam. xxiii, 3.

does when magistrates do hurt to society instead of good), the other argument, which is taken from their being the ordinance of God, must necessarily fail also, no person of a civil character being *God's minister* in the sense of the Apostle any farther than he performs God's will by exercising a just and reasonable authority and ruling for the good of the subject.

This is in general. Let us now trace the Apostle's reasoning in favor of submission to the *higher powers* a little more particularly and exactly. For by this it will appear, on one hand, how good and conclusive it is for submission to those rulers who exercise their power in a proper manner; and, on the other, how weak and trifling and unconnected it is if it be supposed to be meant by the Apostle to show the obligation and duty of [25] obedience to tyrannical, oppressive rulers in common with others of a different character.

The Apostle enters upon his subject thus: *Let every soul be subject unto the higher powers. For there is no power but of God: the powers that be are ordained of God.*‡ Here he urges the duty of obedience from this topic of argument, that civil rulers, as they are supposed to fulfill the pleasure of God, are the ordinance of God. But how is this an argument for obedience to such rulers as do not perform the pleasure of God by doing good but the pleasure of the devil by doing evil, and such as are not, therefore, *God's ministers* but the devil's! *Whosoever, therefore, resisteth the power, resisteth the ordinance of God; and they that resist, shall receive to themselves damnation.*§ Here the Apostle argues that those who resist a reasonable and just authority which is agreeable to the will of God do really resist the will of God himself, and will, therefore, be punished by Him. But how does this prove that those who resist a lawless, unreasonable power, which is contrary to the will of God, do therein resist the will and ordinance of God? Is resisting those who resist God's will the same thing with resisting God? Or shall those who do so *receive to themselves damnation! For rulers are not a terror to good works, but to the evil. Wilt thou then not be afraid of the power? Do that which is good and thou shalt have praise of the same. For he is the minister of God to thee for good.*‖ Here the Apostle argues more explicitly [26] than he had before done for revering and submitting to magistracy, from this consideration: that such as really performed the duty of magistrates would be enemies only to the evil actions of men and would befriend and encourage the good and so be a common blessing

‡ Ver. 1.   § Ver. 2.   ‖ Ver. 3d, and part of the 4th.

to society. But how is this an argument that we must honor and submit to such magistrates as are not enemies to the evil actions of men but to the good, and such as are not a common blessing but a common curse to society! *But if thou do that which is evil, be afraid; for he is the minister of God, a revenger to execute wrath upon him that doth evil.*¶ Here the Apostle argues from the nature and end of magistracy that such as did evil (and such only) had reason to be afraid of the *higher powers,* it being part of their office to punish evildoers no less than to defend and encourage such as do well. But if magistrates are unrighteous, if they are *respecters of persons,* if they are partial in their administration of justice, then those who do well have as much reason to *be afraid* as those that do evil: there can be no safety for the good nor any peculiar ground of terror to the unruly and injurious. So that, in this case, the main end of civil government will be frustrated. And what reason is there for submitting to that government which does by no means answer the design of government? *Wherefore ye must needs be subject not only for wrath but also for conscience sake.** Here the Apostle argues the duty of a cheerful and conscientious submission to civil [27] government from the nature and end of magistracy as he had before laid it down, i.e., as the design of it was to punish evildoers and to support and encourage such as do well, and as it must, if so exercised, be agreeable to the will of God. But how does what he here says prove the duty of a cheerful and conscientious subjection to those who forfeit the character of rulers? — to those who encourage the bad and discourage the good? The argument here used no more proves it to be a sin to resist such rulers than it does to *resist the devil,* that he may *flee from us.*† For one is as truly the *minister of God* as the other. *For, for this cause pay you tribute also: for they are God's ministers, attending continually upon this very thing.*‡ Here the Apostle argues the duty of paying taxes, from this consideration, that those who perform the duty of rulers are continually attending upon the public welfare. But how does this argument conclude for paying taxes to such princes as are continually endeavoring to ruin the public? And especially when such payment would facilitate and promote this wicked design! *Render therefore to all their dues: tribute to whom tribute is due; custom to whom custom; fear to whom fear; honor to whom honor.*§ Here the Apostle sums up what he had been saying concerning the duty of subjects to rulers. And his argument stands thus: "Since

¶ Ver. 4th, latter part.   * Ver. 5.   † Jam. iv, 7.   ‡ Ver. 6.
§ Ver. 7.

magistrates who execute their office well are common benefactors to society and may, in that respect, be properly styled *the ministers and ordinance of God,* and since they are constantly employed [28] in the service of the public, it becomes you to pay them tribute and custom and to reverence, honor, and submit to them in the execution of their respective offices." This is apparently good reasoning. But does this argument conclude for the duty of paying tribute, custom, reverence, honor, and obedience to such persons as (although they bear the title of rulers) use all their power to hurt and injure the public? — such as are not *God's ministers* but *Satan's?* — such as do not take care of, and attend upon, the public interest, but their own, to the ruin of the public? — that is, in short, to such as have no natural and just claim at all to tribute, custom, reverence, honor, and obedience? It is to be hoped that those who have any regard to the Apostle's character as an inspired writer or even as a man of common understanding will not represent him as reasoning in such a loose incoherent manner and drawing conclusions which have not the least relation to his premises. For what can be more absurd than an argument thus framed? — "Rulers are, by their office, bound to consult the public welfare and the good of society: therefore you are bound to pay them tribute, to honor and to submit to them even when they destroy the public welfare and are a common pest to society by acting in direct contradiction to the nature and end of their office."

Thus, upon a careful review of the Apostle's reasoning in this passage, it appears that his arguments to enforce submission are of such a nature as to conclude only in favor of submission *to such rulers as he himself describes;* [29] i.e., such as rule for the good of society, which is the only end of their institution. Common tyrants and public oppressors are not entitled to obedience from their subjects by virtue of anything here laid down by the inspired Apostle.

I now add, farther, that the Apostle's argument is so far from proving it to be the duty of people to obey and submit to such rulers as act in contradiction to the public good || and so to the design of their office, that it proves *the direct contrary.* For, please to observe, that if the end of all civil government be the good of society, if this be the thing that is aimed at in constituting civil rulers, and if the motive and argument for submission to government be taken from the apparent usefulness of civil

---

|| This does not intend [mean] their acting so in *a few particular instances,* which the best of rulers may do through mistake, etc., but their acting so *habitually,* and in a manner which plainly shows that they aim at making themselves great by the ruin of their subjects.

authority, it follows that when no such good end can be answered by submission there remains no argument or motive to enforce it; and if instead of this good end's being brought about by submission, a *contrary end* is brought about and the ruin and misery of society effected by it, here is a plain and positive reason against submission in all such cases, should they ever happen. And therefore, in such cases a regard to the public welfare ought to make us withhold from our rulers that obedience and subjection which it would, otherwise, be our duty to render to them. If it be our duty, for example, to obey our King merely for this reason, that he rules for the public [30] welfare (which is the only argument the Apostle makes use of), it follows by a parity of reason that when he turns tyrant and makes his subjects his prey to devour and to destroy instead of his charge to defend and cherish, we are bound to throw off our allegiance to him and to resist, and that according to the tenor of the Apostle's argument in this passage. Not to discontinue our allegiance, in this case, would be to join with the sovereign in promoting the slavery and misery of that society the welfare of which we ourselves as well as our sovereign are indispensably obliged to secure and promote as far as in us lies. It is true the Apostle puts no case of such a tyrannical prince; but by his grounding his argument for submission wholly upon the good of civil society it is plain he implicitly authorizes and even requires us to make resistance whenever this shall be necessary to the public safety and happiness. Let me make use of this easy and familiar *similitude* to illustrate the point in hand. Suppose God requires a family of children to obey their father and not to resist him, and enforces his command with this argument: that the superintendence and care and authority of a just and kind parent will contribute to the happiness of the whole family so that they ought to obey him for their own sakes more than for his. Suppose this parent at length runs distracted, and attempts, in his mad fit, to cut all his children's throats. Now, in this case, is not the reason before assigned why these children should obey their parent while he continued of a sound mind, namely, *their common good,* a reason equally conclusive [31] for disobeying and resisting him since he is become delirious and attempts their ruin? It makes no alteration in the argument, whether this parent properly speaking loses his reason, or does, while he retains his understanding, that which is as fatal in its consequences as anything he could do were he really deprived of it. This similitude needs no formal application.

But it ought to be remembered that if the duty of universal obedience and nonresistance to our king or prince can be argued from this passage, the same unlimited submission under a republican or any other form of government and even to all the subordinate powers in any particular state, can be proved by it as well: which is more than those who allege it for the mentioned purpose would be willing should be inferred from it. So that this passage does not answer their purpose, but really overthrows and confutes it. This matter deserves to be more particularly considered. — The advocates for unlimited submission and passive obedience do, if I mistake not, always speak with reference to kingly or monarchical government as distinguished from all other forms and with reference to submitting to the will of the king in distinction from all subordinate officers acting beyond their commission and the authority which they have received from the crown. It is not pretended that any persons besides kings have a divine right to do what they please so that no one may resist them without incurring the guilt of factiousness and rebellion. If any other supreme powers oppress the [32] people it is generally allowed that the people may get redress, by resistance if other methods prove ineffectual. And if any officers in a kingly government go beyond the limits of that power which they have derived from the crown (the supposed original source of all power and authority in the state), and attempt, illegally, to take away the properties and lives of their fellow subjects, they may be *forcibly* resisted, at least till application can be made to the crown. But as to the sovereign himself, he may not be resisted in any case, nor any of his officers while they confine themselves within the bounds which he has prescribed to them. This is, I think, a true sketch of the principles of those who defend the doctrine of passive obedience and nonresistance. Now there is nothing in Scripture which supports this scheme of political principles. As to the passage under consideration, the Apostle here speaks of civil rulers in *general,* of all persons in *common* vested with authority for the good of society, without any particular reference to one form of government more than to another or to the supreme power in any particular state more than to subordinate powers. The Apostle does not concern himself with the different forms of government.¶ This he supposes left entirely to human

¶ The essence of government (I mean *good* government, and this is the *only* government which the Apostle treats of in this passage) consists in the *making* and *executing of good laws* — laws attempered to the common felicity of the *governed*. And if this be, *in fact,* done, it is evidently in itself a thing of no consequence at all what the *particular* form of government is — whether the legislative and executive power be lodged in *one and the same* person or in *different* persons; whether in *one* person, whom we call an *absolute monarch;* whether in a *few,* so as to constitute an *aristocracy;* whether in *many,* so as to

[33] prudence and discretion. Now the consequence of this is that unlimited and passive obedience is no more enjoined in this passage under
monarchical government, or to the supreme power in any state, than
under all other species of government which answer the end of government, or to all the subordinate degrees of civil authority, from the highest
to the lowest. Those, therefore, who would from this passage infer the
guilt of resisting kings in all cases whatever, though acting ever so contrary to the design of their office, must, if they will be consistent, go
much farther, and infer from it the guilt of resistance under all other
forms of government and of resisting *any petty officer* in the state, though
acting beyond his commission, in the most arbitrary, illegal manner possible. The argument holds equally strong in both cases. All civil rulers,
as such, are the *ordinance* and *ministers of God;* and they are all, by
the nature of their office and in their respective spheres and stations,
bound to consult the public welfare. With the same reason, therefore,
that any deny unlimited and passive obedience [34] to be here enjoined
under a republic or aristocracy or any other established form of civil
government or to subordinate powers acting in an illegal and oppressive
manner, with the same reason others may deny that such obedience is
enjoined to a king or monarch or any civil power whatever. For the
Apostle says nothing that is *peculiar to kings;* what he says extends
equally to *all* other persons whatever, vested with any civil office. They
are all, in exactly the same sense, the *ordinance of God* and the *ministers
of God;* and obedience is equally enjoined to be paid to them all. For,
as the Apostle expresses it, *there is* NO POWER *but of God:* and we are
required to *render to* ALL *their* DUES, and not MORE than their DUES.
And what these *dues* are, and to *whom* they are to be *rendered,* the Apostle *saith not* but leaves to the reason and consciences of men to determine.

Thus it appears that the common argument, grounded upon this passage, in favor of universal and passive obedience really overthrows itself
by proving too much, if it proves anything at all; namely, that no civil
officer is, in any case whatever, to be resisted, though acting in express

---

constitute a *republic;* or whether in *three co-ordinate branches,* in such manner as to make
the government *partake* something of *each* of these forms, and to be at the same time
essentially different from them *all.* If the *end* be attained, it is enough. But no form of
government seems to be so unlikely to accomplish this *end* as *absolute* monarchy; nor is
there any one that has so little pretense to a *divine original,* unless it be in this sense,
that God *first* introduced it into and thereby overturned the commonwealth of *Israel* as a
curse upon that people for their *folly* and *wickedness,* particularly in *desiring* such a government. (See 1 Sam. viii chap.) Just so God, before, sent *quails* amongst them as a
plague and a *curse* and not as a *blessing.* Numb. chap. xi.

contradiction to the design of his office; which no man in his senses ever did or can assert.

If we calmly consider the nature of the thing itself, nothing can well be imagined more directly contrary to common sense than to suppose that *millions* of people should be subjected to the arbitrary, precarious pleasure [35] of *one single man* (who has *naturally* no superiority over them in point of authority) so that their estates, and everything that is valuable in life, and even their lives also shall be absolutely at his disposal, if he happens to be wanton and capricious enough to demand them. What unprejudiced man can think that God made ALL to be thus subservient to the lawless pleasure and frenzy of ONE so that it shall always be a sin to resist him! Nothing but the most plain and express revelation from Heaven could make a sober impartial man believe such a monstrous, unaccountable doctrine; and, indeed, the thing itself appears so shocking — so out of all *proportion,* that it may be questioned whether all the *miracles* that ever were wrought could make it credible that this doctrine *really* came from God. At present, there is not the least syllable in Scripture which gives any countenance to it. The hereditary, indefeasible, divine right of kings, and the doctrine of nonresistance, which is built upon the supposition of such a right, are altogether as fabulous and chimerical as transubstantiation or any of the most absurd reveries of ancient or modern visionaries. These notions are fetched neither from divine revelation nor human reason; and if they are derived from neither of those sources, it is not much matter from *whence they come, or whither they go.* Only it is a pity that such doctrines should be propagated in society, to raise factions and rebellions, as we see they have in fact been, both in the *last* and in the *present* REIGN.

But then, if unlimited submission and passive obedience to the *higher powers* in all possible cases be not a [36] duty, it will be asked, "How far are we obliged to submit? If we may innocently disobey and resist in some cases, why not in all? Where shall we stop? What is the measure of our duty? This doctrine tends to the total dissolution of civil government and to introduce such scenes of wild anarchy and confusion as are more fatal to society than the worst of tyranny."

After this manner, some men object; and, indeed, this is the most plausible thing that can be said in favor of such an absolute submission as they plead for. But the worst (or rather the best) of it is that there is very little strength or solidity in it. For similar difficulties may be raised with respect to almost every duty of natural and revealed religion. — To instance only in two, both of which are near akin, and indeed exactly parallel, to the case before us. It is unquestionably the duty of children to submit to their parents, and of servants to their masters. But no one asserts that it is their duty to obey and submit to them in all supposable cases, or universally a sin to resist them. Now does this tend to subvert the just authority of parents and masters? Or to introduce confusion and anarchy into private families? No. How then does the same principle tend to unhinge the government of that larger family, the body politic? We know, in general, that children and servants are obliged to obey their parents and masters respectively. We know, also, with equal certainty that they are not obliged to submit to them in all things without exception, but may, in some cases, reasonably and therefore innocently [37] resist them. These principles are acknowledged upon all hands, whatever difficulty there may be in fixing the exact limits of submission. Now there is at least as much difficulty in stating the measure of duty in these two cases as in the cases of rulers and subjects. So that this is really no objection, at least no reasonable one, against resistance to the *higher powers:* or, if it is one, it will hold equally against resistance in the other cases mentioned. It is indeed true that turbulent, vicious-minded men may take occasion from this principle, that their rulers may, in some cases, be lawfully resisted, to raise factions and disturbances in the state and to make resistance where resistance is needless and therefore sinful. But is it not equally true that children and servants of turbulent, vicious minds may take occasion from this principle, that parents and masters may, in some cases, be lawfully resisted, to resist when resistance is unnecessary and therefore criminal? Is the principle in either case false in itself merely because it may be abused and applied to legitimate disobedience and resistance in those instances to which it ought not to be applied? According to this way of arguing there will be no true principles in the world, for there are none but what may be wrested and perverted to serve bad purposes, either through the weakness or wickedness of men.*

* We may very safely assert these two things in general without undermining government: One is that no civil rulers are to be obeyed when they enjoin things that are inconsistent with the commands of God. All such disobedience is lawful and glorious, particularly if persons refuse to comply with any *legal establishment of religion,* because it is a gross perversion and corruption (as to doctrine, worship, and discipline) of a pure and divine religion brought from heaven to earth by the *Son of God* (the only King and Head of the *Christian* church) and propagated through the world by his inspired apostles. All commands running counter to the declared will of the Supreme Legislator of heaven and earth are null and void: and therefore disobedience to them is a duty, not a crime. (See the

[38] A PEOPLE really oppressed to a great degree by their sovereign cannot well be insensible when they are so oppressed. And such a people (if I may allude to an ancient *fable*) have, like the Hesperian fruit, a DRAGON [39] for their *protector* and *guardian;* nor would they have any reason to mourn if some HERCULES should appear [40] to dispatch him. For a nation thus abused to arise unanimously and to resist their

marginal note [footnote], p. 7.) Another thing that may be asserted with equal truth and safety is that no government is to be submitted to at the *expense* of that which is the *sole end* of all government — the common good and safety of society. Because to submit in this case, if it should ever happen, would evidently be to set up the *means* as more valuable and above the *end,* than which there cannot be a greater solecism and contradiction. The only reason of the institution of civil government, and the only rational ground of submission to it, is the common safety and utility. If, therefore, in any case the common safety and utility would not be promoted by submission to government but the contrary, there is no ground or motive for obedience and submission, but for the contrary.

Whoever considers the nature of civil government must, indeed, be sensible that a great degree of *implicit confidence* must unavoidably be placed in those that bear rule. This is implied in the very notion of authority's being originally a *trust,* committed by the people to those who are vested with it as all just and righteous authority is; all besides is mere lawless force and usurpation, neither God nor nature having given any man a right of dominion over any society independently of that society's approbation and consent to be governed by him. — Now as all men are fallible, it cannot be supposed that the public affairs of any state should be always administered in the best manner possible, even by persons of the greatest wisdom and integrity. Nor is it sufficient to legitimate disobedience to the *higher powers* that they are not so administered, or that they are, in some instances, very ill-managed; for upon this principle it is scarcely supposable that any government at all could be supported or subsist. Such a principle manifestly tends to the dissolution of government, and to throw all things into confusion and anarchy. — But it is equally evident, upon the other hand, that those in authority may abuse their *trust* and power *to such a degree* that neither the law of reason nor of religion requires that any obedience or submission should be paid to them; but, on the contrary, that they should be totally *discarded* and the authority which they were before vested with transferred to others, who may exercise it more to those good purposes for which it is given. Nor is this principle, that resistance to the *higher powers* is, in some extraordinary cases, justifiable, so liable to abuse as many persons seem to apprehend it. For although there will be always some petulant, querulous men in every state — men of factious, turbulent, and carping dispositions — glad to lay hold of any trifle to justify and legitimate their caballing against their rulers and other seditious practices; yet there are, comparatively speaking, but few men of this *contemptible character.* It does not appear but that mankind in general have a disposition to be as submissive and passive and tame under government as they ought to be — witness a great, if not the greatest, part of the known world, who are now groaning, but not murmuring, under the heavy yoke of tyranny! While those who govern do it with any tolerable degree of moderation and justice and, in any good measure, act up to their office and character by being public benefactors, the people will generally be easy and peaceable, and be rather inclined to flatter and adore than to insult and resist them. Nor was there ever any *general* complaint against any administration *which lasted long* but what there was good reason for. Till people find themselves greatly abused and oppressed by their governors, they are not apt to complain; and whenever they do, in fact, find themselves thus abused and oppressed, they must be stupid not to complain. To say that subjects in general are not proper judges when their governors oppress them and play the tyrant and when they defend their rights, administer justice impartially, and promote the public welfare, is as great *treason* as ever man uttered: 'tis treason not against

prince, even to the dethroning him, is not criminal, but a reasonable way of vindicating their liberties and just rights; it is making use of the means, and the only means, which God has put into their power for mutual and self-defense. And it would be highly criminal in them not to make use of this means. It would be stupid tameness and unaccountable folly for whole nations to suffer *one* unreasonable, ambitious, and cruel man to wanton and riot in their misery. And in such a case it would, of the two, be more rational to suppose that they did NOT *resist* than that they who did would *receive to themselves damnation.*

And

This naturally brings us to make some reflections upon the resistance which was made about a century since to that unhappy prince, KING CHARLES I, and upon the ANNIVERSARY of his death. This is a point which I should not have concerned myself about were it not that *some men* continue to speak of it, even to this day, with a great deal of warmth and zeal, and in such a manner as to undermine all the principles of LIBERTY, whether civil or religious, and to introduce the most abject slavery both in church and state: so that it is become a matter of universal concern. What I have to offer upon this subject will be comprised in a short answer to the following *queries,* viz.:

[41] For what reason the resistance to King *Charles* the *First* was made?

By whom it was made?

Whether this resistance was REBELLION † or not?

How the *anniversary* of King *Charles's* death came *at first* to be solemnized as a day of fasting and humiliation?

And lastly,

Why those of the episcopal clergy who are very high in the principles

---

one *single* man but the state — against the whole body politic; 'tis treason against mankind; 'tis treason against common sense; 'tis treason against God. And this impious principle lays the foundation for justifying all the tyranny and oppression that ever any prince was guilty of. The people know for what end they set up and maintain their governors; and they are the proper judges when they execute their *trust* as they ought to do it — when their prince exercises an equitable and paternal authority over them; when from a prince and common father he exalts himself into a tyrant; when from subjects and children he degrades them into the class of slaves, plunders them, makes them his prey, and unnaturally sports himself with their lives and fortunes.

† N.B. I speak of rebellion, treason, saintship, martyrdom, etc., throughout this discourse only in the *scriptural* and *theological sense.* I know not how the *law* defines them; the study of *that* not being my employment.

of *ecclesiastical authority* continue to speak of this unhappy man as a great SAINT and a MARTYR?

For what reason, then, was the resistance to King *Charles* made? The general answer to this inquiry is that it was on account of the *tyranny* and *oppression* of his reign.[4] Not a great while after his accession to the throne he married a *French Catholic;* and with her seemed to have *wedded* the politics, if not the religion, of *France* also. For afterwards, during a reign, or rather a tyranny, of many years, he governed in a perfectly wild and arbitrary manner, paying no regard to the constitution and the laws of the kingdom by which the power of the crown was limited or to the solemn oath which he had taken at his coronation. It would be endless, as well as needless, to give a particular account of all the illegal and despotic measures which he took in his administration, partly from his own natural lust of power and partly from the influence of wicked counselors and [42] ministers. — He committed many illustrious members of both houses of Parliament to the *tower* for opposing his arbitrary schemes. — He levied many taxes upon the people without consent of Parliament, and then imprisoned great numbers of the principal merchants and gentry for not paying them. — He erected, or at least revived, several arbitrary courts, in which the most unheard-of barbarities were committed with his knowledge and approbation. — He supported that more than fiend, Archbishop *Laud,* and the clergy of his stamp, in all their church tyranny and hellish cruelties. — He authorized a book in favor of *sports* upon the *Lord's day,* and several clergymen were persecuted by him and the mentioned *pious* bishop for not reading it to the people after *divine service.* — When the Parliament complained to him of the arbitrary proceedings of his corrupt ministers he told that *august body,* in a rough, domineering, unprincely manner, that he wondered anyone should be so foolish and insolent as to think that he would part with the meanest of his servants *upon their account.* — He refused to call any Parliament at all for the space of twelve years together, during all which time he governed in an absolute lawless and despotic manner. — He took all opportunties to encourage the *papists* and to promote them to the highest offices of honor and trust. — He (probably) abetted the horrid massacre in *Ireland,* in which two hundred thousand Protestants were butchered by the Roman Catholics. — He sent a large sum of money, which he had raised by his arbitrary taxes, into *Germany,* to raise foreign troops in order to force more arbitrary taxes [43] upon his subjects. — He not only by a long series of *actions* but also in *plain terms* asserted an absolute uncontrollable power, saying even in one of his speeches to Parliament that as it was blasphemy to dispute what God might do, so it was sedition in subjects to dispute what the King might do. — Towards the end of his tyranny he came to the House of Commons with an armed force‡ [5] and demanded five of its principal members to be delivered up to him. — And this was a prelude to that unnatural war which he soon after levied against his own dutiful subjects, whom he was bound by all the laws of honor, humanity, piety, and, I might add, of *interest* also, to defend and cherish with a paternal affection. I have only time to hint at these facts in a general way, all which, and many more of the same tenor, may be proved by good authorities: so that the *figurative* language which St. *John* uses concerning the just and beneficent deeds of our blessed Saviour may be applied to the unrighteous and execrable deeds of this prince, viz.: *And there are also many other things which* King Charles *did, the which, if they should be written every one, I suppose that even the world itself could not contain the books that should be written.*§ Now it was on account of King *Charles's* thus assuming a power above the laws in direct contradiction to his coronation oath, and governing the greatest part of his time in the most arbitrary oppressive manner; it was upon this account that that resistance was made [44] to him which at length issued in the loss of his crown and of *that head* which was unworthy to wear it.

But by whom was this resistance made? Not by a private *junto;* not by a small seditious *party;* not by a *few desperadoes* who, to mend their fortunes, would embroil the state; but by the LORDS and COMMONS of *England.* It was they that almost unanimously opposed the King's measures for overturning the constitution and changing that free and happy government into a wretched, absolute monarchy. It was they that, when the King was about levying forces against his subjects in order to make himself absolute, commissioned officers and raised an army to defend themselves and the public; and it was they that maintained the war against him all along, till he was made a prisoner. This is indisputable, though it was not, properly speaking, the Parliament but the army which put him to death afterwards. And it ought to be freely acknowledged that most of their proceeding in order to get this matter effected, and particu-

---

‡ Historians are not agreed what number of soldiers attended him in this monstrous invasion of the privileges of Parliament. Some say 300, some 400; and the author of *The History of the Kings of Scotland* says 500.

§ John xxi, 25.

larly the court by which the King was at last tried and condemned, was little better than a mere mockery of justice.

The next question which naturally arises is whether this resistance which was made to the King *by the Parliament* was properly *rebellion* or not? The answer to which is plain, that it was not; but a most righteous and glorious stand made in defense of the natural and legal rights of the people against the unnatural and illegal encroachments of arbitrary power. Nor was this a rash [45] and too sudden opposition. The nation had been patient under the oppressions of the crown even to *long suffering,* for a course of many years; and there was no rational hope of redress in any other way. Resistance was absolutely necessary in order to preserve the nation from slavery, misery, and ruin. And who so proper to make this resistance as the Lords and Commons — the whole representative body of the people — guardians of the public welfare; and each of which was, in point of legislation, vested with an equal, co-ordinate power with that of the crown? || Here were *two* branches of the [46] legislature against *one:* two which had law and equity and the constitution on their side, against one which was impiously attempting to over-

|| The *English* constitution is originally and essentially *free*. The character which *J. Caesar* and *Tacitus* both give of the ancient *Britons* so long ago is that they were extremely *jealous of their liberties,* as well as a people of a *martial* spirit. Nor have there been wanting frequent instances and proofs of the same glorious spirit (in both respects) remaining in their posterity ever since, in the struggles they have made for liberty, both against foreign and domestic tyrants. Their Kings hold their title to the throne solely by grant of Parliament; i.e., in other words, by the voluntary consent of the people. And, agreeably hereto, the prerogative and rights of the crown are stated, defined, and limited by law, and that as truly and strictly as the rights of any inferior officer in the state, or indeed of any private subject. And it is only in this respect that it can be said that "the King can do no wrong." Being restrained by the law, he cannot, while he confines himself within those just limits which the law prescribes to him as the measure of his authority, injure and oppress the subject. The King, in his coronation oath, swears to exercise only such a power as the constitution gives him; and the subject, in the oath of allegiance, swears only to obey him in the exercise of such a power. The King is as much bound by his oath not to infringe the legal rights of the people as the people are bound to yield subjection to him. From whence it follows that as soon as the prince sets himself up above law, he loses the King in the tyrant: he does to all intents and purposes unking himself by acting out of, and beyond, that sphere which the constitution allows him to move in. And in such cases he has no more right to be obeyed than any inferior officer who acts beyond his commission. The subjects' obligation to allegiance *then* ceases of course; and to resist him is no more *rebellion* than to resist any foreign invader. There is an essential difference betwixt *government and tyranny* at least under such a constitution as the *English*. The former consists in ruling according to law and equity; the latter, in ruling contrary to law and equity. So also, there is an essential difference betwixt resisting a tyrant and rebellion. The former is a just and reasonable self-defense; the latter consists in resisting a prince whose administration is just and legal, and this is what denominates it a crime. Now it is evident that King *Charles's* government was illegal and very oppressive through the greatest part of his reign: and, therefore, to resist him was no more rebellion than to oppose any foreign invader, or any other domestic oppressor.

turn law and equity and the constitution, and to exercise a wanton
licentious *sovereignty* over the properties, consciences, and lives of all
the people: such a *sovereignty* as some inconsiderately ascribe to the supreme Governor of the world. — I say inconsiderately, because God himself does not govern in an absolutely arbitrary and despotic manner. The
power of this Almighty King (I speak it not without caution and reverence); the power of this Almighty King is *limited by law,* not, indeed, by
acts of Parliament but by the eternal *laws* of truth, wisdom, and equity,
and the everlasting *tables* of right reason — tables that cannot be *repealed,*
or *thrown down* and *broken* like those of *Moses.* But King *Charles* sat
himself up above all these as much as he did the written laws of the
realm, and made mere humor and caprice, which are no rule at all, the
only rule and measure of his administration. And now, is it not perfectly ridiculous to call resistance to such a tyrant by the name of *rebellion? — the grand rebellion?* Even that Parliament which brought
King [47] *Charles* II to the throne and which run *loyally mad* severely
reproved one of their own members for condemning the proceedings of
that Parliament which first took up arms against the former King. And
upon the same principles that the proceedings of this Parliament may
be censured as wicked and rebellious, the proceedings of those who, since,
opposed King *James* II and brought the Prince of *Orange* to the throne
may be censured as wicked and rebellious also. The cases are parallel. But
whatever *some* men may *think,* it is to be hoped that, for their own sakes,
they will not dare to *speak* against the REVOLUTION, upon the justice
and legality of which depends (in part) his present MAJESTY'S right to
the throne.

If it be said that, although the Parliament which first opposed King
Charles's measures and at length took up arms against him were not
guilty of rebellion, yet certainly those persons were who condemned and
put him to death, even this perhaps is not true. For he had, in fact, *unkinged* himself long before, and had forfeited his title to the allegiance
of the people. So that those who put him to death were at most only
guilty of *murder;* which, indeed, is bad enough, if they were really guilty
of *that* (which is at least disputable). *Cromwell,* and those who were
principally concerned in the (*nominal*) King's death might possibly have
been very wicked and designing men. Nor shall I say anything in vindication of the reigning *hypocrisy* of those times, or of *Cromwell's* malad-
ministration during the *interregnum* (for it is *truth* and not a *party* that

I am speaking [48] for). But still it may be said that *Cromwell* and his adherents were not, properly speaking, guilty of *rebellion* because he whom they beheaded was not, properly speaking, *their King* but a *lawless tyrant.* Much less are the whole body of the nation at that time to be charged with rebellion on that account, for it was no *national act;* it was not done by a *free* Parliament. And much less still is the nation at present to be charged with the great sin of rebellion for what their *ancestors* did (or rather did NOT) a century ago.

But how came the *anniversary* of King *Charles's* death to be solemnized as a day of fasting and humiliation? The true answer, in brief, to which inquiry is that this last was instituted by way of *court* and *compliment* to King *Charles* II upon the *Restoration.* All were desirous of making their court to him, of ingratiating themselves, and of making him forget what had been done in opposition to his *father,* so as not to revenge it. To effect this, they ran into the most extravagant professions of affection and loyalty to him, insomuch that he himself said that it was a *mad* and *harebrained* loyalty which they professed. And amongst other strange things which his first Parliament did, they ordered the *thirtieth* of *January* (the day on which his father was beheaded) to be kept as a day of solemn humiliation, to deprecate the judgments of Heaven for the rebellion which the nation had been guilty of, in that which was no national thing and which was not rebellion in them that did it. Thus they soothed and flattered their new King at the expense [49] of their liberties, and were ready to yield up *freely* to *Charles* II all that enormous power which they had justly resisted *Charles* I for usurping to himself.

The last query mentioned was, Why those of the *Episcopal clergy* who are very high in the principles of *ecclesiastical authority* continue to speak of this unhappy prince as a *great saint* and a *martyr?* This, we know, is what they constantly do, especially upon the 30th of *January* — a day sacred to the *extolling* of *him* and to the *reproaching* of those who are not of the *established church. Out of the same mouth on this day proceedeth blessing and cursing; therewith bless they their God, even* Charles, *and therewith curse they* the *dissenters:* and their *tongue can no man tame; it is an unruly evil, full of deadly poison.*¶[6] King *Charles* is, upon this solemnity, frequently compared to our Lord Jesus Christ, both in respect of the *holiness* of his life and the greatness and injustice of his

¶ Jam. iii, 8, 9, 10.

sufferings; and it is a wonder they do not add something concerning the *merits* of his death also. But *blessed saint* and *royal martyr* are as humble titles as any that are thought worthy of him.

Now this may, at first view, well appear to be a very strange *phenomenon.* For King *Charles* was really a man black with guilt and *laden with iniquity,** as appears by his crimes before-mentioned. He lived a tyrant; and it was the oppression and violence of his reign that brought him to his untimely and violent end at last. Now what of saintship or martyrdom is there in all this! [50] What of saintship is there in encouraging people to *profane* the *Lord's Day?* What of saintship in falsehood and perjury? What of saintship in repeated robberies and depredations? What of saintship in throwing real saints and glorious patriots into jails? What of saintship in overturning an excellent civil constitution and proudly grasping at an illegal and monstrous power? What of saintship in the murder of thousands of innocent people, and involving a nation in all the calamities of a civil war? And what of martyrdom is there in a man's bringing an immature and violent death upon himself by *being wicked overmuch?* † Is there any such thing as grace without goodness? As being a follower of Christ without following Him? As being his disciple without learning of Him to be just and beneficent? Or as saintship without sanctity? ‡ If not, I fear it will be hard to prove this man a saint. And verily one would be apt to suspect that *that church* must be but [51] *poorly stocked* with saints and martyrs which is forced to adopt such enormous sinners into her *calendar* in order to swell the number.

But to unravel this *mystery of (nonsense* as well as of) *iniquity,* which has *already worked* for a *long time* amongst us,§ or, at least, to give the most probable solution of it, it is to be remembered that King *Charles,*

---

* Isai. i, 4.   † Eccles. vii, 17.

‡ Is it any wonder that even persons who do not *walk after their own lusts* should *scoff* at *such saints* as this, both in the *first* and in the *last days,* even *from everlasting to everlasting?* 2 Pet. iii, 3, 4. But perhaps it will be said that these things are MYSTERIES which (although very true in themselves) *lay understandings* cannot comprehend, or, indeed, any other persons amongst us besides those who, being INWARDLY MOVED BY THE HOLY GHOST, have taken a trip across the *Atlantic* to obtain *episcopal ordination* and the *indelible character.* However, if these *consecrated gentlemen* do not quite despair of us, it is hoped that in the abundance of their charity they will endeavor to *elucidate* these *dark* points, and, at the same time, explain the creed of *another of their eminent saints,* [by] which we are told that unless we *believe faithfully* (i.e., *believingly*) *we cannot be saved:* which creed (or rather *riddle*), notwithstanding all the labors of the *pious* and *metaphysical* Dr. *Waterland,* remains somewhat *enigmatical* still.

§ 2 Thess. ii, 7.

this *burlesque* upon saintship and martyrdom, though so great an oppressor, was a true friend to the *Church* — so true a friend to her that
he was very well affected towards the *Roman Catholics,* and would probably have been very willing to unite *Lambeth* and *Rome.* This appears
by his marrying a true *daughter* of that true *mother of harlots*|| which he
did with a dispensation from the *pope,* that supreme BISHOP, to whom
when he wrote he gave the title of MOST HOLY FATHER. His queen
was extremely bigoted to all the follies and superstitions and to the *hierarchy* of *Rome,* and had a prodigious ascendancy over him all his life. It
was in part owing to this that he (probably) abetted the massacre of the
Protestants in *Ireland,* that he assisted in extirpating the *French* Protestants at *Rochelle,* that he all along encouraged *papists* and popishly-
affected *clergymen* in preference to all other persons, and that he upheld
that monster of wickedness, ARCHBISHOP LAUD, and the bishops of
his stamp, in all their church tyranny and diabolical cruelties. In return to
his kindness and indulgence in which respects they caused many of [52]
the pulpits throughout the nation to ring with the divine, absolute, indefeasible right of kings, with the praises of *Charles* and his reign, and
with the damnable sin of resisting the *Lord's anointed,* let him do what
he would. So that not only *Christ* but *Charles* was commonly preached
to the people. In *plain English,* there seems to have been an impious
bargain struck up betwixt the *scepter* and the *surplice* for enslaving both
the *bodies* and *souls* of men. The King appeared to be willing that the
clergy should do what they would — set up a monstrous hierarchy like
that of *Rome* — a monstrous inquisition like that of *Spain* or *Portugal* —
or anything else which their own pride and the devil's malice could
prompt them to: *provided always* that the clergy would be *tools* to the
crown, that they would make the people believe that kings had God's
authority for breaking God's law, that they had a commission from
heaven to seize the estates and lives of their subjects at pleasure, and
that it was a damnable sin to resist them, even when they did such things
as deserved more than damnation. This appears to be the true key for
explaining the *mysterious* doctrine of King *Charles's* saintship and
martyrdom. He was a saint not because he was in his life a good *man*
but a good *churchman;* not because he was a lover of *holiness* but the
hierarchy; not because he was a friend to *Christ* but the *craft.* And he was
a martyr in his death not because he bravely suffered death in the cause

|| Rev. xvii, 5.

of truth and righteousness but because he died an enemy to liberty and the rights of conscience; i.e., not because he died an enemy to *sin* but *dissenters*. For these [53] reasons it is that all bigoted clergymen and friends to church power paint this man as a saint in his life, though he was such a mighty, such a *royal sinner,* and as a martyr in his death, though he fell a sacrifice only to his own ambition, avarice, and un-bounded lust of power. And from prostituting their praise upon King *Charles* and offering him that incense which is not his due, it is natural for them to make a transition to the dissenters (as they commonly do) and to load them with that reproach which they do not deserve, they being generally professed enemies both to civil and ecclesiastical tyranny. WE are commonly charged (upon the *thirtieth* of *January*) with the guilt of putting the King to death, under a notion that it was our an-cestors that did it; and so we are represented in the blackest colors, not only as schismatics but also as traitors and rebels and all that is bad. And these *lofty* gentlemen usually rail upon this head in such a manner as plainly shows that they are either grossly ignorant of the history of those times which they speak of, or, which is worse, that they are guilty of the most shameful prevarication, slander, and falsehood. But every *petty priest* with a *roll* and a *gown* thinks he must do something in imitation of his *betters* in *lawn* and show himself a *true son* of the church, and thus, through a foolish ambition to appear *considerable,* they only render them-selves *contemptible*.

But suppose *our* forefathers did kill their *mock* saint and martyr a century ago, what is that to *us* now? If I mistake not, these gentlemen generally preach down the doctrine of the *imputation of Adam's sin to his posterity* [54] as absurd and unreasonable, notwithstanding they have solemnly subscribed what is equivalent to it in their own *articles of re-ligion*. And therefore one would hardly expect that they would lay the guilt of the King's death upon *us,* although *our forefathers* had been the only authors of it. But this conduct is much more surprising when it does not appear that *our* ancestors had any more hand in it than *their own*. However, bigotry is sufficient to account for this and many other *phenomena* which cannot be accounted for in any other way.

Although the observation of this *anniversary* seems to have been (at least) superstitious in its *original;* and although it is often abused to very bad purposes by the established clergy, as they serve themselves of it, to perpetuate strife, a party spirit, and divisions in the Christian church; yet it is to be hoped that one good end will be answered by it quite contrary to their intention: it is to be hoped that it will prove a standing *memento* that *Britons* will not be *slaves,* and a warning to all corrupt *counselors* and *ministers* not to go too far in advising to arbitrary, despotic measures.

To conclude: Let us all learn to be *free* and to be *loyal.* Let us not profess ourselves vassals to the lawless pleasure of any man on earth. But let us remember, at the same time, government is *sacred* and not to be *trifled* with. It is our happiness to live under the government of a PRINCE who is satisfied with ruling according to law, as every other *good prince* will. We enjoy under his administration all the liberty that is proper and expedient [55] for us. It becomes us, therefore, to be contented and dutiful subjects. Let us prize our freedom but not *use our liberty for a cloak of maliciousness.*¶ There are men who strike at *liberty* under the term *licentiousness.* There are others who aim at *popularity* under the disguise of *patriotism.* Be aware of both. *Extremes* are dangerous. There is at present amongst *us,* perhaps, more danger of the *latter* than of the *former.* For which reason I would exhort you to pay all due regard to the government over us, to the KING and all in authority, and to lead a *quiet and peaceable* life.* And while I am speaking of loyalty to our *earthly prince,* suffer me just to put you in mind to be loyal also to the supreme RULER of the universe, *by whom kings reign and princes decree justice.*† To which King eternal, immortal, invisible, even to the ONLY WISE GOD‡ be all honor and praise, DOMINION and thanksgiving, through JESUS CHRIST our LORD. AMEN.

¶ 1 Pet. ii, 16.   * 1 Tim. ii, 2.   † Prov. viii, 15.   ‡ 1 Tim. i, 17.

PAMPHLET 2

A LETTER TO THE PEOPLE
OF PENNSYLVANIA

PHILADELPHIA, 1760

INTRODUCTION

On the 29th of September, 1759, the Assembly of Pennsylvania passed a law providing that judges of the county courts of common pleas and justices of the Supreme Court of the colony "shall have, hold, enjoy and exercise their several and respective commissions and offices aforesaid, *quamdiu se bene gesseri[n]t,* and that their respective commissions shall be granted to them accordingly." The Latin phrase, signifying permanence of tenure ("as long as they conduct themselves properly"), rescued the judiciary, as most colonists saw it, from the inferiority imposed by the tenure *durante bene placito* ("as long as it pleases [the prince]"), which was almost universal in the colonies. The enactment was promptly disallowed in England.[1] The disallowance touched off a controversy that lasted for years in Pennsylvania and that was significantly paralleled in other colonies: it persisted through the subsequent years, flaring up repeatedly, providing in the end one of the justifications for the American rebellion. It was in the course of this dispute in Pennsylvania and in defense of the law of 1759 that *A Letter to the People of Pennsylvania* was written. The pamphlet, in all probability the work of Joseph Galloway,[2] is ostensibly an argument for the constitutional necessity of permanent tenure for judges; but it goes beyond that immediate issue to broader questions of constitutionalism. It is, in fact, one of the fullest statements of British constitutionalism written in the colonies on the eve of the Revolution, and it gains rather than loses in importance as a Revolutionary document by virtue of its author's fervent defense, in later years, of the Loyalist cause.

The tenure of judges was an old issue, which, like so many of the constitutional issues that entered into the American Revolution, had an analogue in seventeenth-century English history, and had been resolved, for England, in the Glorious Revolution. The English common law courts, being royal offices, had from their origins been filled by appointment of the crown. In the fifteenth and sixteenth centuries, as before, common law judges, holding office at royal pleasure, were regarded "as servants of the crown, to be dismissed at the King's pleasure"; and dismissed they had been on occasions of crown displeasure. Under James I, the question of judicial tenure became a great public issue, playing into the central struggle over prerogative power. Coke, fanatical in his veneration of law and judicial procedures, staked his career on the independence of the bench — and lost; his dismissal as chief justice in 1616 was the first of the series of assaults upon the judiciary launched by the Stuarts in defense of their prerogative. For a period after the Restoration judicial tenure was secure against the pleasure of the crown; but this was a brief interruption in a line of dismissals that went from that of Coke through that of Chief Justice Heath under Charles I to the wholesale corruption of the bench under Charles II and James II climaxing in the elevation of vicious careerists like Scroggs and Jeffreys and the instant dismissal of the indulgent judges in the trial of the seven bishops.[3]

The reaction, when it came, was extreme and salutary. The Act of Settlement of 1701 concluded a quarter century of absolute and arbitrary executive control of the judiciary by declaring that in the future *"judges commissions be made* quamdiu se bene gesserint, *and their salaries ascertained and established."* It was a guarantee of judicial independence never thereafter violated, either by the crown or by Parliament — a guarantee which was declared by the King himself, in 1761, to be "essential to the impartial administration of justice . . . one of the best securities of the rights and liberties of his subjects; and . . . most conducive to the honor of the Crown." [4]

But this guarantee did not apply to the colonies. There, special circumstances were held to obtain. For over half a century after the Glorious Revolution the standard instruction on the tenure of the judges sent to the colonial governors had been that they were "not [to] express any limitation of time in the commissions you are to grant" — a vague ruling that was generally, though not always, interpreted to mean tenure at the pleasure of the crown. In a few notable cases — in New Jersey and New York particularly — nepotism and the fortunes of politics had led governors to commission certain of the judges on permanent tenure; but such instances were rare, and they led in the early 1750's to a sharp clarification of crown intent. Opinions by the chief legal officers of England resulted in 1754 in new instructions to governors ordering all judicial commissions thereafter to be granted "during pleasure only." A law of contrary intent passed in Jamaica was disallowed in the same year on the grounds that it affected "royal prerogative in a point of great moment" and because "in the situation and circumstances" of the colonies it was neither "for the interest of the plantations themselves or of Great Britain that the judges . . . should hold their places *quam diu se bene gesserint.*" What precisely these special circumstances were was made clear in the disallowance of the defiant act passed by the Assembly of Pennsylvania in 1759 — the act in defense of which the present pamphlet was written.[5]

The analogy of the colonies to England, which was the basis of the colonists' arguments, the Board of Trade wrote the Privy Council, was a false one. Permanent tenure of judges had been made mandatory in England only because there had been "the most conclusive and repeated proofs" of arbitrary assaults upon the constitution and upon individual rights as a result of crown manipulation of the judiciary. In Pennsylvania there had been no such assaults by the executive. Quite the contrary: the proprietary governors had been exemplary in their handling of the judiciary; they had served the people in this connection as well as the people had permitted them to. Moreover, to make an exception in the case of Pennsylvania would be particularly embarrassing since it would extend privileges to the people of a proprietary colony denied to those of the King's own colonies. But most important of all, the change proposed by the Assembly of Pennsylvania would strip from the proprietors the power of replacing incumbents "of inferior knowledge and of secondary capacity" when, by virtue of "the growing wealth of the province, a salary may be advanced more suitable to that station" and better qualified people become available.[6]

The final remark touched on the primary motivation: if the governors did not have the power of dismissal as a counterweight to the control of judicial salaries by the Assemblies, the judiciary would become a political weapon in the hands of the popular, antigubernatorial forces in the colonies, and those powers, thus armed, would become that much more unmanageable. The question in effect was not one of constitutionalism as such but of politics expressed in the language of constitutionalism.

Politics had surrounded the issue from the beginning. The committee of the Pennsylvania Assembly that had drafted the bill had been led by Joseph Galloway, an ambitious twenty-nine-year-old lawyer and politician associated with the antiproprietary faction that controlled the Assembly. This "Franklin-Quaker" party, as it has been called, united in its opposition to the privileges — especially tax exemption — enjoyed by the proprietors, had struggled with the Penn family's government for years before 1759 on a variety of issues. Antagonism had reached a pitch of intensity in 1758 when the Assembly charged two proprietary spokesmen with seditious libel, jailed and fined them, and when the governor in turn had refused assent to a money bill on the grounds that five of the commissioners named in the act, among them Joseph Galloway, had ignored him in expending money under a similar appropriation act some time earlier. The judiciary bill itself was part of a cluster of enactments propelled forward by the antiproprietary faction. After passing through the Assembly it had been vehemently opposed in the Council, four out of five of whose members were office-holders under the Penns; its acceptance by the lieutenant governor, William Denny, was said to be a testimony to his venality and contributed to the causes of his recall.[7]

Politics continued to surround the issue in Pennsylvania and elsewhere in the colonies. The controversial bill on the tenure of judges was revived in Pennsylvania in 1762; this time it occasioned "a violent storm" in the Assembly between Galloway and Chief Justice William Allen, the leaders of the opposing factions. A witness reported that the uproar "broke over all bounds of decency"; even the speaker of the House fell into a "rage" before the issue cooled. Two years later, in 1764, the same arguments were once again revived but this time by a committee on grievances, led by Franklin and Galloway, which did not attempt to force the bill into law but settled for a resolution of the Assembly, which could not be vetoed, stating that the proprietary executive's control of the tenure of judges "who are to determine in all causes between the proprietaries and their tenants, the inhabitants of the province, is unjust, renders the liberties and properties of the subject precarious and dependent on the proprietary will and pleasure, and is by no color of reason supportable." Tenure of judges at the proprietors' pleasure, like the proprietorship itself, survived in Pennsylvania until 1776; but it had come to be a symbol of oppression, a witness of the colonists' limited enjoyment of the liberties to which they considered themselves heir.[8]

Elsewhere a similar insistence by the crown brought similar results, though often at even greater political cost. The death of George II, which legally terminated the life of all existing crown commissions, precipitated the issue in several colonies. In New York the problem contributed to one of the bitterest factional fights in that province's tempestuous political history, and it elicited in the end a comprehensive and revealing response from the home government. The Board of Trade, in supporting the refusal of the acting governor to renew the life tenures of Supreme Court judges after the accession of George III — a refusal explicitly based on the fear of losing a valuable political weapon — repeated the remarks it had made in recommending disallowance of the Pennsylvania law of 1759, and added a new, more frankly political, consideration. Too often in recent years, the Board wrote the Privy Council, colonial governors have been forced to give judgeships to those interested only in "their own private interests, and who, added to their ignorance of the law, have too frequently become the partisans of a factious Assembly upon whom they have been dependent for their support and who have withheld or enlarged that support according as the conduct of the judges was more or less favorable to their interests." So long as judges remain dependent upon the "factious will and caprice" of the Assemblies for their salaries, permanence of tenure will be "subversive of all true policy, destructive of the interests of Your Majesty's subjects, and tending to lessen that just dependence which the colonies ought to have upon the government of the mother country." It was in immediate response to the problem as it arose in New York that, in December 1761, final, irrevocable orders were sent to all governors forbidding them ever after "upon pain of being removed from your government" to assent to any act that attempted in any way to regulate the tenure of judges or to commission any judges on any other terms than that "ancient practice and usage" of the colonies, tenure at the pleasure of the crown.[9]

In other colonies there was less explanation but the same action and the same intensification of political bitterness and sense of deprivation. In New Jersey a newly appointed governor struggled in vain to mediate between his instructions and the demands of a stubborn Assembly. When he gave in to the local pressures and agreed to commission Supreme Court judges on permanent tenure he was immediately dismissed from office despite his last-minute efforts to induce the judges themselves to accept commissions at pleasure. In North Carolina the Assembly forced the governor to accept two acts requiring tenure on good behavior. The disallowance of both enactments settled the issue in law but not in politics. It was revived in 1768; settled to the advantage of the Assembly for a five-year period; and then reopened with even greater acrimony than before: the tenure of judges remained a fierce partisan issue in North Carolina until Independence. In South Carolina the question arose as part of the struggle of the Regulators to introduce judicial processes into the wild, faction-torn back country. The act of 1768 creating circuit courts in the west expressed years of resentment against crown-imposed appointees in its stipulation that the new judgeships should be held on permanent tenure. But neither the strong representations by the colony's energetic agent, Charles Garth, of "the distress of the back people, the disorders committed and unpunished" nor his adroit lobbying could overcome the belief in England that permanent tenure for colonial judges, especially judges dependent on the legislatures for their salaries, was "inadmissible." The badly needed act was vetoed, and had to be rewritten with the offending clause omitted before it was accepted in England.[10]

Jamaica, Pennsylvania, New York, New Jersey, North Carolina, South Carolina: the issue, arising in every region of England's American empire, culminated in the 1770's in Massachusetts, where John Adams, in no less than seven essays — essays characteristically indignant, rhetorical, and learned — addressed himself to the question of the independence of the judiciary. His outburst was occasioned by the verification in 1772 of the long-rumored decision of the crown to pay the salaries of the Massachusetts judges itself, from the customs revenues, and thus to end the Assembly's financial control of the judiciary. The action greatly agitated the current fears "of the designs of administration totally to subvert the constitution and to introduce an arbitrary government into the province," and it provoked in the House in Massachusetts a formal resolution stating that "while judges hold their commissions during pleasure, any one of them who shall accept of . . . the crown for his support . . . will discover to the world that . . . he is an enemy to the constitution and has it in his heart to promote the establishment of an arbitrary government in the province." The sentiment was almost, but not quite, unanimous. Among those who disagreed was William Brattle, a wealthy Cambridge merchant and senior member of the provincial Council. In an essay published in a Boston newspaper he defended the new salary grants on the grounds, in part, that the tenure of judges in Massachusetts was not, as was generally claimed, insecure at all. Judges' commissions, he argued, contain no reference whatever to tenure, and therefore the possession of judicial office was as secure in Massachusetts as it was in England: there was no necessity, he explained, "of having *quamdiu bene se gesserint* [written] in their commissions, for they have their commissions now by that tenure as truly as if the said words were in." In fact, they did not even need commissions. According to the terms of the Massachusetts charter the mere nomination and appointment of a judge was sufficient; commissions merely declared the existing fact of appointment. "The greatest sages of the law" have long since determined that by "the common law of England, the birthright of every man here as well as at home," judges have "an estate for life" in their offices. Why, then, had provision been made for judicial tenure in England in the Act of Settlement of

1701? It had been included, Brattle wrote, not to create a new condition of judicial tenure, but only "in affirmance of the old law, that which was really law before." [11]

This was, to say the least, a curious reading of legal history, and it created a situation ideally suited to the polemical talents, learning, and political interests of John Adams. With evident relish, with a rich outpouring of vituperation and scholarship, he threw himself at the unfortunate Brattle. "With surprise and grief," he reported in the first of his essays against Brattle, published in the *Boston Gazette,* had he read the gentleman's arguments. They were wrong in principle and wrong in fact. They were bad law, bad history, and bad politics. Point by point, in a text bristling with citations and crowded with quotations from lawyers, historians, and political theorists, Adams refuted Brattle's major contentions. "The common law of England," he wrote, "is so far from determining that the judges have an estate for life in their offices, that it has determined the direct contrary." Who are these "greatest sages of the law" Brattle refers to as supporting his view? Let him produce a single one; let him produce "one lawyer in this country who ever before entertained such an opinion or heard such a doctrine" as Brattle was attempting to defend. He refers to Chief Justice Holt; but it was Holt in fact who as much as anyone made clear that the Act of Settlement created precisely what Brattle was attempting to argue it did not, "a new law" on judicial tenure, "a total alteration of the tenure of the judges' commissions . . ."

But it was not only Holt and "My Lord Coke, in his Fourth Institute," and other lawyers and judges who established that "the common law of England has not determined the judges to have an estate for life in their offices provided they behave well." The testimony of history, Adams wrote, established the same point and with it the consequent need for explicit guarantees of permanent tenure. "To enumerate all the struggles of the people, the petitions and addresses to kings praying that the judges' commissions might be granted during good behavior, the bills which were actually brought into one or the other House of Parliament for that purpose, which failed of success until the final establishment in the [Act of Settlement], would be," Adams concluded, "too tedious." Nevertheless, exuberant in his "delightful work of quotation," he persevered, relentlessly citing and quoting ("see Rapin, Burnet, Skinner, Comberbach, State Trials, and Sir Edward Herbert's Vindication of Himself") to prove his case. Page followed page, anecdote followed anecdote ("two or three anecdotes were omitted in my last for want of room, which may be here inserted . . . [Brattle] has been extremely unfortunate in having Bracton, Fortescue, Coke, Foster, Hume, Rapin, and Rushworth directly against him . . .") until he reached, some 10,000 words after the start of the controversy, a peroration that sums up the essential facts, the fears, and the dangers implicit in the entire issue of judicial tenure:

It may be depended on that all the commissions of judges throughout America are without the words *quamdiu se bene gesserint* in them; and, consequently, that this horrid fragment of the feudal despotism hangs over the heads of the best of them to this hour. If this is the case, it is a common and serious concern to the whole continent, and the several provinces will take such measures as they shall think fit to obtain a better security of their lives, liberties, and properties.[12]

It was upon this broad background, including within its scope episodes in nearly every colony, and particularly in Pennsylvania where the pamphlet that follows expressed most fully the common grievance, that Jefferson drew, when, in the Declaration of Independence, he stated as one of the justifications for the colonists' rebellion, that the King, who had once declared that an independent judiciary was one of the best securities of the rights and liberties of the people and an honor to the crown, had himself, in his tyranny, "made judges dependent on his will alone for the tenure of their offices and the amount and payment of their salaries."

A/LETTER,/To the People of/PENNSYLVANIA;/Occasioned by the ASSEMBLY'S passing/that Important ACT,/FOR/CONSTITUTING the JUDGES/OF THE/SUPREAM COURTS and COMMON-PLEAS,/During GOOD BEHAVIOUR./

I charged your Judges at that Time, saying, Hear the Causes between your/ Brethren, and judge Righteously between every Man and his Brother, and the/ Stranger that is with him: Ye shall not Respect Persons in Judgment, but you/ shall hear the Small as well as the Great; you shall not be afraid of the Face of/ Man, for the Judgment is GOD's. Deut. i. 16, 17./

PHILADELPHIA: Printed in MDCCLX./

A
LETTER
To the People of
PENNSYLVANIA, &c.

WHOEVER has made himself acquainted with ancient history and looked into the original design of government will find that one of its chief and principal ends was to secure the persons and properties of mankind from private injuries and domestic oppression.

In forming a plan of government completely to answer these excellent purposes, the fundamental laws and rules of the constitution, which ought never to be infringed, should be made alike distributive of justice and equity, and equally calculated to preserve the sovereign's prerogative and the people's [4] liberties. But power and liberty ever being *opponents,* should the work stop here the constitution would bear a near analogy to a ship without rudder, rigging, or sails, utterly incapable of answering the end of its construction. For though the wisest and best laws were enacted to fix the bounds of power and liberty, yet without a due care in constituting persons impartially to execute them, the former by its influence and encroachments on liberty would soon become tyranny, and the latter by the like extent of its limits might possibly degenerate into licentiousness. In both cases, the condition of mankind would be little mended, scarcely better than in their original state of nature and confusion, before any civil polity was agreed upon.

The men therefore who are to settle the contests between prerogative and liberty, who are to ascertain the bounds of sovereign power and to determine the rights of the subject, ought certainly to be perfectly free from the influence of either. But more especially of the former, as history plainly evinces that it is but too apt to prevail over the ministers of justice by its natural weight and authority, notwithstanding the wisest precautions have been used to prevent it.

[5] The necessity of this independent state of justice is rendered apparent by the slightest consideration of human frailty. Consider men as they really are, attended with innumerable foibles and imperfections, ever liable to err, and you will find but very few who are so obstinately just as to be proof against the enticing baits of honor and interest. The love of promotion and private advantage are passions almost universal, and admit of the most dangerous extremes. The one in excess generally produces the most servile obedience, the other, intolerable avarice and a base dereliction of virtue. That which we love and engages our attention we are ever ready to purchase at any *price*. Thus an inordinate lover of promotion, sooner than part with it, would surrender up his regard for justice, his duty to his country and to his GOD for its preservation. And the avaricious man, sooner than lose his pelf, would part with his honor, his reputation, I had almost said his life. And such is the influence of this dread of parting with that which we esteem, whatever it be, that it so effectually chains down the powers of the human soul that it cannot be said to enjoy freedom of judgment, scarcely freedom of thought.

[6] Of this truth the abject promises and servile conduct of the great Lord *Bacon* exhibit an irrefragable proof. It was but rational to think that a man of his extensive abilities and capacious soul, that could comprehend all the beauties of rectitude and justice at a view, would at least preserve in his public station an independent and unperverted judgment. And yet his virtue fell a victim to his love of promotion. He begged for preferment with the same low servility that the necessitous pauper would beg for daily bread. His promise to the King in order to obtain the chancellor's place was "That when a direction was once given, it should be pursued and performed." [1] And when he succeeded in his wishes, his conduct with respect to the court and its arbitrary measures showed that he strictly fulfilled his engagement.

Whoever has read the form of a commission *during pleasure* and considered its limitations must certainly be surprised that a generous mind would accept of a tenure so servile and so incompatible with the very nature of justice. He can be but a *tenant at will* of a g——r at best, and for the most part of an [7] at——y g——l, or perhaps some other favorite in the several counties. The terms of tenure are *until our further will and pleasure shall be made known,* which by a natural construction, if we may call reason and experience to our aid, is no longer than you gratify us, our favorites and creatures, in your determinations, let our *will and pleasure* therein be ever so illegal, ever so partial and unjust.

That some men of independent circumstances, happy in the possession of virtue, have accepted of those commissions and acted uprightly I will not pretend to dispute. They are remarkable instances of public integrity, and merit the highest commendation. They are among mankind as a comet among the stars, rarely to be seen. But generally to look for strict impartiality and a pure administration of justice, to expect that power should be confined within its legal limits and right and justice done to the subject by men who are dependent, is to ridicule all laws against bribery and corruption, and to say that human nature is insensible of the love or above the lure of honor, interest, or promotion.

[8] With what freedom and justness do the modern writers of a certain great nation complain against the multiplicity of ministerial officers who hold their commissions *during pleasure;* and what renders that freedom so justifiable and those complaints so just but the misfortunes the nation has suffered by the weight these *creatures* have thrown into the scale of power by paying an implicit obedience to its commands and a devoted adherence to its measures. If, then, such are the dangerous effects of a dependency in the ministerial officers whose conduct is circumscribed by positive laws and checked by the superior courts of justice, how much more so must a dependency of the judicial officers be where everything is left in the power and to the discretion of the judge on whose breath the security of all property and the liberty of the people depend? Must it not produce more dangerous consequences? Will it not bring on inevitable ruin?

But further to illustrate the necessity of an independent state of justice in every community where the security of property and the happiness of mankind is the object of its *polity,* [9] numerous instances might be adduced from the histories of *Europe* in which it has been the principal policy of the most arbitrary princes who have conceived a design of quelling the spirit of liberty and enslaving their subjects to their *will and pleasure* to draw over to their party the ministers of the law. By this means, having effectually superseded the execution of the laws and subdued the power which alone could check a tyrannical exercise of prerogative, they have let loose every instrument of oppression and left nothing in the community able to oppose the torrent. Attempts of this kind have frequently succeeded, and sometimes in reigns when the judges have been as independent as the law could make them. If so, how much more easily is this policy pursued and executed when the judges hold their offices on the servile tenure of *during pleasure*.

Without wandering into foreign history, a few examples from that of our mother country and our own province will best suit my purpose, as they are more familiar and adapted to your circumstances.

[10] By this kind of policy, RICHARD II broke over every barrier of law and prostrated the fence which the wisdom of ages had planted round the constitution. Or, as the historian has it, "By the murderous weapons of perverted law." [2]

The opinion subscribed by all the judges in *England* touching the commission for inspecting the public revenues of the same reign is an evincing evidence of this truth. The Parliament, observing the immense profusion of the public treasure by the ministers of RICHARD, the great want of economy in his household, a number of pensions granted to his creatures, his numerous favorites grown rich amidst a national penury and distress, saw the necessity of an inquiry into and reformation of these abuses, and appointed a committee of eleven noblemen for that purpose whose authority was confirmed by an act of Parliament. But this being inconsistent with the King's arbitrary plan, he no sooner received the supplies but in a most solemn manner he protested against it, and pursued every measure in his power to enslave the nation. His detestable scheme was to intimidate [11] and corrupt the several sheriffs to return a packed Parliament of his own tools; the city of *London* was to furnish him with men and money, and the judges of the courts were to *pervert the laws* and sacrifice the *rights of the nation*.

But he failed in all his reliances, save on the prostituted judges: the sheriffs informed him that the people would never give up that *most valuable privilege,* the *freedom of elections.* The city of *London* excused herself from acting her part in the horrid scene. But the judges, overawed and corrupted, justified all his measures. In the opinion I have mentioned above, they declared that the commission and statute aforesaid were derogatory to the King's prerogative; that the persons who moved for them procured or prevailed on His Majesty to assent to them should be punished with *death;* that the King in all matters to be treated of in Parliament had a right to *direct and command* from the beginning to the end thereof; that if they acted contrary to the King's *pleasure* made known therein, they were to be punished as traitors; that he could whenever [12] he pleased remove any of his judges and officers, and *justify* or punish them for their offenses; and that the Lords and Commons could not impeach them for any of their crimes; with many other things equally subversive of the laws of the land and the very being of the constitution. An opinion so evidently infamous and servile that it cannot call for the least remark. I shall therefore only observe that *Belknap,* Chief Justice, after he had signed it, not being resolute enough to be steady nor so vicious as to want remorse for violating his oath, the cause of truth, and his country, declared "that he wanted nothing but a hurdle, a horse, and a halter to bring him to the death he deserved."

The same plan of policy was pursued by CHARLES I. He removed Sir *Robert Heath,* Lord Chief Justice, from his office because he could not approve of and justify his conduct, and Sir *John Finch,* a most abject tool of the court, became his successor.[3]

Thus by removing *at his pleasure* men of virtue and integrity from the courts of law and placing in their stead such as would serve his [13] arbitrary purposes, he procured a set of judges entirely devoted to his will. Under the sanction of their opinion, he issued forth his proclamations, and enforced an obedience to them as the fundamental laws of the land; while those very laws, by which not public and private property only but the very existence of the constitution itself was preserved, were dispensed with. So far did he carry this policy that it was common for the secretaries of state to send letters to the judges to lay aside the laws against papists, while the persons that dared to disobey his arbitrary proclamations were proceeded against with more rigor than if they had violated the fundamental laws of the kingdom.

The same measure was taken to justify and support that infamous violation of the subject's right, the imposition of ship money. The judges were first closeted, flattered, threatened, and intimidated, until they were prevailed on to subscribe to an opinion directly inconsistent with the laws of the land and the liberties of the nation.

No *Englishman* can ever forget the unheard of barbarities committed by Judge *Jeffreys,* [14] that murdering instrument of the court of JAMES II.

Nor will that successful attempt of the same King to procure a set of judges that should determine not according to law but his tyrannical directions ever to be effaced from the minds of *Britons.* He first closeted them agreeable to the example of his predecessor CHARLES, and would have made an express bargain with them *that they should continue in their commissions, provided they would maintain his pretended preroga-tive of dispensing with penal laws.* But four of them discovered great dissatisfaction at the proposal, and particularly Sir *Thomas Jones* plainly told him "He would not do what he required of him." His Majesty answered, "He would have twelve judges of his own opinion." Sir *Thomas* replied, "Twelve judges, Sir, you may possibly find, but not twelve lawyers." But to convince him of his mistake, the King in a few days appointed four such *creatures* from the bar, in the room of the four worthy judges, as effectually answered his purpose; and eleven out of twelve confirmed, as far as their opinions could confirm, his illegal power of dispensing with the laws of their country.[4]

[15] Many other instances of this nature might be brought from the history of your forefathers to demonstrate the necessity of creating the office of a judge *independent of power;* and to show that an increase of prerogative, a perversion of the laws, a suspension of your natural rights, and a violation of the fundamentals of an *English* constitution have often been effected by this kind of policy, this undue and *illegal influence* on the courts of justice.

But permit me to remind you of those notorious instances of violated property, the enlistment of your servants in the late *Spanish* War, who were a part of property as firmly secured by the laws of your country as any you enjoy, as much your right as the ox you have paid for or the inheritance you have purchased. Were they not by an arbitrary stretch of power violently wrested from your hands, without *money and with-out recompense?* What availed all your endeavors to procure the benefit of those laws and a restitution of your rights? Your courts of justice were dependent on and under the direction of the very author of the oppression.[5]

[16] Thus it is evident from the nature of justice, from the slightest consideration of the frailty of human nature, and from ancient as well as modern observation that your rights and properties have been utterly insecure while your judges have been under the influence of and subject to the pleasure of your rulers, and that your welfare and happiness have been merely ideal when the laws of the land, those impregnable bul-warks of your safety, have either been suspended or not executed.

Having shown you that a security of your rights and properties was the chief end of your entering into society, and that that security cannot be obtained without an independent and uninfluenced judicature, it be-comes an indispensable duty to take some pains to convince you that this *security* is your undoubted privilege as *Englishmen,* of which you cannot be divested without violence to your ancient rights and the principles of an *English* government.

To trace this important privilege to its original source, it will be necessary to follow me back to the first dawn of the present constitution of *England,* there to learn the precarious [17] situation of property and the wise remedy that was framed to give it a permanent security.[6]

Before the time of the great ALFRED, that wise founder of the *English* government, the care of the several counties was committed to the nobility. They acted in a double capacity, as leaders of the troops and judges of the people's properties; and, being frequently absent on military duty, they were obliged to leave the administration of their civil affairs to prefects or deputies who, holding their authority during the pleasure of the lords, and the lords being the *creatures* and *dependents* of the crown, in all their determinations paid a devoted obedience to the *directions of their superiors* and the voice of prerogative, while the execution of the laws and the rights of the subject were the least of their concern. The nation at this time had property, but no safety in the enjoyment. They had some degree of liberty, but held it as *tenants at will* of the crown, of the nobility, or their favorites; they had laws, but no protection from the hostile hand of the domestic oppressor. In this unfortunate and desponding situation did the great father [18] of public virtue find liberty and property — the two principal objects of all good laws. A generous compassion for the distressed state of the nation induced him to alter the constitution wherever he found it inconsistent with the welfare and happiness of his people. The *security of property,* without which private felicity is a mere chimera, engrossed his chief attention. He was the author of the excellent institution of trials by jurors, that solid pillar of *English* liberty. He altered the former dependent state of justice by appointing and commissionating judges as *independent of the crown* that they might ever after remain free from its influence and deaf to every solicitation but the convictions of truth. He did not, perhaps, like our modern politicians, see no advantage in an impartial administration of justice, but well knew from late experience that justice must be a stranger to the land whose form of government could not ensure safety to the liberties and properties of the people.

The office of a judge being thus wisely established, numerous instances might be drawn from the *English* history to demonstrate [19] that the ministers of justice were not removable at *the pleasure of the crown.*

EDWARD I, a prince remarkable for his excellent schemes of distributive justice, and as cautious as the good ALFRED lest his prerogative should oppress the law, was determined to purge the civil polity from the gross pollutions it had contracted from former reigns. But before he could displace a set of the most venal and corrupted judges, he was under a necessity from the *nature* of their commissions to impeach them before the nobility and convict them of their offenses.

The like method was taken by the great restorer of *English* liberty, EDWARD III, in order to remove *Green* and *Skipwith* from their offices, who had justly incurred his and the nation's displeasure by their extortion and partiality.

The infamous *Tresilian,* Chief Justice, and his brother judges, the former of whom was punished capitally and the others banished to *Ireland* in the reign of RICHARD II, were first tried and convicted before they were removed from the seat of justice.

[20] In the arbitrary reign of JAMES I, Lord Chief Justice *Coke,* who at that time had become very odious to the King by a virtuous opposition to his measures and had also incurred the public indignation by his extreme avarice, was convicted of one of the most trifling articles exhibited against him, on his own confession, which served *as a pretense* for the removing him from his offices.

Agreeable to this excellent policy of the common law, ever since the latter end of the eighth century the judges have held their commissions *during their good behavior,* a few instances to the contrary made by the encroachments of power excepted: even in the most arbitrary reigns of CHARLES and JAMES II, the judges were commissionated in this legal and constitutional form, reigns in which power had so great an ascendancy that had it not been consistent with the ancient common law and the usage and custom of ages, the rights of the nation had not met with so great a favor. The forms of the commissions of Sir *Robert Hyde* and Sir *Robert Forster,* who held them *during good behavior,* are to be seen in the reports of CHARLES's reign. And [21] Sir *Robert Archer,* some time before having unjustly incurred the displeasure of CHARLES, received a supersedeas to his commission as one of the judges, but with virtuous resolution he refused to surrender his patent without a trial, and continued in his office during his life.

The next thing worthy of your attention is how far this invaluable policy, so often suspended by arbitrary power, was restored and confirmed by your predecessors, the first settlers of this province. They had drank of the bitter cup of despotic authority; they had suffered the mischiefs of perverted law; they had seen their liberties both civil and religious bend under its weight; they resolved therefore to seek a more hospitable country, but would not venture their lives and estates in this *desert* land without some security against any encroachment on this *inestimable part* of their mother constitution. They wisely foresaw great danger of an invasion thereof in a province where an immense quantity of *property* was to attend a large extent of *power,* where the same person who was to enjoy the powers of government was likewise to be an *universal landlord* possessed of many millions [22] of acres with all their increasing advantages and emoluments; that this property at the same time it produced contests would create power and influence, and if those contests were to be decided, though not immediately by the proprietary himself yet mediately by his deputies whose dignity, office, and estate depended on his breath, their conditions and circumstances by their removal would be rendered worse, and the safety of their persons and properties more precarious. It was therefore expressly stipulated and solemnly covenanted by *William Penn* with the first adventurers before their departure from their native country, that "He would nominate and appoint such persons for *judges,* treasurers, masters of the rolls, sheriffs, justices, as were most fitly qualified for those employments; to whom he would make and grant commissions for the said offices respectively, to hold them for so long time as every such person should *well behave himself* in the office or place to him respectively granted, and no longer." [7]

Thus secured, as they thought, in the enjoyment of their liberties and estates, they [23] surrendered up every social connection of their native land under the vain expectation of enjoying this privilege agreed on before their departure. But how righteously this fundamental rule of your constitution has been observed, the late dependent state of your magistracy (whose commissions have been granted during the *governor's pleasure*), the partiality and favor that have been shown to a favorite att——y to whose influence they have been indebted for their offices and on whose will their continuance therein depended,[8] the many instances of men of integrity being displaced from the seat of justice because of their virtuous opposition to the measures of power, and the partial distribution of offices to creatures and tools, are so many incontestable testimonies of a manifest breach of public faith with your predecessors and you their posterity.

If your ancestors here were not wanting in their endeavors to secure you from the mischiefs of perverted law and to transmit to you an up-right administration of justice, the Parliament of your mother country have not been less careful in this respect. At the time of the happy Revolution, that famous opportunity [24] of overcoming the usurpations of former reigns and restoring the constitution to its ancient freedom, many of the national rights were revived and confirmed by the *Bill of Rights*. And yet, such was the haste and zeal of the Parliament to settle the essentials of the present government that many important matters were neglected, among which may be accounted a restitution of the courts of judicature to their ancient *independency*. But this error was not long undiscovered. The Parliament called to mind the mischiefs the nation had suffered in the slavish opinion of the judges in the case of ship money; the arbitrary removal of Justices *Powell* and *Holloway* for acting consistent with their oaths and consciences in the case of the five bishops;[9] they remembered that such was the influence of JAMES II with the judges whom he commissioned *during his pleasure* that juries were packed, the subject held to excessive bail, the laws of liberty violated and dispensed with, expensive fines imposed, cruel punishments inflicted, the spirit of liberty worn out, and many innocents condemned. Without the spirit of divination, they plainly foresaw [25] that the same train of fatal consequences must attend the liberties of the nation should their judges remain subject to the same influence. They therefore, as soon as it became necessary to make a farther limitation of the succession of the crown in the Protestant line, gladly embraced the happy opportunity of rectifying former mistakes and of making a further security for the ancient rights and liberties of the subject. They resolved that the *one* should go hand in hand with the *other*. And by the act which settled the further limitation of the crown, it is, among other things, expressly declared that the judges' commissions shall be made *quam diu se bene gesserint*, or as long *as they should behave themselves well in their offices*, and their salaries shall be ascertained and established.

Here it is worthy your information, *first*, that the rights and liberties claimed and declared by the Bill of Rights, that second Magna Carta, and the Act of Settlement created no innovation of the ancient constitution. The Parliament had no design to change but only to restore the ancient laws and customs of the realm, which were the true and indubitable [26] rights and liberties of the people of *England*. This appears as well from the Bill of Rights and the resolves which preceded the Act of Settlement as from the act itself. From whence it follows that this right

of the people to have their judges indifferent men and independent of
the crown is not of a late date but part of the ancient constitution of your
government and inseparably inherent in the persons of every freeborn
Englishman; and that the granting commissions to the judges *during
pleasure* was then esteemed by the Parliament and truly *was* an arbitrary
and illegal violation of the people's ancient liberties.

SECONDLY, that those excellent laws were *intended* to extend, and actually do extend, to all the King's subjects in *America.* That their faith
and allegiance are bound by them to the present most *excellent* royal
family, and of course that they are entitled to the rights and liberties
therein claimed, asserted, and confirmed. And yet your former g——rs,
as if they had been determined to revive and pursue the wicked policy
of those arbitrary reigns I have mentioned, [27] and to throw aside the
worthy example of his present most gracious Majesty, have acted as if
those excellent laws were not to be executed, and the example of their
sovereign unworthy of influencing their conduct. They have granted all
the commissions of the judges *during their will and pleasure,* and like
CHARLES and JAMES have occasionally removed such as dared oppose their
arbitrary designs, and filled up their places with others who would ratify
and support their measures, however unjust and illegal.

This being the case, what censure and blame would your representatives have merited had they not seized the first opportunity of rendering
your *courts and judges independent.* An opportunity offered; they passed
a law limiting the number of judges, which before was unlimited, and
left it in the power of a bad g——r to create as many dependents as his
measures should call for. It directs that the judges of the Supreme Court
and Common Pleas shall hereafter hold their commissions *during their
good behavior;* which before have often depended on the nod of a g——r
or an at——y g——l. And it ordains that the [28] judges of the Common Pleas shall hold the orphans court; that in no instance your properties exceeding the value of £5 should be determined by men *dependent*
on power or its advocates; and the ministers of justice, who ought to
be the ministers of your protection, may not be prevailed on either to
pervert your laws or to give up your rights.

A law so full of advantages to the people one would imagine could not
have an enemy; and yet we find there is nothing so virtuous but the
enemies of virtue will decry. The principal objection against this law is
that "It brings a great expense on the counties without any benefit accruing from it." Let us inquire what mighty burden will attend it in the

county of *Philadelphia,* where the expense will be greatest. The judges
have never sat above *five* days in the quarter at most, which, at *twenty
shillings* per day, will amount to *one hundred pounds* per annum. *One
hundred pounds* divided among 7000 taxables, which this county contains, will not make it *three pence half penny* per man. Is an expense
so trifling equal to the advantages to be derived from such a law? Is that
expense [29] unnecessary which procures safety to your property and
protection to your persons? Is an impartial administration of justice of
so little moment to the people? For what purpose were the courts of
judicature established? Was it that judgment should be given according
to the nod and direction of a p——y,[10] g——r, or att——y g——l, or as
the last shall happen to be employed? Or was it that they should be
free from all fear, favor, or affection whatsoever? That their determinations might flow from an honest conscience, from an impartial and un-
biased mind?

The enemies to this law, like all other persons who do not act upon
principle, manifestly contradict their own constant practice. What man
among them, who has a controversy with his neighbor, would not choose
to have it determined by arbitrators at least as independent of his opponent as himself? I think I am safe in asserting that no man of common
sense would submit his cause to the judgment of arbitrators who are the
tenants at will or debtors of his antagonist, or to persons who are connected with him by blood or affinity or by obligations and favors conferred. [30] Is it not a common objection at our courts of justice in the
election of referees that the person named is of the same religious persuasion with the other party? Whence arises the objection but from a
well-grounded suspicion that in some men even similitude of sentiments
may create undue favor and attachment to the interest of one side and
bias the private judgment and be the cause of injustice.

If this be the case between neighbor and neighbor, how does it stand
between the proprietaries and the people of this province? Every freeholder is by contract their debtor, and therefore every one of them may,
and many often will, have disputes and lawsuits with them respecting
the many covenants contained in their grants and the quitrents. Does
not the same reason which declares the use of indifferent arbitrators in
the case of private persons loudly proclaim the necessity of independent
men to settle the differences between power and property, between the
proprietaries and the people? Have not men who are clothed with immense property and extensive power by the weight of these alone too

[31] great an opportunity of influencing the courts of justice without this unnatural and unreasonable dependency of the judges *on their pleasure?*

I have shown you in the reigns of CHARLES and JAMES that men of fortune and the most extensive abilities have sacrificed their honor, their oaths, and their consciences on the altar of court influence; that they have violated the sacred office and trust of a judge, which were committed to them for the welfare of the people. Do you think it would be a difficult task to produce you examples of the like immolations in your own government? Have some of your past administrations been less oppressive and arbitrary than those of CHARLES and JAMES? Have not the royal grant and proprietary charter, the foundations of your constitution, been dispensed with and superseded by arbitrary p——y edicts? Have not those edicts, which like the laws of the *Medes* and *Persians* were to alter not, chained down the judgments of your rulers and deprived them of their discretion in matters of legislation?

[32] Have you known a scheme of power to deprive you of your properties in which your m—g—st—es have not been concerned? Have you forgot the attempt to destroy the freedom of your elections, abetted and supported by the men who ought to have suppressed it? Have not your servants, as much your property as the money in your purses, been illegally enlisted by a former g——r, and scarcely any could be found who dared to execute the laws made for its safety? What part did they act in preventing your houses (which by law are to every man a place of refuge and safety) from being made *barracks* for the soldiery? Did they execute the penal statute of our mother country against it, or did not some of them act a *shameful* neutrality while others united with power and in its very council abetted the illegal attempt? [11] How *manfully* and *conscientiously* did they exert themselves in suppressing the rioters, those instruments of power, who were collected to frighten the representatives to surrender up your sacred rights, or were not some of them mixed with the mob, promoting and abetting their wicked design? [12]

[33] Where then is the difference? If CHARLES and JAMES dispensed with penal statutes in order to introduce *popery,* your former g——rs have dispensed with the laws and fundamentals of your liberties and privileges in order to introduce *slavery*. If the former influenced the determinations of the judges and thereby perverted the laws of the country, your p——ries by severe penalties have deprived the head of the execu-

tive as well as legislative authority of his discretion and reason. And your g——rs have so influenced the courts of justice to justify and support their despotic designs that you and your predecessors from the like dangerous policy have suffered equal mischief and the like misfortunes.

Should, then, the same illegal and arbitrary measures hereafter be pursued by some future son of oppression, should a design be formed of dispensing with your laws and of imposing unnecessary taxes and burdens *heavy to be borne* without the assent of your representatives, and the ministers of justice be thought the proper instruments of effecting these horrid purposes, how certain the [34] success! how easy the task! while your judges are dependent on the *will of the oppressor*. Can you doubt that human nature, wearing the yoke engraved with the motto DURING PLEASURE, will not hold and practice the doctrine of *passive obedience* and *nonresistance* with respect to the destruction of your rights and privileges? If it should retain virtue enough not to be active in their ruin, will not the same cause ever produce the same effect? Will that which was once destructive now change its nature and become harmless and innocent? Has the poison of the asp ever lost its virulent quality? Will you then surrender up your sacred rights into the hands of power for protection? Will you suffer the safety of your persons, which is still more precious, to depend on the humor and caprice of your rulers and their favorites?

Consider, my countrymen, farther, are the *Pennsylvanians* men of more independent fortunes or of greater abilities? Do they inherit a greater share of inflexible virtue? And are they less liable to influence and corruption than the people of *England?* Has not fatal experience evidently demonstrated that the private [35] property of your p——ries, and their favorites will daily clash more and more with yours, more frequently and in a much greater degree than the private *interest* of your sovereign possibly can with that of his subjects? And yet has not the wise example and policy of a *British* Parliament thought it indispensably necessary, even there, that the judges should hold their commissions *during good behavior,* as independent of the crown as of the nation?

If those things be so, can the least spark of reason be offered why a *British* subject in *America* shall not enjoy the like safety, the same protection against domestic oppression? Is it because you have left your native land at the risk of your lives and fortunes to toil for your mother country, to load her with wealth, that you are to be rewarded with a loss of your privileges? Are you not of the same stock? Was the blood of your ancestors polluted by a change of soil? Were they freemen in *England* and did they become slaves by a six-weeks' voyage to *America?* Does not the sun shine as bright, our blood run as warm? Is not our honor and virtue as [36] pure, our liberty as valuable, our property as dear, our lives as precious here as in *England?* Are we not subjects of the same King, and bound by the same laws, and have we not the same God for our protector?

What, then, can you think of those abject *Americans,* those slaves by principle, those traitors to their own and posterity's happiness, who, plunging the dagger into the vitals of their own liberty, do not blush at declaring that you are not *entitled to the same security of property, the same rights and privileges of the freeborn subjects of* England? Let me ask those enemies to your welfare, how much thereof are you entitled to? Who will measure out and distribute your poor pittance, your short allowance? Is a tenth, an hundredth, or a thousandth part to be the portion of your liberty? Abject, detestable thought! The poor *African,* who is taken captive in war and dragged an involuntary slave to *Jamaica* calls for your humanity and compassion; but the voluntary wretch that works out his own and posterity's slavish condition for the sake of a little present lucre, promotion, or power is an [37] object deserving your deepest resentment, your highest indignation.

Ye who are not willfully blind to the advantages of this beneficial law, who for want of a little reflection have spoke derogatorily of its merits, let me rouse you from your lethargy and prevail on you to see through the perspective of truth your and your posterity's danger and approaching misery. What will avail the laws which are and shall be made for your protection if they are not impartially executed? What will avail the virtuous struggles, the noble victories of your representatives over the attempts of your intestine enemies? What will avail the heavy taxes you labor under? the thousands you have exhausted? the blood and treasure you have expended to protect your persons and properties from foreign invaders, if they are not safe from the insidious designs of ambition and power, their ever vigilant and active foes, nor even from the artful attempts of a litigious neighbor who is in favor with the *great* or can first employ a favorite attorney?

[38] Whatever, then, be the fate of the law which has occasioned this address to you, let me entreat you to insist on the enjoyment of this your native, your ancient, and indubitable right. 'Tis yours by the usage and custom of ages; 'tis yours by the rules of reason; 'tis yours by covenant

with the first founder of your government; 'tis yours by the united consent of King, Lords, and Commons; 'tis yours by birthright and as *Englishmen*. Complain, and remonstrate to your representatives incessantly, until they shall, like the great and good ALFRED, make a restitution of this your most important and essential right, the first and principal object of their concern; until they prevail on your g——rs to grant the judges commissions to the people of *Pennsylvania* in the same free and constitutional manner as your sovereign grants them to his subjects in *England*.

Be assured, if a privilege thus justly founded, so often ratified and confirmed, if an impartial and independent administration of justice is once wrested from your hands, neither the money in your pockets, nor the clothes on your backs, nor your inheritances, nor even [39] your persons can remain long safe from violation. You will become slaves indeed, in no respect different from the sooty *Africans,* whose persons and properties are subject to the disposal of their tyrannical masters.

PAMPHLET 3

JOHN APLIN, *VERSES ON DOCTOR MAYHEW'S BOOK OF OBSERVATIONS*

PROVIDENCE, 1763

INTRODUCTION

John Aplin's *Verses,* a document in the Mayhew-Apthorp controversy over the role in the colonies of the missionary arm of the Church of England, contains nothing original on the problem of church-state relations upon which it is a commentary. Its importance lies in its slashing style, characteristic of the fiercer exchanges of the Revolutionary era; in its unique construction: vituperative essays printed as "NOTES, critical and explanatory" to a set of polemical verses; and in its reflection of Anglican establishment opinion of the issues involved in the dispute over the Society for the Propagation of the Gospel.

The Mayhew-Apthorp controversy, sketched in the General Introduction, was one of the most extended polemics of the pre-Revolutionary years. Ultimately nine pamphlets, including one by the Archbishop of Canterbury, contributed directly to the melee.[1] Aplin's *Verses* appeared early in the sequence. The central publication of the controversy, Jonathan Mayhew's *Observations on the Charter and Conduct of the Society,* attacking East Apthorp's *Considerations* which had so dangerously stirred New Englanders' fears of the imminent establishment of an Anglican episcopate in America, appeared in the last week of April, 1763. One month later, on the 28th of May, there appeared anonymously in the Providence, Rhode Island, *Gazette* a nine-stanza poem abusing Mayhew, together with four long footnotes and one footnote to a footnote expanding and explaining the meaning of the verses. A week later, on June 4, the fifth stanza of the same poem was reprinted in the *Gazette,* and with it, appended to it as a footnote, was a prose essay of some 2500 words responding to Mayhew's central charge that the Society for the Propagation of the Gospel had violated its trust by expending funds intended to support the conversion of the heathen Indians on "missions in *New England,* where the inhabitants had before the means of religion after the Congregational and Presbyterian modes." On June 11 a final installment of commentary appeared in the same newspaper in the form of annotation to the last four stanzas of the poem; and on June 13 the complete set of verses and commentary was advertised for sale as a pamphlet.[2]

The publication of the *Verses* touched off a secondary polemic in the public prints which for sheer vituperation excels the major controversy from which it sprang. One week after Aplin's pamphlet was advertised, a statement appeared in the *Boston Gazette* claiming that there had so far been published only one attempt to refute Mayhew's *Observations,* and that, the

Verses, was "an anonymous *libel* of the coarsest and lowest kind" written by one who called himself a gentleman but who was "supposed by many to be a certain unprincipled, abandoned *worsted-comber* and *peddler* sometime since degenerated into a more infamous *pettifogger*" who had been hired to write the piece. To this, a fierce response was promptly published — anonymously, but written no doubt by Aplin — in the *Providence Gazette:*

Alas! for the Good Old Cause, Dr. M—— beats the chamade in a drummer's habit: Is this he of *Gath,* the very blunderbuss of controversy? What a soldier is here! that makes the first fire and then demands a parley that he may know the names of the rank and file in the enemy host. Ah Doctor! Cackling is a sure mark of running; and a fortress that can be brought to a parley will surrender. But as you have thought fit to turn tail, pray throw off the *lion's* skin, you are known by your *bray.* I was prepared for this, and more. I knew I had a dirty job upon my hands, and came in a habit fitted for the employment. He who puts a ring in the nose of a swine that has newly wallowed in the mire may expect something more than a noise in his ears; he may stand in need of a clean pair of stockings, but nothing worse is to be feared; and he will more than balance the inconveniency by the satisfaction of hindering an unclean beast from worrying himself and doing mischief. Don't take a new fright, Doctor. I shall make but a moderate use of my victory, and shall not even stoop to gather your infected spoils, but shall leave you in possession of all your implements of war save your *stinkpot,* which I bury to prevent contagion.[3]

Mayhew, or someone else writing in his behalf, was not to be outdone, however. A letter to the printer of the *Boston Gazette,* published on August 1, struck a higher but still shrill note in reply:

About two months after Dr. Mayhew's *Observations* . . . came out, one of the most impudent and profligate persons in the colony of Rhode Island published a piece of *billingsgate* against him entitled *Verses* . . . He did not even pretend to enter into the argument, but expressly desired that what he wrote *might not be mistaken for a defense of the Society.* A needless caution! This dirty fellow's dirty performance (for which, it is supposed, he had a fee from some of the Episcopal party) was treated by Dr. *Mayhew* with the contempt and neglect which every sensible and unprejudiced person thought it deserved; and it is therefore now, at the expiration of about two months, almost buried in the oblivion which is the common fate of such productions, unless they are kept in remembrance by an answer.

What restraint Aplin may have been exercising up to that point was completely lost in his rebuttal to this letter which he published as a separate *Advertisement.* Mayhew's complaints, he wrote, were complaints against those who publish vicious pieces anonymously in the newspapers:

One gentleman in particular belonging to the Colony of *Rhode Island,* of better repute than himself, whom he suspected to have published some remarks on his libel and to which he was not able to make any other reply but such as a fish woman might have done as well or better, he hath endeavored harpylike to foul and besmear with his touch; but the gentleman remains unhurt by

the blast of a foul mouth, and hath received no more damage than if a dog
had belched in his face after feasting upon carrion.

The *Advertisement* ended with a swipe at the sensitive central issue of
church and state, claiming that what Mayhew was saying implied "that a
subordinate, fanatic colony have a right, if they see fit, to compel the people
to dissent from the Church of *England,* and that it is an act of grace and
mere indulgence in them to permit any to profess the religion of the nation." [4]
By then, at least two months after the original appearance of the *Verses,*
the polemical force of the pamphlet was slackening. There were two more
journalistic thrusts in the *Boston Gazette* that summer: a request that money
sent from Rhode Island to advertise the *Verses* be taken back, "the sum
being as trifling as the author's character is esteemed at among his own
townsmen, and therefore too small to purchase a place in this paper"; and
a statement that a £5 award to Aplin, "the great bully of this colony," in a
successful suit for libel on his character "was four pounds, nineteen shillings,
and eleven pence more than its real worth." [5] But by the early fall, when the
first full doctrinal replies to Mayhew were beginning to appear, Aplin's *Verses*
— as ephemeral as it was personal and shrill — had disappeared from public
attention.

The pamphlet remains a witness to the intensity of feeling that accompanied the effort to assert the force of the English state-church more broadly
and more deeply in America. It is a witness too to the amateurism of literary
polemics in the colonies. A clumsy piece, it is the work of one deficient not
so much in talent as in practice. In its awkward combination of forms — in
its slipping from verse, clearly inadequate to express the author's thoughts
and feelings, to flat-handed prose placed in footnotes — there is revealed the
provincial amateur, aware of artful modes of expression but incapable of
imitating them, comfortable only in the artless flow of everyday speech.

Of John Aplin little is known. The prolix inscription on his gravestone is,
in fact, the fullest biography of him we have. From that, and from a few
other scraps of information, it appears that he was born in Taunton, England,
in 1709, and that he remained a loyal member of the Church of England all
his life. In Providence, Rhode Island, he became a successful lawyer, involved
in partisan politics. In 1763, sufficiently respected to be entrusted by the government with compiling an official memorandum on all controversies between
Rhode Island and the English customs officials, he drafted an electioneering
piece for the Ward interests, attacking the "crazed or more than crazed"
governor, Stephen Hopkins, for attempting to rig elections.[6] Then, apparently,
he fell on evil times. Years later an octogenarian who claimed to have known
him explained what had happened. Aplin, he recalled, who had risen from
poor circumstances, had become "very avaricious. A very important case presented, both sides wanted him, he so engaged, and received a fee from each.
This was discovered; he consequently, between two days, up keleg and scud
for Connecticut. I doubt whether he was ever in Rhode Island afterwards."

Aplin then settled in Plainfield, Connecticut, and assisted in the founding of an Episcopal church in the neighboring town of Brooklyn. There, in 1772, he died. Whether it is true, as his gravestone claims, that he not only was learned in history and in law but also "abounded with native humor, in the application of which he was singularly successful," there remains only the present pamphlet to testify.[7]

The following is the whole of Aplin's poem, including the footnote indicators, drawn together from the pages of the pamphlet:

Verses on Dr. MAYHEW's Book* of OBSERVATIONS, &c.

I.

Whilst *Britain* led by Royal *George,*
   New blessings† doth dispense;
And where her sword and treasure sav'd,
   Spreads learning, truth, and sense,

II.

Ungrateful *Mayhew's* desperate hand,
   Foul libels dares to write;
To prove her charities are crimes,
   Her favors all a bite.

III.

Her holy faith he represents
   As bad as that of *Spira;*‡
Her bishops§ deep in sacrilege,
   And guilty as *Sapphira.*

IV.

Her nobles,‖ plotting for our harm,
   Our liberties' invasion;
And dreadfully arm'd against our faith,
   With weapons of persuasion.

V.

Her sages,¶ dignified in law,
   Each ignorant as a *Tartar;*
That none for sixty years last past,
   Could explain an *English* charter.

VI.

O *Mayhew!* hadst thou been reserv'd,
   To curse some future day;
We also might from Britain's sun,*
   Have felt a gladd'ning ray.

VII.

By nature vain, by art made worse,
   And greedy of false fame;
Thro' truth disguis'd, and mobs deceiv'd,
   Thou fain would'st get a name.

VIII.

Spite of thy wrangling head and heart,
   Thy slander all shall die;
Thyself too obscure for punishment,
   Too mad for a reply.

IX.

Thou who can'st hate for bounties past,
   And fresh ones would'st control;
Th' unborn shall curse thy sland'ring pen,
   And scorn thy narrow soul.

VERSES/on/Doctor MAYHEW's/BOOK OF OBSERVATIONS/On the CHARTER and CONDUCT/OF THE/SOCIETY/FOR THE/PROPAGATION of the GOSPEL in FOREIGN/PARTS:/With NOTES, critical and explanatory./By a Gentleman of *Rhode-Island* Colony./

PROVIDENCE, in NEW-ENGLAND:/Printed and sold by WILLIAM GODDARD, at the Sign of/SHAKESPEAR's HEAD. 1763./

Verses on Dr. Mayhew's Book*
of Observations, &c.

I.

Whilst *Britain* led by Royal *George,*
New blessings† doth dispense;
And where her sword and treasure sav'd,
Spreads learning, truth, and sense,

---

[3] * It is easy to discern from a general view of the Doctor's book, and particularly from the text which adorns the title page,[1] that he takes the Society to have invaded the rights of the people of *New England* by aiming to propagate Christianity according to the Church of *England* within its limits, although mere persuasion is only used; and he gives a broad hint that the Congregational plan is by law established there. I desire that what follows may not be mistaken for a defense of the Society, for I mean no such thing, as it would be disparaging them and doing too much honor to so wretched and impertinent an accuser to enter upon their exculpation. In this place I shall only show that this blind bigot is for setting up an inquisition against the religion of the nation within His Majesty's own dominions. In Catholic countries, to prevent the promulgation of any other religion is the sole end of the inquisition; the holy office or court itself is but the means used. Now 'tis plain that since the end is by the Doctor attempted, the means would be used also if they were in his power. But alas for him! the principal part of his apparatus is wanting, *Oliver Cromwell* is not at the head of forty thousand cutthroats, to carry his measures into execution.

† His Majesty has been graciously pleased not only [4] to countenance a subscription for erecting and endowing two colleges for promoting literature, the one at *New York* and the other at *Philadelphia,* but of his royal bounty has subscribed £1000, and the Princess Dowager of Wales £100, for that truly noble and useful purpose.[2]

II.

Ungrateful *Mayhew's* desperate hand,
　　Foul libels dares to write;
To prove her charities are crimes,
　　Her favors all a bite.

III.

Her holy faith he represents
　　As bad as that of *Spira*;‡ [3]
Her bishops§ deep in sacrilege,
　　And guilty as *Sapphira*.

---

‡ In the 155th page of the Doctor's book it is written, "When we consider the real constitution of the Church of *England,* how alien her mode of worship is from the simplicity of the Gospel and the apostolic times; when we consider her enormous hierarchy, ascending by various gradations from the dirt to the skies." And in page 71, speaking of the orthodoxy of Independent ministers, he infers that if the Church of *England* limits that term to the clergy of their own church, "they must deny it to the ministers of the established church of *Scotland* and of all other churches, except, perhaps, that of *Rome*." This is an address of thanks upon the Independent plan, and highly orthodox, presented to the people of [5] *England* by a fanatic preacher in return for a deluge of their blood and millions of their treasure lavished in his defense from slavery. Can it be already forgot how few years have gone over us since we had reason to fear that each day's sun would be the last that should light us in a state of liberty? And who, under GOD, were our deliverers? Hath this ungrateful soil been watered with the precious and noble blood of *Wolfe* and *Howe*[4] only to prepare it for larger crops of mockery and scurrility, that e'er our hearts had done throbbing with fear, gloomy pedants without sense or experience crawl out from their hiding places and from among musty commentators who have wrote to humble Christianity, the pure and ethereal spirit of which fled from their sophistical refinement, and every moral and practical duty died of their dogmatisms and under their hands? With heads stored with

this holy lumber, they now venture abroad, proscribe the religion of their guardians and deliverers, and claim the country as a *deodand*,** [5] for the better celebrating their millennium. Whose dead bodies were they that strewed the plains of *Abraham,* and the field of *Ticonderoga?* And how many *New England* Independents could have been numbered among the slain? Forbear, base ingrate! Forbear to slander the dying faith of *British* heroes fresh slaughtered in your defense lest the living ones rise up and avenge the insult. In the 45th page of the Doctor's book it is also affirmed "that the common people of *New England* are, and have all along been, philosophers and divines in comparison with the common [6] people of *England.*" [6] Who can read this without being put in mind of a bit of red flesh that one often sees growing on the top of a dunghill cock's head?

But the Doctor seems in haste to complete the character of an unrelenting bigot, and bestows his filth and abuse very liberally upon the southern colonies also. In the 110th page of his reveries he speaks of what the Society ought to have "done for the heathen or for the colonies in a state little better than heathenism." And in the 151st page he charges the Society with "neglecting both the *Indians* themselves and those heathenish colonies which are the proper objects of their institution." Here the duplicity of his charge proves that by heathenish colonies he means the *English* of those colonies. I wish the Doctor had thought fit to have given us the names of those heathenish colonies, or told how he came to know they were heathenish. All our colonies are professedly Christians; and if the Doctor will allow morals to be comprehended in Christianity, I mean an obedient and respectful behavior to rulers and magistrates, a civil and peaceable demeanor towards one another and to strangers, a punctual payment of debts, with a laudable industry; if these may be allowed to be marks of Christianity, and the Doctor's two Christian colonies, where he saith the Society have nothing to do, were brought into competition with the southern ones, in these respects the former would suffer greatly by the comparison. Who are they that have been printing scandal for six months last past in newspapers about their best and wisest magistrates? And does the Doctor know of nobody that have countenanced or assisted them? [7] But it seems the southern colonies have no establishment for Independent

---

** In the last page of the *Boston* Almanac for the present year are these words: "We hold our lands under no other lord but he who gave *Canaan* to *Abraham.*" This expression, though in an almanac, would have been noted with some public mark of disapprobation in other colonies upon which the Doctor bestows the epithet of heathenish.

ministers, no solemn dump and grimace in their countenances and behavior, and so are heathens. I think it was the knight's head, in the
Spectator, that by clapping on a pair of whiskers and aggravating a
feature or two was converted into that of a *Saracen,*[8] [7] but less labor
and fewer alterations would convert the Doctor into a *St. Dominic,* marching at the head of an army of fanatics, with a sword in one hand and a
platform in the other.

§ The bishops of *England* are in general of the Society; and the Doctor,
in the 142d page of his book, speaking of the conduct of the Society, has
these words: "And supposing such an unjust thing to be designedly done,
which I am not willing to think, the words of the Apostle to *Ananias,* who
kept back part of the price, etc., would be very applicable to this case."
Now in the foregoing page the Doctor tells us what this unjust thing is
which the Society has done, and that he is not willing to think to be done
designedly, where using the metaphor of a steward he represents them
"abusing their trust and alienating the money committed to them from
the particular designs of it." It seems the Society are not only men of deep
design, but their money is very designing money. No doubt the Doctor
was taught to apply to things inanimate qualities proper only to rational
beings, at the same place where the people of *New England* are all made
philosophers and divines, and has carried it abroad to adorn his style and
to enrich our language. And in the 112th page we are told wherein this
abuse and alienation consists, viz., "in their sinking no inconsiderable sum
in the Episcopal gulf of *New England."* I fancy a small part of this sum
might have put a gown upon the Doctor's back, if the Society could have
thought him worthy of wearing it; and its not being offered, the Doctor
may have construed the omission into a misapplication of the money.
Now could the Doctor think that the Society sent missionaries to *New
England* without designing to do it? Or is he not willing to think it was
designedly done, after he has expressly charged the Church and them, in
his 156th page, with persecuting Independents out of the Old World, and
[8] pursuing them into the New to convert them there? Therefore the
Doctor's hesitating about their design in his charge against them of
sacrilege is only in imitation of others who have wrote scandal of their
superiors. In such performances, dark phrases are to be studied and confused descriptions will be frequent, with a perplexity of expression between
saving what the writer's rancor will not let him withhold, and withholding
what his fear will not let him speak out.

IV.

Her nobles,‖ plotting for our harm,
   Our liberties' invasion;
And dreadfully arm'd against our faith,
   With weapons of persuasion.

V.

Her sages,¶ dignified in law,
   Each ignorant as a *Tartar*;
That none for sixty years last past,
   Could explain an *English* charter.

‖ Amongst the venerable and truly respectable names upon the Society's list as members are these noble ones: JOHN LORD CARTERET, LORD BALTIMORE, Lord DIGBY, Lord Viscount TYRCONNELL, besides Sir JOHN BERNARD, ennobled by his high accomplishments, eminent services, and many virtues. It is these, among others, that the Doctor in his 29th page has charged with "turning their arms, as it were, against other Protestants, and expending a great proportion of their money in supporting a party." And in page 107, that they "have long had a formal design to dissolve and root out all the *New England* churches." Now all these arms and this formal design the Doctor himself explains to mean no more than that they have been instrumental in giving an opportunity to such of the people of *New England* as had a mind to worship GOD according to the Church of *England*.

[9] ¶ The last clause of the Society's charter is in the following words: "And our further will and pleasure is that the said Society shall yearly and every year give an account, in writing, to our Lord Chancellor, or Lord Keeper of the Great Seal of *England,* for the time being, the Lord Chief Justice of the King's Bench, and the Lord Chief Justice of the Common Pleas, or any two of them, of the several sum or sums of money by them received and laid out by virtue of these presents, or any other authority hereby given, and of the management and disposition of the revenues and charities aforesaid."

Now the sole head of charge brought by the Doctor against the Society, and which he sometimes calls a perversion and at other times a misapplication of the money committed to their trust, is that they have spent some part of it upon missions in *New England,* where the inhabitants had before the means of religion after the Congregational or Presbyterian modes, as he calls it; which, the Doctor saith, according to the true meaning and intent of the charter, they are not allowed to do; and to find this meaning in the charter he has spent one hundred and seventy-six pages, which, by the way, is proof enough that it is not to be found at all. The locality of this grant is settled by a positive term which in the law of *England* hath a known and definite meaning; the words are *beyond the seas;* and these words have always been adjudged to comprehend all territories, *Great* [10] *Britain* and *Ireland* only excepted, and sometimes *Ireland* too. Now the legal and known meaning of these words the Doctor would control, and form an exception against them by implication, which should have all the effect of a proviso, and to this purpose has been wandering through the charter, putting to torture every plausible word, even to the seal and device of the Society; but this often happens to men of levity that will be scribbling out of their profession. It can be remembered when setting up intents against the plain words of laws and crown grants was used very successfully by fanatics, even until it became a menstruum for dissolving all regal authority and unhinging the government. But what I chiefly purpose to show in this place is that the Doctor hath been mistaken again in his 12th page, where he saith that "other people have a right to give their opinion about the manner that charitable fund (meaning the Society's fund) is employed, and even publicly to remonstrate against any misapplication of it." [9] Now if by giving opinions and remonstrating the Doctor means charging the Society with a perversion of the charity in a printed address to the people, he is wrong, because the whole demeanor of the Society, whilst they execute the discretionary powers granted them, and particularly their management and disposition of the revenues and charities that should come to their hands, is by the charter put under the inspection and made subject to the control of the three greatest magistrates, and who, from the rank they hold, are always the first lawyers in the nation. And the Society, for their own honor and for the private satisfaction of givers as well as for the preservation of their charter, have been punctual in submitting to this inquiry, and have laid before their lordships, once a year, a very particular and exact account how this charity was disposed of, contained in a printed list upon which were the names and places of abode of every missionary and schoolmaster under their employment, and what each [11] one received for his services; therefore, their lordships, who set at this inquiry, could not be ignorant that there were missions in *New*

England. Nor could their lordships want any information about the provision made for Congregational ministers in the *Massachusetts,* because they are always of His Majesty's Privy Council, where the laws by which this provision was made were ratified. And indeed, it is nothing less than impeaching their lordships' characters as judges to suppose that they would enter upon and finish such an inquiry without being fully informed about every matter of fact which the charter made necessary to be known. But such hath been the conduct of the Society that it has ever met with their lordships' approbation. But it seems they had not a sufficient understanding in the law for explaining the charter, and the Doctor has supplied it to them.

The donations to this charitable purpose were bestowed subject to be disposed of according to the terms of the charter, which were only at the discretion of the Society with the approbation of the Lord Chancellor and Lords Chief Justices of *England;* they have ever been so disposed of; and this satisfies the conditions of the charter, and no contributor has complained. This annual inquiry was all the censure that the Society's conduct was by law subjected to, and every year's approbation of their lordships is their lawful acquittal for that year. This is a *commissum fidei* to the Society; they have rendered the accounts of their trust before their judges, and are discharged by the laws of the land. But it seems Doctor *Mayhew,* an Independent preacher of *New England,* was not consulted upon the application of these monies; and because he thinks they might have been better laid out, he has thought fit to compose and put in print a libel addressed to the people of *New England* impeaching the whole Society and charging them positively with a breach of their trust, and to render them as odious and detestable as possible condemns them as criminals equal in guilt with *Ananias* [12] and *Sapphira,* who were struck dead by divine vengeance. Not the least respect is shown to the judgment of that august court before whom they accounted, nor to the high rank which many of the Society hold in the nation, which, by the way, may bring the author within the reach of those laws that aggravate the crime of writing scandal, however secure he may think himself. He mentions *Scotland* as if he had a secret hope of taking shelter there; but had a clergyman of that church committed such an outrage, he would have been punished with immediate deprivation; for as neither the liberty nor property of any subject could be concerned in this dispute, everyone must see that it could be taken up for no other cause but that of FILLING THE MINDS OF HIS MAJESTY'S SUBJECTS WITH FALSE FEARS, AND TO RENDER THEM UNEASY UNDER HIS GOVERNMENT.

But such is the genius and spirit of fanaticism that if one of these lewd actors can but find a means of entangling his interests or his private prejudices with whatever his frenzy disposes him to call religion, he keeps no measures nor observes either decencies or civilities; his interests are become the cause of GOD, kings are called sceptered tyrants, laws that stand in his way are human ordinances, and dignities conferred by the state are principalities and spiritual wickednesses in high places; on an admonition, he mends upon your hands, and 'tis ten to one but he discharges a volley of Scripture full in the face of his adviser; out of which, allowing him but the same license the Doctor takes in interpreting charters, he shall pick you a text in support of every villainy he is disposed to perpetrate.

In this place also, it may be proper to make an estimate of the intrinsic worth and value of a compliment which the Doctor has made to the King in the latter end of his book, and in these words: "But GOD be praised, we have a King, whom Heaven long preserve and prosper, too wise, just, and good to be put upon any [13] violent measures to gratify men of this turn of mind." This I dare affirm to be true; but how consistent is it with what precedes in the same section, in these words: "When we consider the real constitution of the Church of *England,* and how alien her mode of worship is from the simplicity of the Gospel and the apostolic times, when we consider her enormous hierarchy, ascending by various gradations from the dirt to the skies." Now this religion, which the Doctor affirms to be so alien from the simplicity of the Gospel, he knows to be the religion of this wise, just, and good King; and this good King is the very head of this hierarchy which the Doctor calls enormous and represents as springing out of the dirt and ascending to the skies. And everyone knows that the hierarchy or episcopal government of the Church of *England* was first formed in acts of Parliament, and at present subsists upon them. In the Doctor's metaphor these acts of Parliament must of necessity be represented by the dirt. There is no cool man of the Doctor's own church will call these expressions either decent or prudent, or will tell him that any point is to be gained by using them. Nobody can be deceived by his behavior; one hundred and seventy-six pages are spent in abuse upon His Majesty's religion and administration, and three lines of compliment upon his person are put in to make atonement. But this is not new; for the most pestilent writers that have dared to disturb and insult government have not been wanting on certain occasions to gild over their poison with professions of exact obedience, and now and then with the most nauseous and fulsome flatteries; and this last is a kind of incense which this writer at times offers to his prince, and no doubt expects to find it an excuse for whatever may be laid to his charge on the score of obedience. But these expedients have long since been explored: *To obey is better than sacrifice, and to hearken than the fat of rams.*[10] Many a good man is not of the religion of his prince, [14] but at the same time may be a very useful subject; and if such a one could be questioned authoritatively about his creed, he ought to have leave to answer from his heart, and be excused; and when he is at liberty to profess and practice in religion as he thinks fit, if he cannot commend that of his prince and country he will never allow himself to revile it, and especially if he loves his prince, I mean his person and government, which is the duty of every good subject. What signifies panegyrics in thanksgiving sermons and bedropping the royal character with the foul slaver of insincere praise? What avails it to be with one hand writing encomiums upon His Majesty's piety and with the other to be pouring out contempt upon the religion of his crown and of his heart? Is this the portraiture of a good subject? No. And if this writer's love to his prince was pure, he would study the quiet of his government and be afraid to speak evil of his religion lest it should lessen him in the esteem of his people; for in this very esteem are laid the deepest and most durable foundations of public repose. — But away with his daubing, it is like anointing *Aaron's* head even until the bear's grease runs down upon his beard.

The Doctor seems resolved at all events to render the Church of *England* odious and terrible to His Majesty's subjects of *New England,* and so is not content with publishing slander by wholesale against her guardians of the present age, but goes on to deal out by retail the scandal of two ages past, and brings up to view oppressions suffered from sceptered tyrants, as he calls them. Can what happened then have any relation to these times? But it seems His Majesty's mild and gracious government and the security of dissenters by the toleration have not been able to prevent this writer from sounding an alarm on a pretense of new dangers; and tells the people in his 156th page, "We cannot well think of this church's gaining ground [15] here to any great degree, and of seeing bishops fixed amongst us." This can be said with no other view but to inflame. Now peaceable men that love order and understand the necessity of general obedience (I don't mean unlimited obedience) choose, for the sake thereof, not to expose to view past grievances never like to be repeated, but rather incline to draw a veil over the errors of deceased kings. A *Roman* emperor, I think it was,

VI.

O *Mayhew!* hadst thou been reserv'd,
　To curse some future day;
We also might from *Britain's* sun,*
　Have felt a gladd'ning ray.

VII.

By nature vain, by art made worse,
　And greedy of false fame;
Thro' truth disguis'd, and mobs deceiv'd,
　Thou fain would'st get a name.

---

who had but one eye, was by a good-natured painter drawn in profile to hide the defect. But 'tis long since this venal pen has been employed to insult and trample upon fallen majesty; witness his 30th of *January* sermon, pilfered for the most part from an author whom few either can or choose to imitate, and for which he got neither credit nor thanks where he expected both.[11]

* Whoever reads Doctor *Mayhew's* book, throughout which the genius and temper of the Independent religion is shed abroad very liberally and appears to be untolerating in church matters and engrossing in state ones, will never be at a loss to know why *New England* is overlooked at the bestowing of any national or royal bounty for the endowment of seminaries of learning and science. There can be no merit in propagating bigotry and prejudices any more than in bestowing labor to cultivate a nursery of crabs. The choice which His Majesty has been pleased to make of *Philadelphia* for [16] erecting one of these durable monuments of his glory shows that *New England* was not neglected because there were dissenters in it: *Pennsylvania* abounds with them; but they are men of another make. Their principles don't lead them to be always wrestling with the crown for power and places. They have, of their own accord, opened their arms to embrace the sciences and finer arts without tendering them a creed, and have, of their own liberality, bestowed a palm upon every thriving branch of them. Here houses devoted to the public worship of GOD, in general, rise to adorn their capital by universal encouragement, and often at a common expense; nor is difference of opinion allowed to vent itself in

VIII.

Spite of thy wrangling head and heart,
  Thy slander all shall die;
Thyself too obscure for punishment,
  Too mad for a reply.

---

scurrility. And here the grave of the pious and inoffensive Doctor MILLER, instead of being pointed out in a libel, would have been honored with an inscription.[12]

There are the happy mansions where the graces shall be allowed to dwell together with the muses, cherished by the royal hand, and where youth may receive pure science without the nauseous mixtures of bigotry and arrogance. Here the elegant domes are rising apace which are soon to over-top and cast their shadows upon the idol of the Doctor's folly; when the burning lake, the crystal rock, and the enchanted castle, with all its fairy dominion, shall disappear and be no more.

Show me the man that can read with dry eyes the Doctor's funeral elegy over expiring fanaticism, set [17] and sung to a very solemn and doleful tune, and worthy of being performed at a concert of catcalls. It begins in the 155th page, after describing the Church of *England* in words already quoted. "When we consider," says he, "the visible effects of that church's prevailing among us, in the degree that it has." It is pity he had not told us what these visible effects were, for he has spent one-third part of his book in ridiculing her missions, and in proving that she had not prevailed at all. He goes on: "When we reflect upon what our forefathers suffered from these mitred lordly successors of *the fishermen of Galilee.*" Here I stop a little to inquire of him if any mitred lord of the Church of *England* ever shed the blood of a number of poor QUAKERS for no other crime but "disturbing the peace and religious assemblies," as the Doctor, in his 94th page, confesseth his Puritan predecessors to have done; and also to assure him that a bloody-minded man, bent upon mischief, can do it as effectually with a pumpkin shell upon his head as with a mitre. *Calvin* was without a mitre when he burnt *Servetus.* But the ditty goes on: "When we reflect that one principal motive for their exchanging the fair cities, villages, and delightful fields of *Britain* for the then inhospitable shores and deserts of *America* was that they might enjoy, unmolested, GOD's holy word and ordinances." Yes, and it would have proved but a sorry exchange, for they

IX.

Thou who can'st hate for bounties past,
And fresh ones would'st control;
Th' unborn shall curse thy sland'ring pen,
And scorn thy narrow soul.

---

must have been driven into the sea or enslaved [18] long ago if it had not been for the charity of that church which the Doctor rails at for want of charity; and by means of that charity they now enjoy GOD's word and ordinances unmolested, except they call it a molestation that other people are allowed the same enjoyment in their own way. But it seems the peace of the Independent church is of so fragile a nature that if other people can enjoy peace, theirs is broken. It is not a peace that passeth all understanding, for the Doctor has clearly defined its terms; if they are not allowed to plague everybody else, they become a plague to themselves, the Mussulman [Moslem] and Puritanic faith so requiring. But the singsong goes on: "If this growing party should once get the upper hand and a major vote in our houses of Assembly, in which case the Church of *England* might become the established religion here." But this the Doctor don't pretend is likely to be brought about but by the free votes of the people; and if, upon a fair inquiry and comparison, they should think fit to make choice of it, and establish it, what would the Doctor do to prevent it? Such a choice would be but consistent with a state of liberty. And are the mouths of preachers and the ears of hearers to be stopped lest it should come to pass? It is upon these last terms the Doctor admits a toleration for the Church; and I would undertake to obtain one at *Lisbon, Madrid,* or *Rome* upon the very same. But note here that the Doctor puts in his holy claim for power and places; he is afraid it may "exclude [19] all but conformists from posts of honor and emolument." Is not this claim somewhat "alien from the simplicity of the Gospel in the apostolic times?" The Doctor would do well to cite us to the text where *the fishermen of Galilee* made any such claims or complaints; but give the Doctor and his church all the power and wealth, they would civilly abate us the mitre. But to the text: "What other new world remains as a sanctuary for us from their oppressions in case of need? And where is the *Columbus* to explore one for us, and pilot us to it before we are consumed by the flames or deluged in a flood of episcopacy?" Who can but pity the poor en-

chanted and encaged knight? He thinks himself in danger both of fire
and water. Courage, Doctor, don't run away; the apostolic times afford no
precedent for flying in a day of danger, and the *trial ordeal* is abolished by
act of Parliament. But should you resolve to go off to a new world, I beseech you to take at least one truth with you out of the old one. It is, that
neither *Columbus, González,*[13] or any other world finder ever did or ever
will discover one where a company of fanatics can live at peace or let others
live so, except they have all the power, wealth, and reverence in it.

PAMPHLET 4

RICHARD BLAND,
THE COLONEL DISMOUNTED

WILLIAMSBURG, 1764

INTRODUCTION

Richard Bland's *The Colonel Dismounted* was the most notable production of the "great paper-controversy" that accompanied the Parsons' Cause in Virginia. In it, one of the ablest belleletrists of eighteenth-century America, who was also, Jefferson wrote, "the most learned and logical man of those who took prominent lead in public affairs, profound in constitutional lore," mocked in facetious badinage an able opponent and at the same time confronted for the first time certain key issues of Anglo-American constitutionalism. It is an exaggeration to call the pamphlet, as it has been called, "the great initial paper of the Revolution," but it is surely one of the most distinctive of the era.[1]

The circumstances from which it emerged involved the economy of the Chesapeake tobacco lands, the status of the Church of England in the colonies, and the control of colonial legislation by the English government. A crop failure in Virginia in 1758 threatened to raise the price of tobacco far beyond the figures set for it in the many contracts specifying payment in that commodity instead of in currency. Debts payable in tobacco that had been calculated on the basis of the normal availability of the plant rose rapidly in value. Certain creditors and salaried people — particularly the established clergy, whose salaries had been fixed by a law of 1748 at 17,280 pounds of tobacco a year — stood to profit by the situation, but the overwhelming majority of the people, being debtors in some degree, were hurt by it. Pressure built up for the Assembly to take action, which it did by passing the so-called Two-Penny Act of 1758 (a similar one had been enacted in another such emergency in 1755) which fixed the price of tobacco used in payment for debts at two pence a pound, the market price being then more than twice that. The bill was signed by the governor despite his instruction by the crown not to approve without explicit authorization of the King enactments such as this one that unilaterally altered an existing law (the act establishing the salary of the clergy) that had received royal assent. He did so, he said, because the act was an emergency measure intended "to ease the people from the burden which the country thought too great for them to bear, for one year only."

One group, or rather part of one group, immediately rose in opposition. A number of clergymen of the Church of England interpreted the law as a deliberate act of deprivation. Led by the Reverend John Camm, they met in a rump convention to draft a "Representation" (printed by Bland as Appendix III of *The Colonel Dismounted*) which they commissioned Camm to present in person to the Board of Trade. In it they claimed not only that they were "deprived of that maintainance which was enacted for them by His Majesty" and placed on an "unjust and unequal footing" with others in Virginia, rendering their condition "most distressful, various, and uncertain" — not only this, but, they claimed, the Assembly had exceeded its power in enacting such a law without a "suspending clause, to wait royal judgment and pleasure." They begged the Board to recommend the disallowance of this and the earlier Two-Penny Act and, moreover, that they recommend disallowance *"ab initio"* — retroactively, that is, to the date of passage.

Camm's petition was successful. Working through the Bishop of London, who incorporated the "Representation" in a letter to the Board of Trade full of stinging accusations against the people of Virginia,[2] he obtained the desired disallowance by the King in Council in August 1759. The disallowance created serious problems in Virginia, especially when certain of the clergy sued their vestries for back wages in cases at law which collectively became famous as The Parsons' Cause. But the Virginians' resentment, which flared up instantly when the news of the disallowance arrived, was not directed at the crown, even after the King ignored the colony's petition begging him to understand the crippling effect retroactive disallowances would have on the colony. For the colonists did not then consider the King or even Parliament guilty of deliberate malice toward America. On the contrary, the aura of good will that accompanied the accession of George III persisted. The evil lay not with the King but with certain advisers, twisted plotters pursuing factious aims and corrupting public policy. The King and his Privy Council had been misinformed, deliberately, by persons — one in particular — who nursed grievances against the people of Virginia, and had persuaded, no doubt with little effort, the Bishop of London to act as their spokesman.

It was against that dignitary, consequently, to whose diocese the whole of America was considered to belong, that leaders in Virginia launched their first full assault. It began with a pamphlet, *A Letter to the Right Reverend Father in God, the Lord B——p of L——n . . .* , published in December 1759 by Colonel Landon Carter.[3] This English-educated son of Robert "King" Carter, burgess, churchman, owner of vast land and human properties, had already distinguished himself in the Pistole Fee Controversy of 1754 as an outspoken defender of colonial rights, and also, in the course of a vicious squabble with the rector of his parish (an "old friend and acquaintance" of John Camm's) as a violent anticlerical, pledged to "clip the wings of the whole clergy in Virginia."[4] Now, angered by Camm's defiance of the common good as defined by the Burgesses, and bristling with resentment at the bishop's slurs against Virginia, he answered them both in fifty pages of close argument. The Two-Penny Acts, he insisted, had been neither inequitable nor unconstitutional. They had been passed in humanitarian concern for the welfare of the whole in light of the difficult economic conditions in the colony.

Should not the clergy above all be merciful? As to the legality of the acts, their lack of suspending clauses was made necessary by the immediacy of the problem. It would have defeated the beneficent intent of the laws to have held them up for the year or so it would have taken to discover the royal will. The governor as the King's representative had full power to approve such an act, his flat orders to the contrary applying only when there was time to address the crown "before the evil must take effect." And the Burgesses too had acted wholly within their power, for they were the representatives of the people who paid the clergy's salaries, and were merely acting in their name.

Carter's *Letter* was quickly followed by another, this one by Richard Bland, who, if somewhat less affluent than Carter, was no less a member of the planter aristocracy, and in addition was a successful politician, littérateur, and scholar. This "learned, bookish man," as John Adams described him, had inherited wealth, family connections, and political position. Educated by tutors and at William and Mary College but mainly by extensive reading, he qualified as a lawyer and entered political life as a young man. Vestryman, justice of the peace, militia colonel, and, for more than thirty years (1742–1775), member of the House of Burgesses, he was to that body "what John Selden was in the beginning of the troubles in the reign of Charles the First to the House of Commons"; as much as any one man he kept "the legislative machinery of Virginia's government in motion." He acted in a dozen different capacities, drafting bills, chairing committees, writing official addresses, and participating in a great variety of legislative negotiations. He too, with Carter, had been a spokesman for the Burgesses in the Pistole Fee controversy: it was he, in all probability, who had written the House's statement on the rights of the people in that case, and he had published a pamphlet of his own on the dispute. More recently, as a member of the Board of Visitors of the College of William and Mary, he had participated in the dismissal of three members of the faculty, among them John Camm, in the course of a bitter dispute growing out of the first Two-Penny Act. And it was he, finally, who had drafted the Two-Penny Act of 1758.[5]

His *Letter to the Clergy of Virginia . . .*,[6] following quickly on Carter's *Letter,* raised the temperature as well as the intellectual level of the controversy. The Bishop of London's letter to the Board of Trade, he wrote, was "an evidence of the imbecility of the human mind and a demonstration that at certain periods of life the most learned and pious men are subject to the impositions of the crafty and malevolent." The charge that there were "strong instances of a fixed design in the General *Assembly* to *assume a power to bind the King's hands and to say how far his power shall go . . .* [and] *to draw the people of the plantations from their allegiance to the King"* was simply "a false and invidious accusation." The insinuation that the colony was swarming with dissenters was equally "opprobrious and outrageous," and if the Church of England clergy were treated with little respect, that was no more than the many of them who were "a disgrace to the ministry" deserved. But the pamphlet concentrated on the main charge against the Burgesses, that they were "a set of artful designing men, who proceed *warily and endeavor to bring in their schemes by degrees"*: having seized control of the presentation of clergy to vacant parishes, they were now engaged in arbitrarily reducing the ministers' income by means of the Two-Penny Acts. The accusation, Bland wrote, was completely false. The existing management and conditions of tenure of clerical appointments, he said, were deeply embedded in the history of church-state relations in Virginia, which he reviewed in detail, stressing the way in which the civil authorities had repeatedly supported and advanced the church. As to the constitutionality of the Two-Penny Acts, their apparent defiance of a specific point in the royal instructions was justified by "most pressing necessity," for *"salus populi est suprema lex."* There had been no *"traitorous intent* to lessen the prerogative of the crown and to become absolute masters of the maintenance of the clergy," but only the "very laudable and Christian principle, a desire to relieve these people from the unhappy circumstances they were under." It was not the Act of 1758 that tended to undermine the people's loyalty to the crown but the clergy's memorial against it, the doctrines of which, if followed, would reduce the people "to a state scarce superior to that of galley slaves in *Turkey* or *Israelites* under an *Egyptian* bondage."

The two *Letters,* Carter's and Bland's, were effective, and they were not likely to go unanswered. The reply when it came, was the work of the main agent of opposition to the House of Burgesses in general and to the Two-Penny Acts in particular, John Camm, the English-born rector of York-Hampton Parish, deposed professor of divinity at the College of William and Mary (he would later be its president), "a man of abilities," the governor of Virginia wrote in 1759, "but a turbulent man who delights to live in a flame." [7] For him the struggle over the Two-Penny Acts was the culmination of a decade of antagonism with Virginia's native leaders, and the disallowance had been a great personal victory. It was to defend it against the attacks of Carter and Bland that he wrote in 1763 *A Single and Distinct View of the Act* . . . , a pamphlet that went so far beyond the earlier pamphlets in the dispute not only in the details of the economic analysis but also in violence of language that no printer in Virginia would publish it. Printed finally in Maryland, it argued that the latest Two-Penny Act, far from benefiting the poor planters in time of stress, in actuality further enriched the already rich. He listed out the tax rolls of his own parish to show in the case of each taxpayer "the sum in stealing that each of them was presented with . . . by the late Assembly, out of my salary." Profiteering rising, he claimed, with the wealth of the taxpayer, revenues drawn from the Church ended up feeding "the voracious and unsatiable gaming table." With sarcasm thickening with his documentation of the economics of the problem, he translated Bland's maxim *salus populi est suprema lex* as "to take as much as shall be thought necessary, and as often as thought necessary, from the incomes of the clergy, and dispose of it chiefly among the rich and wealthy and successful." He ended on a note of resigned bitterness: dealing as he was with "hectoring bullies more considerable for fierce language than true spirit," he who had already been so badly abused would no doubt still have to endure "vollies of small shot" that would greet his pamphlet.[8]

He was right, except for the size of the shot. The first reply, a vituperative letter by Bland printed in the *Virginia Gazette* (reprinted as Appendix I of *The Colonel Dismounted*) was indeed small shot, and Camm instantly replied in kind (Appendix II). But the next, Carter's *Rector Detected . . . ,* published in February 1764, was thirty-nine pages of sheer verbal savagery, in the course of which Camm's wittier passages — passages, that is, that had to be separated out "from that filth which he has disgorged upon the occasion from an envenomed stomach" — were compared to the croaking of frogs, and his sanity questioned.[9] Camm had to admit, in his *Review of the Rector Detected . . .* (April 1764) that though he had expected a storm to break over him as a result of his *Single and Distinct View,* it had turned out to be "a bitter blast" indeed, not only political "but also logical, critical, personal, sarcastical, and parasitical." [10] But he had not yet heard the end. In August 1764 Richard Bland published *The Colonel Dismounted: or the Rector Vindicated,* which, he said, he had written eight months or so earlier "purely for amusement."

A glance at the documents Bland printed as appendices to the pamphlet (which might well be read as prefaces to the pamphlet itself, in their chronological order: III, I, II) will show the level and style of the earlier publications in the controversy. In contrast, the opening sentence of the pamphlet announces a mock inversion of roles which, maintained throughout, strikes a new note of sophistication. Bland, writing as a fawning adulator of the "gladiatorian penman" Camm, opens with satirically inverted slurs at the "presumptuous *tithe-pig* Colonel" [Carter], the "infatuated *syllogistical* Colonel" [Bland], and with equally ironic encomiums to the "wonderful genius! [Camm] who with infinite wit and humor can transform . . . the most arrant *trash* into delicious fruit . . ." As a presumed defender of the Rector's reputation, he reports verbatim a public conference between himself and a certain colonel, a *"hot and violent demagogue,"* in the course of which the Colonel makes powerful speeches against the Rector which are either weakly answered by the Rector's advocate or are altogether conceded by him ("I was silent. For . . . what could I say in your vindication . . . ?"). In this manner the controversy is reviewed in detail, and the points, subtle and gross, advanced by Camm in the course of the exchanges are refuted, the Rector's "defense" serving only to make the attack more effective. Then, after twenty pages of this banter, a passing reference to the mock claim that Camm had rescued the constitution from attackers creates an easy transition to the heart of the pamphlet: Bland's effort to explain the workings of the British constitution in America (pp. 19 ff.).

There are several distinctive qualities in Bland's thought in this section, which so significantly prefigures the intense concern for constitutional principles that would dominate the thought of the Revolutionary generation. There is, first, the assertion, supported by references to seventeenth-century legal opinions, that the root principles of the English constitution — that all men under it are "born free, are only subject to laws made with their own consent, and cannot be deprived of the benefit of these laws without a transgression of them" — apply to Englishmen in America exactly as they do to Englishmen in England, the colonists being neither a conquered people nor forfeiters of their rights by virtue of migration. But beyond that there is an effort, in terms that would become characteristic and critically important, to clarify the ambiguity in roles of the English and the colonial governments in applying these principles to the colonial situation. *What* government "constitutionally" governed Virginia? If consent was involved, presumably the answer was the government of Virginia, unless consent was impalpably tacit and indirect. But if that were all, then the colony would be wholly independent of England except for the link to the crown, whose only meaningful actions would of necessity be limitations on the Assembly's legislative power. No one at this point, and few indeed for almost a decade to come, sought to reduce the constitutional relationship exclusively to this. Bland's solution, foreshadowing the long, intricate debate on the divisibility of sovereignty that would follow, was based on a central distinction in spheres of governmental action.

There were, first, he wrote, matters of *internal* government, affecting the domestic affairs, the "various circumstances and occasions," of the people within the geographical boundaries of the colony; and these concerns fall within the exclusive sphere of the colony's government. There were also matters of *external* government, in every instance of which "we are, and must be, subject to the authority of the British Parliament." Just as the colony cannot rightly legislate in the area of external concerns without withdrawing its dependence on England and thus by definition "destroying the constitution," so Parliament had no constitutional right to "impose laws upon us merely relative to our INTERNAL government [without depriving] us, as far as those laws extend, of the most valuable part of our birthright as Englishmen, of being governed by laws made with our own consent." Thus it was that "any tax respecting our INTERNAL polity which may hereafter be imposed on us by act of Parliament is arbitrary, as depriving us of our rights, and may be opposed." [11]

It was a central position, but one still only vaguely adumbrated. Bland did examine a few of the problems that flowed from it: the validity of the existing laws of England in the colonies, and the limited force of crown instructions and of crown assent to internal legislation; and he did attempt to buttress the whole argument with a historical review of the Assembly's authority. But the deeper difficulties of sustaining this position were scarcely glimpsed.

The pamphlet warfare over the Two-Penny Act was almost, but not quite, over. A final shot was fired in 1765 when Camm published *Critical Remarks on a Letter Ascribed to Common Sense . . . with a Dissertation on Drowsi-*

ness.[12] But by then so much had happened, so much ink had been spilled, so many arguments spun, so many positions taken, that the argument was largely out of date. In the context of the debate on constitutional principles raging in the year of the Stamp Act, Bland's early thoughts on the subject, which he himself would elaborate and qualify in 1766,[13] were rudimentary. But they had not been entirely superseded, nor would they be. For the constitutional issue he had exposed and freshly commented on in *The Colonel Dismounted* lay at the heart of the Anglo-American struggle.

THE/*Colonel Dismounted:*/OR THE/Rector Vindicated./In a Letter addressed to His REVERENCE:/CONTAINING/*A Dissertation upon the* CONSTITUTION/*of the* COLONY./*By* COMMON SENSE./

Quodcunque ostendis mihi sic, incredulus odi./HOR./

WILLIAMSBURG:/Printed by JOSEPH ROYLE, MDCCLXIV./

I THINK it necessary to advertise the readers that this letter was drawn up above eight months ago, purely for amusement. But from a motive which has prevailed with me, I NOW make it public. To distinguish His REVERENCE's elegant and polite language, the quotations from his inimitable works are printed in ITALIC characters.

TO THE
Reverend *JOHN CAMM*,
Rector of YORK-HAMPTON

IT MUST be confessed, may it please Your Reverence, that you have erected two noble works, outlasting monumental brass, in honor of your victory over the *patrons of ignorance and irreligion.* The dignity of sentiment that shines with so peculiar a luster in your *Single and Distinct View* and in your *Observations,** the elegant language devoid of sophistry and diversified with the most agreeable tropes that give ornament and strength to those excellent performances, must excite the admiration of the present age and transmit your name, with distinguished éclat, to posterity.

Wonderful genius! who with infinite wit and humor can transform the *unripe crab,* the *mouth-distorting persimmon,* the most arrant *trash* into delicious fruit, nay *wring-jaw cider* into palatable liquor.[1] Presumptuous *tithe-pig* Colonel! Infatuated *syllogistical* Colonel! What humiliating disgrace have they brought upon themselves! But they deserve it. Why did they *inflame* your *resentment?* Did they not know Your Reverence has honesty to represent facts truly, learning to write accurately, and wit to make your lampoons, though loaded with rancor and abuse, agreeable and entertaining? Did they not know that besides these excellent accomplishments you possess in an eminent degree that cardinal virtue†[2] with whose assistance very moderate abilities are capable of making a great figure? What arrogance was it then, even in the *boreas of the*

* *See Appendix, No. 2.*
† *Nullum numen abest si sit impudentia.*

301

Northern Neck, in the *violentus auster,*[3] to enter the lists against such a gladiatorian penman? Could these pygmies expect to triumph over such a redoubted colossus? And in defense too of a cause that was not defensible? In defense of *some particular* Assemblies that had been impeached [4] of high crimes and misdemeanors before the Lords of Trade and Plantations, when Your Reverence was agent for the WHOLE body of the Virginia clergy in England? These high crimes and misdemeanors, it is certain, are accumulated in the impeachment to a surprising degree; but what then? The impeachment may be true, notwithstanding; nay, it is true: Your Reverence has said it is true and that is enough. Indeed the colonels with their *hurly-burly vociferous verbosity* dispute your veracity and pretend that in your representation of the General Assembly's conduct you indulge a language injurious to the truth, that you encourage party contentions, that you break in upon the respect owing to the legislature of the colony, that you construe the worthiest and best intentions into criminal designs against the royal authority, that you prefer the support of your own cause before the truth and the service of the public, and that by a low kind of wit and satire you expect to prevail against reason and argument. But they, you know, *deal in false facts, ill-adapted maxims, confident assertions, imaginary impossible cases, inconsistent notions, sneaking chicanery,* and *voluminous nonsense,* and therefore are not worthy of credit.

May it please Your Reverence, I was pronouncing the other day a sublime *miscellaneous* oration before a numerous audience, and proving that Your Reverence does not deserve these reflections. But before I proceed I must explain what I mean by a *miscellaneous* oration, not that I intend this explanation for Your Reverence's information; this would be presumption, since you have proved indisputably, by your own incomparable writings, that you are a perfect master of the *miscellaneous* manner. But as this letter may fall into the hands of readers less learned than Your Reverence, I think it necessary for their information. A *miscellaneous* oration then is exactly like that kind of *miscellaneous* writing in which, according to a noble author, the most confused head, if fraught with a little commonplace book learning, may exert itself to as much advantage as the most orderly and settled judgment.

An orator in this way draws together SHREDS of learning and FRAGMENTS of wit, and tacks them in any fantastic form he thinks proper; but connection, coherence, design, and meaning are against his purpose, and destroy the very spirit and genius of his oration. In short, may it please

Your Reverence, it is just like the *miscellaneous* remarks in your *Single and Distinct View*.

I say, may it please Your Reverence, I was holding forth to a numerous audience in support of your charge against the General Assembly, when the [5] *hot and violent demagogue,* rushing through the crowd in an attitude that would have frightened the renowned knight of La Manca himself, advanced upon me with hasty strides and *brawled out,* Thou *dealer in general topics,* thou *confounder of justice with injustice,* I will prove this *charge to be contrary to the truth in every instance.*

I had given half a crown, may it please Your Reverence, for your *Single and Distinct View;* and as a subscriber to the *Virginia Gazette* I became possessed of your *Observations,* and another witty paper‡ remarkable for an elegant and polite description of a certain odoriferous knight who has the honor of being distinguished by one of the titles properly belonging to Your Reverence.[4] But Ned the barber, a shrewd inquisitive fellow, while shaving me the other day, cast his eye upon that facetious paper, which I held in my hand, and asked me whether the progenitors of the sweet-scented knight received the honor of knighthood from the monarch who advanced the loin of beef to that dignity or not. I told him I believed this honor must have been conferred by the *British* Solomon, because as history tells us he was very intimate with His Reverence's ancestors, making them the constant companions of his sports and divertisements; and it was probable he created them baronets when he instituted that order, but of this I could not be positive. Well then, said Ned, pray Sir ask the Rector of York-Hampton; he knows all things, all secrets, no prattling gossip,

> Who with an hundred pair of wings
> News from the furthest quarters brings,
> Sees, hears, and tells, untold before,
> All that she knows, and ten times more,

knows so much as this Reverend Rector does; and as nothing can be hid from him, no person is so capable of resolving this question. To oblige Ned the barber, this digression has obtruded itself; and he waits with impatience for your determination.

May it please Your Reverence, as you had declared the *hectoring bullies were more considerable for fierce language than true spirit,*[5] I was under no difficulty *about the manner of my defense;* for, thought I, if Your

‡ *The Over-Hearer, a periodical paper supposed to be written by the Rector of Y——H—— in which a S—r R—— is much celebrated.*

Reverence obliged TWO *bullies to part with their strongholds,* surely the same weapons, [6] though perhaps not managed when in my hands with the same dexterity as when under Your Reverence's conduct, will *dispel the fog which* ONE *Cromwellian preacher* endeavors to *diffuse over the face of truth.* Then by a motion of my left hand, which I was obliged to use upon this occasion, similar to that of a soldier when he is commanded to handle his cartridge, I drew your *Single and Distinct View* from my right pocket, and opposing it to the enemy I found myself more invincible than if armed with Mambrino's celebrated helmet, or the more celebrated shield, forged with Vulcanian art for the son of Thetis.[6] It was, may it please Your Reverence, altogether impenetrable to the *enemy's great guns;* and as for his *small arms,* they made not the least impression upon it. Having this advantage, I advanced, in my turn, upon my antagonist, drove him off the field, and took possession of several *posts the strength of which he had magnified, until they fell into my hands.* He then *shifted his ground,* and by a sudden maneuver which I really did not expect, *entrenched himself in new entrenchments.* These I instantly stormed; but as I could not carry them I was at *a loss how to conduct my attack* until reflecting on the astonishing virtues of your *Single and Distinct View,* I resolved to try if trumpeting it out would not have the effect upon these entrenchments as the sound of the ram's horn had upon the walls of Jericho; and I assure you I had great expectations at first, for the entrenchments were shocked several times, especially upon the repetition of your fine criticisms, and I verily thought they would have been leveled with the ground by the sound of the words *justice, learning, religion, liberty, property, public good,* which compose part of your character, in the panegyric Your Reverence so justly bestows upon yourself.

But as the severest shocks from this *tremendous battery* did not destroy the entrenchments, though they were frequently severe enough to shock my senses, I applied to your *Observations,* and thundering out with a *vociferous contempt* these words of your other encomium upon yourself, *I write for liberty and property, for the rights of commerce, for an established church, for the validity of the King's authority, pro aris et focis,*[7] immediately the enemy beat the chamade and demanded a conference, which I granted him. As this conference relates to Your Reverence, I think it proper to transmit you a particular detail of it, which I choose to do through Mr. Royle's press, that I may be certain of its *coming safe to hand.*

The Colonel opened the conference as followeth:

I make no doubt, Sir, said he, but that you have entered into this controversy from an opinion that everything the Rector has advanced with [7] respect to the General Assemblies, and those whom he distinguishes by the name of his adversaries, is true.

I replied, My motive for espousing His Reverence proceeds from my opinion of his veracity. Then, Sir, said the Colonel, I will convince you that the Rector has neither *truth or ingenuity*. Neither truth or ingenuity in His Reverence's works! replied I, hastily. What do you mean, Colonel? Have you not experienced the wonderful effects of his *Single and Distinct View?* And would you not have felt, perhaps, more fatal effects from his *Observations* had you not implored this conference? I acknowledge, said the Colonel, the Rector's works, like those deep-throated engines Milton makes the apostate angels oppose to the celestial army,

> . . . belched out smoke,
> And with outrageous noise the air
> And all her entrails tore; disgorging foul
> Their devilish glut . . .[8]

but smoke and noise are not evidences of truth. Colonel, said I, interrupting him, I expect you will not treat His Reverence with *scurrility*. I will endeavor to avoid it, answered the Colonel, for I am by no means fond of copying the Rector's style or saintlike phrases; it is by reason and argument, not by blows and insults, that I expect to convince you of the truth.

The Colonel went on: I had determined not to give myself any further trouble about the Rector of York-Hampton. I know it was a Sisyphean labor to engage in a dispute with this man, for, as Pope says,

> Destroy his fib, or sophistry, in vain,
> The creature's at his dirty work again.[9]

I thought too I should be very indifferently employed to reply in form, as Lord Shaftesbury calls it, to his *Single and Distinct View,* which in my opinion carries with it its own ridicule; neither could I be persuaded that so sorry a performance, which perverts the meaning of my most simple expressions, mutilates sentences, and makes me speak words I never uttered would be looked upon by men of sense as a refutation of my *Letter to the Clergy.* And as for his tinsel wit, if it can be worthy of such an epithet, I despised it. But that I may convince you of this writer's sophistry, of his misrepresentation of the plainest facts, and of the constitutional proceedings of the General [8] Assembly, I will examine his legerdemain performances; and I hope irksome as the talk is I shall have the strength to go through with it.

In the apology this Rector makes for his *impudence* or *rudeness* (these are his own words) he says that *in this war which his adversaries* BEGAN, *the manner of his defense has been directed by the conduct of the attack, for he found it too great a difficulty for him to let the merit of their example be entirely thrown away;* so that LEX TALIONIS is the rule of retribution with this peacemaking Rector.[10] However, let that be as it will, let us see whether this eminent divine is a man of *truth and ingenuity. My adversaries* BEGAN *the war,* says this faithful recorder of events. But is he sure of this? Or is it a *false fact, a confident assertion* invented to *persuade men out of their senses,* according to his own elegant expressions? I affirm it is a *false fact, a confident assertion,* which, if I prove, will, I presume, make the scourge he intended for others reverberate with double force upon himself.

At the September session of Assembly in the year 1758, the people represented to the House of Burgesses that "by reason of the short crops of tobacco made that year it would be impossible for them to discharge their public dues and taxes that were payable in tobacco, which would expose them to the vexatious and oppressive exactions of the public collectors; and they prayed that an act might pass for paying all public, county, and parish levies, and officers' fees in money at such price as by the House should be thought reasonable." [11] The short crops made that year, and the impossibility of paying their public tobacco dues as the laws then stood, were the reasons given by the people for desiring, and by the General Assembly, in consequence of this representation, for passing the Two-Penny Act. But though the relief of the people from the general distress of that year could be the only possible motive with the General Assembly for passing that act, yet this discerner of spirits, *this man who knows everybody's thoughts,* discovered other reasons for their conduct. Suffer me to recite them in brief from the impeachment brought against the legislative body of the colony before the Lords of Trade and Plantations in the time of the Rector's agency in England. In that impeachment they are accused with *exercising acts of supremacy inconsistent with the dignity of the Church of England and manifestly tending to draw the people of the plantations from their allegiance,* with *assuming to themselves a power to bind the King's hands,* with *having nothing more at heart than to lessen the influence of the crown and the maintenance of the clergy,* with *attacking the rights of the crown and of the clergy,* with *depriving the King of his royal authority over the clergy, putting them under the power of the* [9] *vestries and* making them subject to the humors of the people, with *never intending any good to the clergy,* with *taking possession of the patronages and wanting to be absolute masters of the maintenance of the clergy,* with *passing acts of Assembly on pretense that only small quantities of tobacco were made in some years that they might render the condition of the clergy most distressful, various, and uncertain after a painful and laborious performance of their functions.* In short, and to sum up the whole in one word, with being *traitors in the legal sense of the word.*[12]

This charge, so heavy and so injurious, occasioned my *Letter to the Clergy;* and I will submit it to your determination whether I had not a right, as a friend to truth, as a member of that body so grossly abused, to obviate the acrimonious invectives contained in this charge. If I had no right, then I am the aggressor; but if I had, then the Rector's want of *truth and ingenuity* in a plain matter of fact is evident, as he must be the author of this controversy.

To this I replied, You certainly have a right, Colonel, *by all legal methods,* to vindicate the conduct of the General Assembly not only as a member of it, but as an honest man, against every unjust accusation; and as this impeachment was brought in a public manner before the Lords of Trade in England, who have the direction and superintendency of the plantation affairs, I must own that your publishing your defense HERE does not make you the *author of this war.* The promoter of this impeachment is, without question, the person who BEGAN it. Well then, Sir, said the Colonel, the Rector BEGAN *the war.* I replied, Be not so hasty, Colonel; His Reverence is innocent. A man of his integrity, of his truth and uprightness of heart, could not invent such a malevolent groundless charge; and as you accuse a clergyman remarkable for his humility and meekness of temper as a promoter of dissension between the legislature and clergy of the colony, you deserve the censure His Reverence has thought proper to pass upon you. Why Sir, asked the Colonel, seemingly astonished, was not the Rector the author of this impeachment? If he was not the CLERK that drew it, still he was the instrument; or, that I may express myself in less ambiguous terms, the INFORMER upon whose evidence it was drawn up. Nay, does not the paper§ presented by him to the Lords of Trade as *The Humble Repre-*

§ *See Appendix, No. 3.*

sentation of the Clergy of the Church of England in His Majesty's Colony and Dominion of Virginia, which in fact composes part of this invidious libel, prove that he ⟦10⟧ was the author of it? And is not this more than *thinking,* according to the pretty proverb so wittily applied in his *Observations?* Is it not *good authority* for charging him with being the author, the forger of the impeachment? Besides, does he not justify it in his *Observations?* Does he not, by a most unfair and disingenuous *comment* upon four acts passed by the General Assembly attempt to prove that they all agree in these *peccant circumstances?* Why really, Colonel, said I, how can you justify *three* of those acts? For by your present *plan of defense,* you only endeavor to prove that the General Assembly were not guilty of the crimes laid to their charge by passing *one* act; their passing *three* others, then, of the same *pernicious tendency,* is *altogether unjustifiable.* I was, may it please Your Reverence, a *little graveled here,* and under some apprehension of *tripping* if I had attempted a further justification of your *truth and ingenuity.* I was therefore desirous to divert the Colonel from pursuing his proofs against you as the *author of the war* by putting him upon his defense of the other three *peccant* acts.

The Colonel replied, I perceive, Sir, by your attempting to divert me from the point I was upon, you are convinced the Rector BEGAN *the war.* The Colonel stopped. I was silent. For, may it please Your Reverence, what could I say in your vindication until I had it from yourself that you was not the INFORMER upon whose evidence this impeachment was drawn up; but if you deny that you was the INFORMER, and will let me know who was, I am resolved to have another bout with the Colonel. I must therefore beseech you to be very explicit in this particular when you favor the public with your next production.

It would be disgustful, even to you, Sir, his friend, resumed the Colonel, was I to take notice of all the fustian contained in his panegyrics upon his own and his *brethren's* loyalty. Don't think, gentlemen of the clergy, said the Colonel, breaking out into a rhapsody upon repeating the word *brethren,* don't think that you ALL have the honor of being *brethren* to this ever-to-be-reverenced Rector. No, gentlemen, the word *brethren,* like the word MANY,‖ *is capable of being taken by two handles.* Do not, therefore, flatter yourselves that the Rector of York-Hampton takes it by the same handle he takes the word ALL¶ (by which single word ALL has pro-

‖ *See Single and Distinct View,* p. 29.
¶ *See the Rector's Observations in the Appendix, No. 2* [pp. xi–xiii below].

duced one of the finest pieces of true genuine original criticism that ever
was invented by the wit of man). I say, gentlemen, the word *brethren*
is not, like the [11] word ALL, to be taken by the BIG handle, but like the
word MANY is to be taken by the LITTLE handle; so that the Rector's
brethren are but few comparatively with the whole body of the Virginia
clergy, perhaps only a quindecemvirate of them, of which he is the chief,
who in a *general* convention of twenty-five carried the vote for appointing him their agent to impeach the General Assembly of their country
of treason. But now I am addressing myself to the clergy, give me leave
to propose a question or two to those fifty-five (for it seems there are at
least eighty parochial clergymen in the colony)* who did not *think
proper to attend the regular summons of the bishop's commissary.*[13] Did
you, gentlemen, when you sent *excuses for want of your appearance* send
also *your concurrence in the measures* that were proposed in the convention? Were you acquainted with these measures before they were
proposed? If you were, who made you acquainted with them? Not your
late commissary. He was one of the traitors; he *was not under the influence of the clergy or in their true interest,* and therefore cannot be
supposed to have given you the information, though he was the only
person who ought to have done it; perhaps he was not let into the secret
designs of the Rector and his *brethren.*[14] And if you were not informed,
could you send your concurrence to measures you knew nothing of?
I am persuaded you could not, but that you would have attended the
regular summons of the bishop's commissary on purpose to have opposed
the measures that were carried by the quindecemvirate had you been acquainted with them before the meeting of the convention. The respect
I bear you, the high sentiments I entertain of your *truth and ingenuity*
(these, gentlemen, are favorite words with the Rector), the piety, candor,
and integrity so conspicuous in the lives of most of you, make me sure
you would have attended on purpose to oppose measures so contrary to
your real interest, so repugnant to truth, and which could only serve to
destroy the harmony and concord it is your inclination as well as duty
to cultivate and maintain between the legislature and the reverend body
of the clergy.

The Colonel resumed his defense: Was I to trace out ALL the Rector's
boasts of his and his *brethren's adhering to and preserving the old constitution,* which *some particular* Assemblies *were* endeavoring to destroy,
of their *sheltering themselves* under the authority of the *British oak,*

* See *Single and Distinct View,* p. 16.

under the *wings of the prerogative,* under the *protection of a most gracious and religious monarch,* from whose allegiance the General Assemblies *were attempting to draw the people of the plantations, it would carry me further than there is any* [12] *need to go on this occasion.* ALL his ostentatious flourishes are to be seen at large in his masterly works, which I suppose are by this time transmitted to Graham Franks, *now* in England,[15] to be laid before the Board of Trade or perhaps a more honorable board, that his unparalleled loyalty may be manifested when his cause against the collector of his parish levy is carried before that high tribunal. But lest the word ALL, which I have taken occasion to use TWICE in this part of my defense, to wit, ONCE when I spoke of the Rector's boasts, and again when I spoke of his ostentatious flourishes, should fling him into labor with another criticism and make him bring forth, like the mountain in the fable, I must inform you which *handle* you are to take it by in these two places. Know then, Sir, that you are to take this word ALL by the BIG *handle,* and not by the LITTLE *handle,* which last mentioned *handle* I took it by when in my *Letter to the Clergy* I explained my sense of it as it stood in the impeachment by making it include the GREATER part of the members of the General Assembly; which I said must be the import of the word in that part of the impeachment I was then considering. But this explanation I suppose the Rector passed over, that he might demonstrate to the world his profundity in critical knowledge.

I will now examine the *three* acts the Rector cites as further instances of the General Assembly's disloyalty.

In the year 1738 two new counties and parishes were erected upon the frontiers of the colony, far distant from navigation. That these counties might be settled and a good barrier be thereby made against the French,† several encouragements were granted to the inhabitants; one of these was that they might pay all levies and officers' fees in money for tobacco, at the rate of three farthings per pound. Under this regulation the salary of the ministers in each of the new parishes was only £152, when the salary of the other parochial ministers was 16,640 pounds of tobacco, as settled by the act of 1727, which was then in force. The ministers of these new parishes continued to receive this salary of £152 until the year 1753, when one of them petitioned the Council for an augmentation of his salary; this petition was sent by the Council to the House of Burgesses, who immediately passed the act for the *frontier* parishes, as the Rector

† *See the act for establishing these counties, anno* 1738.

calls it, whereby the minister's salary in each of these parishes was settled at £100 a year, according to the desire of the minister petitioning. This act, passed upon this consideration, and which was so advantageous to the ministers of these parishes, was one article [13] in the impeachment of high crimes against the majesty of our sovereign and the dignity of the Church of England; and as the colony had no agent at that time in England to represent a true state of the case, was, from the misrepresentation of the agent appointed by fifteen of the Virginia clergy without the participation of the two ministers concerned, repealed by the royal proclamation. For this repeal the ministers of those two parishes returned the Rector their humble and hearty acknowledgments by their petition to the General Assembly for a renewal of the repealed act, without which they must starve; which petition had such an effect upon the humanity of this traitorous Assembly, who had *nothing more at heart than to lessen the maintenance of the clergy and to render their condition most distressful, various, and uncertain,* that regardless of the Rector's resentment they complied with the ministers' request.[16]

As to the Norfolk and Princess Anne Act, I presume I need not repeat what I have said upon it in my *Letter to the Clergy,* where I have given a candid and honest account of the reasons which prevailed with the General Assembly to pass it; to which I can add nothing, except that the petition from the people which gave rise to it was presented to the House of Burgesses at their October session, 1754, and being referred to the next session, did not come under the consideration of the House until the 7th day of May, 1755; so that full time was given for any person to represent against it if it had not been agreeable to him.[17]

From this account of the Frontier and Norfolk acts the Rector's want of *truth and ingenuity,* of decency and good manners in his remarks upon the General Assembly for passing these acts, is sufficiently evident. For him to charge the legislature with *attempting to lessen the influence of the crown and the maintenance of the clergy* because they gave to the ministers of the frontier parishes an increase of salary, without which they must have lived in the greatest indigence, and because they gave relief to the people in one part of the colony from laws which under their particular circumstances were extremely oppressive to them, I say for him to charge the legislature with such attempts is an instance of want of truth and an indecency of behavior which no man could be guilty of but one who was resolved to trudge, with might and main, through dirt and mire to gain his ends.

And now, Sir, may I not say with great justice of this Rector, in his own words, that *he has shown more judgment in suppressing part of the Apostle's account of charity than in giving us what he had quoted; for had he given the* [14] *Apostle's account unmutilated, the reader must have seen that charity* doth not behave itself unseemly, that it rejoiceth not in iniquity, but rejoiceth in the TRUTH. But as the *proverbial account* of TRUTH, that it is not to be spoken at all times, *seemed to be more for the* Rector's *purpose,* he has preferred it in his articles of impeachment.

The general act of 1755 was passed when, I confess, there was not such a PRESSING NECESSITY for it as there was afterwards, in the year 1758; but their passing this act when perhaps there was no great necessity for it does not make the General Assembly guilty of the crimes contained in the Rector's impeachment.[18]

The legislature of this as of all other countries are fallible men, and as such may enact laws which they may think necessary and for the public good but which from experience may be found unnecessary and even destructive of that good they were intended to promote. But is this fallibility to be imputed to them as a crime? Or is their enacting a law to enable the inhabitants of the colony to discharge their tobacco debts in money, in a year, as they thought, of general dearth and scarcity, an evidence of their attempting to restrain the power of their sovereign and to destroy the dignity of the established church? And yet in such a point of view does this Rector place their conduct. Is such a representation honest? Is it such a one as ought to have come from a man who so confidently charges others with a want of *truth and ingenuity?* And is it decent for a clergyman to treat members of the General Assembly for offering a just defense against so aggravated a charge with a language not to be found but amongst those who have prostituted themselves to the lowest dregs and sediments of scurrility? Here I stopped the Colonel and said with some warmth, You forget your promise, Colonel, not to treat His Reverence with hard names. His *scurrility,* indeed, *is provoked defensive scurrility; which consideration will have its due effect with the readers of every degree, who are the judge and jury and everything with* His Reverence. But you, Colonel, have, unprovoked, abused His Reverence in your first defense, and in your letter to him published in a public newspaper you have charged him with a neglect of duty in his parish,[19] which is *one of the most palpable, barefaced, and impudent falsehoods that ever was invented.* I thought, Sir, replied the Colonel, I had convinced you that the Rector was the aggressor, and that his abusive and

unjust charge against the General Assembly had occasioned the controversy between us. As to my abuse of him in my *Letter to the Clergy,* you
must be convinced of the contrary if you will read that letter with attention; for though the manner in which [15] he has detached my words
which seem to have any severity of expression in them from their proper
places, collected them into one view, and taken them to himself, may
show how easy it is for a caviler to give a new sense, or a new nonsense,
to anything, yet as they are applied by me in the several parts of my
Letter to the Clergy in which they stand they will appear to be nothing
more than proper and just expressions relative to the treatment the General Assemblies have received from the Rector and his accomplices. It is
true, in one place of my letter I have disputed the Rector's superiority in
point of learning above other men, which I acknowledge is great sauci-
ness in me, since he has demonstrated by his fine writings that he is as
excellent a critic and as learned a divine as he is a good Christian; but
as I did not know so much at that time, I hope I shall be forgiven. If I
have accused him with a neglect of DUTY in his parish, and can be convinced that this accusation is unjust, in that case I have done him an injury, and will not only ask his forgiveness of my offense, but make an
atonement for it by publicly acknowledging that I have aspersed the
character of a diligent pastor, attentive to and perpetually careful of the
spiritual concerns of ALL the flock committed to his charge. But then, as
I *may differ from him about the precise meaning of the word* DUTY, I
must, to prevent mistakes, have the meaning of it fixed and determined;
for perhaps I may understand it in a more extensive sense than the Rector
doth. It is, you know Sir, according to his own definition of it, a *complex
term,* and consequently must include something more than an excursion
out of the parish where he resides to his church in York-Hampton on a
Sunday when he is not confined at home by pain and sickness. I suppose
the Rector calls himself a MINISTER, a LABORER, a WATCHMAN, a PASTOR, a
STEWARD, an AMBASSADOR, in sacred things. These different characters, then,
must have different heads of DUTY belonging to them. I cannot therefore
agree that he discharges all these duties by only attending his parish
church on a *Sunday;* and if he does nothing more, he may be likened to
a servant who having six talents committed to his management wraps
five of them up in a napkin and only trades with one, or rather a small
part of one of them. Whether such a servant acts justly or not is not for
me to determine. But Colonel, said I, *I have studied to find out what connection there could be between* His Reverence's *neglect of duty in his*

parish and the dispute between you and him about the Two-Penny Act. Exactly as much, Sir, replied the Colonel, as there is between my *officiating as a clergyman in the churches of the parish where I live* and a dispute relating to the power of the General Assembly to enact laws; which is all the reply I shall make to his *windmill and giant* and his other quixotisms. Why Colonel, said I, do you really *officiate as a clergyman in the churches of the parish where you live?* [16] I do not, answered the Colonel; but I officiate sometimes as READER in the church which I frequent in the absence of the minister, being thereto appointed by the vestry. My motive for accepting this appointment, I presume, the Rector has no right to inquire into, since it was not from a pecuniary consideration.[20] Well Colonel, said I, as to that matter, whether right or wrong, I have no business with it; but your resentment against His Reverence *for making use of the happy privilege which every British subject enjoys, of approaching the throne in an humble petition,* is not to be defended. Did I express any resentment against the Rector, replied the Colonel, for making use of this *happy privilege,* I should be blameable because I value it as much as the Rector can, notwithstanding his pompous encomiums upon his own loyalty. But I shall always consider it as an affront to the throne, which under our present illustrious race of kings has been eminently distinguished for truth and justice, to approach it with a petition loaded with calumny and abuse against the King's substitute and every other part of the legislature of the colony. If the Rector thought himself injured by any act of the General Assembly, he had a right to *approach the throne with an humble petition* against it; but then he should have approached it with truth: he should have represented facts with candor and integrity, and not have imputed such act to causes which could not possibly exist; and if he had done so, I assure you, Sir, he and I should have had no dispute.

But Colonel, said I, in your account of the *famous petition‡* you have reflected with great severity upon the clergy, when *I own I can see no mighty harm* in that petition, provided it might stand alone, without *your comment.* Besides, it was the petition of *one* clergyman only, *who did not prefer it from any imagination that there was room to expect success in it, but to evince the contrary by experiment.* Your reflections therefore were very disingenuous; and though the design of the petition *is a piece of secret history, a stratagem, a machination, which it seems you, with all your sagacity and insight into everybody's affairs, have not*

‡ *See Single and Distinct View,* p. 29.

been able to penetrate, yet your inference drawn from it *that if the pro-*
vision for the clergy was made better by an act they would make no com-
plaint concerning encroachments on the authority of the King is no less
ungenerous, since *to make this inference good it should have appeared*
in the petition that the clergy wanted a better provision by an act without
a suspending clause. But there is no such thing in the petition; and I
believe it would be a difficult matter to prove that the clergy, though will-
ing enough to have a better provision, would accept of it by means of an
act without a suspending clause. [17] My account of the *famous* petition,
as the Rector calls it, replied the Colonel, is taken from the Burgesses'
Journals, where it stands as the petition of the clergy, and not as the petition of *one* of them. However, let it be for the present that it was *owned*
by *one* clergyman only. The Rector says this clergyman *designed well;*
and that *one* other clergyman was *privy* to the petition, who, from what
he says about the secret history of it, I conclude must be himself. Now
this petition declares that MANY CLERGYMEN WHO ARE A DISGRACE TO THE
MINISTRY FIND OPPORTUNITIES TO FILL THE PARISHES;[21] and can any expression be found in my *Letter to the Clergy,* torture it how you will, that
reflects with such severity upon them as this declaration doth, which was
made in the most public manner by *one* of their own body abetted by
one other, and he no less a person than the pious Rector of York-Hampton? And if our parishes are filled with so MANY clergymen who are a
disgrace to the ministry, may it not be suspected that such men would
accept of a better provision by an act without a suspending clause? And
that they would not be very nice in examining whether such act was
worded exactly conformable to a royal instruction to the governor for his
own particular conduct, especially when they were not answerable for a
transgression of it? The Rector, in zeal for the royal authority, might,
for aught I know, be willing to refuse *a better provision* under such an
act; but as he has not as yet attained to that degree of supremacy as to
decree by his own authority that his brethren should refuse it, it would
be necessary to determine this matter in a convention. And if the clergymen, distinguished with such excellent characters by the author of the
petition, who are so MANY, should prevail against the self-denying Rector
of York-Hampton upon a question in which their temporal interest might
outweigh the royal authority as in all probability they would, the Rector,
by an established rule of the convention, must submit, and perhaps rather
than be the occasion of a schism, would subscribe to the vote of the majority. But as his conduct in such a case cannot be known, it must re-

main a matter of opinion whether he would accept of *a better provision* or not under such an act.

But notwithstanding the CHANGES the Rector is perpetually RINGING upon an act *with,* and an act *without* a suspending clause, his loyalty will not shine forth with a meridian brightness unless he refuses to accept of a better provision under an act *with* a suspending clause; for the governor is not to give his assent to any act *with* a suspending clause that alters or repeals an act which has received the royal approbation, without first obtaining the King's permission. So that before the Rector ought to accept of a *better provision* under any act of the General Assembly, the clergy should appoint him [18] their agent a second time to *approach the throne with an humble petition* for the royal permission to the governor to give his assent to such act; which appointment, if I dare venture a conjecture, would be extremely pleasing to him, as he would thereby have an opportunity of soliciting a place for himself of the first ecclesiastical dignity in the colony, which I believe is at this time vacant.

And let it not be thought that a convention cannot be held during the vacancy of the commissaryship for appointing him agent; for if an advertisement in the *Virginia Gazette,* signed by him and two or three others, was of sufficient authority, in the late commissary's time, to convene the clergy, certainly now there is no commissary he may by his own power call a convention upon a matter of such importance to himself.[22]

But let all this happen as it may, it is extremely obvious that the Rector's temper *inclines him to inflame his own resentment* into a fixed contempt of the General Assembly; otherwise he could not have approved of the conduct of the author of this petition, if what he says of him is true, that *he did not prefer the petition from any imagination that there was room to expect success in it, but to evince the contrary by experiment:* so that the General Assembly may be used by designing men as instruments to carry on their deep-laid stratagems and machinations on purpose to afford *matter of pleasantry* to the Rector. But it may be that the Rector has *tripped* in his history of this clergyman's conduct, who, I have heard, gave the gentleman on whom he prevailed to present the petition to the House of Burgesses a quite different account of his design; and that gentleman was insulted by a great intimate of the Rector's for presenting it; which insult, I suppose, would not have been given if the author of the petition had expected no other effects from it than what the Rector says he did.

Colonel, said I, your remarks are of a *sour and aggravating cast*. His

Reverence's temper *does not incline him to inflame his own resentment;* he has suffered persecution; he has *missed the president's place at the college;* he has been *forbid, with others, the late governor's house under the title of disturbers of his government;* he has been *recommended by the late governor in conjunction with others to the correction of the Grand Jury for being so audacious as to publish under their names an invitation to as many of their brethren as were willing to attend, for them to meet at a brother's house before he left the country.* He has been *forbid the present governor's palace, when he waited on him with the royal disallowance to several acts of Assembly.* He has, I say, suffered all [19] these persecutions, *cum multis aliis quae nunc prescribere longum est;* and certainly His Reverence, *who has suffered so much for adhering to reason and justice, and the principles of true patriotism,* is excusable *for the freedoms he has used.*[23]

The Rector, replied the Colonel, gives colorings to his imagery as best suit his purpose; but remove the false appearances and his representations will not exhibit so amiable a character. The brother at whose house this meeting was appointed was not a person of that distinction or moral accomplishments as to make it necessary for the clergy to pay their compliments to him in a body upon his leaving the country. The late governor knew, the late commissary knew, as did many other gentlemen, that he was one of the cabal; and they all believed, and, *if it was proper to dwell any longer on this circumstance, a very good account might be given* for their belief, that this meeting was on purpose to raise disturbances in the government, to form stratagems and machinations against the administration and the legislature of the colony, which this brother was to solicit in England. And as Mr. Dinwiddie, the late governor, thought it an affront to his authority as well as to the bishop's commissary for three or four clergymen to assume to themselves a power to call a meeting of the clergy, he resented the insult in a manner becoming his character as the King's substitute. As to the prohibition the Rector received from appearing at the present governor's palace, his affrontive and disrespectful behavior was the occasion of it; for, as I have been informed that contrary to his duty and the respect due to the King's representative, he did not wait on the governor with *the royal disallowance to several acts of Assembly,* with which he was charged by the Lords of Trade, until several weeks after his arrival in the country, though he was in the place of the governor's residence; and when he did wait on him he delivered the dispatch opened after he had communicated it to such of his brethren as he thought proper. So that his own modesty, if he has any, and a consideration of his own character, should, methinks, have prevented his complaining of this prohibition.

And as to his missing the president's place at the college, his contumacious treatment of the Visitors' authority, which is so publicly known, could not entitle him to their favors, even admitting that he was qualified in other respects.

Colonel, said I, this is all prejudice. You *suffer your passion to make a fool of you.* His Reverence has given the strongest proofs of *true patriotism;* he has delivered the constitution from the basest attempts to destroy it; he faces [20] every attack, encounters every danger, despises every obloquy; in short, he may say, with old Siffredi in the play,

> . . . I have preferred my duty,
> The good and safety of my fellow subjects,
> To all those views that fire the selfish race
> Of men . . .[24]

since he has with boldness, and, as he says, with truth justified his impeachment against the General Assemblies who were *attempting to overturn the constitution and to restrain the royal prerogative by passing acts which interfered with acts confirmed by His Majesty, without a suspending clause.* Now, Colonel, how can you exculpate the General Assemblies from this atrocious crime?

The Rector's patriotism, answered the Colonel, is as conspicuous as his modesty and politeness; but it is really *matter of pleasantry,* as this Thersites§ said of the *famous* petition, to hear him haranguing about the constitution, which if he knows anything of, he does not care to make it public.

The constitution cannot be destroyed, nor the royal prerogative restrained by any act of the General Assembly. The King as sovereign possesses an inherent power in the legislature of the colony and can give his allowance or disallowance to any act passed by them; but as the Rector boasts that I am not able to answer his arguments upon this head of accusation, that I am *graveled,* that *he hath caught my gentleman tripping lightly over marshy ground,* you must give me leave to examine

§ *Thersites only clamor'd in the throng,*
  Loquacious, loud, and turbulent of tongue;
  Aw'd by no shame, by no respect control'd,
  In scandal busy, in reproaches bold:
  With witty malice studious to defame;
  Scorn all his joy, and laughter all his aim.
                    Pope's *Iliad* [II, 255–260]

into THE POWER OF THE GENERAL ASSEMBLY TO ENACT LAWS, which I believe will put an end to the Rector's exultations and convince you it was the CONTEMPTIBLENESS and not the WEIGHT of his arguments that prevented my answering them in the letter I thought proper to address to him.

I do not suppose, Sir, that you look upon the present inhabitants of Virginia as a people conquered by the British arms. If indeed we are to be considered [21] only as the savage ABORIGINES of this part of America, we cannot pretend to the rights of English subjects; but if we are the descendants of Englishmen, who by their own consent and at the expense of their own blood and treasure undertook to settle this new region for the benefit and aggrandizement of the parent kingdom, the native privileges our progenitors enjoyed must be derived to us from them, as they could not be forfeited by their migration to America.

One of the greatest lawyers and the greatest philosopher of his age|| [25] tells us, "A country gained by conquest hath no right to be governed by the English laws." And another no less eminent lawyer¶ [26] says, "Where the country of a pagan or infidel is conquered, there, *ipso facto,* the laws of such country are abrogated." And from hence I suppose it was that a learned and upright judge* [27] gave it as his opinion, "That Virginia is to be governed by such laws as the King pleases." But certainly this great judge was not acquainted with Virginia; if he was he never would have given an opinion which with respect either to the original or present inhabitants of this country must be erroneous. It must be erroneous with respect to the original inhabitants because they were never fully conquered, but submitted to the English government upon terms of peace and friendship fixed and settled by treaties; and they now possess their native laws and customs, savage as they are, in as full an extent as they did before the English settled upon this continent. It must be erroneous with respect to the present inhabitants because upon a supposition that their ancestors were conquerors of this country, they could not lose their native privileges by their conquests. They were as much freemen, and had as good a right to the liberties of Englishmen after their conquest as they had before; if they had not, few of them, I believe, would have been induced by so inadequate a reward to endeavor an extension of the English dominions, and by making conquests to become slaves.

Under an English government all men are born free, are only subject to laws made with their own consent, and cannot be deprived of the

|| Lord Chancellor Bacon.   ¶ Lord Coke.   * C. J. Holt.

benefit of these laws without a transgression of them. To assert this is sufficient; to demonstrate it to an Englishman is useless. He not only KNOWS, but, if I may use the expression, FEELS it as a vital principle in the constitution, which places him in a situation without the reach of the highest EXECUTIVE power in the state, if he lives in an obedience to its laws.

[22] If then the people of this colony are freeborn and have a right to the liberties and privileges of English subjects, they must necessarily have a legal constitution, that is, a legislature composed in part of the representatives of the people who may enact laws for the INTERNAL government of the colony and suitable to its various circumstances and occasions; and without such a representative, I am bold enough to say, no law can be made.

By the term INTERNAL government it may be easily perceived that I exclude from the legislature of the colony all power derogatory to their dependence upon the mother kingdom; for as we cannot lose the rights of Englishmen by our removal to this continent, so neither can we withdraw our dependence without destroying the constitution. In every instance, therefore, of our EXTERNAL government we are and must be subject to the authority of the British Parliament, but in no others; for if the Parliament should impose laws upon us merely relative to our INTERNAL government, it deprives us, as far as those laws extend, of the most valuable part of our birthright as Englishmen, of being governed by laws made with our own consent. As all power, therefore, is excluded from the colony of withdrawing its dependence from the mother kingdom, so is all power over the colony excluded from the mother kingdom but such as respects its EXTERNAL government. I do not deny but that the Parliament, as the stronger power, can force any laws it shall think fit upon us; but the inquiry is not what it can do, but what constitutional right it has to do so. And if it has not any constitutional right, then any tax respecting our INTERNAL polity which may hereafter be imposed on us by act of Parliament is arbitrary, as depriving us of our rights, and may be opposed. But we have nothing of this sort to fear from those guardians of the rights and liberties of mankind.

But it may be objected that this general position excludes all the laws of England, so as that none of them are obligatory upon us in our INTERNAL government. The answer to this objection is obvious: the common law, being the common consent of the people from time immemorial, and the "birthright of every Englishman, does follow him wherever he goes," and consequently must be the GENERAL law by which the colony is to be governed. So also the statutes of England in force at the time of our separation, having every essential in their institution to make them obligatory upon our ancestors, that is, their consent by their representatives, and having the same sanction with the common law, must have the same extensive force, and bind us in the same manner the common law does; if it was otherwise [23] it would involve this contradiction, that of two laws made by the same power, one is coercive upon us when the other is not so, which is plainly absurd.

From these principles, which I take to be incontrovertible, as they are deduced from the nature of the English constitution, it is evident that the legislature of the colony have a right to enact ANY law they shall think necessary for their INTERNAL government.

But lest these principles, plain and evident as they are, should be controverted by the Rector or some other of Sir Robert Filmer's disciples, who perhaps may assert that the King by his prerogative can establish any form of government he pleases in the colony, I will examine the power the General Assembly derives from grants from the crown, abstracted from the original rights of the people.

King James I by his charter, under the great seal of England, granted the dominion of Virginia to the Treasurer and Company of Adventurers, and gave them full power and authority to constitute a form of government in the colony as near as might be agreeable to the government and policy of England. Pursuant to this power, the Treasurer and Company by their charter established the legislature in the governor, Council, and representatives of the people, to be called the GENERAL ASSEMBLY, with "free power to treat, consult, and conclude as well of all emergent occasions concerning the public weal of the colony and every part thereof, as also to make, ordain, and enact such general laws and orders for the behoof of the colony and the good government thereof as shall from time to time appear necessary or requisite."

The General Assemblies have continued to exercise this legislative power from that time. King James left them in full possession of this power upon his dissolving the company; and King Charles I in the year 1634 by order in his Privy Council declared that "interests which the colony enjoyed while they were a corporation should not be impeached, but that they should enjoy the same privileges they did before the recalling the company's patent." And in the year 1642 under his sign manual and royal signet he "confirmed the form of government, declared that they should ever remain under the King's immediate protection, and that the form of government should not be changed." [28]

[24] After the Restoration, in the year 1675, the General Assembly sent three agents to England to solicit a new charter from King Charles II. Their petition upon this occasion was referred by the King's order in his Privy Council the 23rd of June to his attorney and solicitor general, who reported their opinion to the Lords of the Committee for Foreign Plantations, "That it would be for His Majesty's service and for the increase of the trade and growth of the plantation of Virginia if His Majesty shall be graciously pleased to grant and confirm, under his great seal, unto his subjects in Virginia the particulars following." And then they recite the several heads of the General Assembly's petition, one of which was "That the power and authority of the General Assembly, consisting of the governor, Council, and Burgesses, may be by His Majesty ratified and confirmed"; but with this proviso, "That His Majesty may, at his pleasure, revoke any law made by them; and that no law so revoked shall, AFTER such revocation and intimation thereof from hence (i.e., from England), be further used or observed." [29]

The Lords of the Committee for Foreign Plantations presented this report to His Majesty in his Privy Council at Whitehall on the 19th of November 1675; which His Majesty approved and confirmed, and ordered a bill to be prepared by the attorney and solicitor general for his signature in order to the passing letters patent "for the settlement and confirmation of all things according to the said report."

A complete charter was accordingly prepared, and received the King's signature; but before it came to the great seal stopped in the hanaper office upon receiving an account of Bacon's insurrection.

But though the charter did not pass the great seal, King Charles II from that time, and his successors ever since, have inserted the several clauses of it relative to the power of the General Assembly in their commissions to their governors, who have "full power and authority, by and with the advice of the Council to call General Assemblies, and by and with the advice and consent of the Council and Assembly or the major part of them respectively, to make, constitute, and ordain laws, statutes, and ordinances for the public peace, welfare, and good government of the colony, and the people and inhabitants thereof." "Which laws, statutes, and ordinances, of what nature or duration soever, are to be within three months or sooner after the making of them transmitted unto the King under the [25] public seal of the colony for the royal approbation or disallowance. And in case all or any of them shall at any time be disallowed and not approved and so signified by the King under his sign manual or by the Privy Council unto the governor or commander-in-chief of the colony for the time being, then such and so many as shall be disallowed and not approved shall from THENCEFORTH cease and determine and be utterly void and of no effect." [30]

From this short review of our constitution it may be observed that the people have an original right to a legal government, that this right has been confirmed to them by charter, which establishes the General Assembly with a general power "to make, ordain, and constitute laws, statutes, and ordinances for the public peace, welfare, and good government of the colony." Which power, by a constant and uninterrupted usage and custom, they have continued to exercise for more than 140 years. And if what Lord Coke says in *Calvin's Case* is true, that "where the King by charter or letters patent grants to a country the laws of England or a power to make laws for themselves, he nor his successors can alter or abrogate the same," we cannot be deprived of this right, even upon the Rector's principles of passive obedience.[31]

But it may be asked if the King's assent is not necessary to give sanction to the acts of the General Assembly. I answer, it is necessary. As sovereign, no law can be made without his assent, but then it is not necessary that he should be present in his royal person to give his assent; this is plainly impossible. He therefore gives power by commission under his great seal to his governor to give his assent, which, to speak in the language of the law, is in this case a TESTE MEIPSO,[32] and gives life and being to the laws in the same manner as if he was present in his royal person.

The King frequently gives his assent to acts of Parliament by commission to persons appointed for that purpose; he does the same thing by his commission to the governor, who thereby becomes the King's representative in his legislative character, so that the governor's assent to laws here is in effect the King's assent. But as the King cannot be informed of the nature of the laws passed by his commissioner while under the consideration of the General Assembly, he reserves to himself a power of abrogating them, notwithstanding his commissioner's assent; and FROM THE TIME of such abrogation, and not BEFORE, they are to cease and determine.

[26] But Colonel, said I, notwithstanding you have deduced your history of the constitution from the royal grants and the established

principles of the English government, His Reverence is in the right. He relies upon the King's instructions to the governor, which ought not to be infringed, but must have the force and obligation of laws upon us.

I have, replied the Colonel, a high reverence for the majesty of the King's authority, and shall upon every occasion yield a due obedience to all its just powers and prerogatives; but submission, even to the supreme magistrate, is not the whole duty of a citizen, especially such a submission as he himself does not require. Something is likewise due to the rights of our country and to the liberties of mankind. To say that a royal instruction to a governor, for his own particular conduct, is to have the force and validity of a law, and must be obeyed without reserve, is at once to strip us of all the rights and privileges of British subjects, and to put us under the despotic power of a French or Turkish government. For what is the real difference between a French edict and an English instruction if they are both equally absolute? The royal instructions are nothing more than rules and orders laid down as guides and directions for the conduct of governors. These may and certainly ought to be laws to them, but never can be thought, consistently with the principles of the British constitution, to have the force and power of laws upon the people. Which is evident from this plain reason: promulgation is essential to the nature of laws, so that no law can bind any people before it is declared and published to them; but the King's instructions are to be kept secret and not published to us, no not even to the Council, unless the governor thinks it for the King's service. "You are to communicate," says one of these instructions to the governor, "unto our Council of Virginia from time to time, such and so many of our instructions as you shall find convenient for our service." So that from the instructions themselves it is evident the King does not intend them as laws to his people. Besides, the royal instructions are drawn up in England by ministers who from their distant situation from us cannot have so full and perfect a view of affairs in the colony as is necessary for those who are to be legislators and supreme directors of them. Sudden emergencies will arise; present occasions will be lost; and such quick and unexpected turns are perpetually happening in all sublunary affairs as require the utmost vigilance and celerity, and can never stay for such a distant guidance and command. The ministers in England see nothing with their own eyes that is passing amongst us and know nothing upon their own knowledge, and therefore are very improper legislators to give laws to the [27] colony. The King's instructions, then, being only intended as guides and directions to governors, and not being obligatory upon the people, the governors are only answerable for a breach of them, and not the General Assembly; and if they are answerable only, they have the only right of determining whether their passing acts upon particular emergent occasions is contrary to the spirit and true meaning of their instructions or not. In short, Sir, the Council and House of Burgesses have a right to present any act relative to the internal government of the colony to the governor for his assent without violating any instruction; and the governor has a right, as the King's commissioner representing the royal person, to give or refuse his assent to such act as he may think it agreeable or contrary to his instructions directing his conduct in this particular. This I say, Sir, the Council and House of Burgesses may do, from the general powers with which they are invested by the constitution, without being guilty of attempts to restrain the power of the royal prerogative; which being committed to the governor, he is to determine how he is to exercise it and no other person has anything to do with it in this case. From hence then it is evident that the General Assembly may pass an act which alters or repeals an act that has received the royal approbation without destroying the *old constitution or attempting to bind the King's hands;* and if such act is passed, it must have the force and obligation of a law until the King declares his royal disallowance of it.

But since the royal instructions are so much insisted on by the Rector, I will examine whether the same doctrine I have endeavored to establish may not be deduced from them.

I have no copy of the instructions relating to this question, nor have I been able to procure one; but as I have formerly read them, I believe I can recite them tolerably exact.

By these instructions the governor is "not to give his assent to any act that alters or repeals any other act without a suspending clause, although the act to be altered or repealed has not had the royal approbation, unless in cases of great emergency; nor is he to give his assent to any act that alters or repeals any other act which has had the royal approbation without first obtaining the King's permission, under the penalty of being removed from his government and incurring the King's highest displeasure." [33] Now I infer from these instructions that, admitting the governor should pass an act contrary to them, he subjects himself to the penalties inflicted on him for [28] a breach of his instructions, but the act so passed by him has the obligation of a law until the King's disallowance of it; for if such act is void, AB INITIO, the instructions would be absurd, because to restrain the governor from passing an act which when passed is as absolutely void as if it had never existed, is absurd and useless.

Our sovereign, therefore, knowing that from the fundamental principles of the constitution such act must have the force of a law when passed by the governor, has restrained him from giving his assent in such a case under particular personal penalties, but has left the act to its course until he thinks proper to repeal it by his disapprobation.

But this is not all; for as the governor may pass an act in a case of great emergency though contrary to the general tenor of the instructions, it would involve a greater absurdity, if possible, should an act be void AB INITIO which he passes by virtue of the general powers given him by his commission under the King's great seal, and another act passed by him under the same authority have the force of a law because the governor is of opinion that the exigencies of the colony make such act necessary. Under such a construction the case is plainly this: the governor passes an act in a case of great exigency contrary to the strict letter of his instructions, which act shall have the force of a law because he thinks the circumstances of the colony require it; but if he passes such an act when he thinks the circumstances of the colony do not require it, such act shall be void AB INITIO. This is like the absolution in the Romish Church, which is of no effect, though proclaimed with a loud voice, unless the intention of the priest accompanies, and is too absurd to deserve any further consideration. And yet into such an absurdity must you fall, Sir, when you contend that such an act is void AB INITIO, from a construction of the royal instructions to the governor.

Neither will the Rector's hearsay account† of one of the *revised* laws make any alteration in the case, for the land law that was altered by this *revised* law never received the royal assent; but the reason why this *revised* law laid *some time dormant and unobserved* was that as it affected the King's grants of his lands, a suspending clause was added to it so that it could have no operation until the royal approbation of it was obtained. And though this approbation was obtained, it was not known to us until several years after, [29] when Mr. Montague, our present agent, by direction from the committee of correspondence, inquiring after it found it in the Council office in England and transmitted it to us, from which time it became in force here.[34]

But Colonel, said I, though all this may be true *I am at a loss to*

† *See Single and Distinct View*, p. 37.

know what good reason can be given for an order of the late Assembly to support the vestries against the appeals of the clergy, and not an order for supporting private contractors against the merchants.[35] When, Sir, answered the Colonel, you can produce an instance of a merchant or any other person except the Rector and two or three of his brethren bringing suits to try the validity of an act of the legislature, I will give you a reason why the merchants were not included in the order of the late Assembly. I suppose from what you say you would insinuate as if the Assembly pointed the clergy out as the particular objects of their resentment; but in this you are mistaken. An action was brought in the General Court by the Rector against the collector of his parish levy on purpose to controvert the power of the General Assembly in making laws, or rather to render their power a mere cipher. It behoved them then to support their own authority and the validity of their own acts against every attempt to destroy it; and from hence it was that by an order of the late Assembly the collector of York-Hampton parish levy was to be defended in the Rector's suit against him at the public expense.

Thus, Sir, I have endeavored to obviate the Rector's arguments and to convince you that the General Assemblies were not setting up the standard of rebellion against the King's authority when they passed the acts which have given this patriot Rector such great offense. The insults offered by him to the legislative body of the colony and to private characters are certainly carried to a great height; but whether this is owing to the panic he is thrown into lest the *old constitution* should be destroyed or to satisfy a malevolent and turbulent temper, is not worth my time to inquire. I have avoided repeating what I said formerly in my letters upon this subject, so must desire you to consider those letters as part of my present defense, since I cannot think that the Rector has given any answer to them.

I know that the plainest demonstration is lost upon men who are under the influence of prejudice or an obstinate disposition of mind. Such men will never want ground for wrangling, especially if they have any bypurposes to serve. But notwithstanding the artful endeavors and invidious representations of such men, I make no doubt that you will, from a sincere desire of promoting truth and the public good, give an impartial decision in this [30] dispute, which I shall submit to you after observing that whoever throws out reflections on the acts of the legislature as plainly tend to weaken their authority, let his profession of patriotism be otherwise ever so specious, is so far an enemy to his country.

Colonel, said I, I have not sufficiently considered this matter to form a just opinion of it; but as His Reverence is a great master of reason and acquainted with the nature and principles of government, I will communicate this conference to him, which, as soon as he has *reconnoitered*,[36] I doubt not will receive a proper reply.

And thus, may it please Your Reverence, the conference broke up of which I have given you this faithful account. I shall be extremely rejoiced if you can find leisure from the *laborious and painful* duties of your pastoral office to send forth a reply to the Colonel's arguments; but

> *Cum tot sustineas et tanta negotia solus,*
> *. . . moribus ornes,*
> *Legibus emendes; in publica commoda peccem,*
> *Si longo sermone morer tua tempora . . .*[37]

I am, may it please Your Reverence, with the utmost deference and esteem,

Your most obedient servant,

COMMON SENSE.

APPENDIX
NUMBER I

To the Rev. Mr. John Camm,
Rector of YORK-HAMPTON.

SIR,

Colonel Landon Carter and myself have at length fallen under your correction. It has been delayed, indeed, a good while; and you tell us in excuse *your intention was not to answer us at all, otherwise than by a trial in the ordinary court of judicature, until you was advised by your friends that this was too long a coming, and the colonels would have reason to think themselves neglected.* But this certainly cannot be a good reason for withholding your chastisement from us for more than three years; however, I should be satisfied with it if I did not believe you had at least another motive for not letting us hear from you until this time. The motive I mean is, I confess, a little JESUITICAL and does no great honor to your candor and integrity; but then it is a strong instance of your sagacity, a virtue in your estimation infinitely more valuable than either of the former. You, Sir, have a cause with the collectors of your parish levy to be determined this General Court; and your pamphlet appears mighty properly for that trial.

But let your reason for appearing in print at this time be what it will, I should think the rude and uncivil language that hath been *brawled* out by Colonel Carter and myself, *too rapid with rage and rancor to be free from foam and froth* should not have been exceeded by a person of your urbanity and [ii] politeness; but you, who always act so consistently with your OWN character, have managed this controversy into which you are pleased to enter with the colonels with a *rage* and *rancor* ten times more *foaming* and *frothy* than those are actuated with on whom you have thought proper to discharge the overflowings of your good nature. But perhaps, Sir, according to the language of your first memorial to the Lords of Trade, you was so diligently employed in *a painful and laborious performance of your function* amongst your parishioners that you had no time to examine your weapons properly; and as scurrility and venomous abuse were nighest at hand and most easily to be come at, you employed them in your defense instead of reason and argument *flowing in a gentle and pellucid stream.*

You, Sir, seem to imitate those reasoners who, to use the words of an *ingenious* divine, are very prolix in invalidating arguments which nobody lays any stress upon; but when they are really strong and impregnable, they would fain slip them over as hastily as they can and take a slight cursory notice of them. Very material objections are to them like marshy ground: a man may make a shift to run lightly and nimbly over it, but if he ever treads leisurely and dwells long upon one place, he infallibly sinks.

This is evident as well from your manner of managing your arguments against the Two-Penny Act, as you call it, as from your way of examining the facts contained in my *Letter to the Clergy.* In the one case you do not give a just account of the tobacco made or the price it sold at in the scarce year, nor do you consider the advantages arising from it to the people in general, in opposition to the disadvantage a few individuals suffered by means of it, which, I presume, ought to be a principal consideration with legislatures in forming of laws. In the other case you jumble into one confused and undigested heap distinct points that have not the least connection with one another, and pronounce with the authority of an overbearing pedagogue that my *rambling declaration* is contrary almost in every instance to the truth, and foreign to the purpose.

Without pursuing you through the maze of your disjointed arguments, I will *exhibit* a specimen of your way of reasoning from your miscellaneous remarks.

The Bishop of London tells the Lords of Trade, in his letter to them, that *within these few years past the people of Virginia were* ALL *members of the Church of England, and* NO *dissenters among them; but these days are over.* [iii] In answer to this part of the bishop's letter, I show that there were dissenters in the colony above 100 years ago; and I say, *unless the memorialists can procure a repeal of the Act of Toleration, and establish a hierarchy upon* ARCHBISHOP LAUD's *principles, I will venture to pronounce we shall always have them.* In another part of my letter I compare the conduct of *some* conventioners to Romish inquisitors, as to the secret manner of carrying on their transactions.

Now in answer to these two distinct and very different parts of my letter, you express your astonishment at my *casting the conduct of* ARCHBISHOP LAUD *in your teeth, and not forgetting to compare you to Romish inquisitors.* And, which must certainly be the strongest and most convincing reason in the world for disproving what I say, you charge upon me, what I am sure you do not know, *my own practice of officiating as a clergyman in the churches of the parish where,* with a sarcasm peculiar to men of your uncommon wit, you say *I make the most conspicuous figure.*

This I must confess is to me a *new* way of reasoning; but if it is a conclusive one, suffer me to try how it will do in another case.

By the statutes against nonresidence, the parson is obliged to reside constantly in his parish to discharge the several duties of his office; but the Rector of York-Hampton hath deserted his parish, and is scarce ever in it to perform the duties of his office.[38]

Therefore his *Single and Distinct View* is *almost* in every instance contrary to the truth and foreign to the purpose.

If this is good logic I will submit it to every impartial person to determine whether I have not the advantage in the argument, since my *major* proposition is known to be true by all the lawyers, and my *minor* is known to be true by all the inhabitants of York-Hampton, let my conclusion be what it will. But your argument is not true in any part of it.

This instance, *cum multis aliis, quae nunc prescribere longum est,* but may be found almost in every page of your masterly work, is sufficient to expose your sophistry in the management of this controversy.

But let me ask you, what has my officiating in the church as a clergyman, suppose it true, or Colonel Carter's founding a free school in his parish for the instruction of the poor and ignorant in the duties of religion, to do in a [iv] question upon the utility of the act of Assembly that gives you so great offense? Are you enraged with us for actions which, without your learned commentary, when truly known, may be commendable? Or do you collect all the trash you can from *shrubs and bushes,* with a purpose to swell your notable performance to the size of a thirty-penny pamphlet, that you may be reimbursed *the large sums you have expended out of your own pocket in contending to make the professors useful at the college.*

I remember to have read in some book or other that, after a long and tedious argument of a cause in one of the courts in England, in which much was said quite foreign to the purpose, the judge, when he came to deliver his opinion, told the counsel they had made the cause like a BANBURY cheese, from which, if the bad and unfound parts were pared, the remaining good would be reduced to a very small size. Your *Single and Distinct View* may then most justly be compared to a BANBURY cheese: pare off the scurrility and abuse, the false reasoning, and more false facts, and it will be reduced to less than the title page.

In answer to your scurrility and personal abuse, as I despise what you can say of me, I shall only observe that, like the Yahoo in Lemuel Gulliver, you fling your filth about you in such a manner that no cleanly person can come within your reach without disgust.

I have before *exhibited a specimen* of your false reasoning, and would in this place produce many more instances of it; but as a particular recital of them will much exceed the limits prescribed me by the printer in his paper, I must content myself with desiring every reader who thinks you or me worthy his notice to compare those parts of your *Single and Distinct View* wherein I am mentioned with my *Letter to the Clergy,* and they will easily discover them without my animadversions.

But though false reasoning can easily be discovered by every intelligent reader, false facts cannot be known but from evidence which every reader may not perhaps be acquainted with; it will be necessary therefore for me to consider particularly those you have advanced. You say you have *met with two* VERY CREDIBLE *accounts of the tobacco shipped in the scarce year to Britain, one of them an* IMPERFECT *one amounting to* 25,000 *hogsheads, the other to* 35,000. The impropriety of your expression in this part of your *remarks,* that an IMPERFECT account should be a CREDIBLE one, would not be worth noticing if I had not to do with a person who writes with so much exactness [v] and precision, and who has employed above three years in composing his mighty work. But, Sir, even this imperfect account exceeds the quantity of tobacco shipped the scarce year if the receiver general's accounts are to be credited. By his accounts, only 24,169 hogsheads were shipped; and if you had inquired, you might have known that at least 5,000 of these hogsheads were of the preceding year's crop and the property of merchants residing in Great Britain in the hands of their factors here, and that full 1,000 hogsheads of the tobacco made in the scarce year were brought from the neighboring provinces; so that upon a just state of the account it will appear that not 20,000 hogsheads were made in this colony that year. But I will suppose 20,000 hogsheads were made. Computing then this number of hogsheads at 1,000 each, and allowing the number of tithables to be 120,000, which is 8,000 less than you suppose them to be, it will appear that the tobacco made in the scarce year does not come to 170 pounds for each tithable. But when the clergy's salaries, the secretary's, county court clerks' and sheriffs' fees, with the expenses of the several parishes exclusive of the clergy's salaries and expenses of the several counties, which at a very moderate computation will be found to exceed 4,650,000 pounds of tobacco, I say when these expenses are deducted it will be found that not 100 pounds of tobacco will be remaining for each tithable to maintain themselves and families and to support the late war in that dreadful year.[39]

The circumstances that the people labored under in that year I have particularly described in my letter, which you have not been hardy enough, now you are upon the spot where truth can be discovered, to deny; though I have been informed by good authority when you was in England you told the Lords of Trade in your second memorial to them that the scarcity complained of was mere pretense.

In answer to what you say of the injury the clergy received by the Two-Penny Act, which is what your long list of names and accurate calculations are intended to show, as I have not as yet been under your tuition to learn confidence enough to contest self-evident facts, I shall admit to be true in part; but then let me examine whether the consequences you mention are justly deducible from thence.

Suppose the rich men who had tobacco due to them from their poor tenants could possibly have acted upon the same principles that seem to govern your conduct. Would not *these* poor tenants have felt the inconveniences of that year [vi] in a more affecting manner than they did under the protection of that act? If you could have compelled these rich men to pay any price for their proportion of your salary you had thought proper to exact from them, could not they have meted the same measure to their poor tenants? And in this case, would not the tenants have been the only sufferers? The same reason extends to all kinds of tobacco debtors, and indeed in a good degree to those money debtors the produce of whose labor was not sufficient to subsist their families; and you yourself must acknowledge, if you will acknowledge any truth, that thousands of the people were under such circumstances.

But allowing that the tobacco creditors had a right to receive their tobacco under the several laws that establish their salaries and fees or a compensation in money adequate to the value of tobacco that year, what ought this compensation to be? And here you will find that your account of the price of tobacco the scarce year is no less false than your other facts. In the beginning of the inspection that year, crop tobacco sold at about 27 or 28 shillings; it did rise afterwards to 35 and 40 shillings, and for a short time was as high as 50, and some of the best crops sold at 52 shillings and six pence, occasioned by a man who commenced a purchaser without any design of paying; but it soon fell, and in the month of June was down as low as 35 shillings. The public collectors could not distrain upon the people until the 10th of April, and the public creditors could not legally demand their tobacco from the collectors until the 10th of June, so that at the time your salary was due, crop tobacco was at 35 shillings; but as yours was transfer tobacco, and not equal to crop in value, it would not have produced that price; and yet in your computation you make your salary worth 50 shillings the hundredweight. *Credat Judaeus Apella, non ego.*[40]

Your insinuations that the General Assembly are attempting to restrain the power of the royal prerogative are too contemptible to deserve any reply; but your charge against me relative to my account of the minister of Norfolk's conversation with me requires a particular answer. You say that gentleman was *always* dissatisfied with the act I mention in that part of my *Letter to the Clergy* where I am speaking of Norfolk and Princess Anne. Now I repeat it here that I myself have heard that gentleman declare he was satisfied with it, and I am ready to produce at least three gentlemen, at this time in this city, who will declare he did not ALWAYS *express an utter dislike of it;* and I can likewise prove, by gentlemen also in this city, that he said he left your convention and refused to contribute towards your agency as he disapproved of your scheme. Could I attain to the sublimity of your diction I might very [vii] justly exclaim out on this occasion, *O John Camm! opprobrious John Camm! no good cometh out of John Camm.*

I assure you my principal design in making you this address is to obviate this reflection, flung out by you with so much malevolence against my private character. Indeed, I did not regard it myself, as it came from you; but I did not know what credit it might meet from persons unacquainted with you or me. For the future, whatever productions you may think proper to send forth against me, I shall treat them as they deserve, with a silent contempt.

I am, as I ought to be,

In every respect, yours.

RICHARD BLAND.

Williamsburg, October 25th, 1763.

NUMBER II

Observations on Colonel BLAND's *Letter to the Reverend* JOHN CAMM, *Rector of* York-Hampton, *published in the Virginia Gazette* October 28, 1763.

To the READERS.

This is humbly to acquaint you that Colonel Richard Bland's letter directed to me in the *Gazette* is come safe to hand; and according to report I am in imminent danger of being knocked down with a folio volume from the other colonel, 50 pages of it being already finished. But this is none of my business at present; for why should I anticipate misfortunes? It is enough to bear them with fortitude when they arrive.

My present antagonist seems to give up several posts, the strength of which was magnified until they fell into the enemy's hands; but now when they are no longer tenable by the original possessor, according to a usual turn in war, they are undervalued as of little consequence. He fights as he runs, to secure as handsome a retreat as possible. He shifts his ground and entrenches himself in new encampments. Well, it is still his place to lead and mine to pursue. Farewell then all attempts to prove an act to be made *in salutem populi* for the very preservation and subsistence of the people, which, whatever the respectable enactors intended, is in its own nature a plain attack upon private property, on the foundations of commerce, on the provision for an established church, on the principles of free government, on the King's authority, on the stability of private and public faith, on everything which a British subject has just cause to value himself upon. Adieu to that most pressing necessity which Colonel Bland told us was the only thing that could justify any departure from the *established rule of right* or the passing certain [ix] acts *without a suspending clause,* which necessity for the act in question wants nothing to make it fit for the Colonel's purpose but a *possibility* of existence. Good night to the famous petition, which as the petition of the whole clergy was to effect terrible things, but as the petition of *one* individual is unable to perform any mighty matter. And lastly, peace to the ashes of the kings of Babylon, Turkish slaves, harpies, beasts of prey, monsters, and tithe pigs. No, I beg Colonel Bland's pardon, the tithe pig belongs to the other colonel, and must be kept cold for his particular entertainment, as I understand him to be a great lover of cold roast pig. I wish among the kings of Babylon, etc., I could have buried Archbishop Laud and the Romish inquisitors; but these obstinate warriors still keep the field, and like some heroes in romance insist upon being killed over again.

The Colonel sets off with detecting a horrible machination of mine in publishing my *Single and Distinct View* at so critical a time, for which he pronounces me to be Jesuitical, and kindly informs me what little value I set upon *candor and integrity, resolving,* I suppose, that the letters which have passed between Mr. Royle and me relative to the time and manner of my publishing are not authentic, and that my pretended voyage to the metropolis of Maryland is all an invented trick. As to my setting little value upon *candor* and *integrity,* I hope the Colonel will be convinced to the contrary by my leaving them in his hands, and desiring

that he will show his regard for them by trying to *hold them fast*. As to
my being Jesuitical, I can only entreat him to give over fancying that to
tease an adversary with *cant* terms and to talk to the purpose are one and
the same thing. Once upon a time terms of this kind would have done
wonders, but at present they are somewhat out of date, and no more
regarded than an old almanac. But the Colonel talks of a cause that I
have with *the collectors of my parish levy*. If it be so as he says, let him
tell whether it be usual for the legislature of a free government to interfere in a private lawsuit by making an order to support one private subject against another. If this be usual, I shall be glad to be better informed.
The Colonel says the above cause is to be determined *this* General Court,
in which I have the misfortune to find him a false prophet. I desire the
readers to take notice that, as I was acquainted by my attorney, then
here but now in England, my vestry would not agree that the collectors
should stand suit with me until they were assured that the General Assembly would bear the expense of an appeal, and that several private
contractors with the merchants gave up the point in dispute for want
of the like assurance.

[x] I cannot help being diverted at the Colonel's *scolding* so bitterly
against *scurrility*. He is pleased to confess that I exceed both Their Worships in *scurrility,* which I assure you is no ordinary victory; and therefore he is entitled to my thanks for so easily ceding to me this honor.
As he has not condescended to particularize any scurrilous words of
mine, I suppose he means his own words, which I have returned to him
in as good condition as I received them. I find the Colonel is of their
turn who like to be very sharp and cutting themselves, but do not like
to be attacked with the same weapons, who will fight anybody in the
way of wit and argument, provided they may be allowed the use of a
small sword against their adversary's penknife. So the *overseer*[41] is
hugely delighted to exercise the cowskin upon others; but if any by-
stander presume to snatch it out of his hand and let him *feel* the weight
of it a little, he takes it very unkindly, grows furious, and strikes the
first person, whether friend or foe, who has the misfortune to be placed
within the reach of his arm. These gentlemen act herein as if they had
obtained an *exclusive* right to the trade of scurrility. If they have, they
have nothing to do but to produce their *patent*. After all, the Colonel
is not the proper person to determine *finally* whether I have been scurrilous or not, but this must be left to the decision of the readers of every
degree; and if they bring me in guilty, as they are the judge and jury and

everything with me at present, I have nothing further to urge but only to recommend myself to their mercy, hoping they will consider that my scurrility was *provoked defensive* scurrility, and suffer this consideration to have its due effect in mitigating the rigor of the penalty.

The Colonel next tells us that his *salus populi,* his *most pressing necessity,* which was once the only thing that could bring him off and justify the act in debate and all the other arguments which I have endeavored to invalidate, he no longer lays any stress upon. That's a good Colonel now! This is very kind; this is meeting me more than half way; we shall be quite agreed presently. But hold, the Colonel has still got some *impregnable* fortresses. He is not indeed so indiscreet a commander as to tell me in what their strength consists, but he makes me in some measure acquainted with their situation; by which I am afraid the *foundation* is *bad* upon which they are erected, for it seems they stand on *marshy* and *rotten* ground. Now if I have *run lightly* over the Colonel's *marshy* ground in saying no more of this *marshy* ground than he has, he has *run as lightly* over it as I have done; and therefore the worst that can be concluded against me from hence is that the Colonel and the Parson of York-Hampton are equally expert in *bog-trotting.*

[xi] The Colonel says that I have not given a just account of the tobacco *made* or the price it sold at in the scarce year. I do not pretend to be exact to a pound of tobacco or to a shilling in money, which I think I have told the public already. Why will the Colonel have me to be infallible when I disclaim any such pretensions? The Colonel talks of what ought to be a principal consideration with legislatures in forming laws. I have already endeavored to show either that the occasion of the dispute between the Colonel and me was not a fit object for the legislature of a free government to consider, or if it was, that things have been most *grievously* and *irregularly* managed, that the remedy for the supposed evil was worse than the disease. The Colonel seems to think that he has nothing to do but to prove that there was some disorder or inconvenience had happened to some members of the community here, whereas it lies upon him to show that a safe and adequate remedy was made use of for their relief. To do some good to a green wound in the extremities by throwing the whole body politic into a declining and hectic condition is no sound nor commendable practice. Whether the Colonel or I jumble most, or ramble most, or are most foreign to the purpose is become a matter of fact which cannot now be amended, but must be left as it is to the examination of the readers.

The Colonel will not pursue me through the maze of my disjointed arguments. He is in the right, for without engaging in that undertaking he is sufficiently bewildered.

There is no pressing necessity for supposing that the late Bishop of London by the words *all* and *no* meant that there was lately a time when there was not a *single* dissenter in the colony; because the Colonel himself, as we shall see by and by, uses the like kind of terms without designing to have them taken in so strict a sense. But supposing that the old and venerable bishop had made some mistake here, what has this to do with repealing the Act of Toleration or Archbishop Laud's hierarchy? Was the Bishop of London any enemy to toleration? Are not the clergy in Virginia friends to toleration? Do they desire anything more than that neither the toleration nor the establishment may be sacrificed the one to the other? Does not the Colonel read the public prayers and deliver sermons in the churches of his own parish whenever he pleases? If his zeal should lead him to turn field-preacher, who will take upon them to hinder him? What more toleration would he have? Why I suppose as he goes halves with the parson in the spiritualities, he thinks it but reason that he should have a share in the temporalities too; [xii] which purpose the frequent repetition of Two-Penny Acts would answer fully. *I hope Archbishop Laud and his hierarchy will not have the assurance to rise up again.* What are these horrible secrets for which the conventioners are to be compared to *Romish inquisitors?* I know of nothing that the conventioners had any occasion to keep secret. I know nothing of their being more secret than any other body of men on similar occasions. If I do not mistake (for I have not the pamphlets at this instant before me) the two colonels fall upon them both for being *too secret* and *too open* in relation to the same article, namely, the Bishop of London's letter. *I beg that these Romish inquisitors may be quiet, and not be so impertinent as to give us any further trouble.* Have I brought nothing to disprove what the Colonel says but *his own practice of officiating as a clergyman in the churches of the parish wherein he makes the most conspicuous figure?* Why did he not put in *delivering sermons* too? The Colonel says I do not *know* him to make use of this practice. He means that I never was one of his congregation. True; but what then? What if I know those who have been made a part of his congregation? Will not their evidence be sufficient?

We must now view the Colonel in his meridian glory, armed at all points in a logical coat of mail, drawing up his majors and his minors and allied army of lawyers, rank and file. With all this apparatus, to do what? To attack a windmill instead of a giant, for there is just as much connection between a windmill and a giant as there is between my residing a *mile or two* out of my parish and the dispute about Two-Penny Acts; and anger makes more Don Quixotes than ever were made by reading romances or books of chivalry. But let us muster these majors and minors with the forces under their command and examine how they can perform their exercise. Upon this the Colonel is so hardy as to risk the fortune of the day; and if he will abide by his own criterion, I am afraid he is in great danger of a total overthrow. First, for the Colonel's major; it is this: "By the statutes against nonresidence the parson is obliged to reside constantly in his parish to discharge the several duties of his office." How does the Colonel prove this major proposition? It is known, he says, to be true by *all* the lawyers. Has the Colonel consulted *all* the lawyers in the universe? Has he consulted *all* or *half* the lawyers in Virginia? If the Colonel does not mean by this expression *all the lawyers* above 50 of that numerous body, then let him learn to forgive that learned, religious, and public-spirited prelate, the late Bishop of London, his *all* and *no*. Be it known to the readers that I have received advice on this point of nonresidence wherewith I am so well satisfied that whenever the Colonel or anybody else shall be pleased to proceed legally [xiii] against me for what is injurious to no living soul, I am willing to contest the matter; and if I cannot support myself against the charge, I know I must suffer the penalty in that behalf made or provided, which I hope to bear with patience. The Colonel justly remarks the use of residence, which is that the parson may discharge the several duties of his office. And what if these be discharged without residing as well as they could be by residence, in any part of my parish? Nay, what if they be discharged better, as I have more opportunity now of getting assistance when confined at home by pain or sickness than I could have if resident in any part of my parish? What foundation then can there be left for complaint? Does the Colonel think that the statutes can oblige those Virginia clergymen to reside in their parishes whose glebes and houses are placed out of their parishes? If the Colonel does not, then he will allow some exceptions in the case of residence, and some good reasons for nonresidence. But it is time to look after the Colonel's minor proposition, which is this: "The Rector of York-Hampton hath *deserted* his parish, and is *scarce ever* in it *to perform the duties of his office.*" How does the Colonel prove this minor proposition? He says it is known to be true by *all* the inhabitants of York-Hampton. *All* again! Why will the Colonel lay himself so open? I am almost ashamed to take this advantage of an *angry* man in single combat. Is it not amazing that in an attempt to clear himself, when questioned in point of veracity, this writer should *utter* one of the *most palpable,* barefaced, and impudent falsehoods that ever was invented? If there be a single Negro in my parish so abandoned as to agree to the Colonel's minor proposition, I will beg his master to let him become one of the Colonel's congregation, for I despair of his ever receiving any good from me. And now let the readers decide whether the Colonel's logical outrage will ever prove him to have the advantage of the argument. If the Colonel pleases to excuse *all* this falsehood by attributing it to *confusion* (which I believe he knows to have been pleaded very lately in excuse for an arrant detected falsehood, at a time too when the person I speak of was in the act of clearing up his character), I have no objection to its going as far as can be desired with the readers. Could the Colonel forget himself so far as to think of *awing,* with a fierce and bullying look, *all* my parishioners into false witnesses? Why must I be continually called upon to put the Colonel in mind of the smallness of that circle within which his domineering influence is, or ought to be, circumscribed? Had the Colonel gone no further than to accuse me of neglect of duty in my parish, and to found this charge upon his believing I was too defective in memory to be able to pronounce the names of half the people in my parish, that is of half the free subjects and half the slaves on perusing [xiv] their faces, I am sorry to say he would have had better authority for this accusation than I could have wished. He would have had that of a very respectable person, to whom I am obliged for several favors, and with whom it gives me pain to have any dispute of this nature. However, this gentleman must excuse me for adding on this occasion in my own defense that in charging me with neglect of duty I think he is mistaken in point of fact; that in bringing this charge behind my back he did not act so handsomely as I had reason to expect from one of his station and character; and that in laying the matter before the Visitors and Governors of the college there appears to me something of absurdity, because these gentlemen have not, that I know of, undertaken to extend their authority over the parochial affairs of York-Hampton. It would grieve me to appear ungrateful for favors; but I must say that if any person understands by doing me the greatest favor that he thereby acquires any right to treat me in other matters as he pleases, he is in an error. I will not purchase favor at any such dear rate. Had this gentleman condescended to be explicit to me on the head of duty, I might either have been better informed concerning my duty, or else I might have found that he and I differ about the precise meaning of the complex term *duty,* just as the colonels and I differ about the ideas which ought to be comprised under the terms *charity, poverty,* and *necessity;* for the syllogistical Colonel must know that most disputes, when thoroughly canvassed, are found to end in mere logomachies. Thus much with regard to the gentleman with whom I wish to be upon good terms. With regard to any others it is sufficient to say that I do not look upon either the clergy or the masters of the college to be purely hired and public butts for the patrons of ignorance or irreligion to shoot their arrows at by way of exercise or amusement.

Having studied to find out what connection there could be between my neglect of duty in my parish and the dispute between the Colonel and me, I have stumbled upon an incident which makes me think that the Colonel *does* believe I went to Annapolis and that Mr. Jonas Green really printed my *Single and Distinct View;* and on this incident, as I take it, is founded the connection which it has cost me so much labor to investigate. For you must know that by going to Annapolis to publish against Colonel Bland (*hinc illae lachrymae*) I was absent one Sunday from one of my churches, and the person engaged to officiate in my room happened to be too sick to attend. It fell the harder upon the parish as there are no colonels in it pragmatical enough to be fond of supplying in my absence and exercising my office. When the press here happens to be shut against me, if the Colonel could keep so tight to the duty of my parish as to prevent my having any intercourse with other presses, who knows but he might be easy?

[xv] The Colonel talks of my collecting *trash* from shrubs and bushes. I suppose he here uses the vulgar idiom, and by the word *trash* means *fruit;* and if I spend three years in gathering this fruit, provided it be eatable at last, I therein show the public more respect than I should have in presenting them with hastily gathered, green, sour productions; as full of verjuice as an unripe crab, and as rough to the palate as a mouth-distorting persimmon, or, as the common planter emphatically expresses it, wring-jaw cider.

The Colonel's Banbury cheese is excellent, and is served up in its proper place, close after the fruit, to cure the teeth set on edge by the trash. It will do again and again, on any other occasion as well as this.

Whether the Colonel's not being able *to come near me* is owing to my *yahoo* nature or to something *more disagreeable* to the Colonel, is left to the readers to determine.

Whereas the Colonel recommends it to the readers to compare what I have said in my *Single and Distinct View* with his *Letter to the Clergy*, I have no objection to the sale of his pamphlet. On the contrary, I wish every brother of the quill may meet with proper encouragement.

The Colonel makes rather too much rout concerning the differences between his 24,169 hogsheads and my 25,000. That this observation of the Colonel's may look the more like something, he dexterously drops the little unfavorable word *about;* for I had said the credible and imperfect account amounts to *about* 25,000.

And now suppose, for argument's sake, that the receiver general's account should be unfinished, putting down some parts of Virginia blank, may not the Colonel get an idea from hence how an account may be credible as far as it goes, and yet be imperfect? My other account I am informed came from England, where it may be as well known as here what tobacco was shipped that year to Britain. I do not know whether the principles of the Colonel's calculation be true by which he reduces the crop in the scarce year to 20,000 hogsheads; but if they be, in that case the income of the whole clergy will not amount to a fifteenth part. And a fifteenth of one article of commerce, and no necessary of life, might be paid to the clergy once in fifty years without any heavy burden upon the people; and if it was, I am sure it would be far enough from putting the other colonel's tithe pig into any kind of [xvi] danger. Against the remainder of the preceding crop, and the hogsheads of tobacco which come from other provinces, if the Colonel will descend into these minutiae, he should have set the quantity smuggled and shipped off without inspection. This I presume is not *all* to be found in the receiver general's accounts, or in any other account; so that every account of tobacco raised or exported in any one year viewed in this very nice light must fail of exactness and be at the best credible and imperfect. And surely if the Colonel will reckon on the one side what comes hither from other provinces, he ought to reckon too on the other side what goes from hence to other provinces. I do not know how to deduct the secretary's, county court clerks', and sheriffs' fees except the Colonel had produced authentic accounts of them; and therefore I am only led into a maze by this part of the Colonel's calculations. If the Colonel will give me the liberty he takes of supposing my premises, I will undertake to secure what conclusions I have a mind; but though I do not know how much the above fees come to, this I know, that the price of the scarce crop more than made up for the defect in quantity, besides its causing the next year's crop to sell better than it otherwise would have done; that the scarce crop was a very valuable crop; that any grievance which could arise from it must arise from the inequality of the shares enjoyed by individuals; that to take from some of the poorest and least gainers and give what was so taken to the richest and greatest gainers by means of the high price and small quantity was augmenting the inequality which caused the grievance if there was any, and thereby augmenting the grievance itself. As to what the Colonel says about supporting the war in that dreadful year, I do not remember whether the war was more dreadful in that year than in other years; but if it was, no exigence of war could give any right or make it expedient and useful for one part of the community to plunder the other, or for some subjects to reimburse themselves for their losses by the war out of the substance of those other subjects who cheerfully contributed their quota towards the expense of the war with the rest of the people. This is like the other colonel's urging that *all* the country was poor, and thence arguing not that money must be some way or other got from other countries to relieve the *general* poverty of this, but that money must be taken from some of the poorest part of the community here and be given to the richest to relieve the *general* poverty of the richest and render frugality unnecessary among the opulent. I pretend to be as great a friend, at least speculatively, to the true and real utility of the *whole* colony as Colonel Bland or anybody else; and I believe (whether the Colonel will believe it or not) that it is an honest zeal of this kind which now prompts me to say that I had rather we had endured almost any evil the Colonel can imagine than that a legislature of a free government should set the example [xvii] of breaking the firmest agreements, not to mention that original compact concerning which some of the best writers on government enlarge with so much pleasure. The Colonel can tell by the event of the scarce year how grievous it sometimes is to many people for *one* single man to fail of complying with his agreements.

Whether the Colonel has good authority or not for my telling the Lords of Trade that the scarcity complained of was mere pretense, I hope he will allow me the benefit of the proverb which tells us that a man cannot be hanged for *thinking;* and he may remember, if he pleases, that the first Two-Penny Act was passed when there was no real scarcity.

What would the Colonel say about an inconsiderable number of tenants? Were *all* the tenants poor? Could none of them bear one hard year by the success of former years? Did none of them raise good crops in the scarce year and thereby find it in itself a happy year for them? Were none of them to be ranked among those who were much profited by the *particular* calamity? Could anybody tell better than the landlord himself whether his tenant was an object of charity? Must the landlords as well as the parsons, must everybody, to serve the Colonel's views, be supposed to be void of compassion, except the *charitable corporation,* I mean the late Assembly? If anybody but the landlord can remit or dispose of his rents in charity, has he the private property of his lands? Was there no way to relieve such as were in want but by unhinging private property? Could not the sufferers have been separated from the prosperous, the sheep from the goats? Could not a collection of voluntary contributions have been made for the really unfortunate through the colony as there was for the sufferers by fire in Boston? [42] Would not this have answered all *just* and *reasonable* purposes much better than *such* an act of Assembly? Would it not have been more agreeable to the practice of free governments? Would the landlords have acquiesced so quietly under the act had they not been reimbursed and found their account in the scheme one way for what they lost in another? Must the landlord be compelled, in a *free* government, to relieve the poor tenant by remitting his rents; and must the parson be compelled to reimburse the landlord? Let the Colonel look over my catalogue once more, and tell me how much of my money went either to *poor men,* or to *poor* tenants, or to *poor* sufferers by any accident whatsoever; and let him not forget that many such catalogues, many such objects of charity, might easily be produced, objects which were rich before the *dreadful* calamity arrived and still more enriched by the *dreadful* calamity itself. If all the *angry* colonels upon earth were to beg me to believe that an act which gives three [xviii] or four or five shillings, whatever it be, to a poor man in Gloucester, and five or six hundred times as much to Mr. Page, was made for the sake of the *poor* man in Gloucester and not for the sake of Mr. Page; or that an act which gives a small amount to a few poor tenants and prodigious sums to a promiscuous crowd (of tenants and no tenants, gainers by the high market and no gainers, not in proportion to the poverty but to the riches of each) was made for the sake of the few *poor* tenants, and not for the sake of the promiscuous crowd; or that Mr. Nicholas, for selling his crop of tobacco in the scarce year for 1500 guineas, and his next crop the better by reason of the preceding scarcity, *ought* to be ranked among *objects of charity;* I am so obstinate in this, as well as other points, while I think I have reason and justice on my side, that the *angry* and imperious colonels might in my mind as well bid me swallow one of the Allegheny Mountains under the pretense that it is but a pill of moderate size which may be gulped down at a single effort with the utmost facility by a patient of any resolution.

If the Colonel cannot prevail for having the Two-Penny Act adjudged law (and GOD forbid he should); if he cannot get *all the lawyers* on his side of the question in this debate, his next petition is that the parsons may have as small a compensation by the way of damages as possible. But what if evidence has been already given in one court that tobacco was sold at 50s. a hundred in May and June, and that tobacco to be delivered in August was sold in May at 50s.? What if some of the parsons either did sell or can prove that they could have sold at 50s. in May or June, provided they could have engaged to deliver the tobacco a month or two afterwards? Must not all these things be considered and settled by the jury? Besides, Colonel Bland should not run the tobacco down too low, because this will prove that the *poor* men, the *poor* tenants, and the *poor* sufferers received so much the less relief. As for the *rich* men and the *great gainers,* they perhaps could make more of the tobacco by selling it at 50s. than the parsons could have done by selling at 35s. a hundred. When the Colonel can prevail with those who sold their tobacco at 52s. 6d. to refund because the high price was partly occasioned by a man who commenced purchaser without any design of paying, then will I agree that the parson ought to have less damages on this account, especially from those who sold their tobacco at 52s. 6d. a hundred.

Colonel Bland is pleased to say, "your insinuations that the General Assembly *are* attempting to restrain the power of the royal prerogative are too contemptible to deserve any reply." Is not the Colonel a little graveled here? Or, in his own phrase, have I not caught my gentleman here *tripping* [xix] *lightly over the marshy ground?* I do not insinuate that the General Assembly *are,* but that some *particular* Assemblies *were,* attempting to restrain the power of the royal prerogative. I do not insinuate that Colonel Bland *is* endeavoring to give the people frightful ideas of the royal prerogative in his letter before me, but that he *was* doing this in his former letter. Is not passing acts which interfere with acts confirmed by His Majesty, without a suspending clause and without any necessity, attempting to restrain the power of the royal prerogative?

Has not Colonel Bland acknowledged that this departure from the *established rule of right* can be justified by the *most* pressing necessity *alone?* Will he eat his own words? I do not believe that Colonel Bland refuses to reply on this head because he thinks my arguments contemptible. For this plain reason I do not believe it, because contemptible arguments are more easily replied to than such as are otherwise. Will the Colonel answer none but *sound* arguments? If he will not, he discovers a strange delight to show his art of disputation on the wrong side of the question. Barely to say anything is contemptible must, in a dispute, pass for nothing. If Colonel Bland was to vary this phrase, *I do not like your arguments,* a thousand ways, he would be more tedious than convincing.

Now comes on the minister of Norfolk's affair. The Colonel repeats it that he heard him say he was *satisfied* with the Norfolk Act, and has three gentlemen to produce who will declare he did not always express an utter dislike of it. Supposing this to be true, if I had an opportunity I should beg leave to ask the gentlemen a few such questions as these: Did the minister of Norfolk say he was *perfectly* satisfied with the act? What might he be supposed to mean by being satisfied with the act, from the occasion and circumstances of the discourse? Did he mean that he thought the act just and reasonable in its own nature, or that he was willing to acquiesce rather than disoblige his parishioners? Which Colonel Bland seems willing to make the criterion of a good clergyman. Might he not mean that he was willing to acquiesce rather than be at any considerable expense about it? As the conversation seems to have been about the time of the last convention: Are you sure the minister spoke of the Norfolk Act and not of the last Two-Penny Act? Observe, Colonel Bland brings this story against the clergy for complaining of an act with which the person immediately concerned was *perfectly* satisfied, on the maxim I suppose of *volenti non fit injuria*.[43] This is representing the minister of Norfolk as if he originally thought the act just and reasonable, or at least had given his consent for it to be proposed to the General Assembly; so that if this matter was searched to the bottom, I am still apprehensive it would appear that the Colonel had added something to what the minister said, [xx] or that if he has not *altogether* invented a speech, he has, what is almost as bad, invented a meaning for the minister of Norfolk, and is a great improver of small tales into matters of consequence. The Colonel says he can prove, by the evidence of gentlemen, that the minister of Norfolk said, "he left our convention, and refused to contribute to my agency, as he disapproved of our scheme." This no doubt augmented the minister's merit with the Colonel; but the Colonel does not now undertake to prove that the minister of Norfolk was ever severely censured by any memorialists for this conduct, which a while ago the Colonel may remember was *believed* by him to be no difficult matter. There is such a striking difference between what the Colonel now says and what he said before, his assertions are so much *rounder* in the one place than in the other, that he who will be at the trouble of comparing the passages will not want reason to conclude that the Colonel did exceed his commission from the minister of Norfolk.

I have no desire to meddle with the Colonel's private character, though he seems to be no sparer of private characters; but if the Colonel will publish daring assertions to the prejudice of others, he makes it the business of everyone injured thereby to dispute his veracity.

And now I endeavor at being as indifferent as I ought to be about either the Colonel's *silent* or his *vociferous* contempt. He is welcome either to amuse himself with the sullens or a more boisterous expression of his resentment. I acknowledge the ancient and undeniable right of a baffled disputant to sit down and dissipate his chagrin by swallowing his own spittle alone, or to give it vent in outrageous exclamations, as he finds it most for his ease and convenience. It must be very grating (and I cannot help being touched with compassion for him) to a *patriot* and a *Churchman* to be caught in such a controversy as this in which Colonel Bland has been a fiery volunteer quite on the wrong side of the question with respect to both these characters.

If anyone thinks me too warm, let him consider the cause in the defense of which I have engaged. I write for liberty and property, for the rights of commerce, for an established church, for the validity of private and public contracts, for free government, for the King's authority, *pro aris et focis*.[44] The forces set in battle array against these are *charity, poverty, necessity, a particular* not a general *calamity,* which are not the natural enemies of the former, but pressed into the service against their inclination. I am as ready to dispute the prize of patriotism with the Colonel, whenever he pleases, as that of veracity. I believe it would puzzle the Colonel to name a man in the [xxi] colony who has suffered more for adhering to what he thinks agreeable to reason and justice and the principles of true patriotism than *opprobrious* John Camm. For engaging so zealously in this contest and in compliance with a public challenge, one worthy gentleman I am told is for having the *flesh pulled off my bones with pincers*. To do the Colonel justice, though he has some time ago appeared inclinable to call upon the secular arm by insinuating that the administration was too *mild* in not punishing our *atrocious* and *infatuated* behavior, I do not believe that he would approve of this short method of argument by the pincers, because it savors too much of the Romish inquisition. Let Colonel Bland say what he will of me, I am far from saying *no good can come out of Colonel Bland*. On the other hand, I believe *some* good may come out of him in his calmer moments, when he does not suffer his passion to make a fool of him. It would be hard if there should not some good come out of him when he is pleased, considering how much evil comes out him when he is disobliged.

At length I think I have got tolerably well rid of this blast from *violentus auster* without much damage to my sails and rigging, on which the furious puff seems chiefly to have spent its force. If I was but as well over the storm which is gathering from the opposite quarter, why then I think I might sleep soundly without breaking my rest half a dozen times in a cold night to inquire which way the wind is, and on being told that it is either north or south, jumping out of bed and preparing for a hurricane. I wish these blustering deities would peruse the Reverend Mr. Giberne's once-admired discourse upon peace,[45] and tell us how much better he agrees with the apostle about peace than a certain gentleman that shall be nameless agrees with him about charity.

> Oh peace! thou source and soul of social bliss . . .
> Oh liberty! thou goddess heav'nly bright . . .
> But what is *Hecuba* to *them*, or *they* to *Hecuba!*

I hope the sublimity of this conclusion will be to the Colonel's taste. Readers, until I shall be called upon again to give you further trouble, farewell.

I am your most humble servant,

JOHN CAMM.

[xxii] P.S. Look at the act of Assembly; you will find it was passed (under the influence of a panic terror raised or promoted perhaps by some designing people) on supposition that *there would not be tobacco made sufficient to answer the common demands of the country* for that year. Look at the Colonel's calculations in his letter to me; you will see he supposes about 100 pounds of tobacco left for each tithable, over and above what would have answered these demands. A hundred and twenty thousand tithables (as the Colonel supposes) multiplied by 100 and again

divided by 1000 will give twelve thousand hogsheads of tobacco of a thousandweight each. Observe the consequences hence arising; that there was more than twice as much tobacco made in the scarce year as the act supposes would be made; that after all the debts of the year deducted, there was more tobacco remaining than the act supposed would be made in the *whole;* that after all the debts of the year deducted (the clergy having been paid among the rest) there would remain in the hands of the owners about ten times as much of tobacco alone as the clergy's allowance comes to. These are the consequences from Colonel Bland's own calculation, taking all his suppositions for granted, whereas several of them may be doubted, and one of them is undoubtedly false, namely, his rating the hogsheads shipped at no more than a thousandweight upon an average.

Besides, the tobacco raised in the scarce year was not divided into equal shares and so distributed among the people according to their number of tithables, but some raised little or none, and some had as much as usual. In this consisted the evil, if there was any, which was not remedied but increased by the act. Had such a division of the whole crop been proposed by the Colonel to the General Assembly, it would have been more to the purpose than the act which passed. It would have been a natural and effectual way to remove the inequality *deemed grievous;* but that they who raised as good crops as they did commonly, and sold them for thrice the usual price, should receive a charitable donation into the bargain, is what occasions one of the most difficult parts of the Colonel's talk in justifying the act, which parts the Colonel wisely refuses to buckle to or approach by reason of the difficulty.

The Colonel expresses himself very strangely when he speaks of the tithables maintaining themselves and their families and supporting the late war in that *dreadful* year as if all the tithables were free subjects, when in truth more than three fourths of them are slaves, not possessors of estates, but estates themselves, and maintained (chiefly at least) out of the grain and other produce, [xxiii] the profits of merchandise, and the advantages made by mechanical businesses.

I do not like the Colonel's affecting to call the scarce year that *dreadful* year or his seeming to grudge the expense of a war (so happy and successful, so interesting and beneficial to Virginia) in that *dreadful* year. I dare say, bating a groundless alarm or two, the Colonel enjoyed his fireside very quietly in that *dreadful* year. And what if he did pay his proportion towards the support of the war in that *dreadful* year? Why should this appear to give him such deep regret? Would he have had the brave fellows who ventured their lives for his defense to have fought for nothing in that *dreadful* year?

Since the above was written, Mr. Smith, the late minister of Norfolk, who, as far as I am able to judge, has been the innocent occasion of a dispute between Colonel Bland and me, has appeared in the *Gazette* in his own justification. From whence it is clear that he said he was satisfied with the Two-Penny Act which did not affect him, but never said he was satisfied with the Norfolk and Princess Anne Act, which proved in the end to be a Three-Half-Penny Act, under the lash of which he was left by the Two-Penny Act. On the other hand, after Colonel Bland has given a particular account of the petition for this Three-Half-Penny Act in his *Letter to the Clergy*, page the 12th, his following words are: "This petition was thought *extremely reasonable* by the *ministers* in those counties, as the House of Burgesses were informed by the representatives, and accordingly an act passed for the relief of those people; and I am persuaded the ministers principally concerned never *once* complained of this act. For I myself have heard the minister of Norfolk (who lives in great harmony with his parishioners, and is much esteemed and respected by them) declare he was *perfectly* satisfied with it; and I believe it would be no difficult matter to prove that he fell under the *severe* censure of these memorialists because he refused to enter into their measures."

Now let anybody reconcile what Colonel Bland has here said or what he has said in his letter to me with what I have said and what Mr. Smith has said in print, if they can. I have only to add that from the nature of the thing it does not appear probable to me either that the ministers in Norfolk and Princess Anne should think a petition for putting it into the breast of a county court and their parishioners to set a price upon their tobacco *extremely reasonable,* or that the representatives of those counties, whoever they were, should inform the House of Burgesses that the *ministers* thought such a petition *extremely reasonable.*[46]

NUMBER III

*To the Right Honorable the Lords Commissioners
for Trade and Plantations.*

The humble representation of the clergy of the Church of England in His
Majesty's colony and dominion of Virginia:

Showeth,

That about the year 1620, in the infancy and first establishment of the
said colony, whilst the same was held under grants from the crown to
the Virginia Company, that company, in making provision for the
clergy, had ordered 100 acres of land in each borough or division to be
laid off for a glebe, and for their further maintenance a certain and standing revenue out of the profits of each parish, so as to make each living
at least £200 sterling per annum, to be raised by a certain quantity of
tobacco and corn per head on tithable persons; and afterwards for a
further encouragement that pious, learned, and painful ministers might
be invited to go over, the said company ordered six tenants to be placed
on each of these glebes at the public expense.

That the said provision for a glebe was enacted into a law by an act
of the governor, Council, and Burgesses in General Assembly in the year
1662, which law was again repealed by another act made the 24th of
September, 1696; and in lieu thereof, by the last-mentioned act it was
enacted that the minister in each parish should have for his maintenance
the yearly sum of 16,000 pounds of tobacco besides his lawful perquisites.
And the vestries were authorized to raise and levy the same in their respective parishes, as also to levy 5 per cent for collecting and paying the
same; and other matters were thereby enacted for purchasing and laying
out a glebe and building a convenient dwelling house for the ministers.
Which provision with other advantages also to the minister have been
enforced by sundry other additional acts of Assembly passed since that
time, and particularly by an act of the year 1727, by which the time for
the vestries' meeting and laying the parish [xxv] levy was to be on or
before the 15th of October yearly. That in the year 1748 an act of Assem-

bly entitled An Act for the Support of the Clergy, and for the Regular Collecting the Parish Levies was passed, which was to take place on the 10th of June, 1751, whereby all former acts relating to provision for the clergy were repealed, and that matter was put upon a new footing, viz., that the sole right of presentation should be in the vestries in the several parishes, and that every minister then already preferred or thereafter to be preferred to any parish should have and receive an annual salary of 16,000 pounds of tobacco and cask, with an allowance of 4 per cent for shrinkage to be levied, assessed, collected, and paid in manner therein directed. That the clergy, hoping that the said regulation was certain, fixed, and determinate, acquiesced under the said act, and His Majesty was graciously pleased to give his royal assent thereto, whereby it became a firm and absolute law not within the power of the Assembly of Virginia of themselves to break through, repeal, or alter, as the clergy conceived; but they very soon found their mistake, for that the same has from time to time since been pretended to be set aside in some instances, partially for some particular parts of the colony, and in others totally, for the whole colony, by a number of acts passed by the Assembly in manifest opposition to His Majesty's royal instructions to his governor, contrary to common justice, and to the great discouragement, loss, and injury of the clergy of the said colony.

For by one act of Assembly passed in —— each of the ministers of the two particular parishes of Frederick and Augusta are to be paid in money at the annual rate of £100 Virginia currency only, in lieu of 16,000 pounds of tobacco and cask. And by another act passed the 26th of June, 1755, as to two other counties of Princess Anne and Norfolk the justices in the county courts are annually to set a price on tobacco not under 10 per cent; and whatever value tobacco may happen to be of, all persons chargeable with tobacco for public dues in those counties are to pay and discharge the same in money at such fixed price. And some other partial acts of the like nature have been pretended to be passed there.

And by another more general short temporary act passed in the same year (1755) entitled An Act to Enable the Inhabitants of This Colony to Discharge Their Tobacco Debts in Money for This Present Year (on a pretense that only a small quantity of tobacco was made), all persons from whom any tobacco was due, by any ways or means whatsoever, were to pay the same either in tobacco according to the directions of another act therein referred to, or else in money at the rate of 16s. 8d. per hundred, at the option of the payer; that act to continue in force for the space of ten months, and no longer.

[xxvi] And again, by another general act passed on the 12th of October, 1758, entitled An Act to Enable the Inhabitants of This Colony to Discharge the Public Dues, Officers' Fees, and Other Tobacco Debts in Money for the Ensuing Year (upon a surmise that the crop might prove deficient), all persons in the colony from whom any tobacco is due, by any ways or means whatsoever, are to pay the same either in tobacco according to the directions of another act therein referred to, or else in money at the rate of 16s. 8d. per hundred, at the option of the payer; this act to continue in force for one year, and no longer.

That by these several acts the condition of the clergy is rendered most distressful, various, and uncertain after a painful and laborious performance of their functions in parishes very wide and extensive, some of them 40 or 50 miles in length, and possessed of numerous inhabitants; and they are deprived of that maintenance which was enacted for them by His Majesty, whose royal authority the said Assembly cannot by law control, and are put upon such unjust and unequal footing that if on the one hand tobacco is plenty and the price low, they are to take the tobacco in kind, but if in other years the price or value is something better, then the clergy are by these short temporary acts stripped of the common benefit and obliged to take money, and that paper currency also at a value to be put upon tobacco by the vestry or the justices, who are the persons that owe and are to pay the greatest parts or shares of the same at a price far beneath the real value; whereby the parishes aim at a power to turn out as well as to nominate the rectors there, it being wholly in their own power to render their provision so very mean as to drive them away from the same, to the great hardship of the clergy, who entered on their function, as they conceived, on the faith of a sure and absolute law, as they imagined, but who find themselves thus unduly deprived of the same not only after the contract made but even after the duty and service performed, which is a singular hardship upon the body of the clergy in Virginia in general.

That the clergy are advised that it is not in the power of the Assembly to break through the laws confirmed by His Majesty's royal authority, and that this matter interferes with the royal prerogative in several respects and is forbid by many of the royal instructions, which have been broke through in order to pass these pretended acts there.

That the said acts complained of are made to commence immediately, and contain no suspending clause to wait the royal judgment and pleasure; and [xxvii] some of them are short temporary acts, made only for 10 or 12 months so as to prevent the possibility of the royal consideration of them whilst in continuance: the better to effect which purpose the same are either not sent over at all or at best not until very near the expiration of the same; and the last of the said acts is not yet sent to Your Lordships' board, though passed on the 12th of October, 1758. But the clergy most humbly present herewith an attested copy of the same: that the convention of the clergy being there most grievously and insupportably injured, have, by their most humble address to His Majesty, implored his royal relief.

And pray of Your Lordships to represent the premises to His Majesty in such manner that not only the said pretended acts may be declared null and void *ab initio,* but also that such explicit instructions and commands may be sent to His Majesty's governor that no act may be pretended to be passed there for the future to repeal, alter, or prejudice in any manner the said fundamental act passed in 1758 and confirmed by His Majesty, whereby a certain and fixed maintenance for the clergy in that colony was settled; and to afford the clergy there all such further and other relief in the premises as to Your Lordships, in your great wisdom and justice, shall seem meet.

And they shall ever pray, etc.

JOHN CAMM,

Agent appointed by the General Convention of the Clergy in Virginia.

PAMPHLET 5

CONSIDERATIONS UPON
THE ACT OF PARLIAMENT

BOSTON, 1764

INTRODUCTION

The Sugar Act, or Revenue Act, of 1764[1] was the first unmistakable proof to the colonists that the Grenville administration had seriously undertaken the revision of existing relationships between England and America; and it evoked the first deliberately organized intercolonial protest. The present pamphlet is the most comprehensive and fully articulated of these early protests.

Grenville's policy, which embodied longfelt desires of English politicians to rationalize the colonial administration,[2] was in fact limited in purpose, and it built pragmatically upon a series of recent wartime changes. The central problem of his administration was to find new sources of revenue to reduce, or at least to service, the national debt which in the course of the Seven Years' War had almost doubled. Faced with the adamant refusal of the landed interests to assume greater financial burdens, and confronted with wholly new and sizable expenses incurred in the organizing and policing of the huge areas in America acquired from France in the peace settlement of 1763, Grenville turned to the colonies for revenue. It was not an entirely original approach. The Molasses Act of 1733, whose modification and enforcement would become the Sugar Act of 1764, had been passed deliberately as "a revenue bill superimposed on an intent to regulate trade . . . a very real money bill."[3] Aimed both at barring the importation to British America of sugar products of the foreign West Indies and at producing an income to the government, it had stipulated that all molasses imported into British territory from the foreign islands would be dutied at the rate of 6d. per gallon; all rum at 9d. per gallon; and all sugar at 5s. per hundredweight. But the law had never been enforced, though not because it was, as was then and afterward claimed, economically prohibitive.[4] It was encumbering, however, and given the structure of relationships that had grown up between crown officers and native Americans in the eighteenth century, that was enough to defeat its enforcement. The duty was either ignored or "compounded" at rates that differed according to the place and personnel involved. James Otis said the Boston merchants were in the habit of settling for "about one tenth" of the full duty; in New York the rate was said to be from a fourth to a half penny a gallon. Everyone knew that thousands upon thousands of gallons of foreign molasses entered the mainland colonies duty free, to feed the American rum distilleries and hence to lubricate trade throughout the entire Atlantic world.[5]

Like much of the looseness of the old colonial system, the traditional evasion of the Molasses Act was temporarily restricted by Pitt's wartime measures aimed at eliminating clandestine assistance to the enemy. Whereas the average official income from the duty on molasses between 1734 and the outbreak of war in 1755 had been an insignificant £259 a year, in 1761 it had risen to £1189.[6] It was hardly surprising, therefore, that Grenville, contemplating not only the existing burdens on the government but such new and continuing expenses as the estimated £225,000 annually needed to maintain the troops stationed in America, turned to the renewal and enforcement of the Molasses Act, which was due to expire in 1764. Under his stimulation the customs commissioners in September 1763 endorsed the commonly heard proposal that the amount of the molasses duty should be lowered in order to "diminish the temptation to smuggling" and that violation of the law thereafter be severely punished. The determination of how far to lower the duty was entrusted to two secretaries to the treasury, Charles Jenkinson and Thomas Whately, who concluded, after estimating the exact point at which the size of an enforced duty would begin to lower consumption, that at 3*d*. per gallon the duty would yield the maximum revenue to the government: an estimated £77,775 per year.[7]

In March 1764 the recommendation was placed before Parliament as one of twenty resolutions aimed at raising an income from the colonies (the fifteenth, calling for stamp duties, was laid aside ostensibly to allow the colonists time to express their views); and on April 5, 1764, together with absolute prohibition on the importation of foreign rum and a fourfold increase in the size of the duty on finished sugar, the new molasses duty — bound up in elaborate new procedures for enforcement — became law.

Word that some such measure was under consideration had reached the colonies almost a year before. As early as the end of March 1763 Jasper Mauduit, the Massachusetts agent in England, warned the colony of a proposal being aired in the Board of Trade to reduce the molasses duty and enforce it.[8] Private correspondence verified the threat, and in response, in April, a group of Boston merchants long accustomed to meet informally on matters of common interest, organized themselves into a formal body, The Society for Encouraging Trade and Commerce within the Province of Massachusetts Bay, for the specific purpose of defeating the proposed renewal of the Molasses Act. It appointed a committee to draw up a "State of the Trade" as a basis for the colony's case, and entered into correspondence with neighboring port towns requesting information on trade and the fisheries that might prove useful. Through the summer and fall the committee continued to gather information, and then, amid broadening public speculation as to what the new duty was likely to be and what might be acceptable, it drew up its report. This "State of the Trade" — a compactly written technical essay arguing that imported molasses "will not bear any duty at all" and that to enforce a duty would ruin the commerce not only of the northern colonies but of the sugar islands and of England itself — in December was submitted as a memorial to the General Court with a request that the colony enter an official protest to the English authorities. Marblehead, Salem, and Plymouth endorsed the idea, and in February 250 copies of the "State," published under the title of *Reasons*

Against the Renewal of the Sugar Act . . . , were sent to England together with orders to the colony's agent to protest the contemplated action.[9]

Meanwhile in December the Boston merchants had written to merchants in other colonies, with significant results. Connecticut's legislature met in special session and appointed a fact-finding committee to prepare material to be sent to the colony's agent; a protest statement by the New York merchants passed through both houses of the legislature and was forwarded to England. In Rhode Island agitation had begun independently as far back as the previous October; after word was received from the Bostonians, the Assembly met in special session and commissioned the drafting of a "Remonstrance" against the renewal of the Molasses Act. The document was written by the governor, Stephen Hopkins, who drew on the Boston "State," on a sketch of a similar statement furnished by the Providence merchants, and on "An Essay on the Trade of the Northern Colonies of Great Britain in North America" which he himself was in the midst of writing for publication in the newspapers. In Philadelphia the merchants petitioned the Assembly — without success, it appears — to instruct the colony's agent to cooperate with other agents in efforts to stop the bill, and Hopkins' "Essay," which had already appeared in three northern newspapers, was published in pamphlet form.[10] It was during these same weeks in early 1764, as part of this rising tide of opposition to the proposed measure, that the Boston printers Edes and Gill issued *Considerations upon the Act of Parliament,* the most comprehensive and readable of all the protests.

These statements of objections to the passage of the Sugar Act were all, in different ways, forceful. The Boston merchants' "State" was a rigorous presentation of the economics of trade and of the fisheries in Massachusetts; Hopkins' "Essay" and "Remonstrance" contain, in addition to some frank figures on the importation of foreign molasses into Rhode Island, expressions of a quiet wit; and the *Considerations* ranges widely across the international scene and places its conclusions within a broad context. Yet none of them had the slightest effect on the course of events in England. The statements of both the Boston merchants and the Rhode Island Assembly arrived in England after the Sugar Act had become law, and the New Yorkers' statement was approved by their own House even later. The colonial agents, aware of the mood of Parliament and of the plans of the administration, wasted no time objecting to the passage of the act and concerned themselves only with calculating appropriate sizes for the duties. No effective representations of colonial opinion ever reached the administration as it prepared its legislation on the sugar duties; Americans' views were never mentioned in the languid debate that preceded the passage of the act.[11]

Yet in the overall development of the Revolutionary movement, these statements of colonial opinion, written before the passage of the Sugar Act, are of considerable importance. For not only do they express the colonists' objections to the economic reorganization of the empire, but they mark the last point at which objections to Parliamentary action affecting them could generally be voiced without reference to ideology. The most striking fact about these addresses and petitions is their entire devotion to economic arguments: nowhere do they appeal to constitutional issues; nowhere was Parliament's right to pass such laws officially questioned. But ideological considerations were just below the surface. They had in fact long been associated with these economic matters, having first been raised thirty years before, in the debate in Parliament on the passage of the original Molasses Act; and they continued to be expressed privately whenever the threat of enforcement appeared.[12] Though in early 1764 such considerations were still subordinated to the appeal to economic self-interest, the feeling was widely shared, if privately voiced, that "this act is . . . of dangerous consequence as it will be conceding to the Parliament's having a right to tax our trade, which we can't by any means think of admitting, as it would be contrary to a fundamental principle of our constitution, viz., that all taxes ought to originate with the people." This feeling would grow as the effects of the act were felt, and it would be intensified by the belated discovery that the act contained, in addition to the new duties, some forty sections detailing new procedures for enforcement — procedures that would not only introduce a new rigidity into the economic relations of the colonies to the mother country but that would require in the end the appointment of "hordes of petty placemen" to do the work of enforcement: harpies, sycophants of power, they would be called, intent on eating out the substance of the land. This realization, emerging from the good faith expressed in statements such as the pamphlet that follows, contributed forcefully to the conviction that a deliberate assault had been launched in the highest circles in England against the liberty Americans had for so long enjoyed.[13]

CONSIDERATIONS/upon/The Act of Parliament,/whereby/A Duty is laid of *six Pence*/Sterling per Gallon on Molasses, and *five*/*Shillings* per Hundred on Sugar of foreign/Growth, imported into any of the British/Colonies./shewing,/ Some of the many Inconveniencies necessa-/rily resulting from the Operation of the/said Act, not only to those Colonies, but/also to the British Sugar-Islands, and/finally to *Great-Britain.*/

BOSTON:/Printed and Sold by Edes and Gill, in Queen/Street, M,DCC,LXIV./

CONSIDERATIONS, &c.

WE HAVE read with the greatest pleasure His Majesty's late proclamation for the improving and better regulating the countries and islands ceded and confirmed to the crown of Great Britain by the last treaty of peace,[1] as therein is most conspicuous the paternal care of the best of sovereigns that his loving subjects in his North American dominions should with all convenient speed avail themselves of the great benefits and advantages which must thence accrue to their manufactures, commerce, and navigation, and that a quiet possession of the territories already granted or that may be hereafter granted should be effectually secured. For this end, we hear, great encouragement has been offered to Protestant foreigners, as well as others, to transport themselves and families into both the old and new colonies, within the latter of which His Majesty has been graciously pleased, for the better security of the liberties and property of the subject, to erect four distinct governments, with provision that the inhabitants [4] should, as soon as circumstances would admit, enjoy the peculiar privilege of electing proper persons to represent them in General Assembly within the said governments respectively, in order to make, constitute, and ordain such laws, statutes, and ordinances as may be needful for the public peace, welfare, and good government of the respective colonies.

These happy effects of His Majesty's wisdom and real concern for the good of his subjects will doubtless contribute vastly to enlarge the present foundation of the British Empire in this western hemisphere: a foundation which we may say (with submission to Providence) no earthly power will be capable of subverting, unless any ill-timed jealousies and consequent mercenary divisions should be so far excited in the body politic as to render it blind to any of its most general and essential interests. This we above all things deprecate, and wish that the American interests may ever continue to be a principal object of the national concern. Such it seemed to be estimated by the most discerning and disinterested persons in Great Britain upon the earliest motion of the enemy for a negotiation of peace, the first prospect of which determined a noble lord, in his *Important Letter to Two Great Men* (whom he expected to be the principal negotiators on our side), earnestly to advise them that our plenipotentiaries at the then-expected congress might be directed, whatever they should agree to restore to France, to guard against restoring any part of His Majesty's conquests in North America, giving it as his most serious opinion that these *"should be the sine qua non of the peace";* and that although we should be obliged to part with what we had gained, or might gain, in the West Indies, Africa, and [5] elsewhere, to obtain the desired settlement of affairs in Germany (where the circumstances of things at that time (1760) were most threatening), he assures those great men that it would be the interest of Great Britain to give up all or most of those conquests, rather than any part of what we had conquered or might conquer in North America.[2] Whether the advice of this great and wise counselor has been at the close of the late war so strictly adhered to, in all respects, as it might have been, we shall not determine; but it's evident from what he has said upon the subject that he esteemed it of the last consequence to Great Britain to preserve all her conquests in North America, and in this he seems to coincide with the political sentiments of the great Monsieur Colbert, minister to Louis the 14th, by which the French court was led into the vast expense of a strong chain of fortifications upon the back of these colonies, which that court flattered themselves would in time be so strengthened and secured by colonizing near each of them as effectually to prevent the growth of our settlements and to render infallible the increase of their own; upon the success of which scheme the said minister assured the French court they might depend, if they continued strictly to observe his maxim of *festina lente:* which, happy for Great Britain and her colonies, they long since lost sight of, and by this loss, in part, they have been the sooner deprived of the prospect (with which they were so apt for some time to please themselves) of universal monarchy. From the concurrence of opinion of the aforementioned two great politicians as to the importance of North America to that power who might finally be in quiet possession of it, we may [6] justly infer that whatever does or may hereafter essentially operate to the disadvantage, discouragement, and consequent weakening and dispiriting of these northern colonies in the improvement of their productions and commerce (unless where any branch of the latter should interfere with the interests of the mother country) must of course in the first place strike at the well-being of the sugar colonies, and by a redoubled stroke eventually prove very detrimental to, if not in a great measure tend to enfeeble, the nation in whose power we know it is, and on the wisdom of whose councils we may rely to point out the method of reconciling the present seemingly different and clashing interests of its *southern* and *northern* colonies. From this misconceived militation of interests, we suppose, the Sugar Act, so called, at first took its rise, and notwithstanding the many and spirited remonstrances against it, which we know have been heretofore made by one or more of our American friends at home, has been continued, and we expect, if the experienced mischievous tendency of it be not timely elucidated and closely urged before a British Parliament, will be continued and carried into execution.

That the northern colonies (in which the operation of the said act was chiefly to take place) will be extremely prejudiced in their general navigation, fishery, and commerce is so very obvious that it seems to reflect upon the good understanding of our fellow subjects in general to advance any argument to clear up so evident a proposition. However, as there are some things which may have escaped the notice of many persons of good heads and hearts but who may have been by their situation [7] in life prejudiced in favor of the act, we will endeavor, as briefly as may be, to exhibit some reasons for the conviction of every such person as they arise from the consideration of a number of facts and their consequences, which, if supported, we doubt not will have the desired effect upon everyone who may impartially weigh the same.

If what may be said upon the subject should prove that the northern colonies will be greatly and essentially injured by the said Sugar Act, it will not be difficult to make it equally apparent that the West India colonies, as well as the mother country, must be finally involved in the like fatal consequences.

We conclude none will deny that the general commerce of these northern colonies is the source of great part of their strength and riches, although some we suppose are of opinion that far the greatest part of their support is derived from their husbandry and few manufactures carried on among them; and this is in some measure true, so far as relates to the bare supply of the necessaries of life (or as the French say, *les premiers biens de la vie*), but let such persons consider that should the produce of the land and manufactures even exceed the necessities of each of the colonies (which they do not), without commerce they would find themselves but very little capable of defending their own, or of assisting their mother country to render abortive any design which their common enemy might form against their peaceable enjoyment of the fruits of their labor. As by the ancient history of England it appears that the hardy and robust inhabitants were often subject to the depredations of their neighbors only more powerful as they had [8] pre-engaged in commerce and thence added a naval force solely dependent upon it; and it's also evident that Great Britain has risen to her present grandeur just in proportion to the attention she has given to her commerce and colonies: and therefore as it would be with that now powerful state without trade, or much declined in it, so we may argue from the greater to the less that these colonies in similar circumstances must become proportionably weak.

But it's time to point out the particular mischiefs arising from the act in question as they relate:

> To the northern colonies,
> To the British sugar islands, and
> To Great Britain in her manufacture, commerce, revenue, and naval force.[3]

That we may show in as clear a light as may be wherein the northern colonies will be essentially prejudiced by the said act, let us consider, in the first place, how it will affect the cod and whale fishery in those colonies, these being two of the three principal branches of commerce of several of the said colonies, which when discouraged must of course be followed by a less demand for *shipbuilding;* prior indeed, as it gives rise and ability to the former in the nature of things, and therefore must be the last of the three in falling.

The cod fishery, being the first of almost any business began in the first settlement of these more northern colonies, was followed soon by the whale fishery, and both these sources of trade have since for many years afforded the principal returns by way of Spain, Portugal, and Italy, and direct to Great Britain for the manufactures we receive from thence. Should they be unhappily obstructed — by the rising [9] charge of equipping our fishermen upon their voyages — the consequence must be that they will decline going out upon them, and will choose to cultivate their lands and support themselves and families by their labor, and manufacturing the produce thereof. The owner must be likewise discouraged, as before the supposed change he scarce had any dependence upon saving himself by his part of the fairs of fish catched through the season had he not some hopes of doing better by adventuring some part of his fish, i.e., the merchantable, to Europe, and the rest, called the refuse, to the West Indies, in which last, when all markets were open to him, it has been common to make his profits, if any, upon the returns home, for seldom

would even the foreign markets afford any advantage upon the cargo out-
ward, much less those of our own islands.* And as to the adventure to
Europe, as the proceeds of that have been chiefly remitted to Great Britain, the loss has been often great, the profit for the most part very moderate as many of the merchants of our mother country have been often
heretofore made so sensible that they have for some years past almost
quitted the trade, and when solicited by their correspondents to be concerned with them, they have generally, as it's well known, declined the
same, and left it to their friends here to take the chance (often a very bad
one) of so precarious a trade. From hence we may conclude that an additional burden upon the fish business must expose this branch of it to a
total decay, to the very great [10] encouragement of our rivals in the
fishery, who would doubtless the next fair opportunity joke us into an
enlargement of their *fishing privileges,* and with a very *good grace,* as
they would be able with truth to assure us *we need not fear their interfering with us.* But not to enlarge at present upon this serious and on
our side melancholy truth — a prospect of which one would imagine
should shock every British subject who gives himself time enough to
think of the deplorable consequence to the British nation, which will be
considered under its proper head — let us proceed to the further consideration of the fish trade as it relates to the sugar colonies. It was said above
that for the most part, although the adventurer carried his cargo to
foreign markets, the price even there would seldom yield him any profit
(freight and other charges deducted), so that he must make his advantage upon the sugar and molasses returned home or be content with
a losing voyage. How much greater loss must he meet with if obliged to
sell at either of the foreign islands for cash, or proceed to the British
islands with his cargo and take their produce? In the first case he must
sell very low or not at all in order to obtain cash; if he chooses the alternative of selling in our own islands (until the fatal time arrives of our
fishery being so far *checked* as to be only sufficient for ourselves and
the British islands), he is very sure to be reduced to the necessity of taking a low and discouraging price, and then of receiving in pay the produce of those islands at so high a rate as at once to damp the thought of
further trading under a complicated disadvantage.

* It is generally supposed that the merchantable fish, if good fairs, will no more than
defray the usual expense of equipping the vessels; so that in case the demand for the refuse
or more ordinary part of the fish be much lessened, a total discouragement to them that catch
and those that cure the fish must be consequent.

[11] From the above consideration, we imagine it's evident that a prohibition or a prohibitory duty on the produce of the foreign sugar islands must in its nature and tendency give the fishery of these colonies, both mackerel and herring as well as the cod fishery, so deep a wound as probably the most wise and serious endeavors of a British Parliament could not easily heal, it being a truth experienced by many cities and countries (needless to specify) in several past centuries that a branch of manufactures or commerce, once lost to or much discouraged in a city or country in general, can scarce with the greatest care, labor, and expense, or even with royal munificence, be recovered; and for this reason especially, that a manufacture or trade so lost or discouraged in one political body (by a kind of *transmigration*) passes into another, and to this last it is, as it were, by its own force, united and fixed — the one being weakened by its loss while the other is proportionably strengthened by the addition; and despair of course on one side must become the inevitable consequence. Such must be the issue of the operation of the act in question with regard to the fisheries which were heretofore thought to be so well established in these northern colonies.

What has been observed of the certain ill tendency of the act as to the cod fishery, etc., may be extended to lumber of all kinds, provisions, and other produce, of which these colonies collectively have a growing surplus sufficient to employ a great number of ships and other vessels, but if confined by the act either to dispose of the said commodities for cash only in the foreign islands or to carry the whole into the British sugar islands, such an heavy embarrassment must lie upon the exportation of [12] every article as will make the profit of the voyage by no means *precarious,* for the loss may in general be very certainly calculated.

As the equipment of the whale fishery likewise demands an equal supply of rum, sugar, and molasses, and other West India produce in proportion to the number of men employed, so the extravagant rise of these articles must equally affect this very interesting branch of commerce by diverting the whalemen from a business in which they are by no means certain of a support if they were personally at no charge; but when they find that the charge of their outsets, which they must chiefly furnish themselves with and so run the risk of, whether good or ill success attends them, is greatly enhanced, the event must be the same as mentioned under the head of the cod fishery: much discouragement will attend them, many will quit the employment and betake themselves to agriculture or manufactures, the rest will demand of the owners of the ships proportionably higher encouragement, which will finally discourage their building and equipping vessels for that business.† It is usual with many of the seamen employed the summer season in the whale and cod fishery to proceed on voyages to the West Indies in the fall, in the fish and lumber vessels, by which they employ themselves the three winter months, and so are ready [13] for the spring voyages: but the discouragements of the cod fishery reducing the number of vessels in the West India trade for want of winter employment, their necessities will oblige them to engage in business on shore, which may show us that the whale fishery in some measure depends upon the cod and mackerel fishery; for without fish from the more northern colonies, the lumber will not in general be worth exporting, which by the way may convince us of part of the mischiefs which we shall in the next place endeavor particularly to point out as immediately or consequentially affecting the interest of the British West India islands in the operation of said act.

What has been offered under the head of the northern colonies, we imagine, has made it evident that the prohibitory duty upon foreign sugar and molasses will operate to the great discouragement of the cod and smaller fishery and of the exportation of lumber and other necessary supplies to the sugar islands, also of the whale fishery and of shipbuilding. This being granted, none will deny that the West India colonies must be of course in a short time deeply affected therewith. For notwithstanding they may be able to purchase for a year or two their plantation supplies at a cheaper rate than usual heretofore, and pay for the same in their produce at a higher rate, and also carry their sugars home in our northern colony ships for less freight, they may assure themselves that the tide of these at-present-seeming advantages will soon turn. For upon the decrease of our fisheries they'll find themselves poorly as well as uncertainly supplied with those absolutely needed articles of fish and lumber, the latter (as has been said) not being worth carrying without [14] the former; and should they appear fond of enhancing the price of those commodities in which they pay for the fish and lumber, they may perhaps oblige their present suppliers, if not confined, to try a foreign market, as it might be more their interest to purchase foreign molasses

† As our more northern colony vessels are now very much employed to the northward of Newfoundland, to killing the long-bone whales, a discouragement would be sensibly felt in the remittance of that article from New England, and it would be thought bad policy again to become obliged to pay the Dutch such immense sums annually for bone as we did before we went into the Greenland whale fishery from Europe as well as from these more northern colonies.

and sugars and pay the duty than give an extravagant price to their old friends for those articles duty free. And should this be the case, as it probably in some measure will, the charge in feeding their slaves, building their sugar mills, houses, stores, and doing other things in which lumber is wanted will be enhanced, as the fish and most of the supplies of lumber now go from the same colonies. It's true they'll receive some provisions and a small quantity of lumber from the more southern colonies, and likewise beef from Ireland; but all these, in the want of fish, will be sold much dearer than heretofore, and, as they'll complain, much too dear to feed their slaves with, the consequence of which is plain: they, being ill fed, will be the less able to perform their labor, if nothing worse! From all which will arise an enhanced charge upon the raising and manufacturing of sugars, in the cheapness of which their neighbors in the French islands have heretofore outdone them. But the increasing charge of maintaining their slaves is not the only mischief consequent upon the act in question. They'll be also in danger of being obliged to give higher prices for the slaves which they may have occasion to purchase. This every unprejudiced person doubtless will easily perceive; but for the conviction of those who appear, at home or in the plantations, fond of the act we will add:

[15] That as our sugar colonies have for many years been supplied with slaves by the Bristol, Liverpool, and northern colony traders upon the African coast, so an interruption of those supplies must necessarily raise the price of the laborers employed in the planting and raising the sugar canes and manufacturing their sugars. The heat of the climate, the hard labor, and numberless casualties which attend the slaves annually lessen the number of them and render an annual supply necessary to the planter. But it's evident from what has been said of the tendency of the Sugar Act that such an interruption will necessarily arise from it, the strict execution of the same being promoted and pressed by some of the most interested owners of estates in the sugar islands, by which they may be said to cut or at least weaken the bough they stand on. For by the act, foreign molasses imported into the northern colonies is clogged with a duty of 6d. sterling per gallon, which molasses being distilled into rum at 75 per cent (the highest West India calculation) makes an artificial addition of 8d. sterling per gallon to the price of New England rum[4] more than what it would be if no duty, which is about 50 per cent advance upon an export attended with no hopes of a more encouraging market than usual, and amounts in reality to a pro-

hibition upon that export. It is certain that the dependence which our islanders have heretofore had upon a partial supply of slaves from the North American traders to Africa must for the above reasons in a great measure if not wholly fail; and hence a rising demand and price of slaves will ensue, which must tend to depreciate their estates already settled, and very much discourage the industrious planter from clearing and subduing [16] the new rich lands in the ceded and conquered countries and islands as the price of labor will increase in proportion to the advanced price of every slave they purchase and the enhanced charge of supporting them. It's well known that the slaves in the West India islands are always esteemed a part, and far the greater part, of the estate or plantation, and not to be severed from it, as land is worth very little without laborers; and for this reason, if no other, it's not a little surprising that the West India promoters of this act should so easily lose sight of their own interest.

But it may be objected to what is said above, that the *Bristol* and *Liverpool* traders to the coast may furnish the sugar islands with all the slaves they need, and likewise all the southern colonies upon this continent which produce rice, indigo, tobacco, and naval stores. That the British corn spirits may be afforded as cheap as the *French* brandy or New England rum, we believe; but the captains and supercargoes of those vessels can inform us that their trade is rendered more certain and profitable by the exchange of part of their brandy for New England rum as it's well known that the *French* brandy proves very destructive, and the British much more so, to the constitutions of the Africans. And this they are become so generally sensible of that they are much less inclined to purchase either of those brandies than rum, and therefore we may reasonably conclude that the export of British brandy will be lessened in proportion to the want of North American spirit, which must continue as long as the duty above-mentioned shall subsist, it being probable, as has been said above, that the duty will in a short time [17] put a period to the African trade from this continent; but if only very much discouraged may we not expect that our rivals in that as well as almost in every other branch of commerce will see their interest in promoting the distilling of rum in their own islands, as well as brandy at home, in order to increase their African trade and by this means the value and produce of those islands in proportion to the increase of the number of their slaves. And if this should prove the effect of an ill-timed prohibition upon the African trade from this continent, it must be, we think,

estimated ten times more detrimental to the interest of the sugar islands
and the newly ceded colonies of East Florida than the most extensive
traffic from this continent to the French islands which could be carried
on in fish and lumber, the produce of which, as we think we have clearly
proved, consequentially tends to increase the number of laborers in our
sugar colonies and to add to the cheapness of their support, and upon
these it's well known the growth and value of those colonies must absolutely depend.

Upon a review of what has been alleged (and we hope in good measure proved) of the ill aspect which the said act has upon the sugar
colonies (for whose benefit alone it was calculated), we can't but hope
that those who are most concerned will combine their endeavors to
prevent the continuance of an act so big with many fatal mischiefs as
not to be confined to any nor even all the British colonies, but (which is
still more to be dreaded) will extend its influence to our mother country;
which brings us to the

Last head, under which we are to show that Great Britain will by the
said act be essentially affected [18] in her manufactures, commerce,
revenue, and naval power — which are indeed reciprocally dependent
upon each other, for whatever may prejudice her manufactures, equally
affect her commerce, whatever tends to lessen the latter must diminish her
revenue, and so her naval strength, and vice versa. That her manufactures will be sensibly injured by the act appears from the consideration
of the dependence which most of the northern colonies have upon their
fisheries, shipbuilding, and general commerce to pay for the prodigious
quantity of those goods (chiefly manufactured in the mother kingdom)
which they annually receive from thence in ships owned partly, if not
wholly, by her merchants. Whatever therefore may eventually tend to
exhaust all or any of those general sources of remittance to Great Britain
from these colonies must of consequence proportionably obstruct the
consumption of British manufactures within the same‡[5] for the most
honest reason that can be in any case assigned, that is, an inability to
pay for them. To say that this inability will by no means be the natural
effect of said act must be deemed *gratis dictum* unless those who say it
are able to prove that the profits of our trade to the foreign sugar colonies
will support the trade under the enormous duty of 5 per cent on sugar

‡ Very large are the imports from Great Britain only for the supply of the great and
small fisheries — in cordage of all sizes, canvas, osnaburgs, ticklenburgs, anchors, hooks,
and lines; also a very great quantity of coarse cloths, hose, caps, checked and white linens,
and many other articles.

and 6d. per gallon on molasses, or that the British sugar islands will afford a sufficient demand and a reasonable price generally for the supplies of the fish, lumber, and provisions which these colonies are able to furnish [19] them with, and will be able to pay for the same, so as to give tolerable encouragement to the adventurer; as we are sure neither of these can be proved, we think that what we have said above must remain in full force against the said act.

It may be said that the trade of the northern colonies is by no means confined to the British and French sugar islands, that their commerce is widely extended, even to Spain, Portugal, and Italy, to the coast of Guinea and many other places; but if the asserter will be pleased to consider what has been said above under the head of the northern colony trade and fisheries, that they depend very much upon what encouragement they may receive from that branch of their commerce with foreign as well as British sugar colonies, he will be sensible that if the latter is embarrassed and interrupted the former can't long subsist.

Although it be ever so apparent that the British trade to the sugar colonies is very advantageous as the produce of those colonies is valuable, it would nevertheless be thought very extraordinary for a well-informed hearty friend of his country to rise up from his seat in a British House of Commons, and upon the subject of the colonies to give his opinion that it would be more the interest of Great Britain even to reduce most of the northern colonies to a necessary dependence upon the productions of the earth and their own labor in working up the suitable materials for their use than to suffer any commerce to be carried on from thence which might any way consequentially prejudice the sugar colonies in their particular interest. We would not willingly make any invidious comparison of the different importance of the said [20] colonies to their mother country; but without any such imputation, we hope we may mention a well-known fact, that one of the northern colonies, only, annually imports more British manufactures than the sugar islands collectively. The imports into all the provinces must amount to more than £2,000,000 in 1759, for we find by an authentic account of the preceding year 1758 the exports from Great Britain to the northern colonies were upwards of £1,800,000 (and it is said by those best acquainted that the year 1759 exceeded any former year by a third): the exports to the West India islands the same year 1758 being but £877,500, the difference was near a million in that year.[6] And may we not suppose the annual difference must greatly increase as these colonies shall increase in *numbers* and *ability* to pay for what British manufactures they may stand in need of; and for this ability each colony to the northward of Maryland must depend chiefly upon their shipbuilding, trade, and fisheries, for it's probable the annual produce of their lands is not equal to one-eighth part of their annual imports from Great Britain. It's true the colonies to the southward of Pennsylvania have a growing staple, either of tobacco, rice, indigo, silk, or naval stores, on which they depend to pay for what goods they may import from Great Britain. But the most of these colonies must, as has been above hinted, soon feel the loss of the northern colony trade to Guinea, as they depend so much upon black slaves for labor in the respective products of each of those colonies. If the merchants of Glasgow only, as is said, exported in the year 1759, 85,000 hogsheads of tobacco from Virginia and Maryland,[7] it's evident those plantations increase [21] much, and [also] of course the demand of the proprietors for slaves, as white servants are seldom to be hired and when hired they are but little to be depended on as constant inducements offer to quit their masters and set up for themselves; so that although the act in question at first view does not seem to affect Great Britain in respect of her more southern colonies as they'll be still enabled to take off large quantities of British manufactures, yet we think everyone who shall consider the said act in its operations must see that it will greatly affect those colonies, though not in all respects equally with the sugar islands.

As we imagine it has been clearly evinced that a continuance and strict execution of the Sugar Act will lessen the ability of these colonies to pay for those British manufactures for which they have so increasing a demand and oblige them to turn their thoughts, though at first very unwillingly, upon the improvement of their own, we beg leave in the next place to consider how the commerce of Great Britain will be affected under such a change as the growing inability of the colony will surely produce.

Necessity has no law; it presses those supposed insuperable difficulties the surmounting of which often creates resolution to proceed further and to undertake to remove still more and greater obstacles. Success herein shows the undertaker an ability before the attempt, to him, inconceivable. Experience of this sort among the colonies should in all good policy be prevented as it might very much affect the British interest respecting both commerce and manufactures; and therefore we have reason to expect that the wisdom of Great Britain will permit and even encourage any branch of trade (not interfering [22] with her products or manufactures) to divert the colonies from all thoughts of manufacturing, even for their own use, those rough materials which their various soils and climates are so capable of producing, iron excepted. However, we apprehend the present disposition of the colonies to pursue their trading interest will in general tend to prevent manufactures until obliged by some unhappy and ill-timed restrictions of their commerce (which is indeed the commerce of Britain), of which, did the advantages center or were like to center in any other kingdom or state but that of the mother country, no restraints would be unreasonable; but as they run into her as the rivers fall into the ocean, the trade of the colonies must rather serve to replenish her vast stores than to add much if anything to their own.

The North Americans are well known, by the gentlemen of the army and others at present and lately residing in the maritime towns, to spend full as much of the luxurious British imports as prudence will countenance, and often much more; and it's most probable that this humor will prevail in proportion to their abilities, which have hitherto near wholly depended upon circular trade. It is very certain that the inland part of a country does not expend so much in British manufactures as two or three opulent traders in a seaport town do in the building and frequent equipment of their ships and smaller vessels upon their foreign trade and fisheries, as also in the goods necessary for themselves, families, and other dependents: and of course every clog upon the trader discourages not only him but his dependents also, who, failing of supplies from commerce and fisheries, are naturally [23] led to turn both head and hands upon the earth and its products for their support. Many hands thus converted to tillage will probably contribute much to the quantity and cheapness of the necessaries of life, the low price whereof in any country otherwise inviting will induce many laborers to settle in it, and some artisans (although the country may be under commercial embarrassments). The price of labor falling in some proportion to the chief support of the laborer affords encouragement to manufactures, which must be much wanted in *new countries under such commercial restrictions,* and perhaps for that reason may render more profit than tillage when the fruits of the earth are plenty and cheap, which is the case for the most part where the soil is good and the inhabitants are much the greater part husbandmen, as those of our mother country once were, and the consequent low price of provisions doubtless gave abundant encouragement to their neighboring artisans to come and settle among them.

An ingenious writer§ of our own, in his sagacious observations upon *The Interest of Great Britain with Regard to Her Colonies,* under the head of manufactures tells us that "those who understand the economy and principles thereof know that it is impossible to establish them in places not populous, and even in those which are populous, hardly possible to establish them to the prejudice of the places already in possession of them."[8] The various reasons he assigns are extremely pertinent, and the author is indisputably right as to manufactures which are designed for exportation among strangers or to distant parts of the same [24] country; but for home consumption they may be so fabricated as to answer the end of the consumer, who, in a new country more especially, considers the strength and durableness of what he makes or procures to be made. And this consideration will lead many of the unemployed fishermen and traders, with their connections and dependents, gradually into methods whereby they may be sure of supplying their otherwise increasing wants, necessity ever being the mother of invention. To this necessity a reduction of all or most of the northern colonies we can't but think would be contrary to all sound policy, as the consequential bad effects might be irretrievable in respect to the British commerce with them. For besides the most part being by restraint on trade drove into manufactures to the lessening of the export from home, many traders would be drawn by their interest to emigrate to other places where they expect to be more courteously treated, and with them great part of the capital stock of the country, which is thereby cramped in its abilities and its weakness rendered very conspicuous: all which, if duly considered, evidently shows that commerce (not interfering with the mother country) no more than agriculture should be discouraged or clogged in the colonies — which Great Britain ought always to esteem as the barrier of her empire on this side the Atlantic, and will doubtless think that this barrier can't be too much strengthened by her affording it every supposable *noninterfering* indulgence in her power, well knowing that the increasing vigor of her colonies, under prudent police, will ever be adding fresh vigor to *herself.* The effects of this vigor in the late war, we doubt not, were very perceptible [25] to every sensible Briton; and we hope and expect it will be more so upon every returning occasion.

But we are yet to show that the Sugar Act in its natural tendency and operation will in too great a degree diminish the *revenue* of Great Britain. And here we apprehend no need of recapitulating the facts and

§ The learned DR. FRANKLIN.

arguments which have been alleged to prove that the valuable productions of the sugar island and the more southern colonies on the continent would be essentially embarrassed by the continuance and rigorous execution of the said act. We choose rather to refer the reader to what has been offered upon this head, being persuaded that if unprejudiced he will agree with us that His Majesty's revenue will be consequentially impaired. But further, we observe that as the continental demand for molasses is very large and annually increasing with the colonies, in case the West India traders are obliged by the act to purchase their supply of that grand article in the British islands, the duty on it, when foreign, will be artificially added to the present price in those islands, which will raise it near 75 per cent; and this will induce the planters to neglect their distill[ing] it and barter their molasses for what they may want of those traders; for it is said that by distilling it they can clear but about 4d. sterling per gallon,[9] and if so, we have reason to fear that Great Britain will not be furnished with such quantities of good spirit from her islands as heretofore, and that His Majesty's revenue will be hereby also much diminished, unless the consumer at home should become willing to pay at least nine pence sterling per gallon more for his rum than formerly; by which piece of condescension it's true they may recover their former supply and His Majesty that [26] branch of his revenue amounting, as it's said, to at least £150,000. But then the consumer must be often reminded that the duty of six pence per gallon on molasses (so much complained of by the northern colonies) will become eventually also a tax on the British consumption of West India spirits, though *prima facie* it appeared to affect only those colonies. However, upon a little reflection, we are persuaded every man in Great Britain will perceive the advocates of the act to have had this advantage in view. It's pity their sagacity had not extended a little further and pointed out to them some of the many mischiefs we think we have shown eventually to result from it to the northern colonies, to their own islands in general, and finally to Great Britain in her manufactures, commerce, and revenue.

We will in the next place mention some of the ill consequences of the said act as they regard the naval powers, a power on which under God our all depends! And here we need not repeat what has been said under the heads of the three former grand objects of the fatal influence of the act in question.

If we have, in any good measure, proved that the act will in its operation not only discourage the northern colonies and prejudice the British sugar colonies but also injure Great Britain in her manufactures, commerce, and revenue, we need not go far for proof that her naval strength will also be much diminished. The solicitude which the French court manifested at the late definitive treaty of peace relative to their fisheries may convince us that they esteemed them at least as one of the best nurseries of seamen; surely ours ought to be estimated full as valuable, as we enjoy at *present* much the largest share in that branch.

[27] We have said much already touching the ill influence of the said act upon our North American fisheries; we need only add that as these colonies have annually employed in the cod and whale fishery about 500 vessels of different burdens, a loss of that branch of business, besides numberless other evils consequent upon it, will deduct from the naval force (chiefly dependent on fisheries and commerce) 6 or 7 thousand men annually improved and, as there may be occasion, ready to be taken into His Majesty's service. And upon this increasing nursery of seamen the act, as we have already said, has the most threatening aspect; but its influence will be still more extensive, as a discouragement of our fisheries operates necessarily upon almost every branch of commerce, and thus we may and must strike out of the list of seamen many thousands more who in want of the fisheries will be unemployed.[10] And will any West India gentleman or planter say that in order to raise the price of all the sugar and molasses produced in the British islands, together with no small quantity in addition to foreign growth (very easily strained through the said islands), the wisdom of Parliament ought to continue an act big with so many fatal consequences to her general interests, and especially to that in which all the rest are eventually comprised? And more especially since a natural effect of our discouragement in the *fisheries* will be the immediate encouragement of the French nation in *theirs,* both as to market for fish abroad and in regard of their naval power, which above all other things is indisputably (and we hope always will be) the good policy of Great Britain by every means to obstruct.

[28] We have before observed that the firmest basis of our national confidence is in our naval force, and the principal of this is in the manufactures and commerce of the nation. Whatever therefore may have been humbly represented as militating with these most important interests will, we hope, be well considered before any resolution be formed relative to it.

Should we be so unhappy as in the foregoing considerations to leave it in any measure doubtful whether the manufactures, commerce, revenue, and naval power of our mother country, the fisheries and general trade of the northern colonies, and growth of the sugar colonies would be eventually much prejudiced by the Sugar Act, we still flatter ourselves that they will be viewed by our superiors as the result of much concern for the real interest of Great Britain and her colonies, and as an honest and seasonable endeavor to place the ill tendency of the act in such point of light as might induce them in their great wisdom to resolve upon a discontinuance of it.

APPENDIX

The author acknowledges himself obliged, for the following calculations on the state of the cod and whale fisheries belonging to the province of the Massachusetts Bay.[11]

300 vessels in the cod fishery catched last year 102,265 quintals merchantable fish, at 12s. sterling per quintal	£61,359	0 0
137,794 ditto, West India fish, at 9s.	62,007	6 0
90 mackerel vessels at 200 barrels each, is 18,000 barrels, at 18s.	16,200	0 0
Shad, alewives, and other pickled fish, 10,000 barrels, at 10s.	5,000	0 0
12 barrels oil to each cod fishing vessel, is 3,600 barrels, at 30s.	5,400	0 0
15,000 hogsheads for packing the West India fish, at 6s.	4,500	0 0
West India codfish from *Nova Scotia* and *Newfoundland,* in return for provisions, rum, sugar, and molasses	10,000	0 0
Total of the cod fishery, sterling	£164,466	6 0
180 sail of whale fishing vessels, the exportations to Great Britain amounting in oil and bone to	75,000	0 0
To the West Indies and the continent in ditto	3,500	0 0
	£242,966	6 0

PAMPHLET 6

THOMAS FITCH, *ET AL.,*
REASONS WHY THE BRITISH COLONIES
IN AMERICA SHOULD NOT BE CHARGED
WITH INTERNAL TAXES

NEW HAVEN, 1764

INTRODUCTION

If objections to the portion of Grenville's budget of March 1763 that became known as the Sugar Act failed to vault into constitutional theory and did not fully mobilize the energies of the colonial agents in London, opposition to the clauses providing for a stamp tax was from the start vociferous, based on high points of principle, and well organized. The idea of stamp taxes was not new, either in England or America. Stamp duties had been levied in England without objection since 1670 and had yielded a considerable income to the government. The colonies of Massachusetts, New York, and Maryland had themselves levied stamp taxes on their people in 1755 and 1756 to help support the burdens of the war. Nor was the idea of a Parliamentary stamp tax on all the colonies unfamiliar: it had been proposed by informed officials in 1722, 1726, 1728, 1742, 1755, 1757, 1761, and at least twice in 1763 independent of the planning then under way in the treasury. And this form of taxation was generally understood to be what Grenville considered it to be, "equal, extensive, not burdensome, likely to yield a considerable revenue, and collected without a great number of officers." It was hardly surprising, therefore, that Grenville, convinced of both the absolute necessity of raising revenue in the colonies and the absolute right of Parliament to do so, included this form of excise in his budget of 1763. Yet from the time he first broached the subject in the House of Commons in March 1764 and found "many members warmly opposing it" to the time, two years later, when under the auspices of another administration, the Stamp Act was repealed, it was the source of bitter opposition and the cause of an exhaustive examination of the constitutional relationship between England and America. Rising in the colonies like a sheet of flame, opposition to the proposal and then outright defiance of the tax when imposed roared through the colonies, scorching everything it touched, leaving behind a world reduced in its respect for constituted authority, confident equally of its right and of its power to impose limitations on the jurisdiction of Parliament.[1]

Opposition was given ample opportunity to develop. In part because he needed time to gather detailed information upon which to base the intricacies of stamp duties, in part because he wished if not, as he professed, "to give the provinces their option to raise that or some equivalent tax" then at least to gain their endorsement of what had already been determined upon, Grenville postponed the vote on the bill one year from the time he offered it to the House of Commons in the form of a general resolution.² From March 1764 therefore, until March 1765 when the bill became law, it lay heavily on the minds of the colonists, the subject of general discussion, public agitation, and official pronouncements. Opinion matured rapidly as the logic of the difficulties created by the pending tax was revealed. The present pamphlet, written in the summer of 1764, was one of the first official protests against the tax measure, and it introduces one of the most important of the constitutional problems encountered in this phase of the Revolution by the opposition to Parliamentary authority.

Connecticut was particularly sensitive to the effects of new taxation, for its economy was chronically weak, and it was kept especially well informed of developments in England by its agent, Richard Jackson, a key figure in Anglo-American communications. Agent for Massachusetts and Pennsylvania as well as for Connecticut, and a member of Parliament, Jackson immediately informed Connecticut of Grenville's stamp tax resolution. The Connecticut legislature formed a committee at the first opportunity, in May 1764, "to collect and set on the most advantageous light all such arguments and objections as may justly and reasonably [be] advanced against creating and collecting a revenue in America, more particularly in this colony, and especially against effecting the same by stamp duties, etc." The present pamphlet is the result of that committee's work. Approved by the legislature in October, it was distributed widely in America and England. Over one hundred copies were sent to members of Parliament and to the ministry. Grenville himself read it, disdaining of course its central contention concerning Parliamentary taxation but conceding to it at least "good temper" and, somewhat vaguely, "good arguments." ³

Had he been able to guess the future he might well have been willing to concede it more, for this pamphlet, expressing the official views of one of the most independent-minded colonies in America, took perhaps the least advanced position on the constitutional issues ever assumed by an official body in the colonies and one that only a few years later the English government itself would gladly have accepted. It is in effect the starting point in the development of American thought on the constitutional relationship between England and the colonies. For though it spells out in some detail the premises of British constitutionalism as they bear on property rights and taxation, it does not in the end deny the right of Parliament by the determination of its own will to raise public revenues in America despite the fact that "the colonies may not, they cannot, be represented in Parliament" and that no laws, particularly laws depriving subjects of their property, "CAN BE MADE OR ABROGATED WITHOUT THE CONSENT OF THE PEOPLE BY THEIR REPRESENTATIVES." ⁴

The reasoning by which this paradoxical conclusion was reached rested on the belief, already well expressed by Bland, that there were two spheres of government affecting the colonies: a sphere within the jurisdiction of the local assemblies that included "internal," that is, domestic, matters; and a sphere of the competence of the home government comprised of "external" affairs, that is, the regulation of exterior commerce and relations with foreign states. Faced now with the specific question of Parliamentary taxation which Bland in the Two-Penny Act controversy had not had to confront, the drafters of this statement for the Connecticut government assumed a cognate distinction in public revenue. Limiting their definition of taxation to "internal" taxes — excises, stamp taxes, and the like — they declared taxation to be beyond the competence of Parliament to impose on the colonies; but that did not mean that Parliament could not, if "it shall be judged necessary," raise revenue in America. It might do so not by taxing but by levying duties on the commerce of the colonies, which, falling within the sphere of "external" government, was legitimately within Parliament's province. Such a form of revenue-raising, not encroaching on the proper jurisdiction of the representative assemblies in the colonies, would "leave the legislatures of the colonies entire, and the people in the full possession and enjoyment of their just rights and immunities." The committee even named the duties they would especially favor for this purpose: duties on the importation of slaves and on the exportation of furs, both, naturally, safely distant from the interests of the Connecticut merchants.[5]

Yet if this was a concession that would cost Connecticut little, it was still a concession, and one that gradually came to be seen as crucial. A "conservative," cautious position, it was particularly attractive to the members of the committee that drew up the document for Connecticut. The chairman and chief draftsman was Thomas Fitch, then serving his eleventh year as governor of the colony, who had long stood with the establishment in the controversies that had rent the colony. He had opposed the extensive claims to land in Pennsylvania of the Susquehannah Company, formed by a group of speculators in the land-hungry eastern part of Connecticut, a group which by the early 1760's constituted a powerful political lobby that spoke, it seemed, for dissidence itself. And he had at the same time opposed the New Light assault on the standing order, with its ecclesiastical structure so carefully constructed in the Saybrook Platform and shored up by the punitive legislation of 1742. By instinct conservative, a lawyer by profession (he had drawn up a comprehensive revision of Connecticut's laws), and a magistrate by occupation, Fitch saw the sharp edges of the constitutional issues and the threat they posed to the bonds of authority. His chief assistant on the committee, Jared Ingersoll, was no more eager to draw extreme conclusions. Ingersoll had risen from humble origins to attain distinction as a lawyer in Connecticut and the friendship of influential officials in England, among them Thomas Whately, the draftsman of the Stamp Act, with whom he corresponded amiably and saw frequently in those years. Ingersoll too had stood with the Old Lights in the tumultuous religio-politics of the mid-century; he too had opposed the Susquehannah Company. And he had served since 1751 as king's attorney in New Haven County, in which capacity he had prosecuted evildoers in the name of "the King, our sovereign lord." Like Fitch, inclined by character and position to support constituted authority — "so much an Englishman," he rather proudly confessed to Whately, "so much an advocate for you on your side of the water . . . that I have very much brought upon me the jealousy of my own countrymen; they suspect me of being rather too much a favorer of court interest" — he hoped to mediate the conflict of constitutional interpretation he saw rising like "clouds of darkness." Nor were the lesser members of the committee — Ebenezer Silliman, governor's assistant since 1739 and judge of the Superior Court since 1743, and George Wyllys, then serving his thirty-fourth year as secretary of the colony, both future loyalists — eager to turn the statement in more radical directions.[6]

They were aware of the meaning of the position they were taking. Fitch could hardly have been more explicit. There was nothing in what Connecticut was saying, he correctly explained to Jackson, that he as agent "and our other friends at home" could not have said for the colony. They were submitting the document merely to express in their own words "the feeling sense they have of their rights, how highly they value them, and how grievous it will be to them to be deprived of them" — a direct expression of feeling more likely to be effective "than arguments from other hands" made in their behalf.

> For these reasons we have avoided all pretense of objection against the authority or power of the Parliament, as the supreme legislature of all the King's dominions, to tax the colonies, and have therefore endeavored only to show that the exercise of such power in that particular instance or in like cases will take away part of our ancient privileges, etc. (which it is presumed the Parliament, who are also guardians of our liberties, will not do), and in the whole have endeavored to express our sentiments with becoming modesty, decency, and submission, and, we trust, as was intended, without offense.

If Parliament, he wrote two months later (February 1765), "in their superior wisdom shall judge it expedient to, and accordingly does, pass an act for laying those burdens upon us, we must submit. We never pretend in the least to question whether acts of Parliament expressly extended to the plantations are binding, but always submit to them as binding."[7]

Similarly, Ingersoll, though he reported to Whately the universal hatred of such internal levies as stamp taxes — taxes which would establish a precedent by which "you will have it in your power to keep us just as poor as you please" — made quite clear, in a long, confidential letter, that external duties were acceptable. Nor did he include himself among the extreme opponents of internal taxation: though he was not now, he might one day become "convinced of the propriety as well as the necessity of such a step" as the enactment of the Stamp Act. His warning concentrated on the difficulties of enforcement in face of the "dreadful apprehensions" that filled other people's minds. Any internal tax, he explained, "other than such as shall be laid by the legislative bodies here, to say no more of them, would go down with the people like chopped hay." Nowhere, speaking for himself, did he directly challenge the propriety of internal taxes ("I vent no such speeches"); everywhere he conceded to Whately the right of Parliament to collect revenue in the colonies in the form of trade duties.[8]

And if the third member of the committee, Ebenezer Silliman, was not himself fully aware of the importance of the concession that had been made in Connecticut's statement he was soon informed of it. Thomas Hutchinson, lieutenant governor and chief justice of Massachusetts, in a letter to Silliman mocked the distinction "between duties upon trade and internal taxes" that the Connecticut legislature had drawn, though it was precisely the distinction that he himself had imposed on the Massachusetts legislature as a formula for moderating its extremism. He had done so, he wrote, because people in England believe the distinction to be meaningful, and it therefore served to

> strengthen us in our claim to exemption from internal taxes. Really, there is no difference, and the fallacy of the argument lies here: it is your supposing duties upon trade to be imposed for the sake of regulating trade, whereas the professed design of the duties by the late act is to raise a revenue . . . If they stop where they are, I would not dispute their distinction with them; but if they intend to go on, there will be a necessity of doing it, for they may find duties on trade enough to drain us so thoroughly that it will not be possible to pay internal taxes as a revenue to them or even to support government within ourselves.[9]

Hutchinson would in the end repudiate the distinction which he knew from the start to be indefensible, but not in order to rule out all forms of revenue raising in the colonies by Parliament. Consistent in denying any logic to half-way positions, he would choose to concede to Parliament all power over America rather than none. Fitch and Ingersoll, less logical, struggling to live with the compromise they had constructed, ended in catastrophe. Ingersoll, in England at the end of 1764 and in 1765, joined with the colonial agents in protest against the Stamp Act; but when it was passed he became so "confoundedly begad and beswompt, as we say in Connecticut," that he used his connection to obtain the position of stamp collector in Connecticut. It almost cost him his life. Burned and hanged in effigy upon his return to the colony, he was forced to repudiate the office by the action of an angry mob, and with that post went all hope of a continuing career of consequence in Connecticut. He died, in 1781, a loyalist, still seeking to serve America while holding offices of the British crown. Fitch, condemning the treatment Ingersoll received, took the oath required of governors to uphold the Stamp Act, though only four councilors (one of them Silliman) could be found to witness the deed. No amount of explanation would ever justify this decision, and his defeat at the polls in 1766 was irreversible.[10]

The peculiar significance of this pamphlet lies in its presumably minor concession rather than its major opposition to the authority of Parliament in America. It illustrates something of the way in which a central constitutional problem of the Revolutionary controversy — whether and in what way public authority might be divided among different units of government — unfolded. The distinction between unacceptable internal taxes and permissible trade duties imposed by Parliament that Fitch and his committee drew was not unique with them. Hutchinson at one point reported that "the opinion of most people" in Massachusetts accepted it, and he was able to persuade the legislature of Massachusetts to eliminate the words "we look upon these duties as a tax" from an address to the King and Parliament and to lead them to accept a petition that referred only to internal taxes. Rhode Island too, in its condemnation of the stamp taxes as internal taxes, questioned not the right but the wisdom of Parliament's creating an income from colonial trade duties; Virginia did the same, as did private groups elsewhere in the colonies. And Franklin, an astute student of public opinion, wrote to Jackson from Philadelphia in February 1764 not merely agreeing to revenue-raising duties but suggesting tea and other commodities as additions to the list of such dutiable items if Parliament really intended to persist in seeking a revenue in America.[11]

These concessions to Parliament's right to raise revenue in one way but not another were more the result of the desire not to give offense, to show good will and common sense by conceding something in order to retain the rest, than they were of a conscious determination to assert and maintain the distinction involved. Allowed by implication rather than by explicit pronouncement, it was not thought of or referred to, save by those who opposed it, as the concession of one form of taxation — "external," but not another — "internal." This phraseology was used mainly in England where the distinction was seized upon and articulated with an explicitness it had never had in America as an admission by the colonists of Parliament's right to tax them. By 1766 the colonists awoke to discover that the distinction, which for most people who were aware of it had evolved from the vague sense that spheres of governmental authority might be separated in the colonial situation, was said — by Franklin, most prominently, in his famous testimony before Commons — to be their central proposition. But the weakness of such a position, of which Hutchinson had so clearly warned Silliman in 1764, was by then generally apparent, and while Townshend, who mocked it, cynically proceeded to erect a new system of taxes on it, Americans flatly and finally repudiated it. No one, in England or America, presuming to speak for American opinion could accept such a notion after the publication in 1768 of John Dickinson's Farmer's Letters. [12]

REASONS/why/The *BRITISH* Colonies,/in/*AMERICA,*/Should not be charged with/Internal TAXES,/By authority of/PARLIAMENT;/Humbly offered,/For consideration,/In Behalf of the Colony of/*CONNECTICUT.*/

NEW-HAVEN:/Printed by B. Mecom. m,dcc,lxiv./

REASONS, &c.

B Y THE constitution, government, and laws of Great Britain, the English are a free people. Their freedom consists principally if not wholly in this general privilege, that "NO LAWS CAN BE MADE OR ABROGATED WITHOUT THEIR CONSENT BY THEIR REPRESENTATIVES IN PARLIAMENT."

By the common law of England every commoner hath a right not to be subjected to laws made without his consent, and because such consent (by reason of the great inconvenience and confusion attending numbers in such transactions) cannot be given by every individual man in person, therefore is the power of rendering such consent lodged in the hands of representatives by them elected and chosen for that purpose. Their subjection, then, to their laws is not forced but voluntary.

As the chief excellency of the British constitution consists in the subjects' being bound only by such laws to which they themselves consent, as aforesaid, and as, in order to their enjoying that right, they are (agreeable to the constitution) necessarily vested [4] with the power of electing their representatives, so this right or power is a fundamental privilege and so essential a part of the constitution that without it the subject cannot be said to be free: therefore, if he be hindered from voting in such election or obstructed in the lawful use of that real right or privilege, a suit will lie for him at common law.

None of the privileges included in those general rights (which in an especial manner denominate the British subjects a free people) is maintained with greater care and circumspection, and of which they are more jealous, than this particular, known, approved, and fixed one, that no tax, loan, or benevolence can be imposed on them but with their own consent by their representatives in Parliament. This privilege is of ancient date, and whenever it hath been encroached upon has been claimed, struggled for, and recovered as being essential for the preservation of the liberty, property, and freedom of the subject. For if the privilege of not being taxed without their consent be once taken from them, liberty and freedom are certainly gone with it. That power which can tax as it shall think proper may govern as it pleases; and those subjected to such taxations and government must be far, very far from being a free people. They cannot, indeed, be said to enjoy even so much as the shadow of English liberties.

Upon these general and fundamental principles, it is conceived that the Parliament (although it hath a general authority, a supreme jurisdiction over all His Majesty's subjects, yet as it is also the high and safe guardian of their liberties) doth not extend its [5] taxations to such parts of the British dominions as are not represented in that grand legislature of the nation; nor is it to be presumed that this wise and vigilant body will permit such an essential right, which is as the very basis of the constitution, in any instance ever to be violated. And upon the same principles (as is apprehended) those subordinate jurisdictions or governments which by distance are so separated from Great Britain that they are not and cannot be represented in Parliament have always been permitted to have and enjoy privileges similar to those of their fellow subjects in the mother country, that is, of being subjected only to taxations laid by the particular legislatures wherein they are or may be represented by persons by them elected for that purpose, and consequently of not being taxed without their consent. Thus, in Ireland, taxes are laid by the Parliament of that kingdom; and in the colonies or plantations in America by the several Assemblies or legislatures therein.

These being the essential rights and privileges of the British constitution, founded on the principles of the common law, though in diverse respects particularly regulated by sundry statutes, *the King's subjects in the plantations* claim a general right to the substance and constitutional part of them as their birthright and inheritance. This claim is founded on such considerations as follow, viz.:

First. The people in the colonies and plantations in America are really, truly, and in every respect as much the King's subjects as those born and living in Great Britain are. "All persons born in any [6] part of the King's dominions and within his protection are his subjects, as all those born in Ireland, Scotland, Wales, the King's plantations, or on the English seas, who by their birth owe such an inseparable allegiance to the King that they cannot by any act of theirs renounce or transfer their subjection to any foreign prince." 4 *Bac.* 166.[1]

Secondly. All the King's subjects, both in Great Britain and in the colonies and plantations in America, have right to the same general and essential privileges of the British constitution, or those privileges which denominate them to be a free people.

As protection necessarily demands and binds to subjection and obedience to that authority and those laws whereby a people are protected, so subjection and obedience as necessarily and justly entitle to protection: these mutually imply, require, and support each other. The King, as political head of his subjects, stands equally related to them in that capacity, and is as really obligated to protect one subject as well as another; and as he has an interest in all his subjects, so they have an interest in him, regulated according to the political constitution. Though the particular and formal parts of the governments of the colonies may be various one from another and diverse from that of Great Britain, and such diversity of forms or establishments necessarily arise from their different situations and circumstances, yet both law and equity agree in this general principle, that all the King's subjects ought to be supported and protected in their rights and liberties, and especially in such as are fundamental and essential to their freedom. [7] The subjects in Great Britain are under no greater or stronger obligations of submission and obedience to the crown than those in the colonies are; and surely, if the colonists are under the same obligations to submission and obedience with other their fellow subjects, it will not be easy to show that they have not the same right to be protected and secured in the enjoyment of every just and legal privilege.

Though the subjects in the colonies are situated at a great distance from their mother country, and for that reason cannot participate in the general legislature of the nation nor enjoy some particular formal immunities possessed by those at home, yet as they settled at this distance by royal license and under national encouragements and thereby enlarged the British dominions and commerce, which add riches and strength to the nation, and as they brought with them and constantly claimed the general principles, those fundamental principles which contain the essence and spirit of the common law of the nation, it may not be justly said they have lost their birthright by such their removal into America; for to suppose that those settlements, that the performance of such important and public services, should be prejudicial to the claim of the colonies to the general privileges of British subjects would be inconsistent both with law and reason, would naturally lead to unjust and absurd conclusions, inasmuch as those public national advantages would not have been promoted unless some of the King's subjects had planted, settled, and dwelt in his colonies [8] abroad, and yet that such planting, settling, and living should subject the inhabitants to the loss of their essential rights as Englishmen would be to reward great, public, and meritorious services with great and unspeakable losses and disadvantages. And how inconsistent such measures and principles are with the honor and justice of the British crown and government may well deserve consideration. It therefore seems apparent that the King's subjects in the plantations have a right, and that it is for the honor of the crown and law that they should have a right, to the general and essential privileges of the British constitution, as well as the rest of their fellow subjects. And with regard to the colony of Connecticut in particular, there can be no question of its having such right, as these general privileges and immunities are fully and explicitly granted and declared to belong to them by the royal charter of incorporation given to the said colony by King Charles the Second in the fourteenth year of his reign, in which is contained this paragraph, viz.: "And further our will and pleasure is, and we do for us, our heirs and successors, ordain, declare, and grant unto the said governor and company and their successors that all and every the subjects of us, our heirs or successors, which shall go to inhabit within the said colony, and every of their children which shall happen to be born there, or on the seas in going thither or returning from thence, shall have and enjoy all liberties and immunities of free and natural subjects within any of the dominions of us, our heirs or [9] successors, to all intents, constructions, and purposes whatsoever, as if they, and every of them, were born within the realm of England." Now whether these words are to be understood only as declarative of the principles of the ancient common law of England and of the common rights of Englishmen settled by royal license and under the protection of the crown in a colony or plantation abroad and so evidential of the rights and immunities belonging to all the King's subjects in America, or whether they are to be considered as a grant and confirmation of such privileges and immunities to His Majesty's subjects of the colony of Connecticut in particular, they equally evince (as far as a royal declaration and grant can operate to that purpose) the truth of what is here pleaded for so far as respects the people of the said colony. Indeed these words (on the general principles of the common law) ought (as is apprehended) to be construed as containing a full declaration of the rights of the subject, and in order to remove all doubts about the same, a confirmation of them is annexed to or joined therewith. It may also be further observed that by this paragraph can't be meant or intended that the King's subjects within all his dominions should have or be governed by the same particular and formal laws or regulations, because their situations are in distant parts of the world, and their circumstances are so widely different that the same particular establishments and formal regulations which in one place might be good and wholesome for the people, in another would be unwholesome, prejudicial, and [10] by no means answer the end of laws. But this declaration and confirmation denotes and imports (as is conceived) that all those general and essential rights which the free and natural subjects in the mother country are possessed of and vested with by virtue of the main, leading, and fundamental principles of the common law or constitution of the realm, the King's subjects in the said colony of Connecticut shall have and enjoy to all intents, constructions, and purposes whatsoever, that is, in such plenitude as always to be, and ever to be treated as, free and natural subjects.

Thirdly. In order that the King's subjects in the colonies and plantations in America might have and enjoy the like liberties and immunities as other their fellow subjects are favored with, it was and is necessary the colonies should be vested with the authority and power of legislation; and this they have accordingly assumed and exercised from their first regular settlement down to this time, and have been constantly owned and acknowledged therein, treated as having such authority, and protected in the same by the crown and the supreme legislature of the nation. Those corporations which by their situation and circumstances are privileged with the right of electing their representatives to bear a proportionable part in the general legislature of the nation, although they may be vested with authority to make bylaws and regulations within their own jurisdictions agreeable to the bounds and limits of the charters which institute and give them existence, indeed are, and ought to be, immediately subject to [11] the laws, orders, and taxes of such general legislature, as well as others, and that even without being expressly named, for this obvious and solid reason: because they are legally represented therein. But with regard to those corporations or governments which by their distance and situation have no possible opportunity of such a representation, the case is far otherwise. Whenever, therefore, acts are formed by the supreme legislature that are, in any respect, to extend to the governments abroad, they are made to be so extended by express words; and even such as are so extended to subjects who are not admitted a representation, or to bear a part in the legislation, may not improperly be said to be *sovereign acts,* or acts supported by the sovereign dominion of the makers of them. And as the exercise of such sovereign authority may be said (as is humbly conceived) to be in some measure an exception from the general rule by which British subjects (according to the constitution) are governed, it is most justly to be presumed and relied upon that the supreme guardians of the liberties of the subjects will never extend that authority further than may be done without depriving any of the King's subjects of those privileges which are essential to their liberty and freedom or leave them in possession of such rights and liberties. It is a clear point that the colonies may not, they cannot, be represented in Parliament; and if they are not vested with legislative authority within themselves where they may be represented by persons of their own electing, it is plain they will not be represented in [12] any legislature at all, and consequently if they are subjected to any laws it must be to such as they have never consented to either by themselves or any representatives, which will be directly contrary to that before-mentioned fundamental principle of the British constitution that "NO LAW CAN BE MADE OR ABROGATED WITHOUT THE CONSENT OF THE PEOPLE BY THEIR REPRESENTATIVES." It therefore appears that for the crown to govern the colonies and plantations abroad by and with the consent of the people represented in Assemblies or legislative bodies is properly and truly to govern them agreeable to the British constitution of government; and although this may not in every form and manner be exactly similar to the government at home, yet as near as the different situation and circumstances admit will it agree with the fundamental principles thereof. That the colony of Connecticut (agreeable to these general principles) is vested with such a legislative authority appears by their charter full to that effect. By this charter the colony are empowered to meet in a General Assembly, consisting of a governor or deputy governor, assistants, and deputies, annually to be chosen by the freemen;[2] and such Assembly is vested with authority from time to time to make, ordain, and establish all manner of wholesome and reasonable laws, statutes, and ordinances, directions and instructions not contrary to the laws of the realm of England; and every officer appointed for putting such laws, ordinances, etc., from time to time into due execution is sufficiently warranted and discharged [13] against the King's Majesty, his heirs and successors, by a special clause in the same charter express to that purpose. By this royal patent it is therefore evident that a full power of legislation is granted to the colony, limited with a restriction that they conform or are not to act contrary to the general principles of the laws of the nation; and consequently, as when they exceed the bounds and limits prescribed in the charter their acts will be void, so when they conform and regulate their acts agreeable to the intent and meaning of it their acts may properly be said to have the royal approbation and assent. And these powers, rights, and privileges the colony has been in possession of for more than a century past. This power of legislation necessarily includes in it an authority to impose taxes or duties upon the people for the support of government and for the protection and defense of the inhabitants, as, without such authority, the general rights of legislation would be of no avail to them. These privileges and immunities, these powers and authorities, the colony claims not only in virtue of their right to the general principles of the British constitution and by force of the royal declaration and grant in their favor, but also as having been in the possession, enjoyment, and exercise of them for so long a time, and constantly owned, acknowledged, and allowed to be just in the claim and use thereof by the crown, the ministry, and the Parliament, as may evidently be shown by royal instructions, many letters and acts of Parliament, all supposing and being predicated upon the [14] colony's having and justly exercising these privileges, powers, and authorities; and what better foundation for, or greater evidence of, such rights can be demanded or produced is certainly difficult to be imagined.

These points being thus rendered so clear and evident, may it not thence be very justly inferred,

Fourthly, that charging stamp duties or other internal taxes on the colonies in America by Parliamentary authority will be an infringement of the aforementioned rights and privileges, and deprive the colonists of their freedom and inheritance so far as such taxations extend? The charging a tax on any particular part of the subject's estates in the plantations by authority of Parliament will doubtless be found nothing less than taking from them a part of their estates on the sole consideration of their being able to bear it, or of having a sufficiency left notwithstanding. It must certainly be admitted that the people thus charged do not consent, nor have any opportunity so to do. An express consent, either by themselves or representatives, can by no means be pretended; neither can their consent be argued from implication, as their subjection and allegiance to the crown are supposed to be according to the tenor of the laws of the nation, for although the King is styled the head of the commonwealth, supreme governor, *parens patriae,* etc., yet he is still to make the law of the land the rule of his government, that being the measure as well of his power as of the subject's obedience; for as the law asserts, maintains, and provides [15] for the safety of the King's royal person, crown, and dignity, and all his just rights, revenues, powers, and prerogatives, so it likewise declares and asserts the rights and liberties of the subject. (4 *Bac.* 149).[3] Therefore, in this case, as there can be no other implied consent than what the general principles of the law or constitution implies or what is included in the obligations to submission and obedience to laws, and as the general, fundamental principles of the British constitution or laws, which the Americans claim the privilege of, are quite the reverse of such implications and really imply and suppose the contrary, it follows that charging such taxes will be to take part of their estates from the people without their consent, either expressed or implied. It can't be said such charging would be founded on contract, as it might be where the subjects are represented in the legislature; neither may it be founded on a forfeiture, as there is no pretense of that kind in these cases; surely, then, there can be no right either to demand or receive a man's estate where both these are wanting.

If these internal taxations take place, and the principles upon which they must be founded are adopted and carried into execution, the colonies will have no more than a show of legislation left, nor the King's subjects in them any more than the shadow of true English liberty; for the same principles which will justify such a tax of a penny will warrant a tax of a pound, an hundred, or a thousand pounds, and so on without limitation; and if they will warrant a tax on one article, they will support [16] one on as many particulars as shall be thought necessary to raise any sum proposed. And all such subjections, burdens, and deprivations, if they take place with respect to the King's subjects abroad, will be without their consent, without their having opportunity to be represented or to show their ability, disability, or circumstances. They will no longer enjoy that fundamental privilege of Englishmen whereby, in special, they are denominated a free people. The legislative authority of the colonies will in part actually be cut off; a part of the same will be taken out of their own Assemblies, even such part as they have enjoyed so long and esteem most dear. Nay, may it not be truly said in this case that the Assemblies in the colonies will have left no other power or authority, and the people no other freedom, estates, or privileges than what may be called a tenancy at will; that they have exchanged, or rather lost, those privileges and rights which, according to the national constitution, were their birthright and inheritance, for such a disagreeable tenancy? Will not such deter-

minations amount to plain declarations to the colonies that although they
have enjoyed those immunities and privileges heretofore, and been acknowledged and encouraged in the possession and use of them, yet now
they must expect, for reasons of state, for some public utility, to part with
them, and be brought under a kind of subjection not far from the very
reverse of that freedom they justly claim and so highly value? May it
not be inquired what reasons are or may be assigned for so different
treatment of [17] the subjects of the same most gracious King, of the
same general state or community? May it not, upon the whole, be concluded that charging stamp duties or other internal duties by authority
of Parliament, as has been mentioned, will be such an infringement of
the rights, privileges, and authorities of the colonies that it may be
humbly and firmly trusted and even relied upon that the supreme
guardians of the liberties of the subject will not suffer the same to be
done, and will not only protect them in the enjoyment of their just rights
but treat them with great tenderness, indulgence, and favor?

Objection

Perhaps it may be here objected that these principles, if allowed, will
prove too much, as the Parliament by its supreme dominion has a superintendency over all the colonies and plantations abroad, and right to
govern and control them as shall be thought best and most conducive to
the general good of the whole, and accordingly hath passed divers acts
for regulating their trade and navigation and in other respects directed
their conduct, limited the exercise of their authorities, etc.

Answer

To objections and observations of this kind it may be answered that as
the Parliament of Great Britain is most certainly vested with the supreme
authority of the nation, and its jurisdiction and power most capacious
and transcendent, the colonies will be far, very far from urging or even
attempting anything in derogation of the power or authority [18] of
that august Assembly, or pretending to prescribe bounds or limits to the
exercise of their dominion; nothing in the foregoing observations, be
sure, is intended by way of objection but that the crown by its prerogative
or the Parliament by its supreme and general jurisdiction may justly
order and do some things which may affect the property of the American
subjects in a way which, in some sense, may be said to be independent
upon or without the will or consent of the people, as by regulations of
trade and commerce and the like, and by general orders relative to and
restrictions of their conduct for the good of the whole. For as the colonies

are so many governments independent on each other, or not subjected
the one to the other, they can only establish regulations within and for
themselves respectively; and as they are all subordinate to and dependent
upon the mother country, and propriety, conveniency, and even necessity
require that they should be subject to some general superintendency and
control in order that the general course of their trade and business should
be so uniform as to center in some general national interest, it becomes
plainly expedient that there should be some supreme director over all
His Majesty's dominions; and this character and authority all men must
acknowledge and allow properly belong to the British Parliament.
Against the exercise of such general jurisdiction for the common interest
and advantage of the mother country and of the plantations, collectively
taken, the before-mentioned observations are in no measure intended; for
it is humbly conceived that the subjects in the colonies [19] may enjoy
their rights, privileges, and properties as Englishmen, and yet, for political
reasons, be restrained from some particular correspondence or branches of
trade and commerce, or may be subjected therein to such duties, charges,
and regulations as the supreme power may judge proper to establish as
so many conditions of enjoying such trade. Reasons of state may render
it expedient to prohibit some branches of trade and to burden others as
aforesaid. And as such regulations will doubtless appear, upon examination, rather to be a preventing the subject from acquiring property than
taking it from him after it is legally become his own, the objections relative to such establishment ought to be only against those that may be
supposed unequal, unprofitable, or not expedient, the determination of
which must nevertheless be left to the supreme authority of the nation.
What therefore is designed to be urged from these general principles of
the British constitution is that the legislatures of the colonies ought to
be left entire, and that His Majesty's good subjects in them should be
permitted the continued enjoyment of their essential rights, immunities,
and privileges, which will not, as is supposed, by any means be the case
if the internal taxations before-mentioned should take place. But if restrictions on navigation, commerce, or other external regulations only are
established, the internal government, powers of taxing for its support, an
exemption from being taxed without consent, and other immunities
which legally belong to the subjects of each colony agreeable to their
own particular constitutions [20] will be and continue in the substance
of them whole and entire; life, liberty, and property, in the true use of
the terms, will then remain secure and untouched.

OBJECTION

On this distinction it may perhaps be further said, by way of objection, that a stamp duty differs from a tax as it will oblige the subjects only to pay for paper, parchment, etc., which they are at liberty to use or not to use at pleasure; and so, if they choose to make use of it they voluntarily submit to the charge, and can't be said to be taxed without their consent.

ANSWER

This by no means will obviate the arguments; for a regulation which necessarily obliges a man to part with any certain portion of his estate amounts to the same thing as the actual taking such portion from him. It must be supposed that the people in America will buy and sell their lands, nay, in a multitude of instances they would not know how to subsist without such dispositions. They will also be necessitated to give and take obligations, and to use paper for various other purposes, or there will be of course so great a stagnation of business as almost to bring on a dissolution of their civil and political existence. These things will be found as necessary as the use of agriculture itself. They will therefore be as certainly taxed by a duty charged on the transfer of their lands as by a tax laid directly on the land itself. If lands were to be taxed it might as well be said people are not obliged to have lands [21] (and indeed some have none), so that such as do acquire them voluntarily submit to the charge — which is really saying nothing to the purpose, for the use and improvement of lands, barter, and transmutation of property are as necessary in civilized countries as food and raiment are to the body natural. Indeed, the supposition of the necessity and certain use of the articles to be charged can be the only foundation to render a revenue arising therefrom worthy of notice, as otherwise the effect would be altogether precarious.

Fifthly. Another reason offered as an objection against charging stamp duties, etc., in the colonies may be drawn from the consequence of such a measure, as it is most probable if not certain it will, in the event, prove prejudicial to Great Britain itself. The colonies and plantations in America are indeed of great importance to their mother country and an interest worthy of her most tender regard. The more they prosper and increase in number, riches, and commerce the greater will be the advantage not only to them but also to the nation at home. In the colonies there is a vent for and a consumption of almost all sorts of British manufactures, and of many and various kinds of goods of the produce of other countries first imported into Britain and from thence brought into the plantations, whereby the revenue of the crown and wealth of the nation are much increased at the expense of the colonies; for these goods the colonies make remittances with what monies they are able to collect in a variety of their own produce, and by circular trade; and [22] taking the whole trade together, it amounts to a very great sum, the profits of which in general center in Great Britain. If the plantations are encouraged and prosper, this will be an increasing interest and become more and more of importance; but if measures should be taken which, in regard to them, would have a natural tendency to abate their vigor, spirit, and industry, or to turn them into some other channel to supply the necessaries of life, what can be expected but a decrease of the colonies' wealth and prosperity, and consequently a decay of an important national interest? And as, on the one hand, depriving the colonies of part of their powers and privileges and rendering the tenures of them and of their liberties and properties precarious, as by charging stamp duties or other internal taxes upon them by act of Parliament, etc., will naturally produce that unhappy effect of causing the colonies to languish and decrease, so, on the other hand, upholding and continuing the freedom of their governments, maintaining their authority, their laws, securing their properties, considering and treating their privileges and immunities as matters too sacred to be violated will naturally tend to invigorate, enliven, and encourage the people and keep up in them a spirit of industry in all kinds of dealing and business, and of emulation in the service of their mother country, whereby they will become more able and zealous to promote the national interest. This will doubtless be found almost universally to be the case of a people where they enjoy liberty, and their lives, properties, and privileges are secure, and the reverse [23] of it as generally to be the consequence of a contrary treatment; for what encouragement hath the merchant to expose his interest to chances and dangers, the farmer, the mechanic, and the common laborer to weary themselves in their fatiguing toilsome employments, if, after all, part of their estates (and how great a part is to to them altogether uncertain) may be taken from them, and in such ways and manner as they have heretofore been led to think are inconsistent with their essential rights and liberties? Surely, then, if subjecting the colonies to burdens which will discourage and abate their industry will eventually prove disadvantageous to the mother country, and the charging of stamp duties or other internal taxes on them will, in the end, have that effect (as has been endeavored to be shown and evinced), the taking such a measure must be inconsistent with good policy and the true interest of the nation.

Sixthly. Furthermore to enforce the objections against stamp duties or other internal taxations, it is conceived that a summary representation of the settlement, special services, and circumstances of the colony of Connecticut may be here with great propriety adduced, from whence very cogent reasons may be drawn in their favor.

The first settlers of the colony, who were derived from England, their native country, planted here in the year 1636, and having purchased their lands, or rather a right of pre-emption of the crown or the King's patentees, they were obliged to purchase the greatest part of them again of the native claimers, possessors, and [24] proprietors of the country, and some other part was obtained at a much dearer rate, which was by conquest; for the people of these new settlements, scarce of one year's date, and very small, were forced, for the defense of their lives and those settlements which in a fair and equitable manner they had made, to enter into a war with the principal tribe of Indians then in this part of the country, who rose with all their barbarous, insidious, crafty force and cruelty to rout these new settlers out of the country as the first effort of their set and declared design to break up and prevent the settlement of New England. Against this numerous and powerful tribe enraged with jealousy at the English, these planters, who were able to raise but about fourscore men, took up arms, and, by the smiles of Heaven, in sundry severe conflicts, overthrew, conquered, and effectually subdued these their crafty, bloody, and inveterate enemies. And as this was the first Indian war in New England, and issued so successfully on the part of the English, whose courage, force, and conduct in war now became the dread and terror of the natives throughout the land, it laid a foundation for tranquillity in general for almost forty years after, which gave a most favorable opportunity for the settlements in the country to multiply and increase in strength and vigor.[4]

The plantation and settlement of the colony by the year 1661 being considerably increased, they made application to the crown for a charter of incorporation with powers of government founded [25] on the general principles of the English, now British, constitution, that is to say, that they might be governed with the consent of the people represented in an Assembly composed of members elected for that purpose; and in consequence of such application, King Charles the Second, in the 14th year of his reign, granted his royal charter to the said colony, the preamble of which is worthy of special notice, as in it are these words, viz.:

"Whereas, by the several navigations, discoveries, and successful plantations [of] divers of our loving subjects of this our realm of England, several lands, islands, places, colonies, and plantations have been obtained and settled in that part of the continent of America called New England, and thereby the trade and commerce there hath been of late years much increased: And whereas we have been informed by the humble petition of our truly and well-beloved John Winthrop, John Mason, etc., being persons principally interested in our colony or plantation of Connecticut in New England, that the same colony, or the greatest part thereof, was purchased and obtained for great and valuable considerations, and some other part thereof gained by conquest and with much difficulty and at the only endeavors, expense, and charges of them and their associates and those under whom they claim, subdued and improved and thereby become a considerable enlargement and addition to our dominions and interest there: Now, know ye, that IN CONSIDERATION THEREOF," *etc.*

Hereby it appears that this charter was granted upon valuable considerations, which adds weight [26] and strength to the title on which the claim of the colony to the rights, immunities, and franchises therein granted and confirmed are founded, for here are the considerations of large sums of money advanced, conquest made at the expense of the blood and treasure of the planters, eminent public national services performed and to be performed, and all to the enlargement of the King's dominions and for the increase of the national commerce, which the charter is a clear and full evidence of. The powers and privileges granted by this charter were properly the purchase of the people, and the granting was an instance of royal justice to them, though the grace and favor of the crown assuredly ought to be and hath been at all times humbly and gratefully acknowledged therein. Therefore, as there really were valuable considerations which were proper foundations for such a grant, it was doubtless judged to be for the honor of the crown to grant the powers of government with such ample and beneficial immunities and privileges as are allowed and given in and by the charter aforesaid; and these the people indeed look upon as the purchase of their ancestors, as a gracious and royal reward of the merit and services of their forefathers, and as one of the best inheritances they left to their children. Whether, therefore, it can be consistent with law or equity they should be deprived of such an inheritance or any part thereof, may be worthy of serious consideration; for if the right of a single person to vote in the election of a member of Parliament be so sacred in the eye of the law that to deprive him [27] of it entitles to an action at common law for his damages and the violation of his privileges, as was adjudged in the House of Lords in the case of Ashby and White,[5] how sacred then ought the powers, privileges, and immunities of a whole colony of loyal people, of all the freemen in it, to be looked upon and considered? And of what importance is it they should be defended and protected therein? As the enjoyment of such privileges and liberties, of such a free constitution of government, naturally tends to promote loyalty and obedience in a people, so the inhabitants of the colony of Connecticut (without arrogating) may, with the strictest veracity, say and insist that none of the colonies in the British dominions have approved themselves more loyal and obedient to the King's Majesty or more forward and zealous for promoting his service than they have constantly done. These principles of loyalty and zeal, the natural result of liberty and freedom, have influenced the colony to exert itself with a becoming vigorous spirit and resolution in public and benevolent services whenever they have been called upon or applied to for that purpose. It hath not only defended itself in its infant state against the violent insurrections of the Indians who formerly lived near or dwelt among them, and at all times down to the present day against all its enemies, but also, as it increased in numbers and strength, hath from time to time afforded aid, succor, and relief to the neighboring colonies. It is found by ancient memorials that the colony of Connecticut united with, and, at large expense and to most remarkable effect, [28] assisted the other colonies in carrying on the famous Indian war called the Narragansett War, which raged about the year 1675,[6] when (after a shocking destruction of the English people, their infant towns and settlements) those barbarians were totally subdued and the distressed country thereby saved from impending ruin.

From the year 1688 to about 1695 Connecticut, at sundry times and as occasions required, furnished expeditious aid and succor to the province of New York for the defense and protection of Albany and other places then exposed to frequent irruptions of the French and Indians; in which service, at the several times of their distress, were employed about five hundred men at the charge and expense of the colony, the amount whereof appears to be about five thousand pounds. Within the same times, help and relief were repeatedly raised and sent forward with great expedition for the defense of the frontiers in the county of Hampshire in the province of the Massachusetts Bay, which often happily tended to the safety, encouragement, and support of the people there, and was gratefully acknowledged and certified by some of the principal men in those parts. The expense of these services to the colony of Connecticut (besides the loss of lives in several encounters) amounted to near two thousand pounds.[7]

It appears also that the colony of Connecticut, in the years 1703, '04, '05, and '06, on repeated alarms occasioned by irruptions of the enemy on the frontier towns and places in the province of the [29] Massachusetts Bay, raised and sent numbers of men for the relief, succor, and defense of the inhabitants in those parts. These men were generally sent on horse-back for the sake of expedition, the occasions being urgent, though at some times on foot. And as those alarms were frequent, the succors were sent in, about twenty several parties succeeding one another. The number of men employed in those services was about seventeen hundred and of horse near nine hundred. And the total expense occasioned thereby to the colony (as may be still shown by the accounts thereof) amounted to near eleven thousand pounds. The currency in those times was about three fourths the value of sterling money. All these services were voluntarily performed by the small colony of Connecticut for the relief and protection of their fellow subjects in the other colonies (one of which in particular was under the immediate government of the crown) without receiving either money or any other aid from the crown or from the neighboring provinces.

In the expedition in 1710 against Port Royal, now Annapolis, when it was taken from the French, and the costly, disastrous expeditions set on foot against Canada in 1709 and 1711, the colony of Connecticut bore a full proportion of expense and sustained a very great loss of men. And the colony failed not likewise of bearing a large share in that memorable expedition formed by the New England governments against Cape Breton, in 1745, when it was reduced to the obedience of the British crown. This was a seasonable and important conquest, and [30] will not be forgotten while the principal articles which served as a basis for restoring the peace to Europe that followed it are had in remembrance.[8]

But the more recent instances of the loyalty, zeal, and serviceableness of the colony of Connecticut are such as follow.

In the year 1755, when forces were raised by the northern colonies for removing encroachments made on His Majesty's territories in America by the French, Connecticut raised a thousand men for that service, and also two thousand more the same year to reinforce the army at Lake George, then apprehended too weak to withstand the enemy. This number was two or three times the proportion of Connecticut compared with some other colonies concerned in that expedition. In 1756 it raised two thousand five hundred men, which was double the number proposed by the King's commander-in-chief for the colony's proportion in the service of that year. This was done by the colony, as it was supposed the southern colonies would fail of the proportion allotted for them to raise, and lest the service should suffer, it exerted itself in such duplicate proportion. In 1757 the proportion demanded by His Majesty's commander-in-chief for the service of that year being fourteen hundred men, the colony not only raised that number, but also, on intelligence of the attack on Fort William Henry, speedily sent forward about five thousand of the militia for the relief of that fortress and protection of the country, then in great consternation in those parts. And in 1758 an expedition was set on foot [31] for the reduction of Canada, and the colonies being called upon by the crown to raise as many men as the number of their inhabitants would admit of, and as it was apprehended that in case of success an end would be put to the war in these parts by that year's campaign, Connecticut exerted itself beyond all former efforts in hopes of its being the finishing stroke, and accordingly agreed to raise five thousand men, and actually had but few short of that number in the field. But as this important design failed of accomplishment at that time, the colony, by royal direction, was called upon strenuously to exert itself in the like service in 1759 and even until the end of the war. And as what hath been done by the colonies on that extraordinary occasion in 1758 seemed constantly to be made the rule of demand upon them afterwards, the annual requisition of the crown proved exceeding heavy upon the colony of Connecticut, for it had indeed exerted itself vastly beyond its ability and any just proportion in that year; yet nevertheless they agreed to raise the number demanded in every succeeding year of the war, being spirited as far as possible to yield the strictest obedience to the King's commands, and determined to persevere in his service with the utmost efforts. And in the present year, 1764, the colony hath raised upwards of two hundred and fifty men for the annoyance of the Indians and protection of His Majesty's subjects in other governments. These troops are now out on service at the direction of the King's commander-in-chief in North America.[9]

In these services, from the year 1755 to the year [32] 1762 inclusive, the expenses of the colony, over and above the Parliamentary grants (which have been received with the most sensible and humble gratitude), amounts to upwards of four hundred thousand pounds, the large arrears of which sum will remain a heavy, distressing burden upon the people for many years to come.[10] Moreover, several thousands of the hardiest and most able young men, the hope and strength of the farmers, have been destroyed, lost, and enervated in the many distant arduous campaigns during the course of this terrible war. The husbandry of the country (its only resource) has suffered and still suffers extremely hereby; and the colony will not recover itself from these disadvantages in a long tract of time. And although by the success of the military operations in America, large, extensive, and most valuable acquisitions have been made to the British dominions, yet the colony of Connecticut gains nothing thereby further than as it may be said to be concerned in the common cause and general interest of the whole. It had no lands to recover or even to secure from the enemy, as some other governments had; it hath no immediate trade with the Indians, nor will its situation admit of any but what may, by some individuals, be carried on through and so subject to the control of other colonies. The profits of this trade have ever been mostly in the hands of those whose proximity gave them peculiar advantages for it. Nay, instead of receiving particular benefit by these events, the colony will rather suffer disadvantage thereby in the emigration of its inhabitants, already thinned, for [33] settlement of the vacant lands in other provinces which are now secure from the enemy who formerly annoyed them. Therefore principles of loyalty and zeal for the King's service, principles of benevolence, humanity, and compassion for their fellow subjects in danger and distress, and the agreeable prospect, a laudable desire of enjoying quiet and peace in consequence of a general tranquillity in the land, must be considered as the genuine motives and springs inducing the colony of Connecticut to exert itself in the manner and to the degrees before-mentioned.

And now, when all these things are duly considered and viewed in a proper light, will it not be thought that the colony has good reason to hope and expect, in return for and in consequence of such services, if not to be indulged with greater and more extensive favors from the crown and nation, at least to be protected and secured in the full enjoyment of the rights and privileges essential to the freedom of Englishmen, instead of having those rights curtailed or infringed by charging on them a stamp duty, as proposed, or any other the like new and unprecedented taxation?

OBJECTION

Perhaps, after all that hath been offered, it will be objected by some that America ought, and is able, to bear a just proportion of the American expense, and that as the duty already charged will, they suppose, not be sufficient to defray that expense, it becomes necessary to make additions to the duties already laid.

[34]   ANSWER

First. In order to obviate and answer this objection it may be necessary to enter a little into a consideration of the occasion and nature of those charges which by some are denominated American expenses. That expense which is occasioned merely for the defense and protection of the new governments and acquisitions, it is conceived, ought not to be charged upon the colonies in general, as it is truly no other than a national interest, or an interest of the particular new governments or acquisitions, and consequently ought, where it is not purely national, to be laid on those whose immediate profit is advanced thereby. The old colonies, especially New England, were at the sole charge of settling and defending themselves, and that they should now be compelled to contribute towards settling others under much better advantages in that regard than they were, will not fail of being esteemed hard and injurious. If the expense arises in defending and securing the fur trade and the outposts requisite for carrying on the same, to oblige these colonies which receive no immediate advantage by it to bear a proportionable part of the burden will also be hard and unequal, and especially if that trade is sufficiently profitable to support itself; if otherwise, why is there so much care and mighty attention constantly exercised towards it? If the expense occurs in holding and protecting the new and large acquisitions, wherefore should the colonies bear that when they have no interest [35] in them? They do indeed properly belong to the crown, and will finally be disposed of and settled for the benefit of the crown and the nation in general, and not for the advantage of the colonies in particular. But,

Secondly. What America's proportionable part in the American expense will be is somewhat uncertain and difficult to determine. And in order to form any tolerable judgment in the case, it will be necessary to consider the wealth of the colonies compared with the mother country; their number of inhabitants compared with the extent of their own country; the nature of their climates, in some of which the cold seasons are of such long continuance as to occasion a consumption of the greatest part of their produce; their trade and commerce, the profits of which in general center in Great Britain; their business, advantages and disadvantages and other circumstances, such as their being, in a general way, obliged to spend so great a proportion of their labor in clearing, fencing, and preparing their lands for improvement; and that the surplus of their labor in many instances is but very little and in some nothing at all. The clear profits, therefore, to the colonies being so very inconsiderable, it must surely be found, on a just and reasonable computation, that their proportion of any general national expense, if anything, will be very small. But,

Thirdly. If, notwithstanding, it shall be judged necessary (which is even a difficult supposition) to [36] make an addition to the charges on America, yet is it humbly conceived, for the reasons already offered, it will not by any means ever be thought proper or just, in order to effect that purpose, it should be done in a way that shall be an infringement on the constitutions of the colonies or that will deprive the subjects in them of some of those important liberties and privileges which, as Englishmen and freemen, they so justly value, and have a legal and equitable right to, as well as the rest of their fellow subjects. Revenues are never raised in Great Britain by a violation of the constitution or any part of it, but the liberties and privileges of the subjects are always saved and maintained in those cases. And why the Americans should not value their privileges at as high a rate as their fellow subjects in Great Britain do theirs, and wherefore the same justice is not due to the one as to the other, what sufficient reasons can possibly be assigned? Therefore, whatever may be done in this matter it is humbly trusted will surely be effected in such manner as to leave the legislatures of the colonies entire, and the people in the full possession and enjoyment of their just rights and immunities. This, it is conceived, might be effected by a duty (if thought necessary and proper) on the importation of Negroes and on the fur trade, etc.; for although that on slaves may and doubtless will fall with most weight where the greatest numbers are imported, yet will none be charged thereby but such as voluntarily submit [37] to it; and was such importation lessened, which might indeed be some disadvantage to a few individuals, yet probably it would be attended with many salutary effects both with respect to Great Britain and her colonies in general. And as a principal article of the expense in America must be for protecting and securing the fur trade, what good reasons can be adduced wherefore that trade should not be so charged as to support itself? For (as hath been already hinted) if it will not bear this charge, why is it still held and maintained at such great expense?

Having thus shown that the English are a free people; that their freedom consists in these general privileges, that no laws can be made or abrogated without their consent by representatives, *and for that purpose have right to elect their representatives; that the American colonists are as really the King's subjects, as loyal, and have as much right to the general and fundamental privileges of the British constitution and to protection in the enjoyment thereof as the rest of their fellow subjects in the mother country; that, in consequence hereof, the colonies and plantations in America, according to the general principles of the national constitution, are vested with authority of legislation and have right to be represented in their Assemblies, in whom that authority is lodged, and with whose consent they are to be governed by the crown; that for the crown to govern these colonies* [38] *and plantations by and with the consent of the people in such legislative assemblies is properly and truly to govern them agreeable to the national constitution, or that it is as conformable to the fundamental principles of the British government that the subjects in the colonies should be represented in Assemblies or legislative bodies as that the subjects in Great Britain should be represented in Parliament or the supreme legislature of the nation, and that the government of the subjects, with the consent of their respective representatives, is founded on the same general and essential principles of liberty; that charging stamp duties, or internal taxes on the colony, by authority of Parliament, will be inconsistent with those authorities and privileges which the colonies and the people in them legally enjoy, and have, with the approbation of the supreme power of the nation, been in the use and possession of for a long course of years; as also the probability that such measures will, in the event, prove prejudicial to the national interest as well as hurtful to the colonies; together with some matters and circumstances more directly and peculiarly in favor of the colony of Connecticut, and the especial public and benevolent services performed by it on many occasions, which may justly merit some favorable considerations; and answered such objections as might probably be made against the tenor of the reasonings and representations herein offered and laid down; it is now concluded* that on account of these and such other [39] weighty reasons as may occur, a British Parliament whose design is to keep up that constitution, support the honor and prerogative of the crown, and maintain the privileges of the people, will have a tender regard for the rights and immunities of the King's subjects in the American colonies, and charge no internal taxations upon them without their consent.

PAMPHLET 7

JAMES OTIS, *THE RIGHTS OF THE BRITISH COLONIES ASSERTED AND PROVED*

BOSTON, 1764

INTRODUCTION

Of all the pronouncements issued by the colonists in the agitated year between the passage of the Sugar Act and that of the Stamp Act (April 1764–March 1765) none was more widely known or commented upon than James Otis' *The Rights of the British Colonies Asserted and Proved*. Written in the same conjunction of events, at approximately the same time, as Connecticut's *Reasons Why* (JHL Pamphlet 6), Oxenbridge Thacher's *Sentiments of a British American* (JHL Pamphlet 8), and Stephen Hopkins' *Rights of Colonies* (JHL Pamphlet 9), it surpassed them all in fame, and also in ambiguity of meaning and in the variety of interpretations given to it. It was printed originally in Boston with two important appendixes: the Boston Town Meeting's instructions to its representatives in the General Court, May 1764, which had been drafted by Samuel Adams; and the memorial presented by the Boston representatives to the General Court, which, written by Otis, was transmitted in turn by the House to the colony's agent in London "to be improved as he may judge proper." Before the year was out the pamphlet was reprinted in London, where it was advertised as "universally approved" of in the colonies and "highly necessary for the perusal of the members of both houses and of such who choose to make themselves masters of an argument so little understood but of great consequence to every British subject and lover of constitutional liberty." Reprinted at least three more times before the Stamp Act crisis was over, it was known by all who kept abreast of affairs on both sides of the Atlantic. And it was as widely misunderstood as it was praised and abused.[1]

The pamphlet stated baldly that "the power of Parliament is uncontrollable but by themselves, and we must obey . . . let the Parliament lay what burdens they please on us, we must, it is our duty to submit and patiently bear them." Yet the Massachusetts House of Representatives formally endorsed the pamphlet; extreme radicals in England declared it to be a "noble piece" that applied in original ways "all the great and glorious principles of government . . . which ever warmed Milton, Locke, or any patriot head"; and John Dickinson, praising Otis' "indefatigable zeal and undaunted courage" in defending American rights, sent the manuscript of his *Farmer's Letters* to him "to be disposed of as you think proper."[2] But others spoke of it with contempt. Its conclusions agreed almost completely with those of Thomas Hutchinson; but Hutchinson called it "a loose unconnected performance." On the other hand, though it denied Parliament's right to tax America so long as the colonies were unrepresented, Roger Sherman believed that it "conceded away the rights of Americans." Lord Mansfield in a speech in the House of Lords pointed out that the *Rights* everywhere admitted "the supremacy of the crown over the colonies" — a position he himself supported; but he defended Otis and the *Rights* only on the grounds of their "consequence among the people there." Nor has a consensus developed among modern historians. Some find the pamphlet "a closely reasoned statement"; but others say it is "diffuse and contradictory." And it is generally agreed that Otis repudiated the entire pamphlet in his later writings on American rights.[3]

Yet, properly understood, the pamphlet is not self-contradictory, nor did Otis repudiate it. The confused reaction to it was a response to the subtle, and politically untenable, position it attempted to maintain. The bold and original if somewhat slap-dash effort of a provincial American to define the limitations of Parliament's power over the colonies in terms of a comprehensive theory of the British constitution, it moved into new regions of thought, and marks an important stage in the growth of a revolutionary frame of mind and in the history of American constitutionalism. Otis' untenable subtleties — the result of an unsure, incomplete application of seventeenth-century doctrines to eighteenth-century issues — exposed the central problem of Anglo-American relations, and dramatized in their failure the inescapable imperative of the colonists' claims.

James Otis (1725–1783), the son of a politically ambitious lawyer, was educated at Harvard College with the class of 1743, thus preceding Jonathan Mayhew in that institution by one year. Like Mayhew, Otis participated in Whitefield's revival of 1740–41, and thereafter turned studiously to his books. He spent two postgraduate years at the college reading ancient and modern languages and literature. Several years as apprentice to the leading scholar of the Massachusetts bar, Jeremiah Gridley, followed, and in 1748 he began practice as a lawyer for himself. By the mid-fifties he had settled in Boston, and enjoyed not only an increasingly successful practice at the bar but membership in the literary and intellectual circle that so impressed John Adams when he first arrived as a fledgling lawyer in the provincial capital. Otis, Adams later recalled, had been an indefatigable student in college and after:

> He was well versed in Greek and Roman history, philosophy, oratory, poetry, and mythology. His classical studies had been unusually ardent, and his acquisitions uncommonly great . . . He was a passionate admirer of the Greek poets, especially of Homer; and he said it was in vain to attempt to read the poets in any language without being master of their prosody. This classic scholar was also a great master of the laws of nature and nations. He had read Pufendorf, Vattel, Heineccius; and, in the civil law, Domat, Justinian, and, upon occasions, consulted the *Corpus Juris* at large. It was a maxim which he inculcated on his pupils, as his patron in profession, Mr. Gridley, had done before him, '*that a lawyer ought never to be without a volume of natural*

or public law, or moral philosophy, on his table or in his pocket.' In the history, the common law, and statute laws of England he had no superior, at least in Boston.

His first publication (1760) was, significantly, not a political tract but a treatise on Latin prosody, which was recognized for its learning in England as well as in the colonies. A companion piece on Greek prosody may also have been written at that time, but if so it remained in manuscript.[4]

Yet, though a scholar in literature and law, Otis was scarcely a recluse. Besides his involvement with the everyday problems of the law, he followed and supported his father in the search for political preferment. Favored by the political organization built up in the 1750's by Governor Shirley and his son-in-law and successor Thomas Pownall, Otis was appointed justice of the peace in 1756 and advocate general of the vice-admiralty court two years later. But he wanted more, for himself and for his family. His father, speaker of the House of Representatives, had sought appointment to the Superior Court bench, and though he had not succeeded, he had obtained the promise of the next vacancy. But when it appeared, in September 1760, the governorship had rotated, and the new incumbent, Francis Bernard, then only one month in office and intent on building his own political machine on the interest of the lieutenant governor, Thomas Hutchinson, ignored the promise and appointed Hutchinson instead. "A more deliberate, cool, studied, corrupt appointment never was made," John Adams later wrote much in the mood of the time. Fortified by such a belief, and "most enthusiastically and frenzically" devoted to his father, the younger Otis turned on the administration in fury, assaulting it ruthlessly in print and in conversation. Finally, in absolute defiance, he resigned his post in the vice-admiralty court to attack the government's efforts to enforce the navigation acts.[5] The result was a series of court cases, the most famous of which, concerning writs of assistance, was tried in February 1761.

This dramatic suit heard by a Superior Court presided over by Hutchinson and in which Otis and his colleague Oxenbridge Thacher opposed none other than the venerable Jeremiah Gridley, turned in law on the right of the Superior Court to act as a court of exchequer in issuing the disputed search warrants, and on whether or not such writs were still authorized in law in England. But Otis' speech before the court soared beyond these technicalities into the realm of political and social theory and the principles of British constitutionalism. Here, in the argument he reached at the peak of his peroration, and in the authorities he cited in support — recorded in notes scribbled by the intent eye-witness John Adams — there lies revealed the peculiar tendency of thought which would shape, and alone explains, the intended meaning of *The Rights of the British Colonies Asserted and Proved.* The ultimate problem, Otis said, was not so much the writs as the laws of Parliament controlling the American economy that made such writs necessary. These navigation laws and the writs issued to enforce them invaded the invaluable "privilege of house" by which every subject of English laws was rendered "as secure in his house as a prince in his castle." Both navigation laws and writs of as-

sistance, therefore, violate "the fundamental principles of law"; both, therefore, run against the constitution, and they are, consequently, void. For "an
act against the constitution is void: an act against natural equity is void: and
. . . the executive courts must pass such acts into disuse," the common law
having the power to control an act of Parliament.[6]

It was a doctrine familiar to English law; and to substantiate it Otis cited
Coke's celebrated judgment in *Bonham's Case* (1610) that "it appears in our
books that in many cases the common law will control acts of Parliament, and
sometimes adjudge them to be utterly void: for when an act of Parliament is
against common right or reason, or repugnant, or impossible to be performed,
the common law will control it, and adjudge such act to be void" — to which
Otis would add for further support the dicta of other seventeenth-century
justices endorsing Coke's words and also, significantly, the comments of the
Swiss political theorist Emmerich de Vattel, who, approaching the same question from a different point of view, arrived at a closer approximation to the
modern idea of judicial review than Coke had.[7] For Coke had not meant
that positive, statute laws were restricted to areas defined by a higher law
binding on Parliament and that they could be nullified — declared to be
legally nonexistent — by the judges as custodians of the higher law when
they exceeded these bounds.[8] Nor had Coke conceived of his dictum as going
beyond private law considerations into the realm of constitutional construction. Coke had meant only that the basis of statute law, like that of common
law, was reason and justice, and that when laws created unreasonable or
manifestly unjust or self-contradictory situations — situations wherein law
violated the principles of law — it was the duty of the courts, not to annihilate the statutory provisions, but, as Coke's successor Hobart put it, "to mold
them to the truest and best use." Coke's concern had been the traditional one
of interpreting statutes strictly when reason and justice required it, adjusting,
that is, in the lower courts inequities and impracticalities created by decrees
of the highest court, Parliament.[9]

It was upon the judicial nature of Parliament, and its presumed devotion
to the same principles of justice and reason that animated all courts of law
that Coke's doctrine ultimately rested. And it was, consequently, the great
historic shift in the understanding of Parliament's role that took place in the
mid- and later seventeenth century that gave a new meaning to Coke's doctrine, and that created for James Otis, a century later, the central intellectual
problem of his life. In the course of the searing controversies of the English
Civil War — controversies that destroyed the foundations of public order and
touched off a series of penetrating discussions of public authority — Coke's
assumption that Parliament was animated by the same sense of justice and
reason as other courts, and that its pronouncements were susceptible to equitable interpretation by judges, fell away before a conception of Parliament as
the monopolist of absolute sovereign power, the creator not the discoverer of
law, unbound by any rulings but its own. In the Glorious Revolution, which
secured the absolute supremacy of Parliament over all other agencies of gov-

ernment, Coke's presumptions in *Bonham's Case* were, in effect, abandoned, and the location of an absolute and arbitrary legislative authority fixed firmly and indisputably in Parliament.[10] — *In effect* abandoned: but not in law; for Coke's words, reinforced by later, more expansive pronouncements, remained on the books, to the bewilderment of those who would apply them to an absolute, unchallengable legislative sovereign distinct from courts of law. So in 1701 Chief Justice Holt declared that "what my Lord *Coke* says in *Dr. Bonham's Case* . . . is a very reasonable and true saying"; but he added that "an act of Parliament can do no wrong, though it may do several things that look pretty odd." And then for fourteen folio pages the great jurist wavered, in the words of a modern commentator, "helplessly between two incompatible opinions . . . [:] that the validity of an act of Parliament cannot be questioned; but that all the same it may be void if it enacts . . . something contrary to the axioms of natural justice in all laws." [11] The dilemma was even more acute for Otis seeking leverage against the consolidated power of Parliament than it had been for Holt, for in the intervening half century opinion in England had hardened. By 1761, when Otis introduced the doctrine of *Bonham's Case* into the discussion of Anglo-American relations, the dominant understanding of English jurists and scholars — an understanding which colonial resistance would only confirm — was classically phrased by Blackstone, who admitted that the rule was familiar in law that acts of Parliament contrary to reason are void; "but if the Parliament will positively enact a thing to be done which is unreasonable, I know of no power that can control it." So too Lord Camden, who would oppose the Stamp Act on the ground that "there are some things" a sovereign body cannot rightfully do, in the end concluded that once Parliament did declare its will against right "he did not think himself, nor any man else, at liberty to call it any more in question." [12]

How powerful this view was, how fully it had superseded Coke's doctrine, and how untenable it had rendered compromises like Holt's, remained for the colonists in 1761 still to be discovered. That it was discovered, quickly and decisively, was in large part the result of Otis' insistent refusal to see the radical tendencies implicit in the use of Coke's words in such altered circumstances: to see the significance of the fact that it was no longer primarily private-law considerations but, rather, the organization of government that was under discussion, and that courts were now assumed to be distinct from legislative bodies. The surface applicability of Coke's words was sufficient for Otis. He would never grasp — and this would be his tragedy — what Thomas Hutchinson saw so clearly, that Parliament's power, as it was conceived in the eighteenth century, created legal right,

> the Parliament being beyond dispute the supreme legislature of the British dominions; but our friends to liberty take advantage of a maxim they find in Lord *Coke* that an act of Parliament against Magna Carta or the peculiar rights of Englishmen is *ipso facto* void. This, taken in the latitude the people are often enough disposed to take it, must be fatal to all government.[13]

In the three years between the introduction of *Bonham's Case* into the Writs controversy and the publication of *The Rights of the British Colonies,* Otis' reputation as an irresponsible malcontent intent on the destruction of government grew rapidly. His attacks on the administration became wild, it was said, "beyond all bounds of common decency." His enemies called him a "thoughtless madman" whose election to the General Court threatened to "shake this province to its foundations." And there were in fact signs of mental instability. Even those who sympathized with his politics grew fearful. John Adams as early as 1759 had noted not only that Otis was "extremely quick and elastic" and that "his apprehension is as quick as his temper," but that he "springs, and twitches his muscles about in thinking." Six years later his description darkened: Otis was then

> fiery and feverous. His imagination flames, his passions blaze. He is liable to great inequalities of temper — sometimes in despondency, sometimes in a rage. The rashness and imprudences into which his excess of zeal have formerly transported him have made him enemies whose malicious watch over him occasion more caution and more cunning and more inexplicable passages in his conduct than formerly.[14]

But if he was mad it was in a way that most politicians would envy. For, as Lord Mansfield remarked in a comment on Otis, "one madman often makes many. Massaniello was mad, nobody doubts it; yet for all that, he overturned the government of Naples. Madness is catching in all popular assemblies, and upon all popular matters." Otis' political effectiveness grew; and while he was erratic in politics to the point of being believed to have sold out to the administration, "betraying his friends and rant[ing] on the side of the prerogative for an whole year" in exchange for certain appointments for members of his family, he was only too consistent in his vilification of prerogative.[15] His first political pamphlet, *A Vindication of the Conduct of the House of Representatives of the Province of the Massachusetts-Bay* . . . (Boston, 1762) was an attack on the governor for expending public money without authorization of the House; it is described even by his most disapproving biographer as "a clear, brilliant, and powerful statement of Whig political theory." [16]

He was the acknowledged leader of the popular forces in Massachusetts when the Sugar Act was passed, and he participated fully in the deliberations of the House in the spring and summer of 1764 when the colony's objections to Grenville's taxation program were being formulated. *The Rights of the British Colonies Asserted and Proved,* published in July of that year and adopted by the House as a semiofficial statement,[17] is the effort of a learned, erratic man, to constrict the sovereignty of a supreme Parliament with the legal logic of the age of Coke.

Though in a formal sense the pamphlet has a clear and logical organization — discussions first of the nature of government as such, then of the nature of colonies, then of the natural rights of colonists, and finally of the specific question of the political and civil rights of the British colonists — it is heavily disbalanced in its emphasis on the first and fourth sections, and within each, jumbled in the progression of thought. It abounds with digressions and apparent irrelevancies. In some places it is slowly paced, carefully reasoned, and thickly documented; in others it appears to have been thrown together in a wild rush without regard for proof, logical coherence, or even syntax. But the central point, however paradoxical, is never in doubt. In the British world the "supreme absolute power [which] is *originally* and *ultimately* in the people" and which "*must* exist in and preside over every society" was entrusted to Parliament in the Convention of 1688 "and assented to by the first representative of the nation chosen afterwards, and by every Parliament and by almost every man ever since but the bigots to the indefeasible power of tyrants civil and ecclesiastic." The power of Parliament, thus grounded in necessity and right, "is uncontrollable but by themselves, and we must obey. They only can repeal their own acts . . . let the Parliament lay what burdens they please on us, we must, it is our duty to submit and patiently bear them, till they will be pleased to relieve us." Yet Parliament, though it can impose an absolute prohibition on colonial trade, cannot, for all its power, tax the colonies, for the colonies are not represented in that body. "The imposition of taxes . . . is absolutely irreconcilable with the rights of the colonists as British subjects and as men . . . The very act of taxing exercised over those who are not represented appears to me to be depriving them of one of their most essential rights as freemen, and if continued seems to be in effect an entire disfranchisement of every civil right." [18]

Thus Parliament can do anything, but there are some things it cannot do. It is hardly surprising that Otis' contemporaries were confused and drew from the pamphlet conflicting conclusions. Yet for Otis this doctrine was not self-contradictory. For he insisted that Coke's considerations were still valid, though applied in these different circumstances. He insisted that prohibitions on Parliament were part of its very nature as an organ of the constitution; they were not imposed from without but developed from within out of the necessities of logic, reason, and justice. Parliament can no more tax unrepresented people, he wrote in a crucial passage of the pamphlet, than it can "make 2 and 2, 5: omnipotency cannot do it." Parliament cannot alter a law of God or of logic. Its function is to act for the "good of the whole," but it does not create that good: God does. It does not create law, it articulates it: "*jus dicere* only," he wrote, directing to Parliament the precept Coke's contemporary Francis Bacon had applied to judges and courts of law, "*jus dare*, strictly speaking, belongs alone to GOD." [19]

But suppose, as in the present situation, by misinformation and misunderstanding — for members of Parliament were, after all, human — Parliament did declare something "contrary to eternal truth, equity, and justice." What then? Such a declaration would, necessarily, be void,

and so it would be adjudged by the Parliament itself when convinced of their mistake. Upon this great principle Parliaments repeal such acts as soon as they find they have been mistaken in having declared them to be for the public good when in fact they were not so. When such mistake is evident and palpable, as in the instances in the Appendix, the judges of the executive courts have declared the act "of a whole Parliament void." See here the grandeur of the British constitution! See the wisdom of our ancestors! The supreme *legislative* and the supreme *executive* are a perpetual check and balance to each other. If the supreme executive errs it is informed by the supreme legislative in Parliament. If the supreme legislative errs it is informed by the supreme executive in the King's courts of law . . . This is government! This is a constitution! to preserve which . . . has cost oceans of blood and treasure in every age; and the blood and the treasure have upon the whole been well spent.[20]

In the light of such a view, both an explanation of and the solution for the present problem of threatening Parliamentary taxation became clear. Parliament could scarcely have wished to violate a law of nature or of reason. It had been deceived; and it was not difficult to see by whom. "Gentlemen have had departments in America the functions of which they have not been fortunate in executing." Their ill-advised measures have created popular opposition, and in reports home they have found it useful to characterize the colonists as "factious, seditious, and inclined to democracy whenever they have refused passive obedience to provincial mandates as arbitrary as those of a Turkish bashaw." These bizarre stories, Englishmen of all ranks have unfortunately swallowed like "a bottle bubble or any other story of a cock and a bull"; but in fact the colonists were dutiful subjects who "revere our mother country, and adore our King." Let Parliament be undeceived, and it will repeal acts that "through mistake or other human infirmities" may have been passed in violation of the constitution or of the common good. The solution, therefore, is for the colonists dutifully to petition Parliament and the King, to inform them of the truth concerning America, and to point out the errors Parliament has inadvertently made and has in contemplation. No more than that, by the very nature of the constitution, was needed.[21]

It was a benign position, counselling protest and patience but no more until the self-equilibrating constitution corrected its own errors. But the sense of danger and constitutional innovation officialdom derived from the pamphlet was realistic enough, for the ancient doctrines applied to current problems took on new and challenging meanings — too new and too challenging for Otis himself to accept. An unjust law must be obeyed, he wrote, but if it is clearly against "*natural* equity, the executive courts will adjudge such act void. If there is not a right of private judgment to be exercised, so far at least as to petition for a repeal or to determine the expediency of risking a trial at law, the Parliament may make itself arbitrary, which it is conceived it cannot by the constitution." So too he added, after quoting a cautionary legal comment of 1712 to the effect that "judges will strain hard rather than interpret an act void, *ab initio*," that "*This is granted, but still [Parliament's] authority is not boundless if subject to the control of judges in any case.*" Was this not to restrict the power of Parliament by a higher law, a fundamental law, enforced by ordinary courts? Others would conclude that it was, and repudiate it as heretical and anarchical. But Otis himself would stand amazed at such charges. His meaning was still close to that of his sources, though applied in these altered circumstances. He did not mean that courts could nullify statutory enactments, but only that the courts, in interpreting statutes in cases that came before them, may indicate their belief that "the Parliament have erred or are mistaken in a matter of fact or of right . . ." Courts, Otis meant, are like public-spirited citizens, who have the obligation "to show [Parliament] the truth," but they have no authority to impose compliance; only Parliament could declare what is and what is not law.[22]

From these central positions an array of secondary but important considerations flowed: Otis' explicit denial of any distinction between internal and external taxation; his repeated assertion that the colonists ought to be allowed representatives in Parliament, and that once they had such representatives, Parliament would have the right to tax them; and his view that not only the regulation but the total annihilation of colonial trade lay well within the powers of Parliament. Related too were lesser points, some mere curiosities, some significant in the development of American political theory: the argument that autocracy decreases in effectiveness as the size of the polity increases; the view that the ultimate sovereignty of the people was not something merely conceptual but quite concrete and real: that in fact it had, in recent history — in the Convention Parliament of 1688 — been exercised; the uneasy denial of a Lockean state of nature and of a Lockean social contract combined with the reiterated endorsement of the idea of a governmental contract and of a fiduciary government; the repudiation of the colonial agents as true representatives of the colonies; the deduction of the colonies' rights and constitutional status from the example of Ireland.

Remarkably rich in ideas, though ill-balanced and erratic in composition, the pamphlet made a logical whole in the context of Otis' primary beliefs. Yet, whatever the fine logic of these beliefs may have been — logic that allowed Otis to claim at one and the same time that Parliament was all powerful but that there were things it could not do, that Parliament, if absolute, could not be arbitrary, and to claim this on the authority of the greatest names in English law — their congruence with reality was doubtful. Better politicians than Otis sensed this at once. For Hutchinson, for Adams, for Camden, for Blackstone — for all those who grasped more firmly than Otis the reality of power in the eighteenth-century world — the idea of an automatic, inner self-correction of Parliamentary error was a dangerous fiction. Parliament was sovereign; its legal powers were unlimited. Was there nothing to do but obey?

Within a year Otis was challenged by writers from left and right who claimed both that he was a craven sycophant of the administration and a dangerous revolutionary. In the ensuing controversies, recorded in Pamphlet 11, Otis — sensitive, wildly impetuous, convinced of a logic no one else would see and frantic to explain it — was destroyed as a spokesman for America.

THE/RIGHTS/OF THE/*British Colonies*/Asserted and proved./*By* James Otis, *Esq;/*

*Hæc omnis regio et celsi plaga pinea montis/Cedat amicitiæ Teucrorum: et fœderis æquas/Dicamus leges, sociósque in regna vocemus./Considant, si tantus amor, et mœnia condant./*VIRG./

BOSTON:/Printed and Sold by EDES and GILL, in Queen-Street./M,DCC,LXIV./

Introduction

Of the Origin of Government

The origin of *government* has in all ages no less perplexed the heads of lawyers and politicians than the origin of *evil* has embarrassed divines and philosophers, and 'tis probable the world may receive a satisfactory solution on *both* those points of inquiry at the *same* time.

The various opinions on the origin of *government* have been reduced to four. 1. That dominion is founded in *grace*. 2. On *force* or mere *power*. 3. On *compact*. 4. On *property*.

The first of these opinions is so absurd, and the world has paid so very dear for embracing it, especially under the administration of the *Roman pontiffs,* that mankind seem at this day to be in a great measure cured of their madness in this particular, and the notion is pretty generally exploded and hissed off the stage.

To those who lay the foundation of government in *force* and mere *brutal power* it is objected that their system destroys all distinction between right and wrong; that it overturns all morality, and leaves it to every man to do what is right in his own eyes; that it leads directly to *skepticism,* and ends in *atheism*. When a man's will and pleasure is his only rule and guide, what safety can there be either for him or against him, but in the point of a sword?

[4] On the other hand the gentlemen in favor of the *original compact* have been often told that *their* system is chimerical and unsupported by reason or experience. Questions like the following have been frequently asked them, and may be again.

"When and where was the original compact for introducing government into any society, or for creating a society, made? Who were present and parties to such compact? Who acted for infants and women, or who appointed guardians for them? Had these guardians power to bind both infants and women during life and their posterity after them? Is it in nature or reason that a guardian should by his own act perpetuate his power over his ward and bind him and his posterity in chains? Is not every man born as free by nature as his father? Has he not the same natural right to think and act and contract for himself? Is it possible for a man to have a natural right to make a slave of himself or of his posterity? Can a father supersede the laws of nature? What man is or ever was born free if every man is not? What will there be to distinguish the next generation of men from their forefathers, that they should not have the same right to make original compacts as their ancestors had? If every man has such right, may there not be as many original compacts as there are men and women born or to be born? Are not women born as free as men? Would it not be infamous to assert that the ladies are all slaves by nature? If every man and woman born or to be born has and will have a right to be consulted and must accede to the original compact before they can with any kind of justice be said to be bound by it, will not the compact be ever forming and never finished, ever making but never done? Can it with propriety be called a compact, original or derivative, that is ever in treaty but never concluded?"

When it has been said that each man is bound as soon as he accedes, and that the consent may be either express or tacit, it has been asked, "What is a *tacit* consent or compact? Does it not appear plain that those who refuse their assent cannot be bound? If one is at liberty to [5] accede or not, is he not also at liberty to *recede* on the discovery of some intolerable fraud and abuse that has been palmed upon him by the rest of the high contracting parties? Will not natural equity in several special cases rescind the original compacts of great men as effectually as those of little men are rendered null and void in the ordinary course of a court of chancery?"

There are other questions which have been started and a resolution of them demanded which may perhaps be deemed indecent by those who hold the prerogatives of an earthly monarch and even the power of a plantation government so sacred as to think it little less than blasphemy to inquire into their origin and foundation, while the government of the supreme *ruler* of the universe is every day discussed with less ceremony and decency than the administration of a petty German prince. I hope the reader will consider that I am at present only mentioning such questions as have been put by highfliers and others in church and state who would exclude all compact between a sovereign and his people, without offering my own sentiments upon them; this however I presume I may be allowed hereafter to do without offense. Those who want a full answer to them may consult Mr. Locke's discourses on government, M. De Vattel's law of nature and nations, and their own consciences.

"What state were Great Britain, Ireland, and the plantations left in by the abdication of James II? Was it a state of nature or of civil government? If a state of civil government, where were the supreme legislative and executive powers from the abdication to the election of William and Mary? Could the Lords and Commons be called a complete Parliament or supreme power without a King to head them? Did any law of the land or any original compact previous to the abdication provide that on such an event the supreme power should devolve on the two houses? Were not both houses so manifestly puzzled with the novelty and strangeness of the event, and so far from finding any act of Parliament, book case, or precedent to help them that they disputed in solemn conference by what name to call the action, and at last gave it [6] one as new in our language and in that of Parliament as the thing itself was in fact?" * 1

If on this memorable and very happy event the three kingdoms and the dominions fell back into a state of *nature,* it will be asked "Whether every man and woman were not then equal? If so, had not every one of them a natural and equitable right to be consulted in the choice of a new King or in the formation of a new original compact or government if any new form had been made? Might not the nation at that time have rightfully changed the monarchy into a republic or any form that might seem best? Could any change from a state of nature take place without universal consent, or at least without the consent of the *majority* of the individuals? Upon the principles of the original compact as commonly explained and understood, could a few hundred men who before the dissolution of the government had been called, and in fact were, lords, knights, and gentlemen have lawfully made that glorious deliverer and defender William III rightful King?" Such an one he certainly was, and such have been all his illustrious successors to the present happy times, when we have the joy to see the scepter swayed in justice, wisdom, and mercy by our lawful sovereign, George the Third, a prince who glories in being a Briton born, and whom may God long preserve and prosper.

"If upon the abdication all were reduced to a state of nature, had not

---

* On King James's leaving the kingdom and *abdicating* the government, the Lords would have the word *desertion* made use of, but the Commons thought it was not comprehensive enough, for that the King might then have liberty of returning. The Scots rightly called it a forfeiture of the crown, and this in plain English is the sense of the term *abdication* as by the Convention and every Parliament since applied. See the history and debates of the Convention, and the acts then made.

apple women and orange girls as good a right to give their respectable suffrages for a new King as the philosopher, courtier, *petit-maître,* and politician? Were these and ten millions of others such ever more consulted on that occasion than the multitude now are in the adjustment of that real modern farce, an election of a King of the Romans, which serves as a contrast to the grandeur of the ancient republics, and shows the littleness of the [7] modern German and some other gothic constitutions in their present degenerate state?

"In the election of William III, were the votes of Ireland and the plantations ever called for or once thought of till the affair was settled? Did the Lords and Commons who happened to be then in and about Westminster represent and act for the individuals not only of the three kingdoms but for all the *freeborn and as yet unconquered possessors and proprietors of their own money-purchased, blood-purchased plantations, which, till lately, have been defended with little or no assistance from Great Britain?* Were not those who did not vote in or for the new model at liberty upon the principles of the compact to remain in what some call the delectable state of nature, to which by the hypothesis they were reduced, or to join themselves to any other state whose solemn league and covenant they could subscribe? Is it not a first principle of the original compact that all who are bound should bind *themselves?* Will not common sense without much learning or study dictate obvious answers to all the above questions? And, say the opposers of the original compact and of the natural equality and liberty of mankind, will not those answers infallibly show that the doctrine is a piece of *metaphysical* jargon and *systematical* nonsense?" Perhaps not.

With regard to the fourth opinion, that *dominion is founded in property,* what is it but playing with words? Dominion in one sense of the term is synonymous with property, so one cannot be called the foundation of the other but as one *name* may appear to be the foundation or cause of another.

Property cannot be the foundation of dominion as synonymous with government; for on the supposition that property has a precarious existence antecedent to government, and though it is also admitted that the security of property is one end of government but that of little estimation even in the view of a *miser* when life and liberty of locomotion and further accumulation are placed in competition, it must be a very absurd way of speaking to assert that *one* end of government is the foundation of government. If the ends of government are to be considered as its foundation, it cannot with truth or propriety be [8] said that government is founded on any *one* of those ends; and therefore government is not founded on property or its security *alone,* but at least on something else in conjunction. It is however true in fact and *experience,* as the great, the incomparable *Harrington* has most abundantly demonstrated in his *Oceana* and other divine writings, that empire follows the balance of *property.* 'Tis also certain that *property* in fact generally *confers* power, though the possessor of it may not have much more wit than a mole or a musquash: and this is too often the cause that riches are sought after without the least concern about the right application of them. But is the fault in the riches, or the general law of nature, or the unworthy possessor? It will never follow from all this that government is *rightfully* founded on *property* alone. What shall we say then? Is not government founded on *grace?* No. Nor on *force?* No. Nor on *compact?* Nor *property?* Not altogether on either. Has it *any* solid foundation, any chief cornerstone but what accident, chance, or confusion may lay one moment and destroy the next? I think it has an everlasting foundation in the *unchangeable will of* God, the author of nature, whose laws never vary. The same omniscient, omnipotent, infinitely good and gracious Creator of the universe who has been pleased to make it necessary that what we call matter should *gravitate* for the celestial bodies to roll round their axes, dance their orbits, and perform their various revolutions in that beautiful order and concert which we all admire has made it *equally* necessary that from *Adam* and *Eve* to these degenerate days the different sexes should sweetly *attract* each other, form societies of *single* families, of which *larger* bodies and communities are as naturally, mechanically, and necessarily combined as the dew of heaven and the soft distilling rain is collected by the all-enlivening heat of the sun. *Government* is therefore most evidently founded *on the necessities of our nature.* It is by no means an *arbitrary* thing depending merely on *compact* or *human will* for its existence.

We come into the world forlorn and helpless; and if left alone and to ourselves at any one period of our lives, we should soon die in want, despair, or distraction. So kind is that [9] hand, though little known or regarded, which feeds the rich and the poor, the blind and the naked, and provides for the safety of infants by the principle of parental love, and for that of men by government! We have a King who neither slumbers nor sleeps, but eternally watches for our good, whose rain falls on the just and on the unjust: yet while they live, move, and have their being in Him, and cannot account for either or for anything else, so stupid and wicked are some men as to deny his existence, blaspheme his most evident government, and disgrace their nature.

Let no man think I am about to commence advocate for *despotism* because I affirm that government is founded on the necessity of our natures and that an original supreme, sovereign, absolute, and uncontrollable *earthly* power *must* exist in and preside over every society, from whose final decisions there can be no appeal but directly to Heaven. It is therefore *originally* and *ultimately* in the people. I say this supreme absolute power is *originally* and *ultimately* in the people; and they never did in fact *freely,* nor can they *rightfully* make an absolute, unlimited renunciation of this divine right.† It is ever in the nature of the thing given in *trust* and on a condition the performance of which no mortal can dispense with, namely, that the person or persons on whom the sovereignty is conferred by the people shall *incessantly* consult *their* good. Tyranny of all kinds is to be abhorred, whether it be in the hands of one or of the few or of the many. And though "in the last age a generation of men sprung up that would flatter princes with an opinion that *they* have a *divine right* to absolute power," yet "slavery is so vile and miserable an estate of man and so directly opposite to the generous temper and courage of our nation that 'tis hard to be conceived that an *Englishman,* much less a *gentleman,* should plead for it," ‡ [2] especially at a time when the finest [10] writers of the most polite nations on the continent of *Europe* are enraptured with the beauties of the civil constitution of *Great Britain,* and envy her no less for the *freedom* of her sons than for her immense *wealth* and *military* glory.

But let the *origin* of government be placed where it may, the *end* of it is manifestly the good of *the whole. Salus populi suprema lex esto*[3] is of the law of nature and part of that grand charter given the human race (though too many of them are afraid to assert it) by the only monarch in the universe who has a clear and indisputable right to *absolute* power, because he is the *only* ONE who is *omniscient* as well as *omnipotent.*

It is evidently contrary to the first principles of reason that supreme *unlimited* power should be in the hands of *one* man. It is the greatest

---

† The power of GOD Almighty is the power that can properly and strictly be called supreme and absolute. In the order of nature immediately under him comes the power of a simple *democracy* or the power of the whole over the whole. Subordinate to both these are all other political powers, from that of the French monarch to a petty constable.

‡ Mr. Locke.

"idolatry begotten by *flattery* on the body of *pride"* that could induce one to think that a *single mortal* should be able to hold so great a power if ever so well inclined. Hence the origin of *deifying* princes: it was from the trick of gulling the vulgar into a belief that their tyrants were *omniscient,* and that it was therefore right that they should be considered as *omnipotent.* Hence the *dii majorum et minorum gentium,* the great, the monarchical, the little, provincial, subordinate, and subaltern gods, demigods, and semidemigods, ancient and modern. Thus deities of all kinds were multiplied and increased in *abundance,* for every devil incarnate who could enslave a people acquired a title to *divinity;* and thus the "rabble of the skies" was made up of locusts and caterpillars, lions, tigers, and harpies, and other devourers translated from plaguing the earth! § [4]

The *end* of government being the *good* of mankind points out its great duties: it is above all things to provide for the security, the quiet, and happy enjoyment of life, liberty, and property. There is no one act which a government can have a *right* to make that does not tend to the advancement of the security, tranquillity, and prosperity of the people. If life, liberty, and property could be [11] enjoyed in as great perfection in *solitude* as in *society* there would be no need of government. But the experience of ages has proved that such is the nature of man, a weak, imperfect being, that the valuable ends of life cannot be obtained without the union and assistance of many. Hence 'tis clear that men cannot live apart or independent of each other. In solitude men would perish, and yet they cannot live together without contests. These contests require some arbitrator to determine them. The necessity of a common, indifferent, and impartial judge makes all men seek one, though few find him in the *sovereign power* of their respective states or anywhere else in *subordination* to it.

Government is founded *immediately* on the necessities of human nature and *ultimately* on the will of God, the author of nature, who has not left it to men in general to choose whether they will be members of society or not, but at the hazard of their senses if not of their lives. Yet it is left to every man as he comes of age to choose *what society* he will continue to belong to. Nay, if one has a mind to turn *hermit,* and after he has been born, nursed, and brought up in the arms of society, and

§ Kingcraft and priestcraft have fallen out so often that 'tis a wonder this grand and ancient alliance is not broken off forever. Happy for mankind will it be when such a separation shall take place.

acquired the habits and passions of social life is willing to run the risk of starving alone, which is generally most unavoidable in a state of hermitage, who shall hinder him? I know of no human law founded on the law of *nature* to restrain him from separating himself from all the species if he can find it in his heart to leave them, unless it should be said it is against the great law of *self-preservation:* but of this every man will think himself *his own judge.*

The few *hermits* and *misanthropes* that have ever existed show that those states are *unnatural.* If we were to take out from them those who have made great *worldly* gain of their *godly* hermitage and those who have been under the madness of *enthusiasm* or *disappointed* hopes in their *ambitious* projects for the detriment of mankind, perhaps there might not be left ten from *Adam* to this day.

The form of government is by *nature* and by *right* so far left to the *individuals* of each society that they may alter it from a simple democracy or government of all over all to any other form they please. Such alteration may [12] and ought to be made by express compact. But how seldom this right has been asserted, history will abundantly show. For once that it has been fairly settled by compact, *fraud, force,* or *accident* have determined it an hundred times. As the people have gained upon tyrants, these have been obliged to relax *only* till a fairer opportunity has put it in their power to encroach again.

But if every prince since *Nimrod* had been a tyrant, it would not prove a *right* to tyrannize. There can be no prescription old enough to supersede the law of nature and the grant of GOD Almighty, who has given to all men a natural right to be *free,* and they have it ordinarily in their power to make themselves so if they please.

Government having been proved to be necessary by the law of nature, it makes no difference in the thing to call it from a certain period *civil.* This term can only relate to form, to additions to or deviations from the substance of government: this being founded in nature, the superstructures and the whole administration should be conformed to the law of universal reason. A supreme legislative and a supreme executive power must be placed *somewhere* in every commonwealth. Where there is no other positive provision or compact to the contrary, those powers remain in the *whole body of the people.* It is also evident there can be but *one* best way of depositing those powers; but what that way is, mankind have been disputing in peace and in war more than five thousand years. If we could suppose the individuals of a community met to deliberate whether it were best to keep those powers in *their own* hands or dispose of them in *trust,* the following questions would occur: — Whether those two great powers of *legislation* and *execution* should remain united? If so, whether in the hands of the many or jointly or severally in the hands of a few, or jointly in some one individual? If both those powers are retained in the hands of the many, where nature seems to have placed them originally, the government is a simple *democracy* or a government of all over all. This can be administered only by establishing it as a first principle that the votes of the majority shall be taken as the voice of the whole. If those powers are lodged in the hands of a few, [13] the government is an *aristocracy* or *oligarchy.*|| Here too the first principles of a practicable administration is that the majority rules the whole. If those great powers are both lodged in the hands of one man, the government is a *simple monarchy,* commonly though falsely called *absolute* if by that term is meant a right to do as one pleases. — *Sic volo, sic jubeo, stet pro ratione voluntas* belongs not of right to any mortal man.[5]

The same law of nature and of reason is equally obligatory on a *democracy,* an *aristocracy,* and a *monarchy:* whenever the administrators in any of those forms deviate from truth, justice, and equity, they verge towards tyranny, and are to be opposed; and if they prove incorrigible they will be *deposed* by the people, if the people are not rendered too abject. Deposing the administrators of a *simple democracy* may sound oddly, but it is done every day and in almost every vote. A, B, and C, for example, make a *democracy.* Today A and B are for so vile a measure as a standing army. Tomorrow B and C vote it out. This is as really deposing the former administrators as setting up and making a new King is deposing the old one. *Democracy* in the one case and *monarchy* in the other still remain; all that is done is to change the administration.

The first principle and great end of government being to provide for the best good of all the people, this can be done only by a supreme legislative and executive ultimately in the people or whole community where God has placed it; but the inconveniences, not to say impossibility, attending the consultations and operations of a large body of people have made it necessary to transfer the power of the whole to a *few.* This necessity gave rise to deputation, proxy, or a right of representation.

|| For the sake of the unlettered reader 'tis noted that monarchy means the power of one great man, aristocracy and oligarchy that of a few, and democracy that of all men.

A power of legislation without a power of execution in the same or other hands would be futile and vain. On the other hand, a power of execution, supreme or subordinate, without an *independent* legislature would be perfect despotism.

[14] The difficulties attending an universal congress, especially when society became large, have brought men to consent to a delegation of the power of all: the weak and the wicked have too often been found in the same interest, and in most nations have not only brought these powers *jointly* into the hands of one or some few of their number, but made them *hereditary* in the families of despotic nobles and princes.

The wiser and more virtuous states have always provided that the representation of the people should be *numerous*. Nothing but life and liberty are *naturally* hereditable: this has never been considered by those who have *tamely* given up both into the hands of a tyrannical oligarchy or despotic monarchy.

The analogy between the natural, or material, as it is called, and the moral world is very obvious; GOD himself appears to us at some times to cause the intervention or combination of a *number* of simple principles, though never when *one* will answer the end; gravitation and attraction have place in the revolution of the planets, because the one would fix them to a center and the other would carry them off indefinitely; so in the moral world the first simple principle is *equality* and the power of the whole. This will answer in small numbers; so will a tolerably virtuous *oligarchy* or a *monarchy*. But when the society grows in bulk none of them will answer well *singly,* and none worse than absolute monarchy. It becomes necessary therefore as numbers increase to have those several powers properly combined, so as from the whole to produce that harmony of government so often talked of and wished for but too seldom found in ancient or modern states. The grand political problem in all ages has been to invent the best combination or distribution of the supreme powers of legislation and execution. Those states have ever made the greatest figure, and have been most durable, in which those powers have not only been separated from each other but placed each in more hands than one or a few. The *Romans* are the most shining example; but they never had a balance between the Senate and the people, and the want of this is generally agreed by the few who know anything of the matter to have been the cause of their fall. The *British* constitution in theory and [15] in the present administration of it in general comes nearest the idea of perfection of any that has been reduced to practice;

and if the principles of it are adhered to it will, according to the infallible prediction of *Harrington,* always keep the *Britons* uppermost in *Europe* till their *only* rival nation shall either embrace that perfect model of a commonwealth given us by that author or come as near it as *Great Britain* is.[6] Then indeed, and not till then, will that rival and our nation either be eternal confederates or contend in greater earnest than they have ever yet done, till one of them shall sink under the power of the other and rise no more.

Great Britain has at present most evidently the advantage and such opportunities of honest wealth and grandeur as perhaps no state ever had before, at least not since the days of *Julius Caesar,* the destroyer of the Roman glory and grandeur, at a time when but for him and his adherents both might have been rendered immortal.

We have said that the form and mode of government is to be settled by *compact,* as it was rightfully done by the Convention after the abdication of *James* II, and assented to by the first representative of the nation chosen afterwards, and by every Parliament and by almost every man ever since but the bigots to the indefeasible power of tyrants, civil and ecclesiastic. There was neither time for nor occasion to call the whole people together. If they had not liked the proceedings it was in their power to control them, as it would be should the supreme legislative or executive powers ever again attempt to enslave them. The people will bear a great deal before they will even murmur against their rulers; but when once they are thoroughly roused and in earnest against those who would be glad to enslave them their power is *irresistible.*¶ [7]

At the abdication of King *James* every step was taken that natural justice and equity could require; and all was done that was possible, at least in the wretched state in which he left the nation. Those very noble and worthy patriots, the lords spiritual and temporal of that day, and the principal persons of the commons, advised the prince, who in consequence thereof caused letters to be "written to the lords spiritual and temporal, being Protestants, and other [16] letters to the several counties, cities, universities, boroughs, and Cinque Ports for the choosing such persons to represent them as were of right to be sent to Parliament to meet at Westminster upon the 22d of January 1688 in order to such an establishment as that their religion, laws, and liberties might not again be in danger of being subverted." See Wm. and M. sess. [2], c.[2].

Upon this, elections were made, and thereupon the said lords spiritual

¶ See Mr. Locke on the dissolution of government.

and temporal and commons met and proceeded to assert their rights and liberties, and to the election of the Prince and Princess of Orange to be King and Queen of England, France, and Ireland, and the dominions thereto belonging. The kingdom of Scotland agreed in the same choice. These proceedings were drawn into the form of acts of Parliament, and are the basis of the Acts of Union and Succession since made, and which all together are the sure foundation of that indisputable right which his present Majesty has to the crown of *Great Britain* and the dominions thereto belonging, which right 'tis the greatest folly to doubt of, as well as the blackest treason to deny. The present establishment founded on the law of GoD and of nature was began by the Convention with a professed and real view in all parts of the *British* empire to put the liberties of the people out of the reach of arbitrary power in all times to come.

But the grandeur as well as justice, equity, and goodness of the proceedings of the nation on that memorable occasion never have been nor can be so well represented as in the words of those great men who composed the Convention; for which reason partly, but principally because they show the rights of all British subjects, both at home and abroad, and should therefore be in as many hands as possible, I have transcribed the following clauses.

1 Wm. and M. sess. 1, c.1, preamble and sec. 1 — entitled —
"An Act for Removing and Preventing All Questions and Disputes Concerning the Assembling and Sitting of This Present Parliament."

For preventing all doubts and scruples which may in any wise arise concerning the meeting, sitting, and proceeding of this present Parliament, be it declared and enacted [17] by the King's and Queen's Most Excellent Majesties, by and with the advice and consent of the lords spiritual and temporal, and commons, now assembled, and by authority of the same:

IIdly. That the lords spiritual and temporal, and commons, convened at Westminster the two and twentieth day of January A.D. 1688 and there sitting the 13th of February following, are the two Houses of Parliament, and so shall be and are hereby declared, enacted, and adjudged to be, to all intents, constructions, and purposes whatsoever, notwithstanding any want of writ or writs of summons or any other defect of form or default whatsoever, as if they had been summoned according to the usual form."

1 of Wm. and M. sess. 2, c.2, secs. [1, 2], 4, 5, 6, 11, 12.
"An Act Declaring the Rights and Liberties of the Subject, and Settling the Succession of the Crown."

Whereas the lords spiritual and temporal, and commons, assembled at Westminster, lawfully, fully, and freely representing all the estates of the people of this realm, did upon the 13th of February A.D. 1688 present unto Their Majesties, then called and known by the names and title of William and Mary, Prince and Princess of Orange, being present in their proper persons, a certain declaration in writing made by the said lords and commons in the words following; viz.:

Whereas the late King James II, by the assistance of divers evil counselors, judges, and ministers employed by him, did endeavor to subvert and extirpate the Protestant religion and the laws and liberties of this kingdom:

1. By assuming and exercising a power of dispensing with and suspending of laws, and the execution of laws, without consent of Parliament.

2. By committing and prosecuting divers worthy prelates for humbly petitioning to be excused from concurring to the said assumed power.

3. By issuing and causing to be executed a commission under the great seal for erecting a court called the Court of Commissioners for Ecclesiastical Causes.

4. By levying money for and to the use of the crown, by pretence of prerogative, for other time and in other [18] manner than the same was granted by Parliament.

5. By raising and keeping a standing army within this kingdom in time of peace, without consent of Parliament, and quartering soldiers contrary to law.

6. By causing several good subjects, being Protestants, to be disarmed, at the same time when papists were both armed and employed, contrary to law.

7. By violating the freedom of election of members to serve in Parliament.

8. By prosecutions in the Court of King's Bench for matters and causes cognizable only in Parliament, and by divers and other arbitrary and illegal courses.

9. And whereas of late years, partial, corrupt, and unqualified persons have been returned and served on juries in trials, and particularly divers jurors in trials for high treason, which were not freeholders.

10. And excessive bail hath been required of persons committed in criminal cases, to elude the benefit of the laws made for the liberty of the subjects.

11. And excessive fines have been imposed, and illegal and cruel punishments inflicted.

12. And several grants and promises made of fines and forfeitures before any conviction or judgment against the persons upon whom the same were to be levied.

All of which are utterly and directly contrary to the known laws and statutes and freedom of this realm —

And whereas the said late King *James* II having abdicated the government, and the throne being thereby vacant, His Highness the Prince of Orange (whom it hath pleased Almighty God to make the glorious instrument of delivering this kingdom from popery and arbitrary power) did (by the advice of the lords spiritual and temporal, and divers principal persons of the commons) cause letters to be written to the lords spiritual and temporal, being Protestants, and other letters to the several counties, cities, universities, boroughs, and Cinque Ports for the choosing of such persons to represent them as were of right to be sent to Parliament to meet and sit at Westminster upon the two-and-twentieth of January in this year 1688 in order to such an establishment as that their religion, laws, and liberties might not again be in danger of being subverted. Upon which letters, elections having been accordingly made:

[19] And thereupon the said lords spiritual and temporal, and commons, pursuant to their respective letters and elections, being now assembled in a full and free representative of this nation, taking into their most serious consideration the best means for attaining the ends aforesaid, do in the first place (as their ancestors in like cases have usually done) for the vindicating and asserting their ancient rights and liberties declare:

1. That the pretended power of suspending of laws, or the execution of laws, by regal authority, without consent of Parliament, is illegal.

2. That the pretended power of dispensing with laws, or the execution of laws, by regal authority, as it hath been assumed and exercised of late, is illegal.

3. That the commission for creating the late Court of Commissioners for Ecclesiastical Causes and all other commissions and courts of like nature, are illegal and pernicious.

4. That levying money for or to the use of the crown, by pretense of prerogative, without grant of Parliament, for longer time or in other manner than the same is or shall be granted, is illegal.

5. That it is the right of the subjects to petition the King, and all commitments and prosecutions for such petitioning are illegal.

6. That the raising or keeping a standing army within the kingdom in time of peace, unless it be with consent of Parliament, is against law.

7. That the subjects which are Protestants may have arms for their defense suitable to their conditions and as allowed by law.

8. That election of members of Parliament ought to be free.

9. That the freedom of speech and debates or proceedings in Parliament ought not to be impeached or questioned in any court or place out of Parliament.

10. That excessive bail ought not to be required, nor excessive fines imposed, nor cruel and unusual punishments inflicted.

11. That jurors ought to be duly impaneled and returned, and jurors which pass upon men's trials for high treason ought to be freeholders.

[20] 12. That all grants and promises of fines and forfeitures of particular persons before conviction are illegal and void.

13. And that for redress of all grievances and for the amending, strengthening, and preserving of the laws Parliaments ought to be held frequently.

And they do claim, demand, and insist upon all and singular the premises as their undoubted rights and liberties, and that no declarations, judgments, doings, or proceedings to the prejudice of the people in any of the said premises ought in any wise to be drawn hereafter into consequence or example:

To which demand of their rights they are particularly encouraged by the declaration of His Highness the Prince of Orange, as being the only means for obtaining a full redress and remedy therein —

Having therefore an entire confidence that his said Highness the Prince of Orange will perfect the deliverance so far advanced by him, and will still preserve them from the violation of their rights which they have here asserted, and from all other attempts upon their religion, rights, and liberties:

II. The said lords spiritual and temporal, and commons assembled at Westminster do resolve that William and Mary, Prince and Princess of Orange, be, and be declared, King and Queen of England, France, and Ireland, and the dominions thereunto belonging, to hold the crown and royal dignity of the said kingdoms and dominions to them, the said prince and princess during their lives and the life of the survivor of them; and that the sole and full exercise of the regal power be only in and executed by the said Prince of Orange, in the names of the said prince and princess, during their joint lives; and after their deceases the said crown and royal dignity of the said kingdoms and dominions to be the heirs of the body of the said princess, and for default of such issue, to the Princess Anne of Denmark and the heirs of her body, and for default of such issue to the heirs of the body of the said Prince of Orange. And the lords spiritual and temporal, and commons, do pray the said prince and princess to accept the same accordingly.

[21] IV. Upon which their said Majesties did accept the crown and royal dignity of the kingdom of England, France, and Ireland, and the dominions thereunto belonging, according to the resolutions and desire of the said lords and commons contained in the said declaration.

V. And thereupon Their Majesties were pleased that the said lords spiritual and temporal, and commons, being the two Houses of Parliament, should continue to sit and with Their Majesties' royal concurrence make effectual provision for the settlement of the religion, laws, and liberties of this kingdom, so that the same for the future might not be in danger again of being subverted; to which the said lords spiritual and temporal, and commons, did agree and proceed to act accordingly.

VI. Now in pursuance of the premises, the said lords spiritual and temporal, and commons, in Parliament assembled for the ratifying, confirming, and establishing the said declaration and the articles, clauses, matters, and things therein contained, by the force of a law made in due form by authority of Parliament, do pray that it may be declared and enacted: That all and singular the rights and liberties asserted and claimed in the said declaration are the true, ancient, and indubitable rights and liberties of the people of this kingdom, and so shall be esteemed, allowed, adjudged, deemed, and taken to be; and that all and every the particulars aforesaid shall be firmly and strictly holden and observed as they are expressed in the said declaration, and all officers and ministers whatsoever shall serve Their Majesties and their successors according to the same in all times to come.

XI. All which Their Majesties are contented and pleased shall be declared, enacted, and established by authority of this present Parliament, and shall stand, remain, and be the law of this realm forever; and the same are by their said Majesties, by and with the advice and consent of the lords spiritual and temporal, and commons, in Parliament assembled, and by the authority of the same, declared, enacted, and established accordingly.

XII. And be it further declared and enacted by the authority aforesaid that from and after this present session of Parliament no dispensation by *non obstante* of or to [22] any statute or any part thereof shall be allowed; but that the same shall be held void and of no effect, except a dispensation be allowed in such statutes, and except in such cases as shall be specially provided for by one or more bill or bills to be passed during this present session of Parliament.

12 and 13 of Wm. III c. 2, secs. 3 and 4.

Whereas it is necessary that further provision be made for securing our religion, laws, and liberties after the death of His Majesty and the Princess Anne of Denmark, and in default of issue of the body of the said princess and of His Majesty respectively, it is enacted:

That after the said limitation shall take effect judges' commissions be made *quamdiu se bene gesserint*, and their salaries ascertained and established; but upon the address of both houses of Parliament it may be lawful to remove them.

That no pardon under the Great Seal of England be pleaded to an impeachment by the Commons in Parliament.

Whereas the laws of England are the birthright of the people thereof, and all the Kings and Queens who shall ascend the throne of this realm ought to administer the government of the same according to the said laws, and all their officers and ministers ought to serve them according to the same, all the laws and statutes of this realm for securing the established religion and the rights and liberties of the people and all other laws and statutes now in force are by His Majesty with the advice and consent of the lords spiritual and temporal, and commons, ratified and confirmed.

I shall close this introduction with a passage from Mr. Locke.

"Though," says he, "in a constituted commonwealth standing upon its own basis and acting according to its own nature, that is, acting for the preservation of the community, there can be but one supreme power which is the legislative, to which all the rest are and must be subordinate, yet the legislative being only a fiduciary power, to act for certain ends, there remains still *'in the people, a supreme power to remove, or alter, the legislative when they find the legislative act contrary to the trust reposed in them.'* For all power given with trust for the attaining an [23] end being limited by that end, whenever that end is manifestly neglected or opposed, the trust must necessarily be forfeited, and the power devolve into the hands of those who gave it, who may place it anew where they shall think best for their safety and security. And thus the *community* perpetually retains a supreme power of saving themselves from the attempts and designs of anybody, even of their legislators whenever they shall be so foolish or so wicked as to lay and carry on designs against the liberties and properties of the subject. For no man or society of men having a power to deliver up their preservation or consequently the means of it to the absolute will and arbitrary dominion of another, whenever anyone shall go about to bring them into such a slavish condition, they will always have a right to preserve what they have not a power to part with, and to *rid* themselves of *those* who invade this fundamental, sacred, and unalterable law of self-preservation for which they entered into society.

"And thus the community may be said in this respect to be always the supreme power, but not as considered under any form of government, because this power of the people can never take place till the government be dissolved." Locke on government, bk. II, chap. 13.

This he says may be done "from without by conquest; from within, first, when the legislative is altered. Which is often by the prince, but sometimes by the whole legislative. As by invading the *property* of the subject and making themselves arbitrary disposers of the lives, liberties, and fortunes of the people; reducing them to slavery under arbitrary power, they put themselves into a state of war with the people, who are thereupon absolved from any further obedience, and are left to the common refuge which God hath provided for all men against force and violence. Whensoever, therefore, the legislative shall transgress this fundamental rule of society, and either by ambition, fear, folly, or corruption endeavor to gain themselves or put into the hands of any other an absolute power over the lives, liberties, and estates of the people, by this breach of trust they forfeit the power the *people* had put into their hands for quite contrary ends, and it devolves to the *people,* who have a right to *resume* their [24] original liberty and by the establishment of a *new* legislative (such as they shall think fit) provide for their own safety and security, which is the end for which they are in society." *Idem,* chap. 9.[8]

Of Colonies in General

This subject has never been very clearly and fully handled by any modern writer that I have had the good fortune to meet with, and to do it justice would require much greater abilities than I pretend to, and more leisure than I ever expect will fall to my share. Even the *English* writers and lawyers have either entirely waived any consideration of the nature of *colonies* or very lightly touched upon it, for the people of England never discovered much concern for the prosperity of the *colonies* till the Revolution; and even now some of their great men and writers, by their discourses of and conduct towards them, consider them all rather as a parcel of *little insignificant conquered islands* than as a very extensive settlement on the continent. Even their law books and very dictionaries of law, in editions so late as 1750, speak of the *British* plantations abroad as consisting chiefly of islands; and they are reckoned up in some of them in this order — *Jamaica, Barbados, Virginia, Maryland, New England, New York, Carolina, Burmudas.* At the head of all these *islands* (for there is no distinction made) stands *Jamaica,* in truth a *conquered* island; and as such this and all the other little West India islands deserve to be treated for the conduct of their inhabitants and proprietors with regard to the northern colonies: divers of these colonies are larger than all those islands together, and are well settled, not as the common people of *England* foolishly imagine, with a compound mongrel mixture of *English, Indian,* and *Negro,* but with freeborn *British white* subjects, whose loyalty has never yet been suspected.

There is a man now living, or but lately dead, who once was a secretary of state, during whose *wonderful* conduct of national affairs, without knowing whether *Jamaica* lay in the Mediterranean, the Baltic, or in the moon, letters [25] were often received directed to the governor of the *island* of New England. Which *island* of New England is a part of the *continent* of North America, comprehending two provinces and two colonies, and according to the *undoubted* bounds of their charters, containing more land than there is in the three kingdoms. But I must confine myself to matters of more importance than detecting the geographical blunders or refuting the errors of dead, superannuated, or any otherwise stupefied secretaries of state who are now all out of place.

If I were to define the *modern* colonists, I should say *they are the noble discoverers and settlers of a new world,* from whence as from an endless source, *wealth* and *plenty,* the means of *power, grandeur,* and *glory,* in a degree unknown to the hungry chiefs of former ages, have been pouring into *Europe* for 300 years past: in return for which those colonists have received from the several states of *Europe,* except from *Great Britain* only since the Revolution, nothing but ill-usage, slavery, and chains, as fast as the riches of *their own* earning could furnish the means of forging them.

A plantation or colony is a settlement of subjects in a territory *disjoined* or *remote* from the mother country, and may be made by private adventurers or the public; but in both cases the colonists are entitled to as *ample* rights, liberties, and privileges as the subjects of the mother country are, and in some respects *to more.*

Of the Natural Rights of Colonists

Those who expect to find anything very satisfactory on this subject in particular or with regard to the law of nature in general in the writings of such authors as *Grotius* and *Pufendorf* will find themselves much mistaken. It is their constant practice to establish the matter of right on the matter of *fact:* this the celebrated *Rousseau* expressly says of *Grotius,* and with the same reason he might have added an hundred others. "The learned researches into the laws of nature and nations are often nothing more than the history of ancient abuses, so that it is a ridiculous infatuation [26] to be too fond of studying them." * "This was exactly the case with *Grotius*." † [9] The sentiments on this subject have therefore been chiefly drawn from the purer fountains of one or two of our *English* writers, particularly from Mr. *Locke,* to whom might be added a *few* of

---

* Marquis D'A.   † Rousseau.

other nations; for I have seen but a few of any country, and of all I have seen there are not ten worth reading. *Grotius,* bk. I, chap. 3, sec. 21, discoursing of confederates on unequal terms according to his manner says, "to the inequality in question may be referred some of those rights which are now called right of protection, right of patronage, and a right called *mundiburgium,* as also that which mother cities had over their colonies among the Grecians. For as *Thucydides* says, those colonies enjoyed the same rights of liberty with the other cities, but they owed a *reverence* to the city whence they derived their origin, and were obliged to render her respect and certain expressions of honor *so long as the colony was well treated."* Grotius, *De jure belli,* etc., bk. I, chap. 3, sec. 21.

"Hitherto also," says he, "may be referred that separation which is made when people *by one consent* go to form colonies. *For this is the original of a new and independent state. They are not content to be slaves, but to enjoy equal privileges and freedom* says *Thucydides.* And King *Tullus* in Dion[ysius of] Hali[carnassus] says, *we look upon it to be neither truth nor justice that mother cities ought of necessity and by the law of nature to rule over their colonies."* Bk. II, chap. 9, sec. 10.[10]

"Colonies," says Pufendorf, "are settled in different methods. For either the colony continues a part of the commonwealth it was sent out from, or else is obliged to pay a dutiful respect to the mother commonwealth and to be in readiness to defend and vindicate its honor and so is united to it by a sort of unequal confederacy, or lastly is erected into a separate commonwealth and assumes the same rights with the state it is descended from." Pufend. [*De jure natural et gentium*] bk. VIII, chap. 11, sec. 6.

"Different commonwealths may be formed out of one by common consent, by sending out colonies in the manner usual in old Greece. For the Romans afterwards when [27] they sent a colony abroad continued it under the jurisdiction of the mother commonwealth, or greater country. But the colonies planted by the Greeks, and after their method, constituted particular commonwealths, which were obliged only to pay a kind of deference and dutiful submission to the mother commonwealth." Pufend. bk. VIII, chap. 12, sec. 5.

From which passage 'tis manifest that these two great men only state facts and the opinions of others, without giving their own upon the subject: and all that can be collected from those facts or opinions is that Greece was more generous and a better mother to her colonies than Rome. The conduct of Rome towards her colonies and the corruptions and oppressions tolerated in her provincial officers of all denominations was one great cause of the downfall of that proud republic.

Dr. Strahan says, "there is a great affinity between the British colonies and those of the Spaniards and other nations who have made settlements among the Indians in those parts. For the grants made by our Kings of tracts of lands in that country, for the planting of colonies and making settlements therein appear to have been made in imitation of grants made by the Kings of Spain to the proprietors of lands in the Spanish colonies upon the very same conditions and in consideration of the same services to be performed by the grantees. So that the *government* of the Spanish colonies and the rights of the proprietors of lands therein depending chiefly on the rules of civil and feudal law, as may be seen by the learned treatise of Solorzanus, *De Indiarum Jure,* the knowledge of the said laws must be of service likewise for determining any controversy that may arise touching the duties or forfeitures of the proprietors of lands in our English colonies." Pref. to translat. of Domat.[11]

With submission to so great an authority as Dr. Strahan, 'tis humbly hoped that the British colonists do not hold their lands as well as liberties by so slippery a tenure as do the Spaniards and French. The will of the prince is the only tenure by which *they* hold; and the government of the Spanish and French settlements is in every respect despotic.

[28] 'Tis well known that the first American grants were by the bulls of the popes. The Roman pontiffs had for ages usurped the most abominable power over princes: they granted away the kingdoms of the earth with as little ceremony as a man would lease a sheepcote. Now according to Dr. Strahan's logic it may be inferred that the canon law and the pope's bulls must be of *service likewise for determining any controversy that may arise touching the duties or forfeitures of the proprietors of lands in the British colonies.* And indeed it must be owned, if we were to judge of some late proceedings ‡ by this rule, we must allow that they savor more of modern Rome and the Inquisition than of the common law of England and the constitution of Great Britain.

In order to form an idea of the natural rights of the colonists, I presume it will be granted that they are men, the common children of the same Creator with their brethren of Great Britain. Nature has placed all such in a state of equality and perfect freedom to act within the bounds of the laws of nature and reason without consulting the will or regarding

‡ Of some American courts of admiralty, if the reader pleases.

the humor, the passions, or whims of any other man, unless they are formed into a society or body politic. This it must be confessed is rather an abstract way of considering men than agreeable to the real and general course of nature. The truth is, as has been shown, men come into the world and into society at the same instant. But this hinders not but that the natural and original rights of each individual may be illustrated and explained in this way better than in any other. We see here, by the way, a probability that this abstract consideration of men, which has its use in reasoning on the principles of government, has insensibly led some of the greatest men to imagine some real general state of nature agreeable to this abstract conception, antecedent to and independent of society. This is certainly not the case in general, for most men become members of society from their birth, though separate independent states are really in the condition of perfect freedom and equality with regard to each other, and so are any number of individuals who separate themselves from a society of which they have formerly been [29] members, for ill treatment or other good cause, with express design to found another. If in such case there is a real interval between the separation and the new conjunction, during such interval the individuals are as much detached and under the law of nature only as would be two men who should chance to meet on a desolate island.

The colonists are by the law of nature freeborn, as indeed all men are, white or black. No better reasons can be given for enslaving those of any color than such as Baron Montesquieu has humorously given as the foundation of that cruel slavery exercised over the poor Ethiopians,[12] which threatens one day to reduce both Europe and America to the ignorance and barbarity of the darkest ages. Does it follow that 'tis right to enslave a man because he is black? Will short curled hair like wool instead of Christian hair, as 'tis called by those whose hearts are as hard as the nether millstone, help the argument? Can any logical inference in favor of slavery be drawn from a flat nose, a long or a short face? Nothing better can be said in favor of a trade that is the most shocking violation of the law of nature, has a direct tendency to diminish the idea of the inestimable value of liberty, and makes every dealer in it a tyrant, from the director of an African company to the petty chapman in needles and pins on the unhappy coast. It is a clear truth that those who every day barter away other men's liberty will soon care little for their own. To this cause must be imputed that ferocity, cruelty, and brutal barbarity that has long marked the general character of the sugar islanders. They can in general form no idea of government but that which in person or by an overseer, the joint and several proper representative of a creole § and of the d——l, is exercised over ten thousand of their fellow men, born with the same right to freedom and the sweet enjoyments of liberty and life as their unrelenting taskmasters, the overseers and planters.[13]

Is it to be wondered at if when people of the stamp of a creolean planter get into power they will not stick for a little present gain at making their own posterity, white [30] as well as black, worse slaves if possible than those already mentioned?

There is nothing more evident, says Mr. Locke, than "that creatures of the same species and rank, promiscuously born to all the same advantages of nature and the use of the same faculties, should also be equal one among another without subordination and subjection, unless the master of them all should by any manifest declaration of his will set one above another and confer on him by an evident and clear appointment an undoubted right to dominion and sovereignty." "The natural liberty of man is to be free from any superior power on earth, and not to be under the will or legislative authority of man, but only to have the law of nature for his rule."[14] This is the liberty of independent states; this is the liberty of every man out of society and who has a mind to live so; which liberty is only abridged in certain instances, not lost to those who are born in or voluntarily enter into society; this gift of God cannot be annihilated.

The colonists, being men, have a right to be considered as equally entitled to all the rights of nature with the Europeans, and they are not to be restrained in the exercise of any of these rights but for the evident good of the whole community.

By being or becoming members of society they have not renounced their natural liberty in any greater degree than other good citizens, and if 'tis taken from them without their consent they are so far enslaved.

They have an undoubted right to expect that their best good will ever be consulted by their rulers, supreme and subordinate, without any partial views confined to the particular interest of one island or another. Neither the riches of Jamaica nor the luxury of a metropolis should ever have weight enough to break the balance of truth and justice. Truth and faith belong to men as men from men, and if they are disappointed in their just expectations of them in one society they will at least wish for

§ Those in England who borrow the terms of the Spaniards, as well as their notions of government, apply this term to all Americans of European extract; but the northern colonists apply it only to the islanders and others of such extract, under the Torrid Zone.

them in another. If the love of truth and justice, the only spring of sound policy in any state, is not strong enough to prevent certain causes from taking place, the arts of fraud and force will not prevent the most fatal effects.

[31] In the long run, those who fall on arbitrary measures will meet with their deserved fate. The law of nature was not of man's making, nor is it in his power to mend it or alter its course. He can only perform and keep or disobey and break it. The last is never done with impunity, even in this life, if it is any punishment for a man to feel himself depraved, to find himself degraded by his own folly and wickedness from the rank of a virtuous and good *man* to that of a brute, or to be transformed from the friend, perhaps father, of his country to a devouring lion or tiger.

The unhappy revolutions which for ages have distressed the human race have been all owing to the want of a little wisdom, common sense, and integrity in the administration of those whom, by their stations, God had in kindness to the world rendered able to do a great deal for the benefit of mankind with the exertion of a small portion of private and public virtue.

Of the Political and Civil Rights
of the British *Colonists*

Here indeed opens to view a large field; but I must study brevity. — Few people have extended their inquiries after the foundation of any of their rights beyond a charter from the crown. There are others who think when they have got back to old *Magna Carta* that they are at the beginning of all things. They imagine themselves on the borders of chaos (and so indeed in some respects they are), and see creation rising out of the unformed mass or from nothing. Hence, say they, spring all the rights of men and of citizens. But liberty was better understood and more fully enjoyed by our ancestors before the coming in of the first Norman tyrants than ever after, till it was found necessary for the salvation of the kingdom to combat the arbitrary and wicked proceedings of the Stuarts.

The present happy and most righteous establishment is justly built on the ruins which those princes brought on their family, and two of them on their own heads. The last of the name sacrificed three of the finest kingdoms in [32] Europe to the counsels of bigoted old women, priests, and more weak and wicked ministers of state. He afterward went a-grazing in the fields of St. Germaine, and there died in disgrace and poverty, a terrible example of God's vengeance on arbitrary princes!

The deliverance under God wrought by the Prince of Orange, afterwards deservedly made King William III, was as joyful an event to the colonies as to Great Britain: in some of them steps were taken in his favor as soon as in England.

They all immediately acknowledged King William and Queen Mary as their lawful sovereign. And such has been the zeal and loyalty of the colonies ever since for that establishment and for the Protestant succession in his present Majesty's illustrious family, that I believe there is not one man in a hundred (except in Canada) who does not think himself under the best national civil constitution in the world.

Their loyalty has been abundantly proved, especially in the late war. Their affection and reverence for their mother country is unquestionable. They yield the most cheerful and ready obedience to her laws, particularly to the power of that august body, the Parliament of Great Britain, the supreme legislative of the kingdom and its dominions. These I declare are my own sentiments of duty and loyalty. I also hold it clear that the act of Queen Anne which makes it high treason to deny "that the King with and by the authority of Parliament is able to make laws and statutes of sufficient force and validity to *limit* and *bind* the crown and the descent, limitation, inheritance, and *government* thereof" [15] is founded on the principles of liberty and the British constitution: and he that would palm the doctrine of unlimited passive obedience and non-resistance upon mankind, and thereby or by any other means serve the cause of the Pretender, is not only a fool and a knave, but a rebel against common sense as well as the laws of God, of nature, and his country.

☞ I also lay it down as one of the first principles from whence I intend to deduce the civil rights of the British colonies, that all of them are subject to and dependent on Great Britain, and that therefore as over subordinate [33] governments the Parliament of Great Britain has an undoubted power and lawful authority to make acts for the general good that, by naming them, shall and ought to be equally binding as upon the subjects of Great Britain within the realm. This principle, I presume, will be readily granted on the other side the Atlantic. It has been practised upon for twenty years to my knowledge, in the province of the *Massachusetts Bay;* and I have ever received it that it has been so from the beginning in this and the sister provinces through the continent.|| [16]

I am aware some will think it is time for me to retreat, after having expressed the power of the British Parliament in quite so strong terms. But 'tis from and under this very power and its acts, and from the common law, that the political and civil rights of the colonists are derived: and upon those grand pillars of liberty shall my defense be rested. At present, therefore, the reader may suppose that there is not one provincial charter on the continent; he may, if he pleases, imagine all taken away, without fault or forfeiture, without trial or notice. All this really happened to some of them in the last century. I would have the reader carry his imagination still further, and suppose a time may come when instead of a process at common law the Parliament shall give a decisive blow to every charter in America, and declare them all void. Nay it shall also be granted that 'tis barely possible the time may come when the real interest of the whole may require an act of Parliament to annihilate all those charters. What could follow from all this that would shake one of the essential, natural, civil, or religious rights of the colonists? Nothing. They would be men, citizens and British subjects after all. No act of Parliament can deprive them of the liberties of such, unless any will contend that an act of Parliament can make slaves not only of one but of two millions of the commonwealth. And if so, why not of the whole? I freely own that I can find nothing in the laws of my country that would justify the [34] Parliament in making one slave, nor did they ever professedly undertake to make one.

Two or three innocent colony charters have been threatened with destruction a hundred and forty years past. I wish the present enemies of those harmless charters would reflect a moment and be convinced that an act of Parliament that should demolish those bugbears to the foes of liberty would not reduce the colonists to a state of absolute slavery. The worst enemies of the charter governments are by no means to be found in England. 'Tis a piece of justice due to Great Britain to own they are and have ever been natives of or residents in the colonies. A set of men in America, without honor or love to their country, have been long grasping at powers which they think unattainable while these charters stand in the way. But they will meet with insurmountable obstacles to

---

|| This, however, was formally declared as to Ireland but so lately as the reign of *George* I. Upon the old principles of conquest, the Irish could not have so much to say for an exemption as the unconquered colonists.

their project for enslaving the British colonies should those [obstacles] arising from provincial charters be removed. It would indeed seem very hard and severe for those of the colonists who have charters with peculiar privileges to lose them. They were given to their ancestors in consideration of their sufferings and merit in discovering and settling America. Our forefathers were soon worn away in the toils of hard labor on their little plantations and in war with the savages. They thought they were earning a sure inheritance for their posterity. Could they imagine it would ever be thought just to deprive them or theirs of their charter privileges! Should this ever be the case, there are, thank God, natural, inherent, and inseparable rights as men and as citizens that would remain after the so much wished for catastrophe, and which, whatever became of charters, can never be abolished *de jure,* if *de facto,* till the general conflagration.¶ [17] Our rights as men and freeborn British subjects give all the colonists enough to make them very happy in comparison with the subjects of any other prince in the world.

[35] Every British subject born on the continent of America or in any other of the British dominions is by the law of God and nature, by the common law, and by act of Parliament (exclusive of all charters from the crown) entitled to all the natural, essential, inherent, and inseparable rights of our fellow subjects in Great Britain. Among those rights are the following, which it is humbly conceived no man or body of men, not excepting the Parliament, justly, equitably, and consistently with their own rights and the constitution can take away.

First. *That the supreme and subordinate powers of legislation should be free and sacred in the hands where the community have once rightfully placed them.*

Secondly. *The supreme national legislative cannot be altered justly till the commonwealth is dissolved, nor a subordinate legislative taken away without forfeiture or other good cause.* Nor then can the subjects in the subordinate government be reduced to a state of slavery and subject to the despotic rule of others. A state has no right to make slaves of the conquered. Even when the subordinate right of legislature is forfeited and so declared, this cannot affect the natural persons either of those who were invested with it or the inhabitants so far as to deprive

¶ The fine defense of the provincial charters by *Jeremy Dummer,* Esq., the late very able and learned agent for the province of the *Massachusetts Bay,* makes it needless to go into a particular consideration of charter privileges. That piece is unanswerable but by power and might and other arguments of that kind.

them of the rights of subjects and of men.* [18] The colonists will have an equitable right notwithstanding any such forfeiture of charter to be represented in Parliament or to have some new subordinate legislature among themselves. It would be best if they had both. Deprived, however, of their common rights as subjects they cannot lawfully be while they remain such. A representation in Parliament from the several colonies — since they are become so large and numerous as to be called on not to maintain provincial government, civil and military among themselves (for this they have cheerfully done) but to contribute towards the support of a national standing army, by reason of the heavy national debt, when they themselves owe a large one contracted in the common cause — can't be thought an unreasonable thing, nor if asked [36] could it be called an immodest request. *Qui sentit commodum sentire debet et onus*[19] has been thought a maxim of equity. But that a man should bear a burden for other people as well as himself without a return never long found a place in any law book or decrees but those of the most despotic princes. Besides the equity of an American representation in Parliament, a thousand advantages would result from it. It would be the most effectual means of giving those of both countries a thorough knowledge of each other's interests, as well as that of the whole, which are inseparable.

Were this representation allowed, instead of the scandalous memorials and depositions that have been sometimes, in days of old, privately cooked up in an inquisitorial manner by persons of bad minds and wicked views and sent from America to the several boards, persons of the first reputation among their countrymen might be on the spot from the several colonies truly to represent them. Future ministers need not, like some of their predecessors, have recourse for information in American affairs to every vagabond stroller that has run or rid post through America from his creditors, or to people of no kind of reputation from the colonies, some of whom, at the time of administering their sage advice, have been as ignorant of the state of this country as of the regions in Jupiter and Saturn.

No representation of the colonies in Parliament alone would, however, be equivalent to a subordinate legislative among themselves, nor so well answer the ends of increasing their prosperity and the commerce of Great Britain. It would be impossible for the Parliament to judge so well of their abilities to bear taxes, impositions on trade, and other duties and

---

* See Magna Carta, the Bill of Rights. 3 Mod. [159]; 2 Salkeld 411; Vaughan 300.

burdens, or of the local laws that might be really needful, as a legislative here.

Thirdly. *No legislative, supreme or subordinate, has a right to make itself arbitrary.*

It would be a most manifest contradiction for a free legislative, like that of Great Britain, to make itself arbitrary.

Fourthly. *The supreme legislative cannot justly assume a power of ruling by extempore arbitrary decrees, but is bound to dispense justice by known settled rules* and by duly *authorized independent judges.*

[37] Fifthly. *The supreme power cannot take from any man any part of his property,* without his consent *in person or by representation.*

Sixthly. *The legislature cannot transfer the power of making laws to any other hands.*

These are their bounds, which by God and nature are fixed; hitherto have they a right to come, and no further.

1. *To govern by stated laws.*

2. *Those laws should have no other end ultimately but the good of the people.*

3. *Taxes are not to be laid on the people but by their consent in person or by deputation.*

4. *Their whole power is not transferable.*†

These are the first principles of law and justice, and the great barriers of a free state and of the British constitution in particular. I ask, I want, no more. Now let it be shown how 'tis reconcilable with these principles, or to many other fundamental maxims of the British constitution, as well as the natural and civil rights which by the laws of their country all British subjects are entitled to as their best inheritance and birthright, that all the northern colonies, who are without one representative in the House of Commons, should be taxed by the British Parliament.

That the colonists, black and white, born here are freeborn British subjects, and entitled to all the essential civil rights of such is a truth not only manifest from the provincial charters, from the principles of the common law, and acts of Parliament, but from the British constitution, which was re-established at the Revolution with a professed design to secure the liberties of all the subjects to all generations.‡

In the 12 and 13 of Wm. cited above, the liberties of the subject are spoken of as their best birthrights. No one ever dreamed, surely, that

---

† See Locke on government, bk. II, chap. 11.

‡ See the Convention and acts confirming it.

these liberties were confined to the realm. At that rate no British subjects in the dominions could, without a manifest contradiction, be declared entitled to all the privileges of subjects born within the realm to all intents and purposes which are rightly given foreigners by Parliament after residing seven years. These expressions of Parliament as well as of the charters must be [38] vain and empty sounds unless we are allowed the essential rights of our fellow subjects in Great Britain.

Now can there be any liberty where property is taken away without consent? Can it with any color of truth, justice, or equity be affirmed that the northern colonies are represented in Parliament? Has this whole continent of near three thousand miles in length, and in which and his other American dominions His Majesty has or very soon will have some millions of as good, loyal, and useful subjects, white and black, as any in the three kingdoms, the election of one member of the House of Commons?

Is there the least difference as to the consent of the colonists whether taxes and impositions are laid on their trade and other property by the crown alone or by the Parliament? As it is agreed on all hands the crown alone cannot impose them, we should be justifiable in refusing to pay them, but must and ought to yield obedience to an act of Parliament, though erroneous, till repealed.

I can see no reason to doubt but that the imposition of taxes, whether on trade, or on land, or houses, or ships, on real or personal, fixed or floating property, in the colonies is absolutely irreconcilable with the rights of the colonists as British subjects and as men. I say men, for in a state of nature no man can take my property from me without my consent: if he does, he deprives me of my liberty and makes me a slave. If such a proceeding is a breach of the law of nature, no law of society can make it just. The very act of taxing exercised over those who are not represented appears to me to be depriving them of one of their most essential rights as freemen, and if continued seems to be in effect an entire disfranchisement of every civil right. For what one civil right is worth a rush after a man's property is subject to be taken from him at pleasure without his consent? If a man is not his *own assessor* in person or by deputy, his liberty is gone or lays entirely at the mercy of others.

I think I have heard it said that when the Dutch are asked why they enslave their colonies, their answer is that the liberty of Dutchmen is confined to Holland, and that it was never intended for provincials in America or anywhere else. A sentiment, this, very worthy of modern [39] Dutchmen; but if their brave and worthy ancestors had entertained such narrow ideas of liberty, seven poor and distressed provinces would never have asserted their rights against the whole Spanish monarchy, of which the present is but a shadow. It is to be hoped none of our fellow subjects of Britain, great or small, have borrowed this Dutch maxim of plantation politics; if they have, they had better return it from whence it came; indeed they had. Modern Dutch or French maxims of state never will suit with a British constitution. It is a maxim that the King can do no wrong; and every good subject is bound to believe his King is not inclined to do any. We are blessed with a prince who has given abundant demonstrations that in all his actions he studies the good of his people and the true glory of his crown, which are inseparable. It would therefore be the highest degree of impudence and disloyalty to imagine that the King, at the head of his Parliament, could have any but the most pure and perfect intentions of justice, goodness, and truth that human nature is capable of. All this I say and believe of the King and Parliament in all their acts, even in that which so nearly affects the interest of the colonists, and that a most perfect and ready obedience is to be yielded to it while it remains in force. I will go further, and readily admit that the intention of the ministry was not only to promote the public good by this act, but that Mr. Chancellor of the Exchequer had therein a particular view to the "ease, the quiet, and the good will of the colonies," he having made this declaration more than once. Yet I hold that 'tis possible he may have erred in his kind intentions towards the colonies, and taken away our fish and given us a stone. With regard to the Parliament, as infallibility belongs not to mortals, 'tis possible *they* may have been misinformed and deceived. The power of Parliament is uncontrollable but by themselves, and we must obey. They only can repeal their own acts. There would be an end of all government if one or a number of subjects or subordinate provinces should take upon them so far to judge of the justice of an act of Parliament as to refuse obedience to it. If there was nothing else to restrain such a step, prudence ought to do it, for forceably resisting the Parliament and the King's laws [40] is high treason. Therefore let the Parliament lay what burdens they please on us, we must, it is our duty to submit and patiently bear them till they will be pleased to relieve us. And 'tis to be presumed the wisdom and justice of that august assembly always will afford us relief by repealing such acts as through mistake or other human infirmities have been suffered to pass, if they can be convinced that their proceedings are not constitutional or not for the common good.

The Parliament may be deceived, they may have been misinformed of facts, and the colonies may in many respects be misrepresented to the King, his Parliament, and his ministry. In some instances, I am well assured the colonies have been very strangely misrepresented in England. I have now before me a pamphlet called the *Administration of the Colonies,* said to be written by a gentleman who formerly commanded in chief in one of them.[20] I suppose this book was designed for public information and use. There are in it many good regulations proposed which no power can enforce but the Parliament. From all which I infer that if our hands are tied by the passing of an act of Parliament, our mouths are not stopped, provided we speak of that transcendent body with decency, as I have endeavored always to do; and should anything have escaped me or hereafter fall from my pen that bears the least aspect but that of obedience, duty, and loyalty to the King and Parliament, and the highest respect for the ministry, the candid will impute it to the agony of my heart rather than to the pravity of my will. If I have one ambitious wish, 'tis to see Great Britain at the head of the world, and to see my King, under God, the father of mankind. I pretend neither to the spirit of prophecy nor any uncommon skill in predicting a crisis, much less to tell when it begins to be *"nascent"* or is fairly midwived into the world. But if I were to fix a meaning to the two first paragraphs of the *Administration of the Colonies,* though I do not collect it from them, I should say the world was at the eve of the highest scene of earthly power and grandeur that has been ever yet displayed to the view of mankind. The cards are shuffling fast through all Europe. Who will win the prize is with God. This however I know, [41] *detur digniori.*[21] The next universal monarchy will be favorable to the human race, for it must be founded on the principles of equity, moderation, and justice. No country has been more distinguished for these principles than Great Britain, since the Revolution. I take it every subject has a right to give his sentiments to the public, of the utility or inutility of any act whatsoever, even after it is passed, as well as while it is pending. The equity and justice of a bill may be questioned with perfect submission to the legislature. Reasons may be given why an act ought to be repealed, and yet obedience must be yielded to it till that repeal takes place. If the reasons that can be given against an act are such as plainly demonstrate that it is against *natural* equity, the executive courts will adjudge such act void. It may be questioned by some, though I make no doubt of it, whether they are not obliged by their oaths to adjudge such act void. If there is not a right of private judgment to be exercised, so far at least as to petition for a repeal or to determine the expediency of risking a trial at law, the Parliament might make itself arbitrary, which it is conceived it cannot by the constitution. I think every man has a right to examine as freely into the origin, spring, and foundation of every power and measure in a commonwealth as into a piece of curious machinery or a remarkable phenomenon in nature, and that it ought to give no more offense to say the Parliament have erred or are mistaken in a matter of fact or of right than to say it of a private man, if it is true of both. If the assertion can be proved with regard to either, it is a kindness done them to show them the truth. With regard to the public, it is the duty of every good citizen to point out what he thinks erroneous in the commonwealth.

I have waited years in hopes to see some one friend of the colonies pleading in public for them. I have waited in vain. One privilege is taken away after another, and where we shall be landed God knows, and I trust will protect and provide for us even should we be driven and persecuted into a more western wilderness on the score of liberty, civil and religious, as many of our ancestors were to these once inhospitable shores of America. I had formed great expectations from a gentleman who published his [42] first volume in quarto on the rights of the colonies two years since; but, as he foresaw, the state of his health and affairs have prevented his further progress.[22] The misfortune is, gentlemen in America the best qualified in every respect to state the rights of the colonists have reasons that prevent them from engaging. Some of them have good ones. There are many infinitely better able to serve this cause than I pretend to be; but from indolence, from timidity, or by necessary engagements they are prevented. There has been a most profound and I think shameful silence, till it seems almost too late to assert our indisputable rights as men and as citizens. What must posterity think of us? The trade of the whole continent taxed by Parliament, stamps and other internal duties and taxes as they are called, talked of, and not one petition to the King and Parliament for relief.

I cannot but observe here that if the Parliament have an equitable right to tax our trade, 'tis indisputable that they have as good an one to tax the lands and everything else. The taxing trade furnishes one reason why the other should be taxed, or else the burdens of the province will be unequally borne, upon a supposition that a tax on trade is not a tax on the whole. But take it either way, there is no foundation for the distinction some make in England between an internal and an external tax on the colonies. By the first is meant a tax on trade, by the latter a tax on land and the things on it. A tax on trade is either a tax of every man in the province, or 'tis not. If 'tis not a tax on the whole, 'tis unequal and unjust that a heavy burden should be laid on the trade of the colonies to maintain an army of soldiers, customhouse officers, and fleets of guard-ships, all which the incomes of both trade and land would not furnish means to support so lately as the last war, when all was at stake, and the colonies were reimbursed in part by Parliament. How can it be sup-posed that all of a sudden the trade of the colonies alone can bear all this terrible burden? The late acquisitions in America, as glorious as they have been and as beneficial as they are to Great Britain, are only a security to these colonies against the ravages of the French and Indians. Our trade upon the whole is not, I believe, [43] benefited by them one groat. All the time the French islands were in our hands, the fine sugars, etc., were all shipped home. None as I have been informed were allowed to be brought to the colonies. They were too delicious a morsel for a North American palate. If it be said that a tax on the trade of the colonies is an equal and just tax on the whole of the inhabitants, what then becomes of the notable distinction between external and internal taxes? Why may not the Parliament lay stamps, land taxes, establish tithes to the Church of England, and so indefinitely? I know of no bounds. I do not mention the tithes out of any disrespect to the Church of England, which I esteem by far the best *national* church and to have had as ornaments of it many of the greatest and best men in the world. But to those colonies who in general dissent from a principle of conscience it would seem a little hard to pay towards the support of a worship whose modes they cannot conform to.

If an army must be kept up in America at the expense of the colonies, it would not seem quite so hard if after the Parliament had determined the sum to be raised, and apportioned it, to have allowed each colony to assess its quota and raise it as easily to themselves as might be. But to have the whole levied and collected without our consent is extraordinary. 'Tis allowed even to *tributaries* and those laid under *military* contribution to assess and collect the sums demanded. The case of the provinces is certainly likely to be the hardest that can be instanced in story. Will it not equal anything but downright military execution? Was there ever a trib-ute imposed even on the conquered? A fleet, an army of soldiers, and another of tax gatherers kept up, and not a single office either for securing or collecting the duty in the gift of the tributary state.

I am aware it will be objected that the Parliament of *England,* and of Great Britain since the union, have from early days to this time made acts to bind if not to tax Ireland: I answer, Ireland is a *conquered* country. I do not, however, lay so much stress on this; for it is my opinion that a *conquered* country has, upon submission and good behavior, the same right to be free under a conqueror as the rest of his subjects. But the old notion of the *right of conquest* [44] has been in most nations the cause of many severities and heinous breaches of the law of nature: if any such have taken place with regard to *Ireland* they should form no precedent for the colonies. The subordination and dependency of *Ireland* to Great Britain is expressly declared by act of Parliament in the reign of George I. The subordination of the *colonies* to Great Britain never was doubted by a lawyer, if at all, unless perhaps by the author of the *Administration of the Colonies*: he indeed seems to make a moot point of it, whether the colony legislative power is as independent "as the legislative Great Britain holds by its constitution and under the great charter." [23] The *people* hold under the great charter, as 'tis vulgarly expressed from our law books: but that the King and Parliament should be said to hold under *Magna Carta* is as new to me as it is to question whether the colonies are *subordinate* to Great Britain. The provincial legislative is unquestionably subordinate to that of Great Britain. I shall endeavor more fully to explain the nature of that subordination which has puzzled so many in their inquiries. It is often very difficult for great lovers of power, and great lovers of liberty, neither of whom may have been used to the study of law in any of its branches, to see the difference between subordination, absolute slavery, and subjection on the one side, and liberty, independence, and licentiousness on the other. We should endeavor to find the middle road, and confine ourselves to it. The laws, the proceedings of Parliament, and the decisions of the judges relating to *Ireland* will reflect light on this subject, rendered intricate only by *art.*

"Ireland being of itself a distinct dominion, and no part of the kingdom of England (as it directly appeareth by many authorities in *Calvin's Case*) was to have PARLIAMENTS holden there as in England." [Coke], 4 *Inst.* 349.

Why should not the colonies have, why are they not entitled to, their Assemblies or Parliaments at least as well as a conquered dominion?

"Wales, after the conquest of it by Edward the First, was annexed to England *jure proprietatis,* 12 Edw. I, by the statute of Rutland only, and after, more really by 27 Hen. VIII and 34, but at first received laws from England as [45] Ireland did; but writs proceeded not out of the English chancery, but they had a chancery of their own, as Ireland hath; [Wales] was not bound by the laws of England, unnamed, until 27 Hen. VIII no more than Ireland is.

"Ireland in nothing differs from it but having a parliament *gratia regis* (i.e., upon the old notion of conquest) subject (truly however) to the Parliament of England. None doubts Ireland as much conquered as it, *and as much subject to the Parliament of England, if it please.*" Vaughan 300.

A very strong argument arises from this authority in favor of the *unconquered* plantations. If since Wales was annexed to England, they have had a representation in Parliament, as they have to this day, and if the Parliament of England does not tax *Ireland,* can it be right they should tax *us,* who have never been *conquered,* but came from England to *colonize,* and have always remained *good subjects* to this day?

I cannot find any instance of a tax laid by the English Parliament on *Ireland.* "Sometimes the King of England called his nobles of Ireland to come to his Parliament of England, etc., and by special words the Parliament of England may bind the subjects of Ireland." [4] *Inst.* 350.

The following makes it clear to me, the Parliament of Great Britain do not tax *Ireland.* "The Parliament of Ireland having been prorogued to the month of August *next, before they had provided for the maintenance of the government in that kingdom a project* was set on foot here to supply that defect by retrenching the drawbacks upon goods exported thither from England. According to this scheme, the 22d, the House in a grand committee considered the present laws with respect to drawbacks upon tobaccos, muslins, and East India silks carried to Ireland, and came to two resolutions, which were reported the next day, and with an amendment to one of them agreed to by the House as follows, viz.: "1. That three pence per pound, part of the drawback on tobacco to be exported from Great Britain for Ireland, be taken off.

"2. That the said diminution of the drawback do take effect upon all tobacco exported for Ireland after the 24 of March 1713, and continue until the additional duty of three pence half penny per pound upon tobacco in Ireland, [46] expiring on the said 24th of March, be *regranted:* And ordered a bill to be brought in upon the said resolutions." *Proceedings of House of Commons,* vol. V, 72.[24]

This was constitutional; there is an infinite difference between taking off British drawbacks, and imposing Irish or other provincial duties.

"Ireland is considered as a provincial government, subordinate to but no part of the realm of England," Mich., 11 Geo. II in case of Otway and Ramsay — "Acts of Parliament made here (i.e., in England) extend not to Ireland, unless particularly named, much less judgments obtained in the courts here; nor is it possible they should, because we have no officers to carry them into execution there." *ib.*[25]

The first part seems to be applicable to the plantations in general, the latter is not; for by reason of charter reservations and particular acts of Parliament some judgments in England may be executed here, as final judgments, before His Majesty in Council on a plantation appeal, and so from the admiralty.

It seems to have been disputed in Ireland so lately as the 6 Geo. I, whether any act of the British Parliament bound Ireland; or at least it was apprehended that the undoubted right of the British Parliament to bind Ireland was in danger of being shaken. This, I presume, occasioned the act of that year which declares that "the kingdom of Ireland ought to be subordinate unto and dependent upon the imperial crown of Great Britain, as being inseparably united thereto. And the King's Majesty, with the consent of the Lords and Commons of Great Britain in Parliament, hath power to make laws to bind the people of Ireland." [26] This Parliamentary power must have some bounds even as to *Ireland,* as well as the colonies, who are admitted to be subordinate *ab initio* to Great Britain, not as *conquered,* but as *emigrant* subjects. If this act should be said to be a declaration not only of the general but of the universal power of Parliament, and that they may tax Ireland, I ask why it has never been done. If it had been done a thousand times, it would be a contradiction to the principles of a free government, and what is worse, destroy all subordination consistent with *freedom* and reduce the people to *slavery*.

[47] To say the Parliament is absolute and arbitrary is a contradiction. The Parliament cannot make 2 and 2, 5: omnipotency cannot do it. The supreme power in a state is *jus dicere* only: *jus dare,* strictly speaking, belongs alone to GOD. Parliaments are in all cases to *declare* what is for the good of the whole; but it is not the *declaration* of Parliament that makes it so. There must be in every instance a higher authority, viz., GOD. Should an act of Parliament be against any of *his* natural laws, which are *immutably* true, *their* declaration would be contrary to eternal truth, equity, and justice, and consequently void: and so it would be adjudged by the Parliament itself when convinced of their mistake. Upon this great principle Parliaments repeal such acts as soon as they

find they have been mistaken in having declared them to be for the public good when in fact they were not so. When such mistake is evident and palpable, as in the instances in the Appendix, the judges of the executive courts have declared the act "of a whole Parliament void." See here the grandeur of the British constitution! See the wisdom of our ancestors! The supreme *legislative* and the supreme *executive* are a perpetual check and balance to each other. If the supreme executive errs it is informed by the supreme legislative in Parliament. If the supreme legislative errs it is informed by the supreme executive in the King's courts of law. Here the King appears, as represented by his judges, in the highest luster and majesty, as supreme executor of the commonwealth; and he never shines brighter but on his throne, at the head of the supreme legislative. This is government! This is a constitution! to preserve which, either from foreign or domestic foes, has cost oceans of blood and treasure in every age; and the blood and the treasure have upon the whole been well spent. British America hath been bleeding in this cause from its settlement: we have spent all we could raise, and more; for notwithstanding the Parliamentary reimbursements of part, we still remain much in debt.[27] The province of the *Massachusetts,* I believe, has expended more men and money in war since the year 1620, when a few families first landed at Plymouth, in proportion to their ability than the three kingdoms together. The same, I believe, may be truly [48] affirmed of many of the other colonies; though the *Massachusetts* has undoubtedly had the heaviest burden. This may be thought incredible: but materials are collecting; and though some are lost, enough may remain to demonstrate it to the world. I have reason to hope at least that the public will soon see such proofs exhibited as will show that I do not speak quite at random.

Why then is it thought so heinous by the author of the *Administration of the Colonies,* and others, that the colonists should aspire after "a one whole legislative power" not independent of but subordinate to the laws and Parliament of Great Britain? It is a mistake in this author to bring so heavy a charge as *high treason* against some of the colonists, which he does in effect in this place§ by representing them as "claiming in fact or in deed the same full free independent unrestrained power and legislative will in their several corporations, and under the King's commission and their respective charters, as the government and legislature of Great Britain holds by its constitution and under the great charter." No

§ Page 39 of the *Administration.*

such claim was ever thought of by any of the colonists. They are all better men and better subjects; and many of them too well versed in the laws of nature and nations and the law and constitution of Great Britain to think they have a right to more than a *provincial subordinate legislative*. All power is of GOD. Next and only subordinate to Him in the present state of the well formed, beautifully constructed British monarchy, standing where I hope it ever will stand, for the pillars are fixed in judgment, righteousness, and truth, is the King and Parliament.[28] Under these, it seems easy to conceive subordinate powers in gradation, till we descend to the legislative of a town council or even a private social club. These have each "a one whole legislative" subordinate, which, when it don't counteract the laws of any of its superiors, is to be indulged. Even when the laws of subordination are transgressed, the superior does not destroy the subordinate, but will negative its acts, as it may in all cases when disapproved. This right of negative is essential, and may be enforced. But in no case are the essential rights of the subjects inhabiting the subordinate dominions to be [49] destroyed. This would put it in the power of the superior to reduce the inferior to a state of slavery; which cannot be rightfully done even with *conquered* enemies and *rebels*. After satisfaction and security is obtained of the former and examples are made of so many of the latter as the ends of government require, the rest are to be restored to all the essential rights of men and of citizens. This is the great law of nature: and agreeable to this law is the constant practice of all good and mild governments. This lenity and humanity has nowhere been carried further than in Great Britain. The colonies have been so remarkable for loyalty that there never has been any instance of rebellion or treason in them. This loyalty is in very handsome terms acknowledged by the author of the *Administration of the Colonies*. "It has been often suggested that care should be taken in the administration of the plantations lest, in some future time, these colonies should become independent of the mother country. But perhaps it may be proper on this occasion, nay, it is justice to say it, that if by becoming independent is meant a revolt, nothing is further from their nature, their interest, their thoughts. If a defection from the *alliance* of the mother country be suggested, it ought to be and can be truly said that their spirit abhors the sense of such; their attachment to the Protestant succession of the House of Hanover will ever stand unshaken; and nothing can eradicate from their hearts their natural and almost mechanical affection to Great Britain, which they conceive under no other sense nor call by any other name than that of *home*. Any such suggestion, therefore, is a false and unjust aspersion on their principles and affections, and can arise from nothing but an entire ignorance of their circumstances." || [29] After all this loyalty, it is a little hard to be charged with claiming, and represented as aspiring after, independency. The inconsistency of this I leave. We have said that the loyalty of the colonies has never been suspected; this must be restricted to a just suspicion. For it seems there have long been groundless suspicions of us in the minds of individuals. And there have always been those who have endeavored to magnify these chimerical fears. I find Mr. Dummer complaining of this many years since. [50] "There is," says he, "one thing more I have heard often urged against the charter colonies, and indeed 'tis what one meets with from people of all conditions and qualities, though with due respect to their better judgments, I can see neither reason nor color for it. 'Tis said that their increasing numbers and wealth, joined to their great distance from Britain, will give them an opportunity, in the course of some years, to throw off their dependence on the nation and declare themselves a free state if not curbed in time by being made *entirely subject to the crown."* ¶

This jealousy has been so long talked of that many seem to believe it really well grounded. Not that there is danger of a "revolt," even in the opinion of the *author of the Administration,* but that the colonists will by fraud or force avail themselves, in "fact or in deed," of an independent legislature. This, I think, would be a revolting with a vengeance. What higher revolt can there be than for a province to assume the right of an independent legislative or state? I must therefore think this a greater aspersion on the colonists than to charge them with a design to revolt in the sense in which the gentleman allows they have been abused: it is a more artful and dangerous way of attacking our liberties than to charge us with being in open rebellion. That could be confuted instantly: but this seeming indirect way of charging the colonies with a desire of throwing off their dependency requires more pains to confute it than the other; therefore it has been recurred to. The truth is, gentlemen have had departments in America the functions of which they have not been fortunate in executing. The people have by these means been rendered uneasy at bad provincial measures. They have been represented as factious, seditious, and inclined to democracy whenever they have refused passive obedience to provincial mandates as arbitrary as those of

|| *Administration,* pp. 25, 26.   ¶ *Defence,* 60.

a Turkish bashaw: I say provincial mandates, for to the King and Parliament they have been ever submissive and obedient.

These representations of us many of the good people of England swallow with as much ease as they would a bottle bubble or any other story of a cock and a bull; and the worst of it is, among some of the most credulous have been [51] found stars and garters. However, they may all rest assured, the colonists, who do not pretend to understand themselves so well as the people of England, though the author of the *Administration* makes them the fine compliment to say they "know their business much better," yet will never think of independency. Were they inclined to it, they know the blood and the treasure it would cost, if ever effected; and when done, it would be a thousand to one if their liberties did not fall a sacrifice to the victor.

We all think ourselves happy under Great Britain. We love, esteem, and reverence our mother country, and adore our King. And could the choice of independency be offered the colonies or subjection to Great Britain upon any terms above absolute slavery, I am convinced they would accept the latter. The ministry in all future generations may rely on it that British America will never prove undutiful till driven to it as the last fatal resort against ministerial oppression, which will make the wisest mad, and the weakest strong.

These colonies are and always have been "entirely subject to the crown," in the legal sense of the terms. But if any politican of "tampering activity, of wrong-headed inexperience, misled to be meddling," * means by "curbing the colonies in time" and by "being made entirely subject to the crown" that this subjection should be absolute and confined to the crown, he had better have suppressed his wishes. This never will nor can be done without making the colonists vassals of the crown. Subjects they are; their lands they hold of the crown by common socage, the freest feudal tenure by which any hold their lands in England or anywhere else. Would these gentlemen carry us back to the state of the Goths and Vandals, and revive all the military tenures and bondage which our forefathers could not bear? It may be worth noting here that few if any instances can be given where colonies have been disposed to forsake or disobey a tender mother; but history is full of examples that armies stationed as guards over provinces have seized the prey for their general and given him a crown at the expense of his master. Are all ambitious generals dead? Will no [52] more rise up hereafter? The danger

* *Administration*, 34.

of a standing army in remote provinces is much greater to the metropolis than at home. Rome found the truth of this assertion in her Sullas, her Pompeys, and Caesars; but she found it too late. Eighteen hundred years have rolled away since her ruin. A continuation of the same liberties that have been enjoyed by the colonists since the Revolution, and the same moderation of government exercised towards them will bind them in perpetual lawful and willing subjection, obedience, and love to Great Britain: she and her colonies will both prosper and flourish. The monarchy will remain in sound health and full vigor at that blessed period when the proud arbitrary tyrants of the continent shall either unite in the deliverance of the human race or resign their crowns. Rescued human nature must and will be from the general slavery that has so long triumphed over the species. Great Britain has done much towards it: what a glory will it be for her to complete the work throughout the world!

The author of the *Administration* (page 54) "describes" the defects of the "provincial courts" by a "very description," the first trait of which is "the ignorance of the judges." Whether the description, or the description of the description, are *verily* true, either as applied by Lord Hale or the Administrator, is left to the reader. I only ask, Who makes the judges in the provinces? I know of but two colonies, viz., Connecticut and Rhode Island, where they are chosen by the people. In all other colonies they are either immediately appointed by the crown or by His Majesty's governor with the advice of what the Administrator calls the "governor's Council of State." And if they are in general such ignorant creatures as the Administrator describes them, 'tis the misfortune, not the fault, of the people in the colonies. However, I believe justice in general is as well administered in the colonies as it will be when everything is devolved upon a court of admiralty, general or provincial. The following is very remarkable. "In those popular governments, and where every executive officer is under a dependence for a temporary, wretched, and I had almost said arbitrary support on the deputies of the people." † [30]

[53] Why is the temporary support found fault with? Would it be wise to give a governor a salary for a longer time than his political life? As this is quite as uncertain as his natural life, it has been granted annually. So every governor has the chance of one year's salary after he is dead. All the King's officers are not even in the charter provinces "dependent on the people" for support. The judges of the admiralty, those

† *Administ.*, 56.

mirrors of justice, to be trusted when none of the common law courts are, have all their commissions from home. These, besides other fees, have so much per cent on all they condemn, be it right or wrong, and *this by act of Parliament.* Yet so great is their integrity that it never was suspected that 50 per cent, if allowed, would have any influence on their decrees.

Customhouse officers universally, and naval officers in all but two or three of the colonies, are, I believe, appointed directly from home or by instruction to the governor; and take just what they please, for any restraint they are under by the provincial acts. But on whom should a governor depend for his honorable support but the people? Is not the King fed from the fields and from the labor of his people? Does not His Majesty himself receive his aids from the free grant of his Parliament? Do not all these originate in the House of Commons? Did the House of Lords ever originate a grant? Do not our law books inform us that the Lords only assent or dissent, but never so much as propose an amendment on a money bill? The King can take no more than the Parliament will give him, and yet some of his governors have thought it an insufferable hardship that they could not take what they pleased. To take leave of the Administrator, there are in his book some good hints, but a multiplicity of mistakes in fact and errors in matters of right, which I have not time to mention particularly.

Ireland is a conquered kingdom, and yet have thought they received very hard measure in some of the prohibitions and restrictions of their trade. But were the colonies ever conquered? Have they not been subject and obedient and loyal from their settlement? Were not the settlements made under the British laws and constitution? But if the colonies were all to be considered as conquered, they are [54] entitled to the essential rights of men and citizens. And therefore, admitting the right of prohibition in its utmost extent and latitude, a right of taxation can never be inferred from that. It may be for the good of the whole that a certain commodity should be prohibited, but this power should be exercised with great *moderation* and impartiality over dominions which are not *represented* in the national Parliament. I had, however, rather see this carried with a high hand to the utmost rigor than have a tax of one shilling taken from me without my consent. A people may be very happy, free, and easy among themselves without a particular branch of foreign trade. I am sure these colonies have the natural means of every manufacture in *Europe,* and some that are out of their power to make or produce. It will scarcely be believed a hundred years hence that the American manufactures could have been brought to such perfection as they will then probably be in if the present measures are pushed. One single act of Parliament, we find, has set people a-thinking in six months more than they had done in their whole lives before. It should be remembered that the most famous and flourishing manufactures of wool in *France* were begun by *Louis* XIV not an hundred years ago, and they now bid fair to rival the *English* in every port abroad. All the manufactures that Great Britain could make would be consumed in America and in her own plantations if put on a right footing, for which a greater profit in return would be made than she will ever see again for woolen sent to any part of Europe.

But though it be allowed that liberty may be enjoyed in a comfortable measure where *prohibitions* are laid on the trade of a kingdom or province, yet if *taxes* are laid on either *without* consent, they cannot be said to be free. This barrier of liberty being once broken down, all is lost. If a shilling in the pound may be taken from me against my will, why may not twenty shillings; and if so, why not my liberty or my life? Merchants were always *particularly* favored by the common law. "All merchants, except enemies, may safely come into *England,* with their goods and merchandise." 2 *Inst.* [57]. And why not as well to the *plantations?* Are they not entitled to all the [55] British privileges? No, they must be confined in their imports and exports to the good of the metropolis. Very well, we have submitted to this. The act of navigation is a good act, so are all that exclude foreign manufactures from the plantations, and every honest man will readily subscribe to them. Moreover, "Merchant strangers are also to come into the realm and depart at pleasure; and they are to be friendly entertained." 2 Rich. II c. 1. But to promote the manufacturers of *England* 'tis thought best to shut up the *colonies* in a manner from all the world. Right as to Europe: but for God's sake, must we have no trade with other colonies? In some cases the trade between *British* colony and colony is prohibited, as in wool, etc. Granting all this to be right, is it not enough? No, duties and taxes must be paid without any *consent* or *representation* in Parliament. The common law, that inestimable privilege of a jury, is also taken away in all trials in the colonies relating to the revenue if the informers have a mind to go the admiralty, as they ever have done and ever will do for very obvious reasons.[31] "It has ever been boasted," says Mr. Dummer in his *Defence of the Charters,* "as the peculiar privilege of an Englishman, and the security of his property, to be tried by his country and the laws of the land. Whereas this admiralty method deprives him of both, as it puts his estate in the disposal of a single person and makes the civil law the rule of judgment, which though it may not properly be called foreign, being the law of nations, yet 'tis what he has not consented to himself nor his representative for him. A jurisdiction, therefore, so founded ought not to extend beyond what *necessity* requires." "If some bounds are not set to the jurisdiction of the admiralty beyond which it shall not pass, it may in time, like the element to which it ought to be confined, grow outrageous and overflow the banks of all the other courts of justice." I believe it has never been doubted by one sound common lawyer of England, whether a court of admiralty ever answered many good ends; "the Court of King's Bench has a power to restrain the court of admiralty in England; and the reasons for such restraining power are as strong in New England as in Great Britain," and in some respects more so: yet Mr. Dummer mentions a [56] clamor that was raised at home by a judge of the admiralty for New England, who complained "that the common law courts by granting prohibitions weaken, and in a manner suppress, the authority of this court and all the good ends for which it was constituted." [32] Thus we see that the court of admiralty long ago discovered no very friendly disposition towards the common law courts here; and the records of the House of Representatives afford us a notable instance of one who was expelled the House, of which he had been an unworthy member, for the abusive misrepresentations of the province by him secretly made.

Trade and traffic, says Lord Coke, "is the livelihood of a merchant, the life of the commonwealth, wherein the King and every subject hath interest; for the merchant is the good bailiff of the realm, to export and vent the native commodities of the realm and to import and bring in the necessary commodities for the defense and benefit of the realm" — 2 *Inst.* 28, reading on Magna Carta c. [14]. And are not the merchants of British America entitled to a livelihood also? Are they not British subjects? Are not an infinity of commodities carried from hence for *the benefit of the realm,* for which in return come an infinity of *trifles* which we could do without? Manufactures we must go into if our trade is cut off; our country is too cold to go naked in, and we shall soon be unable to make returns to England even for necessaries.

"When any law or custom of Parliament is broken, and the crown possessed of a precedent, how difficult a thing is it to restore the subject again to his former freedom and safety?" 2 *Inst. On the Confirmation of the Great Charter,* which provides in these words: "And for so much as divers people of our realm are in fear that the aids and tasks which they have given to us before time towards our wars and other business of their own grant and good will (howsoever they were made) might *turn to a bondage* to them and their heirs because they might be at another time found in the rolls and likewise for the prices taken throughout the realm by our ministers, we have granted for us and our heirs that we shall not draw such aids, tasks, nor prices *into a custom* for anything that hath been done heretofore, be it by roll or any other precedent that may be founden."

[57] By the first chapter of this act the great charter is declared to be the common law. I would ask whether we have not reason to fear that the great aids freely given by these provinces in the late war will in like manner turn *to our bondage* if they are to be kept on and *increased* during a *peace* for the maintenance of a *standing army* here? If 'tis said those aids were given for *our own* immediate defense and that England spent millions in the same cause, I answer, the names of his present Majesty and his royal grandfather will be ever dear to every loyal British American for the protection they afforded us and the salvation, under God, effected by their arms; but with regard to our fellow subjects of Britain, we never were a whit behind hand with them. The New England colonies in particular were not only settled without the least expense to the mother country, but they have all along defended themselves against the frequent incursions of the most inhuman savages, perhaps, on the face of the whole earth, at *their own cost.* Those more than brutal *men,* spirited and directed by the most inveterate as well as most powerful enemy of Great Britain, have been constantly annoying our infant settlements for more than a century, spreading terror and desolation, and sometimes depopulating whole villages in a night; yet amidst the fatigues of labor and the horrors of war and bloodshed, Heaven vouchsafed its smiles. Behold, an extensive territory settled, defended, and secured to His Majesty, I repeat it, *without the least expense to the mother country* till within twenty years past! When *Louisbourg* was reduced to his late Majesty by the valor of his *New England* subjects, the Parliament, it must be owned, saw meet to refund *part* of the charges; and everyone knows the importance of *Louisbourg* in the consultations *Aix-la-Chapelle.* But for the loss of our young men, the riches and strength of a country, not indeed slain by the enemy but overborne by the uncommon hardships

of the siege and their confinement in garrison afterwards, there could be
no recompense made.[33] In the late war the *northern colonies* not only
raised their full quota of men but they went even beyond their ability:
they are still deeply in debt, notwithstanding the Parliamentary grants
annually made them *in part* of their expenses [58] in the common
national cause. Had it not been for those grants, they had all been bankrupt long ago; while the *sugar colonies* have borne little or no share in
it. They indeed sent a company or two of *Negroes* and *mulattoes,* if
this be worth mentioning, to the sieges of Guadeloupe, Martinique, and
the Havana. I do not recollect anything else that they have done; while
the flower of *our* youth were annually pressed by ten thousands into the
service and there treated but little better, as we have been told, than
hewers of wood and drawers of water. Provincial acts for impressing
were obtained only by letters of requisition from a secretary of state to
a governor requiring him to use his influence to raise men; and sometimes more than were asked for or wanted were pressed, to give a figure
to the governor and show his influence, a remarkable instance of which
might be mentioned.[34] I would further observe that Great Britain was
as immediately interested in the late war in America as the colonies were.
Was she not threatened with an invasion at the same time we were?
Has she not an immense trade to the colonies? The British writers say
more than half her profitable trade is to *America:* all the profits of our
trade center there, and is little enough to pay for the goods we import.
A prodigious revenue arises to the crown on American exports to Great
Britain, which in general is not murmured at. No manufacture of Europe
besides British can be lawfully brought here; and no honest man desires
they ever should, if the laws were put in execution upon all. With regard
to a few Dutch imports that have made such a noise, the truth is, very
little has been or could be run before the apparatus of guardships; for
the officers of some ports did their duty, while others may have made a
monopoly of smuggling for a few of their friends, who probably paid
them large contributions. For it has been observed that a very small
office in the customs in America has raised a man a fortune sooner than
a government. The truth is, the acts of trade have been too often evaded;
but by whom? Not by the American merchants in general, but by some
former customhouse officers, their friends and partisans. I name no man,
not being about to turn informer; but it has been a notorious grievance
that when [59] the King himself cannot dispense with an act of Parliament, there have been customhouse officers who have practiced it for

years together in favor of those towards whom they were graciously disposed.

But to return to the subject of taxation: I find that "the Lords and Commons cannot be charged with anything for the defense of the realm, for the safeguard of the sea, etc., unless by their *will* in Parliament." Ld. Coke, on Magna Carta c. 30 [2 *Inst.* 61].

"Impositions neither in time of war, or other the greatest necessity or occasion that may be, much less in the time of peace, neither upon foreign or inland commodities, of what nature soever, be they never so superfluous or unnecessary, neither upon merchants, strangers, nor denizens, may be laid by the King's absolute power without assent of Parliament, be it never for so short a time." Viner, Prerogative of the King, Ea. 1. cites 2 Molloy 320. chap. 12, sec. 1.[35]

"In the reign of Edward III, the Black Prince of Wales, having *Aquitaine* granted to him, did lay an imposition of fuage or focage *a foco* upon his subjects of that dukedom, viz., a shilling for every fire, called hearth silver, which was of so great discontentment and odious to them that it made them revolt. And nothing since this time has been imposed by pretext of any prerogative upon merchandises imported into or exported out of this realm until Queen Mary's time." 2 *Inst.* 61.

Nor has anything of that kind taken place since the Revolution. King Charles I his shipmoney everyone has heard of.

It may be said that these authorities will not serve the colonists because the duties laid on them are by Parliament. I acknowledge the difference of fact, but cannot see the great difference in equity while the colonists are not represented in the House of Commons. And therefore with all humble deference I apprehend that till the colonists are so represented the spirit of all these authorities will argue strongly in their favor. When the Parliament shall think fit to allow the colonists a representation in the House of Commons, the equity of their taxing the colonies will be as clear as their power is at present of doing it without, if they please.[36] [60] When Mr. Dummer wrote his *Defense of the Charters* there was a talk of taking them away by act of Parliament. This defense is dedicated to the right honorable the Lord Carteret, then one of His Majesty's principal secretaries of state, since Earl of Granville. His third proposition is that "it is not for the interest of the crown to resume the charters, if forfeited." This he proves, as also that it would be more for the interest of Great Britain to enlarge rather than diminish the privilege of all the colonists. His last proposition is that it "seems inconsistent with justice to disfranchise the charter colonies by an act of Parliament."

"It seems therefore," says he, "a severity without a precedent that a people who have the misfortune of being a thousand leagues distant from their sovereign, a misfortune great enough in itself, should, unsummoned, unheard, in one day, be deprived of their valuable privileges, which they and their fathers have enjoyed for near a hundred years." 'Tis true, as he observes, "the legislative power is absolute and unaccountable, and King, Lords, and Commons may do what they please; but the question here is not about *power* but *right*" (or rather equity) "and shall not the supreme judicature of all the nation do right?" "One may say that what the Parliament cannot do justly they cannot do at all. *In maximus minima est licentia*. The higher the power is, the greater caution is to be used in the execution of it, because the sufferer is helpless and without resort." [37] I never heard that this reasoning gave any offense. Why should it? Is it not exactly agreeable to the decisions of Parliament and the determinations of the highest executive courts? (See the Appendix.) But if it was thought hard that charter privileges should be taken away by act of Parliament, is it not much harder to be in part or in whole disfranchised of rights that have been always thought inherent to a British subject, namely, to be free from all taxes but what he consents to in person or by his representative? This right, if it could be traced no higher than Magna Carta, is part of the common law, part of a British subject's birthright, and as inherent and perpetual as the duty of allegiance; both which have been brought to these colonies, and have been hitherto held sacred and inviolable and I hope and trust ever will. 'Tis humbly conceived that the British colonists [61] (except only the conquered, if any) are, by Magna Carta, as well entitled to have a voice in their taxes as the subjects within the realm. Are we not as really deprived of that right by the Parliament assessing us before we are represented in the House of Commons as if the King should do it by his prerogative? Can it be said with any color of truth or justice that we are represented in Parliament?

As to the colonists being represented by the provincial agents, I know of no power ever given them but to appear before His Majesty and his ministry. Sometimes they have been directed to petition the Parliament. But they none of them have, and I hope never will have, a power given them by the colonists to act as representatives and to consent to taxes; and if they should make any concessions to the ministry, especially without order, the provinces could not by that be considered as represented in Parliament.

Hibernia habet Parliamenta et faciunt leges et nostra statuta non ligant eos, quia non mittant milites ad Parliamentum. Sed personae eorum sunt subjecti regis, sicut inhabitantes calinae Gasconiae et Guienae. 12 Rep. 111. cites Rich. III c. 12.

"Ireland hath parliaments and make laws, and our statutes do not bind them *because they send no knights to Parliament;* but their persons are subjects of the King as the inhabitants of Guienne, Gascony, etc." [38]

Yet if specially named, or by general words included as within any of the King's dominions, Ireland, says Lord Coke, might be bound. 4 *Inst.* 351.

From all which it seems plain that the reason why Ireland and the plantations are not bound unless named by an act of Parliament is because they are *not represented* in the British Parliament. Yet in special cases the British Parliament has an undoubted right as well as power to bind both by their acts. But whether this can be extended to an indefinite taxation of both is the great question. I conceive the spirit of the British constitution must make an exception of all taxes, until it is thought fit to unite a dominion to the realm. Such taxation must be considered either as uniting the dominions to the realm or disfranchising them. If they are united they will be entitled to a representation as well as Wales; if they are so taxed without a union or representation, they are so far disfranchised.[39]

[62] I don't find anything that looks like a duty on the colonies before the 25th of Chas. II c. 7, imposing a duty on enumerated commodities. The liberty of the subject was little attended to in that reign. If the nation could not fully assert their rights till the Revolution, the colonies could not expect to be heard. I look on this act rather as a precedent of power than of right and equity; if 'tis such it will not affect my argument. The act appointing a tax on all mariners, of a certain sum per month to be deducted out of their wages, is not to be compared with this. Mariners are not inhabitants of any part of the dominions: the sea is their element till they are decrepit, and then the hospital is open to all mariners who are British subjects without exception. The general post office established through the dominions is for the convenience of trade and commerce: it is not laying any burden upon it; for besides that it is upon the whole cheaper to correspond in this way than any other, everyone is at liberty to send his own letters by a friend. The act of the 6th

of his late Majesty, though it imposes a *duty* in terms, has been said to be designed for a *prohibition,* which is probable from the sums imposed; and 'tis pity it had not been so expressed, as there is not the least doubt of the just and equitable right of the Parliament to lay prohibitions through the dominions when they think the good of the whole requires it.[40] But, as has been said, there is an infinite difference between that and the exercise of unlimited power of taxation over the dominions without allowing them a representation. It is said that the duties imposed by the new act will amount to a prohibition: time only can ascertain this. The utility of this act is so fully examined in the Appendix, that I shall add nothing on that head here. It may be said that the colonies ought to bear their proportion of the national burdens: 'tis just they should, and I think I have proved they have always done it freely and cheerfully, and I know no reason to doubt but that they ever will.

Sometimes we have been considered only as the corporations in England; and it may be urged that it is no harder upon us to be taxed by Parliament for the general cause than for them, who besides are at the expense of their corporate [63] subordinate government.‡ I answer: 1. Those corporations are *represented* in Parliament. 2. The colonies are and have been at great expense in raising men, building forts, and supporting the King's civil government here. Now I read of no governors and other officers of His Majesty's nomination that the city of London taxes its inhabitants to support; I know of no forts and garrisons that the city of London has lately built at its own expense, or of any annual levies that they have raised for the King's service and the common cause. These are things very fitting and proper to be done by a subordinate dominion, and 'tis their duty to do all they are able; but it seems but equal they should be allowed to assess the charges of it themselves. The rules of equity and the principles of the constitution seem to require this. Those who judge of the reciprocal rights that subsist between a supreme and subordinate state or dominion by no higher rules than are applied to a corporation of button makers will never have a very comprehensive view of them. Yet sorry am I to say it, many elaborate writers on the *administration of the colonies* seem to me never to rise higher in their notions than what might be expected from a secretary to one of the *quorum.* If I should be ranked among this number I shall have this consolation, that I have fallen into what is called very good company and among some who have seen very high life below stairs. I agree with the

‡ See *Administration of the Colonies,* [pp. 31–33].

Administrator that of whatever revenues raised in the colonies, if they must be raised without our consent, *"the first and special appropriation of them ought to be the paying the governors and all the other crown officers,"* [41] for it would be hard for the colonists to be obliged to pay them after this. It was on this principle that at the last Assembly of this province I moved to stop every grant to the officers of the crown, more especially as I know some who have built very much upon the fine salaries they shall receive from the plantation branch of the revenue. Nor can I think it "injustice to the frame of human nature" § to suppose, if I did not know it, that with similar views several officers of the crown in some of the colonies have been pushing for such an act for many years. They have [64] obtained their wish, and much good it will do them. But I would not give much for all that will center neat [net] in the exchequer after deducting the costs attending the execution of it and the appropriations to the several officers proposed by the Administrator. What will be the unavoidable consequence of all this, suppose another war should happen and it should be necessary to employ as many provincials in America as in the last? Would it be possible for the colonies, after being burdened in their trade, perhaps after it is ruined, to raise men? Is it probable that they would have spirit enough to exert themselves? If 'tis said the French will never try for America, or if they should, regular troops are only to be employed, I grant our regular troops are the best in the world, and that the experience of the present officers shows that they are capable of every species of American service; yet we should guard against the worst. If another trial for Canada should take place, which from the known temper of France we may judge she will bring on the first fair opportunity, it might require 30 or 40 thousand regulars to secure His Majesty's just rights. If it should be said that other American duties must then be levied, besides the impossibility of our being able to pay them, the danger recurs of a large standing army so remote from home; whereas a good provincial militia, with such occasional succors from the mother country as exigencies may require, never was and never will be attended with hazard. The experience of past times will show that an army of 20 or 30 thousand veterans, half 3000 miles from *Rome,* were very apt to proclaim *Caesars.* The first of the name, the assassin of his country, owed his false glory to stealing the affections of an army from the commonwealth. I hope these hints will not be taken amiss; they seem to occur from the nature of the subject

§ *Adm.,* p. 57.

I am upon; they are delivered in pure affection to my King and country, and amount to no reflection on any man. The best army and the best men we may hereafter have may be led into temptation; all I think is that a prevention of evil is much easier than a deliverance from it.

The sum of my argument is: that civil government is of God; that the administrators of it were originally the whole people; that they might have devolved it on whom they [65] pleased; that this devolution is fiduciary, for the good of the whole; that by the British constitution this devolution is on the King, Lords and Commons, the supreme, sacred and uncontrollable legislative power not only in the realm but through the dominions; that by the abdication, the original compact was broken to pieces; that by the Revolution it was renewed and more firmly established, and the rights and liberties of the subject in all parts of the dominions more fully explained and confirmed; that in consequence of this establishment and the acts of succession and union, His Majesty GEORGE III is rightful King and sovereign, and, with his Parliament, the supreme legislative of Great Britain, France, and Ireland, and the dominions thereto belonging; that this constitution is the most free one and by far the best now existing on earth; that by this constitution every man in the dominions is a free man; that no parts of His Majesty's dominions can be taxed without their consent; that every part has a right to be represented in the supreme or some subordinate legislature; that the refusal of this would seem to be a contradiction in practice to the theory of the constitution; that the colonies are subordinate dominions and are now in such a state as to make it best for the good of the whole that they should not only be continued in the enjoyment of subordinate legislation but be also represented in some proportion to their number and estates in the grand legislature of the nation; that this would firmly unite all parts of the British empire in the greatest peace and prosperity, and render it invulnerable and perpetual.[42]

APPENDIX

The City of *Boston*, at Their Annual Meet[ing]
in May 1764, Made Choice of *Richard
Dana, Joseph Green, Nathaniel Bethune,
John Ruddock*, Esquires; and Mr.
Samuel Adams to Prepare INSTRUCTIONS
for Their REPRESENTATIVES.[43]

The Following Instructions Were Reported by Said
Committee and Unanimously Voted.
To *Royal Tyler*,* *James Otis, Thomas Cushing*
and *Oxenbridge Thacher*, Esquires.

GENTLEMEN,

Your being chosen by the freeholders and inhabitants of the town of
Boston to represent them in the General Assembly the ensuing year affords you the strongest testimony of that confidence which they place
in your integrity and capacity. By this choice they have delegated to you
the power of acting in their public concerns in general as your own prudence shall direct you, always reserving to themselves the constitutional
right of expressing their mind and giving you such instruction upon
particular matters as they at any time shall judge proper.

[67] We therefore your constituents take this opportunity to declare
our just expectations from you:

That you will constantly use your power and influence in maintaining
the invaluable rights and privileges of the province, of which this town
is so great a part: as well those rights which are derived to us by the
royal charter as those which, being prior to and independent on it, we
hold essentially as freeborn subjects of Great Britain.

That you will endeavor as far as you shall be able to preserve that independence in the House of Representatives which characterizes a free
people, and the want of which may in a great measure prevent the happy
effects of a free government: cultivating as you shall have opportunity

---

* Now of the honorable Board [the Council]; in whose room was returned Mr. *Thomas
Gray*, merchant.

that harmony and union there which is ever desirable to good men when founded in principles of virtue and public spirit, and guarding against any undue weight which may tend to disadjust that critical balance upon which our happy constitution and the blessings of it do depend. And for this purpose we particularly recommend it to you to use your endeavors to have a law passed whereby the seats of such gentlemen as shall accept of posts of profit from the crown or the governor while they are members of the House, shall be vacated, agreeable to an act of the British Parliament, till their constituents shall have the opportunity of re-electing them, if they please, or of returning others in their room.

Being members of the legislative body, you will have a special regard to the morals of this people, which are the basis of public happiness; and endeavor to have such laws made, if any are still wanting, as shall be best adapted to secure them. And we particularly desire you carefully to look into the laws of excise, that if the virtue of the people is endangered by the multiplicity of oaths therein enjoined, or their trade and business is unreasonably impeded or embarrassed thereby, the grievance may be redressed.

As the preservation of morals, as well as property and right, so much depends upon the impartial distribution of justice agreeable to good and wholesome law, and as the judges of the land do depend upon the free grants of the General Assembly for support, it is incumbent upon you at all times to give your voice for their honorable maintenance [68] so long as they, having in their minds an indifference to all other affairs, shall devote themselves wholly to the duties of their own department and the further study of the law by which their customs, precedents, proceedings, and determinations are adjusted and limited.

You will remember that this province hath been at a very great expense in carrying on the war, and that it still lies under a very grievous burden of debt: you will therefore use your utmost endeavor to promote public frugality as one means to lessen the public debt.

You will join in any proposals which may be made for the better cultivating the lands and improving the husbandry of the province; and as you represent a town which lives by its trade, we expect in a very particular manner that you make it the object of your attention to support our commerce in all its just rights, to vindicate it from all unreasonable impositions, and promote its prosperity. Our trade has for a long time labored under great discouragements; and it is with the deepest concern that we see such further difficulties coming upon it as will reduce it to the lowest ebb, if not totally obstruct and ruin it. We cannot help expressing our surprise that when so early notice was given by the agent of the intentions of the ministry to burden us with new taxes, so little regard was had to this most interesting matter that the Court was not even called together to consult about it till the latter end of the year; the consequence of which was that instructions could not be sent to the agent, though solicited by him, till the evil had got beyond an easy remedy.

There is now no room for further delay: we therefore expect that you will use your earliest endeavors in the General Assembly that such methods may be taken as will effectually prevent these proceedings against us. By a proper representation, we apprehend it may easily be made to appear that such severities will prove detrimental to Great Britain itself; upon which account we have reason to hope that an application, even for a repeal of the act, should it be already passed, will be successful. It is the trade of the colonies that renders them beneficial to the mother country. Our trade, as it is now and always has been conducted, centers in Great Britain, and in return for her manufactures [69] affords her more ready cash, beyond any comparison, than can possibly be expected by the most sanguine promoters of these extraordinary methods. We are in short ultimately yielding large supplies to the revenues of the mother country while we are laboring for a very moderate subsistence for ourselves. But if our trade is to be curtailed in its most profitable branches, and burdens beyond all possible bearing laid upon that which is suffered to remain, we shall be so far from being able to take off the manufactures of Great Britain that it will be scarce possible for us to earn our bread.

But what still heightens our apprehensions is that these unexpected proceedings may be preparatory to new taxations upon us: for if our trade may be taxed, why not our lands? Why not the produce of our lands and everything we possess or make use of? This we apprehend annihilates our charter right to govern and tax ourselves. It strikes at our British privileges, which, as we have never forfeited them, we hold in common with our fellow subjects who are natives of Britain: if taxes are laid upon us in any shape without our having a legal representation where they are laid, are we not reduced from the character of free subjects to the miserable state of tributary slaves?

We therefore earnestly recommend it to you to use your utmost endeavors to obtain in the General Assembly all necessary instruction and advice to our agent at this most critical juncture; that while he is setting forth the unshaken loyalty of this province and this town — its unrivaled exertion in supporting His Majesty's government and rights in this part of his dominion, its acknowledged dependence upon and subordination to Great Britain, and the ready submission of its merchants to all just and necessary regulations of trade — he may be able in the most humble and pressing manner to remonstrate for us all those rights and privileges which justly belong to us either by charter or birth.

As His Majesty's other northern American colonies are embarked with us in this most important bottom, we further desire you to use your endeavors that their weight may be added to that of this province, that by the united application of all who are aggrieved, all may happily obtain redress.

[70] Substance of a Memorial Presented the Assembly in Pursuance of the Above Instructions; and by the House Voted to be Transmitted to JASPER MAUDUIT, Esq., Agent for This Province,* to be Improved As He May Judge Proper.[44]

The public transactions from William I to the Revolution may be considered as one continued struggle between the prince and the people, all tending to that happy establishment which Great Britain has since enjoyed.

The absolute rights of Englishmen, as frequently declared in Parliament, from Magna Carta to this time, are the rights of *personal security, personal liberty,* and of *private property.*

The allegiance of British subjects being natural, perpetual, and inseparable from their persons, let them be in what country they may, their rights are also natural, inherent, and perpetual.

By the laws of nature and of nations, the voice of universal reason, and of God, when a nation takes possession of a desert, uncultivated, and uninhabited country, or purchases of savages, as was the case with far the greatest part of the British settlements, the colonists, transplanting themselves and their posterity, though separated from the principal establishment or mother country, naturally become part of the state with its ancient possessions, and entitled to all the essential rights of the mother country. This is not only confirmed by the practice of the ancients but by the moderns ever since the discovery of America. French-

* Only as a State drawn up by one of the House.

men, Spaniards, and Portugals are no greater slaves abroad than at home; and hitherto Britons have been as free on one side of the Atlantic as on the other: and it is humbly hoped that His Majesty and the Parliament will in their wisdom be graciously pleased to continue the colonists in this happy state.

It is presumed that upon these principles the colonists have been by their several charters declared natural subjects [71] and entrusted with the power of making *their own local laws,* not repugnant to the laws of England, and with *the power of taxing themselves.*

This legislative power is subject by the same charter to the King's negative as in Ireland. This effectually secures the *dependence* of the colonies on Great Britain. By the *thirteenth* of *George* the *Second, chapter the* [*seventh*], even foreigners having lived seven years in any of the colonies are deemed natives on taking oaths of allegiance, etc., and are declared by the said act to be His Majesty's natural-born subjects of the kingdom of Great Britain to all intents, constructions, and purposes, as if any of them had been born within the kingdom. The reasons given for this naturalization in the preamble of the act are "that the increase of the people is the means of advancing the wealth and strength of any nation or country; and that many foreigners and strangers, from the lenity of our government, the purity of our religion, the benefit of our laws, the advantages of our trade, and the security of our *property,* might be induced to come and settle in some of His Majesty's colonies in America if they were partakers of the advantages and privileges which the natural-born subjects there enjoy." †

The several acts of Parliament and charters declaratory of the rights and liberties of the colonies are but in affirmance of the common law and law of nature in this point. There are, says my Lord Coke, regularly three incidents to subjects born. (1) Parents under the actual obedience of the King. (2) That the place of his birth be within the King's dominions. (3) The time of his birth to be chiefly considered: for he cannot be a subject born of one kingdom that was born under the allegiance of the King of another kingdom, albeit afterwards the kingdom descends to the King of the other kingdom. See *Calvin's Case* and the several acts of Parliament and decisions on naturalization from Edward the Third to this day. The common law is received and practiced upon here and in the rest of the colonies, and all ancient and modern acts of Parliament that can be considered as part of or in amendment of the common law, together with all such [72] acts of Parliament as expressly name the

† 13 Geo. II c. 7.

plantations; so that the power of the British Parliament is held as sacred and as uncontrollable in the colonies as in England. The question is not upon the general power or right of the Parliament, but whether it is not circumscribed within some equitable and reasonable bounds. 'Tis hoped it will not be considered as a new doctrine that even the authority of the Parliament of *Great Britain* is circumscribed by certain bounds which if exceeded their acts become those of mere *power* without *right,* and consequently void. The judges of England have declared in favor of these sentiments when they expressly declare that *acts of Parliament against natural equity are void.* That *acts against the fundamental principles of the British constitution are void.*‡ [45] This doctrine is agreeable

‡ "A very important question here presents itself. It essentially belongs to the society to make laws both in relation to the manner in which it desires to be governed, and to the conduct of the citizens: this is called the *legislative power.* The nation may entrust the exercise of it to the prince or an assembly, or to the assembly and the prince jointly, who have then a right of making new and abrogating old laws. It is here demanded whether if their power extends so far as to the fundamental laws they may change the constitution of the state. The principles we have laid down lead us to decide this point with certainty that the authority of these legislators does not extend so far, and that they ought to consider the fundamental laws as sacred if the nation has not in very express terms given them the power to change them. For the constitution of the state ought to be fixed; and since that was first established by the nation, which afterwards trusted certain persons with the legislative power, the fundamental laws are excepted from their commission. It appears that the society had only resolved to make provision for the state's being always furnished with laws suited to particular conjunctures, and gave the legislature for that purpose the power of abrogating the ancient civil and political laws that were not fundamental, and of making new ones: but nothing leads us to think that it was willing to submit the constitution itself to their pleasure.

"When a nation takes possession of a different country and settles a colony there, that country, though separated from the principal establishment, or mother country, naturally becomes a part of the state equally with its ancient possessions. Whenever the political laws or treaties make no distinction between them everything said of the territory of a nation ought also to extend to its colonies." De Vattel.

"An act of Parliament made against natural equity, as to make a man judge in his own cause, would be void; for *jura a naturae sunt immutabilia.* Hob. 87. Trin[ity Term], 12 Jac. [I], *Day v. Savadge,* S. C. and P. [same case and point] cited Arg[uendo] 10 Mod. 115 Hil[ary Term], 11 Anne C.B. [Common Bench] in the case of Thornby and Fleetwood, "but says, that this must be a clear case, and judges will strain hard rather than interpret an act void, *ab initio." This is granted, but still their authority is not boundless if subject to the control of the judges in any case.*

"Holt, Chief Justice, thought what Lord Coke says in *Doctor Bonham's Case* a very reasonable and true saying, that if an act of Parliament should ordain that the same person should be both party and judge in his own cause, it would be a void act of Parliament, and an act of Parliament can do no wrong, though it may do several things that look pretty odd; for it may discharge one from the allegiance he lives under and restore to the state of nature, but it cannot make one that lives under a government both judge and party: per Holt C. J., 12 Mod. 687, Hil., 13 Wm. III B.R. [King's Bench] in the case of the *City of London v. Wood.* — It appears in our books that in several cases the common law shall control acts of Parliament and sometimes adjudge them to be utterly void; for when an act of Parliament is against common *right* and *reason,* or repugnant to the law of nature [73] and nations, and to the divine dictates of natural and revealed religion. It is contrary to reason that the supreme power should have right to alter the constitution. This would imply that those who are entrusted with sovereignty by the people have a right to do as they please. In other words, that those who are invested with power to protect the people and support their rights and liberties have a right to make slaves of them. This is not very remote from a flat contradiction. Should the Parliament of Great Britain follow the example of some other foreign states§ and vote the King absolute and despotic, would such an act of Parliament make him so? Would any minister in his senses advise a prince to accept of such an offer of power? It would be unsafe to accept of such a donation, because the Parliament or donors would grant more than was ever in their power lawfully to give. The law of nature never invested them with a power of surrendering their own liberty; [74] and the people certainly never entrusted any body of men with a power to surrender theirs in exchange for slavery.||

---

or impossible to be performed, the common law shall control it and adjudge it to be void, and therefore 8 Edw. III c. 30. *Thomas Tregor's Case* upon the statute of Wm. II c. 38 and Art. sup. Cart. 9. Herle said that sometimes statutes are made contrary to law and right, which the makers of them perceiving will not put them in execution. 8 Rep. 118, Hil., 7 Jac. [I], *Dr. Bonham's Case.*

§ Sweden, Denmark, France, etc.

|| "But if the whole state be conquered, if the nation be subdued, in what manner can the victor treat it without transgressing the bounds of justice? What are his rights over the conquest? Some have dared to advance this monstrous principle, that the conqueror is absolute master of his conquest, that he may dispose of it as his property, treat it as he pleases, according to the common expression of *treating a state as a conquered country;* and hence they derive one of the sources of despotic government. But enough of those that reduce men to the state of transferable goods or use of them like beasts of burden, who deliver them up as the property or patrimony of another man. Let us argue on principles countenanced by reason and becoming humanity. The whole right of the conqueror proceeds from the just defense of himself, which contains the support and prosecution of his rights. Thus when he has totally subdued a nation with whom he had been at war, he may without dispute cause justice to be done him with regard to what gave rise to the war, and require payment for the expense and damage he has sustained; he may, according to the exigency of the case, impose penalties on it as an example; he may, should prudence so dictate, disable it from undertaking any pernicious designs for the future. But in securing all these views the mildest means are to be preferred. We are always to remember that the law of nature permits no injury to be done to an enemy unless in taking measures necessary for a just defense and a reasonable security. Some princes have only imposed a tribute on it; others have been satisfied of stripping it of some privileges, dismembering a province, or keeping it in awe by fortresses; others, as their quarrel was only with the sovereign in person, have left a nation in the full enjoyment of all its rights, only setting a sovereign over it. But if the conqueror thinks proper to retain the sovereignty of the vanquished state and has such a right, the manner in which he is to treat the state still flows from the same principles. If the sovereign be only the just object of his complaint, reason declares that by his conquest he acquires only such rights as actually belonged to the dethroned sovereign, and on the submission of his people he is to govern it according

It is now near three hundred years since the continent of North America was first discovered, and that by British subjects.¶ Ten generations have passed away through infinite toils and bloody conflicts in settling this country. None of those ever dreamed but that they were entitled at least [75] to equal privileges with those of the same rank born within the realm.

British America has been hitherto distinguished from the slavish colonies around about it as the fortunate Britons have been from most of their neighbors on the continent of Europe. It is for the interest of Great Britain that her colonies should be ever thus distinguished. Every man must willfully blind himself that don't see the immense value of our acquisitions in the late war; and that though we did not retain all at the conclusion of the peace that we obtained by the sword, yet our gracious sovereign, at the same time that he has given a divine lesson of equitable moderation to the princes of the earth, has retained sufficient to make the British arms the dread of the universe and his name dear to all posterity.

To the freedom of the British constitution and to their increase of commerce 'tis owing that our colonies have flourished without diminishing the inhabitants of the mother country, quite contrary to the effects of plantations made by most other nations, which have suffered at home in order to aggrandize themselves abroad. This is remarkably the case with Spain. The subjects of a free and happy constitution of government have a thousand advantages to colonize above those who live under despotic princes. We see how the British colonies on the continent have outgrown those of the French notwithstanding they have ever engaged the savages to keep us back. Their advantages over us in the West Indies are, among other causes perhaps, partly owing to these: (1) A capital neglect in former reigns in suffering them to have a firm possession of so many valuable islands that we had a better title to than they. (2) The French, unable to push their settlements effectually on the continent, have bent their views to the islands, and poured vast numbers into them. (3) The climate and business of these islands is by nature much better adapted to Frenchmen and to Negroes than to Britons. (4) The labor of slaves, black or white, will be ever cheaper than that of freemen, because

to the laws of the state. If the people do not voluntarily submit, the state of war subsists." "When a sovereign, as pretending to have the absolute disposal of a people whom he has conquered, is for enslaving them, he causes the state of war to subsist between this people and him."   Mr. De Vattel. bk. III, chap. 10, sec. 201.

¶ The Cabots discovered the continent before the Spaniards.

that of the individuals among the former will never be worth so much as with the latter; but this difference is more than supplied by numbers under the advantages above-mentioned. [76] The French will ever be able to sell their West India produce cheaper than our own islanders; and yet while our own islanders can have such a price for theirs as to grow much richer than the French or any other of the King's subjects in America, as is the case, and what the northern colonies take from the French and other foreign islands centers finally in returns to Great Britain for her manufactures, to an immense value and with a vast profit to her: it is contrary to the first principles of policy to clog such a trade with duties, much more to prohibit it, to the risk if not certain destruction of the fishery. It is allowed by the most accurate British writers on commerce, Mr. Postlethwayt in particular, who seems to favor the cause of the sugar islands, that one half of the immense commerce of Great Britain is with her colonies.[46] It is very certain that without the fishery seven eighths of this commerce would cease. The fishery is the center of motion upon which the wheel of all the British commerce in America turns. Without the American trade, would Britain, as a commercial state, make any great figure at this day in Europe? Her trade in woolen and other manufactures is said to be lessening in all parts of the world but America, where it is increasing and capable of infinite increase from a concurrence of every circumstance in its favor. Here is an extensive territory of different climates, which in time will consume and be able to pay for as many manufactures as Great Britain and Ireland can make, if true maxims are pursued. The French, for reasons already mentioned, can underwork and consequently undersell the English manufactures of Great Britain in every market in Europe. But they can send none of their manufactures here; and it is the wish of every honest British American that they never may; 'tis best they never should. We can do better without the manufactures of Europe, save those of Great Britain, than with them; but without the French West India produce we cannot; without it our fishery must infallibly be ruined. When that is gone our own islands will very poorly subsist. No British manufactures can be paid for by the colonists. What will follow? One of these two things, both of which it is the interest of Great Britain to prevent. (1) The northern [77] colonists must be content to go naked and turn savages. Or (2) become manufacturers of linen and woolen to clothe themselves, which, if they cannot carry to the perfection of Europe, will be very destructive to the interests of Great Britain. The computation has been made, and that within bounds, and it can be demonstrated that if North America is only driven to the fatal necessity of manufacturing a suit of the most ordinary linen or woolen for each inhabitant annually, which may be soon done when necessity the mother of invention shall operate, Great Britain and Ireland will lose two millions per annum, besides a diminution of the revenue to nearly the same amount. This may appear paradoxical, but a few years' experience of the execution of the Sugar Act will sufficiently convince the Parliament not only of the inutility but destructive tendency of it, while calculations may be little attended to. That the trade with the colonies has been of surprising advantage to Great Britain notwithstanding the want of a good regulation is past all doubt. Great Britain is well known to have increased prodigiously both in numbers and in wealth since she began to colonize. To the growth of the plantations Britain is in a great measure indebted for her present riches and strength. As the wild wastes of America have been turned into pleasant habitations and flourishing trading towns, so many of the little villages and obscure boroughs in Great Britain have put on a new face, and suddenly started up and become fair markets and manufacturing towns and opulent cities. London itself, which bids fair to be the metropolis of the world, is five times more populous than it was in the days of Queen Elizabeth. Such are the fruits of the spirit of commerce and liberty. Hence it is manifest how much we all owe to that beautiful form of civil government under which we have the happiness to live.

It is evidently the interest, and ought to be the care, of all those entrusted with the administration of government to see that every part of the British empire enjoys to the full the rights they are entitled to by the laws and the advantages which result from their being maintained with impartiality and vigor. This we have seen reduced to practice in the present and preceding reigns, and have the [78] highest reason, from the paternal care and goodness that His Majesty and the British Parliament have hitherto been graciously pleased to discover to all His Majesty's dutiful and loyal subjects, and to the colonists in particular, to rest satisfied that our privileges will remain sacred and inviolate. The connection between Great Britain and her colonies is so natural and strong as to make their mutual happiness depend upon their mutual support. Nothing can tend more to the destruction of both, and to forward the measures of their enemies than sowing the seeds of jealousy, animosity, and dissension between the mother country and the colonies.

A conviction of the truth and importance of these principles induced

Great Britain during the late war to carry on so many glorious enterprises for the defense of the colonies, and those on their part to exert themselves beyond their ability to pay, as is evident from the Parliamentary reimbursements.

If the spirit of commerce was attended to, perhaps duties would be everywhere decreased, if not annihilated, and prohibitions multiplied. Every branch of trade that hurts a community should be prohibited for the same reason that a private gentleman would break off commerce with a sharper or an extorsive usurer. 'Tis to no purpose to higgle with such people, you are sure to lose by them. 'Tis exactly so with a nation, if the balance is against them and they can possibly subsist without the commodity, as they generally can in such cases, a prohibition is the only remedy; for a duty in such case is like a composition with a thief, that for five shillings in the pound returned, he shall rob you at pleasure, when if the thing is examined to the bottom you are at five shillings expense in traveling to get back your five shillings, and he is at the same expense in coming to pay it, so he robs you of but ten shillings in the pound that you thus wisely compound for. To apply this to trade, I believe every duty that was ever imposed on commerce, or in the nature of things can be, will be found to be divided between the state imposing the duty and the country exported from. This if between the several parts of the same kingdom or dominions of the same prince can [79] only tend to embarrass trade and raise the price of labor above other states, which is of very pernicious consequence to the husbandman, manufacturer, mariner, and merchant, the four tribes that support the whole hive. If your duty is upon a commodity of a foreign state, it is either upon the whole useful and gainful and therefore necessary for the husbandmen, manufacturer, mariner, or merchant, as finally bringing a profit to the state by a balance in her favor; or the importation will work a balance against your state. There is no medium that we know of. If the commodity is of the former kind, it should be prohibited; but if the latter, imported duty free, unless you would raise the price of labor by a duty on necessaries, or make the above wise composition for the importation of commodities you are sure to lose by. The only test of a useful commodity is the gain upon the whole to the state; such should be free. The only test of a pernicious trade is the loss upon the whole or to the community; this should be prohibited. If therefore it can be demonstrated that the sugar and molasses trade from the northern colonies to the foreign plantations is upon the *whole* a loss to the *community,* by which term is here meant the three kingdoms and the British dominions taken collectively, then and not till then should this trade be prohibited. This never has been proved, nor can be, the contrary being certain, to wit, that the nation upon the whole hath been a vast gainer by this trade in the vend of and pay for its manufactures; and a great loss by a duty upon this trade will finally fall on the British husbandman, manufacturer, mariner, and merchant, and consequently the trade of the nation be wounded, and in constant danger of being eat out by those who can undersell her.

The art of underselling, or rather of finding means to undersell, is the grand secret of thrift among commercial states, as well as among individuals of the same state. Should the British sugar islands ever be able to supply Great Britain and her northern colonies with those articles, it will be time enough to think of a total prohibition; but until that time both prohibition and duty will be found to be diametrically opposite to the first principles of policy. [80] Such is the extent of this continent and the increase of its inhabitants that if every inch of the British sugar islands was as well cultivated as any part of Jamaica or Barbados, they would not now be able to supply Great Britain and the colonies on this continent. But before such further improvements can be supposed to take place in our islands, the demands will be proportionably increased by the increase of the inhabitants on the continent. Hence the reason is plain why the British sugar planters are growing rich and ever will, because the demand for their produce has and ever will be greater than they can possibly supply so long as the English hold this continent and are unrivaled in the fishery.

We have everything good and great to hope from our gracious sovereign, his ministry and his Parliament, and trust that when the services and sufferings of the British American colonies are fully known to the mother country, and the nature and importance of the plantation trade more perfectly understood at home, that the most effectual measures will be taken for perpetuating the British Empire in all parts of the world. An empire built upon the principles of justice, moderation, and equity, the only principles that can make a state flourishing, and enable it to elude the machinations of its secret and inveterate enemies.

P. S. By ancient and modern gods, p. 10, I mean all idols, from those of old Egypt to the canonized monsters of modern Rome; and by kingcraft and priestcraft, civil and ecclesiastic polity as administered in general till the Revolution. I now recollect that I have been credibly informed that the British sugar colonists are humane towards their slaves in comparison with the others. Therefore in page 29, let it be read, foreign sugar islanders and foreign creoles.

PAMPHLET 8

OXENBRIDGE THACHER,
THE SENTIMENTS OF A BRITISH AMERICAN

BOSTON, 1764

INTRODUCTION

The colonists' original objection to the Sugar Act of 1764, expressed in pamphlets such as *Considerations upon the Act of Parliament* (JHL Pamphlet 5), were directed almost exclusively to the economic difficulties that were expected to arise from the taxes on the importation of foreign sugar products specified in the act. But by the summer of 1764, several months after the act was passed, it was discovered that the statute was a far more complicated and important piece of legislation than the colonists had suspected. It contained, they found, in addition to the revenue provisions, some forty sections providing the means for the strict enforcement of customs regulations. These provisions, building on the wartime measures Pitt had introduced to prevent clandestine traffic with the enemy, threatened in themselves to revolutionize the traditionally loose administrative relationship between England and America. But they threatened more. They raised issues of constitutionalism, of individual rights, and of the administration of justice; and they raised, also, profoundly disquieting suspicions of the motivations of the people responsible for such legislation in England. Oxenbridge Thacher's "pretty little pamphlet," as John Adams called it,[1] published in the summer of 1764 shortly after the appearance of Otis' *Rights of the British Colonies* (JHL Pamphlet 7) called attention to the problem of motives, and showed its bearing on the ideological issues central to the developing Anglo-American controversy.

Thacher was peculiarly well prepared to deal with a combination of economic, judicial, and ideological questions. Several years older than Otis and Mayhew, he had graduated from Harvard College with the class of 1738 and had remained there as a student of divinity until 1741. But though pious and devoted to traditional New England Congregationalism, he failed as a minister and turned to the law, in which he eventually succeeded despite an initial disinclination for the work of that profession. In 1759 John Adams found him, a man of forty, easily accessible, willing to spend whole evenings talking "upon original sin, origin of evil, the plan of the universe, and at last upon law." But despite the ambivalence of his attitude to his profession, and despite also what Adams viewed as a disconcerting tendency toward impetuous flights in conversation, he made himself an authority on law and a leading member of the Massachusetts bar. He was repeatedly drawn into cases concerning maritime affairs, most conspicuously as Otis' colleague in the writs of assistance controversy and in an important customs case of 1763. His role in the writs case was businesslike and unspectacular: he dwelt on the lack of precedents, and questioned the right of the Superior Court to act as a court of exchequer. But his plea in the customs case, in which goods allegedly imported directly from Europe instead of via England had been seized for violating the navigation laws, had profound implications, as Governor Bernard, among others, quickly realized. For Thacher challenged directly not only the legal right of a customhouse officer to seize such goods but also the all-important technicality that goods brought to an American port and not opened there were legally considered to have been "imported" and hence subject to the restrictions of the law. His argument that such goods do not come under the law "till landing or bulk broken," Governor Bernard wrote the home authorities, threatened to undermine the whole structure of England's commercial system. The failure of Thacher's plea in this case was a blow, Bernard wrote, at what he said was a conspiracy "to distress and embarrass [the customs officials] by appeals and actions at common law." [2]

Nothing could be more revealing of the atmosphere of the time than this interpretation of Thacher's argument by Governor Bernard. For if the governor was convinced that a "confederacy [had been] formed against the ordinary customhouse officers of this port about three years ago," Thacher was equally convinced that Bernard himself was plotting: plotting against the survival of liberty. Like Adams and Otis and the other popular leaders in the Bay Colony, Thacher feared and hated Bernard and his administration, and singled out for particular abuse Bernard's lieutenant governor, the chief justice, Thomas Hutchinson. This "Summa Potestatis," as Thacher called him, was known to have devised a "strict alliance, offensive and defensive, with the monarch of [Hampshire County] and his dominions," to have used insidious Parliamentary tactics to thwart the will of the Massachusetts House, to have silenced the press by a kind of legal blackmail, and above all to be a gluttonous monopolist of high office. From the time Thacher argued against writs of assistance until his death in 1765, John Adams later recalled — characteristically highlighting an essentially accurate story with his own dramatic coloring — Thacher

> considered the King, ministry, Parliament, and the nation of Great Britain as determined to new-model the colonies from the foundation, to annul all their charters, to constitute them all royal governments, to raise a revenue in America by Parliamentary taxation, to apply that revenue to pay the salaries of governors, judges, and all other crown officers . . . and further, to establish bishops and the whole system of the Church of England, tithes and all, throughout all British America. This system, he said, if it was suffered to prevail, would extinguish the flame of liberty all over the world; that America would be employed as an engine to batter down all the miserable remains of liberty in Great Britain and Ireland, where only any semblance of it was left in the world. To this system he considered Hutchinson, the Olivers, and all their connections, dependents, adherents, shoelickers, etc., entirely devoted. He asserted that they were all engaged with all the crown officers in America and the understrappers of the ministry in England, in a deep and treasonable conspiracy to betray the liberties of their country, for their own private, personal, and family aggrandizements.[3]

Thacher's fear of this burgeoning oligarchy, based on the undeniable fact that Hutchinson and his family had engrossed more offices than any faction in the colony's history, was first expressed publicly in the spring of 1761 in anticipation of the May elections to the Council. In a vigorous pamphlet, reprinted in 1762, he urged the public to exclude the Superior Court judges from the Council on the grounds that these offices were incompatible and that the exercise of them by the same individuals was a threat to liberty. Lecturing from Montesquieu on the separation of powers, he pointed out that "where the powers lose their checks, run into one another, or one branch of powers swallows up other branches, it becomes a tyranny, be the external form of government what it will." [4] Thacher reinforced his attack on Hutchinson's plural office-holding the next year in a controversy over monetary policy brought on by a sudden rise in the value of sterling abroad that threatened to drain the colony of silver altogether. The House's solution, for which Thacher became a spokesman, was to declare gold legal tender at the value it was then circulating. But the Council's and Hutchinson's position, that only the scarce and expensive silver, at the established rates, should continue to be acceptable as legal tender, prevailed. Not, however, before the popular leaders had condemned this argument as deliberately vindictive to debtors, favorable only to the rich; and not before Thacher had published a pamphlet attacking Hutchinson's view as "pernicious, and his reasoning inconclusive," referring sarcastically to the "many high offices he with so much dignity sustains," and expressing his shock at the idea that a chief justice "should publicly, in such peremptory and strong terms, declare his opinion on a question which in all probability . . . will one day or other come judicially before him." [5]

Thus when the Massachusetts legislature began its deliberations on the new revenue measures, Thacher had achieved distinction as a lawyer particularly interested in cases bearing on the enforcement of the navigation laws and as a public controversialist known to be a defender of popular liberties against the encroachments of an arbitrary and voracious prerogative. Elected in 1763 a representative of Boston to the General Court, he moved immediately, in his first appearance in the House, to block the appointment of Hutchinson as special agent of the colony to England for the purpose of arguing against the Sugar Act, and in the next session, in the spring of 1764, was appointed, with Otis and three others, to the House's committee to consider the reports of the colony's regular agent and to draft new instructions. These instructions, sent to the agent with a copy of Otis' Memorial (printed as the second appendix to Otis' *Rights,* JHL Pamphlet 7), condemned the agent for having failed to protest vigorously against the principle of Parliamentary taxation (yet quibbled with him about whether 2d. or 1d. per gallon duty on molasses could not have been striven for and attained); touched on the colonies' military and financial contributions to the wars; and argued against the alleged necessity of maintaining regular troops in the colonies. But nowhere did it mention the enforcement provisions of the Sugar Act; nowhere did it consider the revolu-

tion in imperial relations those regulations created. It was to this topic, together with the more familiar ones of representation and taxation and the
economic consequences of the revenue law, that Thacher turned in his *Sentiments of a British American,* written in the summer of 1764 after the ad-
journment of the General Court.[6]

The enforcement provisions of the Sugar Act which Thacher here called
attention to occupy the overwhelming majority of the forty-seven sections of
the act, which spreads over twenty pages of the *Statutes at Large,* and they
represent an effort at a significant tightening of the customs administration.
Included among them was the cumbering — in some cases almost crippling —
requirement that every trading vessel, whether coastal, inland, or overseas,
have a complete cargo list and other papers approved by a customs officer in
advance of the vessel's departure from port. Another section enlarged the
number of articles restricted to shipment in bond to British territory to the
point where almost every vessel would contain at least one of them and hence
be required to undergo the special bonding procedures. In addition, bonds
against illegal shipment of foreign molasses were required of all shippers. To
facilitate prosecution of violators of the navigation laws, the burden of proof
was shifted to the defendant in cases brought by the customs officials; whatever
the outcome of such cases, the defendant was obliged to pay costs; and the
defendant was, in effect, prevented from entering retaliatory suits against
customs officials. Above all, the law allowed all suits involving alleged violations of the navigation laws to be tried, if the "informer or prosecutor"
wished, in the juryless admiralty courts: either the vice-admiralty court in
the colony concerned "or in any court of vice-admiralty which may . . . be
appointed over all *America"* — an alternative that referred to a projected new
tribunal with jurisdiction over all the colonies, concurrent with that of the
provincial vice-admiralty courts, which was created in fact in June 1764 in the
remote hamlet of Halifax, Nova Scotia.[7]

Anticipating in *The Sentiments of a British American* what would become
major irritants in Anglo-American relations in the decade before Independence[8] Thacher inveighed against the deprivation of trial by jury in the admiralty courts; made clear the nature of the threat posed by the removal of
cases to the Halifax court; and pointed out the significance of relieving customs officials of the burden of paying the costs of the trials they lost. If the
arguments in the rest of the pamphlet were familiar to its readers, these passages clearly distinguished it, and served to elevate Thacher still further as a
tribune of the people. A few weeks after the publication of the pamphlet he
was appointed to the committee of the House charged with drafting a petition to the King and Parliament. He wrote the document the committee submitted, and included in it, among the usual charges against unconstitutional
taxation and the much commented-on statement "we look upon those duties
as a tax," two paragraphs on the admiralty courts and the enforcement regulations which he lifted, in certain phrases verbatim, from the pamphlet he
had just published. These passages survived the surgery performed on the

draft by the Council, under the leadership of Thomas Hutchinson, and entered into the final, official petition transmitted by Massachusetts to the House of Commons in November 1764.[9]

The drafting of this petition, and of a memorandum for the colony's agent detailing Massachusetts' contributions to the support of England in her colonial wars, were Thacher's final public actions. Responding poorly to a smallpox inoculation he received early the next year, he weakened rapidly, and on July 9, 1765, he died. Years later John Adams, in his rambling recollections of past heroics, recalled Thacher confined by his fatal illness, longing to be out and doing. "I will go out," Adams recalled him saying. "I will go out. I will go into court and make a speech which shall be read after my death, as my dying testimony against this infernal tyranny which they are bringing upon us."[10]

THE/SENTIMENTS/OF A/*British American.*/

*Asellum in prato timidus pascebat senex./Is, hostium clamore subito territus,/ Suadebat asino fugere, ne possent capi./At ille lentus: quaeso num binas mihi/ Clitellas impositurum victorem putas?/Senex negavit. Ergo quid refert mea/Cui serviam? clitellas dum portem meas./*PHÆDRUS./

BOSTON:/Printed and Sold by EDES & GILL, next to the/Prison in Queen-Street. 1764./[Price Six Pence.]/

THE
SENTIMENTS of a *British American*

I T WELL becomes the wisdom of a great nation, having been highly
successful in their foreign wars and added a large extent of country
to their dominions, to consider with a critical attention their internal
state lest their prosperity should destroy them.

Great Britain at this day is arrived to an heighth of glory and wealth
which no European nation hath ever reached since the decline of the
Roman Empire. Everybody knows that it is not indebted to itself alone
for this envied power: that its colonies, placed in a distant quarter of the
earth, have had their share of efficiency in its late successes, as indeed
they have also contributed to the advancing and increasing its grandeur
from their very first beginnings.

In the forming and settling, therefore, the internal polity of the kingdom, these have reason to expect that *their* interest should be considered
and attended to, that *their* rights, if they have any, should be preserved
to them, and that *they* should have no reason to complain that they have
been lavish of their blood and treasure in the late war only to bind the
shackles of slavery on themselves and their children.

[4] No people have been more wisely jealous of their liberties and
privileges than the British nation. It is observed by *Vattel* that "their
present happy condition hath cost them seas of blood; but they have not
purchased it too dear." [1]

The colonies, making a part of this great empire, having the same
British rights inherent in them as the inhabitants of the island itself,
they cannot be disfranchised or wounded in their privileges but the
whole body politic must in the end feel with them.

The writer of this, being a native of an English colony, will take it for
granted that the colonies are not the mere property of the mother state;
that they have the same rights as other British subjects. He will also suppose that no design is formed to enslave them, and that the justice of the
British Parliament will finally do right to every part of their dominions.

These things presupposed, he intends to consider the late act made in the fourth year of his present Majesty entitled *An Act for Granting Certain Duties in the British Colonies and Plantations in* America, etc.,[2] to show the real subjects of grievance therein to the colonists, and that the interest of Great Britain itself may finally be greatly affected thereby. There is the more reason that this freedom should be indulged after the act is passed inasmuch as the colonies, though greatly interested therein, had no opportunity of being heard while it was pending.

[I.] The first objection is that a tax is thereby laid on several commodities, to be raised and levied in [5] the plantations, and to be remitted home to England. This is esteemed a grievance inasmuch as the same are laid without the consent of the representatives of the colonists. It is esteemed an essential British right that no person shall be subject to any tax but what in person or by his representative he hath a voice in laying. The British Parliament have many times vindicated this right against the attempts of Kings to invade it. And though perhaps it may be said that the House of Commons, in a large sense, are the representatives of the colonies as well as of the people of Great Britain, yet it is certain that these have no voice in their election. Nor can it be any alleviation of their unhappiness that if this right is taken from them, it is taken by that body who have been the great patrons and defenders of it in the people of Great Britain.

Besides, the colonies have ever supported a subordinate government among themselves.

Being placed at such a distance from the capital, it is absolutely impossible they should continue a part of the kingdom in the same sense as the corporations there are. For this reason, from their beginning there hath been a subordinate legislature among them subject to the control of the mother state; and from the necessity of the case there must have been such, their circumstances and situation being in many respects so different from that of the parent state they could not have subsisted without this. Now the colonies have always been taxed by their own representatives and in their respective legislatures, [6] and have supported an entire domestic government among themselves. Is it just, then, they should be doubly taxed? That they should be obliged to bear the whole charges of their domestic government, and should be as subject to the taxes of the British Parliament as those who have no domestic government to support?

The reason given for this extraordinary taxation, namely, that this war was undertaken for the security of the colonies, and that they ought therefore to be taxed to pay the charge thereby incurred, it is humbly apprehended is without foundation. For —

(1) It was of no less consequence to Great Britain than it was to the colonies that these should not be overrun and conquered by the French. Suppose they had prevailed and gotten all the English colonies into their possession: how long would Great Britain have survived their fate! Put the case that the town of *Portsmouth* or any other seaport had been besieged and the like sums expended in its defense, could any have thought that town ought to be charged with the expense?

(2) The colonies contributed their full proportion to those conquests which adorn and dignify the late and present reign. One of them in particular raised in one year seven thousand men to be commanded by His Majesty's general, besides maintaining many guards and garrisons on their own frontiers. All of them by their expenses and exertions in the late war have incurred heavy debts, which it will take them many years to pay.[3]

[7] (3) The colonies are no particular gainers by these acquisitions. None of the conquered territory is annexed to them. All are acquisitions accruing to the crown. On account of their *commerce,* they are no gainers: the northern colonies are even *sufferers* by these cessions.* It is true they have more security from having their throats cut by the French while the peace lasts; but so have also all His Majesty's subjects.

(4) Great Britain gaineth immensely by these acquisitions. The command of the whole American fur trade and the increased demand for their woolen manufactures from their numerous new subjects in a country too cold to keep sheep: these are such immense gains as in a commercial light would refund the kingdom, if every farthing of the expense of reducing Canada were paid out of the exchequer.

But to say the truth, it is not only by the taxation itself that the colonists deem themselves aggrieved by the act we are considering. For —

II. The power therein given to courts of admiralty alarms them greatly. The common law is the birthright of every subject, and trial by jury a most darling privilege.[4] So deemed our ancestors in ancient times, long before the colonies were begun to be planted. Many struggles had they with courts of admiralty, which, like the element they take their

---

*I desire this may not be misunderstood. In this view I suppose them sufferers, namely, that as the West Indies were not large enough to take off the produce the northern colonies could export to them before the conquest of Canada, now [that] that country is added it makes the disproportion much greater.

name from, have divers times [8] attempted to innundate the land. Hence the statutes of *Richard* II, of *Henry* IV, and divers other public acts.[5] Hence the watchful eye the reverend sages of the common law have kept over these courts. Now by the act we are considering, the colonists are deprived of these privileges: of the common law, for these judges are supposed to be connusant only of the civil law; of juries, for all here is put in the breast of one man. He judges both law and fact, and his decree is final; at least it cannot be reversed on this side the Atlantic. In this particular the colonists are put under a quite different law from all the rest of the King's subjects: jurisdiction is nowhere else given to courts of admiralty of matters so foreign from their connusance. In some things the colonists have been long subject to this cruel yoke, and have indeed fully experienced its galling nature. Loud complaints have been long made by them of the oppressions of these courts, their exhorbitant fees, and the little justice the subject may expect from them in cases of seizures. Let me mention one thing that is notorious: these courts have assumed (I know not by what law) a commission of five per cent to the judge on all seizures condemned. What chance does the subject stand for his right upon the best claim when the judge, condemning, is to have an hundred or perhaps five hundred pounds, and acquitting, less than twenty shillings?[6] If the colonists should be thought partial witnesses in this case, let those of the inhabitants of Great Britain [9] who have had the misfortune to be suitors or to have any business in these dreadful courts be inquired of.

There have been times when the legislature of Great Britain appeared to be as sensible of the bad conduct of these courts as we are now. I mean when the statute of 6 Anne c. 37 and some later ones to the same purpose were made, wherein the remedy they have given is as extraordinary as the power given those courts.[7] For in those statutes the judge of admiralty is subjected to a penalty of five hundred pounds, to be recovered by the aggrieved suitor at common law. These only refer to cases of prizes, and give no remedy in cases of seizures, where their power is not only decisive but in many respects uncontrollable. Meantime, can the colonists help wondering and grieving that the British legislature should vest with such high powers *over them* courts in whom they appear to have so little confidence?

But in the act we are considering, the power of these courts is even much enlarged and made still more grievous. For it is thereby enacted that the seizor may inform in any court of admiralty for the particular colony, or in any court of admiralty to be appointed over all America, at his pleasure. Thus a malicious seizor may take the goods of any man, ever so lawfully and duly imported, and carry the trial of the cause to a thousand miles distance, where for mere want of ability to follow, the claimer shall be incapable of defending his right. At the same time an hardship is laid upon the claimer; his claim is not to be admitted [10] or heard until he find sureties to prosecute, who are to be of known ability in the place where security is given. And he, being unknown in a place so distance from home, whatever be his estate, shall be incapable of producing such sureties.[8]

III. The empowering commanders of the King's ships to seize and implead, as is done in this act and a former act and by special commission from the commissioners of the customs, is another great hardship on the colonies.[9] The knowledge of all the statutes relating to the customs, of the prohibitions on exports and imports, and of various intricate cases arising on them, requires a good lawyer. How can this science ever be expected from men educated in a totally different way, brought up upon the boisterous element and knowing no law aboard their ships but their own will? Here perhaps it will be said, this is not peculiar to the colonies. The power to these commanders is given in all parts of the dominions as well as in the colonies: why should they complain of being under the same law as the other subjects? I answer, There is this great essential difference between the cases: in Great Britain no jurisdiction is given to any other than the common law courts; there too the subjects are near the throne, where, when they are oppressed, their complaints may soon be heard and redressed; but with respect to the colonies, far different is the case! Here it is their own courts that try the cause! Here the subject is far distant from the throne! His complaints cannot soon be heard and redressed. The boisterous commander may take for his motto, [11] *Procul a Jove, a fulmine procul.*[10]

The present decree, however unjust, deprives him even of the means of seeking redress. The judge with his troop and the proud captain have divided his wealth; and he hath nothing to do but to hang himself or to go a-begging in a country of beggars.

There is yet another very great objection the colonists make to this act, of no less weight than the other three. It is this:

IV. Whereas it is good law that all officers seizing goods seize at their peril, and if the goods they seize are not liable to forfeiture they must pay the claimant his cost, and are liable to his action besides, which two things have been looked upon as proper checks of exorbitant wanton power in the officer: both these checks are taken off. They, the officers, may charge the revenue with the cost, with the consent of four of the commissioners of the customs. And if the judge of admiralty will certify that there was probable cause of seizure, no action shall be maintained by the claimant though his goods on trial appear to be ever so duly imported and liable to no sort of forfeiture, and he hath been forced to expend ever so much in the defense of them. This last regulation is in the act peculiarly confined to America.[11]

Much more might be said on these subjects, but I aim at brevity.

Let it now be observed that the interest of Great Britain is finally greatly affected by these new regulations. We will not here insist on the [12] parental tenderness due from Great Britain to us and suggest she must suffer from sympathy with her children, who have been guilty of no undutiful behavior towards her but on the contrary have greatly increased her wealth and grandeur and in the last war have impoverished themselves in fighting her battles. We will suppose her for this little moment to have forgot the bowels of a mother.

Neither will we dwell long on the importance of the precedent. The consideration of a million and half of British subjects disfranchised or put under regulations alien from our happy constitution: what pretense it may afford to after ministers to treat the inhabitants of the island itself after the same manner. We will suppose for the present that at a thousand leagues distance, across the water, the inhabitants of the capital will not be endangered by a conflagration of all the colonies.

Nor will we mention any possible danger from the alienation of the affections of the colonies from their mother country in case of a new war. We will suppose them to have that reverence for the English name they are allowed to retain that they will be as lavish of what blood and treasure remains to them now they are cut off from all these privileges as when they could please themselves with the surest hope of holding them inviolable.

What we are now considering is how the mere present self-interest of Great Britain is affected by these new regulations.

[13] Now everybody knows that the greatest part of the trade of Great Britain is with her colonies. This she enjoyeth, exclusive of any other European country, and hath entirely at her own command. Further, it may be made out that the greatest part of the profits of the trade of the colonies, at least on the continent, centers in Great Britain. The

colonists, settled in a wide and sparse manner, are perpetually demanding the linen, woolen, and other manufactures of Great Britain. They are not yet settled in so contiguous a manner as to be able to manufacture sufficient for their own supplies. And while they can pay for those of Great Britain with any proper remittances, their demands will be perpetually increasing. Great Britain, besides, is the mart which supplieth the colonies with all the produce of the other countries in Europe which the colonies use.

Considering the vast numbers supported by these manufactures vended in the colonies, and by the articles of foreign trade brought into the kingdom and thence exported and consumed in the plantations, doubtless even the luxury of the colonists is the gain of Great Britain. So thought wise ministers in the late reign: on which ground they repealed two or three sumptuary laws made in the colonies for restraining that luxury.[12]

Now as the colonies have no gold or silver mines in them, it is certain that all their remittances they make must be from their trade. And it is obvious that when the sources of their remittances are cut off, the demands for these goods, [14] by which so many thousands are supported, must cease. And whoever considereth with any degree of attention the new regulations and is acquainted with the state of the colonies must see that the evident tendency of them is to cut off all these sources and to destroy altogether the trade of the colonists.

One grand source of these remittances is the fishery, which by the duty of three pence a gallon on molasses must entirely be at an end. That branch can never bear the high duties imposed, nor subsist without the molasses which the trade to the foreign islands furnisheth. Not only by their connection with this but by the mere effect of the new regulations, all the other trade of the colonists must be at an end. These regulations must break and subdue the hearts of the traders here. TRADE is a nice and delicate lady; she must be courted and won by soft and fair addresses. She will not bear the rude hand of a ravisher. Penalties increased, heavy taxes laid on, the checks of oppression and violence removed; these things must drive her from her present abode.

Hence, one or other of these consequences will follow: either (1) the colonies will universally go into such manufactures as they are capable of doing within themselves, or (2) they will do without them, and being reduced to mere necessaries, will be clothed like their predecessors the Indians with the skins of beasts, and sink into like [15] barbarism. They must then adopt Jack Straw's verses,

When Adam delved, and Eve span,
Who was then the gentleman? †[13]

Now, either of these events taking place, how will it affect the island of Great Britain? The answer is obvious. The exports to the colonies wholly stopped or greatly diminished, the demands for those manufactures in Great Britain must be in proportion lessened. The substance of those manufacturers, merchants, and traders whom this demand supports is then gone. They who live from supplying these manufacturers, etc., must decay and die with them. Lastly, as trade may be compared to a grand chain made up of innumerable links, it is doubtful whether the British trade, great as it is, can bear the striking out so many without greatly endangering the whole.

What now is the equivalent for all this to the nation? A tenth part of one year's tax, at the extent two years' tax upon the colonies (for after that time all their money will be gone) to be lodged in the exchequer and thence issued as the Parliament shall direct.[14] Doth not this resemble the conduct of the good wife in the fable who killed her hen that every day laid her a *golden egg?*

[16] THESE are the sentiments of a British American, which he ventures to expose to the public with an honest well-meant freedom. Born in one of the colonies and descended from ancestors who were among the first planters of that colony, he is not ashamed to avow a love to the country that gave him birth; yet he hath ever exulted in the name of Briton. He hath ever thought all the inhabitants in the remotest dominions of Great Britain interested in the wealth, the prosperity, and the glory of the capital. And he desireth ever to retain these filial sentiments.

If the objections he proposeth are of any weight, he trusts the meanness and distance of the proposer shall not diminish that weight — that those great minds who can comprehend the whole vast machine in one view will not deem it below them to inspect a single small wheel that is out of order.

He concludes all with his most ardent wishes that the happy island of Great Britain may grow in wealth, in power, and glory to yet greater degrees; that the conquests it makes over foreign enemies may serve the

† I imagine many sanguine readers on the British side the water will think this is all exaggeration. Such may be informed that even now these things begin to appear. For two or three years past, exchange from the Massachusetts to England has been above par, and bills earnestly bought up. Now the bills the government have to dispose of, though set at a less exchange than the last year and though certain advice is received that the money is in the bank, cannot vend.

more to protect the internal liberties of its subjects; that her colonies now happily extended may grow in filial affection and dutiful submission to her their mother; and that she in return may never forget her parental affections. That the whole English empire, united by the strongest bands of love and interest, formidable to the tyrants and oppressors of the earth, may retain its own virtue, and happily possess immortality.

PAMPHLET 9

STEPHEN HOPKINS, *THE RIGHTS OF COLONIES EXAMINED*

PROVIDENCE, 1765

INTRODUCTION

The Rights of Colonies Examined, written by Stephen Hopkins, the governor of Rhode Island, in November 1764, and published with the endorsement of the Rhode Island Assembly in December of that year, is intellectually a less ambitious and a less complicated effort than Otis' *Rights of the British Colonies Asserted and Proved* (JHL Pamphlet 7) which in important ways it resembles, but it displays more typically the central convictions and the surrounding confusions of the early objections to England's new colonial policy. Emerging from one of the most faction-ridden colonies in America, it sparked a series of polemical explosions, among which were the first comprehensive defense of the new English policies (Martin Howard, Jr.'s *Halifax Letter,* JHL Pamphlet 10) and the major effort of James Otis (in *A Vindication of the British Colonies,* JHL Pamphlet 11) to explain the meaning of his *Rights of the British Colonies,* and to justify its doctrine.[1]

Resistance to the new measures had begun early in Rhode Island, with the calling in October 1763 of a meeting of merchants which resulted in the drafting of a remonstrance by the Rhode Island legislature explaining in detail the economic consequences of the proposed Sugar Act and in the writing, by Stephen Hopkins, of the widely reprinted "Essay on the Trade of the Northern Colonies." [2] Protest against the pending Stamp Act followed more slowly, however, and when it came it seemed almost to be a party statement. For factionalism, endemic in all the colonies, had been especially virulent in Rhode Island ever since 1755 when Stephen Hopkins and Martin Howard, Jr. had returned from the Albany Congress, where together they had represented the colony, and Hopkins had run for governor. A self-educated farmer's son who had risen to the colony's chief-justiceship, Hopkins, then 49 years of age, had won that election, and in so doing had completed a monopoly of high public offices that even Thomas Hutchinson might have envied. Adroit and enterprising in politics, capable of charming even the hypercritical John Adams, he had forged a remarkable public career as the leader of the new economic forces in the colony, centering in Providence, which had struggled for years to wrest control of the colony's government from the well-entrenched mercantile leadership of Newport. Personified in the celebrated Ward-Hopkins controversy, this bitterly fought campaign between an established mercantile faction defending established sources of supply and routes of trade, and newcomers drawing on a fresh hinterland and threatening to wrench the economic and ultimately the social structure of the colony out of its familiar frame,

500

dominated politics in Rhode Island for over a decade after Hopkins' victory of 1755. But though this series of political battles was fought with every weapon of publicity, vote-corralling, and wire-pulling available to eighteenth-century Americans, it was devoid of ideological meaning. The clash of ideas and beliefs that took place in the colony after 1763 developed independent of this controversy — developed, indeed, around the question of whether such politics should be permitted to exist at all.[3]

In Newport, long the local center of both the Church of England and English officialdom in the colony, a dozen or so crown officers, English business agents, Anglican lawyers, and natives who identified themselves strongly with England, formed a group — a "junto," a "cabal," it was called by some; a "little, dirty, drinking, drabbing, contaminated knot of thieves, beggars, and transports," James Otis called it — devoted themselves to the elimination of Rhode Island's charter, under whose protective immunities Rhode Island's factious politics had flourished. Through the spring and summer of 1764 they published in the *Newport Mercury* a series of attacks on the Rhode Island government, in which they reiterated the familiar argument that excessive weight in "the democracy" of a government threatened to create chaos, and urged as a solution the intercession of a greater "monarchical" influence in the form of a royal governor and Council. They rejoiced in the overhaul of the imperial administration then in progress, approved of the Sugar Act, and condemned the pamphlets and resolutions that had recently been published against it. By mid-September 1764 it was publicly stated in Providence that the Newport clique had formally petitioned the crown to revoke the Rhode Island charter and hence was "actually conspiring against the liberties of the colony." [4]

Suspicion of the motives behind the new revenue measures, which the Newport group supported, deepened in Rhode Island. For just as in Massachusetts, where Thomas Hutchinson was widely believed to head a power-hungry faction intent on destroying local liberties, so in Rhode Island questions of the motivation behind the new imperial program could be answered in terms of the conspiratorial plotting of Martin Howard, Jr., Thomas Moffat, and the others of the "contaminated knot" in Newport. Governor Hopkins' address to the Assembly at an emergency session held in November to consider "the plan formed by the British ministry" included the Newport petition for the revocation of the charter among the matters that needed immediate attention; and the same set of votes that set up a committee to draft an address to the King for a redress of grievances directed the colony's agent "to use his utmost endeavors to prevent the evil intended" by the Newport petitioners, and to send back immediately "the names of the subscribers." [5]

It was at that time, in November 1764, in the midst of these alarms and resolutions, in this context of fear created not only by the new impositions but also by the clandestine efforts of the local royalists to destroy the century-old chartered government of Rhode Island, that Governor Hopkins, autodidact and veteran of years of public controversy, wrote and published, with the approval of the Rhode Island legislature, his *Rights of Colonies Examined*.

It is a revealing document, for while its central meaning is perfectly clear, it is nevertheless crowded with both stated uncertainties and latent ambiguities resulting from a failure to resolve, or on some points even to grasp, problems implicit in the major propositions. Like almost every American, Hopkins believed the colonists, having lost nothing in their migration from England, had full claim to all the rights and privileges of Englishmen at home, including the right of retaining property until they themselves or their elected representatives voluntarily relinquished it. Therefore Parliament, in which the colonies were not represented, could not tax the colonies. But was not Parliament the "supreme and overruling authority," the absolute sovereign entity that must exist somewhere in every state? Hopkins endorsed this traditional eighteenth-century notion, stating that it is "the indispensable duty of every good and loyal subject cheerfully to obey and patiently submit to all the acts, laws, orders, and regulations that may be made and passed by Parliament for directing and governing all . . . general matters" — *general* matters, that is, as opposed to local police and the "internal government" of the colonies, which was the preserve of the provincial legislatures. But what if Parliament, exercising its rightful "power to make laws and form regulations for the good of all, and to compel their execution and observation," should decide to deal with matters of local concern? Should the colonists resist? If they did, they would be disregarding their "indispensable duty . . . to obey and patiently submit"; if they did not, they would allow themselves to be deprived of precious rights. Lacking Otis' learning and imagination, Hopkins did not attempt to resolve the dilemma in terms of a theory of a systematically benign Parliament that would, of its own inner necessities, correct its errors; nor did he mindlessly insist that a presumably supreme Parliament must keep hands off whatever Americans chose to call their internal affairs. He left the question open, hinting at, but not developing, the argument that "the empire of Great Britain" is "an imperial state, which consists of many separate governments each of which hath peculiar privileges . . . no single part, though greater than another part, is by that superiority entitled to make laws for or to tax such lesser part; but all laws and all taxations which bind the whole must be made by the whole." [6]

Other even more obvious questions were also ignored. If the colonies were not represented, should they be? This difficult problem, Hopkins wrote, "we will pass by"; all he chose to argue was that the colonies ought in some way to be kept informed about matters in Parliament that concern them and, one way or another, be allowed to express their opinion to that body. Similarly, one might ask whether revenues raised by Parliament in the colonies through trade duties were not as much violations of American rights as internal taxes levied by the same body. Hopkins did not face the question squarely; he admitted though, that Parliament had the right to regulate the trade of the empire and hence "full power, by this means, to draw all the money and all the wealth of the colonies into the mother country at pleasure." So, too, he avoided stating flatly the interpretation of the motives behind the new imperial policies that lurked in his thought: whether the change in American policy had been "induced by a jealousy of the colonies, by false informations, or by some alteration in the system of political government, we have," he wrote, "no information." What he did explain clearly and unequivocally was the eonomic damage that would be wrought in America by the Sugar Act and the manifest inequities of the new admiralty court system. On these points he dwelt at length and with the assurance he had shown months before in his "Essay on the Trade of the Northern Colonies." [7]

But the unresolved questions could not be ignored. On all of them Hopkins was vulnerable to anyone with the motive to oppose him and the wit to perceive the difficulties he faced. It is scarcely surprising that shortly after the appearance of Hopkins' pamphlet the leader of the Newport "knot," Martin Howard, Jr., attacked him. His *Letter from a Gentleman at Halifax* (JHL Pamphlet 10) pointed out the inconsistencies in Hopkins' view of Parliamentary supremacy, mocked his handling of the question of representation, disputed his citation of laws, refuted his historical examples, and ridiculed his poetical adornments. In addition, Howard explicitly and without qualification defended both the Sugar Act and the new admiralty regulations. To ignore such a challenge would be an admission of defeat, and Hopkins quickly replied in three lengthy articles entitled "A Vindication of a Late Pamphlet . . . ," which he published in the *Providence Gazette* on February 23, March 2 and 9, 1765.

In the first of these pieces, which together form an addendum to *The Rights of Colonies*, Hopkins considered the question of Parliamentary sovereignty in America. A glance not only at his own pamphlet but at all the others published in defense of American rights, reveals, Hopkins assured his readers, that "it would have been the height of madness and folly to have supposed or mentioned" withdrawing allegiance from England. All he had meant to say in the passages of his pamphlet which *"Don Cholerico Teste Snapshorto"* complained about was simply that Parliament had no right to tax America, but that if, despite this, "Parliament should proceed to tax them, it was their *'indispensable duty cheerfully to obey, and patiently to submit thereto.'* " This was scarcely the "state little better from that of rebellion" it had been pictured. Nor had he ever alleged, as Howard said he had, that behind it all lay "a design of enslaving the colonies." He meant only to point to the historical fact that "raising money upon British subjects without their consent is the first step that those kings who have aimed to change the *British* constitution into a tyranny have ever taken in order to effect it." He had not even claimed that the colonies had natural rights as against Parliament. His view, he now explained, was that the colonists' freedom from Parliamentary taxation was not a right but "an immunity," and had been created not by nature but by policy. Howard's own theory of rights, based on an alleged distinction between personal and political rights, Hopkins dismissed as "unmeaning jargon" handled with the skill of a surgeon dissecting "with a *cleaver.*" Howard was the "successor in nonsense" to such arch-Tory apologists as Hickes and Leslie, whose help he no doubt needed in his attempt to put out "the eyes of a whole continent of people, and then swear to them that they were born blind." Never, he repeated, had he doubted the authority of Parliament. What he had meant in *The Rights of Colonies,* he explained again, was simply that "taxing the plantations, in their interior police, would be, in his opinion, such an exercise of that authority as was not conformable to the *British* principles of government" — "interior police," not "foreign importations, which is a matter of general commerce and can be regulated in Parliament only . . . yet our letter writer can see no difference between such a law [as the Molasses Act] and a stamp duty." Howard's notion that Parliament's right and power flow from the same source — the common law — as do individual rights, and hence that the one cannot be denied without denying the other, amounted to a denial, by this would-be defender of authority, of the supremacy of Parliament, since it reduced that supreme body to a mere voice and executor of the common law: "He may as well maintain that the King derives his authority from a constable." And Howard's argument on representation was riddled with errors, five of which Hopkins took the trouble to enumerate. The author of such trash, Hopkins concluded, must be a "madman (for he can be no better) . . . This must be someone who wants to be established a petty tyrant amongst us: — Drunk with rage at some disappointment, he has retired into the dark, and, grasping the dagger in his assassin hand, seems at a stand whether he shall plunge it into his country's bowels or into his own."

These were vigorous essays whose slashing manner must have delighted Hopkins' partisans. But, as Howard promptly made clear, they were far from impressive as glosses on *The Rights of Colonies Examined.*[8] In both *The Rights* and the "Vindication" Hopkins had hedged on central questions: the limits of Parliamentary sovereignty in America, the nature of representation, and the motivations behind the change of policy in England. Convinced that Americans were being wronged, he had strongly protested; but the logical grounds for his protestations were weak, and his historical and legal documentation incomplete. His sense of the tendency of his own thought was keen, however, and knowing no intellectually coherent way of qualifying the extreme conclusions Howard accused him of, he drew back, praising those like Samuel Adams whom he believed to be bolder than he.[9]

Yet if he could not devise or sustain the arguments he needed, he never gave up the convictions that had stimulated the writing of *The Rights of Colonies Examined.* "Throughout his life a man of deeds rather than words," as his biographer describes him, he remained the leader in Providence and in Rhode Island of opposition to British authority. He presided over the town's committee to instruct the representatives to the Assembly called in protest against the Stamp Act; led in supporting the Massachusetts Circular Letter of 1768; refused, as chief justice, to apprehend the destroyers of the customs schooner *Gaspée;* and, as a participant in both Continental Congresses, signed the Declaration of Independence and aided in drafting the Articles of Confederation. In Philadelphia in 1774 Hopkins "kept us all alive," John Adams later recalled, not only with his sagacious judgment but with his "wit, humor, anecdotes, science, and learning . . . The flow of his soul made all his reading our own, and seemed to bring to recollection in all of us all we had ever read." Drinking grog through long evenings of conversation, Hopkins not only converted everything he consumed "into wit, sense, knowledge, and good humor," Adams said, "but inspired us all with similar qualities." He died in 1785, the best known Rhode Islander of his generation, famed as an early and unfaltering defender of American rights.[10]

THE/RIGHTS/OF/COLONIES/EXAMINED./PUBLISHED BY AUTHORITY./
PROVIDENCE:/PRINTED BY *WILLIAM GODDARD*./M.DCC.LXV./

THE RIGHTS OF COLONIES
EXAMINED

Mid the low murmurs of submissive fear
And mingled rage, my Hampden rais'd his voice,
And to the laws appeal'd . . .

Thomson's *Liberty*[1]

LIBERTY is the greatest blessing that men enjoy, and slavery the heaviest curse that human nature is capable of. This being so makes it a matter of the utmost importance to men which of the two shall be their portion. Absolute liberty is, perhaps, incompatible with any kind of government. The safety resulting from society, and the advantage of just and equal laws, hath caused men to forego some part of their natural liberty, and submit to government. This appears to be the most rational account of its beginning, although, it must be confessed, mankind have by no means been agreed about it. Some have found its origin in the divine appointment; others have thought it took its rise from power; enthusiasts have dreamed that dominion was founded in grace. [4] Leaving these points to be settled by the descendants of Filmer, Cromwell, and Venner,[2] we will consider the British constitution as it at present stands, on Revolution principles, and from thence endeavor to find the measure of the magistrate's power and the people's obedience.

This glorious constitution, the best that ever existed among men, will be confessed by all to be founded by compact and established by consent of the people. By this most beneficent compact British subjects are to be governed only agreeable to laws to which themselves have some way consented, and are not to be compelled to part with their property but as it is called for by the authority of such laws.[3] The former is truly liberty; the latter is really to be possessed of property and to have something that may be called one's own.

On the contrary, those who are governed at the will of another, or of others, and whose property may be taken from them by taxes or otherwise without their own consent and against their will, are in the miserable condition of slaves. "For liberty solely consists in an independency upon the will of another; and by the name of slave we understand a man who can neither dispose of his person or goods, but enjoys all at the will of his master," says Sidney on government.[4] These things premised, whether the British American colonies on the continent are justly entitled to like privileges and freedom as their fellow subjects in Great Britain are, shall be the chief point examined. In discussing this question we shall make the colonies in New England, with whose rights we are best acquainted, the rule of our reasoning, not in the least doubting but [that] all the others are justly entitled to like rights with them.

New England was first planted by adventurers who left England, their native country, by permission of King CHARLES I, and at their own expense transported themselves to America, with great risk and difficulty settled among [5] savages, and in a very surprising manner formed new colonies in the wilderness. Before their departure the terms of their freedom and the relation they should stand in to the mother country in their emigrant state were fully settled: they were to remain subject to the King and dependent on the kingdom of Great Britain. In return they were to receive protection and enjoy all the rights and privileges of freeborn Englishmen.

This is abundantly proved by the charter given to the Massachusetts colony while they were still in England, and which they received and brought over with them as the authentic evidence of the conditions they removed upon. The colonies of Connecticut and Rhode Island also afterwards obtained charters from the crown, granting them the like ample privileges. By all these charters, it is in the most express and solemn manner granted that these adventurers, and their children after them forever, should have and enjoy all the freedom and liberty that the subjects in England enjoy; that they might make laws for their own government suitable to their circumstances, not repugnant to, but as near as might be agreeable to the laws of England; that they might purchase lands, acquire goods, and use trade for their advantage, and have an absolute property in whatever they justly acquired. These, with many other gracious privileges, were granted them by several kings; and they were to pay as an acknowledgment to the crown only one-fifth part of the ore of gold and silver that should at any time be found in the said colonies, in lieu of, and full satisfaction for, all dues and demands of the crown and kingdom of England upon them.

There is not anything new or extraordinary in these rights granted to the British colonies. The colonies from all countries, at all times, have enjoyed equal freedom with the mother state. Indeed, there would be found very few people in the world willing to leave their native country [6] and go through the fatigue and hardship of planting in a new uncultivated one for the sake of losing their freedom. They who settle new countries must be poor and, in course, ought to be free. Advantages, pecuniary or agreeable, are not on the side of emigrants, and surely they must have something in their stead.

To illustrate this, permit us to examine what hath generally been the condition of colonies with respect to their freedom. We will begin with those who went out from the ancient commonwealths of Greece, which are the first, perhaps, we have any good account of. Thucydides, that grave and judicious historian, says of one of them, "they were not sent out to be slaves, but to be the equals of those who remain behind"; and again, the Corinthians gave public notice "that a new colony was going to Epidamnus, into which all that would enter, should have equal and like privileges with those who stayed at home." This was uniformly the condition of all the Grecian colonies; they went out and settled new countries; they took such forms of government as themselves chose, though it generally nearly resembled that of the mother state, whether democratical or oligarchical. 'Tis true, they were fond to acknowledge their original, and always confessed themselves under obligation to pay a kind of honorary respect to, and show a filial dependence on, the commonwealth from whence they sprung. Thucydides again tells us that the Corinthians complained of the Corcyreans, "from whom, though a colony of their own, they had received some contemptuous treatment, for they neither payed them the usual honor on their public solemnities, nor began with a Corinthian in the distribution of the sacrifices, which is always done by other colonies." From hence it is plain what kind of dependence the Greek colonies were under, and what sort of acknowledgment they owed to the mother state.[5]

[7] If we pass from the Grecian to the Roman colonies, we shall find them not less free. But this difference may be observed between them, that the Roman colonies did not, like the Grecian, become separate states governed by different laws, but always remained a part of the mother state; and all that were free of the colonies were also free of Rome, and had right to an equal suffrage in making all laws and appointing all officers for the government of the whole commonwealth. For the truth

of this we have the testimony of St. Paul, who though born at Tarsus, yet assures us he was born free of Rome. And Grotius gives us the opinion of a Roman king concerning the freedom of colonies: King Tullus says, "for our part, we look upon it to be neither truth nor justice that mother cities ought of necessity and by the law of nature to rule over their colonies." [6]

When we come down to the latter ages of the world and consider the colonies planted in the three last centuries in America from several kingdoms in Europe, we shall find them, says Pufendorf, very different from the ancient colonies, and gives us an instance in those of the Spaniards.[7] Although it be confessed these fall greatly short of enjoying equal freedom with the ancient Greek and Roman ones, yet it will be said truly, they enjoy equal freedom with their countrymen in Spain: but as they are all under the government of an absolute monarch, they have no reason to complain that one enjoys the liberty the other is deprived of. The French colonies will be found nearly in the same condition, and for the same reason, because their fellow subjects in France have also lost their liberty. And the question here is not whether all colonies, as compared one with another, enjoy equal liberty, but whether all enjoy as much freedom as the inhabitants of the mother state; and this will hardly be denied in the case of the Spanish, French, or other modern foreign colonies.

[8] By this it fully appears that colonies in general, both ancient and modern, have always enjoyed as much freedom as the mother state from which they went out. And will anyone suppose the British colonies in America are an exception to this general rule? Colonies that came out from a kingdom renowned for liberty, from a constitution founded on compact, from a people of all the sons of men the most tenacious of freedom; who left the delights of their native country, parted from their homes and all their conveniences, searched out and subdued a foreign country with the most amazing travail and fortitude, to the infinite advantage and emolument of the mother state; that removed on a firm reliance of a solemn compact and royal promise and grant that they and their successors forever should be free, should be partakers and sharers in all the privileges and advantages of the then English, now British constitution.[8]

If it were possible a doubt could yet remain, in the most unbelieving mind, that these British colonies are not every way justly and fully entitled to equal liberty and freedom with their fellow subjects in Europe, we might show that the Parliament of Great Britain have always understood their rights in the same light.

By an act passed in the thirteenth year of the reign of his late Majesty, King GEORGE II, entitled An Act For Naturalizing Foreign Protestants, etc., and by another act, passed in the twentieth year of the same reign, for nearly the same purposes, by both which it is enacted and ordained "that all foreign Protestants who had inhabited and resided for the space of seven years or more in any of His Majesty's colonies in America" might, on the conditions therein mentioned, be naturalized, and thereupon should "be deemed, adjudged, and taken to be His Majesty's natural-born subjects of the kingdom of Great Britain to all intents, constructions, and purposes, as if they, and every one of them, had been or were born [9] within the same." No reasonable man will here suppose the Parliament intended by these acts to put foreigners who had been in the colonies only seven years in a better condition than those who had been born in them or had removed from Britain thither, but only to put these foreigners on an equality with them; and to do this, they are obliged to give them all the rights of natural-born subjects of Great Britain.

From what hath been shown, it will appear beyond a doubt that the British subjects in America have equal rights with those in Britain; that they do not hold those rights as a privilege granted them, nor enjoy them as a grace and favor bestowed, but possess them as an inherent, indefeasible right, as they and their ancestors were freeborn subjects, justly and naturally entitled to all the rights and advantages of the British constitution.[9]

And the British legislative and executive powers have considered the colonies as possessed of these rights, and have always heretofore, in the most tender and parental manner, treated them as their dependent, though free, condition required. The protection promised on the part of the crown, with cheerfulness and great gratitude we acknowledge, hath at all times been given to the colonies. The dependence of the colonies to Great Britain hath been fully testified by a constant and ready obedience to all the commands of his present Majesty and his royal predecessors, both men and money having been raised in them at all times when called for with as much alacrity and in as large proportions as hath been done in Great Britain, the ability of each considered. It must also be confessed with thankfulness that the first adventurers and their successors, for one hundred and thirty years, have fully enjoyed all the freedoms and immunities promised on their first removal from England. But here the scene seems to be unhappily changing: the British ministry, whether induced by a jealousy of the colonies by false informations, or by some alteration in the system of political [10] government, we have no information; whatever hath been the motive, this we are sure of: the Parliament in their last session passed an act limiting, restricting, and burdening the trade of these colonies much more than had ever been done before, as also for greatly enlarging the power and jurisdiction of the courts of admiralty in the colonies; and also came to a resolution that it might be necessary to establish stamp duties and other internal taxes to be collected within them. This act and this resolution have caused great uneasiness and consternation among the British subjects on the continent of America: how much reason there is for it we will endeavor, in the most modest and plain manner we can, to lay before our readers.

In the first place, let it be considered that although each of the colonies hath a legislature within itself to take care of its interests and provide for its peace and internal government, yet there are many things of a more general nature, quite out of the reach of these particular legislatures, which it is necessary should be regulated, ordered, and governed. One of this kind is the commerce of the whole British empire, taken collectively, and that of each kingdom and colony in it as it makes a part of that whole. Indeed, everything that concerns the proper interest and fit government of the whole commonwealth, of keeping the peace, and subordination of all the parts towards the whole and one among another, must be considered in this light. Amongst these general concerns, perhaps, money and paper credit, those grand instruments of all commerce, will be found also to have a place. These, with all other matters of a general nature, it is absolutely necessary should have a general power to direct them, some supreme and overruling authority with power to make laws and form regulations for the good of all, and to compel their execution and observation. It being necessary some such general power should exist somewhere, every man of the least knowledge of the British [11] constitution will be naturally led to look for and find it in the Parliament of Great Britain. That grand and august legislative body must from the nature of their authority and the necessity of the thing be justly vested with this power. Hence it becomes the indispensable duty of every good and loyal subject cheerfully to obey and patiently submit to all the acts, laws, orders, and regulations that may be made and passed by Parliament for directing and governing all these general matters.[10]

Here it may be urged by many, and indeed with great appearance of reason, that the equity, justice, and beneficence of the British constitution will require that the separate kingdoms and distant colonies who are to obey and be governed by these general laws and regulations ought to be represented, some way or other, in Parliament, at least whilst these general matters are under consideration. Whether the colonies will ever be admitted to have representatives in Parliament, whether it be consistent with their distant and dependent state, and whether if it were admitted it would be to their advantage, are questions we will pass by, and observe that these colonies ought in justice and for the very evident good of the whole commonwealth to have notice of every new measure about to be pursued and new act that is about to be passed, by which their rights, liberties, or interests will be affected. They ought to have such notice, that they may appear and be heard by their agents, by counsel, or written representation, or by some other equitable and effectual way.

The colonies are at so great a distance from England that the members of Parliament can generally have but little knowledge of their business, connections, and interest but what is gained from people who have been there; the most of these have so slight a knowledge themselves that the informations they can give are very little to be depended on, though they may pretend to determine with confidence [12] on matters far above their reach. All such kind of informations are too uncertain to be depended on in the transacting business of so much consequence and in which the interests of two millions of free people are so deeply concerned. There is no kind of inconveniency or mischief can arise from the colonies having such notice and being heard in the manner above mentioned; but, on the contrary, very great mischiefs have already happened to the colonies, and always must be expected, if they are not heard before things of such importance are determined concerning them.

Had the colonies been fully heard before the late act had been passed, no reasonable man can suppose it ever would have passed at all in the manner it now stands; for what good reason can possibly be given for making a law to cramp the trade and ruin the interests of many of the colonies, and at the same time lessen in a prodigious manner the consumption of the British manufactures in them? These are certainly the effects this act must produce; a duty of three pence per gallon on foreign molasses is well known to every man in the least acquainted with it to be much higher than that article can possibly bear, and therefore must operate as an absolute prohibition. This will put a total stop to our exportation of lumber, horses, flour, and fish to the French and Dutch sugar colonies; and if anyone supposes we may find a sufficient vent for these articles in the English islands in the West Indies, he only verifies what was just now observed, that he wants truer information. Putting an end to the importation of foreign molasses at the same time puts an end to all the costly distilleries in these colonies, and to the rum trade to the coast of Africa, and throws it into the hands of the French. With the loss of the foreign molasses trade, the cod fishery of the English in America must also be lost and thrown also into the hands of the French. That this is the real state of the whole business is not fancy; this, nor any part of it, is not exaggeration but a sober and most melancholy truth.

[13] View this duty of three pence per gallon on foreign molasses not in the light of a prohibition but supposing the trade to continue and the duty to be paid. Heretofore there hath been imported into the colony of Rhode Island only, about one million one hundred and fifty thousand gallons annually; the duty on this quantity is fourteen thousand three hundred and seventy-five pounds sterling to be paid yearly by this little colony, a larger sum than was ever in it at any one time. This money is to be sent away, and never to return; yet the payment is to be repeated every year.[11] Can this possibly be done? Can a new colony, compelled by necessity to purchase all its clothing, furniture, and utensils from England, to support the expenses of its own internal government, obliged by its duty to comply with every call from the crown to raise money on emergencies; after all this, can every man in it pay twenty-four shillings sterling a year for the duties of a single article only? There is surely no man in his right mind believes this possible. The charging foreign molasses with this high duty will not affect all the colonies equally, nor any other near so much as this of Rhode Island, whose trade depended much more on foreign molasses and on distilleries than that of any others; this must show that raising money for the general service of the crown or of the colonies by such a duty will be extremely unequal and therefore unjust. And now taking either alternative, by supposing, on one hand, the foreign molasses trade is stopped and with it the opportunity or ability of the colonies to get money, or, on the other, that this trade is continued and that the colonies get money by it but all their money is taken from them by paying the duty, can Britain be gainer by either? Is it not the chiefest interest of Britain to dispose of and to be paid for her own manufactures?

And doth she not find the greatest and best market for them in her own colonies? Will she find an advantage in disabling the colonies to [14] continue their trade with her? Or can she possibly grow rich by their being made poor?

Ministers have great influence, and Parliaments have great power — can either of them change the nature of things, stop all our means of getting money, and yet expect us to purchase and pay for British manufactures? The genius of the people in these colonies is as little turned to manufacturing goods for their own use as is possible to suppose in any people whatsoever; yet necessity will compel them either to go naked in this cold country or to make themselves some sort of clothing, if it be only the skins of beasts.

By the same act of Parliament, the exportation of all kinds of timber or lumber, the most natural produce of these new colonies, is greatly encumbered and uselessly embarrassed, and the shipping it to any part of Europe except Great Britain prohibited.[12] This must greatly affect the linen manufactory in Ireland, as that kingdom used to receive great quantities of flaxseed from America; many cargoes, being made of that and of barrel staves, were sent thither every year; but as the staves can no longer be exported thither, the ships carrying only flaxseed casks, without the staves which used to be intermixed among them, must lose one half of their freight, which will prevent their continuing this trade, to the great injury of Ireland and of the plantations. And what advantage is to accrue to Great Britain by it must be told by those who can perceive the utility of this measure.

Enlarging the power and jurisdiction of the courts of vice-admiralty in the colonies is another part of the same act, greatly and justly complained of. Courts of admiralty have long been established in most of the colonies, whose authority were circumscribed within moderate territorial jurisdictions; and these courts have always done the business necessary to be brought before such courts for trial in [15] the manner it ought to be done and in a way only moderately expensive to the subjects; and if seizures were made or informations exhibited without reason or contrary to law, the informer or seizor was left to the justice of the common law, there to pay for his folly or suffer for his temerity. But now this course is quite altered, and a customhouse officer may make a seizure in Georgia of goods ever so legally imported, and carry the trial to Halifax at fifteen hundred miles distance; and thither the owner must follow him to defend his property; and when he comes there, quite beyond the circle of his friends, acquaintance, and correspondents, among total strangers, he must there give bond and must find sureties to be bound with him in a large sum before he shall be admitted to claim his own goods; when this is complied with, he hath a trial and his goods acquitted. If the judge can be prevailed on (which it is very well known may too easily be done) to certify there was *only* probable cause for making the seizure, the unhappy owner shall not maintain any action against the illegal seizor for damages or obtain any other satisfaction, but he may return to Georgia quite ruined and undone in conformity to an act of Parliament. Such unbounded encouragement and protection given to informers must call to everyone's remembrance Tacitus' account of the miserable condition of the Romans in the reign of Tiberius their emperor, who let loose and encouraged the informers of that age. Surely if the colonies had been fully heard before this had been done, the liberties and properties of the Americans would not have been so much disregarded.[13]

The resolution of the House of Commons, come into during the same session of Parliament, asserting their rights to establish stamp duties and internal taxes to be collected in the colonies without their own consent, hath much more, and for much more reason, alarmed the British subjects in America than anything that had ever been done before. [16] These resolutions, carried into execution, the colonies cannot help but consider as a manifest violation of their just and long-enjoyed rights. For it must be confessed by all men that they who are taxed at pleasure by others cannot possibly have any property, can have nothing to be called their own. They who have no property can have no freedom, but are indeed reduced to the most abject slavery, are in a condition far worse than countries conquered and made tributary, for these have only a fixed sum to pay, which they are left to raise among themselves in the way that they may think most equal and easy, and having paid the stipulated sum the debt is discharged, and what is left is their own. This is much more tolerable than to be taxed at the mere will of others, without any bounds, without any stipulation and agreement, contrary to their consent and against their will. If we are told that those who lay these taxes upon the colonies are men of the highest character for their wisdom, justice, and integrity, and therefore cannot be supposed to deal hardly, unjustly, or unequally by any; admitting and really believing that all this is true, it will make no alteration in the nature of the case. For one who is bound to obey the will of another is as really a slave though he may have a good master as if he had a bad one; and this is stronger in politic bodies than in natural ones, as the former have perpetual succession and remain the same; and although they may have a very good master at one time, they may have a very bad one at another. And indeed, if the people in America are to be taxed by the representatives of the people in Britain, their malady is an increasing evil that must always grow greater by time. Whatever burdens are laid upon the Americans will be so much taken off the Britons; and the doing this will soon be extremely popular, and those who put up to be members of the House of Commons must obtain the votes of the people by promising to [17] take more and more of the taxes off them by putting it on the Americans. This must most assuredly be the case, and it will not be in the power even of the Parliament to prevent it; the people's private interest will be concerned and will govern them; they will have such, and only such, representatives as will act agreeable to this their interest; and these taxes laid on Americans will be always a part of the supply bill, in which the other branches of the legislature can make no alteration. And in truth, the subjects in the colonies will be taxed at the will and pleasure of their fellow subjects in Britain. How equitable and how just this may be must be left to every impartial man to determine.

But it will be said that the monies drawn from the colonies by duties and by taxes will be laid up and set apart to be used for their future defense. This will not at all alleviate the hardship, but serves only more strongly to mark the servile state of the people. Free people have ever thought, and always will think, that the money necessary for their defense lies safest in their own hands, until it be wanted immediately for that purpose. To take the money of the Americans, which they want continually to use in their trade, and lay it up for their defense at a thousand leagues distance from them when the enemies they have to fear are in their own neighborhood, hath not the greatest probability of friendship or of prudence.

It is not the judgment of free people only that money for defending them is safest in their own keeping, but it hath also been the opinion of the best and wisest kings and governors of mankind, in every age of the world, that the wealth of a state was most securely as well as most profitably deposited in the hands of their faithful subjects. Constantine, emperor of the Romans, though an absolute prince, both practiced and praised this method. "Diocletian sent persons on purpose to reproach him with his neglect of the public, and the poverty to which he was [18] reduced by his own fault. Constantine heard these reproaches with patience; and having persuaded those who made them in Diocletian's name, to stay a few days with him, he sent word to the most wealthy persons in the provinces that he wanted money and that they had now an opportunity of showing whether or no they truly loved their prince. Upon this notice everyone strove who should be foremost in carrying to the exchequer all their gold, silver, and valuable effects; so that in a short time Constantine from being the poorest became by far the most wealthy of all the four princes. He then invited the deputies of Diocletian to visit his treasury, desiring them to make a faithful report to their master of the state in which they should find it. They obeyed; and, while they stood gazing on the mighty heaps of gold and silver, Constantine told them that the wealth which they beheld with astonishment had long since belonged to him, but that he had left it by way of depositum in the hands of his people, adding, the richest and surest treasure of the prince was the love of his subjects. The deputies were no sooner gone than the generous prince sent for those who had assisted him in his exigency, commended their zeal, and returned to everyone what they had so readily brought into his treasury." *Universal Hist., vol. XV, p. 523.*[14]

We are not insensible that when liberty is in danger, the liberty of complaining is dangerous; yet a man on a wreck was never denied the liberty of roaring as loud as he could, says Dean Swift. And we believe no good reason can be given why the colonies should not modestly and soberly inquire what right the Parliament of Great Britain have to tax them. We know such inquiries by a late letter writer have been branded with the little epithet of *mushroom policy;* and he insinuates that for the colonies to pretend to claim any privileges will draw down the [19] resentment of the Parliament on them.[15] Is the defense of liberty become so contemptible, and pleading for just rights so dangerous? Can the guardians of liberty be thus ludicrous? Can the patrons of freedom be so jealous and so severe? If the British House of Commons are rightfully possessed of a power to tax the colonies in America, this power must be vested in them by the British constitution, as they are one branch of the great legislative body of the nation. As they are the representatives of all the people in Britain, they have beyond doubt all the power such a representation can possibly give; yet great as this power is, surely it cannot exceed that of their constituents. And can it possibly be shown that the people in Britain have a sovereign authority over their fellow subjects in America? Yet such is the authority that must be exercised in taking people's estates from them by taxes, or otherwise without their consent. In all aids granted to the crown by the Parliament, it is said with the greatest propriety, "We freely give unto Your Majesty"; for they give their own money and the money of those who have entrusted them with a proper power for that purpose. But can they with the same propriety give away the money of the Americans, who have never given any such power? Before a thing can be justly given away, the giver must certainly have acquired a property in it; and have the people in Britain justly acquired such a property in the goods and estates of the people in these colonies that they may give them away at pleasure?

In an imperial state, which consists of many separate governments each of which hath peculiar privileges and of which kind it is evident the empire of Great Britain is, no single part, though greater than another part, is by that superiority entitled to make laws for or to tax such lesser part; but all laws and all taxations which bind the whole must be made by the whole. This may be fully verified by the empire of Germany, which consists of many states, some [20] powerful and others weak, yet the powerful never make laws to govern or to tax the little and weak ones, neither is it done by the emperor, but only by the diet, consisting of the representatives of the whole body. Indeed, it must be absurd to suppose that the common people of Great Britain have a sovereign and absolute authority over their fellow subjects in America, or even any sort of power whatsoever over them; but it will be still more absurd to suppose they can give a power to their representatives which they have not themselves. If the House of Commons do not receive this authority from their constituents it will be difficult to tell by what means they obtained it, except it be vested in them by mere superiority and power.[16]

Should it be urged that the money expended by the mother country for the defense and protection of America, and especially during the late war, must justly entitle her to some retaliation from the colonies, and that the stamp duties and taxes intended to be raised in them are only designed for that equitable purpose; if we are permitted to examine how far this may rightfully vest the Parliament with the power of taxing the colonies we shall find this claim to have no sort of equitable foundation. In many of the colonies, especially those in New England, who were planted, as before observed, not at the charge of the crown or kingdom of England, but at the expense of the planters themselves, and were not only planted but also defended against the savages and other enemies in long and cruel wars which continued for an hundred years almost without intermission, solely at their own charge: and in the year 1746, when the Duke D'Anville came out from France with the most formidable French fleet that ever was in the American seas, enraged at these colonies for the loss of Louisbourg the year before and with orders to make an attack on them; even in this greatest exigence, these colonies were left to the protection of Heaven and their own efforts.[17] These colonies [21] having thus planted and defended themselves and removed all enemies from their borders, were in hopes to enjoy peace and recruit their state, much exhausted by these long struggles; but they were soon called upon to raise men and send out to the defense of other colonies, and to make conquests for the crown. They dutifully obeyed the requisition, and with ardor entered into those services and continued in them until all encroachments were removed, and all Canada, and even the Havana, conquered. They most cheerfully complied with every call of the crown; they rejoiced, yea even exulted, in the prosperity and exaltation of the British empire. But these colonies, whose bounds were fixed and whose borders were before cleared from enemies by their own fortitude and at their own expense, reaped no sort of advantage by these conquests: they are not enlarged, have not gained a single acre of land, have no part in the Indian or interior trade. The immense tracts of land subdued and no less immense and profitable commerce acquired all belong to Great Britain, and not the least share or portion to these colonies, though thousands of their men have lost their lives and millions of their money have been expended in the purchase of them, for great part of which we are yet in debt, and from which we shall not in many years be able to extricate ourselves. Hard will be the fate, yea cruel the destiny, of these unhappy colonies if the reward they are to receive for all this is the loss of their freedom; better for them Canada still remained French, yea far more eligible that it ever should remain so than that the price of its reduction should be their slavery.

If the colonies are not taxed by Parliament, are they therefore exempted from bearing their proper share in the necessary burdens of government? This by no means follows. Do they not support a regular internal government in each colony as expensive to the people here as the internal government of Britain is to the people there? Have not [22] the colonies here, at all times when called upon by the crown, raised money for the public service, done it as cheerfully as the Parliament have done on like occasions? Is not this the most easy, the most natural, and most constitutional way of raising money in the colonies? What occasion then to distrust the colonies

— what necessity to fall on an invidious and unconstitutional method to compel them to do what they have ever done freely? Are not the people in the colonies as loyal and dutiful subjects as any age or nation ever produced; and are they not as useful to the kingdom, in this remote quarter of the world, as their fellow subjects are who dwell in Britain? The Parliament, it is confessed, have power to regulate the trade of the whole empire; and hath it not full power, by this means, to draw all the money and all the wealth of the colonies into the mother country at pleasure? What motive, after all this, can remain to induce the Parliament to abridge the privileges and lessen the rights of the most loyal and dutiful subjects, subjects justly entitled to ample freedom, who have long enjoyed and not abused or forfeited their liberties, who have used them to their own advantage in dutiful subserviency to the orders and interests of Great Britain? Why should the gentle current of tranquillity that has so long run with peace through all the British states, and flowed with joy and happiness in all her countries, be at last obstructed, be turned out of its true course into unusual and winding channels by which many of those states must be ruined, but none of them can possibly be made more rich or more happy?

    Before we conclude, it may be necessary to take notice of the vast difference there is between the raising money in a country by duties, taxes, or otherwise, and employing and laying out the money again in the same country, and raising the like sums of money by the like means and sending it away quite out of the country where it is raised. Where the former of these is the case, although the sums raised may be [23] very great, yet that country may support itself under them; for as fast as the money is collected together, it is again scattered abroad, to be used in commerce and every kind of business; and money is not made scarcer by this means, but rather the contrary, as this continual circulation must have a tendency to prevent, in some degree, its being hoarded. But where the latter method is pursued, the effect will be extremely different; for here, as fast as the money can be collected, 'tis immediately sent out of the country, never to return but by a tedious round of commerce, which at best must take up much time. Here all trade, and every kind of business depending on it, will grow dull, and must languish more and more until it comes to a final stop at last. If the money raised in Great Britain in the three last years of the late war, and which exceeded forty millions sterling, had been sent out of the kingdom, would not this have nearly ruined the trade of the nation in three years only? Think, then, what must be the condition of these miserable colonies when all the money proposed to be raised in them by high duties on the importation of divers kinds of goods, by the post office, by stamp duties, and other taxes, is sent quite away, as fast as it can be collected, and this to be repeated continually and last forever! Is it possible for colonies under these circumstances to support themselves, to have any money, any trade, or other business, carried on in them? Certainly it is not; nor is there at present, or ever was, any country under Heaven that did, or possibly could, support itself under such burdens.

We finally beg leave to assert that the first planters of these colonies were pious Christians, were faithful subjects who, with a fortitude and perseverance little known and less considered, settled these wild countries, by God's goodness and their own amazing labors, thereby added a most valuable dependence to the crown of Great Britain; were ever dutifully subservient to her interests; so taught their children [24] that not one has been disaffected to this day, but all have honestly obeyed every royal command and cheerfully submitted to every constitutional law; have as little inclination as they have ability to throw off their dependency; have carefully avoided every offensive measure and every interdicted manufacture; have risked their lives as they have been ordered, and furnished their money when it has been called for; have never been troublesome or expensive to the mother country; have kept due order and supported a regular government; have maintained peace and practiced Christianity; and in all conditions, and in every relation, have demeaned themselves as loyal, as dutiful, and as faithful subjects ought; and that no kingdom or state hath, or ever had, colonies more quiet, more obedient, or more profitable than these have ever been.

May the same divine goodness that guided the first planters, protected the settlements, inspired Kings to be gracious, Parliaments to be tender, ever preserve, ever support our present gracious King; give great wisdom to his ministers and much understanding to his Parliaments; perpetuate the sovereignty of the British constitution, and the filial dependency and happiness of all the colonies.

P——.

PROVIDENCE, in NEW ENGLAND
　NOVEMBER 30, 1764.

PAMPHLET 10

MARTIN HOWARD, JR., *A LETTER FROM A GENTLEMAN AT HALIFAX*

NEWPORT, 1765

INTRODUCTION

Very little is known of the life of Martin Howard, Jr., before the eruption of the controversy surrounding the publication of this pamphlet. Son of an English emigrant of the 1720's, he studied law with James Honyman, Jr., member of a leading Anglican family, successively attorney general and king's attorney of the colony. By the 1740's Howard was prominent as a lawyer representing the interests of shipowners and merchants of Newport. An Anglican, he married into the affluent Brenton family, landowners and merchants long associated with the customs administration in Rhode Island; but until 1754, when he was chosen with Stephen Hopkins to represent Rhode Island in the Albany Congress, he does not appear to have been involved in public affairs. Even after that appointment by the colony's Assembly, which fell to him after two others had refused it, he remained aloof from the furious political struggles of the time except for a single unsuccessful bid for the attorney-generalship on the Ward ticket.[1] When in 1763 he emerged permanently from private life, it was not as an active politician seeking office under the government of Rhode Island but as a critic of the constitutional basis of that government and as an outspoken defender of England's new colonial policies. For, inclined by parentage, church affiliation, and — to judge from the brilliantly expressive portrait of him by Copley — temperament as well, to associate himself with England and authority, he was by then involved with a small group in Newport — Otis' "contaminated knot" — consciously devoted to advancing the interests of England and to reducing the chartered independence of Rhode Island.[2]

Certain members of this group have been identified: the newly arrived collector of customs in Rhode Island; an agent of an English commercial firm; the leading colonial architect, brother of a customs official; a Scottish physician and intellectual; a retired officer of the British army; and possibly also the attorney general of the colony.[3] Disdainful of the petty politics of Rhode Island and disposed to sympathize with the policies of the Grenville administration, they published in the *Newport Mercury*, after the passage of the Sugar Act, a series of articles which form the immediate background of the present pamphlet and are in themselves important expressions of a segment of public opinion in the colonies.

These essays, touching fundamentals of political theory as they relate to the emerging conflict in Anglo-American affairs, express attitudes and ideas that would become staples of Tory thought; they would not reappear in

such blatant form — such was the chastening effect of the Stamp Act controversy — until the Tea Party had led to an almost hopeless impasse. They
began with an attack on politics as it was practiced in Rhode Island, factional
struggles for the control of public office, which violated central principles of
eighteenth-century political theory. Such politics, Howard and his friends
argued — in terms so traditional and widely accepted that their most violent
opponents could not have disagreed [4] — was to be avoided at all costs. Everywhere reducing those who were caught up in it to the helpless tools of designing men, it had almost ruined England, and was in the most manifest
way destroying the colony of Rhode Island.

> The baleful influence of party extends to every transaction, public or private.
> Our courts of judicature, which should be the sacred fountains of law and
> justice, are often but mere instruments to execute the particular designs of
> party; and hence it comes to pass that we have neither confidence in nor re
> spect for our judges. Law, instead of being a permanent and uniform rule to
> society, is ever vague and transitory, and adjusted to the annual complexion
> and passions of a party.

Factious politics, "the bane of industry and the nurse of idleness," bred falsehood and insincerity; it contaminated the most private recesses of society.
Even children were affected, for they "imbibe the narrow and illiberal sentiments of those with whom they are nearly connected," learn to consider those
who disagree with their parents as fools and knaves, and develop in their
tender minds "disgusts, antipathies, and hatreds that scarcely ever wear out." [5]

But politics, for all its evils, was the symptom, Howard and his colleagues
wrote, not the disease itself. At the root of the troubled condition of public
life in Rhode Island lay an unbalanced constitution, which, like analogous disbalances in the physical body, led necessarily to repeated breakdowns. There
was in Rhode Island an obvious excess in the influence of the "democratical"
order of society, resulting from and protected by the royal charter that had
been granted by the crown a century earlier. Such a charter, providing for an
elected governor and Council and hence lodging all power in the people, may
be reasonable, they conceded, "in the beginning or infancy of a state, when
its members are few and virtuous and united together by some peculiar ideas
of freedom or religion." In such pristine years there is scarcely need for
government at all: "the people have yet acquired no passion but the love of
their infant country, and simplicity and integrity of heart and manners answer the design of laws." But when the availability and attractiveness of
power increases in society, and increasing maturity and sophistication of the
people transform "simplicity of heart and mutual confidence . . . to licentiousness of manners and universal distrust" then the constitution of the infant state must be changed: "a superior force is necessary and a coercive power
should be increased to regulate and keep it within bounds." If such a change
is not made — if a popular government is allowed to continue in a mature
society — the corrupting evils of faction will inevitably spring up, with fatal
consequences. It was a rigorously predictable development. All of history
proved, they wrote, that

the people, in almost every age and country, have been incapable, collectively, of acting with any degree of moderation or wisdom. It was ever impracticable to combine the various passions, humors, and interests of a multitude so as to produce harmony, order, and subordination in a state. From this incapacity and disorder of the people, particular men of artful and ambitious minds have ever derived their advantage; and by a display of talents fitted to the caprice of the ignorant populace obtained by degrees the authority over them.

One person having risen to demagogic power by satisfying the capricious whims of the people, another, consumed by envy and "thinking himself equally entitled to command, begins an opposition, and thus a party is formed." The result was the kind of factionalism, only too well illustrated in the Ward-Hopkins controversy in Rhode Island, that tears a community to pieces:

> The leaders of these opposite parties having nothing in view but to keep or acquire to themselves and adherents all the profits and emoluments of the government, it follows that the interest of each party becomes its ruling passion to which everything else must submit; and as the suffrages of the people settle and determine everything, these are to be gained by gratifying and humoring all their demands and expectations, however scandalous or extravagant.

For Rhode Island the necessary solution was obvious. "The present folly and riot," lamented by every person in the colony uncorrupted by party, cannot be corrected "by any strength or wisdom among ourselves. A change of rulers hath been, in general, no other than a change of faction . . . Our distemper is radical, and so must be the remedy." An act of Parliament abolishing the charter of the colony and placing the government in the hands of the crown was the only solution. This "coercive power from home" was not to be feared, for the constitution of England, which limited the action of the prince, was famous for its justice and tenderness. "Do we see any marks of tyranny or arbitrary power in the neighboring governments more immediately under the crown?" And in any case, in a crisis created by a tyrant a charter would provide pitifully little protection. "An arbitrary prince never wants a pretext to invade the rights of his people . . . no charter would be any obstacle at all: his single order, with a regiment of dragoons, would dissolve all the charters in his dominions." [6]

This argument, most fully enunciated in April 1764, was followed in successive issues of the *Mercury* by exhortations to Rhode Islanders to forget their political preoccupations and turn to virtuous enterprises such as growing hemp (subsidized, the writers pointed out, by a premium stipulated in the Sugar Act) and raising sheep as a basis for local industries. Week after week bucolic visions of virtuous, hemp-raising yeomen free from corruption and intrigue were conjured up, and factious politicians condemned.[7] But by the early fall, with vigorous pamphlets on the rights and wrongs of Anglo-American relations appearing on all sides, essays on the joys and techniques of hemp production were losing whatever appeal they might once have had. The attention of Howard and his junto turned to the new polemical literature.

In September they commented on Thacher's *Sentiments* (JHL Pamphlet 8), ridiculing the motto on its title page and promising, by way of commentary on it, that anyone who withdraws allegiance from England will be recalled to his duty by "a small fleet and a few regiments." Others of these publications, the writers said, "we have wished . . . had been either suppressed or purged, as perhaps they may be construed to the disadvantage of all the colonies . . . It is to be wished that the indecency and illiberal abuse of sovereign and supreme power had been either restrained or prevented." Writings that presume to whisper into the ear of ministers of state may have "a direct and manifest tendency to represent the colonies in a very offensive and unfavorable light." What can be the "necessity or use of reviling our superiors, or of teaching the people to despise or think slightly of them"? Selfish interest, if not gratitude and duty, ought to teach these pamphleteers "more moderation and civility, more meekness and better manners." Rhode Island too was guilty of this "pernicious and graceless writing," which, it was fervently hoped, would never appear "on the other side of the Atlantic lest the temper or disposition of the people here might be supposed to resemble the complexion of these inflammatory and very undutiful writings." It was all false patriotism and facile declamation, and it was as deserving of condemnation as idleness, dissipation, and "the tyranny of a mob." [8]

The climax came on January 7, 1765, when one of the writers, presumably Howard, fell upon Hopkins' recently published *Rights of Colonies Examined* (JHL Pamphlet 9). The pretentiousness of the pamphlet, the writers said, was perhaps the most offensive thing about it. Rising from amid a pack of "little curs" in Providence, it had been written by one who

> does not know a noun substantive from an adjective, and yet has the astonishing impudence, the most assuming impertinence, to pretend to judge of polite writing: hugs and admires himself in his stupidly profound ignorance; is stared at by those sycophants that nightly guzzle and swill in his company, where, like a bashaw, he presides as the sovereign sole judge of merit, his attendants fawning and slavering him.[9]

But it was not enough to mock the style and abuse the author of the piece; the arguments must be answered. *A Letter From a Gentleman at Halifax,* published in mid-February 1765 was written by Howard for that purpose.

Effectively allusive (every reader recognized Halifax as the seat of the new superior vice-admiralty court that had been created by the Sugar Act), chillingly supercilious, and full of stinging vituperation, the *Halifax Letter* scored debating points left and right. But basically it presented three arguments, which, touching central issues of the constitutional controversy, would be heard again and again in the years that followed.

Howard argued, first, that there was no natural relation between colonies and mother country by which colonists' rights could be abstractly defined. True, Americans were entitled to all the rights of Englishmen; but rights are of two kinds, personal and political. The former, comprehending life, liberty, and estate, are guaranteed to colonists as to all Englishmen by the common law which was "every subject's birthright." But political rights, which pertain to powers of government, are creations of positive law; in the colonies they are limited and defined by the charters which first created the governments. Individually the colonists enjoy all the blessings of the English constitution; collectively "they are confined within the primitive views of their institution" expressed in the charters; once having accepted those terms, they cannot subsequently complain about them.

As to Parliament's power, "it is attached to every English subject, wherever he be," for, Howard argued, the jurisdiction of Parliament flows from the same source — the common law — that gives rise to personal rights; the rights of the individual and the power of Parliament were equally part of the constitution. "Can we claim the common law as an inheritance and at the same time be at liberty to adopt one part of it and reject the other? Indeed we cannot . . . in denying [Parliament's] jurisdiction we at the same time take leave of the common law, and thereby, with equal temerity, and folly, strip ourselves of every blessing we enjoy as Englishmen."

Finally, as to representation, Howard asked the question that would ring through debates on American rights until Independence was a fact: "is the Isle of Man, Jersey, or Guernsey represented? What is the value or amount of each man's representation in the kingdom of Scotland, which contains near two millions of people and yet not more than three thousand have votes in the election of members of Parliament?" [10]

These still fresh arguments (they would soon become threadbare), and the sharp digs at Hopkins and his *Rights* that fill out the pamphlet, hit their mark. In England, Thomas Whately, Grenville's influential secretary and the draftsman and ideologist of the Stamp Act, declared the pamphlet to be "very sensible, and fully confutes [Hopkins'] arguments"; he was glad, he wrote, "to find that there are men in America who have considered the true state of the case, and do not run away with the general current into a proposition so untenable as that an acknowledged sovereign legislature cannot lay taxes." In Rhode Island, Hopkins' supporters in the General Assembly sought to have the pamphlet declared a libel, the printer called to account, and the document itself burned by the common hangman; more moderate views prevailed, however, though the Superior Court did subject the printer to an interrogation. The controversy continued with great heat in the newspapers. The *Newport Mercury* unctuously praised the author of the *Halifax Letter* as having "rendered his country more service than all the leaders and subalterns of both parties," and castigated scurrilous pamphleteers who attempted to inculcate in the common people "such wicked tenets as necessarily tend to weaken the ties of allegiance and a due reverence for supreme authority under the mask or disguise of liberty." [11] At the same time the *Providence Gazette* published detailed replies to the *Halifax Letter*. On February 23, ten days after the publication of Howard's pamphlet, the *Gazette* carried in two and a half columns "Some Account of a Pamphlet Lately Published in Newport," which identified the *Halifax Letter* as the work of "disappointed persons in Newport, noted for their disaffection to the government of the colonies in general and to this of Rhode Island in particular," who had "settled a correspondence with some creatures of the ministry" to whom they send "the most false and scandalous accounts of His Majesty's good and loyal subjects here." Convinced that all of America was "superlatively ignorant, rude, and ungovernable, and slaves by birth," they seek "the highest exercise of severity and arbitrary power over us, and that the laws for our government ought to be written in blood." But why? What motivation could they have? Those who knew them best, the writer explained, offered two explanations: first, that having lost all esteem in the colonies by their "astonishing malevolence and perverseness of heart," they find themselves barred from all public offices except those that will be paid out as rewards upon "the total subversion of the constitution" — an eventuality they therefore seek to bring about; and second, "not being able to bear any superior," they slander Governor Hopkins' pamphlet in the hope that the electorate will turn him out at the next election.

Having offered these explanations, the author turned to the arguments themselves, branding them "a set of idle distinctions and metaphysical quirks," and refuted them one by one. He concluded that the *Halifax Letter*, "like a skunk . . . will discover its extreme filthiness" wherever it appears, and become known for what it is, the product of "a few graceless wretches . . . of most execrable principles, and who are actually conspiring to reduce whole provinces to the depth of slavery and misery."

But this "Account," extensive as it was, was a mere introduction to Hopkins' own reply, "A Vindication of a Late Pamphlet," which ran to 10,000 words in three issues of the *Providence Gazette*.[12] This three-part essay, the contents of which, like those of the "Account," are detailed in the annotation to the present pamphlet, also contained a personal attack on Howard; but its tone was reasonable, and its effect was to explain away as exaggerations the extreme interpretation Howard had put upon the words of *The Rights of Colonies Examined*. It was more a defense than an attack or rebuttal, and it must have appeared to contemporaries, as it has to historians, a retreat on the part of the governor; Howard must have read it with satisfaction.[13]

Hopkins was, nevertheless, revenged, and not merely by his subsequent *Letter to the Author of the Halifax Letter* . . . ([Newport], 1765) or by James Otis' *Vindication* (JHL Pamphlet 11). Through the spring and early summer of 1765, as the date for the beginning of enforcement of the Stamp Act approached, popular hostility to the Newport clique rose to a dangerous pitch. In August, the smoldering situation, fanned by continued polemics in the newspapers and fed by additional pamphlets, exploded. News arrived that rioting had taken place in Boston against the Bay Colony's collector of stamp duties, and word circulated that similar action would soon be undertaken in Rhode Island. Howard, realistically fearful of the designs of any mob that might assemble, appealed in the *Mercury* for freedom from intimidation; he stated that he still stood by every word he had written in the *Halifax Letter*, and claimed the right to publish his opinions. But on August 27 his effigy, identified by a placard bearing Otis' description of him as "that fawning, insidious, infamous parricide, Martinus Scriblerus," was dragged through the streets of Newport, and, together with the effigies of Dr. Moffat and the Rhode Island collector of stamp duties, was hanged and burned. The next night his house, along with Moffat's, was gutted by the mob, and he fled to the protection of the royal man-of-war in the harbor.[14]

He never returned to Rhode Island. Leaving behind him property he later claimed was worth £970, he sailed for England, where he contacted Whately and set about retrieving his fortunes. A winter of maneuvering landed him, as reward for his loyalty, the chief justiceship of North Carolina, which he immediately took up. Confirmed by his recent experiences in his low opinion of "the democracy," he quickly acquired in North Carolina the same reputation for imperiousness and authoritarianism that he had had in Rhode Island. He presided over the special court that tried the Regulators for treason after the battle of the Alamance, and personally handed down the death sentence to twelve of the leaders, six of whom were actually executed. When the break with England came his decision was never in doubt. Refusing to acknowledge the jurisdiction of the Revolutionary court that summoned him for a test of loyalty, he was proscribed, and was forced once more to abandon his home and property to the forces in society that he had for so long and with such apparent justification feared. Destitute in 1777, he was granted a small pension by Parliament. He died in England in 1781, still claiming recompense for the loss he had suffered in Rhode Island in the year of the Stamp Act.[15]

A/LETTER/from a/Gentleman at *Halifax,*/to his/FRIEND in *Rhode-Island,*/containing/REMARKS upon a PAMPHLET,/entitled,/the rights of colonies/examined./

NEWPORT:/Printed and sold by S. HALL. m.dcc.lxv./

A
LETTER, &c.

MY DEAR SIR,

I thank you very kindly for the pamphlets and newspapers you was so obliging as to send me. I will, according to your request, give you a few miscellaneous strictures on that pamphlet, wrote by Mr. *H—p—s,* your governor, entitled *The Rights of Colonies Examined.*

His Honor reminds me of the Roman poet:

> *Est genus hominum, qui esse primos se omnium rerum volunt,*
> *Nec sunt.*[1]

He seems to give a solemnity to his performance, as if the subject had not been sufficiently handled by [4] any other before him, but I am of opinion he falls very short of Mr. ———, who, though unhappily misled by popular ideas and at the head of the *tribunitian veto,* yet appears to be a man of knowledge and parts;[2] whereas *The Rights of Colonies Examined* is a labored, ostentatious piece, discovers its author to be totally unacquainted with style or diction, and eagerly fond to pass upon the world for a man of letters.

I cannot forgive the honorable author in adopting for his motto the three lines from Thomson, so little applicable are they to the present times. I might challenge all the sons of discontent and faction in the British dominions to show the least similitude between the years one thousand six hundred and forty-one and one thousand seven hundred and sixty-four. How cruel and invidious is it to insinuate the most distant likeness between the two periods? How much like sedition does it seem to associate the present transactions of the nation with those of one thousand six hundred and forty-one, which soon after kindled into a civil war, and in the end overturned the English constitution? [3]

The honorable author might perhaps flatter himself that in future editions of Thomson's *Liberty,* commentators may insert *variae lectiones* of the text, and the three lines run thus:

> Mid the low murmurs of submissive fear,
> And mingled rage, my *H — p — s* rais'd his voice,
> And so the laws appeal'd.

Or perhaps some future bard may sing the present times and HE be made the hero of the song. The aptness is easy and striking, and the idea too pleasing [5] to be resisted. Narcissus in contemplating his own image was turned into a daffodil. Who can think of this and feel no pity for the pride and weakness of *man that is born of a woman.*

> So have I seen, on some bright summer's day,
> A calf of genius, debonair and gay,
> Dance on the brink, as if inspired by fame,
> Fond of the pretty fellow in the stream.
> *Love of Fame, the Universal Passion.*[4]

I would fain hope that His Honor's motto is not a true portrait of the general temper and conduct of the Americans; I would rather think *"the low murmurs of submissive fear, and mingled rage"* delineate only a few disappointed traders. It were to be wished that some friend of the colonies would endeavor to remove any unfavorable impressions this and other pamphlets of the like kind may have occasioned at home, lest those in power form the general character of the colonies from such notices as these convey, and from thence be inclined to increase their dependence rather than to emancipate them from the present supposed impositions. Depend upon it, my friend, a people like the English, arrived to the highest pitch of glory and power, the envy and admiration of surrounding slaves, who hold the balance of Europe in their hands and rival in arts and arms every period of ancient or modern story, a nation who, for the defense and safety of America only, staked their all in the late war — this people, I say, justly conscious of their dignity, will not patiently be dictated to by those whom they have ever considered as dependent upon them. Happy will it be for the colonies, yea happy for the honorable author, [6] if his pamphlet should meet with nothing more than contempt and neglect; for should it catch the attention of men in power, measures may be taken to stifle in the birth *"the low murmurs of submissive fear,"* and crush in embryo *"the mingled rage,"* which now so prettily adorns the head of His Honor's pamphlet.

However disguised, polished, or softened the expression of this pamphlet may seem, yet everyone must see that its professed design is sufficiently prominent throughout, namely, to prove *that the colonies have rights independent of, and not controllable by the authority of Parliament.* It is upon this dangerous and indiscreet position I shall communicate to you my real sentiments.

To suppose a design of enslaving the colonies by Parliament is too presumptuous; to propagate it in print is perhaps dangerous. Perplexed between a desire of speaking all he thinks and the fear of saying too much, the honorable author is obliged to entrench himself in obscurity and inconsistency in several parts of his performance: I shall bring one instance.

In page eleven he says, "It is the indispensable duty of every good and loyal subject cheerfully to obey, and patiently submit to, all the laws, orders, etc., that may be passed by Parliament."

I do not much admire either the spirit or composition of this sentence. Is it the duty *only* of good and loyal subjects to obey? Are the wicked and disloyal subjects absolved from this obligation? [5] Else why is this passage so marvelously penned? Philoleutherus Lipsiensis[6] would directly pronounce this a figure in rhetoric called nonsense. Believe me, my friend, I did not quote this passage to show my skill [7] in criticism, but to point out a contradiction between it and another passage in page twenty, which runs thus: "It must be absurd to suppose that the common people of Great Britain have a sovereign and absolute authority over their fellow subjects of America, *or even any sort of power whatsoever over them;* but it will be still more absurd to suppose they can give a power to their representatives which they have not themselves," etc. Here it is observable that the first cited passage expresses a full submission to the authority of Parliament; the last is as explicit a denial of that authority. The sum of His Honor's argument is this: the people of Great Britain have not any sort of power over the Americans; the House of Commons have no greater authority than the people of Great Britain who are their constituents; *ergo,* the House of Commons *have not any sort of power over the Americans.* This is indeed a curious invented syllogism, the sole merit of which is due to the first magistrate of an English colony.[7]

I have endeavored to investigate the true natural relation, if I may so speak, between colonies and their mother state, abstracted from compact or positive institution, but here I can find nothing satisfactory. Till this relation is clearly defined upon a rational and natural principle, our reasoning upon the measure of the colonies' obedience will be desultory and inconclusive. Every connection in life has its reciprocal duties; we know the relation between a parent and child, husband and wife, master and servant, and from thence are able to deduce their respective obligations. But we have no notices of any such precise natural relation between a mother state and its colonies, and therefore cannot reason with so much [8] certainty upon the power of the one or the duty of the others.[8] The ancients have transmitted to us nothing that is applicable to the state of modern colonies because the relation between these is formed by political compact, and the condition of each, variant in their original and from each other. The honorable author has not freed this subject from any of its embarrassments: vague and diffuse talk of rights and privileges, and ringing the changes upon the words liberty and slavery only serve to convince us that words may affect without raising images or affording any repose to a mind philosophically inquisitive. For my own part, I will shun the walk of metaphysics in my inquiry, and be content to consider the colonies' rights upon the footing of their charters, which are the only plain avenues that lead to the truth of this matter.[9]

The several New England charters ascertain, define, and limit the respective rights and privileges of each colony, and I cannot conceive how it has come to pass that the colonies now claim any other or greater rights than are therein expressly granted to them. I fancy when we speak or think of the rights of freeborn Englishmen, we confound those rights which are personal with those which are political: there is a distinction between these which ought always to be kept in view.[10]

Our personal rights, comprehending those of life, liberty, and estate, are secured to us by the common law, which is every subject's birthright, whether born in Great Britain, on the ocean, or in the colonies; and it is in this sense we are said to enjoy all the rights and privileges of Englishmen. The political rights of the colonies or the powers of government communicated [9] to them are more limited, and their nature, quality, and extent depend altogether upon the patent or charter which first created and instituted them. As individuals, the colonists participate of every blessing the English constitution can give them: as corporations created by the crown, they are confined within the primitive views of their institution. Whether, therefore, their indulgence is scanty or liberal can be no cause of complaint; for when they accepted of their charters they tacitly submitted to the terms and conditions of them.

The colonies have no rights independent of their charters; they can claim no greater than those give them; by those the Parliamentary jurisdiction over them is not taken away, neither could any grant of the King abridge that jurisdiction, because it is founded upon common law, as I shall presently show, and was prior to any charter or grant to the colonies: every Englishman, therefore, is subject to this jurisdiction, and it follows him wherever he goes.[11] It is of the essence of government that there should be a supreme head, and it would be a solecism in politics to talk of members independent of it.

With regard to the jurisdiction of Parliament, I shall endeavor to show that it is attached to every English subject wherever he be, and I am led to do this from a clause in page nine of His Honor's pamphlet, where he says "That the colonies do not hold their rights as a privilege granted them, nor enjoy them as a grace and favor bestowed, but possess them as an inherent, indefeasible right." This postulatum cannot be true with regard to political rights, for I have already shown that these are derived from your charters, and are held by force of [10] the King's grant; therefore these inherent, indefeasible rights, as His Honor calls them, must be personal ones, according to the distinction already made. Permit me to say that inherent and indefeasible as these rights may be, the jurisdiction of Parliament over every English subject is equally as inherent and indefeasible: that both have grown out of the same stock, and that if we avail ourselves of the one we must submit to and acknowledge the other.

It might here be properly enough asked, Are these personal rights self-existent? Have they no original source? I answer, They are derived from the constitution of England, which is the common law; and from the same fountain is also derived the jurisdiction of Parliament over us.

But to bring this argument down to the most vulgar apprehension: The common law has established it as a rule or maxim that the plantations are bound by British acts of Parliament if particularly named; and surely no Englishman in his senses will deny the force of a common law maxim. One cannot but smile at the inconsistency of these inherent, indefeasible men: if one of them has a suit at law, in any part of New England, upon a question of land, property, or merchandise, he appeals to the common law to support his claim or defeat his adversary, and yet is so profoundly stupid as to say that an act of Parliament does not bind him when perhaps the same page in a law book which points him out a remedy for a libel or a slap in the face would inform him that it does. In a word, the force of an act of Parliament over the colonies is predicated upon the common law, the origin and basis of all those inherent rights and privileges which constitute the boast and felicity of a Briton.[12]

[11] Can we claim the common law as an inheritance, and at the same time be at liberty to adopt one part of it and reject the other? Indeed we cannot. The common law, pure and indivisible in its nature and essence, cleaves to us during our lives and follows us from Nova Zembla to Cape Horn; and therefore, as the jurisdiction of Parliament arises out of and is supported by it, we may as well renounce our allegiance or change our nature as to be exempt from the jurisdiction of Parliament. Hence it is plain to me that in denying this jurisdiction we at the same time take leave of the common law, and thereby, with equal temerity and folly, strip ourselves of every blessing we enjoy as Englishmen: a flagrant proof, this, that shallow drafts in politics and legislation confound and distract us, and that an extravagant zeal often defeats its own purposes.

I am aware that the foregoing reasoning will be opposed by the maxim "That no Englishman can be taxed but by his own consent or by representatives."

It is this dry maxim, taken in a literal sense and ill understood, that, like the song of "Lillibullero," has made all the mischief in the colonies; and upon this the partisans of the colonies' rights chiefly rest their cause.[13] I don't despair, however, of convincing you that this maxim affords but little support to their argument when rightly examined and explained.

It is the opinion of the House of Commons, and may be considered as a law of Parliament, that they are the representatives of every British subject, wheresoever he be. In this view of the matter, then, the aforegoing maxim is fully vindicated in practice, and the whole benefit of it, in substance and effect, extended and applied to the *colonies*. Indeed the maxim [12] must be considered in this latitude, for in a literal sense or construction it ever was, and ever will be, impracticable. Let me ask, Is the Isle of Man, Jersey, or Guernsey represented? What is the value or amount of each man's representation in the kingdom of Scotland, which contains near two millions of people, and yet not more than three thousand have votes in the election of members of Parliament? But to show still further that in fact and reality this right of representation is not of that consequence it is generally thought to be, let us take into the argument the moneyed interest of Britain, which, though immensely great, has no share in this representation. A worthless freeholder of forty shillings per annum can vote for a member of Parliament, whereas a merchant, though worth one hundred thousand pounds sterling, if it consist only in personal effects, has no vote at all. But yet let no one suppose that the interest of the latter is not equally the object of Parliamentary attention with the former. Let me add one example more. Copy-holders in England of one thousand pounds sterling per annum, whose estates in land are nominally but not intrinsically inferior to a freehold cannot, by law, vote for members of Parliament; yet we never hear that these people *"murmur with submissive fear, and mingled rage."* They don't set up their private humor against the constitution of their country, but submit with cheerfulness to those forms of government which providence, in its goodness, has placed them under.[14]

Suppose that this Utopian privilege of representation should take place. I question if it would answer any other purpose but to bring an expense upon the colonies, unless you can suppose that a few American [13] members could bias the deliberations of the whole British legislature. In short, this right of representation is but a phantom, and if possessed in its full extent would be of no real advantage to the colonies; they would, like Ixion, embrace a cloud in the shape of Juno.[15]

In addition to this head, I could further urge the danger of innovations. Every change in a constitution in some degree weakens its original frame, and hence it is that legislators and statesmen are cautious in admitting them. The goodly building of the British constitution will be best secured and perpetuated by adhering to its original principles. Parliaments are not of yesterday; they are as ancient as our Saxon ancestors. Attendance in Parliament was originally a duty arising from a tenure of lands, and grew out of the feudal system, so that the privilege of sitting in it is territorial and confined to Britain only. Why should the beauty and symmetry of this body be destroyed and its purity defiled by the unnatural mixture of representatives from every part of the British dominions? *Parthians, Medes, Elamites, and the dwellers of Mesopotamia, etc.,* would not, in such a case, speak the same language. What a heterogeneous council would this form? What a monster in government would it be? In truth, my friend, the matter lies here: the freedom and happiness of every British subject depends not upon his share in elections but upon the sense and virtue of the British Parliament, and these depend reciprocally upon the sense and virtue of the whole nation. When virtue and honor are no more, the lovely frame of our constitution will be dissolved. Britain may one day be what Athens and Rome now are; but may Heaven long protract the hour! [16]

[14] The jurisdiction of Parliament being established, it will follow that this jurisdiction cannot be apportioned; it is transcendent and entire, and may levy internal taxes as well as regulate trade. There is no essential

difference in the rights: a stamp duty is confessedly the most reasonable and equitable that can be devised, yet very far am I from desiring to see it established among us; but I fear the shaft is sped and it is now too late to prevent the blow.[17]

The examples cited by His Honor with regard to ancient colonies may show his reading and erudition, but are of no authority in the present question. I am not enough skilled in the Grecian history to correct the proofs drawn from thence, though they amount to very little. If the Grecian colonies, as His Honor says, "took such forms of government as themselves chose," there is no kind of similitude between them and the English colonies, and therefore to name them is nothing to the purpose. The English colonies take their forms of government from the crown; hold their privileges upon condition that they do not abuse them; and hold their lands by the tenure of common socage, which involves in it fealty and obedience to the King. Hence it is plain His Honor's argument is not strengthened by the example of the Grecian colonies; for what likeness is there between independent colonies, as those must be which "took such forms of government as themselves chose," and colonies like ours, which are in a manner feudatory, and holden of a superior?

With regard to the Roman colonies, I must beg leave to say that the honorable author, either ignorantly or willfully, mistakes the facts. A little more inquiry or a little more candor would have [15] convinced him that the Roman *coloniae* did not enjoy all the rights of Roman citizens; on the contrary, they only used the Roman laws and religion and served in the legions, but had not the right of suffrage or of bearing honors. In these respects our English colonies exactly resemble them; we enjoy the English laws and religion but have not the right of suffrage or of bearing honors in Great Britain, and indeed our situation renders it impossible.[18]

If the practice of the ancients was of any authority in this case, I could name examples to justify the enslaving of colonies. The Carthaginians were a free people, yet they, to render the Sardinians and Corsicans more dependent, forbade their planting, sowing, or doing anything of the like kind under pain of death, so that they supplied them with necessaries from Africa: this was indeed very hard. But there is something extremely weak and inconclusive in recurring to the Grecian and Roman history for examples to illustrate any particular favorite opinion: if a deference to the ancients should direct the practice of the moderns, we might sell our children to pay our debts and justify it by the practice of the Athenians. We might lend our wives to our friends and justify it from the example of Cato, among the Romans. In a word, my dear sir, the belly of a sow, pickled, was a high dish in ancient Rome; and I imagine as you advance in the refinements of luxury this will become a capital part of a Rhode Island feast, so fond you seem of ancient customs and laws.[19]

Instead of wandering in the labyrinth of ancient colonies, I would advise His Honor to read the debates in Parliament in the year one thousand seven hundred and thirty-three, when Mr. Partridge, your agent, [16] petitioned the Commons against the then sugar bill; he will there find more satisfaction upon the subject of colonies than in Thucydides' *History of the Peloponnesian War*. It was declared in the course of that debate that the colonists were a part of the people of Great Britain, and, as such, fully represented in that House. The petition then presented by Mr. Partridge was of a very different temper from those now sent home by the colonies; it was extremely modest, and only intimated that the sugar bill if passed into a law might be prejudicial to their charter. At the bare mention of this Sir William Yonge took fire and said, *"It looked like aiming at an independency, and disclaiming the jurisdiction of that House, as if,"* says he, *"this House had not a power to tax the colonies."* Mr. Winnington, with equal warmth, added, *"I hope they have no charter which debars this House from taxing them as well as any other subject of the nation."* Here you have the opinion of two of the most eminent members of that time; they spoke the sentiments of the whole House, and these sentiments still continue the same.[20] And from hence you may perceive how little prospect there is of the colonies' gaining any point upon the footing of these new supposititious rights; broaching such opinions will excite the jealousy of the Parliament, and you will be looked upon with an evil eye. The promoters of such doctrines are no friends to the colonies, whatever may be their pretensions. Can His Honor be so vain as to imagine that ten thousand such pamphlets as his will influence the Parliament, or that they will be persuaded, by the force of his elocution, to give up their supremacy and right of taxing the colonies? What purpose then can be served by these pamphlets but to embitter the minds of a simple, credulous, and hitherto loyal people, [17] and to alienate their affections from Great Britain, their best friend, their protector, and alma mater? A different behavior would be much more prudent and politic. If we have anything to ask, we should remember that diffidence and modesty will always obtain more from generous minds than frowardness and impertinence.

The act of the thirteenth of his late Majesty, entitled An Act for Naturalizing of Foreign Protestants, had better have been omitted by His Honor; for if that act is to be the measure of the colonists' rights they will be more circumscribed than he would willingly choose. In that act there is a proviso that no person who shall become a natural-born subject by virtue of that act should be of the Privy Council, or a member of either house of Parliament, or capable of enjoying in Great Britain or Ireland any place of trust, civil or military, etc. This statute confirms the distinction I have set up between personal and political rights. After naturalization, foreign Protestants are here admitted subjects to all intents and purposes, that is, to the full enjoyment of those rights which are connected with the person, liberty, or estate of Englishmen; but by the proviso they are excluded from bearing offices or honors.[21]

Enlarging the power of the court of admiralty is much complained of by the honorable author. I shall open my mind to you freely on this head.

It is notorious that smuggling, which an eminent writer calls a crime against the law of nature, had well nigh become established in some of the colonies.[22] Acts of Parliament had been uniformly dispensed with by those whose duty it was to execute them; corruption, raised upon the ruins of duty and virtue, had almost grown into a system; courts of admiralty, confined [18] within small territorial jurisdictions, became subject to mercantile influence, and the King's revenue shamefully sacrificed to the venality and perfidiousness of courts and officers. If, my friend, customs are due to the crown; if illicit commerce is to be put an end to as ruinous to the welfare of the nation; if by reason of the interested views of traders and the connivance of courts and customhouse officers, these ends could not be compassed or obtained in the common and ordinary way, tell me, what could the government do but to apply a remedy desperate as the disease? There is, I own, a severity in the method of prosecution in the new established court of admiralty under Doctor *SPRY* here;[23] but it is a severity we have brought upon ourselves. When every mild expedient to stop the atrocious and infamous practice of smuggling has been tried in vain, the government is justifiable in making laws against it, even like those of Draco, which were written in blood. The new instituted court of admiralty and the power given to the seizor are doubtless intended to make us more circumspect in our trade, and to confine the merchant, from motives of fear and dread, within the limits of a fair commerce. "The English constrain the merchant, but it is in favor of commerce," says the admired Secondat.[24] This is the spirit of the new regulations both with regard to the employing of cutters and the enlarged power of the admiralty; and both measures are justifiable upon the same principles as is the late act for preventing murder, which executes and dissects the murderer at Surgeons Hall in twenty-four hours after conviction.

But notwithstanding the severity of this act, let me add that no harm can accrue to the honest and fair [19] trader so long as the crown fills the admiralty department with an upright judge; such a one is Doctor *SPRY*, an able civilian, and whose appointments place him above any kind of influence. Yet the honorable author of the pamphlet before me has told us to this effect, that it is very well known this judge *can be prevailed on, very easily* to certify upon the acquittal of a seizure that there was a probable cause for making it. So shamefully intemperate is His Honor's zeal and opposition to every measure adopted by the government at home that he spares not even private characters, however worthy and respectable. I fear he knows not the high value of a good name, and how dear it is to men of sentiment and honor.

> He who filches from me my good name,
> Robs me of that which not enriches him,
> But makes me poor indeed.
> SHAKESPEARE[25]

To suspect the integrity of others is not the effusion of a virtuous mind. Those who have been long used to traffic with judges and juries are, from the depravity of their own hearts, easily led to believe others even as themselves.

This libel upon Doctor *SPRY*, contained in a pamphlet *published by authority* may spread over the British dominions, and however false and scandalous it be, yet may leave a shade upon his character which can never be effaced. With what grace, let me ask you, do such reflections as these come from the governor of a colony where, all the world agree, the law has scarcely yet dawned, and where all your legal rights are decided by the strength of that faction which happens to be uppermost?

[20] I am not enough skilled in trade to know whether the act so much complained of will do most good or most harm; and I wish others were as diffident of their knowledge in this particular. To comprehend the general trade of the British nation much exceeds the capacity of any one man in America, how great soever he be. Trade is a vast, complicated system, and requires such a depth of genius and extent of knowledge to understand it that little minds, attached to their own sordid interest and long used to the greatest licentiousness in trade are, and must be,

very incompetent judges of it. Sir Andrew Freeport is no inhabitant of Rhode Island colony. For my own part, I am still willing to leave the management of trade with that people who, according to the same admired author just quoted, "know better than any other people upon earth how to value at the same time these three great advantages, religion, commerce, and liberty." [26]

Here I would just observe that, from the intelligence I have gained, the beloved article of molasses is now plentier and cheaper in all the New England colonies than when it was avowedly smuggled; and so far is the linen manufacture of Ireland from being ruined, as His Honor intimates, that never was a greater demand for flaxseed than during the last fall, notwithstanding the clause in the act relating to lumber. How senseless is it to imagine that the prohibiting a few dunnage staves to be carried to Ireland will ruin the manufactures of that kingdom.

Believe me, my friend, it gives me great pain to see so much ingratitude in the colonies to the mother country, whose arms and money so lately rescued them from a French government. I have been told that some have gone so far as to say that they [21] would, as things are, prefer such a government to an English one. Heaven knows I have but little malice in my heart, yet, for a moment, I ardently wish that these spurious, unworthy sons of Britain could feel the iron rod of a Spanish inquisitor or a French farmer of the revenue; it would indeed be a punishment suited to their ingratitude. Here I cannot but call to mind the adder in one of the fables of Pilpay, which was preparing to sting the generous traveler who had just rescued him from the flames.[27]

You'll easily perceive that what I have said is upon the general design of His Honor's pamphlet; if he had divided his argument with any precision, I would have followed him with somewhat more of method. The dispute between Great Britain and the colonies consists of two parts: first, the jurisdiction of Parliament, and, secondly, the exercise of that jurisdiction. His Honor hath blended these togther, and nowhere marked the division between them. The first I have principally remarked upon. As to the second, it can only turn upon the expediency or utility of those schemes which may, from time to time, be adopted by Parliament relative to the colonies. Under this head, I readily grant, they are at full liberty to remonstrate, petition, write pamphlets and newspapers without number, to prevent any improper or unreasonable imposition. Nay, I would have them do all this with that spirit of freedom which Englishmen always have, and I hope ever will, exert; but let us not use our liberty for a cloak of maliciousness. Indeed I am very sure the loyalty of the colonies has ever been irreproachable; but from the pride of some and the ignorance of others the cry against mother country has spread from colony to colony; [22] and it is to be feared that prejudices and resentments are kindled among them which it will be difficult ever thoroughly to soothe or extinguish. It may become necessary for the supreme legislature of the nation to frame some code, and therein adjust the rights of the colonies with precision and certainty, otherwise Great Britain will always be teased with new claims about liberty and privileges.[28]

I have no ambition in appearing in print, yet if you think what is here thrown together is fit for the public eye you are at liberty to publish it.[29] I the more cheerfully acquiesce in this because it is with real concern I have observed that, notwithstanding the frequent abuse poured forth in pamphlets and newspapers against the mother country, not one filial pen in America hath as yet been drawn, to my knowledge, in her vindication.

I am, very affectionately,

Your most faithful and obedient servant,

* * * * * *

PAMPHLET II

JAMES OTIS, *A VINDICATION OF THE BRITISH COLONIES*

BOSTON, 1765

INTRODUCTION

James Otis' motives for publishing this attack on Martin Howard, Jr., and his *Halifax Letter* (JHL Pamphlet 10) are not difficult to understand. Howard's tract was the first and for almost a decade the only full-fledged justification of official English policy written in America, and as such it stood as a direct challenge to Otis, then the leading spokesman for America by virtue of his *Rights of the British Colonies* (JHL Pamphlet 7). In addition, Stephen Hopkins, the immediate victim of Howard's attack, was a friend of Otis, and in a well-known case at law he had been his client; the two respected each other, and though Otis did not hesitate to correct Hopkins publicly when he thought he was in error, he continued to believe that they were both saying essentially the same thing.[1] Most important of all, Howard, in the course of his *Halifax Letter,* had incidentally attacked Otis himself. The Bostonian was, he had admitted, "a man of knowledge and parts," but he was "unhappily misled by popular ideas, and at the head of the *tribunitian veto.*" In addition to this charge of demagoguery, Howard had insinuated that Otis' *Rights* constituted a refusal to acknowledge the authority of Parliament and was responsible for spreading such an attitude through the colonies, kindling prejudices and resentments difficult, perhaps impossible, to extinguish.[2] To Otis this accusation made it clear beyond doubt that the arguments in his *Rights* had been dangerously misunderstood. His desire to defend Hopkins merged with the necessity of defending himself and of explaining what he had meant in his famous pamphlet of 1764.

Otis was on any occasion a formidable polemicist, being sharp-witted, informed, and utterly uninhibited: there was always a fierceness in his expression even when he was not, as John Adams found him to be later in 1765, unnaturally "fiery and feverous." But in answering Howard he had two additional advantages: knowledge of the recently published first volume of Blackstone's *Commentaries,* which Howard had used clumsily and inaccurately in discussing the nature of rights; and a position on the sources of personal liberty more harmonious with tradition and current opinion in America than Howard's. *A Vindication,* jumbling citations of Locke, Coke, and Blackstone together with *tu quoque* arguments and incriminating innuendoes, was undeniably effective as an attack on the *Halifax Letter;* but as a defense and explanation of Otis' *Rights* it succeeded only at the expense of permanently compromising its author's reputation as a spokesman for the colonies.[3]

Stripped of its redundancies, verbal tangles, and vituperation, *A Vindica-*

tion may be seen to consist of four related arguments. It asserts, first, that the relations between England and the colonies are rooted in nature and natural law as well as in the particular specifications of charters and statute laws. Second, it claims that though Parliament (as opposed to the House of Commons) has supreme power over the colonies and by definition of the constitution represents them, nevertheless it can exercise that power justly and equitably only if it allows the colonies an actual representation. From this it follows that while Parliament can tax the colonies, externally and internally, without exceeding the bounds of its rightful authority, it would be "a matter of wonder and astonishment" if it in fact did so when the colonies were not actually represented. The pamphlet states, finally, that neither Otis nor Hopkins had ever denied that Parliament had absolute authority over the colonies — accusations to the contrary being malicious falsifications of what the two had in fact written in their recent pamphlets.

These major points flow from the same single, central source of ideas that had supplied the arguments of *The Rights of the British Colonies Asserted and Proved.* Otis presumed, here as in the earlier pamphlet, an identification of the real and the ideal in the functioning of the British constitution — an identification of such a nature that excesses would be self-correcting in the system as a whole. The great edifice of government and law was, to be sure, man-made, a time-bound creation of history; but its pillars, Otis quoted from his *Rights,* "are fixed in judgment, righteousness, and truth." Thus he disputes Howard's claim that the relations between the colonies and England are defined only by positive law and charters, arguing that those documentary instruments merely enlarge the basic rights guaranteed Britons "by the laws of God and nature as well as by the common law and by the constitution of their country." Only the rights of *corporate* persons, he insists, accurately paraphrasing Blackstone, "are matters of the mere favor and grace of the donor or founder"; the rights of natural persons should be, and those of "Britons and all British subjects" in fact are, guaranteed by institutions and laws "built on the principles of . . . the laws of God and nature." Power, this constitution must have: if Parliament did not have "a supreme sovereign power . . . the colonies would be independent, which none but rebels, fools, or madmen will contend for." And of its power over the colonies Parliament "remains the supreme judge, from whose final determination there is no appeal." Parliament could, indeed, "abrogate and annihilate all colony or subordinate legislation and administration" if it chose; but that did not mean that Parliament was entitled to act "needlessly and wantonly," for, again — the point could not be repeated too often — its foundations rested squarely on principles of natural law and right.[4]

It was a point of view consistent with the central position taken in the *Rights.* The arguments in both pamphlets arose from the same belief in Parliament's instinct for and power of self-correction within the general working of a benevolent constitution. But the emphasis had shifted; for where in the earlier pamphlet Otis' main effort had been placed on explaining the self-criticism and self-limitation of the constitution, in *A Vindication,* responding to the charge that he had denied the power of Parliament in America, he stressed instead his "very clear admission and acknowledgment of the jurisdiction, power, and authority of Parliament over the colonies." Exaggerated by characteristically extreme language, imputed extravagantly to "all the pamphlets that have been published in America upon the new regulations of the colonies," and documented by an unbalanced selection of quotations from *The Rights of the British Colonies,* this reiterated acknowledgment of Parliament's authority, sprung from ideas that had been liberating in an age when the force of Parliament had been directed against an oppressive crown, could only prove embarrassing to one who claimed to speak for the rights of the individual.[5]

It proved embarrassing even in the course of writing the pamphlet, for it led to a thorough confusion on the important question of representation. Did or did not Parliament's right to tax the colonies depend on the presence of actual representatives from America? If it did, Parliament was scarcely the "supreme sovereign power" Otis claimed it to be; if it did not, it was violating the ancient principle of justice, endorsed by Otis, that an individual's property may be alienated from him only with his own or his delegate's consent. There were only two possible ways of dealing with the problem: either to agree with Howard and the government's apologists that representation was virtual rather than actual, or to say that representation did not really limit Parliament's authority. The former reasoning Otis scorned: if virtual representation, he wrote, made sense, why not reduce the number of electoral units still further? Why not reduce the House of Commons "to a single member . . . This would be a shorter cut to absolute and unlimited monarchy than ever Filmer was fortunate to invent." [6] But in seven pages of detailed and indignant argumentation (pp. 14–20), he did not succeed in making clear the extent to which he believed representation was necessary to legitimize the use of Parliamentary power over the colonies.

More embarrassing than the intellectual confusion created by Otis' stress on Parliament's authority was the public reception the pamphlet met. Howard, as would have been expected, flung himself on it joyously. In his comprehensive response to his critics, *A Defence of the Letter from a Gentleman at Halifax . . .* , published in Newport a month after Otis' *Vindication* appeared, he struck at the "Boston writer" from all directions. He first thanked him for having, characteristically, betrayed a friend in having pointed out the fundamental error of Hopkins' *Rights,* and then reported generally that the "dark and gloomy" experience of reading Otis' "dreary waste of thirty-two pages" had "fitted him for any misfortune or disappointment of life. Pain, he will no longer consider as an evil. Nay, should he be forced to pass the Stygian river and drink its poisonous vapors, it would be more than Elysian compared with the misery of reading through this pamphlet." Yet it had had its rewards, for he had found it to be nothing less than a total surrender by Otis of his central position and a betrayal of his whole party, containing as it did "a most unreserved and solemn recognition of the absolute, unlimited authority of Parliament over the colonies." Otis, he claimed, had been converted; shunning "all ambiguity," he now endorsed total Parliamentary sovereignty with the same "warmth of expression" with which he had once rejected it. Howard suggested that the Bostonian use his new-found faith and wisdom to come to some agreement with Hopkins on the basic issue of Parliamentary authority before they started attacking the Halifax gentleman again.[7]

This rejoinder and the impending passage of the Stamp Act stung Otis into a blind frenzy of self-defense. Desperate to affirm his constancy and his loyalty, he published, a bare two weeks after the appearance of Howard's *Defence,* yet another reply to the Rhode Island royalist, this one a wild jumble of Latin quotations, constitutional arguments, sarcasms, innuendoes, and flat-handed abuse. Entitled *Brief Remarks on the Defence of the Halifax Libel on the British-American-Colonies,* it repeated the arguments of the *Vindication,* but with an intensity that made them nightmarish and that exposed more glaringly than ever their inner ambiguities. For though Otis continued to vilify Howard and his Newport junto — he now called them worshipers of "J[im]m[e]y S[tuar]t" and, in a boiling outburst of abuse, a "little, dirty, drinking, drabbing, contaminated knot of thieves, beggars, and transports . . . collected from the four winds of the earth, and made up of Turks, Jews, and other infidels, with a few renegado Christians and Catholics" — though he scalded these "Jacobites and Jew-jobbers" as sycophants of power, he once again defended a view of the constitution that led to conclusions indistinguishable from theirs. Howard, he pointed out again, had asserted the "infinite nonsense and unparalleled absurdity" that the New England charters *"limit* the respective rights and privileges of each colony" and that the colonies had no rights independent of these charters. The Rhode Islanders had insisted, moreover, that because Parliament was itself an outgrowth and extension of the common law it could not be controlled by the common law. Both were nonsensical and vicious ideas: "the source of Parliamentary authority," Otis repeated from the *Rights,* "is clearly derived from God, the author of all things, principalities, and powers." To say that it flows only from the common law is the same as saying "that Lewis XV . . . was created by the Count d'Estaing, his governor and lieutenant general of his islands and dominions in America." Anyone but the "poor maze-headed, clodpated" Halifax writer would know that Parliament's rootage in right and justice conferred upon that body *"a just, clear, equitable, and constitutional right, power, and authority, to bind the colonies by all acts wherein they are named."* It was the essence of Parliament that it "can do no wrong": subjects of such a sovereignty must presume that "the inmost intentions of the supreme power have ever for their favorite object the good of the whole community." Without such a presumption and the acknowledgment that government itself is "the dernier resort for law and justice" no government could subsist. Yet that did not put an end to "modest and humble inquiries after truth and reason." "The whole science of law and the fair and just practice of it," he wrote in a passage reminiscent of his use of *Bonham's Case* in the writs controversy four years earlier, is "founded in the study, interpretation, and right application and execution of the reason, meaning, and intention of the laws, and consequently of the legislative." [8]

It was essentially the same delicately balanced argument of the *Rights* pamphlet, with the emphasis thrown on the side of obedience. How much the weight had shifted, and how confused and confusing the whole performance must have appeared, is suggested by the fact that in writing the *Brief Remarks* Otis took the occasion to endorse enthusiastically the administration's quasi-official pamphlet, *The Regulations Lately Made,* which had been written by Grenville's secretary, Howard's correspondent, Thomas Whately. Howard and Whately were presumably saying the same thing; but while Otis excoriated Howard, he praised Whately as "very ingenious, learned, polite, and delicate" — a person who treated the colonists "not only . . . like men, but gentlemen, and British subjects," acknowledging them to be "an essential part of the empire of Great Britain, and a beloved part, entitled to every benefit of the best constitution on earth." More than that: his knowledge of "our constitution, laws, political interests, internal police, and state of trade and commerce" was nothing less than perfect; and it was an honor, Otis wrote, to agree with him "that the *colonists are virtually, constitutionally, in law and in equity, to be considered as represented in the honorable House of Commons.*" [9]

By now, with this remarkable concession on the question of representation, the argument was distended almost beyond coherence. It took a closer and more sympathetic reading of Otis' jumbled pronouncements than contemporaries — or later historians — were inclined to give them to see the considerable element of truth in Otis' insistence that the *Vindication* was "positively consistent with itself and also with the doctrine advanced in *The Rights of the* [*British*] *Colonies Asserted.*" Governor Bernard interpreted the *Brief Remarks* as Howard had the *Vindication,* as an apology for past errors; and while John Adams' later statement that Otis "was called a reprobate, an apostate, and a traitor in every street in Boston" is a characteristic exaggeration of the ex-President's romantic old age, his contemporary diary notation that views of the administration were thought to "mingle now with his patriotism" expressed a widely shared suspicion. Otis' seat in the General Court as representative from Boston was so far endangered that he felt obliged to publish an effusive piece in the *Boston Gazette* just before the May 1765 election, dilating on the sacrifices he had made for the public, describing his tenacity in upholding the rights and privileges of his "ever beloved and honored constituents," and explaining that his words had been wilfully misconstrued. Even "the little chit chat of the coffee house and the jest cracked merely for the pleasure of cracking it, hath been . . . worked up to infidelity, treason, and rebellion." [10]

He won the election, however — though barely; but his anxieties were scarcely relieved. Once re-established in the House he attempted another full vindication of his writings, this time in the form of a speech from the floor; and then in July began publication of a series of articles in the *Boston Gazette* which he later published as a pamphlet under the title *Considerations on Behalf of the Colonists in a Letter to a Noble Lord*. Here again he reiterated his belief in the "undoubted power, authority, and jurisdiction" of Parliament over all parts of the realm and the empire, and his conviction "that every Englishman, as 'tis his interest, really wishes and means well to the colonies." But now he stressed the reasonableness, if not the constitutional necessity, of an actual colonial representation into the House of Commons. For though it was true, he said, that "King, Lords, and Commons, conjointly, as the supreme legislative, in *fact* as well as in *law,* represent and act for the realm, and all the dominions, if they please," it was nevertheless also true that in a free constitution actual representation serves as a check on the universal "lust of power and unreasonable domination" of officeholders and provides a mechanism for reliably informing them of the interests and desires of the people. "No good reason . . . can be given in any country why every man of sound mind should not have his vote in the election of a representative . . . To what purpose is it to ring everlasting changes to the colonists on the cases of Manchester, Birmingham, and Sheffield, who return no members? If those now so considerable places are not represented, they ought to be." [11]

This was Otis' final effort, in a series that had begun with his plea in the writs case, to apply to the political realities of the eighteenth century, conceptions of power and law that had promoted the cause of liberty in the age of Edward Coke. He had failed, but his failure was dramatically instructive. It proved beyond question the necessity of confronting the problem of Parliament's power directly. This power existed, entire and absolute, and it would not be constrained by legal niceties. Some effective principle of limitation would have to be found, some line drawn between powers it could in right exercise and those it could not, and some machinery devised to enforce such a limitation. To the task of defining this line in defiance of the commonly accepted principle, endorsed by Otis, that sovereignty was by its nature indivisible, American leaders turned in the years that followed, while Otis gradually retired from the developing conflict.[12]

By the fall of 1765 the crest of his tumultuous career as spokesman for the colonies had passed. Elected a delegate to the Stamp Act Congress in June of that year, he played only a minor role in its deliberations. On his return from New York he composed the last of his formal statements on colonial rights, no less repetitive and ambiguous than the others.[13] Thereafter he confined his efforts to the political manipulation rather than the justification of the opposition to the administration. In this he was less ambiguously successful. For though the apparent contradictions in the arguments of his pamphlets were again aired before the election of 1766 — this time by both administration and anti-administration writers — not only was he re-elected to the House by a large majority and chosen Speaker but he led the thoroughly effective purge of the loyalists from the provincial Council. While others took over the ideological battles, Otis remained prominent as a local politician, until in 1769 a physical injury suffered in a brawl with John Robinson, one of the members of the newly created American Board of Customs Commissioners, destroyed the precarious balance of his mind. He lived on until 1783, committed as insane for long periods of time but fitfully lucid. It was said that in his final years he retained wit and charm, and was impressive still in his erudition.[14]

A/VINDICATION/of the/*British Colonies,*/against/The Aspersions of/the/ *Halifax* Gentleman,/in/His Letter to a *Rhode-Island* Friend./

Sed fugite, ô miseri, fugite, atque ab litore funem/Rumpite!/Clamorem immensum tollit, quo pontus et omnes/Intremuere undæ penitúsque exterrita tellus/ Italiæ curvísque immugiit Ætna Cavernis./—— fluit æs rivis, auríque metallum/ Vulnificúsque chalybs vastâ fornace liquescit/—— Alii ventosis follibus auras/Accipiunt reddúntque, alii stridentia tingunt/Æra lacu: gemit impositis incudibus antrum./Illi inter sese multâ vi brachia tollunt/In numerum versántque tenaci forcipe massam. virgil./

BOSTON:/Printed and Sold by Edes and Gill, in Queen-Street, 1765./

A Vindication of the *British Colonies*, against the Aspersions of the *Halifax* Gentleman, in His Letter to a *Rhode Island* Friend

IT HAD been long expected that some American pen would be drawn in support of those measures which to all thinking men must appear to be very extraordinary. Those who are above party can peruse the speculations of a Whig or a Tory, a Quaker or a Jacobite, with the same composure of mind. Those who confine themselves within the bounds of moderation and decency are so far respectable. All who grow outrageous are disgustful. The "head of a *tribunitian veto*" with a mob at his heels and a grand *Asiatic* monarch with a shoal of sycophants clinging about him, like the little wretches in the well-known print of Hobbe's Leviathan, may be objects of equal diversion, derision, and contempt.[1] Mankind ever were, are, and will be, divisible into the great and small vulgar. Both will have their respective heads. The laws of nature are uniform and invariable. The same causes will produce the same effects from generation to generation. He that would be a great captain must for a season exult in the honor of being a little one.

> Bred on the mountains had *proud* Julius been,
> He'd *shone* a *sturdy* wrestler on the green.[2]

The Halifax gentleman having discovered that Governor *H—pk—ns* is "totally unacquainted with style and diction," and yet "eagerly fond to pass upon the world for a man of letters," great perfection might be reasonably expected in the composition of the friendly epistle. Instead of this are found inaccuracies in abundance, declamation and false logic without end; *verse* is retailed in the shape of *prose*, solecisms are attempted to be passed off for good grammar, [4] and the most indelicate fustian for the fine taste. The whole performance is truly *Filmerian*. The

554

picture is very well charged with shade and thick darkness, intermixed
with here and there a ray of light, now and then a flash, and once in a
while is heard a little rumbling thunder from a few distant broken clouds.

> Some future bard may sing the present times,
> And HE be made the hero of the song.

These two lines are crowded together in one short sentence in a prosaic
form (p. 4).

The gentleman (p. 5) has given us a portrait of the English nation.
It contains but a dozen lines, and expresses or plainly implies the following wonderful group of ideas, viz., "A high pitch of glory and power,
envy and admiration of surrounding slaves, holding fast the balance of
Europe, a rival in arts and arms of every period, ancient and modern,
impatience, jealousy, pride and folly, prodigality, particularly in laying
wagers to the value of kingdoms, and a quick sensibility and consciousness of dignity, which renders plain simple truth intolerable." As the
English nation expired about sixty years since in the union of the two
kingdoms, 'tis needless to inquire whether this be a just character of that
once brave and generous, free and loyal people; but if this should be intended for a filial compliment to Great Britain, 'tis a very indifferent one.
In the late war America joined in the stakes: the bet was not for the
safety of the colonies alone; it was for the salvation of Great Britain as
well as the plantations, i.e., for the whole community. Cornwall raises
and pays one company of dragoons, Devonshire another. Is Cornwall
more obliged to Devonshire than Devonshire is to Cornwall? They are
both obliged by the strongest ties of duty and loyalty to the gracious
prince who protects and defends both; to each other they owe but love
and good will.

I cannot think Mr. *H—k—s* or any other of the writers who have the
misfortune to fall under the sore displeasure of the Halifax gentleman
ever really intended to encourage so groundless a claim as an independent,
uncontrollable provincial legislative. Most of them 'tis well known expressly disavow such a claim. It is certain that the ⟦5⟧ Parliament of
Great Britain hath a just, clear, equitable, and constitutional right, power,
and authority to bind the colonies by all acts wherein they are named.
Every lawyer, nay, every tyro, knows this. No less certain is it that the
Parliament of Great Britain has a just and equitable right, power, and
authority to *impose taxes on the colonies, internal and external, on lands
as well as on trade*.[3] This is involved in the idea of a supreme legislative

or sovereign power of a state. It will, however, by no means from thence follow that 'tis always expedient and in all circumstances equitable for the supreme and sovereign legislative to tax the colonies, much less that 'tis reasonable this right should be practiced upon without allowing the colonies an actual representation. An equal representation of the whole state is, at least in theory, of the essence of a perfect parliament or supreme legislative.

There is not the least color of a contradiction between the passages from the *Rights of the Colonies* cited pages 6 and 7. It must indeed be confessed and lamented that the last citation involves a sophism unworthy the pen from whence it fell.[4] But the critic with all his sagacity has not pointed where the fallacy lies. He has reduced His Honor's argument to the form of a syllogism, which is conclusive. "The people of Great Britain have not any sort of power over the Americans; the House of Commons have no greater authority than the people of Great Britain who are their constituents; *ergo,* the House of Commons have not any sort of power over the Americans." This I take to be literally true. Yet by the following reduction the fallacy of His Honor's argument will appear: "The common people of Great Britain have no sovereign absolute authority over their fellow subjects in America"; the House of Commons alone have no greater authority than the common people of Great Britain; *ergo,* the British Parliament, the King's Majesty, Lords, and Commons, have no sovereign absolute authority over the subjects in the colonies. Who does not see the fallacy of this conclusion? The inquiry was not of the sole and separate power and authority of the House of Commons, but of the authority of that august and transcendent body the Parliament, [6] which is composed of the three branches of the grand legislature of the nation considered as united. But all this shows that the last citation at most is but an implicit, and is far from an "express denial of the authority of Parliament," and should by that candor that is inseparable from a liberal mind have been imputed to mere inadvertency.

We come now to the *rationale* of the epistle. "I have endeavored," says the gentleman, "to investigate the *true, natural relation,* if I *may so speak,* between the colonies and their mother state, *abstracted* from *compact* or *positive institution."* What a parade is here? What "a solemnity" does "he give to his performance"? "If I may so speak." Who would not think the world was about to be favored with some extraordinary discovery too mighty for the powers and precision of language?

Let us attend the course of the bubble. "But here," adds he, "I can find nothing satisfactory. Yet till this *relation* is clearly defined upon *rational* and *natural principles* our *reasoning* upon the *measures* of the colonies' obedience will be *desultory* and inconclusive. Every connection or relation in life has its reciprocal duties; we know the relation between a parent and a child, husband and wife, master and servant, and from thence are able to deduce their respective obligations. But we have no notices of any *such* precise natural relation between a *mother state* and its colonies, and therefore cannot reason with so much certainty upon the *power* of the one or the *duties* of the other." If, as the gentleman tells us, he could not find anything satisfactory, he could only guess what reasoning would follow; and I leave it to his readers to determine whether he has not proved that he guessed very rightly. He has placed the relation of master and servant among what he calls natural relations. In a state of nature, where all are equal, I believe the gentleman would be as much puzzled to find his master or servant as others now may be to find his equal. 'Tis a little strange he should attempt to reason on a subject of which he confesses he could find no "satisfactory notices." But he seems determined to flounder on through thick and thin, be his reasonings "desultory" or conclusive.

[7] "The ancients," says he, "have *transmitted* (for handed down; 'tis a wonder it had not been *transported*) to us nothing that is applicable to the state of the modern colonies, because the *relation* between these ('and their mother state' should have been added) is formed by *political compact*." *Brave!* "And the *condition* of each variant in their original and from each other." Better and better still! If *condition* means the present state, and I think it can mean nothing else, what a delectable piece of jargon does the close of this period make. It amounts to this: "The present state of each modern colony is variant in its original, and from each other." Be this as it may, if the *relation* of modern colonies to their mother states is founded on *political compact,* how came the gentleman to beat his brains to find out "their *natural relation abstracted from compact or positive institution*"? To what purpose he has done this he tells us when he confesses he can find nothing *"satisfactory"* about it. Are not *natural* and merely *political or civil relations* different things? Is it not a little jargonical and inconsistent in one breath to talk of "investigating the *true, natural, clearly defined* relation of the colonies to their mother state, abstracted from compact or positive institution," and in the next to affirm that so far as relates to modern colonies this relation depends or "is founded on political compact"? Was there a natural relation

between ancient states and their colonies and none between the modern states and their colonies? Is not a "political compact" the same thing with a "positive institution"? Is this "freeing a subject from embarrassment"? Well might the gentleman "shun the walk of metaphysics." I wish he had not so much avoided that of logic. He everywhere seems to consider *power* and *duty* as correlates. Surely he should be the last man to charge his adversary with "vague and diffuse talk of" those leveling notions, "rights and privileges." He bewilders himself for half a poor creeping page more, abruptly sings a *requiem* to his sweet soul, composes the surges of his "philosophically inquisitive mind" fatigued with its late flight after natural and political relations, and very gravely contents himself with considering the "colonies' [8] rights upon the footing of their charters." This foothold, by a new and bold figure in rhetoric, he calls "the only plain avenues that lead to the truth of this matter."

> . . . *facilis descensus Averni.*[5]

The gentleman is at a loss (p. 8) to "conceive how it comes to pass that the colonies now claim *any other or greater* rights than are expressly granted to them" by charter. Is the gentleman a British-born subject and a lawyer, and ignorant that charters from the crown have usually been given for enlarging the liberties and privileges of the grantees, not for limiting them, much less for curtailing those essential rights which all His Majesty's subjects are entitled to by the laws of God and nature as well as by the common law and by the constitution of their country?

The distinction (p. 8) between personal and political rights is a new invention, and, as applied, has perplexed the author of it. He everywhere confounds the terms rights, liberties, and privileges, which in legal as well as vulgar acceptation denote very different ideas. This is a common mistake with those who cannot see any difference between power and right, between a blind, slavish submission and a loyal, generous, and rational obedience to the supreme authority of a state.

The rights of men are *natural* or *civil*. Both these are divisible into *absolute* and *relative*. The natural absolute personal rights of individuals are so far from being opposed to political or civil rights that they are the very basis of all municipal laws of any great value. "The absolute rights of individuals regarded by the municipal laws compose what is called *political* or *civil liberty*." "The absolute liberties of Englishmen, as frequently declared in Parliament, are principally three: the right of *personal* security, personal *liberty,* and private property." "Besides these three *primary rights,* there are others which are *secondary* and *subordi-*

nate (to preserve the former from unlawful attacks): (1) The constitution or power of Parliament; (2) The limitation of the King's prerogative (and to vindicate them when actually violated); (3) The regular administration of justice; (4) The right of petitioning for redress of grievances; (5) The right of having and using arms for self-defense." [9] See Mr. Blackstone's accurate and elegant analysis of the laws of England.[6] The gentleman seems to have taken this and some other of his distinctions from that excellent treatise very ill understood. The analysis had given this general view of the *objects* of the laws of England: I. Rights of persons; II. Rights of things; III. Private wrongs; IV. Public wrongs. Rights of persons are divided into these: (1) of natural persons; (2) of bodies politic or corporate, i.e., artificial persons or subordinate societies. The rights of these are by the Letter Writer strangely confounded with the political and civil rights of natural persons. And because corporate rights so far as they depend upon charter are matters of the mere favor and grace of the donor or founder, he thence infers (p. 9) that "the colonies have no rights independent of their charters," and that "they can claim no greater than those give them." This is a contradiction to what he admitted in the preceding page, viz., that "by the common law every colonist hath a right to his life, liberty, and property." And he was so vulgar as to call these the "subject's birthright." But what is this birthright worth if it depends merely upon a colony charter that, as he says rightly enough, may be taken away by the Parliament? I wish the gentleman would answer these questions. Would he think an estate worth much that might be taken from him at the pleasure of another? Are charters from the crown usually given for enlarging the liberties and privileges of the grantees in consideration of some special merit and services done the state, or would he have his readers consider them like the ordinances of a French monarch, for limiting and curtailing those rights which all Britons and all British subjects are entitled to by the laws of God and nature, as well as by the common law and the constitution of their country so admirably built on the principles of the former? By which of these laws in contradistinction to the other are the rights of life, liberty, and estate, personal?

The gentleman's positions and principles that "the several New England charters ascertain, define, and limit the respective *rights* and privileges of each colony," and that "the colonies have no rights independent of their charter," [10] and that "they can claim no greater than those give them," if true, would afford a curious train of consequences. Life, liberty, and property are by the law of nature as well as by the common law secured to the happy inhabitants of South Britain, and constitute their *primary* civil or political rights. But in the colonies these and all other rights, according to our author, depend upon charter. Therefore those of the colonies who have no charter have no right to life, liberty, or property. And in those colonies who have charters, these invaluable blessings depend on the mere good will, grace, and pleasure of the supreme power, and all their charters and of course all their rights, even to life, liberty, and property, may be taken away at pleasure. Thus every charter in England may be taken away, for they are but voluntary and gracious grants of the crown of certain limited, local, political privileges superadded to those of the common law. But would it be expedient to strike such a blow without the most urgent necessity? "In all states there is (and must be) an absolute supreme power, to which the right of *legislation* belongs: and which by the singular constitution of these kingdoms is vested in the King, Lords, and Commons." * [7] Now Magna Carta is but a law of their making, and they may alter it at pleasure; but does it thence follow that it would be expedient to repeal every statute from William the Conqueror to this time? But by the gentleman's principles this may be done wantonly and without any reason at all. Further, by his logic the Parliament may make the monarchy absolute or reduce it to a republic, both which would be contrary to the trust reposed in them by the constitution, which is to preserve, not destroy it; and to this all are sworn, from the King's Majesty in his coronation oath to the meanest subject in the oath of allegiance. Into such absurd and treasonable doctrines must the gentleman run in order to be consistent. Nay, all the vagaries of Filmer, Mainwaring, and Sibthorpe, and of the whole tribe of King Adam's subjects will follow.[8] As 1. That Adam was the first monarch of this earth. No prince has a title to his crown but he who can prove himself to be the eldest heir male of the [11] body of Adam. That all other princes are usurpers and tyrants. That according to Filmer, God hath given to every father over his children, and much more to every prince over his subjects, a power "absolute, arbitrary and unlimited, and unlimitable over the lives, liberties, and estates of such children and subjects; so that he may take or alienate their estates, sell, castrate, or use their persons as he pleases, they being all his slaves, and the father or prince, lord proprietor of everything, and his unbounded will their law." This is the substance of one of Mr. Locke's inferences from these words of Filmer, "God hath given to the father a right or liberty to alien his

* Blackstone.

power over his children to any other; whence we find the sale and gift of children to have been much in use in the beginning of the world when men had their servants for a possession and inheritance as well as other goods (and chattels), whereupon we find the power of *castrating* and making eunuchs (for singing songs like "Lillibullero," etc.) much in use in old times." *Obs.* 155. "Law is nothing else but the will of him that hath the power of the *supreme* father." † [9] Horrid blasphemy! The Lord omnipotent reigneth, but to whom hath he committed his supreme power and authority? The pope claims to be but lord lieutenant of Heaven, and before Sir Robert none but the devil ever had vanity or folly enough to contend for the whole power of the supreme father. According to Filmer and his followers, among which the Halifax gentleman is a close imitator, "they that shed innocent blood, even the blood of their sons and their daughters whom they sacrificed unto the idols of Canaan," [10] did no more than they had a right to do. Upon such principles Pharoah was a pious, virtuous prince. And the drowning the infants in the Nile was as justifiable a piece of preventive policy as seizing the ships of the French without a declaration of war. The Philistine rulers too acted very commendably in depriving the Hebrews of the use of iron, it being very certain that any [of] the most polite people without the free use of this invaluable metal would in one century return to the savage state of the Indians. "If the example of what hath been done," says [12] Mr. Locke, "be the rule of what ought to be, history would have furnished our author with instances of this absolute fatherly power in its height and perfection, and he might have showed us in Peru people that begot children on purpose to fatten and eat them." Mr. Locke has recited a story of this kind, so horrid that I would for the honor of the human species think it incredible and but the mere flight of imagination in *Garcilaso de Vega;* like Swift's proposal to the people of Ireland, to fatten their children for sale in Leadenhall market, as almost the only branch of commerce that would give no offense to the good people of England. See the story cited by Mr. Locke in his treatise on government, chaps. II and VI.[11] The Filmerians often preach the principles of anarchy in one breath and those of despotism in another. The gentleman (p. 9) says, "The individuals of the colonists participate of every blessing the English constitution can give them. As corporations created by the crown they are confined within the primitive views of their institution. Whether therefore their *indulgence* is *liberal* or *scanty* can be no cause of complaint;

† *Observ.* p. 223.

for when they accepted of their charters they *tacitly* submitted to the terms and conditions of them." This is admirable! To be sure a liberal indulgence could be no cause of complaint. I have heard of a scanty allowance, and it often happens in a transportation across the Atlantic; but what is a *scanty indulgence?* I am in doubt under what species of Hellenism to rank it. Is it Doric or Ionic? Attic I am sure it is not. But at present I am content it should pass as very good English for a poor pittance of bread, water, stinking beef, and coarse clothes instead of the roast beef of Old Engand praised and sung by such authors as delight in compositions like "Lillibullero." Has a servant no reason to complain that his allowance is scanty, that he is half naked and more than half starved, while his less faithful and less loyal fellow servant is well-fed, plump, gay, and clothed in purple and scarlet and fine linen, faring sumptuously every day upon the spoils of his neighbor? But admitting the former has no right to complain or utter a single sigh, the forced effect of "submissive fear and mingled rage," [12] I [13] cannot for the heart of me conceive how he "participates of every blessing" of his fellow servant; unless the gentleman will contend that half a loaf is equal to a whole one, and that *Martyn* and *Jack* were really a couple of scoundrels for denying that the crusts Lord Peter would have palmed upon them were very good Banstead-down mutton.[13] That "the colonists do not hold their rights as a privilege granted them nor enjoy them as a grace and favor bestowed, but possess them as an inherent indefeasible right," as Mr. H—k—s very justly asserts, is a self-evident proposition to everyone in the least versed in the laws of nature and nations, or but moderately skilled in the common law, except the learned gentleman of Halifax. Even the King's writs are divided into those which the subject hath a right to *ex debito justitiae* and those which depend upon mere grace and favor. These may be denied, the others cannot. The essential rights of British colonists stand on the same basis with those of their fellow subjects of the same rank in any of the three kingdoms.

What the gentleman adds, viz., "that this postulatum of Mr. H—pk—s cannot be true with regard to political rights," by which he evidently means the peculiar privileges of subordinate powers granted by charter, is (asking his pardon) mere impertinence, and in a gentleman of his sense could arise only from a certain set of prejudices having so far blinded him as to make him confound the ideas of corporate subordinate privileges with essential, natural, and civil rights, as is above most abundantly demonstrated, and clearly appears from his own words (p. 10):

"The force of an act of Parliament over the colonies is *predicated* upon the common law, the origin and basis of all those inherent *rights* and *privileges* which constitute the boast and felicity of a Briton." I wish he had said the justly boasted felicity of a Briton, because in that case I should not have suspected him of a Filmerian sneer in this place, which jealousy his dogmas elsewhere will justify. The inherent, indefeasible rights of the subject, so much derided and despised in other parts of the performance, are here admitted, in jest or in earnest, I care not which. The [14] origin of those rights is in the law of nature and its author. This law is the grand basis of the common law and of all other municipal laws that are worth a rush. True it is that every act of Parliament which names the colonies or describes them as by the words "plantations or dominions" binds them. But this is not so strictly and properly speaking by the common law as by the law of nature and by the constitution of a parliament or sovereign and supreme legislative in a state. 'Tis as true that when the colonies are not named or described by an act of Parliament, they are not bound by it.

What is the reason of all this? *Qui haeret in litera haeret in cortice.*[14] Surely the bare naming of the colonies hath no magical charm or force in it. That the colonies should be bound by acts of Parliament wherein they are named is an exception from a general rule or maxim. What is that rule or maxim? It is that the colonies being separate dominions and at a distance from the realm, or mother state, and in fact unrepresented in Parliament shall be governed by laws of their own making; and unless named in acts of Parliament shall not be bound by them. *"Quia non mittunt milites ad parliamentum,"* says Lord Coke.[15] Yet as a mark of, and to preserve their dependency on, and subordination to, the mother state, and to prevent *imperium in imperio,* the greatest of all political solecisms, the mother state justly asserts the right and authority to bind her colonies where she really thinks the good of the whole requires it; and of this she remains the supreme judge, from whose final determination there is no appeal. The mother state hath also an undoubted right to unite a colony to itself and wholly to abrogate and annihilate all colony or subordinate legislation and administration if such alteration shall appear for the best interest of the whole community. But should this be done needlessly and wantonly and without allowing the colonies a representation, the exercise of the power that would otherwise be just and equitable would cease to be distinguished by those amiable qualities. Should a mother state even think it reasonable to impose internal as well as external taxes on six millions of subjects in

their remote dominions without allowing them one voice, it would be
[15] matter of wonder and astonishment; but it could not be said that
the supreme legislative had exceeded the bounds of their power and
authority, nor would this render a petition undutiful and seditious. Those
six millions must on such an event, unless blind, see themselves reduced
to the mortifying condition of mere ciphers and blanks in society. Should
all this ever happen to the British colonies, which God forbid, might it
not be truly and safely affirmed that the representation in the House of
Commons would be very unequal? The right of a supreme power in
a state to tax its colonies is a thing that is clear and evident; and yet
the mode of exercising that right may be questionable in point of reason
and equity. It may be thought to be unequal and contrary to sound
policy to exercise the right, clear as it is, without allowing a representation to the colonies. And though a representation would avail the colonies
very little in this generation, yet to posterity it might be an invaluable
blessing. It may also in future ages be very beneficial to Great Britain.
Is it to be believed that when a continent of 3000 miles in length shall
have more inhabitants than there are at this day in Great Britain, France,
and Ireland, perhaps in all Europe, they will be quite content with the
bare name of British subjects, and to the end of time supinely acquiesce
in laws made, as it may happen, against their interest by an assembly
3000 miles beyond sea, and where, should they agree in the sentiments
with the Halifax gentleman, it may be thought that an admission of an
American member would "sully and defile the purity of the whole
body"? [16] One hundred years will give this continent more inhabitants
than there are in the three kingdoms.

Many great and good men have complained of the inequality of the
representation in Great Britain. This inequality can never be a reason
for making it more so; which, however, is the method of reasoning
adopted by the Halifax gentleman. At his rate, it would be just that
half the counties and boroughs in Great Britain which now return members should be curtailed of their right. If so, why not half the remainder,
and so on till the House of Commons will be reduced to a single member, and when he was [16] split, one branch of the legislature would
be annihilated. By a like process the House of Lords, the second branch
of the legislature, might be destroyed. This would be a shorter cut to
absolute and unlimited monarchy than ever Filmer was fortunate enough
to invent. This brings us to the consideration of the maxim that "no
Englishman can be taxed but by his own consent, in person or by his

representative. This dry maxim, taken in a literal sense and little understood *like* the song of "Lillibullero" has made all the mischief in the colonies," says the gentleman (p. 11). I cannot conceive how this or any other dry maxim, or the song of "Lillibullero" like it, well or ill understood, can make any mischief in the colonies. What notable harm has the song of "Lillibullero" wrought in the colonies, or what like it has this "dry maxim" effected? "It is," says the gentleman (p. 11), "the opinion of the House of Commons and *may* be considered as a law of Parliament that they are the representatives of every British subject wheresoever he be." *Festina lente domine!* This may be true in one sense. The supreme legislative indeed represents the whole society or community, as well the dominions as the realm; and this is the true reason why the dominions are justly bound by such acts of Parliament as name them. This is implied in the idea of a supreme sovereign power; and if the Parliament had not such authority the colonies would be independent, which none but rebels, fools, or madmen will contend for. God forbid these colonies should ever prove undutiful to their mother country! Whenever such a day shall come it will be the beginning of a terrible scene. Were these colonies left to themselves tomorrow, America would be a mere shambles of blood and confusion before little petty states could be settled. How many millions must perish in building up great empires? How many more must be ruined by their fall? Let any man reflect on the revolutions of government, ancient and modern, and he will think himself happy in being born here in the infancy of these settlements, and from his soul deprecate their once entertaining any sentiments but those of loyalty, patience, meekness, and forbearance under any hardships that in the course of [17] time they may be subjected to. These, as far as may be consistent with the character of men and Christians, must be submitted to. If it is the opinion of the present honorable House of Commons that they in *fact represent* the colonies, it is more than I know. Should this be their opinion, the gentleman may if he pleases "consider it as a law of Parliament." But I should rather choose to consider it only as the very respectable opinion of one branch of the supreme legislative. The opinion of the House of Lords and then above all the sanction of the King's Majesty must be superadded, and the concurrence of both is absolutely necessary to make any opinion of the House of Commons an act or law of *Parliament.* 'Tis humbly conceived that it was not as representatives in *fact* of the colonies that the House of Commons granted His Majesty an external tax on the colonies in the instance of the late act. Nor, if before this time an act for granting internal taxes on the colonies should be passed, could I conceive that the House of Commons are our representatives in fact. As one branch of the supreme legislative, they have an undoubted right to originate any bills that, by naming them, shall bind the colonies when passed into an act, let it be for levying internal or external taxes, or for any other regulation that may appear needful. But I cannot find it affirmed or declared in one act of Parliament, history, or journal of Parliamentary proceedings, nor in one English law book, that a British House of Commons are in *fact* the representatives of all the plebeian subjects, without as well as within the *realm*. Lord Coke indeed says that "the House of Commons represent all the commons of *England,* electors and nonelectors";[17] but he nowhere asserts that the House of Commons in *fact* represent the provincials of Ireland and other dominions out of the *realm*. He says, however, the people of Ireland are not represented in the English Parliament, and assigns that as the very reason why, in general, acts of Parliament are confined to the realm. Though from the necessity of the thing, in several cases, by naming them the provinces are bound. In the *Fourth Institute,* speaking of the truly high and most honorable court on earth, and never more so than in the [18] present state of the British Parliament and nation, his lordship says, "This court consisteth of the King's Majesty, sitting there as in his royal political capacity and of the three estates of the *realm,* viz., of the lords spiritual, archbishops and bishops, being in number 24, who sit there by succession in respect of their counties, or baronies parcel of their bishoprics, which they hold also in their politic capacity; and every one of these, when any Parliament is to be holden, ought, *ex debito justitiae,* to have a [writ of] summons. The lords temporal, dukes, marquises, earls, viscounts, and barons, who sit there by reason of their dignities which they hold by descent or creation, in number at this time 106, and likewise every one of these being of full age, ought to have a writ of summons *ex debito justitiae.* The third estate is the *commons* of the *realm,* whereof there be knights of shires or counties, citizens of cities, and burgesses of burghs. All which are respectively elected by the shires or counties, cities, and burghs by force of the King's writ *ex debito justitiae,* and none of them ought to be omitted; and *these represent all the commons of the whole realm, and trusted for them, and are in number at this time* 493." 4 *Inst.* 1.

Here is not one word of the House of Commons representing or being trusted by or for the provincials of Ireland or the colonists in America.

And though in page 4 of the same *Institute* he says, *"in many cases multitudes are bound by acts of Parliament which are not parties to the election of knights, citizens, and burgesses, as all they that have no freehold or have freehold in ancient demesne, and all women, having freehold or no freehold, and men within the age of twenty-one years etc."* — this "etc." may be supplied with female infants, lunatics, idiots, and bedlamites in general. Yet this will not prove that these nonelectors are in *fact* represented and in *fact* trust the representatives in the House of Commons. In estimation of law they are justly deemed as represented. They have all fathers, brothers, friends, or neighbors in the House of Commons, and many *ladies* have husbands there. Few of the members have any of these endearing ties to America. We are as to any personal knowledge they have of us as perfect strangers [19] to most of them as the savages in *California*. But according to our Letter Writer we are not only in *law* but in *deed* represented in the House of Commons. How does he support this? Why, he has dreamt that some one House of Commons in some former reign once thought they were *in fact* our representatives. That "the opinion of a House of Commons is a law of Parliament," therefore " 'tis determined by act of Parliament that we are and shall believe we are in *fact* represented in the House of Commons." Here's more logic. Suppose some future House of Commons should be of opinion that they were the true and proper representatives of all the common people upon the globe; would that make them so and oblige all mankind to believe and submit to it? Would a fiction of the common law of England satisfy the innumerable multitudes on the face of the whole earth that they were in *fact* represented and consenting to all such taxes and tributes as might be demanded of them? Will any man's calling himself my agent, representative, or trustee make him so in fact? At this rate a House of Commons in one of the colonies have but to conceive an opinion that they represent all the common people of Great Britain, and according to our author they would in *fact* represent them and have a right to tax them. 'Tis strange the gentleman can see no difference between a literal sense of a fundamental principle or "dry maxim" as he calls it, and no sense at all. Does it follow because it is "impracticable that each individual should be in *fact* represented" that therefore there should be no representation at all, or a very unequal one? Because the little insignificant isles of Jersey, Guernsey, and Man have never obtained a representation, is it reasonable that the whole kingdom of Ireland and the plantations should be forever excluded from returning members to the British Parliament, even should the Parliament impose external and internal taxes on them and take from them every subordinate power of local legislation? If this would be equal and rational why might not Wales have been excluded from returning members, why may they not be excluded now, and Devonshire and Cornwall, and every other county and [20] borough share the same fate? Matter of fact is one thing, matter of right another. The people of a state may in *fact* be very unequally represented; but few men would, like our author, in effect contend that it were best they should not be represented at all. Has the gentleman forgot the maxim "that equity is equality." 'Tis hoped he will not consider this as a leveling principle, as it has been more than once called. How astonishing is it that the instances (p. 12) of the unequal representation in Great Britain, to which he might have added those of "ten Cornish barns and an ale house," should be brought as an argument to prove that "the right of being represented in Parliament" is "an *utopian privilege*," a "phantom," a "cloud in the shape of Juno"? This is far from a fine compliment to the honorable House of Commons, of which as one of the branches of the supreme legislative and of the privilege of sitting with them it would have been more decent to have made a different choice of expressions. To atone for this indelicacy, the next moment the pendulum vibrates as far the other way.

In page 13, the Parliament is represented as so pure and perfect that *"the beauty and symmetry of this body would be destroyed and its purity defiled by the unnatural mixture of representatives from* every part of the British dominions. Parthians, Medes, Elamites, and the dwellers of Mesopotamia, etc., *would not in such a case speak the same language.* What a heterogeneous council would this form? What a monster in government would it be?" Let me add, was ever insolence equal to this? Are the inhabitants of British America all a parcel of transported thieves, robbers, and rebels, or descended from such? Are the colonists blasted lepers, whose company would infect the whole House of Commons? There are some in the colonies who value themselves on their descent. We have the names of *Tudor* and of *Stuart,* of *Howard, Seymour,* and of *Russell,* who boast an unsullied descent from our ancient princes and nobles, or at least claim the honor of being of the same blood. Can none of these be returned [21] as members without breeding a plague in the House? If this writer is a European, his insults upon the British colonies are quite unpardonable; if he be a native he is an ungrateful parricide. Is he a venal hireling of a party, his employers on either side the Atlantic should discard him as a mere Sir Martyn Marplot? [18] Depend upon it, one such letter as his, if known to breathe the sentiments of the great, would tend more to disgust the colonies against the conduct of their superiors than a hundred thousand such pamphlets as the author scolds at. Parliaments are not only "as ancient as our Saxon ancestors" but as old as the commonwealths of Israel, Greece, and Rome;‡ nay as old as the first compact for changing a simple democracy into any other form of government. "Attendance in Parliament" is not, therefore, as the gentleman conceives, a "duty arising from a tenure of lands or the feudal system" but from the nature of man, of society, and of all original, just, social, and civil compacts for forming a state. "So that the privilege of sitting in it," i.e., in a parliament or grand council of a nation, is not "territorial" in the sense of the Letter Writer, nor in its nature "confined to Great Britain." What is there, what can there be that should naturally and necessarily confine the privilege of returning members to the inhabitants of Great Britain more than to those of London and Westminster?

The gentleman (p. 14) says "the Parliament may levy internal taxes as well as regulate trade, there is no essential difference." By regulating trade I suppose he means, according to the common sophism, taxing trade. Even in this sense 'tis admitted the Parliament have the same right to levy internal taxes on the colonies as to regulate trade, and that the right of levying both is undoubtedly in the Parliament. Yet 'tis humbly conceived and hoped that before the authority is fully exerted in either case it will be thought to be but reasonable and equitable that the dominions should be in *fact* represented. Else it will follow that the provincials in Europe, Asia, Africa, and America ought to all generations to content themselves with having no more share, weight, or influence, even in the provincial government [22] of their respective countries, than the Hottentots have in that of China, or the Ethiopians in that of Great Britain.

I should be glad to know how the gentleman came by his assurance that "a stamp duty is confessedly the most reasonable and equitable that can be devised" (*ibid.*). Some few may be of this opinion, and there never was a new invented tax or excise but its favorers and partisans would highly extol as the most just and equitable device imaginable. This is a trite game "at ways and means." But bold assertions will not pass for clear proofs with "philosophically inquisitive minds." If "the

‡ 4 *Inst.* 2, 3.

shaft is sped" and the aim so good, I wonder the gentleman should even
faintly pretend to "desire not to see a stamp duty established among us,"
or "wish to prevent the blow." Were I convinced, as he is, that it is
reasonable and best that the colonies should be taxed by Parliament
without being allowed a representation, and that it is become not only
necessary to levy internal taxes on them but that the art of man could
not devise so equitable and reasonable a tax as a stamp duty, I should
heartily pray for its establishment.

The gentleman nowhere discovers his temper more plainly than in
his comparison of Greece and Rome in their conduct towards their colonies. 'Tis well known the Grecians were kind, humane, just, and generous
towards theirs. 'Tis as notorious that the Romans were severe, cruel,
brutal, and barbarous towards theirs. I have ever pleased myself in
thinking that Great Britain since the Revolution might be justly compared to Greece in its care and protection of its colonies. I also imagined
that the French and Spaniards followed the Roman example. But our
Letter Writer tells quite a different story. He compliments the nation
and comforts the colonies by declaring that these "exactly resemble those
of Rome. The *Roman coloniae,*" says he, "did not enjoy all the rights of
Roman citizens. They only *used* the Roman laws and religion and served
in their legions, but had no right of suffrage or bearing honors." "In
these respects," adds he, "our English colonies exactly resemble them. We
enjoy the English laws and religion but not the right of suffrage or of
bearing honors in Great Britain."

[23] Is this enjoying the rights, liberties, and privileges of British-born
subjects within the realm to all intents, constructions, and purposes? I
find all this confirmed to the colonists, not only by the common law
and by their charters, but by act of Parliament. Where does the gentleman find it decreed that the British *"coloniae* have no right of bearing
honors in Great Britain"? Has not the King's Majesty, the fountain of
honor, an undoubted right by his prerogative to confer any rank he may
be graciously pleased to bestow on his American subjects, as well as on
those in Great Britain? Cannot the word of a King as easily make even
a Halifaxian Letter Writer or his Rhode Island friend a knight of the
garter or thistle as if either of them had been dropped and drawn their
first breath in one of the three kingdoms?

The gentleman may in his anger wish for the laws of "Draco to be
enforced on America," and in his fierce anger, for the "iron rod of a
Spanish inquisitor." These may be sudden gusts of passion, without

malice prepense, that only hurt his cause, and which his employers will not thank him for. But hard, very hard must his heart be who could employ all his stock of learning in a deliberate attempt to reduce the rights of the colonists to the narrow bound of a bare permission to "use the English laws and religion without a suffrage in things sacred or civil and without a right to bear honors in Great Britain," "except that of being shot at for six pence a day in her armies at home as well as abroad." What is the English religion? Pray wherein does it differ from that of Scotland, Ireland, and the plantations? If it differs, and the colonies are obliged to *use* the religion of the metropolis on her embracing paganism, so must the colonies. Since the Revolution all dissenters, both at home and abroad, papists only excepted, have enjoyed a free and generous toleration. Would the gentleman deprive all Protestant dissenters of this invaluable blessing? If he is an American by birth, what does he deserve of his country for attempting to realize to this and to all future generations the dreary prospect of confinement to the use of the laws and religion of a region 3000 miles beyond sea, in framing which laws and in forming the [24] modes of which religion they shall have no voice nor suffrage, nor shall they have any preferment in church or state, though they shall be taxed without their consent to the support of both?

> . . . *aes triplex*
> *Circa pectus erat.*[19]

The gentleman hath been at great pains in order to represent the merchants of America as a parcel of infamous smugglers. He says, "smuggling had well nigh beome established in some of the colonies." 'Tis notoriously known who have been the great abettors and patrons of smugglers and who have shared the greatest part of the profits. All the riot at Ephesus proceeded from certain collectors of the revenues of Diana of the Ephesians; the shrine makers and silversmiths were but their tools. The craft was in danger, but if it had been only that of Demetrius and his journeymen we might not have heard of that day's uproar.[20] 'Tis a very unjust aspersion to charge the American merchants in general with a design to elude and evade the acts of trade. I cannot so well tell how matters have been managed at Halifax or Rhode Island; but in some other colonies only a few favorites have been indulged in the lucrative crime of smuggling, which, after an eminent writer, the gentleman calls a crime "against the law of nature"; 'tis a wonder it had not been recorded from some old commentator *crimen lesae Majestatis, high treason.* The like indulgence, as far as I can learn, has in Rhode Island been confined also to a few choice friends. The article of molasses is everywhere to be excepted. It was known at home that the importation of this was universally tolerated, paying about one tenth of the duties imposed by the old act. The connivance became very general.

I have perused Mr. H—k—s' book over and over but cannot find the least reflection on Dr. Spry; nor do I think any was intended. The Doctor perhaps may thank the gentleman for bringing his name into question, but I doubt, notwithstanding the gentleman's assertions to the contrary, whether the Doctor's "appointments place him above any kind of influence." I believe he is under the influence of honor and conscience, a clear head, and a good heart, all which [25] the gentleman seems too much a stranger to. And should the Doctor also be under that influence which flows from a general aversion and contempt of flattery and falsehood, he must conceive an opinion of his Halifax neighbor that will be very mortifying to one who hopes to make his court to the great, and to the Doctor among the rest, by abusing the colonies. The Doctor hath been in America some months, but I have not heard of one cause that has been tried before him. This is a tolerable proof either that smuggling was not so common a thing as the Letter Writer asserts, or that those who used to be concerned in it are reformed. I think it proves both.[21]

In the 21st and last page but one of the *Letter,* the gentleman bethought himself, and having in a manner finished his epistle, makes an apology for not following Mr. H—k—s "with somewhat more of method." His excuse is that Mr. H—k—s hath not "divided his argument with precision." He then formally proceeds to a curious and, as he doubtless thought, precise division of the argument. "The dispute," says he, "between Great Britain and the colonies consists of two parts. First, the jurisdiction of Parliament; and secondly, the exercise of that jurisdiction. His honor has blended these together, and nowhere marked the division between them. The first I have principally remarked upon." I know of no dispute between Great Britain and her colonies. Who is so hardy as to dispute the jurisdiction of the Parliament? But were there a thousand disputes between Great Britain and the colonies, if the colonists in general were as the Letter Writer represents them, "a simple, credulous, and hitherto loyal people," in danger of "having their minds embittered and their affections alienated from Great Britain by a few pamphlets," and if "from the pride of some and ignorance of others the cry against mother country had spread from colony to colony; and it were to be feared that prejudices and resentments were kindled among them which it will be difficult ever thoroughly to sooth or extinguish," all which insinuations are however very injurious — what would this prove against *The Rights of Colonies Examined* or any other of the pamphlets that have been lately published in America? Mr. H—k—s, [26] pages 10 and 11 of his book, speaking of the general concerns of the whole British Empire, saith, "These it is absolutely necessary should have a general power to direct them, some supreme and overruling authority, with power to make laws and form regulations for the good of all and to compel their execution and observation. It being necessary some such general power should exist somewhere, every man of the least knowledge of the British constitution will be naturally led to look for and find it in the Parliament of Great Britain; that grand and august legislative body must from the nature of their authority and the necessity of the thing be justly vested with this power." Is not this a very clear admission and acknowledgement of the jurisdiction, power, and authority of Parliament over the colonies? What could put it into the gentleman's head to think the jurisdiction of the Parliament was a matter in dispute? I have perused a pamphlet published in Connecticut relating to their rights, but can find no question made of the jurisdiction of the Parliament. *The Rights of the British Colonies Asserted and Proved* I have also read. This was published before either Mr. H—k—s' or that from Connecticut. These, so far as I can find, are all the pamphlets that have been published in America upon the proposed new regulations of the colonies. From the knowledge I have of the sentiments of the "head of the *tribunitian veto,*" as the gentleman is pleased to describe him, I take upon me to declare that I have heard him in the most public manner declare his submission to the authority of Parliament; and that from his soul he detests and abhors the thought of making a question of their jurisdiction.

The following passages from *The Rights of the British Colonies Asserted and Proved* may serve to show how careful a hand the Halifax gentleman is at a matter of fact.

"I also lay it down as one of the first principles from whence I intend to deduce the civil rights of the British colonies that all of them are subject to and dependent on Great Britain, and that therefore as over subordinate governments the Parliament of Great Britain has an [27] undoubted power and lawful authority to make acts for the general good that, by naming them, shall and ought to be equally binding as upon the subjects of Great Britain within the realm." "When the Parliament shall think fit to allow the colonists a representation in the House of Commons, the equity of their taxing the colonies will be as clear as their power is at present of doing it without, if they please." "No such claim (i.e., of an independent legislative) was ever thought of by the colonists. They are all better men and better subjects; and many of them too well versed in the laws of nature and nations and the law and constitution of Great Britain to think they have a right to more than a *provincial subordinate legislative*. All power is of GOD. Next and only subordinate to Him in the present state of the well-formed, beautiful[ly] constructed British monarchy, standing where I hope it ever will stand, for the pillars are fixed in judgment, righteousness, and truth, is the King and Parliament." "From all which it seems plain that the reason why Ireland and the plantations are not bound unless named by an act of Parliament is because they are *not represented* in the British Parliament. Yet in special cases the British Parliament has an undoubted right, as well as power, to bind both by their acts. But whether this can be extended to an indefinite taxation of both is the great question. I conceive the spirit of the British constitution must make an exception of all taxes until it is thought fit to unite a dominion to the realm. Such taxation must be considered either as uniting the dominions to the realm or disfranchising them. If they are united they will be entitled to a representation as well as Wales; if they are so taxed without a union or representation, they are so far disfranchised." "The sum of my argument is: that civil government is of God; that the administrators of it were originally the whole people; that they might have devolved it on whom they pleased; that this devolution is fiduciary, for the good of the whole; that by the British constitution this devolution is on the King, Lords, and Commons, the supreme, sacred, and uncontrollable legislative power, not only in the realm but through the dominions; that by the [28] abdication, the original compact was broken to pieces; that by the Revolution it was renewed and more firmly established, and the rights and liberties of the subject in all parts of the dominions more fully explained and confirmed; that in consequence of this establishment and the act of succession and union, His Majesty GEORGE III is rightful King and sovereign, and, with his Parliament, the supreme legislative of Great Britain, France, and Ireland,

and the dominions thereto belonging; that this constitution is the most free one and by far the best now existing on earth; that by this constitution every man in the dominions is a free man; that no part of His Majesty's dominions can be taxed without their consent; that every part has a right to be represented in the supreme or some subordinate legislature; that the refusal of this would seem to be a contradiction in practice to the theory of the constitution; that the colonies are subordinate dominions and are now in such a state as to make it best for the good of the whole that they should not only be continued in the enjoyment of subordinate legislation but be also represented in some proportion to their number and estates in the grand legislature of the nation; that this would firmly unite all parts of the British empire in the greatest peace and prosperity, and render it invulnerable and perpetual." *Rights of the British Colonies Asserted and Proved,* pp. 32, 48, 59, 61, 64, [65]. Can the gentleman read these passages and say they imply any question of the power and authority of Parliament? Will he not blush when he reflects that he hath indiscriminately asserted that these pamphlets "have a tendency to embitter the minds of a simple, credulous, and hitherto loyal people, and to alienate their affections from Great Britain, their best friend and alma mater"? Can terms expressive of greater loyalty or submission to the jurisdiction and authority of Parliament be conceived than many that are to be found in those pamphlets? Yet the gentleman has the effrontery to talk of the "frequent abuse poured forth in pamphlets against the mother country," and laments that before his, "not one filial pen in America had been drawn in her vindication." How grand we look! Are not his dragoons [29] enough, but he must fight with his pen too? I believe he must be a man of parlous courage; and yet he is modest withal. He says he has "no ambition of appearing in print," though he is the only loyal subject His Majesty hath in his American dominions and master of the only filial pen worth a button. If this be true, well might he call his countrymen a parcel of scoundrels, rebels, smugglers, and traitors. I shall take leave of my gentleman by desiring him to reflect in his cooler hours and well consider what would soon be his fate if the Americans should treat him as he most richly deserves.

I too have seen in all the pride of May,
A flaunting singsong genius toujours gay;
Whose life was one short senseless pretty dream,
Frisk on the margin of a mighty stream,

Till circling dances seize his tender brain:
He falls! he dies! alas a calf is slain! § [22]

POSTSCRIPT

Since the above sheets were finished two or three pieces have been published in the *Providence Gazette*.[23] The first of these hath furnished us with a clear and concise account of the several principal reasonings and arguments upon the subject of internal taxes to be imposed on the colonies by Parliament while they are unrepresented in the House of Commons. The sum is:

1. That it is the incontestible right of the subject in Great Britain not to be taxed out of Parliament; and every subject within the realm is in fact or in law represented there.

2. The British colonists being British subjects, are to all intents and purposes entitled to the rights, liberties, and privileges of the subject within the realm and ought to be represented in fact as well as in law in the supreme or some subordinate legislature where they are taxed, else they will be deprived of one of the most essential rights of a British subject, namely that of being free from all taxes but such as he shall by himself or representative grant and assess.

3. As the colonies have been erected into subordinate dependent dominions with subordinate powers of legislation, particularly that of levying taxes for the support of their respective subordinate governments, and at their own expense have not only supported the civil provincial administration but many of them have, to their utmost ability, contributed both in men and money for the common cause, as well as for their more immediate defense against His Majesty's enemies, it should seem very

---

§ *"Narcissus,* in contemplating his own image, was turned into a daffodil. Who can think of this and feel no pity for the pride and weakness of *man that is born of a woman."*

> So have I seen, on some bright summer's day,
> A calf of genius debonair and gay,
> Dance on the brink, as if inspired by fame,
> Fond of the pretty fellow in the stream.

Four lines of Dr. Young very modestly applied to Governor H—k—s in the 5th page of the letter from Halifax, as above cited with the allusion to *Narcissus.*

hard that they should be taxed also by Parliament, and that before they are allowed a representation in fact and while they are quite unable to pay such additional taxes.

4. The immense commercial advantages resulting to Great Britain from her plantations, the revenues thence arising to the crown, the taxes we pay by the consumption of an infinity of British manufactures may be thought a reasonable return for the protection received, as 'tis really all that at present is in our power to yield.

5. If the colonies could and ought to yield greater aids towards the national expense, yet it should seem but reasonable either to allow them, (1) to raise such further sums as may be required by taxing themselves in the most easy way and manner their several provincial legislatures could devise; or, (2) at least to allow them a representation in the House of Commons. This with some animadversions on the present state of commerce, with the extension and enlargement of the admiralty juris-diction in America, is the substance of all that has so much incensed the Halifax gentleman. Governor H—k—s hath nowhere said that "the colo-nies have rights independent of, and not controllable by, the authority of Parliament." *See Providence Gazette, Feb.* [23, 1765].

[31] According to the gentleman "it will follow that we may enjoy *personal* liberty, and yet be slaves in *a political sense;* and so *vice versa,* we may be *personally slaves* and yet have a political right to liberty. Life, liberty, and estate, being personal rights, are (by the gentleman admitted to be) secured to us by the common law. I do not remember to have heard that the colonies ever contended for more; and yet (by this per-sonal and political distinction) our estates may be taken away from us against our consent without any violation of our personal right, and all this for want of a *political* right." *Providence Gazette, February* [23], 1765.[24]

"The gentleman confidently maintains that acts of Parliament derive their force from the common law; and for that reason he says they are obligatory on the colonies. I ask him how it is possible that the Parliamen-tary power which controls, alters, and amends the common law at will can derive its support from the common law. *Providence Gazette,* [March 2, 1765].

☞ The power and authority of Parliament is from the constitution, and above all other laws but those of God and nature.

"There may be a natural relation between two subjects that exist by nature; but mother country and colony exist only by policy, and may and no doubt have a political relation to each other, but can have no natural one." *Providence Gazette, March* 2, [1765].

This remark is ingenious, and the manner in which 'tis elucidated is diverting; but I fear 'tis not solid. There is nonsense and contradiction enough of all conscience in the Halifax gentleman's attempt to investigate the "natural relation between colonies and their mother state" without denying the existence of such a relation. Our allegiance is natural, and if this be admitted of each individual in a colony, as it must be, it would be strange to deny a natural relation between two whole bodies between all the respective parts of which a natural relation is admitted. Society is certainly natural and exists prior to and independent of any form of civil policy, always excepting family societies and simple democracies. As there is a natural relation between father and son, so is there between their two families, and so is there between a mother state or metropolis and its colonies. The natural relation between two independent states or societies is the basis of the law of nations, and all its obligations are thence deducible. It would be strange that a natural relation should subsist between two neighboring states and none be between a metropolis and a colony. I can see no absurdity in supposing both natural and political relations to subsist between a mother state and its colonies any more than supposing two qualities in one and the same subject. The same man may be choleric and humane, another is calm and inveterate. The same two men may be father and son, fellow men, fellow subjects, fellow citizens, and brother aldermen. Political relations are but modifications of those which are founded in nature, and from whence rise duties of universal obligation.[25]

I cannot suppress all my indignation at a remark in the close of the Halifax letter, which should have been taken notice of before, but it escaped me. "It may become necessary for the supreme legislature of the [32] nation to frame some code (and canons might have been as properly added) and therein adjust the rights of the colonies with precision and certainty, otherwise Great Britain will always be teased with new claims about liberty and privileges" (p. 22).

If I mistake not, there is in the air of this period the quintessence of a mere martial legislator, the insolence of a haughty and imperious minister, the indolence and half-thought of a *petit-maître,* the flutter of a coxcomb, the pedantry of a quack, and the nonsense of a pettifogger. A strange gallimaufry this; but I am not answerable for it or for any other of the exhibitions of a monster monger. We want no foreign codes nor canons here. The common law is our birthright, and the rights and privileges confirmed and secured to us by the British constitution and by act of Parliament are our best inheritance. Codes, pandects, novels, decretals of popes, and the inventions of the d——l may suit the cold, bleak regions [of] Brandenburg and Prussia or the scorching heats of Jamaica or Gambia; but we live in a more temperate climate, and shall rest content with the laws, customs, and usages of our ancestors, bravely supported and defended with the monarchy, and from age to age handed down. These have and ever will finally triumph over the whims of political and religious enthusiasts, the extremes of which are libertinism and despotism, anarchy and tyranny, spiritual and temporal, from all which may God ever preserve us. I must recommend it to the Halifax gentleman before he publishes any more epistles diligently to read over Swift's *Tale of a Tub,* and to take special note of Lord Peter's method of reasoning with his brethren. He will there find all the forms of syllogism from the *sorites* to the categoric. Of the last form he will find this, to prove that a little learning puffeth little men up:

> Words are but wind,
> Learning is nothing but words,
> *Ergo.* Learning is nothing but wind.

Of the former kind of argumentation he will find a species he seems to be peculiarly fond of.

"In the midst of all this clutter and revolution, in comes Lord Peter with a file of dragoons at his heels, and gathering from all hands what was in the wind, he and his gang, after several millions of scurrilities and curses not very important here to repeat, by main force very fairly kicks them (Martyn and Jack) both out of doors, and would never let them come under his roof from that day to this."

Tale of a Tub, 104, 79.

PAMPHLET 12

[BENJAMIN CHURCH], *LIBERTY AND PROPERTY VINDICATED*

HARTFORD, 1765

INTRODUCTION

The role of violence and the threat of violence in the American Revolution is curiously complicated. For in that upheaval, unlike the French Revolution in which thousands were killed, directly or indirectly, as a result of mob action,[1] there was "a singular self-restraint . . . the participants invariably stopped short of inflicting death." Not a single murder resulted from the activities of the Revolutionary mobs in America, and when blood was accidentally spilt, it was made to go a very long way. The Boston Massacre in which five people were killed by confused and intimidated soldiers, was portrayed in the orations of the patriots as a blood bath, and Loyalists saw in such physical intimidation as there was a "reign of anarchy" in which a maddened "canaille," ripping apart the dwellings of respectable people, looked first into the "beds, in order to murder the children." [2]

These are lurid fantasies. Heads did not roll in the American Revolution; mobs did not turn to butchery. Nevertheless physical intimidation was very much a part of the Revolutionary movement. It was present, Professor Schlesinger writes, "at every significant turning point of the events leading up to the War for Independence. Mobs terrified the stamp agents into resigning and forced a repeal of the tax. Mobs obstructed the execution of the Townshend Revenue Act and backed up the boycotts of British trade. Mobs triggered the Boston Massacre and later the famous Tea Party . . . [Later] civilian mobs behind the lines systematically intimidated Tory opponents, paralyzing their efforts or driving them into exile."

These mob actions, associated with the Revolutionary movement at every turn, were not in themselves "revolutionary" — were not, that is, uprisings of oppressed masses inflamed with meliorist aspirations, seeking to destroy the ruling class and to reconstitute the structure of state and society. They were extensions into an ideologically charged situation of a form of public protest that had been resorted to frequently in the colonies for decades before. Just as in England in the seventeenth and eighteenth centuries, where rioting by uncontrolled mobs was widespread and continuous, "there was in this period no movement for social revolution or even social reform, based upon the class consciousness of the poorer sections of the population." Mob protests, the historian of popular disturbances in pre-industrial England writes, were "of an essentially conservative nature . . . animated by no common aim beyond that of immediate revenge upon the nearest personification of the people's enemies, a corn-dealer, an excise-man, or an East India merchant." [3]

So too in the colonies, popular disturbances, occurring almost continuously in the eighteenth century, had been aimed at specific, limited targets and had expressed immediate grievances which the regular processes of government seemed incapable of satisfying. In Boston, perhaps the best policed and most orderly city in colonial America, a mob of women, armed, it was said, with chamber pots, assaulted the troops returning from the abortive Canadian expedition of 1707; there were riots in 1710 and in 1713 in protest against grain exports at a time of shortage, and then again, for equally specific purposes, in 1721, 1725, 1729, 1741, 1745 (when Guy Fawkes Day parades led to a free-for-all in which several rioters were killed), and in 1747 (when a mob numbering thousands, protesting against impressment into the Royal Navy, put an end to all government and law enforcement for several days). So too mobs in Charleston, Newport, Philadelphia, and New York kept law enforcement officers at bay despite the passage of riot acts; in 1759 and 1760 antimilitary riots were so severe in Philadelphia that it was suggested that the commander-in-chief divert forces from the campaigns against the French and Indians to put them down.[4] Nor, throughout the eighteenth century, was rioting only an urban phenomenon. In 1711 several hundred Palatines, enraged at the treatment they had received in their settlement on the upper Hudson, marched against the governor and the landlords, and were kept in control only by a show of force. In New Jersey repeatedly between 1745 and 1754 there were violent uprisings of farmers protesting against the collection of quitrents and the manipulation of land titles: an estimated one third of the farmers in certain counties were involved; jails were thrown open, courts were stopped, and property destroyed. In the fifties violence among contending factions in the Connecticut-New York border area was so intense and continuous that it approached open warfare; and in the Carolina back country, where lawlessness was so widespread that society as such seemed scarcely to exist, the would-be "regulators" of the outlaw proved at times to be indistinguishable from the mobs they sought to control.[5]

These disturbances, far from being wild, anarchic outbursts of the materially deprived — outbursts such as in France created among the *sansculottes* the continuity of social ferment from which the bloody *journées* developed [6] — were either protests by independent farmers seeking to protect claims to small holdings of property against landlords, speculators, or brigands, or, in the urban centers, demonstrations by transient sailors and dock workers, occasionally joined by more substantial elements of the population, against a variety of immediate harassments, none of them expressive of deep-lying social distress. But if they were in fact ideologically inert, these outbursts nevertheless contained within them a powerful political potential, for they were all, in one way or another, anti-authoritarian, and in all of them dissent of some sort was mobilized into direct action against agencies of the law. It is scarcely surprising, therefore, that in the highly charged atmosphere of the late summer of 1765, as opposition to the approaching enforcement of the Stamp Act rose, this long-familiar form of public protest was seized upon by popular leaders and transformed into what distressed officials called "engines of sedition." The first of the long succession of politically effective and physically destructive, though bloodless, mob actions of the Revolution, took place in Boston, on August 14, 1765.

There, a group of artisans and shopkeepers who became known as the Loyal Nine hung an effigy of the Massachusetts stamp master, Andrew Oliver, from a tree in the center of town and rallied around it what proved to be the most destructive crowd that had, up to then, gathered in Boston. It was in a sense a practiced crowd, for many of its members were among those who regularly demonstrated on the streets of Boston on Guy Fawkes Day, and it was led by Ebenezer McIntosh, the shoemaker who led the South End gang in these boisterous, sometimes dangerous affairs. But in a larger sense it was a new phenomenon, for its hitherto diffuse and indeliberate antiauthoritarianism was now sharply focused and clearly articulated in terms that had universal meaning. Liberty was endangered; tyranny threatened — not in the abstract but quite concretely, in the person of a new kind of tax collector believed to be connected with that evil genius of English politics, Lord Bute. The wild riot that ensued, roaring its defiance to the hastily summoned Governor's Council, destroyed Andrew Oliver's shop building from which the stamps were to have been issued, half demolished his home as well, and the next day forced the thoroughly intimated stamp master to resign his office.[7]

It would later be said by the victims of the Boston mob that the rioters, in that town and elsewhere, were mindless instruments, passive tools, of unscrupulous demagogues like McIntosh, who were themselves but tools of hidden cliques of plotters like the Loyal Nine.[8] And in this they were followed by twentieth-century historians who, fascinated by the possibility of applying "our modern knowledge of the technique of propaganda" to the Revolution, assumed, as an English historian of eighteenth-century crowd phenomena put it, all "crowds engaged in riots, strikes, or political demonstrations . . . to be the passive instruments of outside parties and to have no particular motives of their own other than loot, lucre, free drinks, or the satisfaction of some lurking criminal instinct" — that they were, in other words, gangs of antisocial, strong-arm mercenaries available for the use of anyone who could pay their price or otherwise command their mercurial loyalties.[9] And it is true that the mobilization of demonstrators against the Stamp Act, in Boston and elsewhere in the colonies, was planned, and that the planning, being illegal, was clothed in secrecy. But the rioters, among whom were many substantial townsmen as well as crowds of workmen, far from being empty vessels, shared actively the attitudes and fears of the political and intellectual leaders of the Revolutionary movement. They were engaged in precisely such a "fully-fledged political movement in which devotion to a set of political principles is in greater evidence than attachment to the person of a popular leader or hero" that was at that time only embryonic, only faintly visible, in England. The cry "Liberty and No Stamps" was a meaningful political slogan which, more than "Wilkes and Liberty" in London, "stirred the political passions not only of freeholders and freemen but of the unenfranchised craftsmen and journeymen" as well. How thoroughly large numbers of people in the colonies had become "impregnated with a . . . solid body of political ideas and principles" [10] — how widely shared throughout America were the beliefs that animated the Boston rioters — is revealed in the speed with which the resistance movement spread after August 14, and in the variety of circumstances in which similar scenes were enacted. The present pamphlet, *Liberty and Property Vindicated, and the St—pm–n Burnt,* celebrates a climactic moment in the second series of these agitations, which took place in the villages of Connecticut, on August 21 and 22.[11]

The Connecticut stamp master, Jared Ingersoll, whose career has been sketched in the Introduction to Pamphlet 6, had returned from England on July 28. His first impression upon landing was that Connecticut was calm and would quietly submit to the Stamp Act. But in fact the colony was seething with opposition, particularly in the two eastern counties of Windham and New London. There, religious and political dissent in the form of the "secret plots or intrigues" of the revivalist New Lights aimed at shaking loose the ecclesiastical and civil establishment of the colony, together with economic distress focused in the expansionist efforts of the Susquehannah Company and in merchant discontent with England's commercial policy, had all combined to create an explosive atmosphere. News of the Stamp Act lit a fuse which burned steadily through the spring of 1765. Groups pledged to resistance formed themselves into a loose, quasi-military organization under the name of "Sons of Liberty," a phrase which, ironically, Ingersoll himself had transmitted to the colony in reporting a speech of Isaac Barré.[12] Before the summer was out it was said that the resisters, centered in the eastern counties, were ten thousand strong.

The direct attack on Ingersoll started in the newspapers, where Professor Naphtali Daggett of Yale College, an old enemy of Ingersoll's, branded him a "vile miscreant" who had sold out his country for £300 a year and who would be led on "to every cruel and oppressive measure" by the same "rapacious and base spirit" that had prompted him to accept the post of stamp collector. More of the same followed from other pens, and replies were published by Ingersoll's friends. By mid-August threats of physical punishment to supporters of the Stamp Act were appearing in print, and then, on August 21 and 22, Ingersoll was burned in effigy in Norwich and New London.

The ceremony in New London, of which the speech that appears as the present pamphlet claims to have been a part, was particularly elaborate.

On Thursday, the 22d instant, at 6 o'clock P.M. was exhibited on a gallows erected for that purpose, in the most public part of the town, the effigy of a person sustaining the office of distributor of stamps, with a boot [Bute] placed a little back of his right shoulder, wherein was concealed a young imp of the d——l peeping out of the same in order to whisper in his ear. On the breast of the effigy was a Stamp Act, under was an inscription in praise of liberty. In this posture the effigy continued about an hour; it was then taken down and, the inhabitants and others increasing, it was placed on a pole, and in that manner carried through the main street attended by people of all professions and denominations and accompanied with various kinds of music, guns, drums, etc., and incessant acclamations of the multitude, the number far exceeding whatever has been known to assemble in this place on any occasion, an evident demonstration of their thirst for LIBERTY and detestation of STAMP ACTS. After finishing their route through the town and arriving at the place of assignation, a halter was placed around the neck of the effigy, which was again suspended in the air on a gallows, and, a bonfire being erected under it, the same was consumed. During this exhibition the guns on the battery were repeatedly discharged, and even the children crying "THENCE HANGS A TRAITOR, THERE'S AN ENEMY TO HIS COUNTRY," etc., after which the mobility, gentry, etc., dispersed to different taverns, and after some drinking some loyal toasts, the whole was concluded with the greatest decorum.[13]

Ingersoll's fate as stamp master, clearly forecast by that of Andrew Oliver, moved steadily to its conclusion. In the days that followed, effigies were burned in the eastern towns of Windham, Lebanon, and Lyme, and in West Haven; but Ingersoll clung stubbornly to his office even in the face of crowds gathered to intimidate him directly. Finally in mid-September bands gathered in the eastern towns to force the issue. Marching west, they caught up with Ingersoll in Wethersfield as he rode northward to the special session of the Assembly convening in Hartford. Surrounded by leading Sons of Liberty, and after extended discussions and attempted negotiations, Ingersoll submitted to the inevitable, resigned his office and swore never to execute the duties connected with it.[14]

By then the movement of intimidation had swept across the entire seaboard coast of British North America. Between August 22, when Ingersoll was burned in effigy in New London, and September 18, when he resigned his office, scenes similar to those that had taken place in Boston and New London were enacted in New York, Rhode Island, Maryland, New Jersey, New Hampshire, and Pennsylvania; and they would appear also in the other colonies shortly thereafter. By November 1, when the Stamp Act was to have gone into effect, the actions of mobs that had gathered in all the colonies had made clear that enforcement was an impossibility.[15] Force had been introduced into the Revolutionary movement in a form long familiar but now newly empowered by widely shared principles and beliefs. It would never thereafter be absent.

Liberty and Property Vindicated and the St—pm—n Burnt, published first in Connecticut and then reprinted in Boston, is a quasi-ironic oration in the form of a sermon for the times on a text of Exodus concerning sacrifices to false gods, and it presents its readers with an explicit analogy between Biblical and current events: Pitt is like Moses; Bute, Aaron; Ingersoll, "the molten calf made by Aaron of old in the wilderness." Its authorship has never been definitely established, but its literary character supports the traditional attribution to Benjamin Church. For while its central theme is serious and its Biblicism authentic to the culture, its language is ironic in just the way that clever litterateur would have wanted it to be. It purports to have been delivered as a speech from Ingersoll's "gallows" in New London on August 22, but there is no evidence that in fact it was, or, indeed, that Church was even in Connecticut at the time. It is more likely that Church, reading in Boston the newspaper accounts of the Connecticut riots[16] and knowing Ingersoll from his days in London, seized the opportunity both gently to mock the Biblical pedanticism of rural New England and, parsonlike, to "improve" the occasion politically by publishing this pamphlet. If so, it was his greatest literary success, for despite its exaggeration of the genre and its strained plays on words ("a-try . . . tried," p. 13; "mauger . . . soup-mauger," pp. 9, 12), it appears to have been taken with full seriousness.

Thus ambiguous in its meaning, the piece is characteristic not only of Church's writing but of his career. Physician and politician as well as litterateur, he was born in Newport, Rhode Island, in 1734 but grew up in Boston where his father was the public auctioneer. Famous among Harvard undergraduates for his witty verse, he began publishing his writing in 1757 with *The Choice,* an imitation of a poem by the Englishman John Pomfret judged in modern criticism to be more advanced in technique if more traditional in content than its model.[17] Settled in Boston after two years of study in England, where in all probability he came in contact with Jared Ingersoll, then agent for Connecticut, Church in the years that followed the publication of *Liberty and Property Vindicated* became one of the radical leaders. He contributed to the *Boston Gazette,* was active in both the Masonic Lodge and the Boston Town Meeting, corresponded with Wilkes, and wrote verses and songs for the Sons of Liberty. In *The Times,* a 311-line poem published in 1765, he assaulted Governor Francis Bernard, and also, once again, "J—— Ing——l," whose infamy he explained in prose in a footnote. Four years later he returned to the same theme in the 27-stanza *Address to a Provincial Bashaw. O Shame! Where is thy Blush? . . . (Printed in the Tyrannic Administration of St. Francisco).*[18] But his opposition to the administration began to waver in the early 1770's, and though he remained in close contact with the Sons of Liberty, and in 1773 delivered a fiery Massacre Day Oration, he finally turned traitor to the Revolutionary movement, selling to the British information gained in the councils of the Revolutionary leaders. His treachery was discovered in 1775, and he was imprisoned for over two years. Released in an exchange of prisoners in January 1778, he died in the shipwreck of the vessel taking him to exile in England.

Liberty and Property vindicated, and/the St--pm-n *burnt./*A*/DISCOURSE/*Occasionally Made/On burning the *Effige* of the/ST–PM-N./in/*NEW-LONDON,/*
In the Colony of/*CONNECTICUT./*By a Friend to the Liberty of his Country./

BOSTON: Re-printed and Sold at the Newest/Printing-Office in Milk-Street.
1765./

The Epistle Dedicatory,

*To the honorable gentlemen who are
about to pay the* St—pm–n *a visit,
in defense of liberty and property.*

May it please Your Honors,

THIS great work requires the joint assistance of many hands, and calls aloud for the concurrence of every Christian; and all who bear that honorable title may be assistant therein one way or the other, whether it be by their advice, their prayers, or their purse. But to promote the same in the most expeditious manner it is wished that such a glorious undertaking were made a general concern, and a proper fund raised by subscription for defraying the charges arising upon the emergency, which remains to be done. I being fully sensible of the merit of your cause heartily wish you success in your undertakings; at the same time beg leave to advise you that the following DISCOURSE is humbly dedicated to Your Honors by,

Your Honors' most humble and devoted servant,

Elizaphan of *Parnach,*
of *Zebulun's* Tribe.[1]

Liberty and Property *Vindicated,* and the St–pm-n *Burnt*

Introduction; or, the Preface

Give audience, all ye people; hear my words, O ye wise men; give ear unto me, ye that have knowledge; for the ear trieth words as the mouth tasteth meat. Hear me therefore, O ye mothers in Israel, and children, and depart not from the words of my mouth.

Suffer me a little and I will show you that I have yet to speak in behalf of God and my country.

But first I have an apology to make to the reverend doctors of divinity and others who may dispute my authority to undertake a matter of such immense importance, being one of Zebulun, or of the seafaring tribe, whose calling is upon the mighty waters quite remote from the royal priesthood.

To such I answer with the language of Elihu the son of Barachel the Buzite when he waited for an answer from riper age to reprove Job: I thought days should speak and multitude of years teach wisdom; but when I had waited they spake not, but stood still, and answered no more. Then I thought I would answer my part by [4] my showing my opinion; for I am full of matter, and the spirit within me constraineth me to show my opinion, morally, as I am no doctor of divinity; yet am I a dear lover of morality in its clearest shining light, being destitute of which, no man can make any pretensions to that which is divine. And without intruding upon gentlemen of that holy order, I shall proceed to speak to the words selected out of sacred history for our present entertainment, which you may find written:

EXODUS chap. xxxii, 7th and 8th verses.

And the Lord said unto Moses, get thee down, for the people which thou broughtest out of the land of Egypt have corrupted themselves; they have turned aside quickly out of the way which I commanded them, they have made a molten calf, and have worshiped it, and sacrificed thereunto, and said, these be thy Gods, O Israel, which have brought thee up and out of the land of Egypt.

IN SPEAKING unto which words I shall inquire into and explain the words of the text in regard to primitive times, and compare the times present with them, to see how nearly they agree in regard to moral conduct, and draw a few inferences from both, and apply them to your serious consideration; and conclude with a word or two of advice to all concerned in affairs of immense importance. And,

First. My brethren, it would be tautology in me to rehearse the history of the patriarch Moses to you, knowing you, or most of you, to be the children of pious parents, well educated and brought up in the fear of the Lord, as I look upon none of you to be ignorant of the birth, child-hood, and education of him; you have read and your parents have told you the many wonders wrought by Moses in [5] bringing his brethren out of the land of Egypt and out of the house of bondage (he being endowed with a strong and sincere regard for the Israelites and pity for all under that heavy yoke), how that in honor, truth, and fidelity he led his countrymen until he came to Mount Sinai, where he was called of God up into the mount, and commenced lawgiver from the King of Kings; and as this is the highest pitch of honor that can be conferred upon man, I shall omit saying any more of the patriarch Moses but in-quire into what happened in his absence from the people.

Moses, in his absence, left the care of the people to Aaron, for their guide. The poor people, missing their first leader, little thought he was gone their prime minister to the King of Kings and was consulting for their everlasting welfare. Being ignorant of this, they asked Aaron to make them gods to go before them, for they didn't know what became of the man that brought them out of the land of Egypt.

Aaron being fond of government and not having the fear of God be-fore his eyes, he yielded to the people's request, made a calf, worshiped and sacrificed thereunto; which is the corruption spoken of in my text, which kindled the anger of the Lord to speak unto Moses in the manner he did when in the mount, saying, Get thee down, etc., as in the text.

My brethren, having found the author and finisher of the calf, let us inquire into the manner of their worshiping and sacrificing thereunto; in regard to which I don't conceive that they had any set modes of worship as at this day, for being left of [6] God's teacher they fell into all manner of error and confusion, singing and dancing round their molten calf or calves (Indianlike) proclaiming, *These be thy gods, O Israel.* This was the noise which Joshua heard, coming with Moses out of the mount, he said, *It is not the voice of them which shout for mastery, neither is it the voice of them that cry for being overcome, but the noise of them that sing, do I hear.* This was their way of worship, and their sacrifice was much worse.

Every man broke off the golden earrings which were in their own or their wives' and children's ears, and brought them unto Aaron, and Aaron received them at their hands, and fashioned it with a graving tool; and after he had finished the calf, he built an altar and proclaimed a feast to the Lord, and the people brought burnt offerings and peace offerings, sat down to eat and drink, and arose up to play. Thus they went on until Aaron had stripped them of everything valuable, and made them naked to their shame among their enemies. But Moses drew near unto the camp, saw their unwarrantable proceedings; he saw the calf and the dancing, and his anger waxed hot; and he took the calf which they had made, and burnt it in the fire (perhaps a sacred bonfire which they were dancing round, ready made, as I don't read that Moses kindled a fire for that purpose); and when he had burnt the calf, he ground it to powder, and strowed it upon the water. Our text informs us that this corruption happened suddenly and contrary to God's command, which caused many plagues to fall upon the people (which I shall not take notice of at present, as time would fail me). Therefore I must hasten to compare the times present with the former. And,

[7] First. Can we find a Moses in this evil day which we live in? I answer, an equal to Moses upon all accounts is not to be found on earth, but yet we may find a man of a true patriarch spirit who may resemble him in many things. And I think we may dare nominate Secretary PITT to be our Moses, every way qualified, morally, as Moses was, to lead a people, being endowed with honor, love, truth, and fidelity; and in knowledge of things appertaining to this day Pitt must exceed Moses (as Moses is not, neither doth any man know of his sepulcher to this day).

However, Pitt was our prime minister, under whose ministry we flourished; he was the planner of every operation in time of war which proved successful to us in these American wilds. When he was at the helm, our country-ship was steered, the hearts of the people were made glad, and rejoiced in songs of victory and triumph over their barbarous and savage enemies, the Indians, and their associates, the French natives of Canada and the borders adjacent. By the blessing of God and Pitt's superior knowledge and prudent management of affairs in America, the howling wilderness was stopped in immense silence, and a period was put to the most inhuman massacres, which was so frequently heard of amongst us.

Thus the dark, gloomy, melancholy scenes were over, and everything seemed to appear with a smiling aspect in all quarters of the world, as well as in North America. Thus Secretary PITT, taking Moses of old for his example, conducted gloriously, which will redound to his honor in ages to come. — But O, poor Americans, thy friend, being fatigued with the noise of a corrupt set of [8] people, left the helm to the steerage of E——l B——e,[2] who is an emblem of the primitive Aaron, leading the people into all manner of corruption, as I shall endeavor to demonstrate by what happened soon afterwards: for as Aaron led the people into corruption soon after Moses went into the mount, so B——e is said to lead the people into mischief soon after Pitt leaves the helm, by his bad steerage, etc.

No sooner B——e takes hold of the helm but there is a wide difference in government, every action which should tend to promote the freedom of Britons is most notoriously made use of to enslave and plague them.

What happens to us in this day may be said to be worse than Egyptian bondage, for the Hebrews had nothing to subsist upon of their own while in bondage, and therefore could expect nothing but to labor hard for a livelihood; but with us, my brethren, it is not so, for we had won by conquest and had great things in possession. But alas! what we seemed to have is taken away from us, and gave to the enemies of Britain — all the conquest and victories gained in the West Indies, which were of an immense value, together with the free cod fishery (which was of as much or more consequence to them than their Romish creed, for without fish they could not perform the articles of their belief); all this and more, given up to the nations which waged war against us, in a time when we were under no obligations to make peace with [them] on any terms, much less insignificant ones.[3]

I say, given up without any valuable consideration, for mere nothing that I can suggest, but only to have it said by our enemies that slavery becomes [9] Britons more than the enemies to Briton. (Who it was that so craftily befriended the Romish establishment it's hard for anyone to say; but I am well assured that Secretary Pitt had but little or no hand in it.) Suffer me to tell you that the whole western world feels the effects of the mauger terms of peace; I call them mauger because we are like to be starved and cut short of allowance by the means. — See, imposition upon imposition is crowded upon us; and to crown all corruption, the ST—PM—N is coming upon us, who is an emblem of the molten calf made by Aaron of old in the wilderness. See the manner of his coming and the errand come upon, and you will join with me in sentiments that he is the beast spoken of in my text, and whosoever worships or sacrifices unto him will be brought to nakedness and shame as the Hebrews was of old.

The critics will perhaps query how a man can be an emblem of a beast. To such I answer that I don't mean in bodily shape, but he may be said to be like unto a beast by having a beastly disposition, as indecency, ingratitude, etc., is said to be brutish (in man): and we read "that man in honor abiding not is like the beast that perish." [4] If this be true, this very identical St—pm–n was chosen repre——tive to this colony, he was honored and preferred before any of his function, he was sent upon an important errand to England; his grand design and business was to present the colony's humble thanks to the King and Parliament, etc., of Great Britain for their paternal care over us in the late war and thankfully to acknowledge every instance of favor received from them by the colony, also to represent the true state of the constitution of the government, and to make known the [10] extreme poverty which we were reduced to by the calamities of a long war, and our inability of making a meet restitution for their goodness at present (any more than as dutiful subjects ought, so do we possess hearts full of gratitude).

He also was to pray for the continuation of our rights and liberties as at the first and for the security of our properties as at the beginning without the least encroachment on our charter. But, my brethren, upon his arrival in Europe he inhumanly forgot the place of his nativity, and (as it is said) most ungratefully betrayed the liberty of his country; and for the sake of a post in the government of no great value, he commenced executioner to the death warrant of it. As Eliphaz said to Job, "Should a wise man utter vain knowledge and fill his belly with the east wind?" [5]

Surely, my brethren, the ear of that eastern world had a great effect upon him, his belly being filled with the east wind, puffed him up with pride and arrogancy, that he thought himself and countrymen rich as Caesar, forgetting the important errand of the government's humble address, uttering swelling words of vain knowledge when in company with the B—tified gentry, saying that the colony was able to bear taxation, etc., joined with them in killing his country, and commenced executioner himself, to serve his countrymen, as he says (but as executioner, you must mind). O country kill country, O calf, beast, and antidote against liberty. For it is not possible that he can be the man which was chosen to represent our cause and plead for our freedom; but thou art the beast that is returned with a yoke of bondage to put upon our necks, saying we are able to bear all this [11] and more, uttering swelling words of vain knowledge, by misrepresentations and wrong calculations filling our papers full of the confusion and noise of the brute.

Instead of coming home with answers of peace, lenity, and good will towards us, he comes inhumanly with a variety of st—p duties and very deeply ladened with impositions upon us, proclaiming sacrifice, sacrifice unto me according to the decree passed, bring your silver and your gold (for I know not the paper money of your colony); if you are destitute of hard money, you must bring the extravagancy of your colony. O daughters of Connecticut, you must sacrifice your gold beads, jewels, earrings, etc., until you are made bare and naked to your shame (for the beast's sake), for the calf or st—pm–n will make sterling of all.

O *Connecticut, Connecticut!* where is your charter boasted of for ages past; if the beast is worshiped your charter is void and the government put upon the beast's shoulder, who is an ill-bred beast, nursed and brought up to devour you; which must be acknowledged by every friend to liberty and property.

By comparing I find the times present to be in some measure parallel with the former; if there is any difference it is against us, we being more imposed upon than our fathers.

I must proceed to draw a few inferences from what has been said.

[12] First. From what we have heard we may learn the human frailty of man, and when I am exclaiming against others I do not excuse myself, for I am subject to many; we not only learn the human frailty of man, but also the folly of laying too much stress or dependence on his conduct. Applied to this colony, hath it not been the case in regard to the st—pm–n? I hope not entirely so. If it hath been the case, I don't wonder that he proves a curse to us rather than a blessing. For it is writ-

ten, "cursed is man that trusteth in man, and that maketh flesh his arm." [6] But lest I should go beyond my sphere I must stick to morality.   And,

Secondly. We may learn from the train of impositions received from the mother country the folly in glorying in the roast beef of Old England, since we are so notoriously flogged with the spit. A little soup-mauger with contentment is preferable to roast beef and plum pudding, since we are like to pay so dear for the roast.

For being called Englishmen without having the privileges of Englishmen is like unto a man in a gibbet with dainties set before him which would refresh him and satisfy his craving appetite if he could come at them, but being debarred of that privilege, they only serve for an aggravation to his hunger.

O my poor brethren in the gibbet of America that cannot come at the dainties of Europe, I pity you with all my heart and soul.

Thirdly. Have we learned that corruption is at the helm and that our country-ship is badly steered? This also teaches us that the watch must be called, and the helm relieved by a better man.

[13] O PITT, is your watch upon deck? Turn out, take the helm from B——e, for he hath nigh overset us at times; he hath carried such taut sails in the squalls of impositions that our sails are wore threadbare. See the hurricane of stamp duties coming on, shorten sail timely, down with topgallant mast, yards, and sails of pride and vainglory, in with all small kites, and see everything snug to stand the storm like a bold seaman; bend new courses to the yards, and for God's sake don't lay [us] a-try, for we have been tried sufficiently. If the gale comes on very hard, put before the wind for the safety of the ship and our lives. Scud her manfully until the pernicious gale is over and the mountainous sea of corruption is ran down or is broken to pieces by a gentle breeze of liberty arising to refresh our wearied souls, which have been so long fatigued with the thoughts of approaching slavery.

Fourthly. Have we found a calf to be sacrificed to in this our day? Let us all, every living soul here present, or that lives within the precinct or of hearing the noise of the beast, take example by that worthy patriarch Moses of old and make a sacrifice of the calf, rather than to sacrifice thereunto. Burn it in the fire, grind it to powder, and strow it upon the ocean, that the filthy naughtiness of the beast may be cleansed from the earth, and that our plagues and impositions may not be made wonderful.

Time would fail me to tell you of Shadrach, Meshach, and Abednego in the fiery furnace, Daniel in the lion's den, and many other worthies who have been faithful in bearing testimony against unjust decrees, etc., and have been protected by Heaven in it, their cause being just in the sight of [14] God. For woe unto them that decree unrighteous decrees. My brethren, fear not the face of man in regard to justice and equity; keep the truth of your side, let the world do what they will. I speak freely unto you all, for I am not afraid; if I lose my head, I cannot lose my gown or cassock.

A word or two of advice to all concerned in this affair of grand importance, and I have done.

First of all, my brethren, my advice to you is to fear God above all things, honor and love the King and his friends, detest and loathe his enemies, especially his private ones. If you see or hear of any corruption in his ministry, bear testimony against it; for it is treason in subjects for to keep silent when they see their prince dishonored; and if by wrong representations of any corrupt person or persons his subjects become grieved, impoverished, or cut short of their liberty or privileges, let such subjects make known their grievance that they may be relieved, for whatsoever tends to the poverty of the subjects by means of the enemies to freedom is a disgrace to a monarch. For poor subjects cannot make a rich King.

O freemen of the colony of Conneticut! stand fast in the liberties granted you by your royal charter. Plead the injustice of any that means to infringe upon you by curtailing the rights and privileges once given you freely without any design to take them from you again (without [them] your conduct could be deemed rebellious); and my opinion is that it cannot be counted rebelling for the freemen of this colony to stand for their absolute rights and defend them, as a man would his own house when insulted, for I see no [15] difference in regard to the possession of either, whether it be by deed of gift or deed of sale.

Therefore, if any man in this colony hath for the sake of filthy lucre misrepresented matters so that ye are grieved or are like to be cut short of the privileges enjoyed for many years past, go, one and all, go to such a man and make him sensible of his error; if he will be convinced of his folly, forgive him, but if he willfully persists in his wickedness, use him in such a manner that he will be glad to conform to the truth; and if he is in any post that unjustly grinds the face of the poor or that contributes to your slavery, ask him peaceably to resign it, and if he refuses to, use him in such a manner that he will be glad to do anything for a quiet life. For Britons never must be slaves. And as we read, that "he which, being often reproved, hardeneth his neck shall suddenly be destroyed, and that without remedy." Therefore, take care of Mr. St—pm–n, alias the molten calf.   AMEN.

A few verses on the occasion, to the former Minister PITT

For Americans' relief, appear kind Mister PITT,
Who eat nought of your beef, though flogged with the spit;
Intercept that old t——f the Sc—m—n's fav'rite toast,
That feasteth on the beef, and do not pay the roast:
Pray take wit in thy wrath, when met for our relief;
Sc—m—n, you know, love broth, pray let us taste the beef.

To the KING

Long live great GEORGE our King, in peace and harmony,
Of his fame we will sing, if we have liberty;
But if cut short of that, we cannot raise our voice,
For hearts full of regret sure never can rejoice.

PAMPHLET 13

DANIEL DULANY, *CONSIDERATIONS ON THE PROPRIETY OF IMPOSING TAXES IN THE BRITISH COLONIES*

ANNAPOLIS, 1765

INTRODUCTION

For the modern reader there is little on the surface of Daniel Dulany's *Considerations* of 1765 to account for its contemporary fame. It has none of the rhetorical brilliance of Dickinson's writing, none of the wild power of Otis', none of the elegance of Jefferson's or the vividness of John Adams'. It is, in fact, for all its fame and for all the praise that has been heaped on it, a poorly written piece, full of clumsy sentences weighted to the point of collapse by chains of modifying clauses and parenthetical exclamations, and marred by such infelicities as "inerrability," "conjunctly," and "subdolous," and by such archaisms as "under favor" used in the sense of "by your leave." The pamphlet is, in addition, difficult at times to follow both because the over-all structure of the essay, once the central issue is disposed of, is vague, and because, though there are verbose digressions, important arguments are presented with the parsimony of a lawyer's brief. Yet the pamphlet went through five editions in the colonies within three months of its initial appearance, and it was reprinted in London twice within a year as a separate pamphlet and three times in collections of writings on American affairs.[1] The colonists universally paid tribute to it: even Dulany's bitterest enemies praised it; and it played a significant role in the debate in Parliament on the repeal of the Stamp Act. Pitt did it "much honor" in the Commons, citing it "as a textbook of American rights," and Camden praised it in the Lords.[2]

The fame of Dulany's pamphlet resulted from its strategic role in the debate on constitutional principles that sprang up after the receipt and absorption in England of the American writings of 1764 and after publicists like Franklin had begun placing in English newspapers pieces justifying American resistance.[3] In the spring and summer of 1765, while opposition to the enforcement of the Stamp Act was building up in the colonies, the colonial arguments were countered by a number of skillfully written rebuttals published in England by leading apologists for colonial taxation. These writers, publicists and belleletrists who were also authorities on colonial affairs, were formidable controversialists. Their pamphlets, which elicited Dulany's, did much to refine the intellectual problems created by the new regulations.

Thomas Pownall was almost accidentally one of the group. A prolific pamphleteer with a particular interest in political and constitutional theory, he had been associated with colonial affairs for twenty years before the passage of the Stamp Act. In the 1750's he had occupied a number of important official positions in the colonies, including the governorship of Massachusetts. His *Administration of the Colonies,* published anonymously in 1764, was an ambitious work which he wrote not as an apology for the Grenville administration but in response to the "general idea of some revolution of events beyond the ordinary course of things, some general apprehension of something new arising in the world . . . some new crisis forming." His aim was to urge in sweeping terms the creation of "a grand marine dominion . . . of which Great Britain should be the commercial center, to which it should be the spring of power"; and he argued at length for the recasting, the consolidation and rationalization, of the entire colonial administration and for the formal promulgation of the rights, privileges, and responsibilities of the several parts that composed the empire. Sympathetic to the aspirations of the colonists and convinced of England's natural economic superiority in a world of free trade, he included among his proposals a plan for the general revision and relaxation of the navigation laws. But though he had not written the book to defend the administration, he was inevitably drawn into commenting on the new measures. In the spring of 1765 he published a second edition of the work, the title page of which bore his name and a rather overblown list of the colonial offices he had held. It was dedicated to George Grenville, and it elaborated the idea that though the colonial governments should have "full, free, uncontrolled, independent power in the act of legislation," it was necessary to establish "the subordination and dependence of the colony governments on the government of the mother country." He stated flatly that he had always believed that the "supreme legislature of Great Britain" was "the true and perfect representative" not only of Great Britain but of "its dependencies" as well, and that the colonies were in no way exempted "from being subject and liable to be taxed by Parliament." He specified "imposts, excise, or a stamp duty" as proper forms of Parliamentary taxation, explaining that they were "coincident with those regulations which the laws of the realm prescribe to trade in general . . . [and] because they are duties which arise from the general rights and jurisdiction of the realm rather than from the particular concerns of any one colony." [4]

Soame Jenyns, M.P. 1741–1780, client of the powerful Yorke, or Hardwicke, interest — politician, poet, and skilled pamphleteer (his prose style was considered to be a model of ease and elegance; even Dulany was obliged to recognize it) — had been a member of the Board of Trade for a decade before the Stamp Act controversy, and he too was familiar with the problems of colonial administration. While Pownall was making the revisions for the second edition of his book, Jenyns was writing what proved to be a deft and, to the colonists, a particularly annoying little pamphlet. Entitled *The Objections to the Taxation of Our American Colonies . . . Considered,* it appeared in London also in the spring of 1765, and was almost immediately reprinted in colonial newspapers and otherwise distributed in the colonies. Jenyns dealt directly with "the great capital argument" of consent as a justification for taxation — an argument, he wrote, "which, like an elephant at the head of a nabob's army, being once overthrown, must put the whole into confusion."

Enumerating and then eliminating in turn the logical possibilities of the meaning of this notion, he arrived quickly at the heart of the problem. In England, he wrote,

> Copyholders, leaseholders, and all men possessed of personal property only choose no representatives; Manchester, Birmingham, and many more of our richest and most flourishing trading towns send no members to Parliament, consequently cannot consent by their representatives because they choose none to represent them; yet are they not Englishmen? Or are they not taxed? . . . Why does not this imaginary representation extend to America as well as over the whole island of Great Britain? If it can travel three hundred miles why not three thousand? If it can jump rivers and mountains, why cannot it sail over the ocean? If the towns of Manchester and Birmingham sending no representatives to Parliament are notwithstanding there represented, why are not the cities of Albany and Boston equally represented in that assembly?

As to the suggestion that the colonies be permitted to elect their own representatives to Parliament, "the sudden importation," he wrote, of "so much eloquence at once would greatly endanger the safety and government of this country . . . It will be much cheaper for us to pay their army than their orators." [5]

Thomas Whately was less of a wit than Jenyns, but, as his books on gardening and on Shakespeare indicate, he was equally at home in belles-lettres, and he was an even more formidable pamphleteer on colonial questions. For he was the best informed person in England on the intricacies of the laws and regulations governing the colonies. The friend and correspondent of many prominent colonists, he had risen to prominence with Grenville; as Grenville's private secretary and then as secretary to the treasury he had been the chief draftsman of the Stamp Act. Criticism of that statute and of the Sugar Act of 1764 was, consequently, a personal as well as an official matter for him. His 114-page essay, *The Regulations Lately Made Concerning the Colonies and the Taxes Imposed upon Them, Considered,* published in 1765, was a comprehensive justification of the colonial system in general and of the new revenue and administrative measures in particular. Methodical, thorough, and clear throughout, the pamphlet took up in turn the main regulations "made in the different departments of our legislative or executive government . . . scattered through proclamations, statutes, and orders." The principal subjects which he dealt with were the government's land policy in the newly acquired territories, its management of the fur trade, the Currency Act of 1764, and, in great detail, the reasons for the many new duties and controls laid down in the Sugar Act of 1764. He did not reach the question of the Stamp Act until the last few pages, but what he said there set the terms of discussion firmly. Stamp duties, he wrote, were "the easiest, the most equal, and the most certain" of all taxes that could be devised, and "the right of the mother country to impose such a duty . . . cannot be questioned." For the power to tax was inherent in any full legislative body. Tax measures were not different from other species of legislation; they were in no way different from duties imposed on the shipping and purchasing of goods. "The constitution . . .

knows no distinction between impost duties and internal taxation." Efforts by
the colonists to establish such a distinction must inevitably founder on their
long-standing acceptance of internal taxes in the form of postal fees which
had long ago been imposed for the stated purpose of raising a revenue. Not
that taxation required precedents for its justification. Parliament's right to
tax the colonies rested squarely on "the principles of our constitution." The
fact is, Whately wrote,

> that the colonies are represented in Parliament: they do not indeed choose
> members of that assembly; neither are nine tenths of the people of Britain
> electors; for the right of election is annexed to certain species of property,
> to peculiar franchises, and to inhabitancy in certain places.

And he proceeded to list the categories of people and properties denied the
franchise in England: all property not freehold, all monied property, women
and children, the merchants of London, the inhabitants of Leeds, Halifax,
Birmingham, and Manchester, and the East India Company "whose rights
over the countries they possess fall little short of sovereignty." All British
subjects were in the same situation: "none are actually, all are virtually represented in Parliament; for every member of Parliament sits in the House not
as representative of his own constituents but as one of that august assembly by
which all the commons of Great Britain are represented." The fact that the
colonies have their own Assemblies did not affect the situation: the city of
London too had an assembly in its Common Council, but it had no claim
thereby to exemption from Parliamentary taxes. And in any case, why should
anyone want to be exempted from Parliament's authority? From it flowed
the privileges as well as the burdens of Britons: "to deny the authority of a
legislature is to surrender all claims to a share in its councils." [6]

William Knox was less of a public figure than Whately in 1765 — though
later the two men would serve together at the same high level of the under-
secretaryship of state.[7] Like Pownall and Jenyns, Knox had begun his official
career in association with the work of the Board of Trade and under the
patronage of Lord Halifax. In 1757, when Pownall had received the governorship of Massachusetts, Knox had gone to Georgia as provost marshal and
member of the Governor's Council. He too returned in 1761, as agent for
Georgia, and became available, like so many other ex-colonial officials, for
consultation on American affairs. In 1764 he had submitted to the government
a comprehensive scheme of his own for taxing the colonies, and he had been
instrumental in formulating the principle of the Currency Act. In 1765 he
contributed two pamphlets to the bibliography of official justifications of the
new colonial policies, for which service, and others, he was soon favored
with Grenville's patronage. One of these pamphlets, *The Claim of the
Colonies to an Exemption from Internal Taxes . . . Examined,* was, like
Pownall's, Jenyn's, and Whately's writings, quickly picked up in the colonies,
reprinted, and widely circulated. In it Knox did not bother to refute the
colonists' claims that they lacked representation in Parliament, for the weakness of that argument, he said, had been "fully shown" in Whately's *Regula-*

tions Lately Made. But he did take up all the other claims that had been mentioned as grounds for exemption from direct taxation: the common law, the colonial charters, the lack of precedents, "impracticality or public inconvenience," and discriminations among types of taxes ("I confess I cannot clearly understand the distinction said to be between an internal and an external tax"). His conclusion was that there were no grounds whatever for resistance to Parliament's authority. Yet Knox's arguments were not all one-sided. He admitted that the situation of the colonists was not identical with that of the nonelectors in England insofar as no member of Parliament would suffer from injuries imposed on the Americans, and he urged that "a peculiar tenderness be observed in laying taxes upon the colonies." [8]

Thus by the late summer of 1765 the colonists were faced with a formidable array of rebuttals to their first, imprecisely focused objections to the new regulations and to the Stamp Act. Their claim that they could not legally be taxed by Parliament because they were not represented there had been denied on the ground that it misconstrued the nature of representation. And the loose notion some had expressed almost indeliberately that it was not revenue collection as such but only "internal taxation" that was denied to Parliament had been hardened from the colonists' vague allowances into an assertion of a firm "distinction" among species of taxes which the English pamphleteers declared to be incomprehensible, or if comprehensible, inadmissible.

It was to these challenges, thrown down by skillful and well-informed writers, that Daniel Dulany rose in his *Considerations on the Propriety of Imposing Taxes in the British Colonies for the Purpose of Raising a Revenue.* There was probably no one in America better equipped to make this response. Then 44 years of age, Dulany was an experienced politician and lawyer. The son of a wealthy, highly literate Maryland official, politician, and lawyer who had himself, years before, written a notable essay on the rights of the colonists,[9] Dulany had received the best education available in the English-speaking world. Tutored at home as a child, he had been sent to Eton; then, at 18, to Clare College, Cambridge, where he remained for three years acquiring, among other things, the "pretty good notion of the law of nature and nations" which his father believed was so valuable for lawyers; and finally to the Inns of Court where he studied for four more years, emerging in 1746 with the distinction, unusual for a colonial, of being called to the bar. Home in Maryland after these many years abroad, he quickly made the most of the opportunities that lay before him in the practice of law, in the development of his family's large agricultural and business interests, and above all in the exploitation of the proprietary government of the colony. In 1765, allied by marriage to one of the most affluent families in Maryland, he was secretary of the colony, commissary general, and a member of the Governor's Council. And he was acknowledged to be "a man of great parts, of general knowledge indisputably the best lawyer on this continent, [and] a very entertaining companion when he pleases." [10]

"When he pleases" was not an idle phrase, for it was also felt that Dulany was "very vain and proud and designing" and as a politician "not . . . over-scrupulous in the measures he takes to answer his ends." In the early 1760's the tendency of his politics was particularly uncertain: both the popular and the gubernatorial-proprietary interests distrusted him. His officemongering, pursued most avidly and successfully during a two-year stay in England, 1761–1763, had aroused suspicions that he was a sycophant of power, interested only in self-aggrandizement. At the same time his support of certain popular measures concerning the use of public funds had led the governor to condemn him as a "patriot councilor, and rather inclined to serve the people than the proprietary." But he had been firm in his objection to the new colonial regulations from the beginning. On strictly economic grounds, he had argued in September 1764, the tax laws and the trade and currency regulations were mistaken policies — which, he added, was not too surprising: "The wisest legislators are often mistaken, [and] the Parliament of England are often, very often, mistaken even when the subject of their deliberations is relative only to the internal police of that kingdom, which, it may be presumed, they have understood as well as the affairs of America." [11] How deep this misunderstanding went, how far beyond mere matters of economic policy, he explained in the present pamphlet, which he wrote in the late summer of 1765 and published in early October.

The burden of the pamphlet and the main source of its contemporary fame and historical importance lies in its refutation of the English theorists' claims that Parliamentary taxation of the colonies was justified by their "virtual" representation in the House of Commons. This claim, Dulany said, "consists of facts not true and of conclusions inadmissible." The disproof he offered was the lack of identity of interests between the nonelectors in America and the members of Parliament who were said to represent them "virtually." The close interdependence between nonelectors in England and their representatives did not exist for the colonists: no member of Parliament would be injured by any injury imposed on the colonies. It was this mutuality of interest that justified virtual representation; and since it did not exist, the whole structure of ideas the English pamphleteers had erected, Dulany wrote, was inapplicable.

Dulany did not restrict himself to this rebuttal, however. Having disposed of the immediate question, he went on to sketch his own understanding of the proper relationship between the colonies and England; and in this enlarged, more highly conceptualized discussion he measurably advanced the Anglo-American debate and pointed to what would become the ultimate issue. The denial of Parliament's power to tax, Dulany explained, did not destroy the constitutional relationship between England and the colonies. It did not eliminate the colonies' subordination to England, for it was not a case of all or nothing. Parliament may still be supreme over the colonies and yet still be restricted in certain of its powers in America. Parliament's supreme power

> may justly be exercised to secure or preserve [the colonies'] dependence whenever necessary for that purpose . . . But though the right of the superior to use the proper means for preserving the subordination of his inferior is ad-

mitted, yet it does not necessarily follow that he has the right to seize the property of his inferior when he pleases or to command him in everything since, in the degrees of it, there may very well exist a *dependence* and *inferiority* without absolute *vassalage* and *slavery.*

The essence of it could be stated simply: "by the powers vested in the inferior is the superior limited"; and it was undeniable that certain powers had been vested in the colonies, if not in explicit grants then by evident implication. Thus, in the immediate issue, the denial of Parliament's power to levy internal taxes on the colonies did not strip from that body all money-raising powers in America since certain of those powers were essential to the definition of England's supremacy. "There is a clear and necessary distinction between an act imposing a tax for *the single purpose of revenue* and those acts which have been made for the regulation of trade and have produced some revenue *in consequence of their effect* and operation as *regulations of trade."* And he ended the pamphlet on the same note: "I acknowledge dependence on Great Britain, but I can perceive a degree of it without slavery, and I disown all other." [12]

There was involved in this proposition a contradiction with one of the most fundamental principles of eighteenth-century political theory: the indivisibility of sovereignty; and there were those who would soon draw out this problem. Otis, in fact, had already touched on it.[13] But Dulany did not recognize the challenge of what he was saying for the underlying notion of sovereignty, or if he did, he did not choose to discuss it. His aim was to create grounds for mediation by expressing in theoretical terms the divisions between the powers of Parliament and those of the colonial Assemblies that had long existed. From this position he never departed, even when the developing logic of the discussion appeared to make it untenable. Deeply committed to the maintenance of the imperial *status quo,* he had no desire to follow the implications of his own arguments if by doing so he would be forced to choose between all or nothing. He continued to argue against any innovations that might disturb "the balance of power in America," and he continued to serve and to profit from the proprietary interest in Maryland.[14] He was not active in opposition to the Townshend Duties, though his earlier advice that the colonies should resist by boycotting English trade was then being followed. In the early 1770's his political position came under active challenge by the younger, more radical leaders in Maryland, of whom Charles Carroll of Carrollton, scion of a leading Catholic family with whom the Dulanys had been feuding for years, was the dominant figure.

In 1773 Dulany and Carroll clashed directly in a bitter controversy over whether the Assembly or the proprietor should control certain fees. The issue was in its origins quite limited, but as the dispute developed in long columns of print in the *Maryland Gazette,* it spilled over into the larger problems of Anglo-American relations, and ended by defining Dulany's political position once and for all. Declaring himself to be a friend of both liberty and government, Dulany said that, though self-proclaimed *"Friends of the Constitution"* brand a person of independent judgment a "court-hireling and sycophant," nevertheless "the blessings of order will still be preferred to the horrors of anarchy," and he heaped scorn on those who "are eternally crying out as if the enemy were in the gate, and scattering distraction and distrust through the community." How could leading English merchants be involved "in a plot against liberty," he asked, "since commerce is ever engrafted on the stock of liberty"? But his opponents (an unidentified "Independent Whig" joined Carroll at one point in the controversy) continued to dwell on "the *latent purposes* of *designing men*"; and, quoting Tacitus (in Gordon's translation) and other classical authors, they argued pointedly that history is only too full of examples of men who "in the gratification of sensual appetites are apt to overlook their future consequences; thus for the present enjoyment of wealth and power, liberty in reversion will be early given up." As the dispute advanced Carroll became more explicit; he pictured Dulany "dismayed, trembling, and aghast, though skulking behind the strong rampart of governor and Council . . . [and entrenched] chin-deep in precedents, fortified with transmarine opinions drawn round about him . . . in due time to be played off, as a masked battery, on the inhabitants of Maryland." Dulany's responses became in turn more shrill; he was ultimately reduced to arguing that his antagonist, as a Catholic, was barred from participation in government "by the laws and constitution of the country" and hence was not entitled to discuss matters of public concern. In the end Dulany was branded a "crafty minister" and an *"enemy to his country"* whose undeniable talents suggest "the idea of a jewel buried in a dunghill." [15]

By 1774 Dulany was completely alienated from the Revolutionary leadership. Continuing to stand on the position he had marked out in his *Considerations* of 1765, he was bypassed in the selection of delegates to the Continental Congress. He flatly declared Congress' effort to mobilize troops to be a mistake.[16] In 1775 he retired to a country estate, and there he remained, a neutral, throughout the war. Reduced in wealth but still affluent, isolated from his family who were almost all loyalists, he lived on until 1797, never recovering his former prominence.

CONSIDERATIONS/ON THE/PROPRIETY/OF IMPOSING/TAXES/IN THE/*Brit-ish* COLONIES,/For the Purpose of raising a REVENUE, by/ACT OF PARLIAMENT./

—— *Haud Totum Verba resignent/Quod latet arcanâ, non enarrabile, fibrâ./*
NORTH-AMERICA: Printed by a NORTH-AMERICAN./MDCCLXV./

PREFACE

It would now be an unfashionable doctrine, whatever the ancient opinion might be, to affirm that the constituent can bind his representative by instructions; but though the obligatory force of these instructions is not insisted upon, yet their persuasive influence in most cases may be, for a representative who should act against the explicit recommendation of his constituents would most deservedly forfeit their regard and all pretension to their future confidence.

When it is under deliberation whether a new law shall be enacted in which the electors of England are interested, THEY *have notice of it and an opportunity of declaring their sense.* THEY *may point out every dangerous tendency, and are not restrained in their representations from showing in the plainest language the injustice or oppression of it.*

When a law in its execution is found to be repugnant to the genius of liberty or productive of hardships or inconvenience, THEY *may also instruct their deputies to exert themselves in procuring a repeal of it, and in the exercise of this right are not constrained to whine in the style of humble petitioners.* THEY *are exposed to no danger in explaining their reasons.* THEIR *situation does not become so delicate as to make it prudent to weaken by not urging them with their full force and to their utmost extent. But who are the representatives of the colonies? To whom shall* THEY *send their instructions when desirous to obtain the repeal of a law striking at the root and foundation of every civil right should such an one take place? Instructions to all the members who compose the House of Commons would not be proper. To them the application must be by petition, in which an unreserved style would probably be* [4] *deemed indecency and strong expressions insolence, in which a claim of rights may not, perhaps, be explained or even insinuated if to impugn or glance at their authority whose relief is supplicated. To soften and deprecate must be the hope and endeavor, though a guiltless freeman would probably be awkward in ringing all the changes of* parce, precor.[1]

Under these cirumstances the liberty of the press is of the most momentous consequence, for if truth is not allowed to speak thence in its genuine language of plainness and simplicity, nor freedom to vindicate

*its privileges with decent firmness, we shall have too much reason to ac-
knowledge his foresight who predicted that "the constitution of the British government was too excellent to be permanent." The train for the
accomplishment of that prophecy hath not yet catched in America, nor,
I trust, been laid.*

*That there have been laws extremely unjust and oppressive, the declara-
tions of subsequent Parliaments fixing this stigma upon them evince; but
whilst the power which introduced them prevailed it was not prudent to
give them their deserved characters. The Parliament of Henry III or that
of Henry VI need not be cited; there are many other instances, though
not branded with epithets so remarkably opprobrious.*

*In the opinion of a great lawyer, an act of Parliament may be void; and
of a great divine, "all men have natural, and freemen legal, rights, which
they may justly maintain, and no legislative authority can deprive them
of."* [2]

*Cases may be imagined in which the truth of these positions might in
theory be admitted; but in practice, unless there should be very peculiar
circumstances, such as can't be supposed to exist during the prevalence
of the power that introduced it, who would rely upon the authority of
opinions or the principles of them for his protection against the penalties
of any positive law?*

*When the judges were asked by Henry VIII whether a man might be
attainted of high treason by Parliament, though not called to answer, they
declared that it was a dangerous question, and gave the evasive answer
that "the High Court of Parliament ought to give examples of justice to
the inferior courts, none of which could do the like."* [3] *But though it
might be dangerous to declare against the authority of Parliament, we
are not bound to acknowledge its inerrability, nor precluded from examining the principles and consequences of laws, or from pointing out their
improprieties and defects. Upon this ground I have proceeded in the
following considerations, and shall not be disappointed if they should
appear to be too free or too reserved to readers of different complexions.*

VIRGINIA , August 12, 1765.

CONSIDERATIONS, &c.

I N THE constitution of England the three principal forms of government, monarchy, aristocracy, and democracy, are blended together in certain proportions; but each of these orders, in the exercise of the legislative authority, hath its peculiar department from which the others are excluded. In this division the *granting of supplies* or *laying taxes* is deemed to be the province of the House of Commons, as the representative of the people. All supplies are supposed to flow from their gift; and the other orders are permitted only to assent or reject generally, not to propose any modification, amendment, or partial alteration of it.

This observation being considered, it will undeniably appear that in framing the late Stamp Act the Commons acted in the character of representative of the colonies. They assumed it as the principle of that measure, and the propriety of it must therefore stand or fall as the principle is true or false, for the preamble sets forth that the Commons of Great Britain had resolved to *give and grant* the several rates and duties imposed by the act. But what right had the Commons of Great Britain to be thus munificent at the expense of the commons of America? To give property not belonging to the giver and without the consent of the owner [6] is such evident and flagrant injustice in *ordinary cases* that few are hardy enough to avow it; and therefore when it really happens, the fact is disguised and varnished over by the most plausible pretenses the ingenuity of the giver can suggest. But it is alleged that there is a *virtual* or *implied representation* of the colonies springing out of the constitution of the British government; and it must be confessed on all hands that as the representation is not actual it is virtual or it doth not exist at all, for no third kind of representation can be imagined. The colonies claim the privilege, which is common to all *British subjects,* of being taxed *only* with their own consent given by their representatives, and all the advocates for the Stamp Act admit this claim. Whether, therefore, upon the whole matter the imposition of the *stamp duties* is a *proper* exercise of constitutional authority or not depends upon the single question, whether the Commons of Great Britain are *virtually* the representatives of the commons of America or not.

The advocates for the Stamp Act admit, in express terms, that "the colonies do not choose members of Parliament," but they assert that "the colonies are *virtually* represented in the same manner with the nonelectors resident in Great Britain."

How have they proved this position? Where have they defined or precisely explained what they mean by the expression *virtual representation?* As it is the very hinge upon which the rectitude of the taxation turns, something more satisfactory than mere assertion, more solid than a form of expression, is necessary. For how can it be seriously expected that men who think themselves injuriously affected in their properties and privileges will be convinced and reconciled by a fanciful phrase the meaning of which can't be precisely ascertained by those who use it or properly applied to the purpose for which it hath been advanced? They argue that "the right of election being annexed to certain species of property, to franchises, and inhabitancy in some particular places, a very small part of the land, the property, and the people of England are comprehended in those descriptions. All landed property not freehold and all monied property are *excluded*. The merchants of London, the proprietors of the public funds, the inhabitants of Leeds, Halifax, Birmingham, and Manchester, and that great corporation of the East India Company, *none of them* choose their representatives, and yet they are all represented in Parliament, and the colonies being *exactly* in *their* situation are represented in the *same* manner." [4]

[7] Now this argument, which is all that their invention hath been able to supply, is totally defective, for it consists of facts not true and of conclusions inadmissible.

It is so far from being true that all the persons enumerated under the character of *nonelectors* are in that predicament that it is indubitably certain there is *no* species of property, landed or monied, which is not possessed by *very many* of the British *electors*.

I shall undertake to disprove the supposed similarity of situation, whence the same kind of representation is deduced of the inhabitants of the colonies and of the British nonelectors; and if I succeed, the notion of a *virtual representation* of the colonies must fail, which in truth is a mere cobweb, spread to catch the unwary and entangle the weak. I would be understood. I am upon a question of *propriety,* not of power; and though some may be inclined to think it is to little purpose to discuss the one when the other is irresistible, yet are they different considerations; and at the same time that I invalidate the claim upon which it is founded

I may very consistently recommend a submission to the law whilst it endures. I shall say nothing of the use I intend by the discussion, for if it should not be perceived by the sequel, there is no use in it, and if it should appear then, it need not be premised.

Lessees for years, copyholders, proprietors of the public funds, inhabitants of Birmingham, Leeds, Halifax, and Manchester, merchants of the city of London, or members of the corporation of the East India Company are *as such* under no personal incapacity to be electors, for they may acquire the right of election; and there are *actually* not only a considerable number of electors in each of the classes of lessees for years, etc., but in many of them, if not all, even members of Parliament. The interests therefore of the nonelectors, the electors, and the representatives are individually the same, to say nothing of the connection among neighbors, friends, and relations. The security of the nonelectors against oppression is that their oppression will fall also upon the electors and the representatives. The one can't be injured and the other indemnified.

Further, if the nonelectors should not be taxed by the British Parliament they would not be taxed *at all;* and it would be iniquitous as well as a solecism in the political system that they should partake of all the benefits resulting from the imposition and application of taxes and derive an immunity from the circumstance of not being qualified to vote. [8] Under this constitution, then, a double or virtual representation may be reasonably supposed. The electors, who are inseparably connected in their interests with the nonelectors, may be justly deemed to be the representatives of the nonelectors at the same time they exercise their personal privilege in their right of election, and the members chosen, therefore, the representatives of both. This is the only rational explanation of the expression *virtual representation*. None has been advanced by the asserters of it, and their meaning can only be inferred from the instances by which they endeavor to elucidate it, and no other meaning can be stated to which the instances apply.

It is an essential principle of the English constitution that the subject shall not be taxed without his consent, which hath not been introduced by any particular law but necessarily results from the nature of that mixed government, for without it the order of democracy could not exist.

Parliaments were not formerly so regular in point of form as they now are.* [5] Even the number of knights for each shire were not ascertained. The first writs now extant for their choice are 22d Edward I, by which two,

* See Treat. Peerage.

as at this day, were directed to be chosen for each county; but the King not being satisfied with that number, other writs were issued for choosing two more. This discretionary power, being thought inconvenient, was afterwards restrained by the statutes of Richard II, Henry IV, and subsequent acts.

In earlier times there was more simplicity in the rules of government, and men were more solicitous about the essentials than the forms of it. When the consent of those who were to perform or pay anything extra-feudal was fairly applied for and obtained, the manner was little regarded. But as the people had reason to be jealous of designs to impose contributions upon them without their consent, it was thought expedient to have formalities regulated and fixed to prevent this injury to their rights, not to destroy a principle without which they could not be said to have any rights at all.

Before the introduction of those formalities, which were framed with a view to restrain the excursions of power and to secure the privileges of the subject, as the mode of proceeding was more simple, so perhaps this foundation of consent was more visible than it is at present, wherefore it [9] may be of use to adduce some instances which directly point out this necessary and essential principle of *British liberty.*

The Lords and Commons have separately given aids and subsidies to the crown. In 13th Edward III, the Lords granted the tenth of all the corn, etc., growing upon their demesnes, the Commons then granting nothing, nor concerning themselves with what the Lords thought fit to grant out of their own estates. At other times the knights of shires, separating from the rest of the Commons and joining with the Lords, have granted a subsidy, and the representatives of cities and boroughs have likewise granted subsidies to the crown separately, as appears by a writ in 24th Edward I which runs in these words: *Rex, etc., cum comites, barones, milites nobis, etc., secerunt undecimam de omnibus bonis suis mobilibus, et cives et burgenses, etc., septimam de omnibus suis mobilibus, etc., nobis curialiter concesserint, etc.*[6] When an affair happened which affected only some individuals and called for an aid to the crown, it was common for those individuals *alone* to be summoned, to which purpose several writs are extant. In 35th Edward III there is a writ (which Dugdale has printed in his collection of writs of summons to Parliament) directed to the Earl of Northampton, which, after reciting the confusion the affairs of Ireland were in and that he and some other English lords had possessions in that kingdom and were therefore more particularly obliged to the defense of it, follows in these words: *Volumus vobiscum, et cum aliis de eodem regno (Angliae scilicet) terras in dicta terra habentibus colloquium habere, etc.*[7]

But that the reader may perceive how strictly the principle of no person's being taxed without their consent hath been regarded, it is proper to take notice that upon the same occasion writs were likewise directed even to women who were proprietors of land in Ireland to send their deputies to consult and consent to what should be judged necessary to be done on the occasion; e.g., *Rex, etc., Mariae, etc., salutem, etc., vobis, etc., mandamus quod aliquem, vel aliquos de quibus confidatis apud Westmon. mittatis ad loquendum nobiscum super dictis negotiis et ad faciendum et consentiendum nomine vestro, super hoc quod ibidem ordinari contigerit.*[8]

A reflection naturally arises from the instances cited. When on a particular occasion *some* individuals *only* were to be taxed, and not the *whole* community, *their* consent *only* was called for, and in the last instance it appears that they who upon an occasion of a general tax would have been bound by the consent of their *virtual representatives* (for in that case they would have had no *actual representatives*) were in an affair calling for a [10] *particular* aid from them *separate* from the rest of the community required to send their *particular deputies*. But how different would be the principle of a statute imposing duties without *their* consent who are to pay them, upon the authority of *their* gift who should undertake to give what doth not belong to them.

That great King Edward I inserted in his writs of summons as a first principle of law that *quod omnes tangat ab omnibus approbetur*,[9] which by no torture can be made to signify that their approbation or consent *only* is to be required in the imposition of a tax who are to pay *no* part of it.

The situation of the nonelectors in England — their capacity to become electors, their inseparable connection with those who are electors and their representatives, their security against oppression resulting from this connection, and the necessity of imagining a double or virtual representation to avoid iniquity and absurdity — have been explained. The inhabitants of the colonies are *as such* incapable of being electors, the privilege of election being exercisable only in person, and therefore if *every* inhabitant of America had the requisite freehold, not *one* could vote but upon the supposition of his ceasing to be an inhabitant of America and becoming a resident of Great Britain, a supposition which would be impertinent because it shifts the question. Should the colonies not be taxed by *Parliamentary impositions,* their respective legislatures have a regular, adequate, and constitutional authority to tax them, and therefore would not necessarily be an iniquitous and absurd exemption from their not being represented by the *House of Commons.*

There is not that intimate and inseparable relation between the *electors* of Great Britain and the *inhabitants of the colonies* which must inevitably involve both in the same taxation; on the contrary, not a single *actual* elector in England might be immediately affected by a taxation in America imposed by a statute which would have a general operation and effect upon the properties of the inhabitants of the colonies. The latter might be oppressed in a thousand shapes without any sympathy or exciting any alarm in the former. Moreover, even acts oppressive and injurious to the colonies in an extreme degree might become popular in England from the promise or expectation that the very measures which depressed the colonies would give ease to the inhabitants of Great Britain. It is indeed true that the interests of England and the colonies are allied, and an injury to the colonies produced into all its consequences will eventually affect the mother country; yet these consequences being generally remote are not [11] at once foreseen. They do not immediately alarm the fears and engage the passions of the English electors, the connection between a freeholder of Great Britain and a British American being deducible only through a train of reasoning which few will take the trouble or can have the opportunity, if they have the capacity, to investigate. Wherefore the relation between the *British Americans* and the *English electors* is a knot too infirm to be relied on as a competent security, especially against the force of a present counteracting expectation of relief.

If it would have been a just conclusion that the *colonies,* being exactly in the *same* situation with the *nonelectors* of England, are *therefore* represented in the same manner, it ought to be allowed that the reasoning is solid which, after having evinced a total *dissimilarity* of situation, infers that their representation is *different.*

If the Commons of Great Britain have no right by the constitution to GIVE AND GRANT property *not* belonging to themselves but to others without their consent actually or virtually given; if the claim of the colonies not to be taxed *without their consent,* signified by their representatives, is well founded; if it appears that the colonies are not actually represented by the Commons of Great Britain and that the notion of a double or virtual representation doth not with any propriety apply to the people of America; then the principle of the Stamp Act must be given up as indefensible on the point of representation, and the validity of it rested upon the *power* which they who framed it have to carry it into execution.

"Should the Parliament devise a tax to be paid only by those of the people in Great Britain who are neither members of either House of Parliament nor their electors, such an act would be unjust and partial," saith the author of *The Claim of the Colonies, etc.,* who yet allows that the "Nonelectors would have a security against the weight of such a tax, should it be imposed, which the colonies have not, viz., that the members of Parliament and the electors must be relatively affected by it; but the industrious North American and the opulent West Indian may have their properties taxed and no individual in Great Britain participate with them in the burden. On the contrary, the members of Parliament would make their court to their constituents most effectually by multiplying taxes upon the subjects of the colonies." [10]

Is it not amazing that the above author, *with these sentiments,* should undertake the defense of the stamp duties, which, by his own concession, [12] appear to be *more* unjust and *more* partial than the tax he supposes and upon which he bestows, very properly, the epithets of *unjust* and *partial*?

> . . . *Diluit helleborum, certo compescere puncto*
> *Nescius examen.*[11]

But it has been objected that if the inhabitants of America, because represented in their respective assemblies, are *therefore* exempted from a *Parliamentary tax,* then the citizens of London, who are represented in their common council, may plead the *same immunity.* If it were not for the authority upon which this objection is urged, it might be safely passed over without a particular answer; but since it hath been introduced with an appearance of reliance, and the opinion which it retails is said to have been delivered with great gravity and pronounced with decisive confidence, I would not be so wanting in respect to an eminent character as to neglect the ceremony of a direct refutation.

But I must observe that when the opinion of a lawyer is taken in a matter of private concern in which he is under no bias to deceive, a concise declaration of it may generally suffice, he who applies for it being generally obliged to depend upon his counsel's character of integrity and knowledge not only because the expense of a methodical and minute discussion would be too burdensome, but because the force of legal reasoning is not generally understood. But in a question of public concernment the opinion of no *court lawyer,* however respectable for his candor and abilities, ought to weigh more than the reasons adduced in support of it. They ought to be explained, they may be examined. Considering his temptations, credit ought to be cautiously and diffidently given to his assertion of what is his opinion. Considering the consequence of a decision, not to one man only but to millions that exist and myriads that may exist, and the exceeding fallibility of legal knowledge, nothing short of clear conviction, after the fullest explication of the reasons of the opinion and the most accurate and intense consideration of their validity, can justify an acquiescence under it.

On the present occasion, so immensely important, *nullius addictus jurare in verba magistri,*[12] I shall pin my faith upon the *dictum* of no lawyer in the universe; and when his *ipse dixit* is authoritatively urged I shall be at no pains to repress my suspicions that his reasons are concealed, because if fairly produced and held up to the light, many flaws in them would be discovered by a careful examiner. I have lived long enough to remember many opinions of *court lawyers* upon American affairs; they have been all [13] strongly marked with the same character; they have been generally very sententious and the same observation may be applied to them all. They have all declared *that* to be *legal* which the minister for the time being has deemed to be *expedient.* The opinion given by a general of the law in the late war on the question whether soldiers might be quartered in private houses in America must be pretty generally remembered. [13]

The very learned gentleman has, it seems, declared that "upon mature deliberation he has formed his opinion that the colonies are in their nature no more than common corporations, and that the inhabitants of a colony are no more entitled to an exemption from Parliamentary taxations because represented in an American assembly than the citizens of London."[14]

This opinion may be incontestably just in the judgment of that accomplished politician and elegant writer who chooses to distinguish himself by the titles of late G—rn—r of the J—rs—ys, of the M—ss—ch—s—ts B——, and of S——th C—r—l—a, and who does not choose to be distinguished by the title of late *Maitre d'Hotel* of the late Sir D—v—s O—b—e, or that exactly fitting and characteristical appellation† conferred

† See the Hist. of TOM BRAZEN.

on him by an incensed culprit in an American court of star chamber, an appellation rather adapted to signify those powers which are useful in intrigue and that lead to promotion than expressive of respect and dignity.[15] But having considered the subject in the best manner my very slender and limited capacity will allow, neither doth the opinion of the one nor the approbation of it by the other influence my judgment.

Let a great man declare a similitude, and he will soon find a Polonius to acknowledge that *"yonder cloud is, by the mass, like a camel indeed,"* — or *"black like an ouzel,"* — or *"very like a whale."* [16]

The objection having been stated, the answer is obvious and clear.

The colonies have a complete and adequate legislative authority, and are not only represented in their Assemblies but in *no other manner.* The power of making bylaws vested in the common council is inadequate and incomplete, being bounded by a few particular subjects; and the common council are actually represented too, by having a choice of members to serve in Parliament. How then can the reason of the exemption from [14] internal Parliamentary taxations claimed by the colonies apply to the citizens of London?

The power described in the provincial charters is to make laws, and in the exercise of that power the colonies are bounded by no other limitations than what result from their subordination to and dependence upon Great Britain. The term *bylaws* is as novel and improper when applied to the *Assemblies* as the expression *acts of Assembly* would be if applied to the *Parliament of Great Britain;* and it is as absurd and insensible to call a colony a common corporation because not an independent kingdom, and the powers of each to make laws and bylaws are limited though not comparable in their extent and the variety of their objects, as it would be to call Lake Erie a *duck puddle* because not the Atlantic Ocean.

Should the analogy between the *colonies* and *corporations* be even admitted for a moment in order to see what would be the consequence of the *postulatum,* it would only amount to this: the *colonies* are vested with as complete authority to all intents and purposes to tax themselves as any English *corporation* is to make a bylaw in any imaginable instance for any local purpose whatever, and the *Parliament* doth not make laws for *corporations* upon subjects in every respect proper for *bylaws.*

But I don't rest the matter upon this or any other circumstance, however considerable, to prove the impropriety of a taxation by the British Parliament. I rely upon the fact that not one inhabitant in any colony is or can be *actually* or *virtually* represented by the British *House of Commons,* and therefore that the stamp duties are severely imposed.

But it has been alleged that if the right to *give and grant* the property of the colonies by an internal taxation is denied by the House of Commons, the subordination or dependence of the colonies and the superintendence of the British Parliament can't be consistently established — that any supposed line of distinction between the two cases is but "a whimsical imagination, a chimerical speculation against fact and experience." Now, under favor, I conceive there is more confidence than solidity in this assertion; and it may be satisfactorily and easily proved that the subordination and dependence of the colonies may be preserved and the *supreme authority* of the mother country be firmly supported, and yet the principle of representation and the right of the British House of Commons flowing from *it* to *give and grant* the property of the commons of America be denied.

[15] The colonies are dependent upon Great Britain, and the supreme authority vested in the King, Lords, and Commons may justly be exercised to secure or preserve their dependence whenever necessary for that purpose. This authority results from and is implied in the idea of the relation subsisting between England and her colonies; for considering the nature of human affections, the inferior is not to be trusted with providing regulations to prevent his rising to an equality with his superior. But though the right of the superior to use the proper means for preserving the subordination of his inferior is admitted, yet it does not necessarily follow that he has a right to seize the property of his inferior when he pleases or to command him in everything since, in the degrees of it, there may very well exist a *dependence* and *inferiority* without absolute *vassalage* and *slavery.* In what the superior may *rightfully* control or compel, and in what the inferior ought to be at liberty to act without control or compulsion, depends upon the nature of the dependence and the degree of the subordination; and these being ascertained, the measure of obedience and submission and the extent of the authority and superintendence will be settled. When powers compatible with the relation between the superior and inferior have by express compact been granted to and accepted by the latter, and have been, after that compact, repeatedly recognized by the former — when they may be exercised effectually upon every occasion without any injury to that relation — the authority of the superior can't properly interpose, for by the powers vested in the inferior is the superior limited.

By their constitutions of government the colonies are empowered to impose internal taxes. This power is compatible with their dependence, and hath been expressly recognized by British ministers and the British Parliament upon many occasions; and it may be exercised effectually without striking at or impeaching in any respect the superintendence of the British Parliament. May not then the line be distinctly and justly drawn between such acts as are necessary or proper for preserving or securing the dependence of the colonies and such as are not necessary or proper for that very important purpose?

When the powers were conferred upon the colonies they were conferred too as privileges and immunities, and accepted as such; or, to speak more properly, the privileges belonging necessarily to them as British subjects were solemnly declared and confirmed by their charters, and they who settled in America under the encouragement and faith of these charters understood not only that they *might* but that it was their *right* to [16] exercise those powers without control or prevention. In some of the charters the distinction is expressed, and the strongest declarations made, and the most solemn assurances given, that the settlers should not have their property taxed without their own consent by their representatives, though their legislative authority is limited at the same time by the subordination implied in their relation, and they are therefore restrained from making acts of Assembly repugnant to the laws of England. And had the distinction not been expressed, the powers given would have implied it, for if the Parliament may in any case interpose when the authority of the colonies is adequate to the occasion and not limited by their subordination to the mother country, it may in every *case,* which would make *another* appellation more proper to describe their condition than the name by which their inhabitants have been usually called and have gloried in.

Because the Parliament may, when the relation between Great Britain and her colonies calls for an extertion of her superintendence, bind the colonies by statute, therefore a Parliamentary interposition in every other instance is justifiable, is an inference that may be denied.

On some emergencies the King, by the constitution, hath an absolute power to provide for the safety of the state, to take care, like a Roman dictator, *ne quid detrimenti capiat respublica,*[17] and this power is not specifically annexed to the monarchy by any express law; it necessarily results from the end and nature of government. But who would infer from this that the King in every instance or upon every occasion can, upon the principles of the constitution, exercise this supreme power?

The British *ministers* have in the most effectual terms, at different periods, from the reign of Charles II to that of the present King, recognized this distinction in their requisitions transmitted to the colonies to raise and levy men and money by acts of Assembly. And recently, in the course of the last war, they were so far from thinking that it was proper for the British *House of Commons* to *give and grant* the property *of the colonies* to support the military operations in America, upon which not only the immediate protection of that part of the British *dominions* but the most important interests, perhaps the ultimate preservation of Great Britain from destruction, essentially depended — I say, on this great occasion of the most important and national concernment, the British *ministers* were so far from calling upon the *House of Commons* in their *peculiar* department to *give and grant* property belonging neither to themselves nor their constituents, that they directly applied to *the colonies* to tax themselves in virtue of the authority and [17] privilege conferred by their charters, and promised to recommend it to the British *Parliament* to reimburse the expense they should incur in providing for the general service. They made good their promise; and if all the money raised in the colonies by acts of Assembly in pursuance of the requisitions of the British ministers hath not been repaid by Parliament, a very considerable part of it hath.[18]

Could they who made the requisitions I have mentioned, or the Assemblies that complied with them, intend or imagine the faith of the English government was to be preserved by a retribution at one time of the money disbursed at the instance and upon the credit of the British *ministry,* enforced and supported by *royal assurances,* and by taking it back again at another time? Is this method of keeping the faith of government to be ranked among the "improvements which have been made beyond the idea of former administrations, conducted by ministers ignorant of the importance of the colonies, or who impotently neglected their concerns or were diverted by mean pursuits from attending to them"? [19] It is absolutely certain that there never can at any future period arise a crisis in which the exertion of the colonies may be necessary; or, if there should, that it will bring with it an oblivion of all former indirection? But this is a subject fitter for silent meditation than public discussion.

There was a time when measures of prevention might have been taken by the colonies. There may be a time when redress may be obtained. Till then, prudence, as well as duty, requires submission.

It is presumed that it was a notable service done by New England when the militia of that colony reduced Cape Breton, since it enabled the British *ministers* to make a peace less disadvantageous and inglorious than they otherwise must have been constrained to submit to in the humble state to which they were then reduced; that the general exertion *of the colonies* in North America during the last war not only facilitated but was indispensably requisite to the success of those operations by which so many glorious conquests were achieved; and that those conquests have put it in the power of the present illustrious ministers to make a peace upon terms of so much glory and advantage as to afford an inexhaustible subject during their administration and the triumph of Toryism, at least, for their ingenious panegyrists to celebrate.

An American, without justly incurring the imputation of ingratitude, may doubt whether some other motive besides pure generosity did not [18] prompt the British *nation* to engage in the defense of the colonies. He may be induced to think that the measures taken for the protection of the plantations were not only connected with the interests but even necessary to the defense of Great Britain herself, because he may have reason to imagine that Great Britain could not long subsist as an independent kingdom after the loss of her colonies. He may, without arrogance, be inclined to claim some merit from the exertion of colonies, since it enabled Great Britain ultimately to defend herself; I mean that kind of merit which arises from benefits done to others by the operation of measures taken for our own sakes — a merit most illustriously displayed in the generosity of Great Britain when, with their co-operation, she protected the colonies to preserve *herself*.

When an house is in flames and the next neighbor is extremely active and exerts his endeavors to extinguish the fire, which if not conquered would catch and consume his own dwelling, I don't say that if the owner of the house which had been in flames should, after the fire subdued, complaisantly thank his neighbor generally for his services, he would be absurdly ceremonious; but if the assistant should afterwards boast of his great generosity and claim a right to the furniture of the house which he had assisted in saving, upon the merit of his zeal and activity, he would deserve to be put in mind of the motive of his service.

If the advantages gained by the late *most glorious and successful war* have been secured by an *adequate peace* — if the successes that attended the military operations of the British arms were the effect of the conjunct efforts of the British *nation* and her *colonies,* roused by the spirit, excited by the virtue, animated by the vigor, and conducted by the wisdom of the ablest minister that ever served his country, has there been no compensation received for the charges of the war? Are the colonies entitled to no credit for it?

When the design is to oppress the colonies with taxes or calumniate the late patriotic minister, the *expenses of the war* and the *enormity* of the *national debt* are proclaimed. When the present all-accomplished administration is to be celebrated, then is the immense value of the new acquisitions dispayed in the brightest colors,

acquisitions vast in extent, richly productive of the valuable commodities belonging to their several climates. The possession of those in North America ensures the safety of the other colonies there insomuch that our only dangerous neighbors, the French, do not think the pittance left worth retaining, having, by the cession of [19] Louisiana to the Spaniards, avowedly given up forever those great objects for which alone they began the war. The ceded islands are almost of equal advantage for protecting our own and annoying the settlements of the French and Spaniards if they should be again our enemies. Part of Nova Scotia since the removal of the neutral French hath been already settled by 10,000 inhabitants within the compass of six or seven years, a province lately considered as no more than a proper situation for a fortress, whose garrison it could not subsist. Even Cape Breton, that barren appendage to the province of Nova Scotia, is known now to contain treasures so worthy of attention as to be reserved to the crown. The mines there are not veins, they are mountains of coal; vast cliffs of nothing else stand open and accessible, no boring necessary to find it, no pit necessary to come at it, no fire engines requisite for carrying on the works. This island and all the neighboring shores in the Gulf of St. Lawrence have another fund of wealth in their fisheries. Canada is already a very flourishing colony inhabited by 90,000 people, and their demand on Great Britain for a supply of manufactures must be immediately considerable. The peltry will be another great branch of commerce. West Florida is surprisingly fertile and luxuriantly productive in its natural state of everything, and not only promising but actually producing wines and silk and indigo, etc., etc.[20]

Is no part of this description of the ebullition of an exuberant fancy, and shall we not cast one glance of retrospection towards the man who, when his country was despised and insulted and sunk into the most abject condition of despondence, by inspiring her sons with that invincible vigor of patriotism with which himself was animated not only dispelled her fears, secured her safety, and retrieved her honor, but humbled her enemies and tore from them the resources of their strength and the supports of their insolence?

Are the acquisitions of the war retained by the peace so inestimably valuable, and ought not the colonies to have some consideration that were instrumental in the successes whence those acquisitions flowed and strained every nerve in the general service to that degree of exertion that without it all the power of Great Britain, all the amazing abilities of her minister, and all the discipline and unparalleled bravery of her national troops and seamen could not have availed beyond mere defense, if happily so far? If the war was expensive beyond all former example, so were the successes of it beneficial. If the expenses attending the military operations in America are justly to be charged to the sole defense of the colonies, [20] and no part of it to the security of Great Britain or to the views of extending her dominions by conquest, if all the successes of the war have been achieved by the national arms of Great Britain ALONE, without any assistance or co-operation of the plantations, still ought not the claim against the colonies in equity to be mitigated upon reflection of the advantages derived from them and of their contribution to the national revenue for a long course of years, during which their protection put the British nation to very little if any particular expense?

If, moreover, Great Britain hath an equitable claim to the contribution of the colonies, it ought to be proportioned to their circumstances, and they might, surely, be indulged with discharging it in the most easy and satisfactory manner to themselves. If ways and means convenient and conciliating would produce their contribution as well as oppressive and disgusting exactions, it is neither consistent with humanity or policy to pursue the latter. A power may even exist without an actual exercise of it, and it indicates as little good sense as good nature to exercise it only that the subjects of it may feel the rod that rules them. Moderation may be observed and equity maintained at the same time that superiority is asserted and authority vindicated, whatever the apprehensions of pusillanimity or the insolence of usurpation may suggest.

What is the annual sum expected from the colonies — what proportion from each — how far do their abilities extend? These matters have been, without doubt, precisely ascertained, or easily may be, at a time "when the real, the substantial, the commercial interests of Great Britain are preferred to every other consideration, and it is so well known that the trade whence its greatest wealth is derived and upon which its maritime power is principally founded depends upon a wise and proper use of the colonies," [21] which implies, at least, such an understanding of their circumstances as must render it extremely easy to form a reasonable estimate of their comparative wealth and the extent of their abilities. The proportion of each colony being so easily ascertainable at this period of *uncommon* knowledge of their affairs, why has the course observed by *former* ministers when supplies have been expected from America, been neglected by the *present*? Why was there not the usual requisition communicated to the provincial Assemblies, instead of exacting an uncertain and unequal sum from each colony by a law abruptly passed without any previous default of those who are affected by it? I shall not call it a law repugnant to their genius, canceling their charters, infringing the most valuable rights and privileges of British subjects, derogatory from the faith [21] and honor of government, unjust and cruel in its principles, rigorous and oppressive in the means provided for its execution, and as pernicious in its consequences to the mother country as injurious to the colonies in its immediate operation; but I may call it a rigorous and severe law. It is in vain to attempt a palliation of this useless severity (useless, I mean, to the purpose of raising a revenue) by fallaciously pretending that as all the colonies were to be taxed and the authority of each is limited, the interposition of the Parliament became necessary, since nothing can be less disputable than that each colony hath a competent authority to raise its proportion, and consequently nothing is more evident than that all the colonies might raise the whole. The assertion that the colonies would have paid no regard to any requisitions‡ is rash and unauthorized, and had the event actually happened, the trouble and loss of time to the ministers in making the experiment would not have been considerable or detrimental to the nation; and after its failure an act of Parliament might still have been made to compel the contribution, if the power which hath been exercised is defensible upon the principles of the British *constitution*.[22]

A measure so extreme could hardly be at once pursued, because the ministers did not know what to demand, who have made so many regu-

‡ It is asserted in the pamphlet entitled *The Claim of the Colonies, etc.*, that Maryland, availing herself of the protection of Virginia and Pennsylvania, contributed *nothing* to the common defense. This writer from a view of some map of North America imagined, it should seem, that Virginia and Pennsylvania were settled so as to encompass Maryland; but the truth is that the frontiers of Maryland were as much exposed as those of the next colonies, and the fact is moreover false, for I have been well informed that Maryland contributed near £50,000 and incurred besides a considerable expense, which is now a debt upon the public journal of that colony, by putting her militia into actual service, and that an unhappy dispute, attended with a very heavy provincial charge, on some topic of privilege, was the real cause why the grants of Maryland were not more liberal. After all, there have been instances, I speak not of more modern times, in which the parsimony of the Parliament hath been complained of, and the notion of privilege carried to a great length by the House of Commons; but these have not been thought solid reasons for stripping their constituents of their rights.

lations in regard to the colonies "founded upon knowledge, formed with judgment, and executed with vigor."[23] Had the requisitions been communicated, I make no doubt but they would have been entertained with respect and productive of all the effects that could reasonably have been expected from them. A petty American Assembly would not in answer to [22] such requisitions have impertinently recommended the reduction of exorbitant salaries, the abatement of extravagant and the abolition of illegal perquisites, the extinction of useless places, or the disbanding of undeserving or ill-deserving pensioners as a more proper and beneficial method of relieving the public burdens than a new and heavy imposition upon useful and industrious subjects.

Have great things been promised for the ease of the people of England, and hath a measure been fallen upon that, by putting the accomplishment of them at a distance and keeping expectation alive, it may contribute to the prolongation of a power which in the interim will find sufficient opportunities to gratify the views of ministerial avarice or ambition?

If a sum had been liquidated and a precise demand made, it might perhaps have been shown, if proportioned to the circumstances of the colonies, to be of no real consequence to the nation; and, if above their circumstances that it would, with the oppression of the plantations, prove ruinous to the British manufactures. But whilst matters are thus vague and indeterminate, any attempt to show that the *stamp duties* will be inadequate to the promised relief, distress the colonies, and consequently beggar the British manufacturers, may be obviated by saying that "the act is in the nature of an experiment; if inadequate, other methods may be superadded; if inconvenient, it may be repealed as soon as discovered"; and hints may be thrown out at the same time to cherish the hopes of the nation that there are the best grounds to expect the measure will be productive of all that can be desired or wished.§ [24]

The frugal *republicans* of North America (if the British inhabitants there are to be distinguished by a *nickname,* because it implies that they are enemies to the government of England and ought therefore to be regarded with a jealous eye[25]) may be allowed, without derogating from

§ It is asserted by the author of *The Claim of the Colonies, etc.,* that the merchants trading to the several colonies gave an estimate of the debt due to them from the colonies amounting to £4,000,000. It would have been a real public service if he had pointed out how this debt is to be paid under the oppression of new and heavy impositions, or what will be the proper remedy if there should be a stoppage in the payment of £4,000,000, a stagnation of commerce, and want of employment to the British manufacturers.

the vast and [23] prodigious knowledge of a minister, to be acquainted with their own internal circumstances better than a stranger, who must depend upon information, and that too, most frequently, of men not the most eminent for their candor, distinguished by their sagacity, or respectable for their integrity. Had requisitions been made, and the sum demanded been equitable and proportioned to their circumstances, they could have fallen upon ways and means less oppressive than the *stamp duties*. They have frequently taxed themselves; they have tried various methods of taxation; they know by experience the easiest and least expensive. The meaning or construction of their levy act is settled: they can be carried into execution not only at a small expense, without exhausting a considerable part of their produce by the multiplication of officers and their support, but without heavy pains and grievous penalties, without oppression of the innocent, giving countenance to vexation and encouragement to profligate informers, without the establishment of arbitrary and *distant* courts of admiralty.||

The national debt is heavy, and it is a popular scheme to draw from colonies a contribution towards the relief of the mother country. The manner of effecting it is not carefully attended to or nicely regarded by those who expect to receive the benefit. The end is so ardently desired that whether the means might not be more moderate is not scrupulously examined by men who think themselves in no danger of injury or oppression from their severity. It is affirmed to those who cannot detect the fallacy of the assertion that millions have been expended *solely* in the defense of America. They believe it, thence are easily persuaded that the claim of a contribution from the colonies is just and equitable, and that any measure necessary to secure it is right and laudable. It is represented that unless the colonies are stripped of the *trial by jury,* and courts of *admiralty are* established in which judges from England—strangers, without connection or interest in America, removable at pleasure, and supported by liberal salaries — are to preside; unless informers are encouraged and favored, and the accused most rigorously dealt by, that the tax will be eluded — and these severities are excused on account of their supposed necessity. The colonies are described to be a numerous, flourishing, and opulent people. It is alleged that they contribute to the national expense by taxes *there* only the pitiful sum of £1900 per year,

---

|| It was formerly held to be a grievous oppression that instead of having justice at home the English subject was drawn to Rome by APPEALS, but an American is to be drawn from home in the FIRST INSTANCE as well as by appeals.

for the collection of which an [24] establishment of officers, attended with the expense of £7600 per annum, is necessary.[26] Upon these premises, the uneasiness of the colonies at being forced to bring more into the common stock appears to be unreasonable, if not rebellious; and they seem rather to deserve reprehension and correction than favor and indulgence.

The successes of the war were obtained as well by the vigorous efforts of the colonies as the exertion of Great Britain. The faith of Great Britain hath been engaged in the most solemn manner to repay the colonies the monies levied by internal taxations for the support of the war. Is it consistent with that faith to tax them towards sinking the debt in part incurred by that repayment? The immense accession of territory and value of the acquisitions obtained by the peace is the consequence of the successes of the war. The charge of the war is lessened by the advantages resulting from the peace. The colonies for a long course of time have largely contributed to the public revenue, and put Great Britain to little or no expense for their protection. If it were equitable to draw from them a further contribution, it does not therefore follow that it is proper to force it from them by the harsh and rigorous methods established by the Stamp Act, an act unequal and disproportioned to *their* circumstances whom it affects, exempting opulence, crushing indigence, and tearing from a numerous, loyal, and useful people the privileges they had, in their opinion, earned and merited, and justly held most dear. If they are really in debt, the payment of it hath not been refused, it hath not been demanded. If one subject, grown giddy with sudden elevation, should at any future period rashly declare that the colonies should be taxed at all events in the most rigorous manner, and that millions of industrious and useful subjects should be grievously oppressed rather than himself depart from his character of pertinacity and willfulness, check the impulse of a tyrannical disposition, or forego the gratification of his vanity in a wanton display of power, submission would be an admirable virtue indeed, if not the effect of impotence.

That the contribution arising from the *stamp duties* is disproportioned to *their* circumstances from whom it is exacted is manifest; for they will produce in each colony a greater or less sum, not in proportion to its wealth, but to the multiplicity of juridical forms, the quantity of vacant land, the frequency of transferring landed property, the extent of paper negotiations, the scarcity of money, and the number of debtors. A larger sum will be exacted from a tobacco colony than from Jamaica; and it will not only be higher in one of the poorest colonies, and the least able [25] to bear it, than in the richest; but the principal part of the revenue will be drawn from the poorest individuals in the poorest colonies, from mortgagors, obligors, and defendants. If this be true, does the act deserve the encomium of being *a mode of taxation the easiest and the most equal, a duty upon property spread lightly over a great variety of subjects and heavy upon none?* [27]

The *Commons of Great Britain,* moreover, in their capacity of *representative,* not only *give and grant* the property of the colonies, but in my construction of the Stamp Act (however, every reader may examine and judge for himself) *give and grant* also to certain officers of the crown a power to tax them higher still; for these officers will not, I presume, be called *virtual representatives* too; and what they shall think fit to levy, by an ingenious extent of the fiction, will not be considered as levied with the consent of the colonies. The instances, I believe, are *rare* in which the representatives of the people of England have delegated to officers of the crown the power of taxing their constituents, nor hath any distinction yet been advanced to prove that in their capacity of *virtual representatives* of the colonies the House of Commons, not having the same confidence reposed in them, ought to proceed upon peculiar rules. There was a statute of Henry VIII by which, I think, the King's proclamations, with the consent of the Privy Council, were to operate as laws; and another statute of Richard II that the power of the two Houses should be vested in twelve lords; but these acts bear *no resemblance* to the Stamp Act.[28]

The stamping instruments are to be retained in England. Vellum, parchment, and paper are to be sent to America ready stamped. The first commissioner of the treasury, or the commissioners, or any three or more of them are, by the act, empowered to set *any* price upon the vellum, parchment, and paper, and the payment of that price is secured and enforced by the *same* pains and penalties that the stamp duties are.

If the substitution of an arbitrary civil-law court in the place of the legal judicatories and that deserved favorite, the common law trial by jury, would not justify the assertion that the Stamp Act hath stripped the colonies of the guards and securities provided by the constitution against oppression in the execution of laws, I would much less presume to say the vesting in the commissioners of the treasury a power to tax the colonies will amply justify the assertion that the Stamp Act hath not left them even the shadow of a privilege. It is indeed something difficult to imagine how the order of democracy, which is as much a part of the [26] constitution as monarchy or aristocracy, can exist when the people are excluded from a share in the executing and a share in the making of laws; but that is *not* the present case; and though I may not be able to answer a specious objection formed upon general principles, I am not obliged to adopt it till I am convinced of its solidity.

A little examination will find how unfair and deceptive the representation is that the colonies in North America, "two millions of British subjects, an opulent, thriving, and commercial people, contribute to the national expense no more than £700 or £800 per annum by taxes raised *there*," for though it should be acknowledged (which I neither acknowledge nor deny, because I don't know, nor have an opportunity of coming at the fact) that the impositions upon the inhabitants of the colonies do not raise *there* a greater sum than hath been stated, it doth not follow that "the inhabitants of the colonies are indulged at the expense of Great Britain, and that the neediest British cottager, who out of his scanty pittance hardly earned pays the high duties of customs and excise in the price of his consumptions, has reason to complain" if immense sums are raised upon the inhabitants of the colonies *elsewhere*.[29]

By such artifices and sophistry is ignorance misled, credulity deceived, and prejudices excited. Thus oppression gains the credit of equity, cruelty passes for moderation, and tyranny for justice, and the man who deserves reproach is celebrated by adulation and applauded by delusion for his wisdom and patriotic virtues.

The truth is that a vast revenue arises to the British nation from taxes paid by the colonies in Great Britain, and even *the most ignorant British cottager,* not imposed upon by infamous misrepresentation, must perceive that it is of no consequence to his ease and relief whether the duties raised upon America are paid *there* and thence afterwards remitted to Great Britain, or paid *at first* upon the produce of the colonies in Great Britain.

In the article of tobacco, for instance, the planter pays a tax upon that produce of his land and labor consumed in Great Britain more than six times the clear sum received by him for it, besides the expenses of freight, commission, and other charges, and double freight, commission, and charges upon the tobacco re-exported by which the British merchants, mariners, and other British subjects are supported — a tax at least equal to what is paid by any farmer of Great Britain possessed of the same [27] degree of property; and, moreover, the planter must contribute to the support of the expensive internal government of the colony in which he resides.¶

Is it objected that the duties charged upon tobacco fall ultimately upon the consumers of this commodity in the consequential price set upon it? Be it so, and let the principle be established that all taxes upon a commodity are paid by the consumers of it, and the consequence of this principle be fairly drawn and equally applied.

The British consumers, therefore, ultimately pay the high duties laid upon tobacco in proportion to the quantity of that commodity which they consume. The colonies, therefore, in proportion to their consumption of British manufactures pay also the high duties of customs and excise with which the manufacturers are charged in the consequential price set upon their consumptions. In their passage, moreover, from the British manufacturers to the American importers the commodities go through a great many hands, by which their costs are enhanced; the factors, the carriers, the shopkeepers, the merchants, the brokers, the porters, the watermen, the mariners, and others have their respective profits, from which they derive their subsistence and the support of their families, and are enabled to pay the high duties of customs and excise in the price of their consumptions.*

The policy of the late regulations of the colonies is of the same character with their justice and lenity. The produce of their lands, the earnings of their industry, and the gains of their commerce center in Great Britain, support the artificers, the manufactories, and navigation of the nation, and with them the British landholders too.

Great Britain had ALL before, and therefore can have no more from the colonies; but the minister, in the pursuit of a "well digested, consistent, wise, and salutary plan of colonization and government, a plan founded upon the principles of policy, commerce, and finances," [30] chooses to demolish at one blow all their privileges as they have understood them, that he may raise in America a part of what was before paid in Great Britain. But if the execution of it, instead of improving the advantages already possessed, confirming the blessings already enjoyed, and promoting the public welfare, should happen to distress the trade, reduce the navigation, impoverish the manufacturers, and diminish the value of the lands in [28] Great Britain, should it drive the British mechanics and manufacturers to America by depriving them of their best customers at home, and force the colonies upon manufactures they are

¶ See the Appendix.   * See the Appendix.

disabled from purchasing, other topics of eulogy must be discovered by his ingenious encomiasts than his wisdom or his political achievements. Upon such an event an American will have very little reason to exclaim:

> O! me infelicem, qui nunc demum intelligo
> Ut illa mihi profuerint quae despexeram,
> Et illa, quae laudaram, quantum luctus habuerint! [31]

The right of exemption from all taxes *without their consent* the colonies claim as British subjects. They derive this right from the common law, which their charters have declared and confirmed, and they conceive that when stripped of this right, whether by prerogative or by any other power, they are at the same time deprived of every privilege distinguishing freemen from slaves.

On the other hand, they acknowledge themselves to be subordinate to the mother country, and that the authority vested in the supreme council of the nation may be justly exercised to support and preserve that subordination.

Great and just encomiums have been bestowed upon the constitution of England, and their representative is deservedly the favorite of the inhabitants in Britain. But it is not because the supreme council is called *Parliament* that they boast of their constitution of government, for there is no particular magical influence from the combination of the letters which form the word; it is because they have a share in that council, that they appoint the members who constitute one branch of it, whose duty and interest it is to consult their benefit and to assert their rights and who are vested with an authority to prevent any measures taking effect dangerous to their liberties or injurious to their properties.

But the inhabitants in the colonies have no share in this great council. None of the members of it are or can be of their appointment, or in any respect dependent upon them. There is no immediate connection; on the contrary, there may be an opposition of interest. How puerile then is the declamation, "What will become of the colonies' birthright and the glorious securities which their forefathers handed down to them if the authority of the British Parliament *to impose taxes* upon them should be given up? To deny the authority of the British legislature is to [29] surrender all claim to a share in its councils, and if this were the tenor of their charters, a grant more insidious or replete with mischief could not be imagined, a forfeiture of their rights would be couched under the appearance of privilege, etc." [32]

We claim an exemption from all *Parliamentary* impositions, that we may enjoy those securities of our rights and properties which we are entitled to by the constitution. For those securities are derived to the subject from the principle *that he is not to be taxed without his own consent,* and an inhabitant in America can give his consent in no other manner than in Assembly. It is in the councils that exist there, and there *only,* that he hath a share, and whilst he enjoys it his rights and privileges are as well secured as an elector's in England who hath a share in the national councils there; for the words *Parliament* and *Assembly* are in this respect only different terms to express the same thing.

But it is argued that "if the common law of England is to be brought as justifying a claim of exemption in any subject of Great Britain from a Parliamentary tax, it will plead against a tax imposed by a provincial Assembly; for as all the colony Assemblies derive their authority from the mere grant of the crown only, it might be urged that any tax imposed by them is imposed by authority of the prerogative of the crown, and not by full consent of Parliament. That if this right in the crown is acknowledged to exempt the subject from the jurisdiction of Parliament in the case of taxation, its power to dispense with acts of Parliament or to deprive the same subject of the benefit of the common law can't be denied." [33]

One would be inclined to suspect that it is supposed something else than reason may on this occasion conduce to persuasion.

The English subjects who left their *native* country to settle in the wilderness of America had the privileges of *other* Englishmen. They knew their value, and were desirous of having them perpetuated to their posterity. They were aware that as their consent whilst they should reside in America could neither be asked nor regularly given in the national legislature, and that if they were to be bound by laws without restriction affecting the property they should earn by the utmost hazard and fatigue, they would lose every other privilege which they had enjoyed in their native country and become mere tenants at will, dependent upon the moderation of their lords and masters without any other security — that [30] as their settlement was to be made under the protection of the English government they knew that in consequence of their relation to the mother country they and their posterity would be subordinate to the supreme national council, and expected that obedience and protection would be considered as reciprocal duties.

Considering themselves and being considered in this light, they entered into a compact with the crown the basis of which was *that their privileges as English subjects should be effectually secured to themselves and transmitted to their posterity*. And as for this purpose precise declarations and provisions formed upon the principles and according to the spirit of the English *constitution* were necessary, CHARTERS were accordingly framed and conferred by the crown and accepted by the settlers, by which all doubts and inconveniencies which might have arisen from the application of general principles to a new subject were prevented.

By these charters, founded upon the unalienable rights of the subject and upon the most sacred compact, the colonies claim a right of exemption from taxes *not imposed with their consent*. They claim it upon the principles of the constitution, as once English and now British subjects, upon principles on which their compact with the crown was originally founded.

The origin of other governments is covered by the veil of antiquity and is differently traced by the fancies of different men; but of the colonies the evidence of it is as clear and unequivocal as any other fact.

By these declaratory charters the inhabitants of the colonies claim an exemption from *all* taxes not imposed by their own consent; and to infer from their objection to a taxation to which their consent is not nor can be given, that *they are setting up a right in the crown to dispense with acts of Parliament and to deprive the British subjects in America of the benefits of the common law* is so extremely absurd that I should be at a loss to account for the appearance of so strange an argument, were I not apprised of the unworthy arts employed by the enemies of the colonies to excite strong prejudices against them in the minds of their brethren at home, and what gross incongruities prejudiced men are wont to adopt.

Though I am persuaded that this reasoning hath already been sufficiently refuted, and that no sensible and dispassionate man can perceive any force in it, yet I can't help remarking that it is grounded upon a principle which, if it were possible for the Examiner to establish it, would entitle him to the [31] applause of the inhabitants in Great Britain as little as to the thanks of the colonies.

From what source do the peers of England derive their dignity and the share they have in the British *legislature*? Are there no places in England that derive their power of choosing members of Parliament from royal charters? Will this writer argue that the crown may, by prerogative, tax the inhabitants of Great Britain because the peers of England and some representatives of the people exercise a legislative authority under royal patents and charters? It must be admitted that all the members of the House of Commons are freely chosen by the people, and are not afterwards subject to any influence of the crown or the ministry. And are not the members of the lower houses of Assembly as freely chosen also by the people, and in fact as independent as the members of the House of Commons? If the truth were confessed, the objection would not be *that the colonies are too dependent upon the crown* or that their claim of exemption from all taxes not imposed by their own consent *is founded upon a principle leading to slavery*. At one time the North Americans are called *republicans;* at another, *the assertors of despotism*. What a strange animal must a North American appear to be from these representations to the generality of English readers, who have never had an opportunity to admire that he may be neither black nor tawny, may speak the English language, and in other respects seem, for all the world, like one of them!

"The common law, the Great Charter, the Bill of Rights" are so far from "declaring, with one voice, that the inhabitants of the colonies shall be taxed by no other authority than that of the British *Parliament*" [34] that they prove the contrary; for the principle of the common law is *that no part of their property shall be drawn from British subjects without their consent, given by those whom they depute to represent them;* and this principle is enforced by the declaration of the GREAT CHARTER and *the Bill of Rights,* neither the one nor the other introducing any *new* privilege. In Great Britain the consent of the people is given by the House of Commons; and as money had been levied there for the use of the crown *by pretense of prerogative, without their consent,* it was properly declared at the Revolution, in support of the constitution and in vindication of the people's rights, that the levying of money by *pretense of prerogative,* without grant of Parliament, i.e., without their consent who are to pay it, is illegal, which declaration was most suitable to the occasion and effectually establishes the very principle contended for by the colonies.

[32] The word *Parliament* having been made use of, the *letter* of the declaration is adhered to, and the consequence drawn that no British subject can be legally taxed but by the authority of the British *Parliament,* against the spirit and principle of the declaration, which was aimed only

to check and restrain the *prerogative* and to establish the necessity of obtaining *the consent* of those on whom taxes were to be levied. Is not this a new kind of logic, to infer from declarations and claims founded upon the necessary and essential principle of a free government that the people ought not to be taxed without their consent, that therefore the colonies ought to be taxed by an authority in which their consent is not nor can be concerned; or, in other words, to draw an inference from a declaration or claim of privilege subversive of the very principle upon which the privilege is founded? How awkwardly are the principles of the Revolution applied by some men! What astonishment would the promoters of that glorious measure, those patrons and friends of liberty, did they now tread the stage of this world, express that a *word* by which they meant to assert the privileges of the subject and restrain despotic power should be relied upon to demolish the very principle by which themselves were animated, and after all their pains and hazards to establish the generous sentiments of liberty, that those who feel and enjoy the blessings of their successful struggles should not be able to raise a thought beyond the ideas affixed to systematic terms.

It was declared also by the *Bill of Rights* that the elections of *members of Parliament* ought to be free, and the common law laid down the same rule before, which is as applicable to the election of the representatives of the colonies as of the commons of Great Britain. But with the help of the Examiner's logic it might be proved from the *letter* of the *Bill of Rights* that the elections *only* of *members of Parliament* ought to be free; for the freedom expressed in the Bill of Rights is as much attached to elections of members of Parliament as the authority to grant money is to *the British Parliament,* and if the declaration in the one case implies a negative there is the like implication in the other. If, moreover, the common law, the Great Charter, and the Bill of Rights do really, as the Examiner asserts, with one voice declare that the inhabitants of the colonies ought to be taxed *only* by the British Parliament, it is not consistent with that character of vigilance and jealousy of their power commonly ascribed to the British *Parliament* that from their first regular settlement to the reign of George III, the American Assemblies should not only have been suffered, without any animadversion, without one resolve, or even a single motion to restrain them, to encroach upon the jurisdiction and authority [33] of the British *Parliament;* but that the Parliament should never before the late *Stamp Act,* in one instance, have imposed an internal tax upon the colonies for *the single purpose of revenue,* and that even when acts of Assembly passed in consequence of ministerial enforced by royal requisitions have been laid before them, they should be so far from objecting to their validity as actually to recognize the authority of the provincial legislatures, and upon that foundation superstruct their own resolves and acts.

But though it hath been admitted that the *Stamp Act* is the first statute that hath imposed an internal tax upon the colonies *for the single purpose of revenue,* yet the advocates for that law contend that there are many instances of the Parliament's exercising a supreme legislative authority over the colonies and actually imposing *internal taxes* upon their properties — that the duties upon any exports or imports are internal taxes — that an impost on a foreign commodity is as much an internal tax as a duty upon any production of the plantation — that no distinction can be supported between one kind of tax and another, an authority to impose the one extending to the other.

If these things are really as represented by the advocates for the *Stamp Act,* why did the *chancellor of the exchequer* make it a question for the consideration of the House of Commons whether the Parliament could impose an *internal tax* in the colonies or not for the *single purpose of revenue?* † [35]

[34] It appears to me that there is a clear and necessary distinction between an act imposing a tax for *the single purpose of revenue* and those acts which have been made for the regulation of trade and have produced some revenue *in consequence of their effect* and operation as *regulations of trade.*

The colonies claim the privileges of British subjects — it has been proved to be inconsistent with those privileges to tax them *without their own consent,* and it hath been demonstrated that a tax imposed by Parliament is a tax *without their consent.*

†I have presumed to mention this fact upon the authority of private intelligence as well as of the newspapers and other publications; and though the chancellor of the exchequer is not named, yet the fact seems in general to be referred to in the postscript to *the excellent Letter Concerning Libels, Warrants, Seizure of Papers, and Security of the Peace, etc.,* in the following words: "Otherwise (i.e., if it were not right for the Parliament to resolve general warrants to be illegal) let me ask how that *momentous* resolution touching an English Parliament's right of taxing the colonies could be justified? It was an independent substantive resolution, followed by nothing (i.e., that session) and yet was a resolution not only of *extreme magnitude,* but of the most *general* and *highest legal* nature, involving in it a decision of *the first and most fundamental principles of liberty, property, and government, and well worthy,* also as to the temporary policy of it, the most *serious* of *all* consideration. This was resolved too, if I am informed right, at the close of the night and the rising of the House; so that everybody must have taken it as a clear thing that they could at any time come to a resolution upon any general point of law whenever they should see it *expedient* so to do, *sed verbum sapienti sat est.*

The subordination of the colonies and the authority of the Parliament to preserve it have been fully acknowledged. Not only the welfare but perhaps the existence of the mother country as an independent kingdom may depend upon her trade and navigation, and these so far upon her intercourse with the colonies that if this should be neglected there would soon be an end to that commerce whence her greatest wealth is derived and upon which her maritime power is principally founded. From these considerations the right of the British *Parliament* to regulate the trade of the colonies may be justly deduced; a denial of it would contradict the admission of the subordination and of the authority to preserve it resulting from the nature of the relation between the mother country and her colonies. It is a common and frequently the most proper method to regulate trade by duties on imports and exports. The authority of the mother country to regulate the trade of the colonies being unquestionable, what regulations are the most proper are to be of course submitted to the determination of the Parliament; and if an *incidental revenue* should be produced by such regulations, these are not therefore unwarrantable.

A right to impose an internal tax on the colonies without their consent *for the single purpose of revenue* is denied, a right to regulate their trade without their consent is admitted. The imposition of a duty may in some instances be the proper regulation. If the claims of the mother country and the colonies should seem on such an occasion to interfere and the point of right to be doubtful (which I take to be otherwise) it is easy to guess that the determination will be on the side of power and that the inferior will be constrained to submit.‡ [36]

[35] The writer on *The Regulations Lately Made with Respect to the Colonies,* who is said to have been *well informed,* asserts a fact which indisputably proves that the impositions mentioned were *only* regulations of trade and can with no kind of propriety be considered in any other light. The fact he asserts is that "the whole remittance from all the taxes in the colonies, at an average of thirty years, has not amounted to £1900 a year, and in that sum £700 or £800 per annum only have been re-

‡ In the reign of our great deliverer, when the English and the Dutch were at war with France they joined in preventing the northern powers from carrying on a trade with the enemy. M. Groning having formed a design to prove the right of the northern powers to a free trade and navigation, communicated his plan to and desired the opinion of Baron Pufendorf upon it, who observed that as the question had not been settled upon clear and undeniable principles and there was a mixture of fact and right, the confederates might contend that they have a right to distress the enemy, and, as the means to attain that purpose, to restrain the trade of the northern powers, an argument that with superior force would be conclusive.

mitted from North America; and that the establishment of officers necessary to collect that revenue amounts to £7600 per annum." [37]

It would be ridiculous indeed to suppose that the Parliament would raise a revenue by taxes in the colonies to defray part of the national expense, the collection of which taxes would increase that expense to a sum more than three times the amount of the revenue; but the impositions being considered in their true light, as regulations of trade, the expense arising from an establishment necessary to carry them into execution is so far from being ridiculous that it may be wisely incurred.

The author of *The Claim of the Colonies, etc.,* gives (as hath been observed) the epithets of *unjust* and *partial* to a tax which should be imposed upon the nonelectors only in Britain, and in that very instance proves that a tax upon the nonelectors in the colonies is more unjust and partial, and yet undertakes to defend the justice of it; and the writer on *The Regulations of the Colonies* declares that it is in vain to call the acts he has cited as precedents by the name of mere regulations, notwithstanding he hath irrefragably proved that they are ridiculous if considered in any other light. (See *The Regulations of the Colonies, etc.,* page 105, 57, and *The Claim of the Colonies, etc.,* page 28, 29, 30.) § [38]

[36] Though I conceive that the distinction which hath been suggested is sufficiently evident and that the argument from precedents hath been refuted, yet as there have been two or three instances particularly enforced and relied upon, I must beg the reader's patience whilst I examine them separately, without undertaking the task to remove every incongruity to be found in the writings of the enemies of America on this occasion, for it would require an Hercules to cleanse the stable.

The 5th George II, it is alleged, *"abrogates so much of the common law as relates to descents of freeholds in America, takes from the son the right of inheritance in the lands the crown had granted to the father* and his heirs in absolute fee, makes them assets, and applies them to the payment of debts and accounts contracted by the father *without the participation of the son;* it *sets aside* the sort of evidence required by the common law and *established by every court of justice in America* in proof of a debt, and enjoins the admission of an *ex parte affidavit.* The power of

---

§ A grave answer to a little pert pamphlet called *The Objections to the Taxation, etc.,* would be too ludicrous. When the author of it talks of orders to be observed under pains and penalties, he uses the awful style of a L——d of T——, but it was too constrained for him to support, and he therefore very naturally relapsed into the character of a jack-pudding. He had very little reason to apprehend that Locke, Sidney, or Selden would be called upon to pull off his ——cap.

Parliament having been exercised *to take away the lands of the people in America,* the most *sacred* part of any man's property, and *disposing of them for the use of private persons, inhabitants of Great Britain,* who can question," says the Examiner, "the Parliament's right to take away a *small* part of the products of those lands and apply it to the *public service?*"[39]

It is very observable that in applying this statute a language is made use of which gives the idea of violence; and it must be confessed that great aggravation of features and strong coloring were necessary to make it in any degree resemble the impositions of the *Stamp Act.*

It would be useless as well as tedious to point out every misrepresentation in this application, since that will be effectually done by briefly showing the effect of the 5th George II and suggesting the occasion of making that statute.

Lands, Negroes, etc., in the plantations are made assets for the satisfaction of all debts owing to His Majesty or *any of his subjects* in like manner as real estates are by the law of England liable to the satisfaction of debts due by specialty.

If the creditor resides in Great Britain, the affidavits of his witnesses taken there are to be allowed as evidence and to have the same force their testimony would have if given *viva-voce* in open court.

[37] The evidence mentioned in the statute prevailed in most if not all the colonies before the statute, and lands were also liable to the satisfaction of all debts in most instances by the method practiced also in the Court of Chancery in England of marshaling assets. In some of the colonies, without this circuity, lands were immediately liable to simple contract debts.

Independent of the statute, when the creditor obtains a judgment against his debtor, *all* his lands, etc., over which he has a *disposing* power are liable, and since the statute, only *such* lands, etc., are assets as the debtor had a power to dispose of. It appears, then, that all the effects of the statute on this head is to subject real estates to the payment of debts *after* the death of the debtor (for the most part the case before the statute) which might have been made subject *before* his death.

In many of the colonies the provincial creditors of deceased debtors were preferred to the British in the same degree by acts of Assembly which carried the appearance of partiality, though in fact the effect of the laws of England gave rise to them; for upon bankruptcies in Great Britain, the steps required by the statutes to entitle creditors to a satisfaction effectually exclude colony creditors in most cases; and their distance, when their debtors die in Great Britain where colony creditors have not standing agents as the merchants have in the plantations, and there happens a deficiency of assets, shuts them out likewise from all chance of satisfaction in the usual scramble among creditors for the debtor's estate on such events.

In some of the colonies they changed, by acts of Assembly, certain species of personal property, e.g., Negroes, into the nature of real estates by making them descendible and, by this alteration of the common law and confusion of the former distinction of property, very considerably diminished the personal fund liable to *all* debts.

As these circumstances were represented and believed to be great discouragements to the trade of the mother country, after repeated requisitions to provide a remedy in the colonies in which the grievance was most sensibly felt had been disregarded, the statute was finally made.

This was, without doubt, a subject upon which the superintendence of the mother country might be justly exercised, it being relative to her trade and navigation, upon which her wealth and her power depend, [38] and the preservation of her superiority and the subordination of the colonies are secured, and therefore is comprehended in the distinction.

After citing and applying this statute the Examiner takes occasion to insult a gentleman of a most amiable and respectable character because he presumed, it seems, to question the universality of Parliamentary power, and appears to be so totally occupied in the business of defamation as not to be aware of his running into the most egregious inconsistencies.[40] If the Examiner is a lawyer, he has betrayed the most shameful ignorance; if an agent, the most infamous unfaithfulness. Had the American chief justice acted in England as too many of his countrymen have done — had he paid his court to power by mean compliances, and endeavored to recommend himself by inventing accusations against the colonies, by representing the inhabitants in them as a refractory, disloyal, and rebellious people, and by proposing schemes for their depression — had he not firmly maintained his character of honor and probity, we should not have seen this impeachment of his understanding; but he left the task of prostitution to the man of sordid views,

> *Ille superbos aditus regum,*
> *Durasque fores, expers somni*
> *Colat . . .*[41]

"Had the colonies," says the Examiner, "agreed to the imposition of the stamp duties, a precedent would have been established for their being consulted before any imposition upon them by Parliament would hereafter take place." [42] He intimates that they were advised by some of their agents to take this course. If such advice hath been given, it was weak or insidious, and the agents who recommended the measure ought to be removed for their incapacity or their treachery.

How would the precedent have been established, or if it had, what would have been the advantage? This conduct would have admitted that the colonies might be taxed at any time and in any manner without their consent, and consequently would at once have been an effectual surrender of all their privileges as British subjects.

If precedents were to be regarded when a tax in America for the *single purpose of revenue* is required, they are not wanting. Upon such occasions the course hath always and uniformly been, till the imposition of the stamp duties, to transmit requisitions to the colonies; and if the instance cited by the Examiner is in any degree pertinent, he has shown in [39] his appendix that the method of requisition was *in that* pursued; for the Lords of Trade in their report expressly mention the refusal of the colonies to comply with the requisitions transmitted to them to remove the grievance complained of.

The clause in the Mutiny Act during the late war is also relied upon, but with how much propriety few words will evince.

The acts of Assembly of each colony could have no obligatory force beyond the limits of each; but the service of the colony troops was not confined within the same colony in which they were raised. It is therefore evident that the provincial legislatures had not an authority adequate to the great object of the military operations in America, which was not merely the defense of the plantations by measures executed within their boundaries, but the enemy was attacked in his own country, and for this purpose the British and American troops acted conjunctly. On this occasion it was not only convenient that the troops employed in the same service should be subject to the same discipline, but it was indispensably necessary that this discipline should be established by *act of Parliament,* the authority of the *provincial legislatures* being deemed incompetent. And it is to be remarked, moreover, that the provincial troops were raised and paid by the colonies, and that it was in the power of their Assemblies, a power exercised by some of them, to disband or reduce them when they pleased, and therefore their supporting and keeping them up was an effectual consent to the act of Parliament. But as hath been shown, an internal tax may be as completely and adequately laid in every colony by the authority of the *respective Assemblies* as by the British *Parliament,* and therefore there is not the same necessity for the interposition of the mother country in this as in the other instance, and the colonies with reference to the Stamp Act are not called upon to do any act expressive of their assent to it, nor is it in their power to hinder its taking effect in the fullest extent.

The act for *The Establishment of a Post Office in the Colonies* (9 Anne c. 10) comes the nearest to the subject of any regulation that hath been mentioned; but yet it is materially distinguishable from the Stamp Act. For the same reason that an act of Parliament was necessary to secure the discipline of the provincial troops acting in conjunction with the British forces during the late war, the authority of Parliament might be proper for the general establishment of a regular post office, for as the laws of each colony are in their operation confined within the limits of each, [40] prohibitory and compulsive clauses to enforce a general observance, without which the establishment would fail, might be eluded. If a man should maliciously give a wound in one colony and the wounded person die in another, the offender could not be convicted of murder because the whole fact constituting that crime would not be cognizable in the colony where the wound was given or the death happened; and the same principle is applicable to every other inferior offense, and intimates in what manner prohibitory clauses might be evaded. This matter, therefore, of the post office may be referred to the general superintending authority of the mother country, the power of the provincial legislatures being too stinted to reach it. In this view, and upon the consideration of the general convenience and accommodation arising from the establishment, the people of America have not complained of it. But if this instance were more pertinent than it is, it would only prove what hath been too often proved before: when men do not suspect any designs to invade their rights, and subdolous steps taken to that end are productive of immediate convenience without pointing out their destructive tendency, they are frequently involved in ruin before they are aware of danger; or that the conduct flowing from the negligence of innocent intentions may afford an handle to men of different dispositions for the commission of oppression. Of the truth of these observations the histories of all people who have once been blessed with freedom and have lost it exhibit abundant examples.

When instances are urged as an authoritative reason for adopting a new measure, they are proved to be more important from this use of them, and ought therefore to be reviewed with accuracy and canvassed with strictness. What is proposed ought to be incorporated with what hath been done, and the result of both stated and considered as a substantive original question; and if the measure proposed is incompatible with the constitutional rights of the subject, it is so far from being a rational argument that consistency requires an adoption of the proposed measure, that, on the contrary, it suggests the strongest motive for abolishing the precedent. When, therefore, an instance of *deviation* from the constitution is pressed as a reason for the *establishment* of a measure striking at the very root of all liberty, though the argument is inconclusive, it ought to be useful.

Wherefore, if a sufficient answer were not given to the argument drawn from precedents by showing that none of the instances adduced are applicable, I should have very little difficulty in denying the justice of the principle on which it is founded. What hath been done, if wrongful, confers no right to repeat it. To justify oppression and outrage by [41] instances of their commission is a kind of argument which never can produce conviction, though it may *their* acquiescence whom the terror of greater evils may restrain from resisting, and thus the despotism of the East may be supported and the natural rights of mankind be trampled under feet. The question of right, therefore, doth not depend upon precedents, but on the principles of the constitution, and hath been put upon its proper point already discussed, whether the colonies are represented or not in Parliament.

As the name of Hampden occurred to the Examiner in his design of casting an oblique reflection upon the colonies,[43] it is surprising he did not recollect that very numerous precedents have been applied in the defense of an arbitrary and oppressive proceeding, destructive of the essential principle of English liberty. But though mere acts of power prove no right, yet the real opinion entertained of it may be inferred from forbearance; for mankind are generally so fond of power that they are oftener tempted to exercise it beyond the limits of justice than induced to set bounds to it from the pure consideration of the rectitude of forbearance. Wherefore, if I had denied the principle of this kind of reasoning without showing the defects of the artificial painted precedents which have been produced, I might still very consistently urge that the repeated and uniform requisitions of the English ministers, as often as occasions for the *single purpose of revenue* have happened, transmitted to the colonies to tax themselves by provincial acts, and the acts of Parliament regulating the trade of the plantations as well as of Ireland without one instance before the Stamp Act of a tax imposed by Parliament upon either for the *unmixed* purpose of revenue, prove that the imposition of a tax upon them without their consent hath constantly been held to be inconsistent with their constitutional rights and privileges. I have joined Ireland with the colonies, and presume it will hardly be contended that Ireland, over which the courts of justice in England have a superintendent power, is not at least as subject to Great Britain as the colonies are.

A most extraordinary reason hath been given why the method of requisition would have been improper, viz., that "the sums raised must be paid into the exchequer, and if levied by the provincial Assemblies the Parliament would have no right to inquire into the expenditure of them." [44] This is so extremely futile that it would be almost absurd to bestow a serious refutation upon it.

Why must the sums raised be paid into the exchequer? If the intention is to apply them in the colonies to any internal purpose, why must they [42] be remitted to Great Britain? If armies are to be kept up in America to defend the colonies against *themselves* (for it can hardly be imagined that troops are necessary for their protection against any foreign enemy), or are to be employed in the national service of cropping the ears and slitting the nostrils of the civil magistrates as marks of distinction,|| [45] why must the money be paid into the exchequer? Or, if it should be paid into the exchequer in order to be applied towards sinking the national debt, why might not the Parliament inquire into the application of it? Does the Examiner in his idea of the Parliament figure to himself a monster with an hand that can reach to the utmost verge of the British dominions and clutch and crush millions of subjects at a gripe, but when the object is near, apt to be rendered by some magical influence so short and so feeble as not to be able to reach the *exchequer* or to squeeze the *chancellor* of it.

We are assured that there never can be any irregular "attempts of the prerogative upon our rights whilst we are blessed with a prince of the glorious line of Brunswick upon the throne of Great Britain." [46] I have all the confidence in the excellent dispositions of our present most gracious sovereign that an Englishman ought to have, but I cannot penetrate

|| See the narrative of the outrages committed by the soldiery on Mr. Justice Walker in Canada.

into futurity; and as the Examiner hath not yet established the character of a prophet, I must consider this assertion rather as a curious specimen of lip-loyalty, I will not call it extravagant adulation, than as a sober recommendation to surrender all those guards and securities of liberty which the constitution of a free government hath provided; but if the British Americans should ever be reduced to the unhappy necessity of giving up their natural rights and their civil privileges, I believe they would as soon make the surrender to a prince of the *line of Brunswick* as to any other mortal or number of mortals in the universe.

We have seen too a piece in some of our late newspapers all bedaubed with the lace of compliment. There is no end to human ambition! It is perpetually restless and pushing forward. If a little p—ct—r is raised to the title of excellency and the rank of a kind of viceroy, there is still a summit beyond the eminence to which he hath been elevated that he is solicitous to gain.¶

[43] It hath been truly said that "it will be no easy task to persuade the Americans to forsake the culture of their lands, to leave the ways their fathers trod and in which themselves were trained, to drop a business they already understand, in which they have had long experience and by which their families have thriven, to change all their habits of thinking and their manner of life, in order to apply to arts which they do not know, or know but imperfectly, and that where estates may be easily raised by mere tillage the temptations to manufacture are wanting, and men who can depend upon their industry alone will not have recourse to arts for subsistence." [47] But that which persuasion might not effect and to which peculiar circumstances might be adverse, necessity and an alteration of those circumstances may accomplish. When the alternative is proposed, and the one part of it assures success and a comfortable support by a moderate application of industry familiarized by use and rendered easy by practice, and the other affording only an experiment of precarious issue, calling for an application unexperienced and dreaded, attended with perplexity and productive of irksome anxiety, the generality of mankind would not hesitate in choosing the former. But though it would gain the preference of choice, yet if the alternative is taken away and choice yields to necessity, the enterprising will form projects, the judicious improve, the industrious execute them. Success in one instance will animate the timid to make trial of the means which

---

¶ A late notable speech puts me in mind of the ingenuity of the female disputant who used to silence debate by crying out, *God bless the King, and what have you to say to that?*

have succeeded under the direction of others, stimulate the phlegmatic, and rouse the indolent. Should the necessity after a little time cease, new habits may become as strong as the old, and the alternative would therefore be altered, the choice be an act of deliberation rather than of blind impulse; old prejudices would be greatly abated, if not extinguished, new attachments, perhaps, be formed. From this change, different consequences may be conjectured or foretold, and perhaps the most confident might be disappointed by the event. It is not so difficult for men to strike into new employments and methods of life when impelled by the urgency of distress, nor so easy to call them back to their old manner of life and divert them from new pursuits experienced to be profitable and *productive of the best security against oppression* as some seem to apprehend.

It is not contended that the colonies ought to be indulged in a general liberty of exporting and importing everything in what manner they please, but since they are hindered from making all the advantages they might do — and what advantages might they not make if under no checks? — they have a good plea against all rigor and severity not absolutely necessary. That British manufactures come dearer and not so good in quality to America as formerly is a very general complaint, and what effect [44] it may have should they still grow dearer and worse in quality, or the colonies be rendered less able to consume them, is a consideration which concerns Great Britain at least as much as the colonies. An increase of price and falling in the goodness of quality is the usual effect of monopolies; there is no danger of foreigners taking advantage of this circumstance in America whatever they may do in other countries, but the industry it may give rise to in America, when other circumstances concur, is not difficult to be foreseen.

It must be acknowledged that the balance of trade between Great Britain and her colonies is considerably against the latter, and that no gold or silver mines have yet been discovered in the old American settlements or among the *treasures* of the new acquisitions. How then is this balance to be discharged? The former trade of the colonies, which enabled them to keep up their credit with Great Britain by applying the balance they had gained against foreigners, is now so fettered with difficulties as to be almost prohibited. In order therefore to reduce the balance against them upon the trade between the colonies and Great Britain, this trade must be contracted so as to bring the scales to an equilibrium, or a debt will be incurred that can't be paid off, which will distress the creditor as well as the debtor by the insolvency of the latter. The income also of the colonies, which was before invested in their trade, will be diminished in proportion to the produce of the Stamp Act, and therefore the amount of that produce must be drawn out, which will create a further reduction of the trade.

I confess that I am one of those who do not perceive the policy in laying difficulties and obstructions upon the gainful trade of the colonies with foreigners, or that it even makes any real difference to the English nation whether the merchants who carry it on with commodities Great Britain will not purchase reside in Philadelphia, New York, or Boston, London, Bristol, or Liverpool, when the balance gained by the American merchant in the pursuit of that trade centers in Great Britain and is applied to the discharge of a debt contracted by the consumption of British manufactures in the colonies, and in this to the support of the national expense.

If in consequence of the obstructions, or regulations as they are called, of their commerce and the imposition of taxes upon their properties, the colonies should only be driven to observe the strictest maxims of frugality, the consequence would rather be disagreeable than hurtful. Should they be forced to use new methods of industry and to have recourse to arts for a supply of necessaries, the difficulty in succeeding would prove [45] less than the apprehension of miscarrying, and the benefit greater than the hope of it. There are few people of the highest and even of the middle rank but would upon a strict scrutiny into their ordinary disbursements discover some articles that would admit of defalcation.

A prudent man, constrained to abridge his outgoings, will consider what articles of expense may be retrenched or given up without distress or discomfort, and if after this saving he still finds that his expenses exceed his income, he will then consider of what articles he can provide a supply by the application of domestic industry or whether some tolerable substitute may not be fallen upon to answer the purpose of what he can neither buy nor hath skill or ability to fabricate. He will reflect that the expedient, which is at first but an indifferent shift, use and experience will improve into convenience, that practice will confer knowledge and skill, and these facility and satisfaction, and though the progress should be slow and gradual, habit will grow with it and produce reconcilement and content.

What are called in North America luxuries ought for the most part to be ranked among the comforts and decencies of life, but these will not be relinquished if a supply of necessaries may be provided by domestic industry. For food, thank GOD, they do not, and for raiment they need not, depend upon Great Britain.

Any thin covering in the summer to preserve decency and substantial clothing in the winter to repel the cold are sufficient for domestic servants and laborers, and these may be provided without remora to the business of tillage, for there are many intervals in which it is suspended. There are times too when the employment is so slight as to be rather a moderate exercise than a laborious task, when the work that is done might be performed by half the number of laborers without excessive exertion or exhausting fatigue. There are besides in most families those whom the feebleness of immature years, or their sex at particular periods, or the decrepitude of old age discharge from the duties of tillage. Leather, and wool, and cotton, and flax are at hand; how easy then is the necessary clothing provided for those whose station does not require any attention or regard to fashion or elegance; so easy that many have already gone into this manufacture without any other impulse than the spirit of industry, which can't bear inaction, though the savings on this head have afterwards been neglected. In this very considerable branch so little difficulty is there that a beginning is half the work. The path is beaten, there is no danger of losing the way, there are directors to guide every step. But why should they stop at the point of clothing laborers, why [46] not proceed, when vigor and strength will increase with the progression, to clothe the planters? When the first stage is arrived at the spirits will be recruited, and the second should be undertaken with alacrity, since it may be performed with ease. In this too the experiment hath been made and hath succeeded. Let the manufacture of America be the symbol of dignity, the badge of virtue, and it will soon break the fetters of distress. A garment of linsey-woolsey, when made the distinction of real patriotism, is more honorable and attractive of respect and veneration than all the pageantry and the robes and the plumes and the diadem of an emperor without it. Let the emulation be not in the richness and variety of foreign productions, but in the improvement and perfection of our own. Let it be demonstrated that the subjects of the British empire in Europe and America are the same, that the hardships of the latter will ever recoil upon the former.*

* Upon a surmise that a certain noble l——d was the author of some hardships inflicted upon the colonies, a reproachful and mischievous distinction hath been made by some people between the natives of S—t—d and of E—g—d and America, which

In theory it is supposed that each is equally important to the other, that all partake of the adversity and depression of any. The theory is just and time will certainly establish it; but if another principle should be hereafter adopted in practice, and a violation deliberate, cruel, ungrateful, and attended with every circumstance of provocation be offered to our fundamental rights, why should we leave it to the slow advances of time (which may be the great hope and reliance, probably, of the authors of the injury, whose view it may be to accomplish their selfish purposes in the [47] interval) to prove what might be demonstrated immediately? Instead of moping and puling and whining to excite compassion, in such a situation we ought with spirit and vigor and alacrity to bid defiance to tyranny by exposing its impotence, by making it as contemptible as it would be detestable. By a vigorous application to manufactures, the consequence of oppression in the colonies to the inhabitants of Great Britain would strike home, and immediately. None would mistake it. Craft and subtlety would not be able to impose on the most ignorant and credulous; for if any should be so weak of sight as not to see, they would not be so callous as not to feel it. Such conduct would be the most dutiful and beneficial to the mother country. It would point out the distemper when the remedy might be easy and a cure at once effected by a simple alteration of regimen.

Of this measure should there be apprehensions, and ministerial orators and panegyrists endeavor to obviate them by observing that "it would always be easy to reinstate things where they were, and that by easing the colonies of their burdens and giving encouragement to their produce, the establishment of any manufacture in America might be prevented," [48] we should mark well this reasoning and avail ourselves of the instruction given by our enemies, which would point out to us the remedy, and the

---

every judicious friend of the colonies must wish to see abolished, and an *union* rather established than divisions promoted. Every man who has his all and the welfare of his posterity at stake upon the prosperity of America, as he hath an interest in common with the natives of it, ought to be considered as an American. It is an effectual way to make men adversaries, to call and treat them as such. Besides, laying aside this consideration, the distinction is extremely unjust, for though there is too much reason to believe that some natives of America and of E—g—d who have resided in the colonies have been instrumental in bringing upon us the severities we deplore, yet hath it never been even surmised, I speak it to their honor, that any native of S—t—d residing or that ever did reside in America had in any degree a hand in them. It is much to be feared, if the breach which a too eager prosecution of the little views of party hath made among the inhabitants of a colony heretofore the most distinguished for prudence and unanimity should not be closed in consideration of the general calamity, that America as well as Denmark will furnish an instance of the excessive temerity of political animosity.

more speedy the application of it the better, and that would depend upon ourselves.

Besides the urgency of such an occasion (should it happen) there would be another powerful inducement to this simple, natural, easy method: the good or bad success of one attempt to oppress generally produces or prevents future impositions. In common life a tameness in bearing a deprivation of part of a man's property encourages rapacity to seize the rest.

Any oppression of the colonies would intimate an opinion of them I am persuaded they don't deserve, and their security as well as honor ought to engage them to confute. When contempt is mixed with injustice and insult with violence, which is the case when an injury is done to him who hath the means of redress in his power, if the injured hath one inflammable grain of honor in his breast his resentment will invigorate his pursuit of reparation, and animate his efforts to obtain an effectual security against a repetition of the outrage.

If the case supposed should really happen, the resentment I should recommend would be a legal, orderly, and prudent resentment, to be [48] expressed in a zealous and vigorous industry,† [49] in an immediate use and unabating application of the advantages we derive from our situation — a resentment which could not fail to produce effects as beneficial to the mother country as to the colonies, and which a regard to her welfare as well as our own ought to inspire us with on such an occasion.

The General Assemblies would not, I suppose, have it in their power to encourage by laws the prosecution of this beneficial, this necessary measure; but they might promote it almost as effectually by their example. I have in my younger days seen fine sights and been captivated by their dazzling pomp and glittering splendor; but the sight of our representatives, all adorned in complete dresses of their own leather and flax and wool, manufactured by the art and industry of the inhabitants of Virginia, would excite, not the gaze of admiration, the flutter of an agitated imagination, or the momentary amusement of a transient scene, but a calm, solid, heartfelt delight. Such a sight would give me more pleasure than the most splendid and magnificent spectacle the most exquisite taste

---

† The ingenious Mr. Hume observes in his history of James I that the English fine cloth was in so little credit even at home that the King was obliged to seek expedients by which he might engage the people of fashion to wear it, and the manufacture of fine linen was totally unknown in the kingdom. What an encouragement to industry! This very penetrating gentleman also recommends a *mild government* as a proper measure for preserving the dominion of England over her colonies.

ever painted, the richest fancy ever imagined, realized to the view — as much more pleasure as a good mind would receive from the contemplation of virtue than of elegance, of the spirit of patriotism than the ostentation of opulence.

Not only "as a friend to the colonies" but as an inhabitant having my all at stake upon their welfare, I desire an "exemption from taxes imposed *without my consent*," and I have reflected longer than "a moment upon the consequences." ‡ I value it as one of the dearest privileges I enjoy. I acknowledge dependence on Great Britain, but I can perceive a degree of it without slavery, and I disown all other. I do not expect that the interests of the colonies will be considered by some men but in subserviency to other regards. The effects of luxury and venality and oppression posterity may perhaps experience, and SUFFICIENT FOR THE DAY WILL BE THE EVIL THEREOF.

[49]   A P P E N D I X

By the 12th Charles II the colonies are restrained from sending the products enumerated in the act to *any foreign* ports. By the 15th of the same King they are prohibited from importing commodities of the growth or manufacture of Europe *except from* GREAT BRITAIN, saving a few articles mentioned in this act.

A law which restrains one part of the society from *exporting* its products to the most profitable market *in favor of another,* or obliges it to *import* the manufactures of one country that are dear instead of those of another that are cheap, is effectually a tax. For if the profitable *exportation* and the *importation* of the cheaper commodities were permitted, a tax equal to such gain in the former case and to the saving in the latter would leave that part of society in the same state and condition as if under the prohibition and restriction above-mentioned. As for instance in the case of *importation:* Suppose a country, which I will distinguish by the name of A, can purchase commodities of the same kind and equal goodness 20 per cent cheaper of B than she can of C, then it is clear,

‡ See *The Regulations, etc.*, p. 111.

if A is prohibited from taking these commodities of B and obliged to purchase them of C, that A is just in the same state and condition as if she were allowed to purchase the commodities of B on paying thereon a duty of [50] 20 per cent to C. This instance, *mutatis mutandis,* is equally applicable to the case of *exportation.* Hence it appears that the country favored by the prohibition and restriction gains as much thereby as it would do if the proportionate tax were paid to it upon taking off the prohibition and restriction; or, in other words, the profit which the one is hindered from making in consequence of the prohibition and restriction is made by the other, in whose favor they have been introduced.

It hath been observed by a well-received writer on the subject of trade that "a prohibition acknowledges the commodities it is laid on to be good and cheap, otherwise it were needless, and a prohibition on the goods of any one nation gives a monopoly to other nations that raise the like." Again: "A prohibition against any one nation makes other nations having the like commodities take the advantage and raise their price, *and is therefore a tax."* * [50]

If a prohibition extending to one nation only in favor of many confers a monopoly and is therefore a tax, a prohibition extending to all other nations in favor of one is indubitably so.

From Virginia and Maryland are exported, *communibus annis,* 90,000 hogsheads of tobacco to Great Britain, of which it is supposed 60,000 are thence re-exported. But these colonies not being permitted to send their tobacco *immediately* to foreign markets *distributively,* in proportion to their demands, the re-exported tobacco pays double freight, double insurance, commission, and other shipping charges. The whole quantity is, moreover, of course much depreciated, for going all to Great Britain, the *home market* is overdone, by which circumstance the quantity required for *home consumption* is without doubt purchased cheaper than it would be if no more than *that* were imported into Great Britain, and of this glut foreigners and purchasers on speculation also avail themselves. Besides, a great deal of the tobacco getting home late, the rigorous season hinders its being reshipped for some months, during which it is dead on hand, and moreover gives advantage to buyers — a loss to the planter which would be avoided if the tobacco could be immediately sent to its proper market.

The above-quoted author hath computed the duties, excises, etc., on leather at 50 per cent, and the artificial value of a bale of English cloth

* Sir Matthew Decker.

arising from taxes, monopolies, and ill-judged laws at 51 per cent, by which he means that every hundred pounds worth of that species of manufacture includes in that sum £51 of taxes. His computation is without [51] doubt too low now, taxes having been increased very considerably since the time in which he wrote.

	per cent
In the gross sum of the artificial value, he computed the amount of the taxes to be full	31
Monopolies and ill-judged laws therefore stand at	20
	51
A bale of English cloth costing	£100
Includes an artificial value of	51
The artificial value subtracted leaves the natural value	49

But lest the estimate should be objected to on account of its including 20 per cent for monopolies, etc., I will state the artificial value arising from taxes *only* to be £33 6s. 8d., which will hardly be objected to for being too high.

The colonies, it is supposed, take annually manufactures from Great Britain to the amount of	£2,000,000
Therefore they pay an ANNUAL TAX of	666,666: 13: 4
To which must be added freight, insurance, commission, and shipping charges amounting at least to 10 per cent, the half of which, as it might be saved by back freight, etc., were the colonies permitted to import *directly* the manufactures of foreign countries, is computed at	100,000: 00: 0
What may be the amount from the restrictions on all the enumerated commodities (except tobacco) exported from all the colonies, with subsidies retained and duties laid, upon the most moderate computation may, I suppose, be stated at	150,000: 00: 0
	£916,666: 13: 4

Part of the commodities sent from Great Britain to the colonies is first imported into Great Britain from *foreign* countries; but the estimate is not exceptionable on that account, for the general calculation on the advanced price of British manufactures is extremely low. Several of the foreign commodities receive their perfection in Britain; all of them are enhanced [52] by the articles of double freight, insurance, shipping charges, the merchant importer's commission, the English tradesman's profit, the merchant exporter's commission, and subsidies retained. If the colonies were not restrained from directly importing foreign commodities they would, it is presumed, pay less for them, even by 50 per cent, than they do at present.

It hath been already observed that there are shipped from Virginia and Maryland annually, at an average, about 90,000 hogsheads of tobacco, 60,000 of which, or upwards, are re-exported from Great Britain to foreign markets; but they pay to Great Britain, for the reasons above explained, £3 per hogshead, i.e., the sum of £3 upon each hogshead might be saved if the tobacco might be *immediately* and *distributively* sent to the respective markets in proportion to their demands; and an equal sum is paid also to Great Britain upon the same rule of computation, i.e., that these colonies pay what they might save if not restrained. For though the English manufacturer gets the tobacco he wants without the double freight, etc., yet he has the advantage of the glut and an opportunity of buying it as cheap as it is sold in Great Britain for the foreign markets before the charges of double freight, etc., are incurred, and therefore the planter gets no more for his tobacco sold for *home* than that which is sold for *foreign* consumption, and consequently pays as much for it. For there is great reason to imagine that if these colonies were at liberty to send their tobacco *immediately* where they pleased, the market in England would be as profitable as those of France, Holland, etc. But when the tobacco, under the present regulation, is purchased for re-exportation, the purchaser undoubtedly considers the expense he is to be at before it gets to the foreign market as part of the price of the commodity, and therefore lowers his price to the merchant in proportion.

The above sum of £3 for each hogshead makes	£270,000: 00: 0
The amount of the sundry impositions and restrictions before mentioned brought forward	916,666: 13: 4
Total amount of taxes to Great Britain	1,186,666: 13: 4
Besides the above amount of taxes paid to the mother country, the colonies in North America support their own civil establishments, and pay quit rents to the crown and proprietaries to the amount (supposing 600,000 taxables at the moderate rate of 15s. each) of	450,000: 00: 0
Total amount of taxes paid to our mother country and the support of our civil establishment *annually*	1,636,666: 13: 4
[53] Supposing the clear annual rents of the lands in North America (unrestrained by acts of Parliament) would amount to	2,500,000

It appears, then, that the whole tax is upwards of 65 per cent, and if, therefore, the artificial value of one hundred pounds' worth of British manufacture (cloth for instance) is, according to the above computation, £33 6s. 8d., there was, before the *Stamp Act,* a tax paid by the North Americans near double of that which is paid by the inhabitants of England. If the above sum of £33 6s. 8d. is too low and ought to be increased, then the tax on North America on the article of manufactures imported from Britain must also be increased.

It should seem that the maxim of every tax upon labor falling *ultimately* upon the consumer of its product cannot be strictly applied to the product of the North American colonies. For as they are obliged to send their commodities to some port in the British dominions, or (where indulgence is granted to send some of them to other places) deprived in great measure of the benefit of returns, they are by this means subjected to dead freight; and, moreover, being confined in their consumption to a particular manufacture, and the commodities they export being chiefly raw materials, they have not the means generally in the power of other people, by raising the price of labor to throw their burdens upon others, but are for the most part obliged, both in their exports and imports, to submit to an arbitrary determination of their value.

The sanguine genius of one of the anti-American writers brings to my mind the fable of the boy and the hen that laid *golden eggs*. He is not content to wait for the increase of the *public revenue* by that gradual process and circulation of property which an attention to the commercial interests of the nation hath established, but is at once for tearing away the embryo, which in due time might be matured into fullness of size and vigor, without ever reflecting that when the hen is destroyed by his violence there will be no more GOLDEN EGGS. The following passage justifies this observation.

"If we have from the colonies their ALL already, we only have it," says he, "by trade and not by taxes; and surely it is not the same thing whether the wealth be brought into the public coffers by taxes or, coming in by trade, flows into the pockets of individuals, and, by [54] augmenting his influence with his wealth, enables the merchant to plunge us into new wars and new debts for his advantage." † [51]

The man who thinks the gains of the merchant are dangerous and that the welfare of the manufacturers, the landholders, etc., doth not depend upon the trade and navigation of Great Britain is very consistently an advocate for a measure which hath a direct tendency to check them; but whether this opinion and very consistent conduct might not be more

† *The Objections to the Taxations, etc. Considered.*

serviceable in some other employment than in that of a L—— of T—— is submitted to their consideration who are the judges of merit and the dispensers of its rewards.

For a reason which the above opinion suggests I shall subjoin an estimate of the duties upon tobacco consumed in Great Britain and of the profit to the planter on that tobacco. The intelligent reader will not apprehend it to be my meaning that the planter pays out of his pocket all the duties laid on tobacco, or be at a loss to infer that the estimate has been made with no other view than to obviate the principle others by their writings seem to adopt.

The old subsidy is one penny per pound, 25 per cent deducted.

All the other duties are seven pence and one third per pound, 15 per cent deducted.

An hogshead of tobacco, at an average, contains 952 pounds.

The whole duties therefore	£27: 14: 0
The amount of the whole duties on 30,000 hogsheads is	£831,000: 00: 0

The full clear proceeds of an hogshead of tobacco, reckoning 952 pounds in each hogshead, has not, on an average for some years past, exceeded £4;‡ wherefore on 30,000 hogsheads the planters get £120,000. How much of the above sum of £831,000 is net to the revenue I shall not undertake to say; but I presume it may be safely asserted that no part of this or any other public money is touched by any Americans whether *they have* [55] *great powers of speech* or not; though any gentleman who might be affected by it is not to be blamed for his apprehension that a *sudden importation* of a certain commodity might hurt the *home* market.

The sum of the taxes paid in North America will appear enormous to those who, having been told that these colonies pay only £700 or £800 per annum in consequence of taxes laid *there,* might be led, in their dependence upon *ministerial candor,* to believe that they paid no more *elsewhere;* but to others, who are better acquainted with the subject, the computation will appear too low. From these observations it may be inferred what vast wealth, in *taxes only,* the mother country has, in the course of a hundred years, drawn from her colonies, and how *profoundly well informed* the writer is who, with equal pertinency and confidence,

‡ See before, p. 52. The attentive reader will observe that the net proceeds of a hogshead of tobacco, at an average, are £4, and the taxes £3 — together £7. Quere: how much per cent does the tax amount to which takes from the two wretched tobacco colonies £3 out of every £7? And how deplorable must their circumstances appear when their vast debt to the mother country and the annual burden of their civil establishments are added to the estimate? In these two colonies there are upwards of 180,000 taxables.

pronounces "that it is *now* high time for England to draw some *little* profit from her colonies, after the *vast treasure she has expended on their settlement."*

I confess that the above computations are conjectural, but I believe they are probable. I mean that those who are best acquainted with the subject will think the charge upon North America is not exaggerated, and which I think very naturally accounts for the enormous debt she at present labors under to the mother country.

Dr. Davenant observes that "if ever anything great or good be done for the English colonies, industry must have its due recompense, and that can't be without encouragement to it, which, perhaps, is only to be brought about by *confirming their liberties* and establishing good discipline among them, that as they see they are a free people in point of government, so they may, by discipline, be kept free of the mischiefs that follow vice and idleness. And, as great care should be taken in this respect, so without doubt it is advisable that no little emulation of private interests of neighbor governors, nor the petitions of *hungry courtiers* at home should prevail to discourage those particular colonies who in a few years have raised themselves by their *own charge, prudence, and industry* to the wealth and greatness they are now arrived at, *without any expense to the crown;* upon which account, any *innovations* or *breach* of their *original charters* (besides that it seems a *breach* of the *public faith*) may, peradventure, not tend to the King's profit." Excellent observation! But how little it hath been regarded the present deeply afflicting distress of the inhabitants of North America demonstrates — a distress sufficient to drive men into despair who are not animated by the hope that Deus dabit his quoque finem.[52]

PAMPHLET 14

JOHN DICKINSON, *THE LATE REGULATIONS RESPECTING THE BRITISH COLONIES*

PHILADELPHIA, 1765

INTRODUCTION

John Dickinson, a leader of the Revolutionary movement from its inception — author of the Declaration of the Stamp Act Congress and of the *Farmer's Letters* (1768), drafter if not sole author of both the Declaration of the Causes and Necessity of Taking up Arms and of the Articles of Confederation, and chief executive of Pennsylvania and Delaware under their first state constitutions: a luminous ideologist and effective public official — committed three errors for which his contemporaries, and posterity, never forgave him. He defended the proprietors of Pennsylvania against the attacks of a quasi-popular political coalition led by Benjamin Franklin; he refused to sign the Declaration of Independence; and he won the personal enmity of both John Adams and Thomas Jefferson. The latter, who rarely condemned his opponents openly, called Dickinson "a lawyer of more ingenuity than sound judgment, and still more timid than ingenious," and in his autobiograpical notes misrepresented Dickinson's role in the drafting of the Declaration of the Causes of Taking up Arms. Adams believed Dickinson to have been the tool of a reactionary cabal working against Independence, and he described him in a letter of 1775, which the British intercepted and published, as "a certain great fortune and piddling genius . . . [who] has given a silly cast to our whole doings" — a remark for which Dickinson cut him dead, and which has been repeated almost ritualistically by every subsequent commentator.[1] Modern writers have most often viewed Dickinson as a "conservative of conservatives" — a cautious, property-conscious lawyer respectful of England, where he was educated, essentially a defender of the *status quo*.[2] Yet as a young man, with his career before him, he raised his voice repeatedly and ringingly against Parliamentary pretensions, and defended paper money; later he identified himself with the Jeffersonians and defended the French Revolution against the massed opinion of his friends and colleagues.

Yet his career, if complicated, was not a jumble of contradictions. Essentially consistent, it parallels and personifies the Revolutionary movement itself.

It is less significant that John Dickinson failed to sign the Declaration of Independence than that he figured at all in the leadership of the Revolution. For his background, occupation, social position, religious sympathies, and personality all disposed him toward the maintenance of stability, and toward constraining rather than exciting the disruptive forces of society. Born in 1732 the son of a wealthy Maryland landowner and lawyer, he was educated privately, and at the age of eighteen began the study of law in the office of the attorney general of Pennsylvania, the colony's leading lawyer, John Moland. Three years later, in 1753, he went to England where he remained for three years studying law at the Inns of Court. Settled in Philadelphia after 1757, he rose rapidly in his profession; he quickly secured both financial independence and professional eminence. In 1760 he entered politics as a partisan of the proprietary-Quaker party, and from that time on was almost continuously involved in public affairs. The trajectory of his career was still further elevated in 1770 when, at the age of thirty-eight, he married Mary Norris, daughter of the powerful and wealthy Quaker politician, Isaac Norris II. The couple moved into the Norris mansion, Fairhill, and Dickinson thereafter "mingled freely with the Quaker grandees — the Logans, Pembertons, Foxes, Drinkers, Morrises, Emlens." [3]

As much as any group in eighteenth-century America, the Quaker aristocracy had attained Burke's "uncontending ease, the unbought grace of life." They were affluent, though not ostentatious; they were cultivated: Isaac Norris' extensive library, housed in a special building in the garden at Fairhill, reflected the wealth and discriminating taste of two generations of Norrises and Logans; and they were influential, if no longer dominant, in the colony's politics. None of this — position, wealth, grace of life, power — was despised by Dickinson; he accepted it all gladly, and never questioned its economic or social foundations. And his profession served to reinforce and articulate the conservative character of his private life. The law was not merely a vocation for him: it was a form of faith and the basis of a public philosophy. He believed it to be the cornerstone of civilization and the foundation of British liberty. A philosopher of law as well as a legal technician, he drew from the law an elaborate vocabulary and an intricate grammar by which to defend the foundations of property and of the existing order. It was perfectly natural for him to enter politics as a defender of Pennsylvania's proprietary government, for though he had no particular admiration for the Penn family's rule, he understood it to be a part of the legal system of the colony; it flowed from the same empowering document — the Charter of Liberties of 1701 — that secured the remarkable rights and privileges of Pennsylvania. It was inconsistent, he believed, to sacrifice the Charter of Liberties in order to get rid of the proprietors and still claim the rights and privileges embedded in that document. His opposition to the Stamp Act was not a reversal of this position but an extension of it, for if his arguments in provincial politics appeared favorable to established authority and his efforts in the Stamp Act crisis antagonistic to it, both were derived from the same central concern for the maintenance of rights and privileges established in the law.

His religious sympathies, too, led him away from conflict, away from the disruptive forces of life, and toward the maintenance of social and political harmony. Though not himself formally a Quaker, he was influenced by the ideas of the Quaker world into which he had been born and to which he returned after his marriage. In every phase of his life, Frederick Tolles has written, "there was something of the Quaker devotion to peace — the horror of violence, the longing for conciliation, the faith in negotiation, the persistent, undiscourageable effort to find common ground with enemies." Neither a pacifist nor a neutralist in politics, he nevertheless shared the Quakers' "zeal for peace and reconciliation," and continued to seek those goals even at the cost of his public reputation.[4]

That he did so was a consequence, too, of his temperament, for Dickinson was the most fastidious of men, elegant in manner, delicate in appearance, scrupulous in personal relations. Again it is Adams who furnishes the unforgettable phrase: Dickinson, he wrote in 1774, when the two men first met, "is a shadow — tall, but slender as a reed — pale as ashes. One would think at first sight that he could not live a month." He had been a priggish young man. Twenty years before Adams knew him, he had written to his mother from London that "As to the vicious pleasures of London, I know not what they are; I never hear of them and never think of them . . . I hope to return to you not only pure in my morals but improved in everything you desire." The diversions of the theater were "too high seasoned for me; they glare agreeably for a time, but they blunt the sight to more lasting, more sincere pleasures." He was finicky with women, and feared the influence of "private passion" on public affairs. He disliked rashness and hasty innovations all his life. Nothing was more characteristic of him than his insistence on Congress' passing the controversial Olive Branch Petition in 1775; it was a device, he hoped, by which rashness might be restrained and the door kept open to reconciliation. And nothing was more consistent than his speech opposing not independence as such, but a declaration of independence then, in early July of 1776, for, as he said in his fateful speech of opposition on July 1, it would be foolhardy to "brave the storm in a skiff of paper"; proper preparations must be made: measures must be taken that will show "deliberation, wisdom, caution, and unanimity." He was too cautious, Professor Colbourn has written in a notable essay, "too conscious of the past, too aware of previously ill-timed efforts at change, too anxious for complete preparation and thus assured success; he lacked, in brief, the gambling instinct vital to a successful politician."[5]

And yet, for all of this — for all his wealth, position, occupational bias, moral sensibility, and temperamental constraint — Dickinson was a radical: a radical in the vital sense in which the Revolution itself was radical. He was a man of wide reading and scholarly interests, thoroughly acquainted with the history and the political and social science of his day as well as with the law. Indeed, though he was learned in the law, he was more a scholar of history and politics than of the law; the law itself, as he approached it, became a form of history and of political science applicable to the great issues of the time.[6] His mind was soaked in the literature of eighteenth-century radicalism. He knew Trenchard and Gordon's *Cato's Letters* thoroughly, quoting them frequently, and, as in the present pamphlet, at length. He took his history from many sources: from the Whig historians, especially Rapin, whom he cited on Monmouth's Rebellion, on standing armies, and on the Glorious Revolution; from Viscount Molesworth, whose *Account of Denmark* fortified him in his defense of the proprietary government of Pennsylvania; and above all from those key writers of classical antiquity, Tacitus ("that excellent historian and statesman") whose *Germania* Dickinson owned in Gordon's edition, Cicero, and Sallust ("of whom I professed myself an admirer") — from all of whom, and especially from the last, he drew a vivid picture of the decay of virtue and the growth of corruption which had led to the downfall of Rome. Later he read the current application of this ancient experience in Burgh's *Political Disquisitions,* a copy of which arrived for him in Philadelphia with a covering letter from the London bookseller Edward Dilly underscoring Burgh's emphasis on the "bribery and corruption . . . [which] engenders swarms of placemen and pensioners . . . [who] like leeches suck the very vitals of the constitution." [7]

The warnings from Dilly and Burgh, like those from the scores of other authorities Dickinson delighted in citing — Bolingbroke, Locke, Hoadly, Montesquieu, Burlamaqui, Beccaria, Price, Burnet, Coke, Grotius, Pufendorf: the footnotes became larger in successive pamphlets; they completely overwhelm the text of his *Essay* of 1774[8] — such authoritative warnings were useful reinforcements for his own views, but they came to him as no surprise. As a young man he had seen it all at first hand. London had excited him when he arrived there in his twenty-second year; he had been impressed by the majesty of the courts and awed by his sudden proximity to the scenes of English greatness. But he had been profoundly shocked by the corruption — the "impudence and villainy" — of politics. Oaths against bribery, he reported to his mother, were laughed at; voters were "made dead drunk and kept in that state . . . till all is over . . ." Like ancient Rome, England, he wrote, paraphrasing a line of Sallust popular in the colonies, was " 'easy to be bought, if there was but a purchaser.' " Greater familiarity merely deepened his shock and pessimism as he viewed Hogarthian election scenes: ". . . it is ridiculous and absurd to pretend to curb the effects of luxury and corruption in one instance or in one spot without a general reformation of manners, which everyone sees is absolutely necessary for the welfare of this kingdom. Yet Heaven knows how it can be effected. It is grown a vice here to be virtuous . . . People are grown too polite to have an old-fashioned religion, and are too weak to find out a new, from whence follows the most unbounded licentiousness and utter disregard of virtue, which is the unfailing cause of the destruction of all empires . . ." There appeared to be no end to the inroads corruption was making on the ancient constitution. He was "astonished to hear from Englishmen," he reported, the arguments spoken on a militia bill in a House of Lords debate; they indicated what he could only conclude was a favorable opinion of standing armies and of the employments of foreign mercenaries. "But such is the complacency these great men have for the smiles of their prince that they will gratify every desire of ambition and power at the expense of truth, reason, and their country." [9]

Dickinson's social and political philosophy as it developed in the two decades before Independence was a compendium of eighteenth-century radicalism. He feared the use of power: power, he repeated again and again, was "of an encroaching nature, ever on the watch to extend its sway"; it was "like the *ocean,* not easily admitting limits to be fixed in it"; it was "of a tenacious nature: what it seizes it will retain." He feared human weakness in the face of power, feared especially the madness that absolute power, in the form of military might, generated in those who controlled it. And while he venerated the British constitution as the greatest arrangement for the control of power yet known, he doubted, citing the admired Bolingbroke, whether England would be able to avoid the fate of Rome.[10] When the challenge to the proprietary charter of Pennsylvania rose he thought instinctively of the fate of Denmark a century earlier where the Commons, "smarting under the tyranny of their nobility, in a fit of revengeful fury *suddenly* surrendered their liberties to their king; and ever since, with unavailing grief and useless execrations, have detested the *mad moment* which slipt upon them the shackles of slavery, which no struggles can shake off." Already at this early stage, on an issue peripheral to the mounting Anglo-American controversy, he feared the machinations of the ministry. "'Tis true," he admitted, "they don't choose to act arbitrarily, and tear away the present government from us without our consent. This is not the age for such things. But let *us* only furnish them with a pretext by pressing petitions for a change; let us only relinquish the hold we now have, and in an instant we are precipitated from that envied height where we now stand." The Stamp Act fortified his suspicions that a power-hungry ministry was seeking to rivet chains on the colonies. Judge, he warned in November 1765, the use that would be made of American compliance "by the eagerness with which the pack of ministerial tools have hunted for precedents to palliate the horrors of this attack upon American freedom." These men "who designed to oppress us," he pointed out a year later, seeking the plunder of "oppressive offices for themselves and their creatures . . . held up to those whose assistance they were obliged to use, specious pretences of immediate advantage, while every remoter mischief, every disagreeable truth, was artfully concealed from them . . . All was arbitrary, rigid, threatening, dreadful." [11]

There was respite in the repeal of the Stamp Act, but the ease it brought was illusory. The Townshend Duties, passed after all the defiance Americans had shown in 1765, Dickinson wrote, were manifestly "a part of that plan by which [Grenville] endeavored to render himself POPULAR at home." All of history testified to "how eager ministers are to seize upon any settled revenue, and apply it in supporting their own power." The consequences of acquiescence were only too clear. There would be a vast multiplication of lucrative offices exercised by dependents of absentee profiteers, and then "the *army,* the *administration of justice,* and the *civil government* here, with such salaries as the crown shall please to annex, will extend *ministerial influence* as much beyond its former bounds as the late war did the British dominions." It is true, he said, "that a strong spirit of liberty subsists at present in Great Britain, but what reliance is to be placed in the *temper* of a people when the prince is possessed of an unconstitutional power, our own history can sufficiently inform us." Pressure on popular liberties would be maintained; the people's will would soften; and liberty-preserving virtue would decay. In the end there was no safety in the temper of the British. America must rely on its own purity to defend its liberty. The blandishments of the great must be resisted; industry, frugality, and sleepless vigilance must be maintained. " 'SLAVERY IS EVER PRECEDED BY SLEEP,' " he quoted from Montesquieu.[12]

Dickinson's worst fears soon seemed justified. After a brief *detente* came the Tea Act of 1773, whose intent, he wrote, was "not only to *enforce* the *Revenue Act* but to *establish* a *monopoly* for the *East India Company,* who have espoused the cause of the ministry, and hope to repair their broken fortunes by the ruin of American freedom and liberty! . . . Pray have you heard whether *they* and the *minister* have not *made a property* of US, and whether WE, our WIVES and CHILDREN, together with the HARD-EARNED FRUITS OF OUR LABOR, are not *made over* to *this* almost *bankrupt company,* to augment their stock, and to *repair* their *ruined fortunes?* Justice seems to have forsaken the Old World . . . the *East India Company* . . . have now the assurance to step forth in aid of the minister, to execute his plan of enslaving America." The record of the company was only too well known:

> they have, by the most unparalleled barbarities, extortions, and monopolies, stripped the miserable inhabitants of their property, and reduced whole provinces to indigence and ruin . . . having drained the sources of that immense wealth which they have for several years past been accustomed to amass and squander away on their lusts and in corrupting their country, they now, it seems, cast their eyes on America as a new theater whereon to exercise their talents of rapine, oppression, and cruelty . . . It is something of a consolation to be overcome by a lion, but to be devoured by rats is intolerable.[13]

The evidence by then seemed overwhelming; it had led Dickinson step by step toward the conclusion that a conspiracy against freedom in America was under way. But still he hesitated to draw the final conclusion. "I can hardly persuade myself," he wrote in November 1773, "that the ministry are so mad" as to order military enforcement of the Tea Act "at the hazard of losing the affection of the Americans." But after the Intolerable Acts the ultimate conclusion could not be avoided: "a plan has been deliberately framed and pertinaciously adhered to," Dickinson wrote in June 1774, "unchanged even by frequent changes of ministers, unchecked by any intervening gleam of humanity, to sacrifice to a passion for arbitrary dominion the universal property, liberty, safety, honor, happiness, and prosperity of us unoffending yet devoted Americans." He then proceeded, in letters to the press, to lay out the "series of correspondent facts" that would "tear up by the roots and throw out of your bosoms every lurking doubt" that such was in fact the case.[14]

The question thereafter was one of tactics, and in this, in 1774 and 1775, Dickinson's natural caution became controlling while others rushed ahead from conclusions he too had reached. The ministry's success, the severity of the action they had been able to take against America, stemmed in large part,

Dickinson believed, from their "great cunning and labor" in deluding the English people and the King as to the colonists' intentions. They had convinced the people and the crown that "we are in a state of rebellion and aiming directly at a state of independency." Hope lay, therefore, first, in organizing a complete unanimity in colonial opposition to the English government; second, in exerting the full force of economic pressure against England; and third, in appealing directly to the King to free himself from the malign influences that surrounded him and to hold back the impending catastrophe.[15]

It was the last that dictated the wording of Dickinson's Olive Branch Petition, which so enraged the more impatient of the Revolutionary leaders. In it he calmly described the alarm that had been caused by the "new system of statutes and regulations adopted for the administration of the colonies"; he prudently mentioned but did not dilate on "the irksome variety of artifices practiced by many of Your Majesty's ministers, the delusive pretenses, fruitless terrors, and unavailing severities that have from time to time been dealt out by them in their attempts to execute this impolitic plan"; he depicted the colonies' "artful and cruel enemies who abuse your royal confidence and authority for the purpose of effecting our destruction"; and at the end he prayed for relief from the "afflicting fears and jealousies occasioned by the system before-mentioned." But it was all unavailing; the petition was ignored. Thereafter there remained only the question of timing in pronouncing independence. Dickinson's speech in Congress of July 1, 1776, urging postponement of this final act until passions had a chance to cool, until alliances could be contracted, and until a government was firmly constructed, gave, as he knew it would, "the finishing blow to my once too great and, my integrity considered, now too diminished popularity." But it had not resulted from a difference of opinion with the more forthright leaders over the meaning of the events of the time or over the obligation this understanding imposed on the people of America. His refusal to take the final step until full preparations were made was courageous if unimaginative: it was the act of a prudent man, instinctively cautious and always reasonable, seeking hostages of fate.[16]

The present pamphlet, published in December 1765, reveals, as much in its timing as in its contents, the rationality and constraint of Dickinson's approach to the problems of Anglo-American relations. For though it appeared after the publication of notable essays on constitutional theory and on rights, and after the Stamp Act Congress had issued its declarations of principles which Dickinson himself had drafted, it directs its appeal to England on strictly economic grounds, on grounds of material self-interest narrowly defined. Considered only as an essay in economic theory the pamphlet is notable, for its discussions of paper money, of flows of trade, and of the mechanisms and effects of taxation are sophisticated for the time; and they are based on statistical evidence as well as on the arguments of authoritative writers on economics. But the essay is more than a technical treatise. Stylistically, it has the vivid phraseology, the dramatic, exclamatory italicization and paragraphing, and the aptness of illustration that would soon make Dickinson the most widely read pamphleteer in the colonies. And it demonstrates in its effective use of *Cato's Letters* in what would seem to be an unlikely context the universal relevance to Americans of the radical tradition in English political thought.

THE/LATE REGULATIONS/RESPECTING THE/BRITISH COLONIES/ON THE CONTINENT OF/AMERICA/CONSIDERED,/In a Letter from a Gentleman in PHILADEL-PHIA/to his Friend in LONDON./

Prosunt minus recte excogitata; cum alios incitent saltem/ad veritatis investigationem. FULB. A BARTOL./

PHILADELPHIA:/Printed and Sold by WILLIAM BRADFORD, at the Corner of/Market and Front-Streets. M.DCC.LXV./

THE LATE REGULATIONS

Sir,

When I last wrote to you and said "that the late measures respecting America would not only be extremely injurious to the colonies but also to Great Britain," I little thought I was entering into an engagement which would oblige me to exceed the usual limits of a letter; but since you desire to have at large the reasons in support of this opinion, and I always think it my duty to comply with your requests, I will endeavor in the clearest manner I can to lay my sentiments before you.

The American continental colonies are inhabited by persons of small fortunes who *are* so closely employed in subduing a wild country for their subsistence and who *would* labor under such difficulties in contending with old and populous countries which must exceed them in workmanship and cheapness, that they have not [4] time nor any temptation to apply themselves to manufactures.

Hence arises the importance* [1] of the colonies to Great Britain. Her

---

* It has been said in the House of Commons, when complaints have been made of the decay of trade to any part of Europe, "that such things were not worth regard, as Great Britain was possessed of colonies that could consume more of her manufactures than she was able to supply them with."

"As the case now stands, we shall show that the plantations are a spring of *wealth* to this nation, that they *work* for us, that their treasure *centers all here,* and that the laws have tied them fast enough to us; so that it must be through our own fault and mismanagement if they become independent of England." Davenant on the plantation trade.

"It is better that the islands should be supplied from the northern colonies than from England for this reason; the provisions we might send to Barbados, Jamaica, etc., would be *unimproved* product of the earth, as grain of all kinds, or such product where there is little got by the improvement, as malt, salt, beef, and pork; indeed, the exportation of salt fish thither would be more advantageous, but the goods which we send to the northern colonies are such whose *improvement* may be justly said one with another to be near *four fifths* of the value of the *whole commodity,* as apparel, household furniture, and many other things. *Idem.*

"New England is the most prejudicial plantation to the kingdom of England; and yet, to do right to that most industrious English colony, I must confess that though we lose by their unlimited trade with other foreign plantations, yet we are very great gainers by their direct trade to and from Old England. Our yearly exportations of English manufactures, malt, and other goods, from hence thither, amounting, in my opinion, to *ten times* the value of what is imported from thence; which calculation I do not make at random, but upon *mature consideration,* and, peradventure, upon *as much experience in this very trade* as any other person will pretend to; and therefore, whenever reformation of our cor-

prosperity depends on her commerce; her commerce on her manufactures; her [5] manufactures on the markets for them; and the most constant and advantageous markets are afforded by the colonies, as in all others the rest of Europe†[2] interferes with her, and various accidents may interrupt them. The benefit from hence is at *present* immense; but in *future* times when America shall be more fully peopled, must exceed with prudent management the warmest wishes of a British patriot.

Our chief productions are provisions, naval stores, furs, iron, and lumber. A few colonies yield tobacco and indigo. Many of these commodities are necessary to Great Britain; but all that she requires are [6] vastly insufficient to pay for her manufactures which we want. The productions of some of the southern colonies may perhaps be equal to their demands, but the case is widely different with the northern; for in these, the importations from Great Britain are computed to be generally more than double the value of their immediate exportations to that kingdom.

The only expedient left us for making our remittances is to carry on some other trade, whereby we can obtain silver and gold, which our own

---

respondency in trade with that people shall be thought on, it will, in my poor judgment, require GREAT TENDERNESS and VERY SERIOUS CIRCUMSPECTION." Sir Josiah Child's *Discourse on Trade.*

"Our plantations spend mostly our English manufactures, and those *of all sorts almost imaginable,* in *egregious quantities,* and employ near *two thirds of our English shipping;* so that we have *more people* in England by reason of our plantations in America." *Idem.*

Sir JOSIAH CHILD says, in another part of his work, "That not more than fifty families are maintained in England by the refining of sugar." From whence, and from what Davenant says, it is plain that the advantages here said to be derived from the plantations by England must be meant chiefly of the continental colonies. See notes to pages 12 and 13.

"I shall sum up my whole remarks on our American colonies with this observation, that as they are a certain annual revenue of several millions sterling to their mother country, they ought carefully to be protected, duly encouraged, and every opportunity that presents improved for their increment and advantage, as every one they can possibly reap must at last return to us with interest." Beawes's *Lex Merc. Red.*

"We may safely advance that our trade and navigation are greatly increased by our colonies, and that they really are a source of treasure and naval power to this kingdom, since *they work for us,* and *their treasure centers here.* Before their settlement, our manufactures were few, and those but indifferent; the number of English merchants very small, and the whole shipping of the nation much inferior to what now belongs to the northern colonies only. *These are certain facts.* But since their establishment, our condition has altered for the better, almost to a degree beyond credibility. Our MANUFACTURES are prodigiously increased, chiefly by the demand for them in the plantations, where they AT LEAST TAKE OFF ONE HALF, and supply us with many valuable commodities for exportation, which is as great an emolument to the mother kingdom as to the plantations themselves." Postlethwayt's *Univ. Dict. of Trade and Commerce.*

† "Most of the nations of Europe have interfered with us, more or less, in divers of our staple manufactures, within half a century, not only in our woolen but in our lead and tin manufactures as well as our fisheries." Postlethwayt, *ibid.*

country does not afford. Hence it is evident that if our taking off and paying for her manufactures is beneficial to Great Britain, the channels by which we acquire money for that purpose ought to be industriously kept open and uninterrupted.

Our trade with Spain, Portugal, and the foreign plantations in the West Indies have chiefly answered this end, though with much difficulty, the mother country having long since drawn the commercial cords‡ [3] with which the colonies are bound extremely tight upon them. Every thing produced *here* that Great Britain chooses to take to herself must be carried to that [7] kingdom§ [4] only. Everything we choose to import from Europe must be shipped in Great Britain.|| Heavy duties have been laid on our importations from the foreign plantations.

However, under all these restraints and some others that have been imposed on us, we have not till lately been unhappy. Our spirits were not depressed. We apprehended no design formed against our liberty. We for a long time enjoyed peace, and were quite free from any heavy debt, either internal or external. We had a paper currency which served as a

‡ As far as regulations are requisite to confine the commerce of the colonies to British subjects and to British ships; to give Great Britain the preference in being supplied with naval stores, so essential to her strength at sea; with commodities necessary for carrying on her woolen manufactures, or such articles as can bear high duties upon them, and thereby make a considerable addition to the revenue; or as far as they are requisite to prevent the colonies from being supplied with anything in the place of British manufactures, they may be reasonable. These regulations, it is apprehended, establish the basis of the British power, and form such a firm connection between the mother country and her colonies as will produce all the advantages she ought to wish for, or that they can afford her. Any further attempt to shackle *some* of the colonies in favor of *others,* or to advance the revenue in America by restraining its trade, is but regulating by a severe exercise of power what wants no regulation, and losing by too much haste to gain. (See notes to page 15.) *Unnecessary* and *irritating* restrictions will at last cast *contempt* and *hatred* on those *substantial* ones that length of time and the natural reverence of colonies for their mother country would have consecrated, for discontented minds are not apt to distinguish. "Narrow-limited notions in trade and planting are only advanced by, and can only be of use to, *particular* persons, but are always injurious to the *public* interests in preventing the full employment of our own people, and giving our rivals and competitors in trade the opportunity of employing greater numbers of theirs, producing greater quantities of merchandises, and underselling us at foreign markets." Postlethwayt's *Univ. Dict. of Trade and Commerce.*

§ Montesquieu, speaking of the contract made by Poland for selling *all* her corn to Danzig ONLY, and another of the like nature between some Indian princes and the Dutch for spices, says: "These agreements are proper for a poor nation, whose inhabitants are satisfied *to forego the hopes of enriching themselves* provided *they can be secure of a certain subsistence,* or for nations whose SLAVERY consists either *in renouncing the use of those things which nature has given them,* or in being OBLIGED TO SUBMIT TO A DISADVANTAGEOUS COMMERCE."

|| Except salt from any part of Europe for the fisheries of Newfoundland, New England, New York and Pennsylvania; and a few things from Ireland.

medium of domestic commerce and permitted us to employ all the gold and silver we could acquire in trade abroad. We had a multitude of markets for our provisions, lumber, and iron. These allowed liberties, with some others we assumed, enabled us to collect considerable sums of money for the joint benefit of ourselves and our mother country. [8]

But the modern regulations are in every circumstance afflicting. The remittances we have been able to make to Great Britain, with all the license hitherto granted or taken and all the money brought among us in the course of the late war, have not been sufficient to pay her what we owe; but there still remains due, according to a late calculation made by the English merchants, the sum of four millions sterling. Besides this, we are and have been for many years heavily taxed for the payment of the debts contracted by our efforts against the common enemy. These seem to be difficulties severe enough for young colonies to contend with. The last sinks our paper currency very fast.¶ The former sweeps off our silver and gold in a torrent to Great Britain and leaves us continually toiling to supply from a number of distant springs the continually wasting stream.

Thus drained, we are prohibited by new and stricter restraints being laid on our trade from procuring these coins as we used to do and from instituting among ourselves bills of credit in the place of such portions of them as are required in our internal traffic; and in this exhausted condition, our languishing country is to strive to take up and to totter under the additional burden of the STAMP ACT.

In defense of the prohibition to institute *bills of credit* it may be said, "that some few colonies, by injurious emissions of paper currency, did great injury to [9] individuals." It is true: But it is as true that others* always supported the credit of their bills in such a manner that their emissions were of vast benefit both to the provinces and to Great Britain.[5] The inconveniences under which the colonies labored before these emissions are well remembered and were produced by the same cause that distresses us at this time, that is, by Great Britain's taking off all our gold and silver. There was then so little money among several of them that a stop was put in a manner to buying and selling, and then shopkeepers

---

¶ While the quantity of paper currency is proportioned to the uses for it, it must be beneficial; and therefore to sink it below that quantity must be prejudicial.

* No attempt was ever made in this province and some others to pay English debts any otherwise than according to the rate of exchange; and no complaint was ever made of injustice from the depreciation of the currency.

were obliged to barter their goods for food. The effect produced by these emissions was surprising. Trade revived and the remarkable and immediate increase† [6] of our importations showed how advantageous they were to Great Britain. If any [10] inconveniences were feared from this kind of currency, means might have been found to prevent them without utterly abolishing it; but now the apprehension of mischiefs that might have been more easily obviated has deprived us of real benefits.

Perhaps no mode could be devised more advantageous to the public, or to individuals, than our method of emitting bills in this province for our own use. They are lent out upon good security, chiefly real, at the interest of *five per cent*. The borrowers are allowed a long term for pay-

---

† Value of the exports from England to Pennsylvania at different periods.

$$
\begin{array}{lr}
\text{In 1723 they were} & £15,992{:}19{:}4 \\
1730 & 48,592{:}\ 7{:}5 \\
1737 & 56,690{:}\ 6{:}7 \\
1742 & 75,295{:}\ 3{:}4 \\
\end{array}
$$

In the year 1723 the first bills of credit were emitted in Pennsylvania, to the value of £45,000. In 1728, part of the first emission being then sunk, £30,000 more were emitted. It appears from the account above that in seven years from 1723 to 1730 the exports increased £32,599:8:1 sterling. In 1738, great part of the preceding emissions being then sunk, there was an emission and re-emission amounting in the whole to £80,000. In five years afterwards, it appears by the account above, the exports increased over £20,000 sterling.

In later times when larger emissions have been made, the exports have proportionately increased. In 1755 £55,000 were emitted, and in 1756 £30,000. In 1757 the exports amounted to £268,426:6:6. Afterwards our emissions were still greater, and in one year of the war, the exports rose to more than £700,000 sterling.

It is not pretended that the increase of our importations is *solely* owing to the emissions of paper money; but it is thought to be a very great cause of that increase. It is undoubtedly owing in part to the increase of people by propagation and the influx of foreigners. But such *great* and *sudden* increases as have been mentioned in the short space of seven or five years, from 1723 to 1730 and from 1737 to 1742, could not in any great degree proceed from the increase by propagation; and at that time I think foreigners did not flow in upon us in such numbers as they since have done. In the war large sums were brought among us for the maintenance of the fleets and armies, it is true; but that our currency was then of great utility is evident, because when the greatest quantity of it was passing, bills of exchange were lower than they were for a long time before, or have been since.

It may be objected that the complaint of the scarcity of money in America, particularly in this province, cannot be well founded, as we have lately had such large emissions. I am very sensible how liable persons are to errors in questions of this nature, and therefore I think myself obliged to speak with diffidence on the subject. Perhaps the following observations may in some measure answer the objection. 1st. About one half of the emissions is sunk. 2dly. A very great part of the bills now circulating are passing in the neighboring provinces. 3dly. Our gold and silver are sent to Great Britain, so that but small quantities thereof are now current among us—and therefore we must almost entirely rely on our paper for the medium of domestic commerce. Lastly, it does not seem probable that we should have heard such great complaints of the scarcity of money if the extreme restrictions of our commerce had not so generally prevented our usual methods of acquiring it.

ment, and the sums borrowed being divided into equal portions, they are obliged to pay one of these, with the interest of the whole, every year during the term. This renders the payments very easy; and as no person [11] is permitted to borrow a large sum, a great number are accommodated. The consequences of such regulations are obvious. These bills represent money in the same manner that money represents other things. As long therefore as the quantity is proportioned to the uses, these emissions have the same effects that the gradual introduction of additional sums of money would have. People of very small fortunes are enabled to purchase and cultivate land, which is of so much consequence in settling new countries, or to carry on some business that without such assistance they would be incapable of managing: for no private person would lend money on such favorable terms. From the borrowers the currency passes into other hands, increases consumption, raises the prices of commodities, quickens circulation, and communicating a vigor to all kinds of industry, returns in its course into the possession of the borrowers to repay them for that labor which it may properly be said to have produced. They deliver it, according to the original contracts, into the treasury, where the interest raises a fund, without the imposition of taxes, for the public use.

While emissions are thus conducted with prudence, they may be compared to springs whose water an industrious and knowing farmer spreads in many meandering rivulets through his gardens and meadows, and after it has refreshed all the vegetable tribes it meets with and has set them a-growing, leads it into a reservoir where it answers some new purpose.

If it could be possible to establish a currency throughout the colonies on some foundation of this kind, perhaps greater benefits might be derived from it than would be generally believed without the trial. [12]

With respect to the restrictions laid on our trade in foreign plantations, it has been alleged as a reason for them, "that our islands ought to be encouraged." They ought to be; but should the interest of one colony be preferred to that of another? Should the welfare of millions be sacrificed to the magnificence of a few? If the exorbitant profits of one colony must arise from the depression of another, should not such injustice be redressed?

There is a vast difference to be made in calculating the gains of any particular branch of business to the *public* and to *individuals*. The advantages to the last may be small, and yet great to the first, or the reverse. The statutes made to restrain the trade of the continent in favor of the islands‡ [7] seem to tend rather towards [13] promoting

‡ "The agents for New York, in their contest with the sugar colonies, affirmed that their winters being severe, obliged them to take off more of the woollen manufactures of this kingdom (*for which they remitted gold and silver*) than all the *islands* (Jamaica excepted) *put together;* and which I believe has remained uncontradicted." Beawes's *Lex Merc. Red.*

If one province THEN exceeded all our West Indies except Jamaica, in this particular, what proportion would that single island bear NOW to *all the rest of the continental colonies?*

The following account of the exports from ENGLAND to the northern colonies and to the West India islands will show they were nearly equal some time ago; that those to the northern colonies now vastly exceed, and are prodigiously increasing, while those to the islands have continued nearly the same.

From 1744 to 1748, inclusive

Northern Colonies.					West India Islands.		
1744	£640,114:	12:	4		£796,112:	17:	9
1745	534,316:	2:	5		503,669:	19:	9
1746	754,945:	4:	3		472,994:	19:	7
1747	726,648:	5:	5		856,463:	18:	6
1748	830,243:	16:	9		734,095:	15:	3

Total £3,486,268: 1: 2

Total £3,363,337: 10: 10
Difference 122,930: 10: 4

£3,486,268: 1: 2

From 1754 to 1758, inclusive

Northern Colonies.					West India Islands.		
1754	£1,246,615:	1:	11		£685,675:	3:	0
1755	1,177,848:	6:	10		694,667:	13:	3
1756	1,428,720:	18:	10		733,458:	16:	3
1757	1,727,924:	2:	10		776,488:	0:	6
1758	1,832,948:	13:	10		877,571:	19:	11

Total £7,414,057: 4: 3

Total £3,767,841: 12: 11
Difference 3,646,215: 11: 4

£7,414,057: 4: 3

Total for the northern colonies, in the first term £3,486,268: 1: 2
Ditto, in the second term 7,414,057: 4: 3

Increase £3,927,789: 3: 1

Total for the West India islands, in the first term £3,363,337: 10: 10
Ditto, in the second term 3,767,841: 12: 11

Increase, only £0,404,504: 2: 1

The difference between the employment afforded to the manufacturers of England by the northern colonies and by the West India islands is still greater than it may appear to

partial § than *general* interests, and it appears to me no paradox to say that the public would be a great gainer if estates there were so moderate|| [8] that not a tenth part of the West India gentlemen that now sit in the House of Commons could obtain that frequently expensive honor.

It is allowed by those well acquainted with the islands that they cannot supply Great Britain and these colonies [14] with sugar and other articles, and that they can by no means consume the productions of these colonies; yet in favor to them¶ we are almost entirely prevented from sending these productions to any other markets. Hence it follows that we are frequently obliged to sell our commodities to them at so low a price as not to pay the first cost and freight, while we, being in a manner prohibited from getting the West India productions for which we have occasion anywhere else but from them, must pay extravagantly for them.

Nor is this management attended, as it is presumed, with any benefit to the mother country, but with a disadvantage, either where the productions of the foreign plantations are consumed among us or re-exported to Europe. By the compulsion on us to take from our islands, the price of their productions is raised on the people of Great Britain. The revenue would be increased by this restriction being taken off, as we should will-

---

be from the first view of the preceding account, for a much greater quantity of East India goods is exported to the last than to the first; and the English manufactures consumed by them generally derive their value from the richness of the materials, many of which are brought from foreign countries, but those we consume chiefly derive their value from the work bestowed upon them. (Vide note to pages 4 and 5.)

§ Vide note to page 6.

|| "A great advantage which the French have over the English in their sugar colonies is their *agrarian law,* whereby monopolists are prevented from engrossing too much land; so that the number of whites is greatly increased, the land improved, more commodities raised, the planters *obliged to a more frugal way of living,* and *all things rendered cheaper.* By these means Martinique can muster 16,000 fighting men, but Jamaica, which is near three times as large, only 4,000." Tucker on trade.

¶ It is recited in the 6th of Geo. II c. 13, now made perpetual, "that the sugar colonies could not carry on their trade ON AN EQUAL FOOTING with the foreign sugar colonies without some *advantage* and relief given to them by Great Britain." That *advantage* GIVEN by Great Britain was to compel the continental colonies to take their productions at any price they please to ask. In short, to grant them a MONOPOLY for sugars. This was taking *from one* indeed to give *to another,* but goes not to the root of the evil, as the next preceding note evidently shows. For if Great Britain should sacrifice her own interests and those of her continental colonies still more, *if it be possible,* to the interest of these islanders, *they never will* "carry on their trade ON AN EQUAL FOOTING with the foreign sugar colonies" until there is the same moderation in their estates and the same frugality in their living. By a very singular disposition of affairs the colonies of an *absolute monarchy* are settled on a *republican principle,* while those of a kingdom in many respects *resembling a commonwealth* are cantoned out among *a few lords* vested with despotic power over *myriads of vassals* and supported in the pomp of *bassas* by *their* slavery.

ingly pay a moderate duty upon importations from the French and Spaniards without attempting to run them, while a very considerable duty would be paid [15] on the sugars* of our islands, which, instead of coming to us, would then go to Great Britain. Besides, whatever extraordinary price we pay for the productions of our own islands must lessen our demand for British manufactures, since it is an undeniable† [9] truth that what we [16] should save in that way would be chiefly spent in this. It may also justly be added that our commerce with the foreign plantations carries to them very considerable quantities of British manufactures for their consumption.‡

If our importations from them should be re-exported to Europe, the profits would center in Great Britain, according to the usual course of our trade. The statute passed in the twenty-fifth year of Charles the

* The restriction on the trade of the colonies to foreign plantations for molasses is particularly grievous and impolitic as the molasses brought from thence was distilled for the fisheries, the Indian and Guinea trades, the profit of which centered in Great Britain. It is said our vessels now buy spirituous liquors on the coast of Guinea from the Dutch.

† This cannot be disputed by any one who is acquainted with America. This increase of a man's wealth there shows itself in a great consumption of British manufactures of all kinds. This reasoning in favor of the continental colonies trade with foreign plantations is confirmed by what Sir Josiah Child mentions of New England. He says, "England loses by the *unlimited trade* of this colony to other foreign plantations but gains by her direct trade to Old England, from whence she exports manufactures to *ten times* the value of her imports." (See the note to page 4.) What was it then that enabled New England to pay *ten times* the *value* of her *imports* to England but the *profits of her trade to foreign plantations?* This appears to be a direct authority in support of the arguments hereafter used. It seems therefore that Great Britain of late, through too great eagerness to gather golden fruits, has shaken the tree before they were full grown. With a little patience they would ripen and then of themselves drop into her lap.

"The inhabitants of our colonies, by carrying on a trade with their *foreign neighbors,* do not only occasion *a greater quantity of the goods and merchandises of Europe being sent from hence to them,* and a greater quantity of the product of *America* to be sent from them hither, *which would otherwise be carried from and brought to Europe by foreigners,* but an increase of the seamen and navigation in those parts, which is of great strength and security as well as of great advantage to our plantations in general. And though *some of our colonies* are not only for preventing the *importation of all goods of the same species they produce* but suffer particular planters to *keep great runs of land in their possession uncultivated* with design to prevent new settlements, whereby they imagine the prices of their commodities may be affected, yet if it be considered that the markets of Great Britain depend on the markets of ALL Europe *in general,* and that the European markets *in general* depend on the proportion between the *annual consumption* and the *whole quantity* of each species *annually produced* by ALL nations, it must follow that whether we or foreigners are the producers, *carriers,* importers, and exporters of American produce, yet their respective prices in *each colony* (the difference of freight, customs, and importations considered) will always bear proportion to the *general consumption* of the *whole quantity* of each sort *produced in all colonies* and *in all parts,* allowing only for the usual contingencies that trade and commerce, agriculture and manufactures are liable to in all countries." Postlethwayt's *Univ. Dict. of Trade and Commerce.*

‡ See the preceding note.

Second indeed mentions this practice as injurious. It might be so, if regarded without its attendant circumstances; but if *they* are taken into view, and it be considered that if *we* do not carry these productions to Europe *foreigners* will, no mischief seems likely to ensue from our becoming the carriers.§

The restriction also with regard to our iron is thought particularly severe. Whenever we can get a better price in Great Britain than elsewhere, it is unnecessary; whenever we can get a better price in other places, it is prejudicial.|| Cargoes composed of this [17] metal, provisions, and lumber, have been found to answer very well at the Portuguese and some other markets; and as the last articles are frequently very low and our foreign trade is reduced to so few commodities, the taking away any one of them must be hurtful to us. Indeed, to require us to send all our iron to Great Britain is, in the opinion of some of our most judicious merchants, to require an impossibility. For as this article is so heavy and such small quantities can be sent in one vessel, they assert that we cannot find freight directly home for one half of it.

Besides the circumstances already mentioned to prove the injurious consequences of the late restrictions, there is another, which has great force in persuading me that our trade ought by all means to be more encouraged and extended at this time than was formerly necessary. Our settlements then only comprehended a narrow strip along the shore of the ocean; they were less populous, and their distance from the seaports [18] being small, they were supplied with everything they wanted from thence without any length of inland carriage. But now we have penetrated boundless forests, have passed over immense mountains, and are daily pushing further and further into the wilderness, the inhabitants of these remote regions must of necessity hold very little intercourse with

§ See the preceding note.
|| If Great Britain really takes off from Sweden iron to the value of £200,000, according to the calculation that has been made, yet she does not lose all that sum. Not to insist on the merely political advantage of having a commerce with that *Protestant* kingdom, which by being beneficial to her may more firmly attach her to our interest, it may be observed that the trade of Great Britain to Sweden, it is for iron in the gross, which is afterwards worked up, and large quantities of it re-exported: so that money may thereby be brought into the kingdom, and a great number of hands is employed. There is a vast difference between this trade and that to France, from whence the importations into Great Britain are merely for consumption, without affording any employment to her people or any profit by re-exportation. Besides, if the colonies can get more by carrying their iron to foreign ports than to Great Britain (and if they cannot, there is no occasion of a law to compel them to carry it to Great Britain) they will be more able to make larger demands for British manufactures, so that Great Britain will gain the profits of our iron, to make up her loss by what she takes from Sweden.

those which are near the sea, unless a very extensive commerce shall enable these to supply them with such quantities of foreign commodities ¶ as they want, and at such prices as they can afford to pay. Every restriction on our trade seems to be a restriction on this intercourse and must gradually cut off the connection of the interior parts with the maritime and the mother country.

But it is unnecessary to endeavor to prove by reasoning on these things that we *shall suffer,* for we *already suffer.* Trade is decaying, and all credit is expiring. Money is become so extremely scarce that reputable freeholders find it impossible to pay debts which are trifling in comparison to their estates.* If creditors sue and take out executions, the lands and personal estate, as the sale must be for ready money, are sold for a small part of what they were worth when the debts were contracted. The debtors are ruined. The creditors get but part of their debts, and that ruins them. [19] Thus the consumers break the shopkeepers; they break the merchants; and the shock must be felt as far as London. Fortunate indeed is the man who can get satisfaction *in money* for any part of his debt in some counties; for in many instances, after lands and goods have been repeatedly advertised in the public gazettes and exposed to sale, not a buyer appears.

By these means multitudes are already ruined, and the estates of others are melting away in the same manner. It must strike any one with great surprise and concern to hear of the number of debtors discharged every court by our insolvent act. Though our courts are held every quarter, yet at the last term for the county of Philadelphia alone no less than thirty-five persons applied for the benefit of that act. If it be considered that this law extends only to those who do not owe any single debt above £150, that many are daily released by the lenity of their creditors, and that many more remove without their knowledge, it will not be difficult to form a judgment of the condition to which the people are reduced.

If these effects are produced already, what can we expect when the same cause shall have operated longer? What can we expect when the exhausted colonies shall feel the STAMP ACT drawing off, as it were, the

¶ It is apprehended, that if the greatest part of the commodities demanded by the back country should not be British but West Indian, yet it must be beneficial to Great Britain to promote this trade by all means. For if the country nearer the sea grows rich by supplying them with the productions of the West Indies, these will certainly consume greater quantities of British manufactures.

* It is said that in Virginia the sheriffs, instead of raising the annual levies, have been obliged to make returns into the treasury of effects which they have taken in execution but could not sell, as there were no bidders for ready money.

last drops of their blood? From whence is the silver to come with which the taxes imposed by this act and the duties imposed by other late acts are to be paid? Or how will our *merchants* and the *lower ranks of people,* on whom the force of these regulations will fall first and with the greatest violence, bear this additional load? [20]

These last are to be considered in a very different light from those of the same classes in Great Britain. *There* the nature of their employments and the plenty of money gives them very little occasion to make contracts in writing; but *here* they are continually making them, and are obliged to do so. The STAMP ACT, therefore, will be severely felt by *these,* in whose welfare the prosperity of a state is always so much interested; and transfers of property† that ought, in new countries particularly, to be made as easy as possible will be much discouraged. From the necessity they are under of making contracts *to be executed afterwards* the lower ranks of people here are frequently engaged in law suits; and as the law is already a very heavy tax on the subject in all parts of the British dominions, this act will render it destructive here; for the necessaries, the follies, and the passions of mankind will not suffer them to cease from harassing one another in that way.

Neither are the merchants here by any means able to bear taxes as they do at home. A very great number of them there put such stocks into trade as would be thought large fortunes among us; and our merchants would think themselves very happy to leave off business with such estates as the others begin with. I speak of the merchants in general, for we have on the continent individuals who are rich, but their number [21] is too inconsiderable to deserve any notice on this occasion. Besides, the interest of money being lower at home than it is here, those who trade on borrowed stocks can do it to much greater advantage there than we can. Indeed, among us it is almost impossible to get money to trade upon at any rate. How unequal, under the present disadvantages, a merchant's commerce will be to the payment of all the taxes imposed by the STAMP ACT on his policies, fees with clerks, charter parties, protests, his other notarial acts, his letters, and even his advertisements, experience, I am afraid, will unhappily prove.

† In the present scarcity of money, the sellers of lands, Negroes, etc., etc., always insist on having part of the purchase money in hand. The buyers, unless they happen to be rich men, find it impossible to comply with this term unless they borrow money, which cannot now be done but in very small parcels from different persons. Each of these must have a bond; and each of those bonds must pay a stamp duty of one shilling sterling, if the sum be above ten pounds and under twenty — and if above twenty pounds and under forty, one shilling and six pence sterling — besides a duty on the original contract.

Thus I apprehend that this act will be extremely heavy on those who are least able to bear it; and if our merchants and people of little substance languish under it, all others must be affected. Our mode of taxation hath always been by making as exact an estimate as could be formed of each man's estate; by which means our taxes have been proportioned to the abilities of those who were to pay them. Few persons are employed in the collection of them; their allowance is very moderate, and therefore the expense is small. No excessive penalties, no tribes of informers, no dreadful and detestable courts are necessary. This I imagine is the mode of taxation which in young colonies will be found to be least oppressive and destructive, and certainly the most equal. But by the STAMP ACT, the wealthy,‡ who have money to let out at interest or to make purchases and undoubtedly ought to pay the most towards the public charges, will escape these taxes, while the whole [22] weight of them will fall on the necessitous and industrious, who most of all require relief and encouragement.

But it may be said, "that the merchants will not be affected by these taxes because they will raise the prices of their goods in proportion, and that at length *all taxes must arise from lands.*"

This rule seems more applicable to very populous and rich countries where the manufacturers and landholders, through necessity or the force of fashions, have pressing demands upon the merchants, than to such a country as this, where a great majority of the people live on their lands in a very plain way. For by practicing a strict frugality and industry, *we* may render ourselves more independent of the merchants than the circumstances of more populous and wealthy states will permit the other classes of their people to be. The high prices, therefore, which our merchants impose upon their goods will discourage the sale of them, and consequently they must "be affected by the taxes," which oblige them to raise the prices in this manner.

However, granting that all taxes must arise from lands, it follows that where the profits of the lands are small they can bear but small taxes. The more labor is bestowed on them, the greater the profits *will* be, and the taxes *may be.* In old populous countries there is an opportunity of bestowing this labor, and the manner of doing it is well understood. Thus in England the profits of land are so great as to support a very large num-

‡ If a rich man buys land, it is generally from the distressed, and therefore the seller's situation will oblige him to pay for the deed, when the other insists on it; and when a man borrows money, everybody knows who pays for the bonds and mortgages.

ber of nobility and gentry in splendor, and to afford means of raising taxes to an amazing amount. Nor are the workers of the land unrewarded, for the farmers have such long leases and other encouragements that they thrive and live comfortably, and many of them are very wealthy. [23]

How different is the case in America? The inhabitants being scattered thin through the country and laborers being very scarce, they think themselves fortunate if they can clear their land, fence it, and anyhow put their grain into the ground in season. Manuring or improving soils is not known,§ [10] except in some small closes near cities; but everyone must be content with what his land will yield of itself. With this it must be considered that at least four fifths of the people in America live upon farms either of their own or rented, and spend their small profits in maintaining their families; and it frequently happens from the length and severity of our winters that the whole produce of a man's farm is not sufficient to maintain his family and stock.||

We are informed, that an opinion has been industriously propagated in Great Britain that the colonies are wallowing in wealth and luxury ¶ [11]

§ "Further, it may be observed that our lands are not sufficiently cultivated, even where they are capable of great improvement. Hence large tracts serve only to maintain a small number of people. If we ask, why our lands (meaning in Scotland) are so ill cultivated, besides the OBVIOUS CAUSES arising from the POVERTY and UNSKILLFULNESS of many of our farmers, the SHORTNESS OF THEIR LEASES, and other things which will occur upon the least reflection, it is not a little owing to a want of inclination for agriculture, etc." *Dissertation on the Numbers of Mankind*.

|| Small as the value of our land is, it is still daily decreasing, by the number of markets for their produce being lessened; which must in time give the people an inclination to try what they can make by manufactures.

The *riches* of a people are always in proportion to the number of hands employed in works of SKILL and LABOR. Where these are few, there can be but little wealth; and where there is little wealth, but very small taxes can be borne.

¶ "It is certain that from the very time Sir Walter Raleigh, the father of our English colonies, and his associates first projected these establishments, there have been persons who have found an interest in *misrepresenting* or lessening the value of them. The attempts were called chimerical and dangerous. Afterwards many malignant suggestions were made about sacrificing so many Englishmen to the obstinate desire of settling colonies in countries which then produced very little advantage. But as these difficulties were gradually surmounted, those complaints vanished. No sooner were *these lamentations* over but *others* arose in their stead; when it could no longer be said that the colonies were *useless,* it was alleged that they were not *useful enough* to their mother country; that while we were loaded with taxes, they were absolutely free; that the *planters* lived like *princes,* while the inhabitants of England labored hard for a tolerable subsistence. This produced customs and impositions which, if grievous to the plantations, must turn to our disadvantage as well as theirs, and consequently become detrimental to both." Postlethwayt's *Univ. Dict. of Trade and Commerce.*

In pursuance of this design to bring down the pride of these PRINCELY PLANTERS, such

while she is [24] laboring under an enormous load of debt. Never was there a greater mistake. This opinion has arisen from slight observations made in our cities during the late war, when large sums of money were spent here in support of fleets and armies. Our productions were then in great demand, and trade flourished. Having a number of strangers among us, the people, naturally not ungenerous or inhospitable, indulged themselves in many uncommon expenses. But the cause of this gaiety has ceased, and all the effect remaining is that we are to be treated as a rich people when we are really poor. Tully mentions a man who lost an honorable office by the homely entertainment he gave the people of Rome when he could have afforded a better;[12] but we have lost vastly more by the imprudent excess of kindness with which we have [25] treated the people of Great Britain who have come among us, at an expense that did not suit our fortunes.

To all the disadvantages that have been mentioned, it must be added that our markets are much more precarious than those at home. It is computed that one half of the people there live in cities, and consequently there must be a perpetual domestic demand for the productions of the earth; and foreign markets are not far distant for the overplus. Here the quantity sold for consumption among us is small, and most of the foreign markets are very remote.

These reasons induce me to think that the colonies, unless some fortunate event, not to be expected, should happen, cannot bear the restrictions and taxations laid upon them by the mother country without suffering very severely. What then can we do? Which way shall we turn ourselves? How may we mitigate the miseries of our country? Great Britain gives us an example to guide us. SHE TEACHES US TO MAKE A DISTINCTION BETWEEN HER INTERESTS AND OUR OWN. Teaches! She requires — commands — insists upon it — threatens — compels — and even distresses us into it.

We have our choice of these two things — to continue our present limited and disadvantageous commerce — or to promote manufactures among ourselves, with a habit of economy, and thereby remove the necessity we are now under of being supplied by Great Britain.

It is not difficult to determine which of these things is most eligible.

heavy impositions were laid in Great Britain on tobacco that the inhabitants of Maryland and Virginia were discouraged from raising it. Then the mother country FELT her error, and these PRINCES were found to be very poor people. The same *unhappy spirit* is now producing the same mistake. There wants but a very little more weight upon Maryland and Virginia to prevent their raising tobacco, and to make them and all their sister colonies sink under their multiplied burthens.

Could the last of them be only so far [26] executed as to bring our demand for British manufactures below the profits of our foreign trade, and the amount of our commodities immediately remitted home, these colonies might revive and flourish. States and families are enriched by the same means; that is, by being so industrious and frugal as to spend less than what they raise can pay for.

We have examples in this province, which, if imitated by others, must unavoidably produce the most happy effects for us: I mean the examples of the industrious, frugal, honest Germans. Their lands are as well cultivated as they can be in this new country, and they have the good sense to require very little provisions and clothes more than they can get from their own farms and make with their own hands. If we only consider for a moment the consequences of such a conduct, should it be general, we must be convinced it must produce commerce, since all superfluities would be exported, and the owners having few demands in return, *that commerce* would of course produce wealth.

Indeed we shall be compelled, I apprehend, generally to imitate these examples. The late regulations and our constant remittances to Great Britain have extremely lessened the quantity of money among us, and yet these remittances are not sufficient to pay for those things we want from home. Necessity will teach us two ways to relieve ourselves. The one is to keep the British manufactures we purchase longer in use for wear than we have been accustomed to do. The other is to supply their place by manufactures of our own. I don't suppose our difficulties will *immediately* produce expert artists among us; but as the inhabitants here generally [27] reside on their lands and live in a plain rustic way, they will be able to supply themselves with many articles. Some author, and I think Keysler, says that in Switzerland every family has all the trades in it that are necessary for its use. Their work is not, it may be presumed, at all in the taste of London or Paris, but it serves their purpose; and their coarse clothes and simple furniture enable them to live in plenty, and to defend their liberty. Something of this kind will be, nay, already is, practiced by us. It is surprising to see the linen and cloth that have been lately made among us. Many gentlemen in this city dress now in suits produced, manufactured, and made up in this province. The cloth is not equal in fineness to the best broadcloth, but it is warm, strong, and not very homely; and when the British workmen understand that they may meet with better encouragement here than they do at home, I believe in a few years we shall have very different kinds of cloth among us from these we now make. Instances are not wanting to justify the most sanguine expectations on this head. Spain used formerly to be entirely supplied with cloths from England; but in the reigns only of their two last kings, Philip the Fifth and Ferdinand the Sixth, their manufactures have been improved to such a degree, even by that proud and indolent people, that this commerce has entirely ceased in most parts of that kingdom. The same thing has happened in France, notwithstanding the destructive wars in which she has been continually involved. Switzerland some time ago spent large sums of money in foreign commodities; but now they make excellent cloths and good silks, though the scheme at first labored under very great difficulties. That country used also to be supplied by Savoy with [28] wine; but the duke laying a duty upon it, the Switzers remonstrated; but in vain. At last some of the principal men promoted the cultivation of vines, though their predecessors had never planted any. The result exceeded their hopes. "The demand for the Savoyard wine daily decreased, and instead of the precarious advantage arising from this *impolitic duty,* the certain revenue was *irretrievably lost,* and the industrious subject deprived of the benefit of his labor." * [13]

"Before the settlement of these colonies," says Postlethwayt, "our manufactures were few, and those but indifferent. In those days we had not only our naval stores, but our ships from our neighbors. Germany furnished us with all things made of metal, even to nails. Wine, paper, linens, and a thousand other things came from France. Portugal supplied us with sugar; all the products of America were poured into us from Spain; and the Venetians and Genoese retailed to us the commodities of the East Indies at their own price." [14]

The astonishing alterations in all these particulars are too well known to need enumeration.

These instances, and many others that might be mentioned, may convince us that nothing is too difficult for men to effect whose hearts are filled with a generous love of their country; and they may convince the world of the dangers that attend provoking innovations in commerce. A branch of trade once lost is lost for ever. In short, so strong a spirit is raised in these colonies by late measures, and such successful [29] efforts are already made among us that it cannot be doubted that before the end of this century the modern regulations will teach America that she has resources within herself of which she never otherwise would have thought. Individuals, perhaps, may find their benefit in opposing her use

* Keysler.

of these resources; but I hope very, very few will wish to receive benefits by such means. The man who would promote his own interests by injuring his country is unworthy of the blessings of society.

It has hitherto been thought by the people of Great Britain, and I hope it will still be thought, that sufficient advantages are derived by her from the colonies without laying taxes upon them. To represent them as an "expensive appendage of the British Empire that can no other way repay the trouble and treasure they cost her" is certainly one of the greatest errors; and to spend much time in refuting this notion would be unnecessary. Every advantage accruing to the colonies by their connection with the mother country is *amply — dearly —* paid for by the benefits derived to her from them and by the restrictions of their commerce. These benefits have been allowed by the best writers to be immense, and consist † in the various employment and the support they afford her people. If the colonies enable *her* to pay taxes, is it not as useful to her as if *they* paid them? Or, indeed, may not the colonies with the strictest propriety be said to pay a great part of those taxes when they consume the British manufactures loaded with the advanced prices occasioned by such taxes? ‡ [15] Or, further, as the colonies are compelled to take those manufactures thus [[30]] loaded when they might furnish themselves so much cheaper from other countries, may not the difference between these prices be called an *enormous tax* paid by them to Great Britain? May they not also be said to pay *an enormous tax* to her by being compelled to carry their most valuable productions *to her alone* and to receive what she pleases to give for them when they might sell them at other markets to much greater advantage? Lastly, may they not be said to pay a heavy tax to her in being prohibited from carrying on such manufactures as

† Chiefly; even the supplying her with naval stores, etc., being inconsiderable when compared with the other advantages.

‡ "If it be asked, whether foreigners, for what goods they take of us, do not pay on *that consumption* a great portion of our taxes, it is admitted they do." Postlethwayt's *Great Britain's True System.*

By the consumption of British manufactures in America, we pay a heavier tax to Great Britain than if they were consumed at home. For in the bringing them here a vast number of merchants, factors, brokers, and seamen are employed, every one of which must have such a profit as will enable him to support himself and his family, if he has any, in a country where everything is dear by reason of the high taxes.

So far was the Parliament from thinking in the last war that any further taxes should be laid on the colonies, so convinced indeed were they that we had exceeded our abilities in the supplies we gave to the crown, that several sums of money were granted to us as indemnifications for the too heavy expenses in which we had involved ourselves.

The sums thus given paid part of our debts, but we are still laboring under the remainder.

they could have employed themselves in with advantage, and thus being obliged to resort to her for those things with which they might supply themselves? If these things are true, and can they be denied! may not the mother country more justly be called *expensive* to her colonies than they can be called *expensive* to her?

What would France give for such *extensive* dominions? Would she refuse the empire of North America unless the inhabitants would submit to any taxes she should please to impose? Or would she not rather afford them her utmost protection, if ever they should [31] be wretched enough to require it, for one half of the emoluments Great Britain receives from them? In short, the amazing increase of the wealth and strength of this kingdom since the reign of Queen Elizabeth, in whose time the colonies began to be settled, appears to be a sufficient proof of their importance: and therefore I think it may justly be said that THE FOUNDATIONS OF THE POWER AND GLORY OF GREAT BRITAIN ARE LAID IN AMERICA.

When the advantages derived by the mother country from her colonies are so *important* § and *evident,* it is amazing that any persons should venture to assert "that she poured out her wealth and blood in the late war *only for their defense and benefit,* and that she cannot be recompensed for this expense and loss *but by taxing them.*"

If any man who does not choose to spend much time in considering this subject would only read the speeches from the throne during that period, with the addresses in answer to them, he will soon be convinced *for whose benefit* Great Britain thought she was exerting herself. For my part, I should not now be surprised if those who maintain the above-mentioned assertions should contend that Great Britain ought to tax Portugal. For was not that kingdom "defended by the troops and treasure of Great Britain"? And how can she be "otherwise recompensed for this expense and loss"? If the protection of Portugal, though no taxes are received from thence, was beneficial to Great Britain, infinitely more so was the protection of the colonies.

So far I must beg leave to dissent from these gentlemen: that if the colonies by an increase of industry [32] and frugality should become able to bear this taxation, it will, in my apprehension, notwithstanding be injurious to Great Britain. If the sum be trifling, it cannot be worth the discontent and unhappiness the taking it will produce among so many faithful subjects of His Majesty. If it be considerable, it must also be hurtful in another respect.

§ Vide notes to page 4.

It must be granted that it is not merely the bringing money into a nation that makes it wealthy, but the bringing money into it by the general industry of its inhabitants. A country may perpetually receive vast sums and yet be perpetually poor. It must also be granted that almost all the money acquired by the colonies in their other branches of trade is spent by them in Great Britain, and finds employment for her people. Whatever then lessens the sum so spent, must lessen that employment. This I think will be one consequence of the STAMP ACT: for our demand will be as much less for British manufactures as the amount of the sums raised by the taxes. So much the fewer British merchants, artists, seamen, and ships will be employed by us, and so much the more distressed at first, and afterwards so much the more frugal, ingenious, laborious, and independent will the colonists become.||

It is evident from the concurrent testimony of her own most noted authors on this subject that Great Britain is sure of having our money at last ¶; and it appears no difficult matter to determine whether it is better to take it in taxes or trade. Suppose the [33] STAMP ACT, enforced by uncommon penalties and unheard-of jurisdictions, should pick up every piece of gold and silver that shall wander into the plantations, what would Great Britain gain by this measure? Or rather what would she not lose by attempting to advance her revenue by means so distressing to commerce?

But if the late restrictions shall not prove *profitable,* perhaps they may by some be called *prudent* for another reason. We are informed that many persons at home affect to speak of the colonists as of a people designing and endeavoring to render themselves independent, and therefore it may be said to be proper as much as possible to depress them. This method for securing obedience has been tried by many powerful nations and seen to be the constant policy of commonwealths; but the attempt in almost every instance, from Athens down to Genoa, has been unsuccessful. Many states and kingdoms have lost their dominions by severity and an unjust jealousy. I remember none that have been lost by kindness and a generous confidence. Evils are frequently precipitated by imprudent attempts to prevent them. In short, we never can be made an

---

|| Great Britain will not only lose in such case the annual amount of the taxes, but the people of America, establishing manufactures through discontent, will in time entirely withdraw their intercourse with her. And therefore her loss of the whole American trade may be justly attributed to this inauspicious beginning.

¶ See notes to page 4.

independent people except it be by Great Britain herself;* [16] [34] and the only way for her to do it is to make us frugal, ingenious, united, and discontented.† [17]

---

* "If we are afraid that one day or other the colonies will revolt and set up for themselves, as some seem to apprehend, let us not *drive* them to a *necessity* to *feel* themselves independent of us, as they *will* do the moment they perceive that *they can be supplied with all things from within themselves,* and do not need our assistance. If we would keep them still dependent upon their mother country, and in some respects *subservient* to their *views* and welfare, let us make it their INTEREST always to be so." Tucker on trade.

"Our colonies, while they have English blood in their veins, and have relations in England, and WHILE THEY CAN GET BY TRADING WITH US, the *stronger* and *greater they* grow, the *more* this *crown* and *kingdom* will *get* by them; and nothing but such an arbitrary power as shall make them desperate can bring them to rebel." Davenant on the plantation trade.

"The northern colonies are not upon the same footing as those of the south; and having a worse soil to improve, they must find the recompense some other way, which only can be in property and dominion. Upon which score, any innovations in the form of government there should be cautiously examined for fear of entering upon measures by which the industry of the inhabitants be quite discouraged. 'Tis ALWAYS UNFORTUNATE for a people, either by CONSENT or upon COMPULSION, to depart from their PRIMITIVE INSTITUTIONS and THOSE FUNDAMENTALS by which they were FIRST UNITED TOGETHER." *Idem.*

† The most effectual way of *uniting* the colonies is to make it their common interest to oppose the designs and attempts of Great Britain.

"All wise states will well consider how to preserve the advantages arising from colonies, and avoid the evils. And I conceive that there can be but TWO ways in nature to hinder them from throwing off their dependence: *one,* to keep it out of their *power;* and the *other,* out of their *will.* The *first* must be by *force;* and the *latter,* by *using them well* and keeping them employed in such productions and making such manufactures as will support themselves and families comfortably, *and procure them wealth too,* and at least not prejudice their mother country.

"*Force* can never be used effectually to answer the end *without destroying the colonies themselves.* Liberty and encouragement are necessary to carry people thither, and to keep them together when they are there; and violence will hinder both. Any body of troops considerable enough to awe them and keep them in subjection, under the direction too of a needy governor often sent thither to make his fortune, and at such a distance from any application for redress, will soon put an end to all planting, and leave the country to the soldiers alone, and if it did not, *would eat up all the profit of the colony.* For this reason, arbitrary countries have not been equally successful in planting colonies with free ones; and what they have done in that kind has either been by force at a vast expense or *by departing from the nature of their government,* and *giving such privileges to planters* as were *denied to their other subjects.* And I dare say that a few prudent laws and a little prudent conduct would soon give us far the greatest share of the riches of all America, perhaps drive many of other nations out of it, or into our colonies for shelter.

"There are *so many exigencies* in all states, *so many foreign wars* and *domestic disturbances,* that these colonies CAN NEVER WANT OPPORTUNITIES, if they watch for them, *to do what they shall find their interest to do.* And therefore we ought to take all the precautions in our power that it shall never be *their interest* to act against that of their native country, an evil which can no otherwise be averted than by keeping them *fully employed* in such trades *as will increase their own* as well as our wealth; for it is much to be feared, if we do not find employment for *them,* they might find it for *us.* The interest of the mother country is always to keep them dependent, and so employed; and it requires all her address to do it; and it is certainly more *easily* and *effectually* done by *gentle* and *insensible* methods than by *power* alone." *Cato's Letters.*

But if this event shall ever happen, which Providence I hope will never permit, it must when the present generation and the present set of sentiments are extinct. Late measures have indeed excited an universal and unexampled grief and indignation throughout the colonies. What man who wishes the welfare of America can view without pity, without passion, her restricted and almost stagnated trade, with its numerous train of evils — taxes [35] torn from her without her consent — her legislative Assemblies, the principal pillars of her liberty, crushed into insignificance — a formidable force established in the midst of peace, to bleed her into obedience — the sacred right of trial by jury violated by the erection of arbitrary and unconstitutional jurisdictions — and general poverty, discontent, and despondence stretching themselves over his unoffending country?

The reflections of the colonists on these melancholy subjects are not a little embittered by a firm persuasion that they never would have been treated as they are if Canada still continued in the hands of the French. Thus their hearts, glowing with every sentiment of duty and affection towards their mother country and expecting, not unreasonably perhaps, some mark of tenderness in return, are pierced by a fatal discovery that the vigorous [36] assistance which they faithfully afforded her in extending her domains has only proved the glorious but destructive cause of the calamities they now deplore and resent.

Yet still their resentment is but the resentment of dutiful children who have received unmerited blows from a beloved parent. Their obedience to Great Britain is secured by the best and strongest ties, *those of affection,* which alone *can,* and I hope *will,* form an everlasting union between her and her colonies. May no successes or suspicions ever tempt *her* to deviate from the natural generosity of her spirit. And may no dreadful revolution of sentiments ever teach *them* to fear her victories or to repine at her glories. [37]

I am, etc.

POSTSCRIPT

I have omitted mentioning one thing that seems to be connected with the foregoing subject.

With a vast expense of blood and wealth we fought our way in the late war up the doors of the Spanish treasuries, and by the possession of Florida, might obtain some recompense for that expense. Pensacola and the other ports in that country are convenient places where the Spaniards might meet us, and exchange their silver for the manufactures of Great Britain and the provisions of these colonies. By this means a commerce inconceivably beneficial to the British subjects might be carried on. This commerce the Spaniards wish and have endeavored to carry on. Many hundred thousand dollars have been brought by them to Pensacola to lay out there; but the men-of-war at that station have compelled them to take back their cargoes, *the receipt of which,* it may from thence be presumed, *would be destructive to the interests of Great Britain.* Thus we receive less advantage from Florida, now it belongs to us, than we did when it was possessed by our enemies; for then, by permission from the Spanish governors to trade there, we deprived considerable emoluments from our intercourse with them.

Upon what reasons this conduct is founded is not easy to determine. Sure no one considers Florida in the same light with these colonies and thinks that no vessels should be permitted to trade there but British shipping. This would be to apply the acts of navigation [38] to purposes directly opposite to the spirit of them. They were intended to preserve an intercourse between the mother country and her colonies, and thus to cultivate a *mutual affection;* to promote the interests of *both* by an exchange of *their* most valuable productions for *her* manufactures, thereby to increase the shipping of both, and thus render them capable of affording aid to each other. Which of these purposes is answered by prohibiting a commerce that can be no other way carried on? That is, by forbidding the Spaniards to bring their wealth *for us* to Florida, which is an unhealthy sandbank held by a garrison at a great expense of money and a greater of lives, that cannot for ages, if ever it will, yield a single advantage to Great Britain but *that* she refuses to enjoy.

NOTES

MAYHEW, *A DISCOURSE CONCERNING UNLIMITED SUBMISSION*

There is one full-length biography of Mayhew: Charles W. Akers, *Called unto Liberty: A Life of Jonathan Mayhew (1720–1766)* (Cambridge, 1964), which I have had the privilege of consulting in manuscript. There is a valuable sketch of Mayhew's career and a complete bibliography of his writings by Clifford K. Shipton in *Sibley's Harvard Graduates,* XI (Boston, 1960). Clinton Rossiter has written generally of Mayhew's ideas in *W.M.Q.,* 3d ser., 7 (1950), 531–558; and Conrad Wright has analyzed his religious views in *The Beginnings of Unitarianism in America* (Boston, 1955). There are many accounts of Mayhew's famous controversy with East Apthorp over the role of the Society for the Propagation of the Gospel (discussed in General Introduction pp. 61–62, 156–158, and on pp. 274–276); of these, the most useful are Richard J. Hooker, "The Mayhew Controversy," *Church History,* 5 (1936), 239 ff., and Carl Bridenbaugh, *Mitre and Sceptre* (New York, 1962), especially pp. 99–103. One older publication, Alden Bradford's *Memoir of the Life and Writings of Rev. Jonathan Mayhew, D.D. . . . .* (Boston, 1838), remains especially valuable, since it is largely a collection of documents pertaining to Mayhew's life and a digest of his writings. Its quotations from the two main groups of Mayhew manuscripts — the Mayhew Papers at Boston University and in the Massachusetts Historical Society — while not meticulously accurate by the standards of modern scholarship, do not distort the meanings of the quoted passages. The valuable Hollis-Mayhew Correspondence in the Massachusetts Historical Society has been published in its entirety, edited by Bernhard Knollenberg, in the *Proceedings of the Massachusetts Historical Society,* 69 (Boston, 1956), 102–193.

The printing history of *A Discourse* and a location listing of the various printings and editions of the pamphlet will be found in the bibliography to Shipton's biography of Mayhew.

The Latin quotation on the title page combines two passages from the *Aeneid:* bk. viii, lines 483–484 ("Why recount the despot's heinous murders? Why his savage deeds? God keep the like for himself and for his breed!"); and bk. vi, lines 645–646 ("And there, long-robed, the Thracian priest [Orpheus] sings"). *"Rom. Vat. Prin."* may refer to an unidentified anthology of Roman poets.

Notes to Introduction

1. The fragment of Mayhew's Extract Book is in Folder 10 of the Mayhew Papers, Boston University. Both Whitefield's attack on irreligion at Harvard ("Tillotson and Clarke are read instead of Shepard and Stoddard") and Professor Wigglesworth's curious defense (a tutor had just been fired for "corrupt principles" and a professor for "immoral practices," and "writers reckoned evangelical [were] so often borrowed by undergraduates as scarcely ever to be in the library") are revealing of the atmosphere of the college in Mayhew's time. See Josiah Quincy, *History of Harvard University* (Cambridge, 1840), II, 41, 50.

2. For biographical sketches of Experience Mayhew and Ebenezer Gay, see Shipton, *Sibley's Harvard Graduates,* VII (Boston, 1945), 632–639; and VI (Boston, 1942), 59–66. Wright, *Unitarianism,* discusses Gay's religious views; both Wright and Akers, *Mayhew,* trace the development of Mayhew's thought.

3. Bradford, *Mayhew,* pp. 87 ff. On the Dissenting Deputies in the context of American affairs, see Maurice W. Armstrong, "The Dissenting Deputies and the American Colonies," *Church History,* 29 (1960), 298–320; and Bridenbaugh, *Mitre and Sceptre,* chaps. ii and iv.

4. Bradford, *Mayhew,* pp. 88, 94–95.

5. There never was an American Jacobite, a contemporary of Mayhew's explained: "the very air of America is death to such monsters, never any grew there, and if any are transported or import themselves, loss of speech always attends them." [John Joachim Zubly], *An Humble Enquiry into the Nature of the Dependency of the American Colonies . . .* [Charleston?], 1769), p. 24. The Anglican John Checkley, who was convicted of seditious libel in Massachusetts in 1724 for republishing a tract by the nonjuror and leading High Church apologist Charles Leslie (mentioned contemptuously by Mayhew in the Preface and on p. 24) was thought to be a Jacobite and an advocate of authoritarianism generally; other Anglicans too were suspected of divine right leanings, especially in Maryland (William H. Browne, *Maryland,* Boston, 1884, pp. 186, 208–209). But it was not, apparently, until Jonathan Boucher's suppressed sermon of 1775, cited in note 15 below, that a fully elaborated statement of divine right theory appeared in the colonies. On the Checkley case, see Edmund F. Slafter, *John Checkley* (2 vols., Boston, 1897), and Perry Miller, *The New England Mind from Colony to Province* (Cambridge, 1953), pp. 468–473; on the Churchmen and their ideas generally in pre-Revolutionary America, see Bridenbaugh, *Mitre and Sceptre,* chaps. iii-vi.

6. The notes on Charles I's reign in Mayhew's Extract Book, quoted here, are accurate transcriptions of phrases from Bulstrode Whitelocke's *Memorials of the English Affairs . . .* (London, 1682), p. 8. This history of England from the reign of Charles I to the Restoration, though it "swarms with inaccuracies and anachronisms," presented an interpretation sympathetic to the Parliamentary side, and was favored by Whigs in the eighteenth century over Clarendon's *History* as the more accurate and impartial of the two. (Charles Firth, in *D.N.B.,* XXI, 115; Bradford, *Mayhew,* p. 95.) On the history of divine right theorizing in England, see J. N. Figgis, *Divine Right of Kings* (Cambridge, England, 1914 ed.), chaps. vii-x; G. P. Gooch, *Political Thought in England from Bacon to Halifax* (London, 1914), pp. 16 ff.; and George L. Mosse, *The Struggle for Sovereignty in England* (East Lansing, Mich., 1950). Mosse's book has a particularly full exposition (pp. 48 ff.) of the views of Robert Sibthorpe, one of the two prime exponents of divine right, as the colonists saw the seventeenth century; on the other, Roger Mainwaring (or Maynwaring), see Figgis, *Divine Right,* pp. 141, 150. The most comprehensive survey of divine right theorizing available to the colonists was Abednego Seller's *The History of Passive Obedience Since the Reformation* (Amsterdam, 1689), and the same author's *Continuation of the History . . .* (Amsterdam, 1690). Both remain valuable summaries of the literature and convey excellently the quality of the polemics surrounding the issue of divine right and passive obedience which were still so immediate and vital a concern for Americans of the Revolutionary generation. On the reappearance "with pristine vigor" of divine right and nonresistance theories under Anne and their renewed predominance in High Church pulpits, see Norman Sykes, in F. J. C. Hearnshaw, ed., *Social and Political Ideas of Some English Thinkers . . . 1650–1750* (London, 1928), pp. 117, 128; on the curious modification of these theories to justify the accession of William and Mary, see Gerald Straka, "The Final Phase of Divine Right Theory in England, 1688–1702," *English Historical Review,* 77 (1962), 638–658.

Charles Brockwell, the bristly, imperious assistant minister of King's Chapel, Boston, believed — probably correctly — that Mayhew's sermon was directed in the first instance at him. Akers, *Mayhew,* p. 90; Henry W. Foote, *et al., Annals of King's Chapel* (Boston, 1882-1940), II, 23 ff.

7. Martha L. Counts, The Political Views of the Eighteenth Century New England Clergy as Expressed in Their Election Sermons (unpub. Ph.D. diss., Columbia University, 1956), pp. 53, 59, 65, 68–84, 91–92.

8. Mayhew, *A Discourse,* pp. 39n (cf. p. 44), 30, 40; Counts, New England Clergy, p. 92.

9. *Boston Evening-Post,* February 19, 1750.

10. Notices of Mayhew's pamphlet, and articles attacking and defending it, appear in: *Boston Evening-Post,* February 19, 26; March 12, 19; April 2, 16, 23; May 21; June 18; July 9; *Boston Gazette,* February 27; March 13, 20 (2); *Boston Weekly News-Letter,* March 1, 22.

11. Mayhew's letter to Hoadly is in Bradford, *Mayhew,* pp. 96–97.

The character of the plagiarism may be judged by the following examples printed in the *Evening-Post:*

Mayhew:

That you may see the truth and justness of what I assert (viz., that magistracy is the ordinance of God, and that you sin against him in opposing it) consider that even *pagan rulers* are not by the nature and design of their office enemies and a terror to the good and virtuous actions of men, but only to the injurious and mischievous to society . . . For while you do thus, they are by their office as ministers of God obliged to encourage and protect you; it is for this purpose they are clothed with power.

Mayhew:

Since therefore magistracy is the ordinance of God, and since rulers are by their office benefactors to society by discouraging what is bad and encouraging what is good and so preserving peace and order amongst men, it is evident ye ought to pay a willing subjection to them not to obey merely for fear of exposing your selves to their wrath and displeasure, but also in point of reason, duty, and conscience: Ye are under an indispensable obligation as *Christians* to honor their office and to submit to them in the execution of it.

Hoadly:

And that what I have said is true, viz., that magistrates are the ordinance of God and that to resist and oppose them in the execution of their office is a great sin, is evident from the good end and useful nature of their office. For you very much mistake the business even of *heathen magistrates* if you look upon them as enemies by their office to what is truly good and praiseworthy . . . For while you behave yourselves well, they are by their office the ministers of God to protect and encourage you, and invested with power for this very purpose.

Hoadly:

Since therefore the office of magistrates is the ordinance of God as it carries forward his designs in the world, and since their work is so good and beneficial to human society, as they are the punishers of all that is evil and encouragers of all that is good, it is manifest from hence that it is not only a point of interest to show a ready subjection to them for fear of their anger and their punishment if you did not, but a point of duty and conscience, for fear of God's displeasure, whose will they execute and whose work they carry forward in the world.

A close comparison of the whole of Mayhew's gloss on Romans xiii, 1–8 (pp. 4 ff.) with Hoadly's in his *Measures of Submission,* in *Works* (John Hoadly, ed.,

London, 1773), II, 38 ff., makes clear that Mayhew did indeed follow Hoadly line by line and thought by thought; these pages of Mayhew's pamphlet seem, in fact, to be more a gloss on Hoadly than on St. Paul. The alleged plagiarism of [George Coade's] *Letter to a Clergyman* . . . (London, 1746) (compare pp. 33–35 with *Discourse,* pp. 45–46) is much less obvious, as is Mayhew's reliance on Milton's *Pro Populo Anglicano Defensio,* illustrated in quotations in parallel columns in George Sensabaugh, *Milton in Early America* (Princeton, 1964), pp. 61–65. The difference in specificity between Mayhew's reliance on Milton and on Hoadly illustrates well the process of transmission of seventeenth-century ideas described in the General Introduction, Chap. III.

12. Cf. General Introduction, Chap. III, esp. pp. 28–37.

13. *The Snare Broken* (Boston, 1776), p. 35.

14. *Works,* X, 288.

15. William Livingston, *et al., The Independent Reflector* (Milton M. Klein, ed., Cambridge, 1963), papers 38, 39; *Boston Gazette,* May 4, 1761; Aplin, *Verses on Doctor Mayhew's Book of Observations* (JHL Pamphlet 3), p. 15. For examples of the persistence into the Revolution itself of the seventeenth-century formulations of passive obedience and nonresistance, see John Adams, *A Dissertation on the Canon and Feudal Law* (1765), in *Works,* III, 454; [Stephen Johnson], *Some Important Observations* . . . (Newport, 1766), pp. 21, 27–29; [John Dickinson], *Letters from a Farmer* . . . (Philadelphia, 1768), in Paul L. Ford, ed., *Writings of John Dickinson* (*Memoirs of the Historical Society of Pennsylvania,* XIV, Philadelphia, 1895), 387–389, 399–400; Jason Haven, *A Sermon Preached Before His Excellency* . . . (Boston, 1769), p. 40; John Tucker, *A Sermon Preached at Cambridge* . . . (Boston, 1771), p. 32; [John Allen], *The American Alarm, or the Bostonian Plea* . . . (Boston, 1773), *passim,* e.g., first section, pp. 15, 26; [John Allen]. *An Oration upon the Beauties of Liberty* . . . (Boston, 1773), pp. ix, 28; Gad Hitchcock, *A Sermon Preached Before* . . . *Gage* . . . (Boston, 1774), pp. 23 (which reprints a passage from Hoadly's *Measures of Submission*), 27; John Lathrop, *A Sermon Preached to the Ancient and Honorable Artillery-Company* . . . (Boston, 1774), *passim,* esp. p. 31; Peter Whitney, *The Transgression of a Land Punished* . . . (Boston, 1774), pp. 8, 18 ff.; John Carmichael, *A Self-Defensive War Lawful* . . . (Lancaster, [1775]), pp. 10 ff.; Samuel West, *A Sermon Preached* . . . *May 29, 1776* . . . (Boston, 1776), pp. 25 ff. On Boucher and his sermon, which was published twenty-two years after it was delivered, in *A View of the Causes and Consequences of the American Revolution* . . . (London, 1797), see the General Introduction, pp. 199 ff.

16. Caroline Robbins, *The Eighteenth-Century Commonwealthman* (Cambridge, 1959), pp. 259–261, 393; Francis Blackburne, comp., *Memoirs of Thomas Hollis* (London, 1780), II, 573–586.

17. Knollenberg, "Hollis-Mayhew Correspondence." On Hollis, see, besides her *Commonwealthman,* Caroline Robbins' articles in *W.M.Q.,* 3d ser., 7 (1950), 406–453; and *Harvard Library Bulletin,* 5 (1951), 5–23, 181–196.

18. Shipton, "Mayhew," pp. 462, 463, 465; Mayhew, *Two Discourses* . . . (Boston, 1759), pp. 60–61; Akers, *Mayhew,* chaps. xi–xiii.

Notes to Text

1. Charles Leslie (1650–1722), nonjuror, Jacobite, and High Church Anglican apologist, prolific defender of Anglican sacerdotalism and of the autonomy of the

Church hierarchy, fought furiously with Defoe, Hoadly, and others in controversies in which the role of the laity was a major point at issue. A more gifted writer than Hoadly (his periodical *The Rehearsal* [4 vols., 1704-1709] is still remarkably readable) and generally considered to be a more deft theologian, Leslie replied to Hoadly's major treatise, *The Original and Institution of Civil Government Discussed* (London, 1710), in *The Finishing Stroke, Being a Vindication of the Patriarchal Scheme of Government* . . . (London, 1711).

2. "The First Satire of the Second Book of Horace," lines 121-124.

3. Grotius' comment on "tribute" and "custom" referred to by Mayhew in the footnote is in his *Annotationes in Epistolas Apostolicas et Apocalypsin,* in *Operum Theologicorum,* III (Basel, 1732), p. 751 col. a. It is likely, however, that Mayhew found the reference in a compilation of glosses, such as Abraham Calovius' *Biblia Novi Testamenti Illustrata* (Dresden and Leipzig, 1719), III, 217. Hoadly does not cite Grotius in his commentary on Romans xiii, 7.

4. The enumeration of the misdeeds of Charles I that follows summarizes the more lurid account in Coade's *Letter to a Clergyman* (pp. 4 ff.), a portion of which (pp. 33-35) Mayhew was accused of having plagiarized in composing the lengthy footnote on the English constitution which appears on pages 45-46. The meaning of the two passages on the constitution is identical, but the wording, except for a few isolated phrases, is not.

5. Coade, quoting the account of the famous events of 1641 in Edmund Ludlow's *Memoirs,* says "three or four hundred" (p. 59). The book cited has not been identified.

6. The words *"therewith . . . dissenters"* are a play on James iii, 9: "Therewith bless we God, even the Father; and therewith curse we men, which are made after the similitude of God."

7. Daniel Waterland (1683-1740), theologian, fought the spread of latitudinarianism within the Church of England. His most famous tract, *Scripture Vindicated* (1730), was written in reply to Matthew Tindal's deistical *Christianity As Old As the Creation,* published in the same year.

PAMPHLET 2

A LETTER TO THE PEOPLE OF PENNSYLVANIA

There is no general history of judicial tenure — or in fact of the judiciary or of the court systems — in the colonial period, but there are good brief discussions of the problem in Leonard W. Labaree, *Royal Government in America* (New Haven, 1930), pp. 388-401, and in Oliver M. Dickerson, *American Colonial Government 1696-1765* (Cleveland, 1912), pp. 195-209. William S. Carpenter, *Judicial Tenure in the United States* (New Haven, 1918) ignores the colonial period but treats the subsequent history of the problem in detail. The local situation in colonial Pennsylvania is covered in J. Paul Selsam's "A History of Judicial Tenure in Pennsylvania," *Dickinson Law Review,* 38 (January 1934), 168-183. The history of judicial tenure in England may be traced in William S. Holdsworth, *History of English Law* (London, 1903-1952), vols. I, VI, and X. Relevant aspects of Pennsylvania politics in the 1750's are discussed by Theodore Thayer in *Pennsylvania Politics and the Growth of Democracy 1740-1776* (Harrisburg, 1953) and in his article "The Quaker Party of Pennsylvania, 1755-1765," *Pa. Mag.,* 71 (1947), 19-43. At least two of the many biographies of Franklin, those of Verner Crane and Carl Van Doren, also cover the political background well.

Notes to Introduction

1. For the act and its disallowance, see James T. Mitchell and Henry Flanders, comps., *Statutes at Large of Pennsylvania from 1682 to 1801* ([Harrisburg], 1896–1911), V, 462–465, 655, 722–724.

2. Galloway's authorship of the pamphlet seems most likely since he was the key figure in the committee that drafted the bill; he was the leader of the political faction pressing for its enactment; and, most important, he was peculiarly well versed in the constitutional arguments that are developed in the pamphlet, and he expressed them in similar language on other occasions. Much of the substance of *A Letter to the People of Pennsylvania* appears in *A True and Impartial State of the Province of Pennsylvania* . . . (Philadelphia, 1759), which is known to have been written by Galloway. (Lawrence C. Wroth, *An American Bookshelf, 1775*, Philadelphia, 1934, pp. 146–147.) The passage from Penn's Frame of Government of 1682 quoted in *A True and Impartial State*, p. 33, is identical to the passage quoted in *A Letter*, p. 22.

Julian P. Boyd's *Anglo-American Union: Joseph Galloway's Plans To Preserve the British Empire, 1774–1788* (Philadelphia, 1941) contains the best biography of Galloway and includes a discussion and documentation of his constitutional ideas as they relate to the question of imperial organization.

3. Holdsworth, *History of English Law*, I, 194–195; VI, 501 ff., 527 ff.; G. E. Aylmer, *The King's Servants: The Civil Service of Charles I, 1625–1642* (New York, 1961), pp. 106 ff.; J. R. Tanner, *English Constitutional Conflicts of the Seventeenth Century, 1603–1689* (Cambridge, England, 1928), pp. 38 ff., 254, 275, 291.

4. E. Neville Williams, ed., *The Eighteenth-Century Constitution 1688–1815* (Cambridge, England, 1960), p. 59; Holdsworth, *History of English Law*, VI, 234 ff.; X, 644.

5. Dickerson, *Colonial Government*, pp. 195n, 200; Labaree, *Royal Government*, pp. 388–389; W. L. Grant, *et al.*, eds., *Acts of the Privy Council of England, Colonial Series* (Hereford and London, 1908–1912), IV, 217. On the background of the problem in Pennsylvania, see Selsam, "Judicial Tenure in Pennsylvania."

6. *Statutes of Pennsylvania*, V, 724. Cf. Labaree, *Royal Government*, pp. 382–383, 385–386.

7. Thayer, "Quaker Party," pp. 20–23; Verner W. Crane, *Benjamin Franklin and a Rising People* (Boston, 1954), pp. 82, 85; Ernest H. Baldwin, "Joseph Galloway . . . ," *Pa. Mag.*, 26 (1902), 174 ff.; *Pennsylvania Archives*, 8th ser., VI, 2768 ff., 4991–4992, 5038–5040, 5044; *Minutes of the Provincial Council of Pennsylvania* . . . (Harrisburg, 1852), VIII, 399–402; William R. Shepherd, *History of Proprietary Government in Pennsylvania* (New York, 1896), pp. 398–400, 456–458; Nicholas B. Wainwright, "Governor William Denny . . . ," *Pa. Mag.*, 81 (1957), 192–194.

8. The efforts to revive the bill may be traced in *Pennsylvania Archives*, 8th ser., VI; the Resolution of 1764 appears in vol. VII, p. 5593. The report on the "storm" of 1762 is published in "The Pennsylvania Assembly in 1761–2: A Memorandum Kept by Samuel Foulke," *Pa. Mag.*, 8 (1884), 410. John Dickinson, who defended the proprietary interest on certain issues (see Introduction to *The Late Regulations*, JHL Pamphlet 14), agreed wholeheartedly that permanence of tenure for judges was a prerequisite for the preservation of liberty. He devoted most of

Letter IX of his *Letters from a Farmer in Pennsylvania* (Philadelphia, 1768) to the question.

9. Labaree, *Royal Government,* pp. 391–398; E. B. O'Callaghan and Berthold Fernow, eds., *Documents Relative to the Colonial History of the State of New-York . . .* (Albany, 1853–1887), VII, 475; William A. Whitehead, *et al.,* eds., *New Jersey Archives* (Newark, 1880–1941), 1st ser., IX, 322–323, 329–330.

10. Dickerson, *Colonial Government,* pp. 152–153, 205, 207; Labaree, *Royal Government,* pp. 398–400; Richard M. Brown, *The South Carolina Regulators* (Cambridge, 1963), pp. 65–66, 68–69, 79, 80–81.

11. Thomas Hutchinson, *The History of the Colony and Province of Massachusetts-Bay* (Lawrence S. Mayo, ed., Cambridge, 1936), III, 278, 279; Adams, *Works,* III, 517, 518. Adams' and Brattle's essays are published in their entirety in volume III of Adams' *Works,* pp. 513–574. For an earlier episode in Massachusetts, see Ellen E. Brennan, *Plural Office-Holding in Massachusetts 1760–1780* (Chapel Hill, 1945), pp. 49–50.

12. Adams, *Works,* III, 521, 522, 523, 530, 551, 558, 559.

Notes to Text

1. The quotation is from William Guthrie, *A General History of England, from the Invasion of the Romans under Julius Caesar, to the Late Revolution in MDCLXXXVIII . . .* (London, 1744–1751), III, 713. This work, published in three massive volumes, was used repeatedly, as will be seen below, by the author of the pamphlet. Guthrie (1708–1770) was a journalist and political writer as well as historian. His strongly Whiggish interpretation of English history, similar to Rapin's, was continued in two folio volumes by Franklin's friend James Ralph, mentioned in the General Introduction, above p. 13, under the title *The History of England: During the Reigns of K. William, Q. Anne, and K. George I. With an Introductory Review of the Reigns of the Royal Brothers, Charles and James; in Which Are To Be Found the Seeds of the Revolution* (London, 1744–1746). The Introductory Review mentioned in the title occupies the entire first volume (1078 double-columned pages); the second volume concludes with the death of William III.

2. Guthrie, *General History,* II, 340. The quotation concludes a section entitled "The King tampers with the judges and sheriffs to pack a new Parliament," which recounts the subservience of the judges to the tyrannical royal will.

3. The preceding three paragraphs on Richard's reign are a rephrasing of Guthrie, *General History,* II, 335–336, 339–340; III, 969. The remark quoted from Belknap appears on II, 340.

4. Ralph, *History of England,* I, 919, 920, 922. Ralph's account of the "bloodhound" Jeffreys is on pp. 888–892.

5. The reference is to an episode of 1740 that resulted from the zealous efforts of crown recruitment officers to man the disastrous expedition against Cartagena during the War of Jenkins' Ear. The recruiters, faced with a resolutely pacifist Assembly in Pennsylvania, had offered concealment of identity to indentured servants who left their masters for army service, an offer that 276 bondsmen were said to have accepted. The Assembly, already at loggerheads with the governor, protested vehemently, and, given no satisfaction by officials either in America or in England, satisfied itself by appropriating funds not for military purposes as requested but for compensation to masters whose servants had deserted. For ac-

counts of the episode, see Herbert L. Osgood, *The American Colonies in the Eighteenth Century* (New York, 1924–1925), III, 58–61; and Shepherd, *Proprietary Government,* pp. 523–526, especially pp. 523–524n.

6. The next six paragraphs, on the history of judicial tenure in England, are largely based on — indeed, at certain points are lifted directly from — Guthrie's *General History* (see especially I, 221, 907; II, 218, 349; III, 715). Guthrie, in standard Whig form, read the achievements of the seventeenth-centuy Parliamentarians and of the Glorious Revolution back into the immemorial past of "the ancient constitution"; but the author of the pamphlet goes beyond him in this. Guthrie's stress in the passages cited is not on the judicial procedures by which these judges were condemned but upon the fact of their condemnation. On the importance of the concept of the "ancient constitution" in the seventeenth and eighteenth centuries, see General Introduction, pp. 52–54, and works cited there.

7. The quotation is from Penn's Frame of Government (1682). It is accurately quoted except for a few minor details and the addition of the italics. For the subsequent interpretation of this provision, especially in relation to the problem of judicial tenure, see Selsam's article cited above.

8. The reference is probably to William Allen (1704–1780), English-educated lawyer and merchant, councilor, justice of various lower courts from 1737 to 1750, and chief justice of the Supreme Court 1750–1774, who led the proprietary party in Pennsylvania politics for nearly fifty years, and, as indicated in the Introduction above, strongly opposed instituting permanent tenure for judges.

9. The famous trial and acquittal by the jury of the seven bishops charged with seditious libel for petitioning against James II's Declaration of Indulgence favoring Catholics, was held on June 29–30, 1688. Sir John Powell and Sir Richard Holloway were two of the four presiding judges; they summed up the case for the jury in terms favorable to the bishops and were dismissed from the bench as a consequence. Ralph's long and detailed account of the trial (*History of England,* I, 984–994) quotes Powell's and Holloway's speeches to the jury. For a modern account of the trial, see Tanner, *Constitutional Conflicts,* pp. 258–261, 292–294.

10. Presumably "proprietary"; the plural appears below pp. 33 and 35.

11. The reference to the problem of quartering British troops is significant; it touches on major concepts of eighteenth-century constitutional theory as well as on a point of political conflict between the English government and the colonies analogous to one of the great issues of seventeenth-century English history settled definitively at the Glorious Revolution. The problem of quartering troops, closely associated in the colonists' minds with the danger of a standing army, first became acute in 1754 and 1755 when accommodations had to be made for Braddock's army. The Pennsylvania Assembly, unlike the other affected legislatures, refused the military commander's demand that they appropriate funds either to build barracks or to repay those who undertook to house the troops. Instead, the legislature raised the legal point of "the undoubted right" of British subjects, a right confirmed in the Bill of Rights, "not to be burdened with the sojourning of soldiers against their will." It then adopted as the law of the province the arrangement that obtained in times of peace in England and Wales whereby troops were allowed to be billeted only in public houses, the proprieters being repaid for stipulated expenses out of the troops' subsistence funds. (*Statutes at Large,* V, 194.) The act was promptly disallowed in England with the comment by the attorney general that "propositions true in the mother country and rightly asserted in the reigns of

Charles I and Charles II in time of peace, when soldiers were kept up without consent of Parliament," did not apply "to a colony in time of war in case of troops raised for their protection by the authority of the Parliament . . ." (*Acts of the Privy Council, Colonial,* IV, 338.) The distinction was lost on the Pennsylvanians, however, and they proceeded to pass a similar act in 1756 when quarters were again demanded. Public inns proving, as expected, inadequate, the governor moved to requisition private houses, but the Assembly cut him off, disputing with him, through a committee, with "heat, passion, and rudeness." The legislature finally consented to provide the needed facilities only when the commanding general, Lord Loudoun, threatened to march additional troops to Pennsylvania to settle the matter by force. The dispute, paralleled in other colonies and destined to become a great issue in the colonies after 1763 and to result in a clause of the Declaration of Independence, is summarized in Stanley M. Pargellis, *Lord Loudoun in North America* (New Haven, 1933), pp. 187, 191, 201–202; the governor's account of the controversy is printed in *Pennsylvania Archives,* III, 110–112; and other relevant documents are in *Minutes of the Provincial Council,* VII, 271 ff., 361 ff.

12. The reference in all probability is to the "Smith-Moore" affair of 1757–58. During the Assembly's abortive trial for libel of William Moore, a justice of the peace originally charged with extortion, and William Smith, provost of the College of Philadelphia, both loyal to the proprietary interest, friends of Smith began "a loud tumultuous stamping of feet, hissing and clapping of hands" at the conclusion of a dramatic speech Smith delivered to the House in his own defense. The House declared the tumult to be "an high contempt to the authority of this House, a breach of the privileges thereof, and destructive to the freedom and liberties of the representatives of the people." Among those seized by the House and forced to apologize for participating in the affair were the paymaster of the Pennsylvania troops, a Philadelphia alderman, one of the city's justices of the peace and two Philadelphia merchants. Galloway, who had personally prepared the charges against Moore, led the House throughout the affair. Documents of the episode are in *Pennsylvania Archives,* 8th ser., VI, 4715–4724.

PAMPHLET 3

APLIN, *VERSES ON DOCTOR MAYHEW'S BOOK OF OBSERVATIONS*

The main writings on the Mayhew-Apthorp controversy have been listed in the notes to Pamphlet 1. To the references there may be added for the present context Wendell Garrett's detailed account of East Apthorp and his "palace" in *Apthorp House, 1760–1960* (Cambridge, 1960), chaps. i, ii; and the documentation in William S. Perry, ed., *Historical Collections Relating to the American Colonial Church: Volume III, Massachusetts* ([Hartford], 1873).

A full bibliographical description of the *Verses,* together with a location listing of extant copies, will be found in John E. Alden, *Rhode Island Imprints, 1727–1800* (New York, 1949), pp. 112–113. Mr. Alden explains that two editions, distinguished by minor differences in type settings, were printed, both in 1763. The present edition reprints "Edition A."

Notes to Introduction

1. The controversy opened with a satiric obituary of the Reverend Ebenezer Miller, an Anglican missionary who had labored in "the rugged wildernesses and lakes of Braintree [Massachusetts] . . . endeavoring to turn the miserable barbarians 'from darkness to light and from the power of Satan,' " which was published in the *Boston Gazette,* February 21, 1763 (quoted in Carl Bridenbaugh, *Mitre and Sceptre,* New York, 1962, p. 219). Apthorp's *Considerations on the Institution and Conduct of the Society* . . . (Boston, 1763) defended the Society, and led to Mayhew's *Observations.* This book-length tract provoked the following rebuttals: 1) Aplin's *Verses;* 2) *Remarks on Dr. Mayhew's Incidental Reflections* . . . (Portsmouth, N.H., 1763), by Arthur Browne, Rector of Queen's Chapel, Portsmouth; and 3) *A Candid Examination of Dr. Mayhew's Observations* . . . (Boston, 1763), by Henry Caner, Rector of King's Chapel, Boston. To all of these Mayhew replied in his *Defence of the Observations* . . . (Boston, 1763); but when an additional rebuttal to his *Observations* appeared in London in 1764 — *An Answer to Dr. Mayhew's Observations* . . . — and was believed to have been written by Thomas Secker, Archbishop of Canterbury, Mayhew responded once again, in *Remarks on an Anonymous Tract, Entitled an Answer* . . . (Boston, 1764; London, 1765). Tagging along at the end was a final comment by Apthorp, who had already returned to England, entitled *A Review of Dr. Mayhew's Remarks on the Answer to His Observations* . . . (London, 1765).

2. The *Gazette* articles were reprinted in the *Newport Mercury,* June 6, 13, and 20, 1763. The first advertisement for the pamphlet appeared in the *Boston Gazette, Supplement,* June 13, 1763.

3. *Boston Gazette,* June 20, 1763; *Providence Gazette,* June 25, 1763.

4. *Advertisement, A Certain Jonathan Mayhew* [Providence, 1763?].

5. *Boston Gazette,* August 15, 1763. Cf. *ibid.,* August 8, September 5, October 17, November 14 and 21, 1763.

6. The gravestone inscription is printed in Thomas B. Fogg, *A Memorial Sermon Delivered in Old Trinity Church, Brooklyn, Connecticut . . . 1871* [Hartford, 1871], p. 14. The electioneering piece, "Reasons Showing that the Governor, Deputy Governor, and Assistants . . . Ought To Have No Negative . . . for Admitting or Rejecting Freemen . . . ," is in the Foster Papers, Rhode Island Historical Society. For Aplin's other public controversies, see *Boston Gazette,* June 20 and August 15, 1763; *Providence Gazette,* April 9, 1763; John D. Washburn, "Hopkins v. Ward, — An Ante-Revolutionary Lawsuit," *Monthly Law Reporter,* 22 (October, 1859), 336, 338. The memorandum is mentioned in John R. Bartlett, ed., *Records of the Colony of Rhode Island* . . . (Providence, 1856–1865), VI, 350. See also Hopkins, *Rights of Colonies* (JHL Pamphlet 9), Introduction note 7.

7. The reminiscence is part of a long undated letter from Samuel Thurber, "one of our oldest and most respectable citizens, since deceased," written in response to a circular requesting information sent out by the antiquarian William R. Staples, printed in Staples' *Annals of the Town of Providence* . . . (Providence, 1843), pp. 600–607; the quotation is at 603. "Up keleg and scud": weigh anchor and run before the gale.

The claim made by "A. L." in the letter printed in the *Boston Gazette* of August 1, 1763, that Aplin was the author of an attack on the Anglican missionary James

MacSparran and hence had contradicted himself on the validity of episcopacy, is almost certainly false.

Notes to Text

1. The text on the title page of Mayhew's *Observations* is from Galatians ii, 4–5: "Brethren unawares brought in, who came in privily to spy out our liberty which we have in Christ Jesus, that they might bring us into bondage: To whom we gave place by subjection, no, not for an hour; that the truth of the Gospel might continue with you."

2. Sir James Jay and Dr. William Smith both arrived in London at the same moment to solicit funds for King's College, New York, and the College of Philadelphia respectively. George III and his advisers decided that the solicitation should be a joint one. The King personally donated £400 to King's College and £200 to the College of Philadelphia on the ground that Penn was the patron of the Philadelphia institution while King's College had no patron but himself. The Princess Dowager of Wales contributed £100 to the College of Philadelphia. The transactions are recounted in Sir James Jay, *A Letter to the College of New York Respecting the Collection . . . for the Colleges of Philadelphia and New York* (London, 1771).

3. Spira: i.e., Speyer, the Bavarian episcopal city.

4. The reference is to George Augustus Howe, elder brother of Admiral Richard and General William Howe, who led British forces in America during the Revolution. He was killed in action at Lake George in 1758.

5. The quotation in the footnote is taken, accurately, from the essay, "Of the Settlement and Increase of New England," in Nathaniel Ames's *An Astronomical Diary or Almanac for the Year . . . 1763* (Boston, [1763]), last page (unnumbered). It follows a quotation from Genesis xiii, 14–15, in which God promises Abraham and his posterity "all the land which thou seest . . . forever; and I will make thy seed as the dust of the earth . . ."

6. "It may be added, that the common people in New England, by means of our schools and the instructions of our 'able, learned, orthodox ministers' are, and have all along been, philosophers and divines in comparison of the common people in England of the communion of the church there established." Mayhew, *Observations,* p. 45.

7. Aplin is probably referring here to an outburst of feeling in the newspapers in the spring of 1763 regarding the practice of plural office-holding. See Ellen E. Brennan, *Plural Office-Holding in Massachusetts, 1760–1780* (Chapel Hill, 1945), pp. 56–57; *Boston Gazette* and *Boston Evening-Post,* February–June 1763.

8. From Addison's tale of Sir Roger and the inn sign (*Spectator,* No. 122, July 20, 1711), in which Sir Roger declines the honor of having his portrait appear on an inn sign, and orders whiskers added, which, with "a little aggravation to the features," turned his likeness into "the *Saracen's Head.*"

9. Aplin omits the phrase "whether agreeably to the interest of the charter or not," between the two clauses.

10. 1 Samuel xv, 22.

11. The reference is to Mayhew's *Discourse* (JHL Pamphlet 1) and its presumed plagiarism of Bishop Hoadly's *Measures of Submission.*

12. Ebenezer Miller was the Anglican missionary in Braintree, Massachusetts, whose death touched off the Mayhew-Apthorp controversy.

13. The reference may be to Gil González Dávila, Spanish conquistador, who in 1522 explored Nicaragua.

PAMPHLET 4

BLAND, *THE COLONEL DISMOUNTED*

Much has been written about the Two-Penny Acts, the Parsons' Cause, and Richard Bland. The most recent and fullest account of the political history of Virginia in the 1750's and early sixties, containing a detailed chronicle of the events surrounding the Two-Penny Act of 1758 and brief summaries of the main pamphlets, is Richard L. Morton, *Colonial Virginia* (Chapel Hill, 1960), II, chaps. xxvii–xxx. Though the significant relations among events are obscured in this narrative, it has the advantage of unusual breadth and detail. Important events in the history of the College of William and Mary and of the formation of a committee of correspondence in 1759 to direct the work of the Assembly's agent in England are included, though they are not integrated into the history of the Two-Penny Acts and the Parsons' Cause. A brief, focused account of the controversy appears in Bernhard Knollenberg, *Origin of the American Revolution: 1759–1766* (New York, 1960), chap. iii. Constitutional issues involved are described in two articles: Arthur P. Scott, "The Constitutional Aspects of the 'Parsons' Cause,'" *Political Science Quarterly*, 31 (1916), 558–577; and Glenn C. Smith, "The Parsons' Cause, 1755–65," *Tyler's Historical and Genealogical Magazine*, 21 (1940), 140–171, 291–306. A number of important documents bearing on the case are printed in William S. Perry, ed., *Historical Collections of the American Colonial Church: Volume I, Virginia* ([Hartford], 1870). One aspect of the controversy is discussed above, General Introduction, Chap. VII, sec. 2.

The most complete biography of Bland is Clinton Rossiter, "Richard Bland: The Whig in America," *W.M.Q.*, 3d ser., 10 (1953), 33–79. The latest account of Landon Carter is Part Two of Walter R. Wineman, *The Landon Carter Papers* . . . (Charlottesville, 1962); see also Jack P. Greene, "Landon Carter and the Pistole Fee Dispute," *W.M.Q.*, 3d ser., 14 (1957), 66–69. Almost nothing has been written on Camm: the brief notes in *William and Mary College Quarterly*, 19 (1910–1911), 28–30; and in Edward L. Goodwin, *The Colonial Church in Virginia* (Milwaukee, 1927), p. 258 are all we have.

Bibliographical listing of the pamphlets in the controversy will be found in William Clayton-Torrence, *A Trial Bibliography of Colonial Virginia (1754–1776)* (*Sixth Annual Report of the Library Board of the Virginia State Library* [*Part 2*], Richmond, 1910), which is cited below as Torrence, *Bibliography*. In that work *The Colonel Dismounted* appears as entry 310 (p. 36). Evans did not list the pamphlet in his *American Bibliography,* and it does not appear in the Shipton microcard edition of American imprints; there are, however, excerpts from the pamphlet in *William and Mary College Quarterly*, 19 (1910–1911), 31–41. The most recent bibliographical listing of the pamphlet is Adams, "Bibliographical Study," entry 1.

The quotation on the title page is from Horace, *Ars Poetica,* 188: "Whatever you thus show me, I discredit and abhor." (Loeb tr.)

Notes to Introduction

1. Jefferson to William Wirt, August 5 and 14, 1815, in Paul L. Ford, ed., *Writings of Thomas Jefferson* (New York, 1892–1899), IX, 467, 474; Lyon G. Tyler, "The Leadership of Virginia in the War of the Revolution," *William and Mary College Quarterly*, 19 (1910–1911), 25.

2. The text of the letter is printed in Perry, *Historical Collections*, I, 461–463.

3. Torrence, *Bibliography*, pp. 19–20. A summary of this pamphlet will be found in Smith, "Parsons' Cause," pp. 168–170.

4. Morton, *Virginia*, II, 759n, 760.

5. Adams, *Diary and Autobiography*, II, 120; Rossiter, "Bland," pp. 33–44: the quotations are at p. 40. On the College dismissals, see Morton, *Virginia*, II, 774–775. Camm was reinstated in 1763 on order of the Privy Council.

6. Torrence, *Bibliography*, pp. 24–25. The quotations that follow are on pp. 3, 5, 7, 12, 13, 16 of the pamphlet.

7. Morton, *Virginia*, II, 788.

8. Torrence, *Bibliography*, pp. 33–34. The quotations are on pp. 4-11, 14, 22, 41 of the pamphlet.

9. Torrence, *Bibliography*, pp. 37–38. Quotations are on pp. 12–13 of the pamphlet.

10. Camm's reply to Carter was entirely in kind. Answering *The Rector Detected* page by page, he ended in a wild allegorical flight concerning the proper way to keep a pig from squealing, he having been likened at one point by Carter to that animal. The pamphlet is listed by Torrence, *Bibliography*, p. 37; the quotation is at p. 3 of the pamphlet.

11. Quotations are from pp. [3], 5, 10, and 22. It should be noted that no word had yet been received in the colonies that the Grenville administration was contemplating a stamp tax. This argument, therefore, which would play such a central role in American thought in the years to follow, may be seen here evolving from the logic of the effort to distinguish spheres of governmental action rather than being haphazardly thrown together for the immediate purpose of opposing the Stamp Act.

12. Torrence, *Bibliography*, p. 40. The pamphlet, though ineffective as a commentary on the constitutional problems, is remarkable at least for its frenzied effort to top Bland's raillery. It employs a bewildering array of devices, including doggerel verse, to denounce Bland's *"scribendi cacoethes,"* his "haunted and hag-ridden imagination." At points the imagery is so elaborate, the conceits and name-calling so jumbled together, that it is almost impossible to follow the thought.

13. In *An Inquiry into the Rights of the British Colonies . . .* (Williamsburg, 1766).

Notes to Text

1. *Crab . . . persimmon . . . trash . . . cider:* a response to Camm's remarks in his *"Observations,"* Appendix No. II, p. xv, below — which in turn respond to Bland's snipes in his letter to Camm, printed as Appendix No. I, p. iv, below.

2. The Latin phrase quoted in the footnote — "No protecting deity is wanting if there is prudence" — is an adaptation of Juvenal, *Satires*, x, 365.

3. "Angry, or violent south wind." A response to Camm's use of the phrase in his *"Observations,"* Appendix No. II, p. xxi, below.

4. The "witty paper" referred to probably appeared in the *Virginia Gazette* in September or October 1763. The only extant issue of the *Gazette* for 1763, that of November 4, contains a letter to "The Overhearer" from "The Overseer," dated October 16, 1763.

5. Camm, *Single and Distinct View*, p. 41.

6. Mambrino was a pagan king in Ariosto's *Orlando Furioso* who had a helmet of pure gold which rendered the wearer invulnerable. Thetis' son, protected by special armor, was Achilles.

7. Camm, *"Observations,"* Appendix II, p. xx, below.

8. *Paradise Lost*, vi, 586–589.

9. Alexander Pope, *Epistle to Dr. Arbuthnot*, lines 91–92.

10. Camm, *Single and Distinct View*, pp. 40–41.

11. A petition from the inhabitants of Prince George County presented at the September 15, 1758, session of the House of Burgesses. H. R. McIlwaine, ed., *Journal of the House of Burgesses, 1758–1761* (Richmond, 1908), p. 5.

12. Conflated from the report of the Board of Trade to the Privy Council, July 4, 1759, and the letter from the Bishop of London to the Board, June 14, 1759, which was included in the report. Both are reprinted in Perry, *Historical Collections*, I, 458–463.

13. The play on numbers here refers to the few clergy who actually attended Camm's protest conventions in 1757 and 1758. According to Dinwiddie only nine attended the 1757 meeting. A retrospective account of the 1758 convention numbered those in attendance at about thirty-five. Morton, *Virginia*, II, 765, 786.

14. Bland here refers to Commissary Thomas Dawson's repeated refusals to call conventions of the clergy upon Camm's request.

15. Commissary William Robinson referred to Graham Franks, August 12, 1765, as "formerly Mr. Camm's attorney, now a merchant in London." Perry, *Historical Collections*, I, 511, 519.

16. Camm, *Single and Distinct View*, pp. 26–30.

17. *Ibid.*, pp. 26–30.

18. *Ibid.*, p. 14. The tobacco crop for 1755–1756 was much better than expected, with the result that prices rose very little. William Dawson wrote the Bishop of London that the clergy "determined to acquiesce" in the Two-Penny Act of 1755 as the price allowed was nearly equal to the market price. Perry, *Historical Collections*, I, 508.

19. The charge that Camm neglected his parish resulted from his journey to Annapolis in August–September 1763 to have his *Single and Distinct View* printed. The colleague substituting for him became ill, leaving the post empty briefly. Camm was also absent for eighteen months while in England, 1758–1760, petitioning for the disallowance of the Two-Penny Act. Cf. Appendix No. II, below, pp. xii–xiv.

20. Camm brought Bland's lay reading into his argument in *Single and Distinct View*, pp. 21–22: "It is to be sure happy for us to have laymen who are not only infallible judges of a clergyman's duty and merit, but can perform such eminent parts of his office as well as himself, because where this is the case there is the less occasion to provide a good maintenance for the clergy or for being punctual in paying their appointment whether it be great or little, the office being by the same means preserved from that contempt which justly falls upon the person of

the minister. Yet if a parson was to go into a muster field and take upon him to exercise the Colonel's troops in the Colonel's absence, I make no doubt but such an impropriety would be loudly condemned as a heinous offense and unseemly usurpation."

21. "That the small encouragement given to clergymen is a reason why so few come into this colony from the two universities, and that so many who are a disgrace to the ministry find opportunities to fill the parishes . . ." H. R. McIlwaine, ed., *Journals of the House of Burgesses, 1752–1755* (Richmond, 1909), p. 257.

22. Governor Dinwiddie in a letter to the Bishop of London, September 17, 1757 (Perry, *Historical Collections,* I, 456) said such an advertisement appeared in the August 9, 1757, issue of the *Virginia Gazette.* There are, however, no extant issues of the paper between April 22 and September 2, 1757. Camm requested Dawson, the commissary, to call meetings on three different occasions: summer 1757, fall 1758, and summer 1760. Dawson refused each time, whereupon Camm called the meetings himself.

23. For accounts of the "persecutions" suffered by Camm, see Morton, *Virginia,* II, 774–775, 802; and Smith, "Parsons' Cause," p. 159. *Cum multis aliis . . . :* "and many other things which it would now be tedious to describe."

24. From a speech by Matteo Siffredi, Lord High Chancellor of Sicily, in James Thomson's *Tancred and Sigismunda* (V, i, 24–27), first published in London, 1745. The complete fourth line reads: "Of mortal men, and mix them in eternal broils."

25. The views of Bacon and Coke referred to are from their opinions in *Calvin's Case* (1608), which, like *Bonham's Case* (1609), discussed in the Introduction to Otis' *Rights of the British Colonies,* Pamphlet 7 below, was invaluable to the colonists in their search for precedents and arguments to set against the claims of Parliamentary sovereignty. Their interpretations of both cases involved what might be called constructive anachronism in that, posing "a constitutional question of a 'preconstitutional' society," they reached conclusions that would have been alien to the thinking of the early seventeenth-century lawyers they quoted. At issue in *Calvin's Case* was the question, in the matter of a Scotsman's claim to land title in Ireland, of whether naturalization resulted from personal allegiance to the King or from the jurisdiction of English law, hence whether the source of English authority outside the realm lay in the crown or in Parliament. Though Coke in his decision, as well as Bacon in his brief for the crown, supported the claims of the crown, in his analysis of the issues he backed the opposing, Parliamentary view. It is this ambiguity in his opinion that explains why Professors McIlwain and Schuyler, like eighteenth-century interpreters of the case, could reach opposite conclusions from the same evidence in judging the validity of the colonists' claim based on legal precedent. "Both could find support but neither could find victory." Harvey Wheeler, "Calvin's Case (1608) and the McIlwain-Schuyler Debate," *American Historical Review,* 61 (1956), 597. For a particularly clear example of the use later made by the colonists of the opinions in *Calvin's Case,* see [James Wilson], *Considerations on the . . . Legislative Authority of the British Parliament* (Philadelphia, 1774), p. 25, where, like Bland in the present pamphlet, he argues that Coke's assertion of Parliamentary authority over Ireland based on the right of conquest is inapplicable to America; and pp. 29–33, where he adopts Bacon's reasoning to prove that in the colonies as in Ireland allegiance was owed to the King and not to Parliament. For James Otis' discussion of Ireland's relations to England and of the constitutional rights of conquered peoples, see his *Rights of*

the British Colonies (JHL Pamphlet 7), pp. 43-46; for John Adams' more detailed arguments along the same line, see *Novanglus and Massachusettensis* . . . (Boston, 1819), pp. 79-80, 111 ff. Cf. Charles H. McIlwain, *The American Revolution: A Constitutional Interpretation* (New York, 1923), pp. 92 ff.; Robert L. Schuyler, *Parliament and the British Empire* (New York, 1929), pp. 64-65.

In 1763 the issues that would ultimately determine the relevance of the case to American constitutionalism were not clear. Bland here cites, in order to refute them, passages from both Bacon and Coke that appear to justify arbitrary crown rule in the colonies. The quotation from Bacon is a paraphrase. The original reads: ". . . the laws of England are not superinduced upon any country by conquest; but that the old laws remain until the King by his proclamation or letters patent declare other laws; and then if he will he may declare laws which be utterly repugnant and differing from the laws of England." T. B. Howell, comp., *A Complete Collection of State Trials* . . . (London, 1812-1828), II, cols. 591-592.

26. The passage here cited (accurately) from Coke's opinion in *Calvin's Case* suggested a distinction in the extent of prerogative power between Christian and pagan countries taken in conquest which was based on the argument that the laws of infidels are "not only against Christianity but against the law of God and nature contained in the decalogue" and hence that they should fall away immediately upon conquest by a Christian king. The distinction was later repudiated. Howell, *State Trials,* II, col. 638; William Holdsworth, *A History of English Law,* XI (London, 1938), 234-235.

27. The reference is to Holt's opinion in *Smith v. Browne and Cooper* (1707), invalidating a contract for the sale of a Negro in England on the ground that Negroes were free in England. "You should have averred in the declaration that the sale was in Virginia, and, by the laws of that country, Negroes are saleable; for the laws of England do not extend to Virginia; being a conquered country their law is what the King pleases." Holdsworth, *English Law,* XI, 247. The crown's powers by right of conquest were settled in their modern form only, significantly, in 1774, when Lord Mansfield ruled that though the King may legislate for a conquered territory until it becomes "settled" constitutionally, he could do so only "as a part of the supreme legislature in Parliament," and could make no law "contrary to fundamental principles." *Ibid.,* pp. 230-253, esp. pp. 236-238.

28. The quotation from the "Ordinance and Constitution for Council and Assembly in Virginia, July 24, 1621" is essentially correct. The later pronouncements are found in W. L. Grant, *et al.,* eds., *Acts of the Privy Council of England, Colonial Series* (Hereford, 1908-1912), I, 203-204; William W. Hening, ed., *The Statutes at Large . . . of Virginia . . . (1619-1792)* (New York etc., 1819-1823), I, 231.

29. The petition was presented on June 23, 1675, by Francis Moryson, Thomas Ludwell, and Robert Smith. Cf. *Acts of Privy Council, Colonial,* I, 629-630. The report of the attorney and solicitor general are on pp. 636-638.

30. See Leonard W. Labaree, ed., *Royal Instructions to British Colonial Governors, 1670-1776* (New York, 1935), I, Nos. 201, 202, 214, 215. On the significance of the word "THENCEFORTH" and the question of the constitutionality of *ab initio* disallowances, see Scott, "Constitutional Aspects of the 'Parsons' Cause,'" pp. 561 ff.

31. Not a direct quote from *Calvin's Case.* Coke said, "But if a King hath a kingdom by title of descent, there seeing by the laws of that kingdom he doth inherit the kingdom, he cannot change those laws of himself without consent of

Parliament. Also if a King hath a Christian kingdom by conquest, as Henry VI had Ireland, after John had given unto them, being under his obedience and subjection, the laws of England for the government of that country, no succeeding King could alter the same without Parliament." Howell, *State Trials,* II, cols. 638–639.

32. *Teste meipso:* a solemn formula of attestation by the sovereign, used at the conclusion of charters, and other public instruments.

33. On royal instructions to colonial governors, see Leonard W. Labaree, *Royal Government in America* (New Haven, 1920), pp. 94–99, 219; for the exact wording of the passage quoted, see Labaree, *Royal Instructions,* II, Nos. 205, 208.

34. Bland refers here to the Pistole Fee Case of 1752–1754. See Morton, *Virginia,* II, 621–634.

35. The Assembly, acting upon the suggestion of the committee of correspondence, ordered on November 14, 1759, "That it be an instruction to the committee of correspondence to direct the agent for this country that if any appeal should be carried from hence to England relative to the Act entitled, *An Act To Enable the Inhabitants of This Colony To Discharge Their Public Dues, Officers Fees, and Other Tobacco Debts, in Money, for the Ensuing Year,* to use his own endeavors, and to employ proper counsel to support the proceedings of the vestries, of this colony acting under authority of the said law." *Journal of the House of Burgesses . . . 1758–1761,* p. 146; "Proceedings of the Virginia Committee of Correspondence, 1759–67," *Virginia Magazine of History and Biography,* 10 (April 1903), 352–353.

36. *"Reconnoitred"* is a reference to Camm's *A Review of the Rector Detected: or, the Colonel Reconnoitred* (Williamsburg, 1764), written in answer to Landon Carter's *The Rector Detected.*

37. The quotation is from Horace, *Epistles,* II, i, 1–4; which was translated by Christopher Smart in 1756 (brackets indicate words omitted by Bland) as follows: "[O Caesar!] while you alone sustain so many and momentous concerns; [while you defend the state of Italy with your arms, and] adorn it with laws respecting morals, and correct with ordinances, I should offend against the common utility, were I to detain your precious time with a long harangue."

38. Cf. Camm's reply, pp. xii–xiii, and Bland's further comments, above pp. 14–15.

39. Tobacco prices apparently rose from an average of around 1.5 pence per pound Virginia currency to 4.5 pence per pound in 1758. Knollenberg, *Origin,* p. 302.

40. Horace, *Satires,* I, v, 100: "Apella, the Jew, may believe it, not I."

41. On "The Overseer," see above, note 4.

42. An account of the Boston fire of March 10, 1760, by William Cooper, the town clerk, can be found in the *Boston Post-Boy,* March 20, 1760. The General Court on March 22 voted that the governor be asked to request a general contribution for the aid of the sufferers. Peter E. Vose, "The Great Boston Fire of 1760," *New England Historical and Genealogical Register,* 34 (July 1880), 288–293.

43. "An injury cannot be done to a consenting party."

44. "For our altars and our hearths"; i.e., in defense of our religion and our country.

45. The Rev. Isaac W. Giberne, a nephew of the Bishop of Durham, arrived in Virginia in 1759, and served in several parishes before becoming rector of Lunenburg Parish, Richmond County, where he remained from 1762–1795. He

"purchased the disgust of the clergy" soon after his arrival in Virginia by attempting to calm their opposition to the Two-Penny Act. Perry, *Historical Collections,*
I, 522. Of the three verses that follow, the second is from Addison's *Letter from
Italy to the Right Honourable Charles Lord Halifax,* line 119; and the third is based
on *Hamlet,* II, ii, 585. The first line has not been identified, nor has the source of
the cento as a whole.

46. Camm and Bland are here referring to the various attempts of the House
of Burgesses to relieve the clergy of the non-tobacco counties from the obligation
of being paid in tobacco. The royal disallowance of the Two-Penny Act created
hardships for ministers in these counties. They immediately petitioned for assistance
but without success until 1769. Cf. above, pp. 12–13; George M. Brydon, *Virginia's
Mother Church* . . . (Richmond and Philadelphia, 1947–1952), II, 119–120; and
Morton, *Virginia,* II, 801–805.

PAMPHLET 5

CONSIDERATIONS UPON THE ACT OF PARLIAMENT

There are several accounts of the passing of the Sugar Act and of the reaction
to it in the colonies. The fullest is by Gipson, *British Empire,* X, chap. xi. A
briefer version by the same author can be found in *The Coming of the Revolution
1763–1775* (New York, 1954), chap. v. Bernhard Knollenberg adds some useful
details in his *Origin of the American Revolution, 1759–1766* (New York, 1960),
chap. xi. The analysis of the act in Oliver M. Dickerson, *The Navigation Acts and
the American Revolution* (Philadelphia, 1951), chap. vii, is of particular importance; it demonstrates the importance of the elaborate customs regulations written
into the act which in themselves "amounted to a constitutional revolution in the
relations of the colonies to the home country." Details on the English background
of the act will be found in Allen S. Johnson, "The Passage of the Sugar Act,"
W.M.Q., 3d ser., 16 (1959), 507–514. *Jasper Mauduit* . . . (*Collections of the
Massachusetts Historical Society, LXXIV*), contains letters to and from the Massachusetts agent in London concerning the act before and after its passage.

The present pamphlet — entry 2 in Adams' "Bibliographical Study" — appeared
in only one edition, though it may have had a second printing.

Notes to Introduction

1. 4 George III c. 15. Excerpts from the text of the act will be found in Merrill
Jensen, ed., *American Colonial Documents to 1776* (*English Historical Documents,*
IX, London, 1955), pp. 643–648.

2. Alison G. Olson, "The British Government and Colonial Union, 1754,"
W.M.Q., 3d ser., 17 (1960), 22–34; Margaret M. Spector, *The American Department of the British Government, 1768–1782* (New York, 1940), chap. i and ii;
Arthur H. Basye, "The Secretary of State for the Colonies, 1768–1782," *American
Historical Review,* 28 (1922), 13–15; Johnson, "Passage of the Sugar Act," p. 508
n4. For Townshend's compulsive desire to reorganize the colonial administration,
see Lewis B. Namier, *Charles Townshend* (Oxford, 1959), pp. 16–29.

3. Albert B. Southwick, "The Molasses Act — A Source of Precedents," *W.M.Q.,*
3d ser., 8 (1951), 400, 401.

4. Gipson, *Coming of the Revolution,* pp. 63–64. For a detailed account of the

economics of the sugar trade, see Richard Pares, *Yankees and Creoles* (Cambridge, 1956), pp. 53 ff., chap. iv.

5. Knollenberg, *Origin,* p. 139; cf. Gipson, *British Empire,* X, p. 218 for a higher estimate of the rate in New York.

6. George L. Beer, *British Colonial Policy, 1754–1765* (New York, 1907), pp. 115–116. Gipson's figures indicate that in the thirty years after 1733 the income from the mainland colonies under all provisions of the Molasses Act averaged £721 per year. *British Empire,* X, pp. 204–205; cf. p. 219.

7. Johnson, "Passage of the Sugar Act," pp. 510–511. The calculation proved to be quite inaccurate. The total duty collected in the two years after September 29, 1764, averaged less than £9000 per year. Gipson, *British Empire,* X, p. 214; cf. Thomas Hutchinson, *History of the Colony and Province of Massachusetts-Bay* (Lawrence S. Mayo, ed., Cambridge, 1936), III, 78–79.

8. *Mauduit,* p. 159n.

9. Charles M. Andrews, "The Boston Merchants and the Non-Importation Movement," *Publications of the Colonial Society of Massachusetts,* XIX (*Transactions 1916–1917*), pp. 380–390 (the quotation is at 382); a more literal version appears in the *Collections of the Connecticut Historical Society,* XVIII (*Fitch Papers,* II, Hartford, 1920), 262–273.

10. Knollenberg, *Origin,* pp. 145–148; *Fitch Papers,* II, 277–279; Frederick B. Wiener, "The Rhode Island Merchants and the Sugar Act," *N.E.Q.,* 3 (1930), 468–495. The text of the "Remonstrance" is in John R. Bartlett, ed., *Records of the Colony of Rhode Island* (Providence, 1856–1865), VI, 378–383. Hopkins' "Essay" was printed in the *Providence Gazette,* January 14 and 21; in the *Newport Mercury,* February 6 and 13; and in the *Boston Evening-Post,* January 30 and February 6. Apparently only one copy of the Philadelphia reprint of the *Essay* has survived (Gipson, *British Empire,* X, p. 213). The pamphlet was reprinted in London in the same year (Sabin, no. 22970).

11. Wiener, "Rhode Island Merchants," p. 496; Andrews, "Boston Merchants," p. 167; Knollenberg, *Origin,* p. 343 n37; Johnson, "Sugar Act," pp. 512–513.

12. Southwick, "Molasses Act," pp. 401–403; Hutchinson, *History,* III, 78–79.

13. Thomas Cushing to Jasper Mauduit, Boston, January 1764, *Mauduit,* pp. 145–146; Gipson, *British Empire,* X, p. 212. On placemen and the sense of conspiracy, see above, General Introduction, Chap. V.

Notes to Text

1. The Proclamation of October 7, 1763, famous in American history for its attempt to regulate the settlement of the trans-Appalachian west, provided more generally for the government of the areas acquired by Great Britain in the Seven Years' War.

2. The pamphlet referred to is [John Douglas, Bishop of Salisbury], *A Letter Addressed to Two Great Men, on the Prospect of Peace; and on the Terms Necessary To Be Insisted upon in the Negotiation* . . . (London, 1760). The "two great men" were Pitt and Newcastle.

3. This organization of the problem will be found also in *An Essay on the Trade of the Northern Colonies* and in *Reasons Against the Renewal of the Sugar Act.* The latter, however, places particular emphasis on the fishery problem.

4. Some New England distillers were able to produce one gallon of rum from one gallon of molasses, but a 25 per cent loss in the distillation process was common

("molasses being distilled into rum at 75 per cent"). Thus a 6*d*. per gallon duty on molasses, by the author's calculation, becomes an 8*d*. per gallon duty on rum. Cf. p. 25 of the present pamphlet.

5. Osnaburgs and ticklenburgs mentioned in the author's footnote are coarse cloths originally produced in the towns of Osnabrück and Tecklenburg.

6. The figures cited were in all probability taken from Franklin's pamphlet *The Interest of Great Britain Considered, with Regard to Her Colonies, and the Acquisitions of Canada and Guadaloupe . . .* (London, 1760), no doubt in the Boston or Philadelphia reprints of the same year, pp. 58–59 and 46–47 respectively; in Albert H. Smyth, ed., *Writings of Benjamin Franklin* (New York, 1905–1907), IV, 66–67. Franklin, attacking William Burke's arguments for retaining Guadeloupe instead of Canada in the approaching peace negotiations, listed English exports to the northern colonies and to the West Indies year by year 1744–1748 and 1754–1758, pointing out that while exports to the two regions were roughly equal in the first period, the difference in their value in the second period was close to £4,000,000 in favor of the mainland. For a general discussion of this exchange of pamphlets, see Beer, *British Colonial Policy*, pp. 142–152; Gipson, *British Empire*, IX, 233–236. Franklin's figures were used also in Hopkins' *Essay on the Trade of the Northern Colonies*.

7. It was at the end of the fifties that Glasgow became the major distribution center for American tobacco. In 1758 it passed London, and surpassed all the outports combined. Jacob M. Price, "The Rise of Glasgow in the Chesapeake Tobacco Trade, 1707–1775," *W.M.Q.*, 3d ser., 11 (1954), 187, 190. Cf. *The Colonel Dismounted* (JHL Pamphlet 4), Introduction, and Appendix, p. v.

8. Franklin, *Interest of Great Britain Considered*, p. 30 of the first edition; in Smyth, *Writings*, IV, 61.

9. On the pricing of rum and molasses in the British West Indies and the economics of distilling in the islands, see Pares, *Yankees and Creoles*, pp. 126–138; Gipson, *Coming of the Revolution*, p. 63.

10. In *An Essay on the Trade of the Northern Colonies*, p. 26, Hopkins predicted that twenty thousand seamen and fishermen will be "turned out of employ." In *Reasons Against the Renewal*, the Boston merchants presented a most detailed account of the supposed ill effects on the fisheries of the new duties.

11. The figures are taken from the Boston merchants' "State of the Trade," 1763, as published by Andrews in "Boston Merchants," p. 386.

PAMPHLET 6

FITCH, *REASONS WHY THE BRITISH COLONIES IN AMERICA SHOULD NOT BE CHARGED WITH INTERNAL TAXES*

The Stamp Act, with which this pamphlet is primarily concerned, has been the subject of a great deal of historical writing. A selected listing of these works will be found in Oscar Handlin, *et al.*, eds., *Harvard Guide to American History* (Cambridge, 1954), p. 298. The fullest account, which surrounds the immediate narrative of events with biographical chapters on certain leading figures, is in Morgan, *Stamp Act*. Morgan has also published a collection of documents on the Stamp Act: *Prologue to Revolution: Sources and Documents on the Stamp Act Crisis, 1764–1766* (Chapel Hill, 1959). His interpretation of the constitutional issues involved is drawn out more fully in "Colonial Ideas of Parliamentary Power, 1764–1766," *W.M.Q.*, 3d ser., 5 (1948), 311–341. The other two recent works that deal with the subject in detail — Bernhard Knollenberg, *Origin of the American Revolution, 1759–1766* (New York, 1960), and Gipson, *British Empire,* X — had the advantage of Morgan's research and interpretation as a starting point, and, accepting his formulation of the constitutional problem, have reached somewhat different conclusions.

The Connecticut background of the present pamphlet is included in Oscar Zeichner, *Connecticut's Years of Controversy, 1750–1776* (Chapel Hill, 1949), a study that makes a particular effort to relate local politics to the imperial problems. Lawrence H. Gipson's *Jared Ingersoll* (New Haven, 1920) covers much of the same ground from a different point of view. *Mr. Ingersoll's Letters Relating to the Stamp-Act* (New Haven, 1766) is a key document in the entire controversy and bears particularly on the situation in Connecticut. Other selections from Ingersoll's letters of these years are printed in the *Papers of the New Haven Historical Society,* IX (New Haven, 1918). Thomas Fitch's correspondence and miscellaneous writing dating from his governorship, 1754–1766, have also been published, by the Connecticut Historical Society in its *Collections,* XVII-XVIII (Hartford, 1918–1920).

The present pamphlet, printed in five hundred copies, of which 112 were taken to England for distribution by Jared Ingersoll, is entry no. 3 in Adams, "Bibliographical Study." It was reprinted as an Appendix to vol. XII of John H. Trumbull, *et al.,* eds., *Public Records of the Colony of Connecticut . . .* (Hartford, 1850–1890).

Notes to Introduction

1. Gipson, *British Empire,* X, pp. 252, 55–56, 79–80, 253–256, 260, 258.

2. Morgan, *Stamp Act,* pp. 56 ff.; Gipson, *British Empire,* X, chap. xii: the quotation at p. 260.

3. Zeichner, *Years of Controversy,* chap. iii; *Public Records of the Colony of Connecticut,* XII, 256; Gipson, *Ingersoll,* p. 126; *Ingersoll's Letters,* pp. 2n, 44. Cf. Lawrence H. Gipson, "Connecticut Taxation and Parliamentary Aid Preceding the Revolutionary War," *American Historical Review,* 36 (1930–1931), 721–739. On Jackson see Carl Van Doren's Introduction to his edition of the *Letters and Papers of Benjamin Franklin and Richard Jackson 1753–1785* (Philadelphia, 1947).

4. The quotations are from the present pamphlet, pp. 11, 12.

5. *Ibid.,* pp. 35–37. Cf. Knollenberg, *Origin,* p. 203; and Morgan, "Colonial Ideas," pp. 317–318.

6. On Fitch and Connecticut politics of the fifties and sixties, see Zeichner, *Years of Controversy,* chap. iii; Franklin B. Dexter, *Biographical Sketches of the Graduates of Yale College . . .* (New York, 1885–1912), I, 247–251; *D.A.B.* article on Fitch; and the two volumes of Fitch's papers mentioned in the general references above. On Ingersoll, see Gipson, *Ingersoll,* chaps. i–iv; and the *Papers of the New Haven Historical Society,* IX (New Haven, 1918). On Silliman and Wyllys, see Dexter, *Biographical Sketches,* I, 356–358, 399–400; on Whately, see Introduction and notes to Dulany, *Considerations* (JHL Pamphlet 14). The quotations in this paragraph are taken from *Ingersoll's Letters,* p. 8.

7. *Fitch Papers,* II, 304; Zeichner, *Years of Controversy,* p. 50: Jackson agreed with the position stated in Connecticut's pamphlet: Jackson to Franklin, November 12, 1763, in Van Doren, *Letters and Papers,* pp. 113–114.

8. *Ingersoll's Letters,* pp. 9, 10.

9. Knollenberg, *Origin,* pp. 199–201; Morgan, *Stamp Act,* p. 216.

10. On Hutchinson's later position, see especially *The Speeches of . . . Governor Hutchinson . . . at a Session Begun . . . January, 1773 . . .* (Boston, 1773), discussed in the General Introduction, Chap. VI, sec. 3. On Ingersoll's fate, see Gipson, *Ingersoll,* chap xiii, and *Liberty and Property Vindicated . . .* (JHL Pamphlet 12), Introduction. On Fitch's later career, see works cited in note 6 above.

11. Morgan, *Stamp Act,* p. 216; Knollenberg, *Origin,* chaps. xvii, xviii, p. 346; Stephen Hopkins, *Rights of Colonies Examined* (JHL Pamphlet 9); and above, General Introduction, pp. 125–126. Cf. Edmund Morgan, "Thomas Hutchinson and the Stamp Act," *N.E.Q.,* 21 (1948), 478.

12. See General Introduction, above pp. 124–128. Connecticut had shifted its position as early as October 1765; see *Public Records of the Colony of Connecticut,* XII, 424, where "duties" are listed together with "taxes" as special "acts of legislation" which are free gifts of the people not to be granted away by any but "legal and elected representatives."

Notes to Text

1. [Matthew Bacon], *A New Abridgment of the Law* (London, 1736–1766), IV, 166. This standard legal reference work of the later eighteenth century ("a sound digest," Jefferson called it, though he disapproved of its alphabetical arrangement, "the manual of every judge and lawyer") was left unfinished at Bacon's death. The titles after "Sheriff" were completed by Sergeant Sayer and Owen Ruffhead. Volume IV was published in 1759. E. Millicent Sowerby, comp., *Catalogue of the Library of Thomas Jefferson* (Washington, D.C., 1952–1959), II, 223.

2. The Charter of 1662 refers to two "persons" or "freemen" to be elected by each of the towns; the Fundamental Orders of 1639 refers to "deputies." The text of the charter, cited again p. 25 below, is printed in *Public Records of the Colony of Connecticut,* II, 3–11.

3. The passage "is styled . . . liberties of the subject" is taken verbatim from Bacon, *Abridgment,* IV, 149.

4. The conflict referred to is the Pequot War, which began in the summer of 1636 with the murder of the trader John Oldham by Pequot Indians and ended a year later when Capt. John Mason and his men captured a substantial number of the tribe.

5. This famous case arose in the general election of 1700 when Matthew Ashby, a Whig voter at Aylesbury, was prevented from voting by the mayor, William White. Contested into the Court of Queen's Bench, the case precipitated an important jurisdictional conflict. Three out of four judges decided that election disputes were a matter for the House of Commons and not for the courts to decide, but Chief Justice Holt held that though the Commons could decide who had been chosen, the right to vote was in effect "a matter of property" injuries upon which were remediable by the courts. In this he was upheld by the House of Lords where the case was heard on appeal, and the result was a fierce contest between the two Houses. Though the issues were left in doubt for some time, subsequent judgments confirmed Holt's opinion. See E. Neville Williams, *The Eighteenth-Century Constitution, 1688–1815: Documents and Commentary* (Cambridge, England, 1960), pp. 221–222, 225.

6. King Philip's War, 1675–1676.

7. During the course of King William's War, 1689–1697, Connecticut did contribute detachments to the defense of Albany, New York City, and Hampshire

County, Massachusetts, as well as to the joint expedition against Canada in 1690 led by Fitz-John Winthrop which proved to be a fiasco. The historian Benjamin Trumbull estimated the total cost of the war to Connecticut to have been in excess of £12,000: *A Complete History of Connecticut* (Hartford, 1797), I, 398–418; see also Allen W. Trelease, *Indian Affairs in Colonial New York: The Seventeenth Century* (Ithaca, 1960), pp. 299–305.

8. The cost of Connecticut's contribution to these expeditions was approximately £20,000. G. M. Waller, *Samuel Vetch* (Chapel Hill, 1960), p. 164; Trumbull, *History of Connecticut*, I, 457–475. Cf. Gerald S. Graham, ed., *The Walker Expedition to Quebec, 1711* (*Publications of the Champlain Society*, XXXII, Toronto, 1953).

9. The figures cited in this paragraph are essentially correct with the possible exception of the additional 2,000 men said to have been sent as reinforcements to Lake George in 1755.

10. Between 1755 and 1762 Connecticut issued £408,450, including interest, of its so-called lawful money. Of this, £346,500, equivalent to £259,875 sterling, was devoted to war purposes. By the end of 1763 all but £82,000 lawful money had been repaid either by Parliamentary reimbursement or by local taxation. Between 1756 and 1767 Connecticut received a total of £316,788 lawful money in Parliamentary reimbursements for its war effort; the colony levied no taxes at all from 1766 to 1770. Gipson, *British Empire*, X, 73–75.

PAMPHLET 7

OTIS, *RIGHTS OF THE BRITISH COLONIES*

Surprisingly little has been written on that strange but important figure James Otis. The only book-length biography remains William Tudor's *Life of James Otis of Massachusetts* (Boston, 1823), which relies heavily on John Adams' rambling reminiscences in old age (published in vol. X of Adams' *Works*). Of the modern treatments, one may choose between Samuel Eliot Morison's affectionate sketch in *D.A.B.*, XIV, and Shipton's remarkable polemic in *Sibley's Harvard Graduates*, XI (Boston, 1960), 247–287. The latter, full of excellent detail culled from the sources, makes the account of Otis written by his bitter enemy Thomas Hutchinson, in vol. III of his *History of the Colony and Province of Massachusetts-Bay* (Lawrence S. Mayo, ed., Cambridge, 1936), cordial by comparison.

The most detailed and impartial account of Otis' political activities in the sixties will be found in Ellen E. Brennan, *Plural Office-Holding in Massachusetts 1760–1780* (Chapel Hill, 1945), chapters i–iii. There are accounts of Otis' constitutional views by Charles F. Mullett in his edition of Otis' writings (*University of Missouri Studies*, IV, nos. 3 and 4, July and October 1929) and in his *Fundamental Law and the American Revolution 1760–1776* (New York, 1933); by Charles H. McIlwain, in *The American Revolution: A Constitutional Interpretation* (New York, 1923); by Randolph G. Adams, *Political Ideas of the American Revolution* (Durham, North Carolina, 1922); and by Morgan, in *Stamp Act*. A usefully detailed but misleading account of Otis' shifts in political and theoretical position is Ellen E. Brennan, "James Otis: Recreant and Patriot," *N.E.Q.*, 12 (1939), 691–725. For references to the literature on the Stamp Act controversy, see notes to JHL Pamphlet 6.

The standard reprint edition of Otis' pamphlets is that of Mullett, cited above. Documents of the writs of assistance case are collected and fully commented on in the exhaustive Appendix I, by Horace Gray, in Josiah Quincy, Jr.'s *Reports of Cases . . . in the Superior Court of Judicature . . . Between 1761 and 1772 . . .* (Samuel M. Quincy, ed., Boston, 1865). The most recent discussion of the writs case, containing references to the entire literature on that episode, is by Gipson in *British Empire*, X, chap. vi. In contrast to his later garrulous reminiscences of Otis, John Adams' contemporary impressions of him, recorded in his Diary (vols. I and II of *Diary and Autobiography*) are unusually penetrating.

For a bibliographical listing of the five eighteenth-century editions of *The Rights of the British Colonies*, see Adams, "Bibliographical Study," entries 4a–e. The present text reproduces the first (Boston, 1764) edition.

The quotation on the title page is from the *Aeneid*, xi, 320–323: "Let us cede the whole of this area, with its pine-covered mountain ridge/ To gain the goodwill of the Trojans. Let us draw up a treaty, fair to/ Both sides, and invite them to partner us in the kingdom./ If they want it so much, let them found a city and settle down here." (C. Day Lewis, tr., Oxford, 1952).

Notes to Introduction

1. *Boston News-Letter*, April 4, 1765; *Boston Gazette*, April 8, 1765.

2. Morgan, *Stamp Act*, p. 35; Thomas Hollis to Jonathan Mayhew, March 4, 1765, in *Proceedings of the Massachusetts Historical Society*, 69 (1956), 165–166; Shipton, "Otis," p. 272.

3. Hutchinson to Richard Jackson, July 23, 1764, Massachusetts Archives, XXVI, 99–100, quoted in *N.E.Q.*, 12 (1939), 696n; Adams, *Diary and Autobiography*, II, 100; Tudor, *Otis*, p. 172n; *Novanglus and Massachusettensis . . .* (Boston, 1819), pp. 180, 201, 206; Morison, "Otis," pp. 696 ff.; *W.M.Q.*, 3d ser., 14 (1957), 99, 304. The pamphlet was said to have given "great offense to the ministry." *Collections of the Massachusetts Historical Society*, 6th ser., IX, 45.

4. Shipton, "Otis," pp. 247–249; Adams, *Works*, X, 275.

5. Shipton, "Otis," pp. 250, 252; Gipson, *British Empire*, X, 115, 116, 121; Adams, *Works*, X, 291. On the Superior Court appointment and its political repercussions, see Brennan, *Plural Office-Holding*, pp. 29 ff.

6. Gipson, *British Empire*, X, 122–126; Gray, "Appendix I," in Quincy, *Reports of Cases*, pp. 471, 474.

7. T. F. T. Plucknett, "Bonham's Case and Judicial Review," *Harvard Law Review*, 40 (1926–1927), 34; Otis, *Rights*, pp. 72, 73.

8. For the early development of American ideas of judicial review, see Edward S. Corwin, *The 'Higher Law' Background of American Constitutional Law* (Ithaca, 1955), pp. 77–79; and Knollenberg, *Origin*, pp. 163–165. Both Corwin and Knollenberg badly telescope, and hence do not explain, the character of this development, which, as recounted above, General Introduction, pp. 99 ff., was slow and unsure in the 1760's and turned on the correlative development of the idea of a fixed constitution: hence the particular significance of Otis' quotations from Vattel in the present pamphlet, pp. 72, 73. Of the early examples of the actual practice of judicial voidance cited by Knollenberg, only one, the opinion of the Northampton, Virginia, County Court of February 1766 declaring that the Stamp Act was not to "bind, affect, or concern the inhabitants of this colony inasmuch as they conceive the [act] to be unconstitutional" is convincing. *William and Mary College Quarterly*, 19 (1910–1911), 224.

9. The interpretation in this paragraph rests on the construction of the case

by S. E. Thorne, in "Dr. Bonham's Case," *Law Quarterly Review,* 54 (1938), 543–552, and in his Introduction to *A Discourse upon the . . . Statutes . . .* (San Marino, 1942), pp. 85–92. I have benefited particularly from the views of L. Kinvin Wroth, coeditor of the *Legal Papers of John Adams,* whose own careful analysis of Coke and the Writs case, which he generously allowed me to read in manuscript, is to be published in vol. II of that publication. The quotation from Hobart is taken from Plucknett, "Bonham's Case," p. 50. Cf. J. W. Gough, *Fundamental Law in English Constitutional History* (Oxford, 1955), pp. 31–32, 35.

10. General Introduction, above, pp. 116–118; Gough, *Fundamental Law,* chaps. vi–xi; Plucknett, "Bonham's Case," pp. 49–61.

11. Plucknett, "Bonham's Case," p. 55.

12. *Ibid.,* pp. 59–60; T. C. Hansard, *The Parliamentary History of England . . .* (London, 1806–1820), XVI, 168; W. S. Johnson to Roger Sherman, London, September 27, 1758, in Misc. Bound MSS, Massachusetts Historical Society.

13. Hutchinson to Jackson, September 12, 1765, quoted from the Massachusetts Archives, XXVI, 153, by Gray, "Appendix I," in Quincy, *Reports of Cases,* p. 441.

14. Shipton, "Otis," pp. 254, 259; Adams, *Diary and Autobiography,* I, 84, 271.

15. Tudor, *Otis,* p. 172n; on the supposed sellout, see Brennan, *Plural Office-Holding,* pp. 52–54, 57, 67–68; Adams, *Diary and Autobiography,* II, 66, and his *Works,* X, 295; Hutchinson, *History,* III, 69–70.

16. Shipton, "Otis," p. 257. Cf. Adams, *Works,* X, 300 ff.

17. "This work was read in the House of Representatives of Massachusetts, in manuscript, in 1764, and, though not ordered by them to be published, it was printed with their knowledge." Adams, *Works,* X, 293. Cf. *Journal of the Honourable House of Representatives . . . 1764* (Boston, 1764), p. 66.

18. *Rights,* pp. 9, 15, 39, 40, 38.

19. *Ibid.,* p. 47; *Works of Francis Bacon* (Basil Montagu, ed., London, 1825–1834), I, 179.

20. *Rights,* p. 47. The "instances in the Appendix" are the opinions of Hobart and Holt following Coke's dictum in *Bonham's Case;* they appear on pages 72 and 73 of the pamphlet together with quotations from Vattel. For modern discussions of the cases cited by Otis, see Gough, *Fundamental Law,* pp. 9–10, 33, 39; and Plucknett, "Bonham's Case," pp. 49–56.

21. *Rights,* pp. 50, 51, 40 (cf. p. 24).

22. *Ibid.,* pp. 41, 72n. Cf. note 8 above.

Notes to Text

1. It is assumed that this paragraph, like that on p. 4 and those that follow, is not a quotation from another writer but Otis' own phrasing of hypothetical questions. On the political theory of the Glorious Revolution and the Convention Parliament, see E. Neville Williams, ed., *The Eighteenth-Century Constitution 1688–1815* (Cambridge, England, 1960), chap. i, and articles listed pp. 433–434.

2. Locke's words are quoted, essentially correctly, from the *First Treatise of Government,* i, 3 and 1 (pp. 160 and 159 in the Peter Laslett edition of the *Two Treatises of Government,* Cambridge, England, 1960).

3. This well-known adage of classical antiquity — "let the good of the people be the supreme law" — which was conveyed to the colonists through Cicero, among others, and made much of in *Cato's Letters,* was commonly mentioned and discussed in the Revolutionary literature. See, e.g., the play on the phrase between

Bland and Camm, discussed in the Introduction to *The Colonel Dismounted* (JHL Pamphlet 4), above p. 296. Cf. Gough, *Fundamental Law*, pp. 99, 186.

4. See Otis' further explanation of "ancient and modern gods" in his *P.S.*, p. 80.

5. The Latin — "Thus I will it, thus I command it, let my desire serve for reason" — is from Juvenal, *Satires*, vi, 221.

6. The reference is to *Oceana*, p. 197 in the S. B. Liljegren ed. (Heidelberg, 1924): "The first of these nations (which if you stay her leisure will in my mind be *France*) that recovers the health of ancient prudence shall assuredly govern the world . . ." But if Otis meant to imply that Harrington would have approved of the eighteenth-century balance of the British constitution, he had misread Harrington. The central argument of *Oceana* is that the "Gothic balance" was defective both in its monarchy and its overweening nobility, and particularly in the chronic state of warfare between them; the only means of recovering from this "bed of sickness" was to return to the "health of ancient prudence," that is, to classical republicanism as interpreted by Harrington. See Zera S. Fink, *The Classical Republicans* (Evanston, 1945), chap. iii; Charles Blitzer, *An Immortal Commonwealth* (New Haven, 1960), chap. iv.

7. Otis' footnote reference is to the passage of the *Second Treatise* (xix, 225; Laslett ed., p. 433) that echoes so clearly in the Declaration of Independence: "But if a long train of abuses, prevarications, and artifices all tending the same way, make the design visible to the people . . . 'tis not to be wondered that they should rouse themselves . . ."

8. The three paragraphs above are quoted, essentially correctly, from the *Second Treatise*, xiii, 149; xix, 222, except that the words before "them to slavery . . ." in the paragraph immediately above is a brisk paraphrase of xix, 211-212. (The passages referred to are in the Laslett ed., pp. 384-385, 424-425, 430.)

9. The first of the preceding two sentences is a quotation from René Louis de Voyer, Marquis d'Argenson, *Considérations sur le gouvernement ancien et présent de la France comparé avec celui des autres états* . . . (Amsterdam, 1764), ch. ii, which Rousseau used in a footnote in the *Social Contract* (i, 2) by way of dismissing Grotius' denial that all human authority is established for the benefit of the governed. The second sentence is Rousseau's, and follows the first directly.

10. The quotations from Grotius, correct both in wording and citation, were taken from a London, 1738 translation (translator unnamed). The passages from Pufendorf that follow, also essentially correct, are taken from a translation by Basil Kennett and William Percivale, the first edition of which was published in Oxford in 1703. For Stephen Hopkins' use of the same passages, see his *Rights of Colonies Examined* (JHL Pamphlet 9), pp. 6–7.

11. Jean Domat, *The Civil Law in Its Natural Order, Together with the Publick Law . . . With Additional Remarks on Some Material Differences Between the Civil Law and the Law of England* (William Strahan, tr., 2 vols., London, 1722). The quotation is from Strahan's preface, pp. xviii, xix. The translator was not the famous printer and friend of Benjamin Franklin, though the names are the same, but an LL.D. known to history mainly through this translation of Domat.

12. Montesquieu's ironical defense of slavery in *The Spirit of the Laws*, xv, 5, caricatured certain presumed arguments of slave traders and owners: "Sugar would be too dear if the plants . . . were cultivated by any other than slaves. These creatures are all over black, and with such a flat nose that they can scarcely be pitied. It is hardly to be believed that God, who is a wise Being, should place a soul, especially a good soul, in such a black ugly body." (Nugent tr., Franz Neu-

mann, ed., New York, 1949.) It appears that some readers took the arguments seriously. Cf. F. T. H. Fletcher, *Montesquieu and English Politics* (*1750–1800*) (London, 1939), pp. 228–229.

13. See Otis' qualification of this statement in his *P.S.*, p. 80 below.

14. *Second Treatise*, ii, 4; iv, 22 (Laslett ed., pp. 287, 301).

15. The quotation is from the Succession to the Crown Act of 1707 (6 Anne c. 7).

16. The first sentence of this paragraph proved to be particularly valuable to Otis in his later efforts to demonstrate his loyalty to England. See his *Vindication* (JHL Pamphlet 11), pp. 26, 27. The statute referred to in the footnote is An Act for the Better Securing the Dependency of Ireland upon the Crown of Great Britain, 6 George I c. 5. Otis discusses the question of Irish dependence in detail below, pp. 43 ff.; he quotes from the act on p. 46.

17. The reference in the footnote is to Jeremiah Dummer's *A Defence of the New-England Charters* (London, 1721).

18. The cases cited in the footnote are the following: 3 Mod. 159: *Wytham v. Dutton* (1687), in which the Court of King's Bench appears to have denied the claim that "the King is not restrained by the laws of Englnd to govern [Barbadoes] by any particular law whatsoever, and therefore not by common law . . . for those islands were gotten by conquest or by some of the subjects going in search of some prize and planting themselves there . . ." Salkeld 411: *Blankard v. Galdy* (1694), in which Holt reaffirmed Coke's rule that the laws of conquered colonies may be altered by the conqueror, but until they are so altered they remain in force, and that colonists in settled colonies have all the rights of Englishmen. Vaughan 300: *Craw v. Ramsey* (1670), which confirmed the distinction that had been drawn in *Calvin's Case* between Ireland and the plantations on the one hand, as dominions belonging to the "crown of England," and Scotland, a dominion of the "King of England" and hence not subject to Parliament, on the other. On the main issue involved in these cases, see below, note 38; Bland, *Colonel Dismounted* (JHL Pamphlet 4), text notes 25–27; McIlwain, *American Revolution*, pp. 96–104.

19. "He who derives the advantage ought to sustain the burden."

20. The reference is to Thomas Pownall's *The Administration of the Colonies*, of which Otis was using the first (London, 1764) edition. On Pownall, who had been governor of Massachusetts 1758–1760, and his book, see Daniel Dulany's *Considerations* (JHL Pamphlet 13), Introduction. Among the proposals Pownall made which Otis would probably have considered "good regulations" were those to create circuit courts of appeal presided over by trained and experienced jurists, currency reform, and changing the navigation laws to allow direct exportation from the colonies to foreign countries. Otis' statement of Pownall's sense of an impending crisis is quite accurate; Pownall's dramatic words expressing his sense of "something new arising in the world" are quoted in the Introduction to Pamphlet 13. But the sentence "The cards are shuffling fast through all Europe" is not from Pownall.

21. "Let it be given to the more worthy."

22. The reference is to a pamphlet by William Bollan: *Coloniae Anglicanae Illustratae: or, The Acquest of Dominion, and The Plantation of Colonies Made by the English in America, With the Rights of the Colonies Examined, Stated, and Illustrated. Part I* (London, 1762). This 141-page publication was a preface to the projected work; nothing further was published, however. This mild reference to Bollan and his writing is curious in light of Otis' characterization of him two years earlier as a tool of "high church men and dissenters who, for the sake of the

offices they sustain, are full as high in their notions of prerogative as the church-men." According to John Adams, Otis had abused not only Bollan but this very pamphlet, shortly after its publication, in a speech to the Massachusetts House. (Otis to Jasper Mauduit, October 28, 1762, *Mauduit,* p. 77; Adams, *Works,* X, 356.) Bollan (c. 1710–1776), Governor Shirley's son-in-law, had studied law in Boston, and had served as the colony's advocate general and then as its agent in London until he was dismissed in 1762. His later career, particularly his authorship of *Continued Corruption, Standing Armies, and Popular Discontents Considered . . .* (London, 1768), bears out Adams' contention that if Bollan had not been dis-couraged "he would have produced much in illustration of the ecclesiastical and political superstition and despotism of the ages when colonization commenced and proceeded."

23. Pownall, *Administration,* p. 39.

24. The source cited (correctly) is *The History and Proceedings of the House of Commons from the Restoration to the Present Time* (London, 1742–1744), V, 72.

25. The reference is to Michaelmas term of 11 George II. Otis was apparently quoting the case from a secondary source, probably one of the abridgments.

26. On 6 George I c. 5, see above, note 16.

27. On colonial expenditures and Parliamentary reimbursements, see Gipson, *British Empire,* X, chaps. ii–v.

28. This sentence, like that on pp. 32–33 above, was used by Otis to prove his loyalty to England when he came to write his *Vindication* (JHL Pamphlet 11), p. 27.

29. Otis omits from the passage quoted, after the words ". . . nor call by any other name than that of *home,*" Pownall's more hard-headed interpretation: "Besides, the merchants are, and must ever be, in great measure allied with those of Great Britain: their very support consists of this alliance. The liberty and religion of the British colonies are incompatible with either French or Spanish government; and they know full well that they could hope for neither liberty nor protection under a Dutch one; no circumstances of trade could tempt them thus to certain ruin."

30. The passage of Pownall's *Administration* from which Otis quoted at the beginning of the paragraph reads: "I cannot, in one view, better describe the de-fects of the provincial courts in these infant governments than by the very descrip-tion which my Lord Chief Justice Hale gives of our county courts in the infancy of our governments, wherein he mentions, *First,* the ignorance of the judges, who were the freeholders of the county . . ."

31. The references are to the Wool Act (1699), 10 and 11 William III c. 10, which prohibited the export of American woolen products, and to the provisions of the navigation laws, beginning with that of 1696, which allowed suits for violation of the navigation laws to be prosecuted in the vice-admiralty courts, which sat without juries and were presided over by single judges.

32. The quotations are taken from pp. 50–51 and 49 of Dummer's *Defence.*

33. During King George's War, Massachusetts' Governor William Shirley or-ganized an expedition to capture Louisbourg on Cape Breton Island. Supported by Commodore Peter Warren and his English warships which blockaded the harbor, the attack was successful in June 1745. Colonial forces proudly held Louis-bourg despite French attempts to recapture it. England's decision to sacrifice Louisbourg for Madras in the Treaty of Aix-la-Chapelle at the end of the war produced great indignation in the colonies which reimbursement for expenses failed to overcome.

34. While impressment was legal in Great Britain, its legality in the colonies was much in question. An Act of 1708 specifically declared American vessels or those in the American trade out of bounds for press gangs; but the crown attempted to interpret the law as expiring at the conclusion of the War of Spanish Succession. The matter remained an open question and a source of agitation. While Boston was the scene of a famous anti-impressment riot in 1747, the grievance was not confined to New England. See Richard Pares, "The Manning of the Navy in the West Indies, 1702–63," *Transactions of the Royal Historical Society,* 4th ser., 20 (1937), 31–60; Dora Mae Clark, "The Impressment of Seamen in the American Colonies," *Essays in Colonial History Presented to Charles McLean Andrews* (New Haven, 1931), pp. 198–224.

35. Charles Viner, *A General Abridgment of Law and Equity Alphabetically Digested* . . . (23 vols., Aldershot [1741–1751]). Otis' citation is correct: "Prerogative of the King," section Ea1 (vol. XVI, p. 578), where Viner cites Charles Molloy, *De Jure Maritimo et Navali or A Treatise of Affairs Maritime and of Commerce,* book II, chap. xii, section 1, pp. 320–321 (probably using the sixth edition, London, 1707).

36. Otis quotes this sentence in his *Vindication* (JHL Pamphlet 11), p. 27, in attempting to disprove charges of his disloyalty to Parliament's authority.

37. The quotations are from Dummer, *Defence,* pp. 67, 74, 76.

38. The quotation is from the *Merchants of Waterford Case* (1484) in Year Book 2 Richard III, 12, plea 26, which Otis copied from 12 Coke's Reports 112 where it is quoted in an opinion of the chief legal officers of England concerning the operation of Poynings' Law (1494) forbidding the summoning of a Parliament in Ireland without the prior approval of the King and Council. The quotation is accurate; but the question of Parliament's authority over Ireland is remarkably complicated, and has been as hotly contested by modern historians as it was by seventeenth-century lawyers. Prof. Thorne writes that at the time of the *Waterford Case* "there was certainty only that, depending upon content, some statutes bound Ireland, others did not." In Elizabeth's time it was assumed that Ireland was bound if expressly named. In the eighteenth century the consensus of English law appears to have been that "all acts of Parliament bind Ireland, and have always bound it"; but some still disputed the point. Both sides cited historical precedents, "but neither position could be found in the sources, for neither was based upon unambiguous historical authority . . . the theories advanced were superimposed upon the facts rather than drawn from them." Thus Otis could cite this clear-sounding precedent from the fifteenth century as transmitted, presumably with endorsement, by early seventeenth-century lawyers; but it misrepresents the legal realities of both eras, and in any case had been superceded well before 1764. Thorne, *Discourse,* pp. 32–35; Robert L. Schuyler, *Parliament and the British Empire* (New York, 1929), chap. ii, esp. pp. 63–66, 73–74, 89–91. Cf. McIlwain, *American Revolution,* pp. 29–80; Quincy, *Reports,* pp. 514–515n.

39. Otis quotes this entire paragraph in his *Vindication* (JHL Pamphlet 11), p. 27, to clarify his position on Parliamentary authority.

40. 6 George II c. 13 is the Molasses Act of 1733, discussed in the Introduction to *Considerations* (JHL Pamphlet 5).

41. Pownall, *Administration,* p. 68.

42. Otis quotes the entire last paragraph in his *Vindication* (JHL Pamphlet 11), pp. 27–28, to justify and explain his position.

43. These Instructions were drafted by Samuel Adams.

44. The Memorial was almost certainly written by Otis. As the foonote indicates, it

was written as a statement of the claims of the Massachusetts House for the guidance of the colony's agent.

45. The quotations in the first two paragraphs of the footnote are accurate transcriptions of Emmerich de Vattel's *Law of Nations* (I, iii, 34; I, xviii, 210), which appeared originally as *Le droit des gens, ou Principes de la loi naturelle* . . . (London, 1758). Otis was using a London, 1759 translation (translator unnamed). The legal documentation that follows in the footnote consists of quotations from four cases, which are, in order of quotation: Hobart's judgment in *Day v. Savadge* (1614), with the final words "and they are *leges legum*" omitted from the sentence; Sir Thomas Powys' plea in *Thornby, On the Demise of the Duchess of Hamilton, v. Fleetwood* (1712); Holt's decision (with excisions) in *City of London v. Wood* (1701); Coke's opinion (with minor emendations) in *Dr. Bonham's Case* (1610). Otis took the reference to Herle's statement in *Thomas Tregor's Case* (1334) from Coke's opinion in *Bonham's Case*. "Articuli Super Cartas" is the title of a statute of 28 Edw. I confirming particulars of Magna Carta. These cases are discussed, with relevance to Otis' use of them, in Plucknett, "Bonham's Case," pp. 49–50, 54–56, 58; Thorne's writings cited in Introduction note 9 above; and Gough, *Fundamental Law*, pp. 39, 10, 33. The full titles of the reports referred to at the beginning of each of the citations will be found in the list of abbreviations, p. 2.

46. The reference is to Malachy Postlethwayt, author of *Britain's Commercial Interest Explained and Improved* . . . (2 vols., London, 1757).

PAMPHLET 8

THACHER, *SENTIMENTS OF A BRITISH AMERICAN*

The only recent biographical sketch of Oxenbridge Thacher (1719–1765) is by Clifford K. Shipton, in *Sibley's Harvard Graduates*, X (Boston, 1958), 322–328. Like the same author's biography of James Otis, it is informed and based on study of the sources; unlike that remarkable polemic it is impartial, turning partisan only when Otis' name appears. Important details of Thacher's politics in the early 1760's and excellent quotations from his early pamphlets and newspaper writings appear in Ellen E. Brennan, *Plural Office-Holding in Massachusetts 1760–1780* (Chapel Hill, 1945), chap. ii.

A number of recent historical works have made clear the importance of the administrative sections of the Sugar Act which Thacher points to in this pamphlet. Oliver Dickerson makes much of them in chap. vii of his *The Navigation Acts and the American Revolution* (Philadelphia, 1951) — which adopts wholesale the contemporary Whig interpretation of the Revolution as the result of a conspiracy of "King's Friends." Bernhard Knollenberg, *Origin of the American Revolution, 1759–1766* (New York, 1960), chap. xv, also discusses these changes, as does Lawrence H. Gipson in *British Empire*, X, chap. xi; chap. vi of the same work contains valuable background information on the problems of enforcement at the end of the Seven Years' War. A history of the admiralty courts in this period, especially in their enhanced role created by the Sugar Act, will be found in Carl Ubbelohde, *The Vice-Admiralty Courts and the American Revolution* (Chapel Hill, 1960). Writings on the passage of the Sugar Act and on the colonists' initial reaction to it are listed in the Introduction and notes to Pamphlet 5 above.

Thacher's *Sentiments of a British American* was printed only once. It is entered as no. 7 in Adams' "Bibliographical Study."

The quotation on the title page of the pamphlet is from the fabulist Phaedrus' "The Sapient Ass," translated by Christopher Smart in *A Poetical Translation of the Fables of Phaedrus* (London, 1765), i, 15, as follows:

A fearful old man in a mead,
While leading of his ass about,
Was startled at the sudden shout
Of enemies approaching nigh —
He then advis'd the ass to fly,
Lest we be taken in the place;
But loth at all to mend his pace,
"Pray will the conqueror," quoth Jack
"With double panniers load my back?"
"No" says the man — "If that's the thing,"
Cries he, "I care not who is king."

This quotation itself became part of the controversy of the time. It was attacked by "O.Z." (presumably Martin Howard, Jr.) in the *Newport Mercury*, September 17, 1764, as unacceptable to right-minded people. "The ass, we agree, was wise enough in his conclusion, but we humbly think the sickly apprehensions of a *senex pavidus* will not have so great an effect upon the minds of our countrymen as to fright them from their allegiance. If ever this should happen to be the case, our consolation must be that a small fleet and a few regiments will bring them peaceably back again." Howard continued his attack in his *Defence of the Letter from a Gentleman at Halifax* . . . , which was published in Newport in April 1765, claiming that the quotation proves that it was a matter of indifference to Thacher what prince or power ruled him, whether "a George or a Lewis." This brought down on Howard the full weight of James Otis' sarcastic abuse. Howard's reasoning, Otis wrote in his *Brief Remarks on the Defence of the Halifax Libel* . . . (Boston, 1765), pp. 12–13, is "of a piece with the law, the truth, the sincerity, the logic and philanthropy of [his] other productions." The fable was only that "of an old man and his ass, surely none but a jackass could have been offended at it." See also *Boston Gazette*, October 1, 1764. On the Howard-Otis polemic, see JHL Pamphlets 10 and 11.

Notes to Introduction

1. *Works*, X, 292.
2. Shipton, "Thacher," pp. 322–323; Adams, *Diary and Autobiography*, I, 55, 110, and on Thacher's status as a lawyer, pp. 160–161, 236, 238, 251; Josiah Quincy, Jr., *Reports of Cases . . . in the Superior Court of Judicature . . . Between 1761 and 1772* . . . (Samuel M. Quincy, ed., Boston, 1865), pp. 52–55, 469–471, 482, 391, 393–394.
3. Quincy, *Reports*, p. 394; Oxenbridge Thacher to Benjamin Prat [1762], in "Thacher Papers," *Proceedings of the Massachusetts Historical Society*, 20 (1882–1883), 46–48; Adams, *Works*, X, 286.
4. [Oxenbridge Thacher], *Considerations on the Election of Counsellors, Humbly Offered to the Electors* ([Boston], 1761), p. 6. Brennan, *Plural Office-Holding*, chap. i, especially page 32, establishes the facts of Hutchinson's plural office-holding; she discusses Thacher's attack on this near-monopoly in chap. ii, especially pp. 41–46, 59–60, 62–66.
5. George R. Minot, *Continuation of the History of . . . Massachusetts . . .*

(Boston, 1798–1803), II, 102–106; Oxenbridge Thacher, *Considerations on Lowering the Value of Gold Coins* . . . [Boston, 1762], pp. 9, 22. Thomas Hutchinson, *History of . . . Massachusetts-Bay* (L. S. Mayo, ed., Cambridge, 1936), III, 71–72; Brennan, *Plural Office-Holding,* pp. 46–47.

6. Hutchinson, *History,* III, 77; *Journal of the Honourable House of Representatives* . . . *1764* (Boston, 1764), pp. 72–77.

7. The sections of the Sugar Act (4 George III c. 15) referred to are 29 (cf. 20, 21), 27, 28, 23, 45, 46, 47, 41, in *Statutes at Large,* XXVI, 33 ff. Excerpts from the act will be found in Merrill Jensen, ed., *American Colonial Documents to 1776* (*English Historical Documents,* IX, London, 1955), 644–648. Cf. Dickerson, *Navigation Acts,* pp. 179–184; Knollenberg, *Origin,* pp. 176–180; Ubbelohde, *Vice-Admiralty Courts,* pp. 44–54.

8. On the later history of the struggle against the customs administration, see, among the contemporary pamphlets, especially [Henry Laurens], *Extracts from the Proceedings of the Court of Vice-Admiralty, in Charles-town, South Carolina* . . . *with* . . . *Some General Observations on American Custom-house Officers and Courts of Vice-Admiralty* (Charlestown [i.e., Charleston], 1769); and *Observations on Several Acts of Parliament* . . . *and Also on the Conduct of the Officers of the Customs* . . . *Published by the Merchants of Boston* ([Boston], 1769). Cf. Ubbelohde, *Vice-Admiralty Courts,* chaps. iv–viii; Dickerson, *Navigation Acts,* chap. ix; David S. Lovejoy, "Rights Imply Equality: The Case Against Admiralty Jurisdiction in America, 1764–1776," *W.M.Q.,* 3d ser., 16 (1959), 465 ff.

9. Thacher's draft of the Petition is in "Thacher Papers," pp. 49–52; the final document is in *Collections of the Massachusetts Historical Society,* 6th ser., IX, 32–36. Cf. *ibid.,* LXXIV, 170–171; Morgan, *Stamp Act,* p. 35.

10. Adams, *Works,* X, 287.

Notes to Text

1. Emmerich de Vattel, *Law of Nations,* I, ii, 24. The wording in the London 1759 translation is: "Happy constitution: which they did not suddenly obtain; it has cost rivers of blood; but they have not purchased it too dear." Cf. Otis, *Rights of the British Colonies* (JHL Pamphlet 7), text note 45.

2. I.e., the Sugar Act, 4 George III c. 15.

3. On March 11, 1758, the Massachusetts Assembly voted to raise 7000 men for Abercromby's expedition against Canada. According to Hutchinson, "Four thousand five hundred only could be raised by voluntary enlistment, and the remaining twenty-five hundred, by a subsequent act or order of court, were drawn from the militia, and impressed into the service." Hutchinson, *History,* III, 50. These contributions were stressed in the House's draft of the instructions to Mauduit: "a greater levy for a single province than the three kingdoms have made collectively in any one year since the Revolution." *Journal of the Honourable House* . . . *1764,* p. 73.

4. The reference is to section 41, and possibly also to section 46, of the Sugar Act. Thacher used the same sentence in his draft of the Massachusetts House of Representative's Petition to the King, but it does not appear in the final version, as approved by the whole Assembly and addressed to the House of Commons.

5. The statutes referred to are: 13 Richard II c. 5, which declared that "Admirals and their deputies shall not meddle from henceforth of anything done within the realm, but only of a thing done upon the sea"; 15 Richard II c. 3, which added that over all matters "rising within the bodies of the counties, as well by land as

by water, and also of wreck of the sea, the admiral's court shall have no jurisdiction"; and 2 Henry IV c. 11, which confirmed 13 Richard II c. 5.

6. Thacher included this passage almost verbatim in the draft Petition to the King, but it does not appear in the Assembly's final session.

7. 6 Anne c. 37 — An Act for the Encouragement of the Trade to America — removed all prize offices in America, gave officers and seamen the sole property in prize ships, attempted to speed prize procedure in admiralty courts, set limits on the fees to be paid admiralty judges and officers and declared them subject to penalty for neglect of duty, and allowed unsatisfied claimants to appeal to the crown.

8. This paragraph was taken over by Thacher in his draft of the Massachusetts Petition to England, and it appears, largely intact, in the final document.

9. Thacher had aired similar views in his plea in *Bishop v. Brig Freemason* (1763). He particularly attacked Capt. Bishop's commission for its failure to limit his jurisdiction geographically as required by law. Other important aspects of Thacher's argument in this case are referred to in the Introduction to the present pamphlet. Cf. Quincy, *Reports,* pp. 389-391. Thacher included the same charge in his draft of the petition to England.

10. "Far from Jove, far from his thunder."

11. This passage, referring to section 46 of the Sugar Act, was carried over intact into the Massachusetts Petition to the House of Commons.

12. The Privy Council had long been used to disallowing colonial laws placing duties on English imported products or restraining English trade in other ways. Instructions to colonial governors repeatedly emphasized that such laws should be vetoed. Thacher probably had in mind particularly a Massachusetts act of March 1750 (1749-1750 session, c. 21) placing an excise on tea, coffee, arrack, snuff, and china-ware, which was disallowed in June 1752. A similar act was passed in May 1754 (1754-1755 session, c. 3) on "tea, coffee, and East India ware, called china-ware"; this was allowed to stand due to the expenses of war.

13. The verses are John Ball's, from his incendiary sermon at Blackheath in Wat Tyler's Rebellion; Jack Straw was another of Tyler's lieutenants. Thacher's obscurely worded argument in the footnote is probably meant to imply that people in Massachusetts were already refusing to buy English manufactures, and consequently English bills were not in great demand and could not easily be disposed of.

14. According to section 11 of the Sugar Act "all the monies . . . shall be paid into the receipt of His Majesty's exchequer, and shall be entered separate and apart from all other monies paid or payable to His Majesty . . . and shall be there reserved to be from time to time disposed of by Parliament towards defraying the necessary expenses of defending, protecting, and securing the British colonies and plantations in America." According to the original administrative procedures, however, the funds collected were not to leave the colonies. "The paymaster general," Thomas Whately explained to John Temple in connection with the stamp duties, "wanting to remit money for subsistence, etc., will apply to the commissioners of customs or stamps for bills or orders upon their officers in the colonies. These officers will in consequence thereof pay over the money in their hands to the deputy paymasters, and whatever sums shall be thus advanced in America will be paid here by the paymaster general to the commissioners of customs or stamps, who will pay the same into the exchequer as American revenue in conformity to the act." *Collections of the Massachusetts Historical Society,* LXIX, 59. This procedure appears to have lasted only until 1767; thereafter funds collected in America were

consolidated in England and expenses paid on the home budgets. Cf. Edward Channing, *History of the United States* (New York, 1905–1925), III, 43–44, 77–78, 114.

PAMPHLET 9

HOPKINS, *THE RIGHTS OF COLONIES EXAMINED*

The political background of the publication of this pamphlet has been described in detail by David S. Lovejoy in *Rhode Island Politics and the American Revolution 1760–1776* (Providence, 1958), chaps. ii–iv. The central issues at stake in the fierce factional fighting of the 1750's and 1760's are particularly well delineated in an article by Mack E. Thompson, "The Ward-Hopkins Controversy and the American Revolution in Rhode Island: An Interpretation," *W.M.Q.*, 3d ser., 16 (1959), 363–375. The standard works on the Sugar Act and the Stamp Act, listed in the references to Pamphlets 5, 6, and 7, show the place of Rhode Island and its protests in the general scene. Frederick B. Wiener's thorough article, "The Rhode Island Merchants and the Sugar Act," *N.E.Q.*, 3 (1930), 464–500, makes clear the importance of Hopkins' role in drawing up Rhode Island's initial protests against the new regulations.

There is no modern biography of Stephen Hopkins. Besides a sketch by Irving Richman in the *D.A.B.*, the only account of his life is the informative but out-of-date biography by William E. Foster: *Stephen Hopkins, A Rhode Island Statesman* (*Rhode Island Historical Tracts*, no. 19, 2 parts, Providence, 1884). The best source for understanding Hopkins' career is Lovejoy's book mentioned above, which refers repeatedly to his ideas and activities.

The Rights of Colonies Examined, entered as items 14a and 14b in Adams' "Bibliographical Study," was issued twice by the Providence printer William Goddard. Though the first issue, here reprinted, was dated 1765, the pamphlet actually appeared in December 1764. John E. Alden, *Rhode Island Imprints, 1727–1800* (New York, 1949), entry 326, pp. 134–135. Advertised as a treatise that "breathes a true spirit of liberty" and that "must undoubtedly merit the attention of all who are anxious . . . for the freedom and happiness of this country," the pamphlet was read widely in the colonies, and, according to Goddard, was "reprinted from the Providence edition in almost every colony in North America." (He refers, presumably to excerpts printed in the newspapers.) *Boston Evening-Post,* January 7, 1765; *Boston Post-Boy,* January 7, 1765; *Providence Gazette,* May 11, 1765.

Notes to Introduction

1. The order of publications in this polemical succession is as follows: Hopkins' *Rights of Colonies Examined* (JHL Pamphlet 9) was answered by Howard's *A Letter from a Gentleman at Halifax* (JHL Pamphlet 10). To Howard's *Letter* there were three replies: (a) Hopkins' "A Vindication of a Late Pamphlet Entitled *The Rights of Colonies Examined,* from the Censures and Remarks Contained in *A Letter from a Gentleman in Halifax . . . ,*" *Providence Gazette,* February 23, March 2, and March 9, 1765; (b) James Otis' *A Vindication of the British Colonies Against the Aspersions of the Halifax Gentleman* (JHL Pamphlet 11); and (c) an anonymous essay, "Some Account of a Pamphlet Lately Published in *Newport . . . ,*" *Providence Gazette,* February 23, 1765. Howard replied to both Hopkins and Otis in his *A Defence of the Letter from a Gentleman at Halifax . . .*

(Newport, 1765). Hopkins took courteous exception to a central point in his friend James Otis' *Vindication* in a letter to the publisher, printed in the *Providence Gazette*, April 8, 1765, and replied fiercely to Howard's *Defence* in his *A Letter to the Author of the Halifax Letter* . . . (Providence, 1765); Otis' response to Howard's *Defence* was *Brief Remarks on the Defence of the Halifax Libel* . . . (Boston, 1765), which is one of the most abusive pieces published in the pre-Revolutionary years.

2. Bernhard Knollenberg, *Origin of the American Revolution, 1759–1766* (New York, 1960), pp. 146–147, 343; Wiener, "Rhode Island Merchants," pp. 477–495. On the reprinting of Hopkins' "Essay," see *Considerations upon the Act of Parliament* (JHL Pamphlet 5), Introduction note 10.

3. Foster, *Hopkins,* chaps. i–vii; Thompson, "Ward-Hopkins Controversy"; Edward Field, ed., *State of Rhode Island . . . A History* (Boston, 1902), I, chap. xiii. Adams' estimate of Hopkins appears in *Diary and Autobiography*, III, 350. On Hopkins' plural office-holding, see Foster, *Hopkins,* part I, pp. 150–151; part 2, pp. 23, 25, 90, 93, 253–256.

4. Morgan, *Stamp Act,* pp. 47–51; Lovejoy, *Rhode Island Politics,* pp. 49–51; Otis, *Brief Remarks,* p. 5. For further discussion of the group and its ideas and writings, see the Introduction to Howard's *Halifax Letter* (JHL Pamphlet 10).

5. John R. Bartlett, ed., *Records of the Colony of Rhode Island . . .* (Providence, 1856–1865), VI, 414, 411.

6. The passages referred to are on pp. 4–9, 11, 10, 19.

7. *Rights*, pp. 11, 22, 9–10, 12 ff. Hopkins had had a long career of conflict with the admiralty courts, and knew full well the importance of the new regulations. In 1761 on behalf of Rhode Island he had sued the local admiralty judge in a common law court for the third of a condemned cargo that had been assigned to the crown as its due. Accused by the opposing lawyer, John Aplin (author of *Verses,* JHL Pamphlet 3) of having converted the colony's portion to his own use, Hopkins replied with his usual vigor in print. The war of pamphlets that followed may well have contributed to Hopkins' defeat for re-election as governor in May 1762. Frederick B. Wiener, "Notes on the Rhode Island Admiralty, 1727–1790," *Harvard Law Review,* 46 (1932–33), 56–57; *Records of the Colony of Rhode Island,* VI, 370–372. Cf. Dorothy S. Towle, ed., *Records of the Vice-Admiralty Court of Rhode Island 1716–1752* (Washington, D.C., 1936), pp. 338, 381–382.

8. Howard's rebuttal is the furious *A Defence of the Letter from a Gentleman at Halifax,* published in April 1765, a few weeks after Hopkins' "Vindication" appeared. Hopkins responded to this attack with equal savagery in his *Letter to the Author of the Halifax Letter.* These later efforts of Hopkins to deal with Howard's criticism are detailed in the annotation to the *Halifax Letter* (JHL Pamphlet 10).

9. For Hopkins' admiration of the resolves written by Samuel Adams and adopted by the Massachusetts House of Representatives in October 1765, see Adams, *Diary and Autobiography,* I, 300 and 301n4.

10. *Diary and Autobiography,* III, 350.

Notes to Text

1. James Thomson, *Liberty* (1735–1736), iv, 1012–1014. This book-length poem, a "very remarkable attempt at a brief history of civilization," proved to be of particular ideological importance to the colonists of the Revolutionary generation, first, because it radiated a veritable passion for liberty and located its fulfillment

in Britain after the Glorious Revolution; second, because it inveighed against corruption as a threat to liberty in terms that expressed the colonists' feelings about England under George III; and third, because of its specific reference in part v, "The Prospect," to "gay colonies . . . the calm retreat/ Of undeserv'd distress, the better home/ Of those whom bigots chase from foreign lands./ Not built on rapine, servitude and woe/ And in their turn some petty tyrant's prey;/ But, bound by social freedom, firm they rise;/ Such as, of late, an Oglethorpe has form'd,/ And, crowding round, the charm'd Savannah sees." Cf. Bonamy Dobrée, *The Theme of Patriotism in the Poetry of the Early Eighteenth Century* (London, 1949), pp. 10–11; Richard Koebner, *Empire* (Cambridge, England, 1961), pp. 82, 85, 97–104. The few words of the poem Hopkins here quotes were seized on by Howard in his *Halifax Letter* (JHL Pamphlet 10), pp. 4–5, 12, and in his *Defence of the Letter*, pp. 9–10, as evidence of Hopkins' resistance to constituted authority; rebuttals appear in "Some Account," *Providence Gazette,* February 23, 1765, and in Otis' *Vindication* (JHL Pamphlet 11), p. 12.

2. Thomas Venner, a wine cooper, led Fifth Monarchy rebellions against the government in 1657 and 1661, on the latter occasion, under the banner "For King Jesus," terrorizing the city of London for several days.

3. The words "to be governed . . . laws" are repeated verbatim in Rhode Island's Petition to the King, of November 29, 1764. *Records of the Colony of Rhode Island,* VI, 415.

4. Algernon Sidney, *Discourses On Government,* i, 4 — a section entitled "To Depend on the Will of a Man Is Slavery." Howard, in his *Defence of the Letter,* p. 16, quotes passages from this paragraph of Hopkins' pamphlet as evidence of Hopkins' denial of Parliament's authority.

5. The passages are from *The History of the Peloponnesian War,* i, 34, 27, 25. Hopkins was using a translation by William Smith, London, 1753, of which there is a copy listed in *Catalogue of All the Books Belonging to the Providence Library . . .* (Providence, 1768). It seems likely that Hopkins was led to Thucydides, Grotius, and Pufendorf by Otis, *Rights of the British Colonies* (JHL Pamphlet 7), pp. 25–26, where references to the same passages of these authors' writings may be found and where some of the same sentences are quoted.

6. Grotius, *The Rights of War and Peace,* II, ix, 10. Cf. Otis, *Rights of the British Colonies* (JHL Pamphlet 7), p. 26.

7. Pufendorf, *Law of Nature and of Nations,* VIII, xi, 6, after illustrating the way in which colonies were formed in classical antiquity from the "'off-scourings of cities,'" adds only that "colonies may be and usually are planted in different ways. For they either remain a part of the state from which they are sent forth, or they are obligated to show respect to the mother state and to uphold its majesty, and are therefore joined to it by a kind of unequal treaty, or, finally, they treat with it on equal terms and right. Add Garcilaso de la Vega, *Comentarios Reales,* bk. VII, chap. i." Cf. Otis, *Rights of the British Colonies* (JHL Pamphlet 7), pp. 26–27.

8. Cf. Hopkins' "An Historical Account of the Planting and Growth of Providence," which appeared in seven issues of the *Providence Gazette* early in 1765. These sections from an uncompleted history have been published together in *Collections of the Massachusetts Historical Society,* 2d ser., IX, 166–203; cf. *Proceedings of the Massachusetts Historical Society,* 1 (1791–1835), 133n–134n.

9. Howard, in his *Halifax Letter* (JHL Pamphlet 10), p. 9, quotes this "postulatum" and argues that it "cannot be true with regard to political rights." Both Hopkins and Otis subsequently defended the passage and attacked Howard's claims.

10. Passages from the latter half of this paragraph were quoted and commented on adversely by Howard in his *Halifax Letter* (JHL Pamphlet 10), pp. 6–7, and favorably by Otis in his *Vindication* (JHL Pamphlet 11), pp. 5, 26.

11. Cf. *Records of the Colony of Rhode Island,* VI, 380, where the figure is put at 14,000 hogsheads. These figures are particularly interesting in view of the virtual impossibility of establishing even roughly the total quantities imported into the mainland colonies. Officially, only 53,708 gallons of molasses were imported into New England in 1763; 93,314 in 1764; 215,941 in 1765. No accounts at all were received from Rhode Island from 1733 to 1750. Gipson, *British Empire,* X, 241, 242; Frank W. Pitman, *The Development of the British West Indies, 1700–63* (New Haven, 1917), p. 275. On the molasses trade and the Rhode Island economy generally, see James B. Hedges, *The Browns of Providence Plantations* (Cambridge, 1952), chap. ii. On the disposition of moneys collected under the revenue acts, see Thacher, *Sentiments* (JHL Pamphlet 8), text note 14.

12. Section 28 of the Sugar Act provided that no iron or lumber grown, produced, or manufactured in British America could be shipped without bond or surety being provided to the customs officials for double the value of the goods binding the shipper to land the goods only in Great Britain if for Europe and to present a certificate of compliance within eighteen months. If the goods were landed in the colonies, the certificate was due within six months; if in any other place, within twelve months.

13. The reference is to Tacitus' *Annals,* iv, esp. chap. 30. It appears from the letter in the *Providence Gazette,* April 8, 1765, that Hopkins, or whoever was writing for him, was using "the fine English [translation] of Mr. Gordon," a copy of which was in the Providence Library in 1768. Howard, in his *Defence of the Letter,* pp. 11–12, condemned this comparison of Britain to Rome under Tiberius as "not the effusions of a peaceable citizen or of a faithful magistrate."

14. *An Universal History, From the Earliest Account of Time* (21 vols., London, 1745–1754). Cf. Daniel J. Boorstin, *The Mysterious Science of the Law* (Boston, 1958 ed.), pp. 39–40.

15. On Howard's letters to the *Newport Mercury,* see Introduction to his *Halifax Letter* (JHL Pamphlet 10).

16. For Howard's attack on this "curious invented syllogism," see *Halifax Letter,* p. 7. Otis too declared the reasoning in the passage to be fallacious since it confused the House of Commons with Parliament. *Vindication* (JHL Pamphlet 11), pp. 5–6.

17. In the spring of 1746, when an expedition against Quebec was being planned, news arrived that a French fleet led by the Duc d'Anville had escaped to sea with the intention of reconquering Louisbourg and Annapolis Royal, destroying Boston, and ravaging the New England coast. Shirley and Warren, in a high state of excitement, maneuvered what troops and supplies they had to defend Annapolis, where the French were expected to launch their offensive. The failure of the expedition was due to foul weather and d'Anville's lack of experience rather than to British enterprise.

PAMPHLET 10

HOWARD, *LETTER FROM A GENTLEMAN AT HALIFAX*

The bibliography for the background of this pamphlet has been sketched in the general references to Stephen Hopkins' *Rights of Colonies Examined* (JHL Pamphlet 9). The only biographical account of Howard is Henry H. Edes, "Chief-

Justice Martin Howard and his Portrait by Copley," *Publications of the Colonial Society of Massachusetts*, VI (*Transactions, 1899–1900*), 384–402. Inaccurate on many points, this essay is useful mainly for the details it presents on the fortunes of Howard's descendants. The sketch in the present Introduction is based on the scattered sources cited in the notes that follow.

A Letter from a Gentleman at Halifax is listed as item 16 in Adams' "Bibliographical Study" and as item 329 in John E. Alden, *Rhode Island Imprints, 1727–1800* (New York, 1949). It was issued only once, on February 13, 1765, by the Newport printer Hall, who was also the publisher of the *Newport Mercury*.

Notes to Introduction

1. George C. Mason, *Annals of Trinity Church, Newport, Rhode Island, 1698–1821* (Newport, 1890), pp. 91, 53; Dorothy S. Towle, ed., *Records of the Vice-Admiralty Court of Rhode Island 1716–1752* (Washington, D.C., 1936), pp. 516, 523–525, 538–539, 541, 542–543, 544–548; John O. Austin, *Genealogical Dictionary of Rhode Island* (Albany, 1887), p. 257; Sidney S. Rider, ed., *A True Representation of the Plan formed at Albany in 1754 . . .* (*Rhode Island Historical Tracts*, no. 9, Providence, 1880); David S. Lovejoy, *Rhode Island Politics and the American Revolution 1760–1776* (Providence, 1958), pp. 81, 201n3.

2. Cf. Introduction to Hopkins' *Rights of Colonies Examined* (JHL Pamphlet 9), above, p. 501.

3. On the identification of the group, see Morgan, *Stamp Act,* p. 47, and references cited there.

4. For a detailed expression of the notion, commonly held by eighteenth-century Americans, that sustained competition for public power was evil if not seditious, see William Livingston, *et al., The Independent Reflector . . .* (Milton M. Klein, ed., Cambridge, 1963), papers 9, 13, 23, 32, 33.

5. *Newport Mercury*, January 24, April 18, 1763; April 23, 1764. On the writers' question "Whether the King is not more fit to appoint judges than an ignorant and corrupt deputy of a town, a *party-jobber* who dubs a man a judge for his vote and gets him confirmed by his party if it happens to be the majority," and the writers' conclusion that only "a coercive power from home" will solve Rhode Island's problems, see the issue of November 21, 1763.

6. *Newport Mercury,* April 23, 1764.

7. *Ibid.,* August 20, 27; September 3, 10, and 17, 1764.

8. *Ibid.,* September 17, October 1, October 29, November 19, 1764.

9. This passage was, in effect, a reply in kind. The *Providence Gazette* on September 15, 1764, had commented in some detail on the inelegant diction of the "dull and unentertaining pieces" the *Newport Mercury* was printing, comparing them in their crudeness to a "belch in the faces of the company," deserving of "an application of a strong-toed shoe to [the] *posteriors."* "How much can this self-important club think the public interested in their low talk among themselves . . . yawned up at twelve of the clock at night, with the fumes of indigestion"? It was at this point that the *Gazette* recalled "that it is said that some if not all of the members of this wonderful club are at this time actually conspiring against the liberties of the colony, and that they have, with other enemies of the colony, formed a petition, and sent it to the King, praying that our most valuable charter privileges may be taken away . . ."

10. The passages cited are on pp. 9, 11, 12. On representation, see esp. Daniel Dulany's *Considerations* (JHL Pamphlet 13).

11. Thomas Whately to John Temple, May 10, 1765, *Collections of the Massachusetts Historical Society,* 6th ser., IX, 52; Lovejoy, *Rhode Island Politics,* p. 80; *Newport Mercury,* March 11, 1765.

12. February 23, March 2, and 9, 1765, cf. April 8.

13. Lovejoy, *Rhode Island Politics,* pp. 78, 82, 84.

14. These events are recounted in Lovejoy, *Rhode Island Politics,* chap. vi; and in Morgan, *Stamp Act,* pp. 144–148. A letter from Newport printed in the *Boston Evening-Post,* September 2, 1765, describes the effigy of the stamp master as clasping in his right hand "his Halifax Letter, and on his right arm inscribed, *The only filial pen."*

15. On Howard's contacts with Whately, see Whately's letters to John Temple and to Howard, in *Collections of the Massachusetts Historical Society,* 6th ser., IX, 75 ff. For a newspaper report from Boston, dated February 24, 1766, that Howard and Moffat were rudely treated by the ministry in London when they petitioned for redress, see Gipson, *British Empire,* X, 298n42. On the events in North Carolina (including Howard's curious relations with Maurice Moore, author of *The Justice and Policy of Taxing the American Colonies,* Wilmington, N.C., 1765), see Marshall D. Haywood, *Governor William Tryon . . . 1765–1771* (Raleigh, N.C., 1903), pp. 108–110, 144–145; Alonzo T. Dill, *Governor Tryon and His Palace* (Chapel Hill, 1955), pp. 180–181; and Robert O. DeMond, *The Loyalists in North Carolina . . .* (Durham, N.C., 1940), pp. 183, 203. References to Howard's claim for recompense are listed in Gertrude S. Kimball, ed., *The Correspondence of the Colonial Governors of Rhode Island, 1723–1775* (Boston and New York, 1903), II, 387n2; and in Gipson, *British Empire,* X, 298n42.

Notes to Text

1. Terence, *The Eunuch,* ii, 248: "There is a class of men who set up for being the head in everything, and are not." The quotation was replied to both by the author of "Some Account of a Pamphlet" and by Hopkins in his "Vindication," *Providence Gazette,* February 23, 1765, the former dismissing it as false erudition cadged "from a *schoolbook,"* the latter turning it back on Howard.

2. The reference is to James Otis and his *Rights of the British Colonies* (JHL Pamphlet 7). Otis responded directly to the sentence in his *Vindication* (JHL Pamphlet 11), p. 26, though maintaining his anonymity.

3. "Some Account of a Pamphlet," *Providence Gazette,* February 23, 1765, defended Hopkins' use of Thomson's lines by pointing out that Hampden's stand on ship money "was many years before 1641, and at a time when a civil war was no more foreseen or expected than in 1764. When *Hampden* made this noble appeal, taxes were laid on the people of *England* otherwise than by their own representatives. Then it was that the people began to whisper that such taxes were illegal, and to *murmur* at their imposition. In the year 1764, it was proposed to tax the *Americans* without the consent of their own representatives. This occasioned whispers and *murmurs* amongst them. — Now whether there be any resemblance between these cases and times, let every man judge."

4. Edward Young, *Love of Fame, The Universal Passion, In Seven Characteristical Satires . . .* (London, 1728), satire II. Though modern critics have dismissed Young's poetry as, among other things, "sapless drooling," the colonists found his writing, especially the Satires, engaging in its epigrammatic characterization of familiar human types. His *The Merchant. An Ode on the British Trade and Navigation* touched on certain of the themes that made Thomson's poetry so im-

portant. Cf. Bonamy Dobrée, *English Literature in the Early Eighteenth Century,
1700–1740* (Oxford, 1959), p. 523; above, Pamphlet 9, text note 1; Richard Koebner,
Empire (Cambridge, England, 1961), p. 82.

5. To this, Hopkins replied in his "Vindication," *Providence Gazette,* February
23, 1765, that he had "only mentioned some constituent parts essential to the
character of a good subject. He has said nothing of wicked and disloyal ones; but
leaves their characters to be filled up by the letter writer, who may be best acquainted with them."

6. "Philoleutherus Lipsiensis" was the pseudonym of Richard Bentley, English
critic and classical scholar (1661–1742).

7. In his "Vindication," *Providence Gazette,* February 23, 1765, Hopkins answered this charge of contradiction with the explanation that it was his belief "that
according to the British principles of government, the subject of America ought
not to be taxed in Parliament; but that if the Parliament should proceed to tax
them, it was their *'indispensable duty cheerfully to obey and patiently to submit
thereto.'* " For Otis' view of Hopkins' "fallacy," see his *Vindication* (JHL Pamphlet
11), pp. 5–6.

8. Hopkins conceded in his "Vindication," *Providence Gazette,* March 2, 1765,
that "There may be a natural relation between two subjects that exist by nature;
but the mother country and colony exist only by policy, and may, no doubt, have
a political relation to each other; but can have no natural one."

9. For Otis' extensive response to this, see his *Vindication* (JHL Pamphlet 11),
pp. 6–8.

10. For Otis' characterization of the distinctions that follow as confusion compounded, and for his own ideas on the subject based on Blackstone, see *ibid.,* pp.
8–10.

11. "In what sense," Hopkins asked in response, "can the power of the British
Parliament be said to extend to France? If a British subject visits Versailles or
Fontainebleau, does this give the Parliament of Great Britain a temporary jurisdiction in the French King's palaces?" "Vindication," *Providence Gazette,* March 2,
1765. Cf. [Howard's] *Defence of the Letter* . . . (Newport, 1765), p. 19.

12. Hopkins quotes the two paragraphs immediately above in his "Vindication,"
Providence Gazette, March 2, 1765, refuting the argument as follows: "He confidently maintains that acts of Parliament derive their force from the common
law; and for that reason, he says, they are obligatory upon the colonies. If so,
the jurisdiction of Parliament must be subordinate to that of the common law:
otherwise the superior jurisdiction would and must derive its force, and support,
from the inferior; which is absurd." Otis in his *Vindication* (JHL Pamphlet 11),
p. 13, also quoted the last sentence in the paragraph as an admission by Howard
of the colonists' indefeasible rights.

13. "Lillibullero," a watchword of Irish Catholics in 1641, became a popular
political song during the Glorious Revolution. The text by Lord Wharton satirizes
the Earl of Tyrconnel on his going to Ireland in 1686–1687 as the papist lieutenant
of James II; the music was written by Henry Purcell. The song was the basis of
"Jemmibullero," a screed against James Otis printed in March 1765. Clifford K.
Shipton, *Sibley's Harvard Graduates,* XI (Boston, 1960), pp. 263–264. Cf. Otis'
Vindication (JHL Pamphlet 11), p. 16.

14. Hopkins replied to this argument for virtual representation as follows: "The
Parliament of England never assumed the character of representatives of Scotland
before the Union, nor are the Commons of Great Britain at this day the representa-

tive of Ireland so as to tax them, but Ireland is taxed by her own Parliament." The Channel Islands, he claimed, were not taxed by Parliament, and were bound by Parliament only when named. As for money as such not being represented in Parliament, money is not taxed, and its possessors do in fact vote. "Vindication," *Providence Gazette,* March 9, 1765. Otis replied to Howard's argument in *Vindication* (JHL Pamphlet 11), pp. 19–20. On virtual representation generally, see Daniel Dulany's *Considerations* (JHL Pamphlet 13).

15. In the legend, Zeus sent a cloud to Ixion in the form of Hera, the Greek Juno, and the cloud became by him the mother of the Centaurs.

16. Otis' replies to this paragraph appear in *Vindication* (JHL Pamphlet 11), pp. 21, 20.

17. For Otis' response, agreeing with the first sentence in the paragraph but disagreeing that stamp duties were equitable, see *ibid.,* pp. 21, 22.

18. Cf. *ibid.,* pp. 22, 23.

19. To this, Hopkins replied that Sardinia and Corsica were Carthaginian conquests rather than colonies. "Is there any analogy between Britain and Carthage, or between British colonies and Carthaginian conquests? He has not made the application in words, but the malice of the expression supplies the meaning, and it is apparent that it would rejoice his cankered soul to see North America in the situation of his Corsicans and Sardinians." "Vindication," *Providence Gazette,* March 9, 1765.

20. These quotations are taken from the excerpts of the debate on the Molasses Act published in the *Newport Mercury,* January 14, 1765. Hopkins in his reply to this passage pointed out that "the law proposed was only to tax our foreign importations, which is a matter of general commerce and can be regulated in Parliament only . . . yet our letter writer can see no difference between such a law and a stamp duty . . . he could not have been so unjust as to charge the colonies with aiming at an independency by presenting a petition, which is an act that carries in itself all the marks of submission." No one had been aiming at independency, Hopkins wrote, and no one had said the colonies were *"fully"* represented; Winnington merely said that they were *"generally"* represented. "Vindication," *Providence Gazette,* March 9, 1765. For the realities of the debate on the Molasses Act, see Albert B. Southwick, "The Molasses Act — Source of Precedents," *W.M.Q.,* 3d ser., 8 (1951), 389–405; Leo F. Stock, ed., *Proceedings and Debates of the British Parliaments Respecting North America* (Washington, D.C., 1937), IV, 105, 113–116, 120, 129, 159, 170, 189, 208, 209, 211.

21. 13 George II c. 7 provided that all aliens resident seven consecutive years in the colonies could be naturalized upon taking the usual oaths, but they would not thereby be enabled to hold lands or offices in Great Britain or serve as members of Parliament. Cf. Clive Parry, *British Nationality Law and the History of Naturalization* (Milan, 1954), pp. 86–87, 99–101.

22. To this Hopkins replied: "There has been for years past little or no smuggling carried on in the northern colonies but in the article of foreign molasses, and it is well known the duty on this article was imposed by West India influence, not so much to augment the revenue of the crown as to increase the value of sugar estates . . . But what if we should inquire who were at the root of this *venality* and corruption; what *courts* and *officers* were these to whose *perfidiousness* the King's revenue was sacrificed. The colonies have not the collection and care of the King's revenue, so that their officers could not be intended; and it is true also that suits concerning the revenue seldom or never came before their courts.

If corruption had arrived to this height, it was amongst officers of royal or ministerial appointment. They had the whole game in their hands, and played it as they pleased; and how are the colonies answerable for what was won or lost? I have known but two or three applications made by the customhouse to colony courts, and these were upon French seizures, when it was thought there was danger of being outbid at the admiralty." "Vindication," *Providence Gazette,* March 9, 1765. Cf. Otis, *Vindication* (JHL Pamphlet 11), p. 24.

23. In 1764 William Spry, LL.D., a relative by marriage of William Pitt, was appointed judge of the new court of vice-admiralty for all America at Halifax. See Carl Ubbelohde, *The Vice-Admiralty Courts and the American Revolution* (Chapel Hill, 1960), esp. chaps. i–iii. Cf. Otis, *Vindication* (JHL Pamphlet 11), p. 24.

24. Montesquieu, *Spirit of the Laws,* xx, 12 (Franz Neumann, ed., New York, 1949).

25. *Othello,* III, iii, 159–161.

26. Montesquieu, *Spirit of the Laws,* xx, 7. Sir Andrew Freeport was a member of the hypothetical club that launched the *Spectator.* He is described as a London merchant, industrious, generous, and of sound good sense.

27. Of the many versions of the popular *Fables of Pilpay,* first translated into English in 1570, Howard was using a Dublin, 1752, edition; his reference is to "The Man and the Adder," which appears as fable 3 in chap. iv of that edition.

28. For Otis' response to this paragraph, especially to the suggestion of a formal code of rights, see his *Vindication* (JHL Pamphlet 11), pp. 25, 32.

29. For responses to this coy statement, see *ibid.,* p. 29; "Vindication," *Providence Gazette,* February 23, 1765.

PAMPHLET 11

OTIS, *A VINDICATION OF THE BRITISH COLONIES*

A Vindication of the British Colonies is entered as items 20a–c in Adams' "Bibliographical Study." It was published in Boston in the third week of March 1765 by Edes and Gill, and reprinted in London by J. Almon in 1769. Almon included the pamphlet also in volume II of his *Collection of Tracts on the Subjects of Taxing the British Colonies in America* (London, 1773). A full listing of the writings on and by James Otis will be found in the notes to Pamphlet 7.

The lines on the title page are from the *Aeneid,* iii, 639, 640, 672–674; viii, 445, 446, 449–453, describing the escape from the giant Polyphemus and the forging of arms in Vulcan's cave: "But flee, O hapless ones, flee and cut your cables from the shore! [Polyphemus raises] a mighty roar, whereat the sea and all its waves shuddered and the land of Italy was affrighted far within, and Aetna bellowed in its winding caverns. Brass and golden ore flow in streams, and wounding steel is molten in the vast furnace. Some with panting bellows make the blasts come and go, others dip the hissing brass in the lake, while the cavern groans under the anvils laid upon it. They with mighty force, now one, now another, raise their arms in measured cadence, and turn the metal with gripping tongs." (Loeb tr.)

Notes to Introduction

1. Otis had been Hopkins' lawyer in the slander suit Hopkins had brought against Samuel Ward in 1757 as a result of Ward's published accusations that Hopkins had feathered his nest during the war by a series of illegal transactions. William E. Foster, *Stephen Hopkins, A Rhode Island Statesman (Rhode Island*

Historical Tracts, no. 19, Providence, 1884), II, 22, 242n; John D. Washburn, "Hopkins v. Ward, — an Ante-revolutionary Lawsuit," *Monthly Law Reporter,* 22 (October 1859), 327–339.

2. Howard, *Halifax Letter* (JHL Pamphlet 10), pp. 4, 21–22.

3. Adams' impression of Otis in 1765 is recorded in *Diary and Autobiography,* I, 271. On Blackstone, see Howard, *Halifax Letter* (JHL Pamphlet 10), pp. 8–9, and the present pamphlet, pp. 8–9. The disputed section of Blackstone's *Commentaries* is chap. i of book I, "Of the Absolute Rights of Individuals" (pp. 117–141 in the first, 1765, edition of volume I).

4. Pp. 27, 7–8, 9, 16, 14.

5. P. 26.

6. Pp. 15, 16.

7. [Martin Howard, Jr.], *A Defence of the Letter from a Gentleman at Halifax, to his Friend in Rhode Island* . . . (Newport, 1765), pp. 17, 24, 25.

8. [James Otis], *Brief Remarks on the Defence of the Halifax Libel on the British-American-Colonies* (Boston, 1765), pp. 5, 7, 16, 20, 22, 25, 26.

9. *Ibid.,* pp. 10, 11, 27.

10. *Ibid.,* p. 30; Ellen E. Brennan, "James Otis: Recreant and Patriot," *N.E.Q.,* 12 (1939), 711; Adams, *Works,* X, 295; *Diary and Autobiography,* I, 271; *Boston Gazette,* May 13, 1765.

11. On the election of 1765, see Brennan, "Otis," pp. 713–714. Otis' success at the polls that year is traditionally attributed to the boomerang effect of the scurrilous jingle "Jemmibullero," written by the customs officer James Waterhouse and published on May 13, 1765, in the *Boston Evening-Post. Considerations on Behalf of the Colonists in a Letter to a Noble Lord* (London, 1765), pp. 9, 33, 50, 5, 6.

12. See above, General Introduction, pp. 123 ff.

13. Morgan, *Stamp Act,* pp. 104–105. On the six "Hampden Letters," published in the *Boston Gazette* in December 1765, and January 1766, see Brennan, "Otis," pp. 719–720.

14. Brennan, "Otis," pp. 721–724; Ellen E. Brennan, *Plural Office-Holding in Massachusetts 1760–1780* (Chapel Hill, 1945), pp. 81–88; Francis G. Wallett, "The Massachusetts Council, 1766–1774 . . . ," *W.M.Q.,* 3d ser., 6 (1949), 605 ff.; Morgan, *Stamp Act,* pp. 294, 301–302; Clifford K. Shipton, "James Otis," *Sibley's Harvard Graduates,* XI (Boston, 1960), 286.

Notes to Text

1. The typical seventeenth- and eighteenth-century representation of the Leviathan was a giant in clothes patterned with faces. One such appeared on the title page of the original edition; but there were many later variations.

2. Verses unidentified.

3. Howard cites this sentence in his *Defence,* p. 25, as indication of Otis' total surrender to the claims of Parliamentary sovereignty.

4. The reference is to the supposedly contradictory passages of Hopkins' *Rights of Colonies Examined* (JHL Pamphlet 9) cited on pages 6 and 7 of Howard's *Halifax Letter* (JHL Pamphlet 10). Otis' admission that Hopkins' argument involved a sophism was welcomed and made much of by Howard in his *Defence,* pp. 15–16.

5. "Easy the descent to Hell." The quotations in the previous paragraphs are from pages 7 and 8 of Howard's *Halifax Letter* (JHL Pamphlet 10).

6. The words quoted in the sentences above are from Blackstone's *Commentaries,* i, 1 ("Of the Absolute Rights of Individuals"): pp. 117–141 of the first (Oxford, 1765) edition. Otis restates Blackstone's formulation correctly, but the words he quotes are conflations and paraphrases of scattered phrases and sentences. He seems to have written this section from notes he had taken of Blackstone's book rather than from the volume itself. He may well have found it difficult to keep a copy of Blackstone at hand to refer to when he was writing the pamphlet since copies of volume I must just then have begun to arrive in the colonies.

7. The quotation combines phrases from Blackstone's *Commentaries,* i, 2 ("Of the Parliament"), pp. 142–143 of the 1765 edition.

8. On Sibthorpe and Mainwaring, see Mayhew's *Discourse* (JHL Pamphlet 1), Introduction note 6.

9. Locke, *First Treatise,* ii, 9, 8, quoting Filmer's *Directions for Obedience to Government . . . ,* in his *Observations upon Aristotle's Politiques . . .* (1652) and *Patriarcha* (1680) (in the Peter Laslett edition of *Two Treatises of Government,* Cambridge, England, 1960, pp. 166, 165).

10. Psalms cvi, 38, quoted by Locke, *First Treatise,* vi, 58 (Laslett ed., p. 201).

11. *Ibid.,* vi, 57 (Laslett ed., p. 200) where Locke quotes at length Garcilaso de la Vega's account of Peruvian cannibalism.

12. The quotation is from the passage of Thomson's *Liberty* quoted by Hopkins in his *Rights of Colonies* (JHL Pamphlet 9); see esp. text note 1.

13. Martyn, Jack, and Lord Peter — characters in Swift's *Tale of a Tub.*

14. "He who stops with the words does not reach the meaning."

15. The words are not Coke's; see Otis' *Rights of the British Colonies* (JHL Pamphlet 7), p. 61 and note 38.

16. Paraphrased from Howard's *Halifax Letter* (JHL Pamphlet 10), p. 13.

17. 4 *Inst.* 1; see quotation below, p. 18.

18. Otis confused or combined two characters: Sir Martyn Mar-all, from a play of that name by Dryden and William Cavendish, Duke of Newcastle, and Marplot, the hero of two comedies by Mrs. Centlivre, *The Busy Body* and *Marplot in Lisbon.* In the Dramatis Personae of *The Busy Body,* Marplot is described as "a sort of a silly fellow, cowardly, but very inquisitive to know everybody's business, generally spoils all he undertakes, yet without design."

19. "Triple brass around his chest" — Horace, *Carmina,* I, iii, 9.

20. Acts xix, 23–41.

21. On Spry, see Howard, *Halifax Letter* (JHL Pamphlet 10), text note 23.

22. The verses appear to be Otis' lampoon of Howard's quotation from Young's *Love of Fame, ibid.,* p. 5.

23. The reference is to Hopkins' "Vindication" and "Some Account of a Pamphlet" cited in full in Hopkins' *Rights of Colonies* (JHL Pamphlet 9), Introduction note 1.

24. Unlike the other quotations in the Postscript, this paragraph is taken not from Hopkins' "Vindication" but from "Some Account."

25. Cf. Howard's use of this paragraph in his *Defence,* p. 17.

PAMPHLET 12

[CHURCH], *LIBERTY AND PROPERTY VINDICATED*

The fullest account of the life of Benjamin Church, the presumed author of the present pamphlet, is by Clifford K. Shipton in the forthcoming Volume XIII of *Sibley's Harvard Graduates,* of which Mr. Shipton has kindly allowed me to read the manuscript. As indicated in note 18, several of Church's poems have been reprinted in *The Magazine of History.* Documents relating to Church's treason are published in Allen French, *General Gage's Informers* (Ann Arbor, 1932), chap. v. Writings on the Stamp Act and on the situation in Connecticut in 1765 are listed in the notes to Fitch's *Reasons Why* (JHL Pamphlet 6).

Liberty and Property Vindicated, and the St — pm–n Burnt appears in Adams' "Bibliographical Study" as entries 9a, b, and c. As Adams shows, the pamphlet was published first in 1765 without indication of place of publication; but it probably issued from a press in either Hartford or New London. It was then reprinted in Boston in the same year, and again in Boston in 1766. The present edition reproduces an unrecorded Boston 1765 reprint in the American Antiquarian Society, which is identical in text to the original printing but superior in paragraphing.

Notes to Introduction

1. Donald Greer, in *The Incidence of Terror During the French Revolution* (Cambridge, 1935), concludes (p. 37) that "between thirty-five and forty thousand persons, including those who succumbed in the prisons and those killed without any form of trial, lost their lives as a consequence of terrorism."

2. Arthur M. Schlesinger, "Political Mobs and the American Revolution, 1765–1776," *Proceedings of the American Philosophical Society,* 99 (1955), 246; Douglass Adair and John A. Schutz, eds., *Peter Oliver's Origin & Progress of the American Revolution* (San Marino, 1961), pp. 52–53. Oliver included in his history an appendix (pp. 152–157) listing a number of the mobs' "innocent frolics of rebellion" besides those described in the text itself. It is instructive to compare the violence described by even this most vituperative and bitter of loyalists with that recounted by Greer in his *Incidence of Terror During the French Revolution.*

3. Schlesinger, "Political Mobs," p. 244; Max Beloff, *Public Order and Popular Disturbances 1660–1714* (Oxford, 1938), pp. 153, 155 (note also p. 33: "London, indeed, seems to have been a city where the very children were capable of causing a riot"). Cf. George Rudé, *Wilkes and Liberty* (Oxford, 1962), chap. i, and also, among Rudé's other writings on the same general subject, "The London 'Mob' of the Eighteenth Century," *The Historical Journal,* 2 (1959), 1–18.

4. Carl Bridenbaugh, *Cities in the Wilderness* (N.Y., 1955 ed.), pp. 224, 196, 382–383; Carl Bridenbaugh, *Cities in Revolt* (N.Y., 1955), pp. 114–118.

5. Irving Mark, *Agrarian Conflicts in Colonial New York 1711–1775* (N.Y., 1940), chap. iv, especially pp. 111–112, 115–116, 124–126; Richard M. Brown, *The South Carolina Regulators* (Cambridge, 1963), chaps. i, ii; Richard J. Hooker, ed., *The Carolina Backcountry on the Eve of the Revolution . . .* (Chapel Hill, 1953).

6. George Rudé, *The Crowd in the French Revolution* (Oxford, 1959), chap. xiii, especially p. 208.

7. There are good accounts of the Boston riots of August, 1765, in Morgan, *Stamp Act,* chap. viii, and Gipson, *British Empire,* X, chap. xiii.

8. E.g., Peter Oliver's description of McIntosh: ". . . in order to convince the public of that power with which he was invested, he paraded the town with a mob of 2,000 men in two files, and passed by the statehouse when the General Assembly were sitting to display his power. If a whisper was heard among his followers, the holding up his finger hushed it in a moment, and when he had

fully displayed his authority he marched his men to the first rendezvous and ordered them to retire peaceably to their several homes, and was punctually obeyed. This unhappy fellow was always ready for the drudgeries of his employers until by neglecting his business he was induced to part with his *last and all,* took to hard drinking, was thrown into a jail, and died. And to the eternal disgrace of his rich employers, when he supplicated some of them for two or three dollars to relieve his distress, he was refused the small pittance because at that time they had no further service for him . . ." And again: "As for the people in general, they were like the mobility of all countries, perfect machines, wound up by any hand who might first take the winch. . . ." *Peter Oliver's Origin & Progress of the American Revolution,* pp. 54–55, 65. This view of the mob is central to Oliver's interpretation of the Revolution, for like all the Tories, and like the administration itself, it was essential for him to argue that if left alone the populace as a whole would have made no trouble about the enactments of Parliament; opposition, according to this view, was stirred up by malcontents secretly plotting, for purely selfish reasons, to cause a rupture between England and her colonies.

9. Philip Davidson, *Propaganda and the American Revolution 1763–1783* (Chapel Hill, 1941), p. xiii; Rudé, "The London 'Mob,'" pp. 1–2.

10. Rudé, "The London 'Mob,'" p. 17; Rudé, *Wilkes and Liberty,* p. 197.

11. On the circumstances and events in Connecticut summarized in the following paragraphs, see Lawrence H. Gipson, *Jared Ingersoll* (New Haven, 1920), pp. 153 ff.; Oscar Zeichner, *Connecticut's Years of Controversy 1750–1776* (Chapel Hill, 1949), chap. ii; Morgan, *Stamp Act,* chap. xiii. Crucial for the reconstruction of these episodes is the documentary pamphlet *Mr. [Jared] Ingersoll's Letters Relating to the Stamp-Act* (New Haven, 1766).

12. *Ingersoll's Letters,* p. 16. On an earlier appearance of the name in Connecticut, see J. Hammond Trumbull, "Sons of Liberty in 1755," *The New Englander,* 35 (1876), 299–313.

13. *Connecticut Courant,* September 2, 1765. The *Connecticut Gazette* carried the same account on August 30 (Gipson, *Ingersoll,* p. 169).

14. Ingersoll's explanation of the whole episode, including the reasons both for his taking the office of stamp master and for his holding on to it in the face of public disapproval, appears in his *Letters,* pp. 28 ff., especially pp. 31–33, 35–39, 50–54, 56–58. In the same pamphlet, pp. 61–68, Ingersoll republished in full the detailed account of his resignation of the stamp office that appeared in the *Connecticut Gazette* on September 27, 1765.

15. Morgan, *Stamp Act,* chaps. ix, x; Gipson, *British Empire,* X, chaps. xiii, xv.

16. *Boston Evening-Post,* September 2, 9, 16, 30; *Boston Gazette,* September 9; *Boston Post-Boy,* September 9.

17. Edwin T. Bowden, "Benjamin Church's *Choice* and American Colonial Poetry," *N.E.Q.,* 32 (1959), 180.

18. *The Choice,* published first in 1757 and reprinted in 1802, was reprinted again in *Magazine of History,* 17 [Extra Number 68] (1919–1920). *The Times* appears in the same periodical, vol. 21 [Extra Number 84] (1922); *An Address to a Provincial Bashaw* is in vol. 19 [Extra Number 74] (1921); and Church's Massacre oration appears in both vol. 47 [Extra Number 186] (1933) and vol. 48 [Extra Number 192] (1934). The footnote in *The Times* describes Ingersoll as "An ingenious stamp distributor who modestly asserted in the public papers that the Stamp Act was designed to make America happy by her indulgent mother, and that it would certainly prove so if his country would suffer him to continue in office."

Notes to Text

1. Numbers xxxiv, 25.
2. The Earl of Bute.
3. On the discussion of the terms of peace, see above, *Considerations* (JHL Pamphlet 5), text note 6.
4. Psalms xlix, 12.
5. Job xv, 2.
6. Jeremiah xvii, 5.

PAMPHLET 13

DULANY, *CONSIDERATIONS ON THE PROPRIETY OF IMPOSING TAXES*

Details on the Revolutionary movement in Maryland, and on Dulany's role in it, may be found in two exhaustive studies. Charles A. Barker, *The Background of the Revolution in Maryland* (New Haven, 1940) makes particularly clear the bearing of proprietary politics on the Revolutionary movement, and explains the political context of Dulany's career. Aubrey C. Land, *The Dulanys of Maryland* (Baltimore, 1955) traces the lives of Daniel Dulany, Sr. (1685–1753) and of his son, the author of the present pamphlet. Among the voluminous sources listed in Barker's bibliography, those pertaining to Dulany's antagonist, Charles Carroll of Carrollton, are of particular relevance to the ideology of the Revolution in Maryland and, by contrast, to Dulany. The valuable Carroll correspondence has been partially published in many volumes of the *Maryland Historical Magazine,* beginning with volume 10 (1915), and in Thomas M. Field, ed., *Unpublished Letters of Charles Carroll . . .* (New York, 1902). The documents of the sprawling Dulany-Carroll controversy of 1773 have been collected from the *Maryland Gazette* and published by Elihu S. Riley in a volume entitled *Correspondence of "First Citizen" — Charles Carroll of Carrollton, and "Antilon" —Daniel Dulany, Jr., 1773, With a History of Governor Eden's Administration in Maryland. 1769–1776* (Baltimore, 1902).

Considerations on the Propriety of Imposing Taxes is entered in Adams' "Bibliographical Study" as items 11a–g. The bibliographical problems of the Maryland imprints of the pamphlet are discussed in great detail in Lawrence C. Wroth, *A History of Printing in Colonial Maryland 1686–1776* (Baltimore, 1922), entries 255–258. The present edition reproduces the first — Annapolis, 1765 — printing.

The verses on the title page are from Persius, *Satires,* v, 28–29. The New York, 1765 edition of the pamphlet includes translations of all the Latin quotations; the lines on the title page are translated: "Let not my words show all; The hidden mischief cannot be expressed." The translations throughout the pamphlet will be taken from the New York edition even though, as in the present case, they are somewhat less than strictly accurate.

Notes to Introduction

1. Adams, "Bibliographical Study," items 11f–g.
2. Land, *The Dulanys,* p. 267; Julian P. Boyd, ed., *Papers of Thomas Jefferson* (Princeton, 1950–), I, 671.
3. On Franklin's sponsorship of the London reprints of *Considerations,* see

Verner W. Crane, *Benjamin Franklin's Letters to the Press 1758–1775* (Chapel Hill, 1950), p. xlix.

4. *Administration of the Colonies,* first ed. (London, 1764), pp. 1, 2, 6, 9 ff.; second ed. (London, 1765), pp. 41, 49, 89, 90. Pownall's career is traced in John A. Schutz, *Thomas Pownall* (Glendale, Calif., 1951); on Pownall's political ideas, see particularly Caroline Robbins, *The Eighteenth-Century Commonwealthman* (Cambridge, 1959), pp. 311–319. The publishing history of Pownall's *Administration* (of which five editions appeared before 1775) is traced in Adams, "Bibliographical Study," 5a–g. For other replies to Pownall's *Administration* see Otis, *Rights of the British Colonies* (JHL Pamphlet 7) and Richard Bland, *An Inquiry into the Rights of the British Colonies, Intended as an Answer to ["]The Regulations Lately Made ["] . . .* (Williamsburg, 1766).

5. *Objections . . . Considered* (London, 1765), pp. 4–5, 7, 8–9, 18. On Jenyns, see *D.N.B.;* Lewis B. Namier, *The Structure of Politics at the Accession of George III* (London, 1929), I, 273; II, 521. Jenyns' pamphlet is entered in Adams, "Bibliographical Study," as items 16Aa–b. For an example of the annoyance Jenyns' pamphlet created, see, besides the present pamphlet, p. 35n, James Otis' stinging response, *Considerations on Behalf of the Colonists in a Letter to a Noble Lord* (London, 1765), reprinted in Mullett, *Political Writings,* II, 109–125.

6. *Regulations Lately Made . . .* (London, 1765), pp. 4, 101, 104, 105, 106, 108, 109, 111. (Adams, "Bibliographical Study," lists the pamphlet as items 21a–b.) On Whately, see above, Introductions to Pamphlets 10 and 11; *D.N.B.; Collections of the Massachusetts Historical Society,* 6th ser., IX, *passim,* esp. 18n. For another extensive reply to Whately, besides the present pamphlet, see Bland, *An Inquiry,* cited in note 4 above. Whately's pamphlet was excerpted in the *Newport Mercury,* April 22, 1765.

7. Knox was undersecretary of state for America 1770–1782; Whately was undersecretary of state for the Northern Department from June 1771 until his death in May 1772.

8. *Claim . . . Examined* (London, 1765), pp. 16, 3, 14, 27, 30. (Adams, "Bibliographical Study," lists this pamphlet as 17a–b.) The second pamphlet of 1765 usually attributed to Knox is *A Letter to a Member of Parliament, Wherein the Power of the British Legislature, and the Case of the Colonies, Are . . . Considered.* On Knox, see *D.N.B.;* Edmund S. Morgan, "The Postponement of the Stamp Act," *W.M.Q.,* 3d ser., 7 (1950), 377–380; William W. Abbot, *Royal Government in Georgia 1754–1775* (Chapel Hill, 1959), pp. 109, 135–136; Edward Channing, *History of the United States* (New York, 1905–1925), III, 39n; Gipson, *British Empire,* X, 174–175. Knox's *Claim . . . Examined* was answered not only by Dulany in the present pamphlet but, in great detail, by Ebenezer Devotion in *The Examiner Examined . . .* (New London, 1766).

9. Dulany Sr.'s *Right of the Inhabitants of Maryland to the Benefit of the English Laws* (Annapolis, 1728), reprinted in St. George L. Sioussat, *The English Statutes in Maryland* (Baltimore, 1903), pp. 80–104, is a remarkable essay for the time. Anticipating in important respects the dominant configuration of political ideas that would appear in the pamphlets of the Revolutionary period, it mobilized in support of colonial rights Pufendorf, Grotius, and Locke among the theorists; Coke, Holt, and Hale among the lawyers and jurists; Tacitus, Polybius, and Caesar among the classical historians; and among the immediately current libertarians, in addition to *Cato's Letters,* "the book called English liberties," which was probably Henry Care's *English Liberties, or the Freeborn Subject's Inheritance . . .* (London,

[1680?]), a combination casebook in law, guide to legal procedures, and Anglophile propaganda piece, the fifth edition of which was reprinted in Boston by James Franklin in 1721, and the sixth in Providence in 1774.

10. Land, *The Dulanys*, p. 153; E. Alfred Jones, *American Members of the Inns of Court* (London, 1924), p. 68; Charles Carroll Sr. to Charles Carroll of Carrollton, April 17, 1761, *Maryland Historical Magazine*, 10 (1915), 343.

11. *Ibid.*, 10 (1915), 343; Land, *The Dulanys*, p. 251; Dulany to Cecilius Calvert, September 10, 1764, *The Calvert Papers*, II (Maryland Historical Society, *Fund Publication, No. 34*, Baltimore, 1894), 244–247. The Carrolls, being rivals of the Dulanys, were no doubt inclined to dwell on the weaknesses of the leader of the clan. ("C'est un homme bizarre," the younger Carroll wrote of Dulany [*Maryland Historical Magazine*, 11 (1916), 326]; "he cannot bear contradiction or opposition" [Field, *Unpublished Letters*, p. 52].) But the Carrolls' estimations of people were generally realistic, and their views of Dulany check with both the facts of his career and with other appraisals of his character. Cf. *Calvert Papers*, II, 228–229.

12. *Considerations*, pp. 6, 14, 15, 34, 48.

13. James Otis, *Rights of the British Colonies* (JHL Pamphlet 7), pp. 9, 39. Cf. Knox, *Letter to a Member of Parliament*, pp. 5, 8, 14; General Introduction, above, pp. 121 ff.

14. Land, *The Dulanys*, p. 272.

15. Riley, *Correspondence of "First Citizen" . . . and "Antilon,"* pp. 32, 34, 35, 48, 50, 93, 118, 123, 139, 230. The "Independent Whig" article, of which Carroll said "he had not the least intelligence till he read it in the *Maryland Gazette*," appeared on February 11, 1773. Dulany made much of what struck him as the unfortunate aptness of "the signature INDEPENDENT WHIGS," applying it repeatedly to all the "confederates" and "profligate incendiaries" who opposed him. *Correspondence*, pp. 59–63.

16. "D.D., it is said, shakes his head and dreads consequences. He would not advise us to set *puling and moaning*. See his *Considerations*; I think therein he advises a cessation of trade, nothing more I apprehend is intended." Charles Carroll Sr. to Charles Carroll of Carrollton, May 27, 1774, *Maryland Historical Magazine*, 16 (1921), 31; Land, *The Dulanys*, pp. 314–315.

Notes to Text

1. "O spare, I beseech you."

2. The great lawyer is no doubt Coke; see the discussion of *Bonham's Case* in the Introduction to Otis, *Rights of the British Colonies* (JHL Pamphlet 7). The great divine may be Hoadly; the quotation has not been located.

3. Coke, 4 *Inst.* 37.

4. The two foregoing paragraphs paraphrase Whately, *Regulations Lately Made*, pp. 108–109.

5. The treatise on peerage referred to in the footnote has not been located.

6. Translated in the New York edition as "The earls, barons, and knights, having given unto us in Parliament the eleventh part, and the citizens and burgesses the seventh part of their goods and chattels, etc."

7. Translated in the New York edition as "We will confer with you and others of the same kingdom (viz., England) possessed of lands in the said country." The collection of writs referred to is Sir William Dugdale, *A Perfect Copy of All Summons of the Nobility to the Great Councils and Parliaments of the Realm, from the*

XLIX of King Henry the IIId until These Present Times (London, 1685), pp. 263–264.

8. "We command you to send to Westminster some person or persons whom you may confide in, to confer with us on the above-said affair, and to do and assent in your name to whatever shall be there decreed."

9. "What concerns all must be approved by all."

10. Paraphrased from Knox, *Claim of the Colonies,* p. 29.

11. Persius, *Satires,* v, 100–101, translated in the New York edition as "He infuses a dangerous drug, without skill to know the proper point between its good and ill effects."

12. Horace, *Epistles,* I, i, 14, translated in the New York edition as "Unused to swear on any master's word."

13. The reference is to the opinion of the attorney general on the quartering bill passed by the Pennsylvania Assembly in 1755. See *Letter to the People of Pennsylvania* (JHL Pamphlet 2), text note 11.

14. The idea expressed here was a commonplace of the time; the words themselves sound most like those of William Knox, among Dulany's immediate antagonists, in his *Letter to a Member of Parliament,* p. 13.

15. Thomas Pownall on the title page of the second, 1765, edition of his *Administration of the Colonies* printed a rather overblown list of the colonial offices he had held. He had come to America in 1753 as the private secretary of Sir Danvers Osborne, the newly appointed governor of New York, who hanged himself within a week of his arrival. The footnote refers to the title of a satirical essay on Pownall's administration in Massachusetts written by Samuel Waterhouse under the pseudonym Thomas Thumb: *Proposals for Printing by Subscription the History of Vice-Admiral Sir Thomas Brazen . . .* (Boston, 1760).

16. *Hamlet,* III, ii, 361–365.

17. "That the commonwealth may not suffer."

18. On Parliament's reimbursement of the colonies for their wartime expenses, see Gipson, *British Empire,* X, chaps. ii–v.

19. Paraphrased from Whately, *Regulations Lately Made,* p. 3.

20. *Ibid.,* pp. 5, 9–11, 15.

21. *Ibid.,* p. 3.

22. The reference in the footnote is to Knox, *Claim of the Colonies,* p. 19. There is truth in Knox's accusation. Maryland contributed relatively little to the common defense in part at least as a result of a dispute between the lower House of the Assembly and the governor and Council, representing the proprietary interest, over the use of license fees in the operation of ordinaries as a means of raising revenue. Between 1757 and 1761 eight appropriation bills were considered and rejected; the only funds actually voted were in 1754, when the Assembly raised £6000, and in 1756, following Braddock's defeat, when £40,000 was appropriated. Gipson, *British Empire,* VII, 296–298.

23. Whately, *Regulations Lately Made,* p. 44.

24. The note refers to Knox, *Claim of the Colonies,* p. 23.

25. The phrase referred to occurs in Whately, *Regulations Lately Made,* p. 6.

26. *Ibid.,* p. 57; the exact quotation is given below, p. 35.

27. *Ibid.,* p. 101.

28. 31 Henry VIII c. 8: "The King for the time being, with the advice of his council, or the more part of them, may set forth proclamations under such penalties and pains as to him and them shall seem necessary, which shall be observed as though they were made by act of Parliament; but this shall not be prejudicial to

any person's inheritance, offices, liberties, goods, chattels or life . . ." Repealed by
1 Edward VI c. 12.

29. Whately, *Regulations Lately Made*, p. 103.

30. *Ibid.*, p. 5.

31. From the fabulist Phaedrus, I, xii, 13–15; translated in the New York edition
of the pamphlet as: "O! unhappy I, who now at length am sensible/ How the
things I had despised were of advantage to me,/ And how much mourning they
caused, which I had so much approved!"

32. Knox, *Claim of the Colonies*, p. 8.

33. *Ibid.*, p. 4.

34. *Ibid.*, p. 4.

35. The document referred to and quoted in the footnote is [J. Almon], *A
Postscript to the Letter on Libels, Warrants, &c. In Answer to a Postscript in the
Defence of the Majority, and Another Pamphlet, Entitled, Considerations on the
Legality of General Warrants* (London, 1765), pp. 6–7. The words in parentheses
are Dulany's.

36. Dulany's footnote refers to the declaration of England and Holland in 1689
during the War of the League of Augsburg that all vessels trading with France
and its dominions would be subject to attack and confiscation. John Groning, in
his *Tractatus de Navigatio Libera . . .* (1694) defended the trade of the northern
powers, but Pufendorf responded not only with the argument Dulany reports but
with the point that England's and Holland's war aims served the interests of the
complaining states. See Carl J. Kulsrud, *Maritime Neutrality to 1780* (Boston, 1936),
pp. 234–237.

37. Whately, *Regulations Lately Made*, p. 57.

38. The pamphlet referred to in the note is Soame Jenyns' *Objections to the
Taxation of Our American Colonies*, discussed in the Introduction to the present
pamphlet. In the second sentence of the note, read L[or]d of T[rade].

39. Knox, *Claim of the Colonies*, pp. 10, 11. The statute referred to below is 5
George II c. 7: An Act for the More Easy Recovery of Debts in His Majesty's
Plantations and Colonies in America.

40. Knox, *Claim of the Colonies*, pp. 5–6.

41. Seneca, *Hercules Furens*, 164–166; translated in the New York edition as
"Let such a one, without taking sleep,/ Attend the proud levees, and haughty
gates/ Of kings — "

42. Knox, *Claim of the Colonies*, p. 32.

43. *Ibid.*, p. 8.

44. *Ibid.*, p. 20. On the disposition of funds collected in America, see Oxenbridge
Thacher, *Sentiments of a British American* (JHL Pamphlet 8), text note 14.

45. The note refers to an episode of December 6, 1764, in Montreal. A group
of soldiers broke into the house of Thomas Walker, a justice of the peace, and
cut off his right ear. The attack was prompted by Walker's attempts to alleviate
the abuses of the troop billeting system. See Francis Maseres, *The Trial of Daniel
Disney . . . upon an Indictment for a Burglary and Felony in Breaking into Thomas
Walker's House . . . With an Intention of Murder . . .* (New York, 1768).

46. Knox, *Claim of the Colonies*, pp. 3, 4.

47. Whately, *Regulations Lately Made*, p. 66.

48. *Ibid.*, p. 69.

49. David Hume, *The History of Great Britain* (Edinburgh, 1754–1757), I (Containing the Reigns of James I and Charles I), p. 131.

50. [Sir Matthew Decker], *An Essay on the Causes of the Decline of the Foreign*

Trade . . . (London, 1750). Second edition, reprinted in [John R. McCulloch, ed.], *A Select Collection of Scarce and Valuable Tracts on Commerce* (London, 1859), pp. 119, 120.

51. Paraphrased from Jenyns, *Objections to the Taxation of Our American Colonies,* p. 21.

52. The quotation is from [Charles Davenant], *Discourses on the Publick Revenues and on the Trade of England . . .* (London, 1698), II, 249 (a section from Discourse III, "On the Plantation Trade"). The final quotation is from the *Aeneid,* i, 199: "God shall also put an end to these."

PAMPHLET 14

DICKINSON, *THE LATE REGULATIONS*

John Dickinson appears to be the last of the major figures of the Revolution to receive proper attention from historians. The standard account of his life is still Charles Stillé's *Life and Times of John Dickinson* (Philadelphia, 1891). Paul Leicester Ford undertook a complete and careful edition of Dickinson's writings, but he completed only one volume, *Political Writings, 1764–1774,* published in *Memoirs of the Historical Society of Pennsylvania,* XIV (Philadelphia, 1895); for the rest, one must go back to the original publications or to the two-volume edition of Dickinson's political writings which Dickinson himself published in 1801.

Three modern scholars have made available for the first time, and in excellent editions, several hitherto unknown works. John H. Powell has reconstructed from sketchy notes Dickinson's speech against the Declaration of Independence. The heavily edited text is published in *Pa. Mag.,* 65 (1941), 468–481; a reader's version of the speech, omitting the scholarly apparatus, appears in Merrill Jensen, ed., *American Colonial Documents to 1776 (English Historical Documents,* IX, London, 1955), 873–877. Richard J. Hooker, "John Dickinson on Church and State," *American Literature,* 16 (1944–45), 82–98, has identified and edited three newspaper essays by Dickinson written in opposition to Anglican proposals for an American episcopate. And H. Trevor Colbourn has edited from the manuscripts the letters Dickinson wrote to his parents from London during his years as a law student: "A Pennsylvania Farmer at the Court of King George: John Dickinson's London Letters, 1754–1756," *Pa. Mag.,* 86 (1962), 241–286, 417–453. These letters contain valuable details on Dickinson's impressions of England, particularly on his shocked reaction to the corruption of English politics; more generally, they express his personality as a young man and something of his early beliefs.

In addition to these documentary publications there have recently appeared a number of notable essays on Dickinson. H. Trevor Colbourn's "The Historical Perspective of John Dickinson," in *Early Dickinsoniana* (The Boyd Lee Spahr Lectures in Americana, 1957–1961, Dickinson College, Carlisle, Pa., 1961), which broadens a more technical study, "John Dickinson, Historical Revolutionary," *Pa. Mag.,* 83 (1959), 271–292, is a penetrating analysis of Dickinson's character and ideas. John H. Powell's "A Certain Great Fortune and Piddling Genius . . . ," published in the same volume of Spahr Lectures, concentrates on Dickinson's role in the Continental Congress through 1776, and especially on the problem of the Olive Branch Petition. The previous volume in the same lecture series, entitled *"John and Mary's College"* (Carlisle, Pa., 1956) contains an essay by Frederick B. Tolles, "John Dickinson and the Quakers," as well as a paper by James M. Tunnell, Jr., on Dickinson and the Federal Constitution. David L. Jacobson has published a study of Dickinson's defense of the proprietary government of Pennsylvania in *W.M.Q.*, 3d ser., 19 (1962), 64–85, which makes available in more elaborate form a section of his unpublished doctoral dissertation, John Dickinson and Joseph Galloway, 1764–1776: A Study in Contrasts (Princeton University, 1959). Bernhard Knollenberg has brought together the relevant documentation of the antagonism between Adams and Dickinson in "John Dickinson vs John Adams: 1774–1776," *Proceedings of the American Philosophical Society*, 107 (1963), 138–144. Richard M. Gummere has written on Dickinson's classical learning in *Classical Journal*, 52 (1956–57), 81–88; and Dickinson's career as president of Delaware, 1781–1782, has been traced by John H. Powell in *Delaware History*, 1 (1946), 1–54, 111–134. References to writings on the political background in Pennsylvania will be found in the notes to *A Letter to the People of Pennsylvania* (JHL Pamphlet 2).

The Late Regulations . . . is entered as items 10a–c in Adams' "Bibliographical Study." Published first in Philadelphia, the pamphlet was reprinted in London on order of Benjamin Franklin in 1765 (actually issued in 1766) and again in 1773. It appeared also in 1766 in two collections of tracts on taxing the colonies published in London by J. Almon, and again, in a third such collection, in 1773.

The pamphlet has been edited according to the general rules set forth in the Preface, but in addition the uniform italicization of all place names, which appears in the original editions and which was retained in the Ford edition, has been eliminated. All other italics have been retained.

Notes to Introduction

1. Julian P. Boyd, ed., *Papers of Thomas Jefferson* (Princeton, 1950–), X, 378; I, 187–219 (cf. VII, 289); Adams, *Diary and Autobiography*, II, 173, 174n; III, 315, 318.

2. Colbourn, "Historical Perspective," pp. 3–6.

3. Tolles, "Dickinson and the Quakers," p. 69. On the Quaker aristocracy in general, see Tolles, *Meeting House and Counting House* (Chapel Hill, 1948).

4. Tolles, "Dickinson and the Quakers," pp. 81, 82.

5. *Diary and Autobiography*, II, 117; Colbourn, "London Letters," pp. 262, 252, 254, 434, 453; Colbourn, "Historical Perspective," pp. 28–35, 16; Powell, "A Certain Great Fortune"; Jensen, *Documents*, p. 875.

6. Stillé, *Dickinson*, pp. 37, 36; Colbourn, "Historical Perspective," p. 13.

7. Colbourn, "London Letters," pp. 246, 448–449, 453; Gummere, "Classical Penman," pp. 81–87; Colbourn, "Historical Perspective," pp. 15–16, 23.

8. For an enumeration of sixty-three of the authorities cited by Dickinson in his various writings, see John Dickinson, "The Political Thought of John Dickinson," *Dickinson Law Review*, 39 (1934), 3n. Dickinson's *Essay on the Constitutional Power of Great-Britain over the Colonies in America* . . . (Philadelphia, 1774), reprinted in *Pennsylvania Archives*, 2d ser., III, 565 ff., is a remarkable compendium of quotations loosely attached to a brief text; the text itself is submerged for pages, as footnotes and then footnotes on footnotes pile up.

9. Colbourn, "London Letters," pp. 268, 421–422, 445.

10. Hooker, "Dickinson on Church and State," p. 90; Dickinson, *An Address to . . . Barbados* . . . (Philadelphia, 1766), pp. 9–11, in Ford, *Writings*, pp. 266–267; Colbourn, "London Letters," p. 247.

11. *A Speech* . . . *1764* . . . (Philadelphia, 1764), pp. 4, 12; *An Address* . . . *on the Stamp Act* (broadside [Philadelphia, 1765]); *Address to Barbados*, pp. 12, 13, in Ford, *Writings*, pp. 24, 31, 202, 269, 270.

12. *Letters from a Farmer in Pennsylvania* . . . (Philadelphia, 1768), in Ford, *Writings*, pp. 352, 375, 380–381, 382, 393, 402.

13. *A Letter from the Country* . . . (broadside [Philadelphia, 1773]), in Ford, *Writings*, pp. 459–461.

14. *Ibid.; "To the Inhabitants of the British Colonies in America," Pennsylvania Journal*, June 1, 1774 (cf. June 15, 1774), in Ford, *Writings*, pp. 461–462, 473–474, 487 ff.

15. "To the Inhabitants," *Pennsylvania Journal*, June 15, 1774, in Ford, *Writings*, pp. 491, 497–499.

16. Jensen, *Documents*, pp. 848, 873.

Notes to Text

1. The quotations in Dickinson's note are from: [Charles Davenant], *Discourses on the Publick Revenues and on the Trade of England* . . . (London, 1698), II, discourse iii ("On the Plantation Trade"), 204, 226, 255; Josiah Child, *A New Discourse of Trade* . . . (London, 1693), chap. x, secs. 11, 4; Wyndham Beawes, *Lex Mercatoria Rediviva* (Dublin, 1754), p. 554; Malachy Postlethwayt, *The Universal Dictionary of Trade and Commerce* . . . (London, 1751–1755), I, 532–533.

2. Postlethwayt, *Universal Dictionary*, I, 536.

3. Postlethwayt, *Universal Dictionary*, I, 532.

4. Montesquieu, *Spirit of the Laws*, xx, 9.

5. Dickinson's view of the stability of paper currency in the middle colonies was accurate; see E. James Ferguson, "Currency Finance: An Interpretation of Colonial Monetary Practices," *W.M.Q.*, 3d ser., 10 (1953), 153–180.

6. Cf. Benjamin M. Nead, *A Brief Review of the Financial History of Pennsylvania* (Harrisburg, 1881), pp. 6–19.

7. Beawes, *Lex Mercatoria*, p. 542.

8. Dickinson quotes in the footnote: Josiah Tucker, *A Brief Essay on the Advantages and Disadvantages Which Respectively Attend France and Great Britain with Regard to Trade* (3d ed., London., 1753), reprinted in [John R. McCulloch, ed.,], *A Select Collection of Scarce and Valuable Tracts on Commerce* (London, 1859), p. 17.

9. Postlethwayt, *Universal Dictionary*, I, 532.

10. [Robert Wallace], *Dissertation on the Numbers of Mankind* . . . (Edinburgh, 1753), p. 150.

11. Postlethwayt, *Universal Dictionary*, I, 535.

12. Cicero, *De Officiis*, ii, 17, tells of Mamercus who was defeated for the consulship because he failed to provide the magnificent entertainments expected of men in their year of aedileship.

13. John G. Keysler, *Travels Through Germany, Hungary, Bohemia, Switzerland, Italy and Lorrain* . . . (London, 1758), I, 165.

14. Postlethwayt, *Universal Dictionary*, I, 532–533; note Dickinson's earlier quotation of the same passage in the note to his page 4, above.

15. Malachy Postlethwayt, *Great-Britain's True System* . . . (London, 1757), p. 176.

16. Tucker, *Brief Essay*, in McCulloch, *Select Collection*, p. 74; Davenant, *Discourses*, II, 208–209, 244.

17. [John Trenchard and Thomas Gordon], *Cato's Letters* (London, 1724), IV, no. 106 ("Of Plantations and Colonies").

PAMPHLETS TO APPEAR
IN SUBSEQUENT VOLUMES

INDEX

753

THE JOHN HARVARD LIBRARY

*The intent of
Waldron Phoenix Belknap, Jr.,
as expressed in an early will, was for
Harvard College to use the income from a
permanent trust fund he set up, for "editing and
publishing rare, inaccessible, or hitherto unpublished
source material of interest in connection with the
history, literature, art (including minor and useful
art), commerce, customs, and manners or way of
life of the Colonial and Federal Periods of the United
States . . . In all cases the emphasis shall be on the
presentation of the basic material." A later testament
broadened this statement, but Mr. Belknap's interests remained constant until his death.*

*In linking the name of the first benefactor of
Harvard College with the purpose of this later,
generous-minded believer in American culture the
John Harvard Library seeks to emphasize the importance of Mr. Belknap's purpose. The John Harvard
Library of the Belknap Press of Harvard University
Press exists to make books and documents
about the American past more readily
available to scholars and the
general reader.*

DATE DUE

Feb 11			
GAYLORD			PRINTED IN U.S.A.